THE HIRSEL EXCAVATIONS

by

Rosemary Cramp

Including contributions by
Belinda Burke

and

Michael Alexander, Sue Anderson,
Marion Archibald, Arnold Aspinall†, Ian Bailiff,
Paul Bidwell, David Birkett†, Philip Clogg, Derek Craig,
Valerie Dean, Lloyd Edwards, Blanche Ellis, Richard Fawcett,
Louisa Gidney, Pamela Graves, Jacqui Huntley,
Dawn McLaren, Andrew Millard, Susan Mills,
Jennifer Price, Ian Riddler, Graeme Rimer,
Alison Sheridan, John Waller,
Caroline Wickham-Jones,
Robert Young

HISTORIC SCOTLAND
ALBA AOSMHOR

THE SOCIETY FOR MEDIEVAL ARCHAEOLOGY
MONOGRAPH 36

ISSN 0583-9106
ISBN 978-1-909662-35-3

Series editor: Christopher Gerrard
Published by The Society for Medieval Archaeology, London

The Society for Medieval Archaeology is grateful to Historic Scotland for a grant towards this publication

The Society for Medieval Archaeology
www.medievalarchaeology.org

Cramp, R, 2014
The Hirsel excavations,
The Society for Medieval Archaeology Monograph 36,
London

Cover: The site during excavation in 1981, showing the Phase III church and Hirsel House in the background

CONTENTS

LIST OF FIGURES

Appendices

SUMMARY

The surveys and excavations which are the subject of this book began in 1978 with a geophysical survey of a field adjacent to the Hirsel House, Coldstream, Scotland, where grave stones had been revealed by ploughing in 1977. This was followed by five short seasons of excavations in 1979–82, and 1984. Post-excavation analysis began in 1984, and short interim reports were issued up to 1985. Most specialist reports were completed in the 1990s, but there was then a suspension of work on the site until the final preparation for publication.

The site has revealed a long occupation beginning in the Neolithic period, with some later prehistoric evidence from the site and the nearby hillfort Hirsel Law. This hillfort, which is within the boundaries of the historic Hirsel Estate, still played a part in the military and legal activities of the region until the 16th century.

The history and topography of the Estate is first considered, but the main focus of the excavation was on a church which developed from *c*10th to 14th century with an associated cemetery which seems to have existed from *c*12th to 16th with sporadic internments into 17th century. This is the most complete excavation of a proprietary church in Scotland, which developed from a single-cell drystone building into a substantial church of cut and mortared stone. It was granted to the nearby Priory of Coldstream in 1165, only to be put out of ecclesiastical use, ruined, turned to lay use and finally burnt before being firmly sealed over with rubble by the 16th century. Its location was forgotten by the 17th century. This is then a remarkably detailed story of a church at a period when the parochial structure in Scotland was being developed and very little is known about the relationship of estate churches and the monasteries to which they were donated.

Prehistoric pottery and flints, as well as Roman pottery and glass were recovered from the excavation, and the medieval finds are particularly rich for this type of site. They include an important collection of iron work with a significant number of arrowheads, unusual stone tools, and a large amount of pottery dating from the 10th to 16th centuries, as well as a considerable collection of architectural and funerary stone work.

The cemetery is one of the largest medieval rural cemeteries in Scotland, and provides evidence for an interesting range of burial modes and grave markings, as well as the palaeopathology of the skeletons. The life of the people who lived on the estate has been further illuminated by the environmental discussion in the botanical and faunal reports.

RÉSUMÉ

Les prospections et fouilles qui sont le sujet de cet ouvrage ont commencé en 1978 par la prospection géophysique d'un terrain adjacent à la Hirsel House, Coldstream, Ecosse, là où des labours avaient remonté des pierres tombales en 1977. Cinq courtes saisons de fouilles s'en suivirent entre 1979 et 1982, et en 1984. Des analyses post-fouilles ont débuté en 1984 et de courts rapports intermédiaires en ont découlé en 1985. La plupart des rapports d'experts ont été effectués dans les années 1990, suivis d'une suspension d'opération sur le terrain jusqu'à la préparation finale pour la publication.

Le site a révélé une longue occupation qui a débuté à la période néolithique, avec quelques éléments de la fin de la Préhistoire provenant du site et de l'habitat fortifié de hauteur voisin Hirsel Law. Cet habitat fortifié, qui s'inscrit dans les limites de l'Hirsel Estate historique, a continué de jouer un rôle dans les activités militaires et juridiques de la région jusqu'au XVIe siècle.

L'histoire et la topographie du domaine sont ici d'abord considérées, mais l'objectif principal de la fouille réside surtout dans l'étude d'une église qui s'est développée du Xe siècle environ jusqu'au XIVe siècle, et de son cimetière associé qui semble avoir utilisé du XIIe siècle environ jusqu'au XVIe siècle, avec quelques inhumations sporadiques au XVIIe siècle. Il s'agit ici de la fouille la plus complète d'une église privée en Ecosse, qui s'est développée à partir d'une construction en pierres sèches à nef unique pour devenir une église importante en pierres taillées, jointes avec du mortier. Bien qu'acquise par le prieuré voisin de Coldstream en 1165, elle est désacralisée, se délabre, est détournée à des fins laïcs, pour finalement brûler avant d'être condamnée par des remblais au XVIe siècle. Sa localisation est tombée dans l'oubli au XVIIe siècle. Il s'agit donc ici de l'histoire remarquablement détaillée d'une église pendant la période de développement de la structure paroissiale en Ecosse, et pour laquelle la relation entre églises privées et monastères qui ont bénéficié de ces donations était jusqu' à présent peu connue.

Des poteries et silex préhistoriques, ainsi que de la céramique et du verre romains ont été mis au jour lors des fouilles, et les artefacts médiévaux sont particulièrement riches pour ce type de site. Ils comprennent une série importante d'objets en fer avec un nombre important de pointes de flèche, des outils en pierre peu communs, une grande quantité de poteries datant du Xe au XVIe siècle, ainsi qu'une collection considérable d'ouvrages architecturaux et funéraires en pierre.

Le cimetière est un des plus grands ruraux du Moyen Age en Ecosse, et fournit des indices importants sur les différents modes d'inhumation et les gravures des tombes, ainsi que pour la paléopathologie des squelettes. Les rapports sur les études botanique et faunique ont également participé à l'amélioration de nos connaissances sur la vie des personnes liées au domaine.

RIASSUNTO

Le ricognizioni e gli scavi descritti in questo libro ebbero inizio nel 1978 con una prospezione geofisica di un terreno adiacente alla Hirsel House di Coldstream in Scozia, dove alcune pietre tombali erano state portate alla luce dalle arature nel 1977. Questa fu seguita da cinque brevi campagne di scavi nel 1979–82 e nel 1984. Le analisi del post-scavo iniziarono nel 1984 e brevi rapporti preliminari sono stati pubblicati fino al 1985. La maggior parte degli studi degli specialisti fu completata negli anni '90, ma vi fu una sospensione del lavoro sul sito fino alla preparazione finale della pubblicazione.

Il sito ha rivelato una lunga occupazione a partire dall'era neolitica, con alcune attestazioni preistoriche successive nel sito stesso e nei paraggi del forte di Hirsel Law. Questo forte, che si trova entro i confini della storica tenuta Hirsel, partecipò anche alle attività militari e legali della regione fino al XVI secolo.

Viene innanzitutto considerata la storia e la topografia della tenuta, mentre le indagini di scavo si sono concentrate soprattutto in una chiesa utilizzata tra il XII e il XIV secolo circa, insieme all'annesso cimitero che sembra essere utilizzato tra il XII e il XVI secolo, con sporadiche frequentazioni nel XVII secolo. Questo è lo scavo più completo di una chiesa privata in Scozia, evolutasi da un singolo ambiente con muri a secco in un considerevole edificio in pietre tagliate e legate con malta. La chiesa fu assegnata alla Prioria di Coldstream nel 1165, cessò il suo uso liturgico, fu lasciata andare in rovina, convertita per un uso profano e infine incendiata prima di rimanere sepolta sotto le macerie nel XVI secolo. Si perse memoria della sua posizione già nel XVII secolo. Si tratta quindi di una storia di una chiesa eccezionalmente ben dettagliata in un periodo in cui la struttura delle parrocchie in Scozia si stava evolvendo e molto poco si conosce del rapporto tra le chiese private e i monasteri a cui esse vennero donate.

Nello scavo sono state rinvenute ceramica preistorica e selci, così come ceramica e vetri romani. I rinvenimenti di età medievale sono particolarmente ricchi per questo tipo di sito. Essi includono un importante insieme di manufatti in ferro con un numero significativo di punte di freccia, rari utensili in pietra, e una grande quantità di ceramica databile tra il X e il XVI secolo, così come una notevole quantità di elementi architettonici e funerari in pietra.

Il cimitero è tra i più vasti cimiteri rurali medievali e vi è documentata un'interessante in Scozia gamma di tipi di sepoltura e segnacoli tombali nonché la paleopatologia degli scheletri. Grazie alla ricostruzione ambientale negli studi riguardanti i reperti botanici e faunistici, è stata portata ulteriore luce sulla vita degli abitanti della tenuta.

ACKNOWLEDGEMENTS

The final report of this excavation has been long delayed by the principal author's other commitments, and apologies are certainly due to those who contributed to the excavation and to the subsequent reports, and have had to wait disgracefully long for their efforts to be recognised.

The excavation was financed by Durham University, the Douglas and Angus Estates, Historic Scotland, and the Hunter Trust. Historic Scotland also generously supported the post-excavation work and publication, and negotiated a management agreement for the site with the Estate. The Department of Archaeology at Durham University has supported the project throughout, by providing space and facilities even into the days of stringent space costing. Special thanks are due to the Home family at The Hirsel: Lady Caroline Douglas-Home not only drew attention to the site, but supported it throughout excavation by providing and organising accommodation for living and working on the estate, as well as taking part in the fieldwork; the late Lord and Lady Home provided throughout encouragement, support and generous hospitality to the team, and the present Lord Home has provided permission to visit the site and the finds.

For the excavation, the supervisors and volunteers were mainly from Durham University, with a seasoning of volunteers from other universities, and individuals from the USA and France. A listing appears at the end of this section. The smoothness of the whole operation was ensured by a remarkable partnership; Fred Bettess, who not only laid down the site grid and undertook the detailed contour survey of the site, but also instructed undergraduate volunteers in the skills of survey, and Gladys Bettess, who organised the finds recording and the work rotas with military precision. She was aided also in the finds recording by Elizabeth Coatsworth. Life on site was considerably enhanced by the delicious meals produced by our two cooks: Barbara and Ian Harrison. The overall site drawing, as well as many of the finds drawings, was the work of Keith McBarron, and crucial parts of the photography were the work of Tom Middlemass, both from the Durham University Department of Archaeology. I am grateful also to other Durham colleagues such as Michael Alexander and Jacqui Huntley, who not only worked at the site but submitted specialist reports, and to Arnold and Priscilla Aspinall from Bradford University. Arnold deserves special thanks for organising further geophysical recording after the excavation, with the help of Paul Johnson and his team. Arnold cheerfully continued to enhance his findings to the stage of the completion of the text, but sadly he did not live to see the final publication. I am grateful to all the specialists whose reports are published below, not only for their erudition, but for their patience in waiting and in many cases updating their reports.

Post-excavation analysis began during and immediately after the dig by Michael Trueman and Ian Riddler, followed by Derek Craig who sorted and catalogued the archive, prepared the finds lists and contributed a great deal to the context catalogue and the bibliography. The X-ray and conservation of the finds was undertaken by Colin MacGregor, Phillip Clogg and Jennifer Jones. After a hiatus in this work, Belinda Burke as Research Assistant has been the main participant in the final stages of post-excavation and volume production and has contributed much to the final judgments. Her help has been the essential element in the publication, and I can only thank her for her staying power.

Yvonne Beadnell also deserves special thanks since she not only worked on the site but has undertaken the completion and oversight of all the finds and other site drawings to the stage of transfer to Christina Unwin who, arriving into the project in a new age, has digitised and enhanced the line illustrations throughout. The photographs of the site and finds, many of which are the work of the principal author, have been scanned and skilfully enhanced by Jeff Veitch.

My patchy knowledge of later medieval Scottish history has been generously aided by other scholars who are leading specialists in this field. I would like to thank particularly Geoffrey Barrow, Elsa Hamilton and Thomas Clanchy, and for architectural history Richard Fawcett. Michael Hickman has generously shared his knowledge of the history and topography of Coldstream and its Priory. I have also benefited from useful discussions with Roger Miket and Eric Cambridge. A series of Inspectors from Historic Scotland have helpfully provided information and support in particular Roderick McCullagh who has guided the project to the stage of publication. Finally I would like to thank Alejandra Gutiérrez for her meticulous editing of the text and Christina Unwin for her skilfull layout of this book. (RC)

Acknowledgements for specialist reports

In Chapter 10, Jacqui Huntley would like to thank Professor Martin Jones and Professor Marijke van der Veen, both then of the Department of Archaeology, Durham University, for help in the identification of cereal grains and chaff fragments during the original 1985 work. She would also like to thank Professor Brian Huntley and Dr Judith Turner of the then Department of Botany, Durham University, for valuable discussions and for their critical reading of the 1985 manuscript. Finally but by no means least she is grateful to Professor Rosemary Cramp and Belinda Burke for providing updated phasing and grouping of the samples and to Professor Cramp for giving her the opportunity in the first place to study these plant remains — 'they were a wonderful assemblage upon which to cut teeth'.

In Chapter 17, Valerie Dean extends grateful thanks to the following: Dr David H Caldwell for advice and encouragement; Catherine M Brooks, Dr Ewan Campbell, Mark Collard, George Haggarty and Derek Hall for information on fabrics from other sites; Charles J Burnett, Nicholas M McQ Holmes, Nigel Ruckley; June Davidson for checking for sherd joins; Margaret Fairbairn for typing work.

In Chapters 19 and 20, Rosemary Cramp and Belinda Burke would like to thank Jennifer Jones for her helpful comments, and for cleaning and photographing the horseshoe (Fe97). They are grateful to Ian Riddler and Nicola Trzaska-Nartowski for reading the text and providing further suggestions. Belinda Burke also benefitted from discussions with Erik Matthews.

In Chapter 24, Caroline Wickham-Jones would like to thank Ann Clarke, Ann Crone, Jill Harden, Ann MacSween and Olly Owen, who all helped with advice and information relating to the assemblage. The geological identification and discussion was carried out by Diane Dixon. Peter Hill also helped with information and made available the report of the Whithorn material in advance of publication.

Illustrations

After such a long interval between excavation, immediate post-excavation, and the recent preparation for the publication, there has been a considerable amount of redrawing and rescanning of the illustrations. Christina Unwin has rescanned or redrawn most of the site plans to bring them to a common and improved format, and has been credited with this, but the detailed site drawings of the stone work, in particular Keith McBarron's stone by stone drawing of the foundations of the church, were not redrawn in any way and remain his achievement. Yvonne Beadnell's site plans, which appeared in the interim reports, also remain the basis for the new format.

Drawings: Michael Alexander (3.6–11), Arnold Aspinall† (2.12–13, 3.2–5), Fred Bettess (1.7), Yvonne Beadnell (1.1, 1.5, 5.7, 5.16, 12.27, 12.34, 12.37–38, 16.1, 18.1, 19.6, 20.1–5, 20.7–9, 20.12–14, 20.17, 23.3), Belinda Burke (1.8–9, 3.6–11, 4.13, 5.1, 6.3, 6.9, 6.12, 8.10, 20.16), Philip Clogg (5.21), Valerie Dean (17.2, 17.4), Lloyd Edwards (18.1), Louisa Gidney (10.14–15, 10.18, 10.19, 10.21), Jacqui Huntley (10.1–8), Keith McBarron (4.21, 5.22, 12.1, 12.5, 12.15, 12.18, 12.22, 12.30, 12.33, 12.35, 12.37–38, 14.1, 19.1–3, 19.5–7, 20.1–14, 20.17, 21.1, 24.1, 24.3–7, 24.10, 25.1), Marion O'Neil (15.1–4, 17.5–10), Christina Unwin (2.3, 2.5, 4.1–2, 4.5, 4.12, 4.14–16, 4.18–19, 4.21, 5.4–5, 5.7, 5.10, 5.15–16, 5.19, 5.22, 5.26, 5.32, 5.36–37, 5.42, 6.1–2, 6.14, 6.17, 6.44, 7.2, 7.4, 7.6–7, 7.15–17, 7.20, 8.1, 8.5, 27.2).

Photographs: Sue Anderson (11.19, 11.21–22, 11.24–31), BBC North (5.14, 6.34), Belinda Burke (5.43, 12.6, 12.20, 13.1), Philip Clogg (6.43, 19.4), Rosemary Cramp (1.4, 1.6, 3.1, 4.3–4, 4.6–11, 4.17, 4.20, 4.22–23, 5.3, 5.6, 5.8–9, 5.18, 5.23, 5.27–29, 5.31, 5.33–34, 5.38, 5.41, 6.4–7, 6.10–11, 6.15–16, 6.18, 6.20, 6.25–27, 6.29–31, 6.33, 6.35–37, 7.1, 7.3, 7.5, 7.8, 7.10–11, 7.13, 7.19, 8.6–7, 8.9, 8.11, 12.10–14, 12.20, 12.26, 12.31–32, 13.3, 13.5, 13.7–8, 27.1), Caroline Douglas-Home (13.2), Richard Fawcett (12.2), Jennifer Jones (20.10, 20.17), Tom Middlemass (1.10, 5.2, 5.11–13, 5.24–25, 5.30, 5.35, 5.39, 6.8, 6.13, 6.19, 6.21–22, 6.28, 6.38–42, 7.9, 7.12, 7.14, 7.18, 8.2–4, 8.8, 12.3–4, 12.8, 12.16–17, 12.21, 12.24–25, 12.27–29, 12.35, 13.4, 13.6, 14.1, 19.1, 19.6, 22.1, 24.1, 25.1), Christina Unwin (5.40, 13.6), Jeff Veitch (12.7, 12.9, 12.19, 12.23), Sonia Williams (6.23–24).

We are grateful to the following institutions for permission to use their images: RCAHMS for aerial photographs (1.2, 1.3, 2.1, 2.10, 2.11), to the Librarian, University of Glasgow Library, for supplying the illustration of the archer (20.15) and to the National Library of Scotland for supplying the historic maps (2.4 and 2.6–9).

Site supervisors

Martha Ashbrooke, Neil Beagrie, Gareth Binns, Roy Le Hegarat, Susan Mills, Rachel Newman, Rebecca Payne, Deirdre O'Sullivan, Jane Shute, Ian Smith†, Richard Steel, Harvey Watt.

Volunteers

Rochelle Allison, Caroline Arter, Ruth Barach, Josephine Bateson, Georgina Beech, Roger Bettess, Sebastian Birch, Guy de la Bedoyere, Paul Bernot, D Beslich, Andrew Boyd, Andrew Brown, Sheila Brown, Brigitte Camus, Rosemary Carey,

Dido Clark, Giles Cockerill, Jane Coggrave, Morag Colquhoun, Julia Cross, James Daniel, Ashley Deakin, Laura Dermott, Archie Dick, Caroline Douglas-Home, Marion Edwards, Jane Fielding, Trent Foley, H Geizler, Chris Gladstone, Charles Glenn, Peter Harvey, Ellen Hobbie, Birgit Höhn, Peter Hoy, John Hudson, Spencer Hymen, Chris Kelly, Charles Kendall, Peter Kendall, Jill Kerr, Judith Kitching, D Latin, Colin MacGregor, Margaret Meldrum, David Montgomery, Hugh Morgan, John Morgan, Agnes Muirhead, Alison Munro, Nicola Nartowski, Helen Nowell, Jeanette Ratcliffe, Ian Riddler, Sarah Robson, Stewart Satterley/Stuart Slatterly, Michael Sekulla, Katherine Slade, Andrew Slater, Andrew Snell, Greg Speed, Rachael Squire†, Chris Stephens, Jim Summerely†, Janet Swallow, Nick Till, Susan Topping, Sylvia Usher, Paul Watson, Kelly Wickham-Crowley, Jacqueline Williams, Andrew Witham, Louise Williams, Colin Worswick, Robert Wotherspoon, Sarah Wyles, Christine Yardley, Brita Yakes, Lawrence Yates.

1

INTRODUCTION TO THE SITE

Rosemary Cramp

1.1 LOCATION AND NATURE OF THE SITE (NGR: NT 830 406)

The Hirsel site lies 1km north-west of the village of Coldstream, Scotland, on a low-lying sand and gravel terrace on the left bank of the Leet Water, a tributary of the River Tweed (Figure 1.1), and the area investigated lay immediately adjacent to Hirsel House in a field called the Dial Knowe or Low Field. The area excavated was in the north of the field bordering the ha-ha which separated it from the gardens of the house (Figures 1.2–1.5). The area covered by the geophysical surveys was however much more extensive and extended towards the slope on the south of the excavated area (see Chapters 2 and 3).

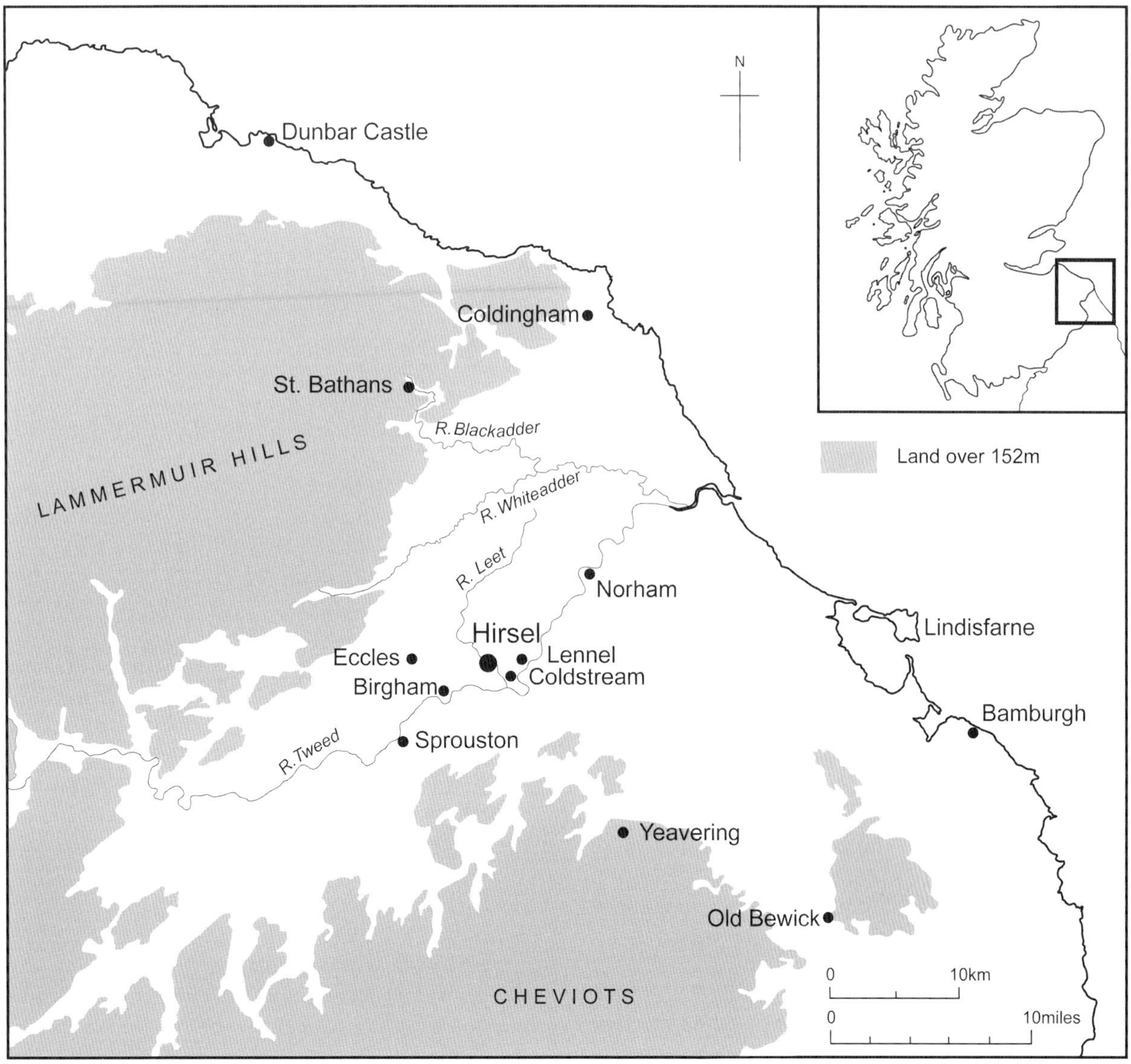

FIGURE 1.1
The location of The Hirsel within its region

FIGURE 1.2
Aerial view looking WNW, showing the line of the River Leet and crossing point. The excavation field lies to the south of Hirsel House with the walled garden adjacent (RCAHMS Aerial Photography Digital DP 013299) © RCAHMS

1.2 CIRCUMSTANCES OF EXCAVATION

In June 1977, when the Dial Knowe was chisel-ploughed, a number of carved stones were unearthed together with a large amount of stone debris. The carved stones included a cross head and shaft; cross-marked grave-markers and architectural fragments (Cramp and Douglas-Home 1980, pls 13–17; and Chapters 13 and 14 below), and clearly indicated an ecclesiastical site. The find was reported by Lady Caroline Douglas-Home, the then Factor of the estate, and the author visited the site and proposed a geophysical survey, since because of the plough drag it was not possible to locate the exact position from which the carved stones derived, although it was clearly in the northern half of the field.

Before any larger scale excavation there was a period of exploratory fieldwork. The 1978 geophysical survey, directed by Arnold Aspinall of Bradford University (Figure 1.6), concentrated on an area north of a break of slope bounded on the east by terraces leading down to the River Leet (see Chapter 2). Fred Bettess then recorded the site in a detailed contour survey which also established the site grid at 10m squares, aligned six minutes east of the National Grid north and eight minutes west of True North (Figure 1.7). This survey provided the basis for all subsequent work.

The geophysics identified what seemed to be a perimeter or some form of enclosure to the north of the area and, within it, other areas of high resistance (see Chapter 3), and since historical sources identified a parcel of land donated by the Earl of Dunbar for the foundation of Coldstream Priory which included a chapel, in existence by 1165–66, and a graveyard still in use in 1627 (Rogers 1879; Cramp and Douglas-Home 1980; and Chapter 2), this seemed a hopeful explanation for gravestones together with the anomalies revealed on the northern ridge of the field, although other features were noted on the higher ground to the south.

In order to test the nature of the geophysical anomalies and to provide some information to assist the estate in the management of the field, a

FIGURE 1.3
Aerial view of Hirsel House and the site in course of excavation in 1979, viewed from the north (Berwickshire NT 84 54. 1980 BW/3031) © RCAHMS

FIGURE 1.4
View of the site looking south from Hirsel House

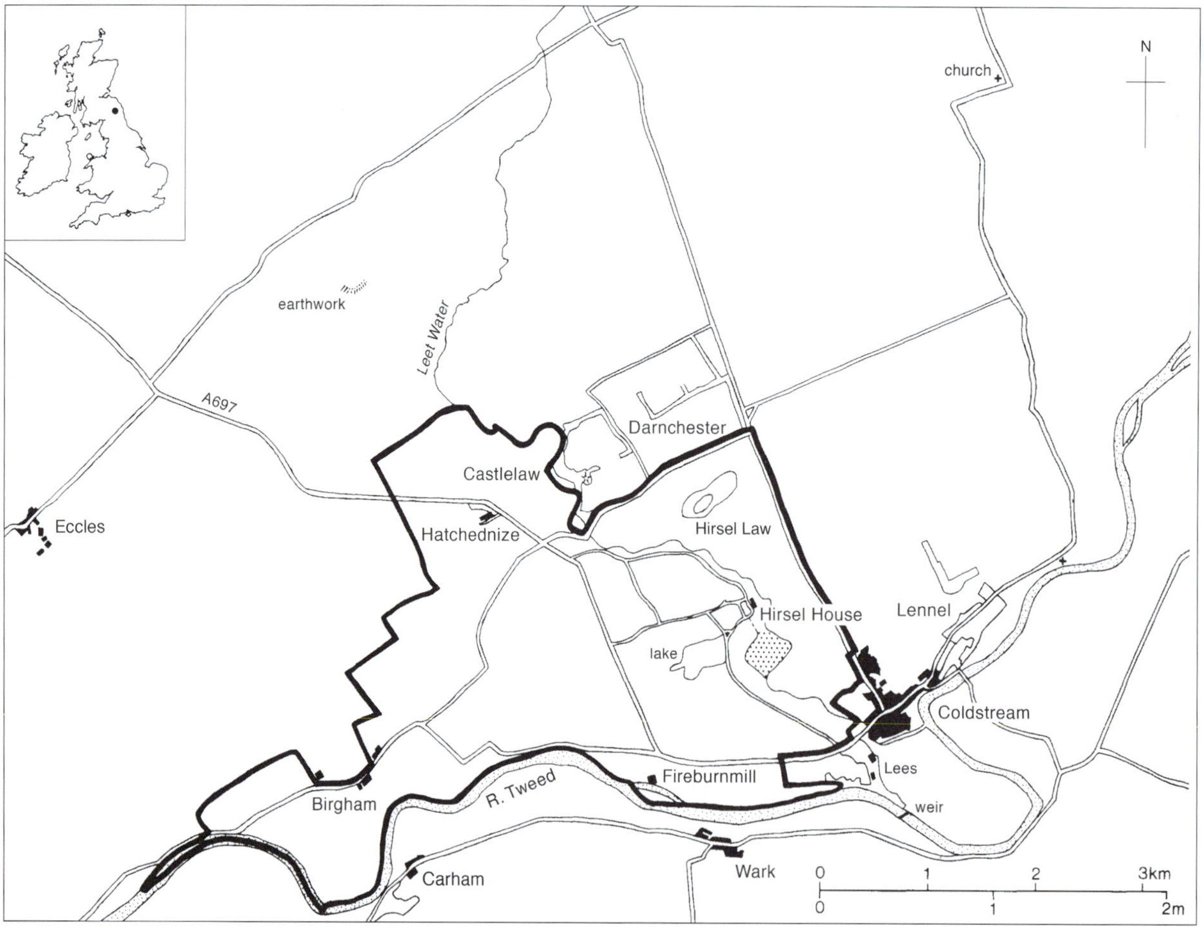

FIGURE 1.5
The Hirsel estate

FIGURE 1.6
Resistance survey in 1978; Arnold and Priscilla Aspinall in foreground

limited excavation was undertaken in 1979 by the Department of Archaeology, Durham University, under the direction of Rosemary Cramp. Four cuttings, identified as A–D (Figure 1.8) were opened and, concomitantly, a series of soil samples were taken across the site to test for the survival of pollen and organic remains (Chapter 10). Unfortunately the area proved unsuitable for pollen survival.

The excavation revealed Neolithic occupation in the western half of D, cut by medieval terracing; medieval structures and walling in B with, to the south, burials which extended into cutting C as far south as a wall. In cutting A, the 'boundary line', visible on the resistance survey, proved to be the edge of a gravel terrace, which had been partly reshaped by human action. In the north of the cutting was a section of palisade trench of uncertain date. The season's excavation was accompanied by further geophysical survey conducted by Arnold and Priscilla Aspinall and phosphate survey conducted by Michael Alexander and Gladys Bettess (see Chapter 3).

In 1980 the objective of the work was to examine a larger area of the burial ground revealed in the small cuttings of 1979, and to try to determine its western extent, also to investigate the nature of the small area of pitched stone foundations, discovered in cutting C in 1979. The northern sector, B, was reopened and extended eastwards, and a block (183–190/830–850) was opened up (from 1980 onwards the excavated areas on the site were defined by the grid references, see Figure 1.9). The 1980 excavations revealed the outlines of a small stone building (which by its form was reasonably identified as a church), and an extensive burial ground to the north of it. In 1981 the area around the church was extended west and south with a test cutting down the terraced slope to the river. The problems of photographing this scale of site were solved by a variety of ingenious means (Figure 1.10). In 1982 and 1984 this area (175–210/820–840) was further excavated. There was no excavation in 1983, which was assigned to post-excavation analysis.

The context for the discovery of the carved stones was therefore revealed and, in addition, there was evidence on the site for Neolithic, later prehistoric, Romano-British, and medieval occupation, this last beginning at an uncertain post-Roman date, although certainly by the 10th–11th century and extending through the 14th. There was also evidence for a limited use of the site extending to the end of the 17th–beginning of 18th century. After that the area seems to have been put down to pasture until the ploughing which occasioned the excavation.

The site record was kept on context sheets which were filled in on site by the supervisors and backed by their personal daybook records. Finds were checked and entered by context into a finds register on site. The phased plans were constructed during the post-excavation process and periods were loosely assigned to the activities identified. It has not been possible, because of the lack of closely dated pottery and other finds and the relatively few radiocarbon dates, to be very precise in dating the phases but see Figure 1.11. The absence of any pottery which can in current thinking be dated before around the 10th century and the lack of excavation under the nave of the church, and to the west and south where the surveys indicate activity may explain the lack of dated phases between the Roman period and the 10th century.

1.3 LOCATION OF RECORDS AND FINDS

All of the records will be deposited with the National Monuments Record for Scotland. The total finds record is to be held by National Museums Scotland as well as the major collections of environmental and artefactual material. A number of finds are displayed in the exhibition centre at The Hirsel.

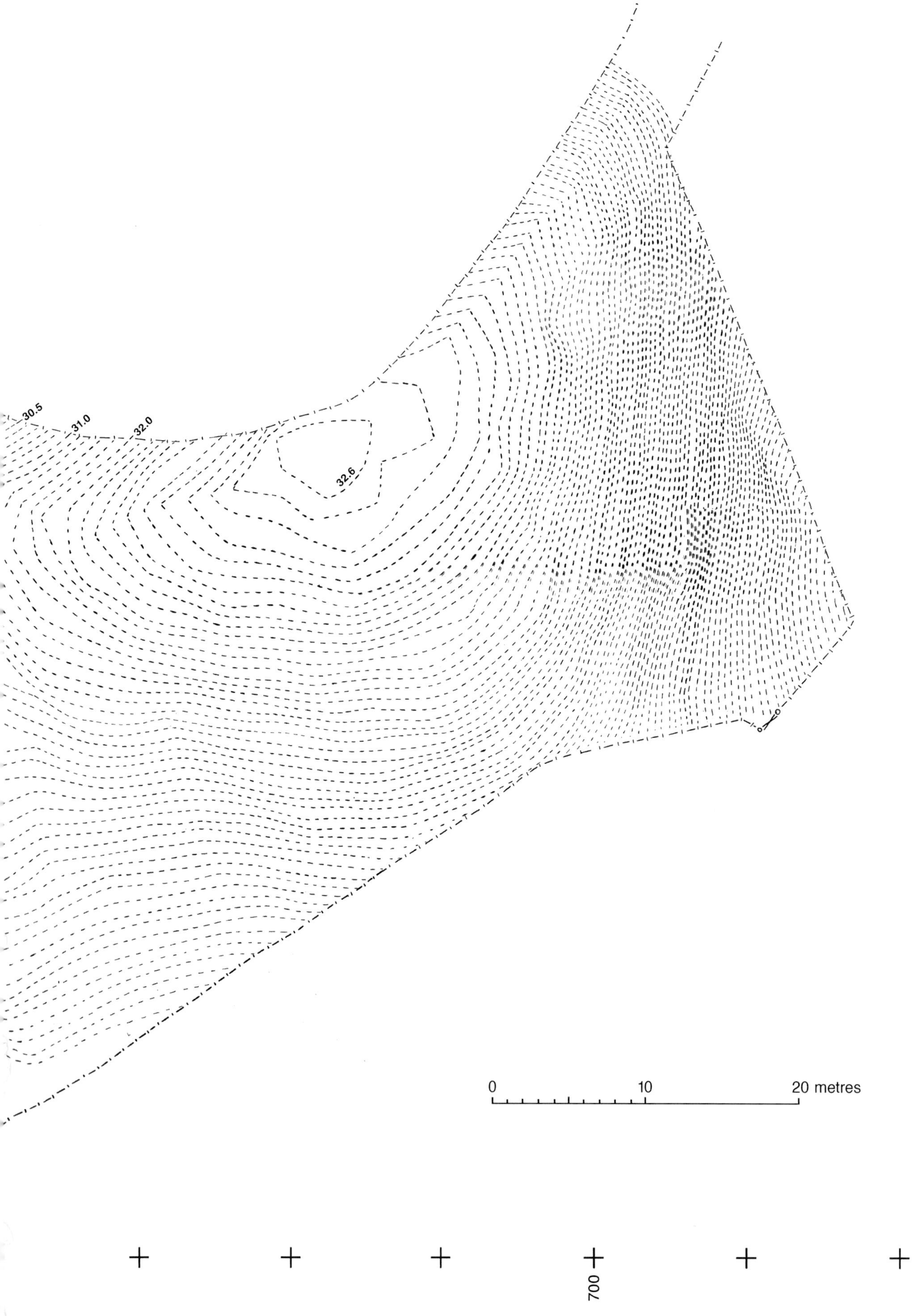
30.5
31.0
32.0
32.6
0
10
20 metres
700

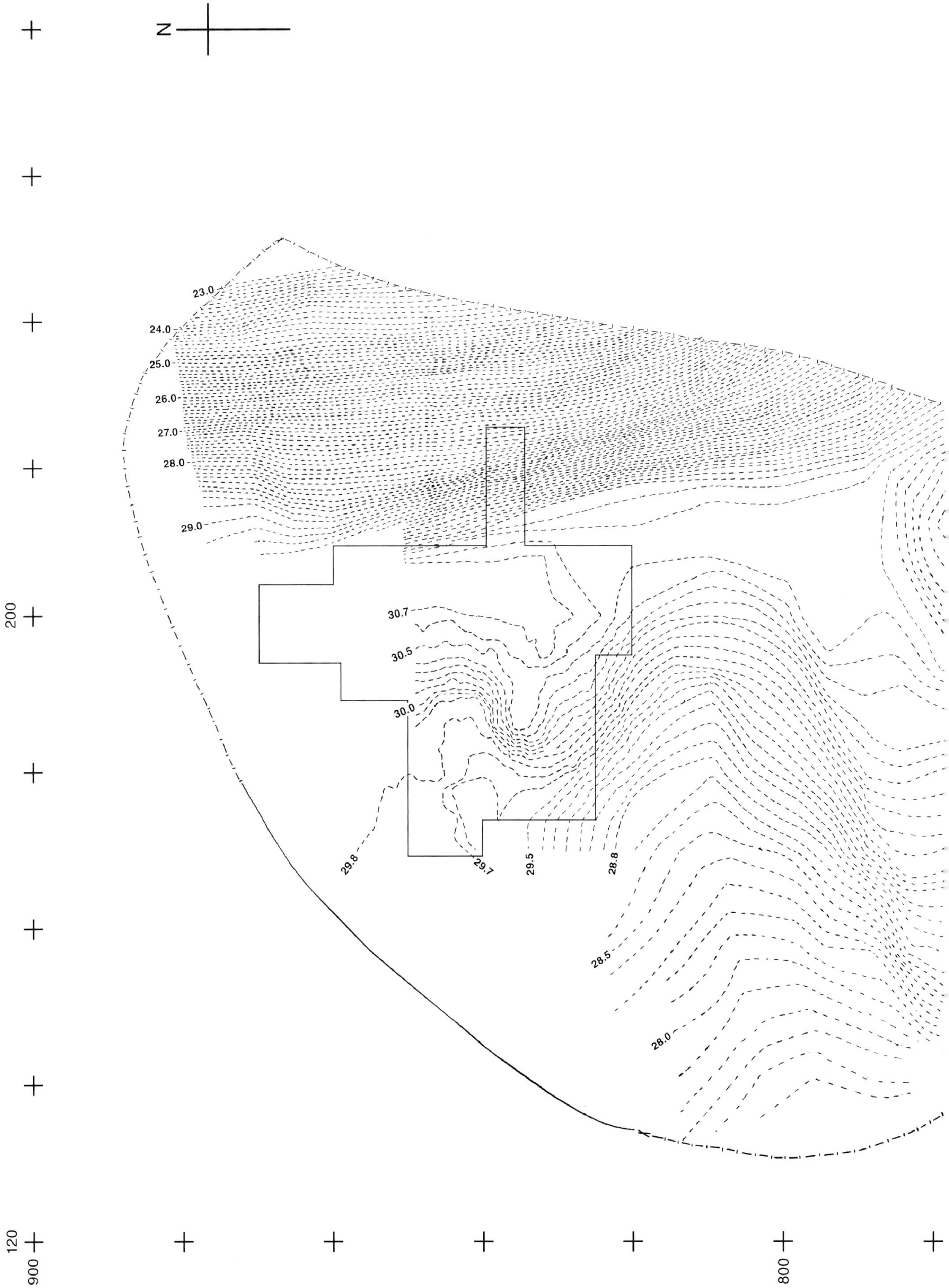

FIGURE 1.7
Contour survey with excavated area (Fred Bettess)

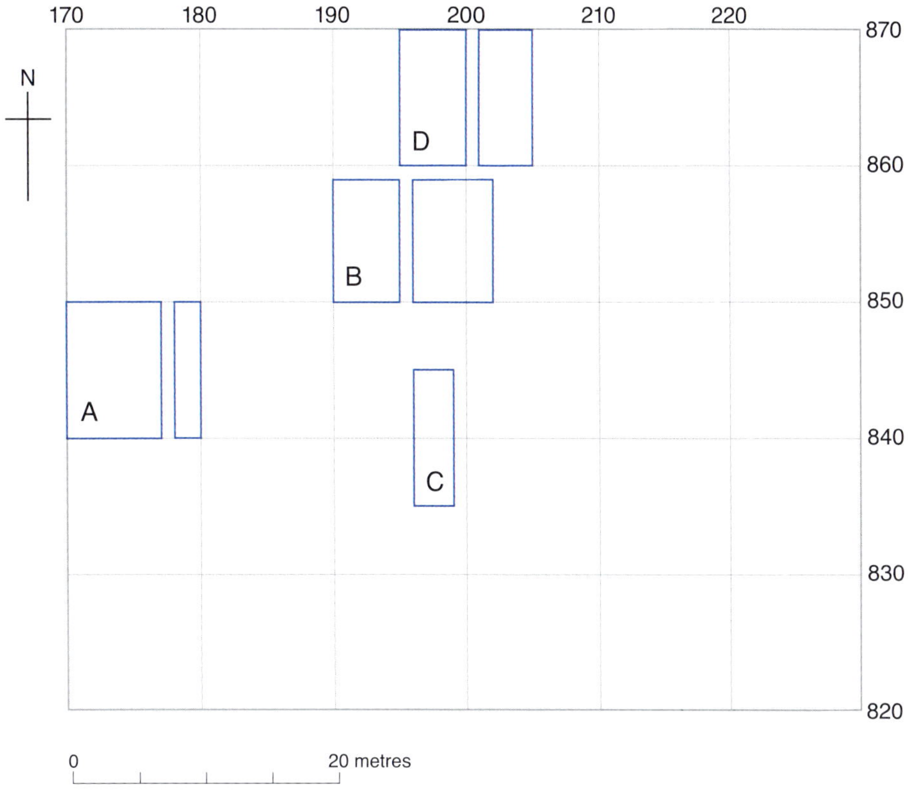

FIGURE 1.8
Location of excavation trenches in 1979

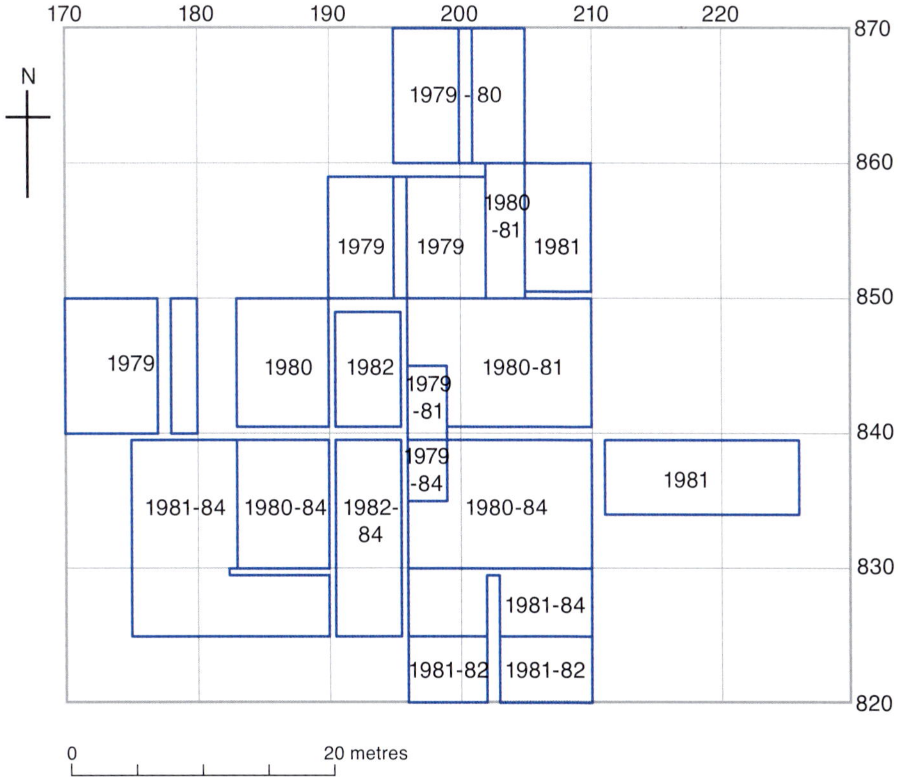

FIGURE 1.9
Areas excavated between 1979 and 1984

FIGURE 1.10

Three ways to take a site photograph: mobile (the haylift and climbing spikes), everyday use; the easy way (a one-day television visit); the fixed point (a tower for the 1981 season)

Phase	Period		Date	Activity
0	Natural			
1a	Neolithic	(Neol)		Settlement
1b	Later prehistoric	(LP1)	?	Woodland growth
2	Late Prehistory	(LP2)	Bronze Age/Iron Age	Presence
3	Roman/sub-Roman	(R)	1st–2nd century?	Presence nearby
4	Early medieval 1	(EM1)	9th–10th century	Beginning of church site
5	Early medieval 2	(EM2)	10th–12th century	Development of church and burial
6	Medieval	(Med)	12th–14th century	Church and settlement, burial ground developed
7	Late medieval	(LM)	14th–16th century	Robbing of church and use of nave
8	Early post-medieval	(EPM)	17th–18th century	Disuse of cemetery, construction of enclosure
9	Late post-medieval	(LPM)	18th–19th century	Site given over to pasture

FIGURE 1.11

Site phasing

2
THE ESTATE

2.1 THE REGION

Rosemary Cramp

The territory in south-east Scotland in which The Hirsel estate was embedded is the Berwickshire Merse, a low-lying area from the base of the Lammermuir Hills to the foothills of the Cheviots (Figure 1.1). The underlying rocks are carboniferous sandstones and in places igneous masses protrude forming natural strong points such as Hirsel Law (discussed below). The area physically is a prolongation of the Northumbrian plain with the Lammermuirs constituting the major physical barrier between England and Scotland, rather than the River Tweed, which despite its width and strong currents, is fordable at Norham and Coldstream.

The soils of the Merse are light and fertile (Figure 2.1), and in the later Middle Ages it was a notable corn producing area (RCAHMS 1915,

FIGURE 2.1
The ploughed out land of The Merse, with the north-west corner of the Hirsel estate marked by the tree line (RCAHMS Aerial Photography SC 973206) © RCAHMS

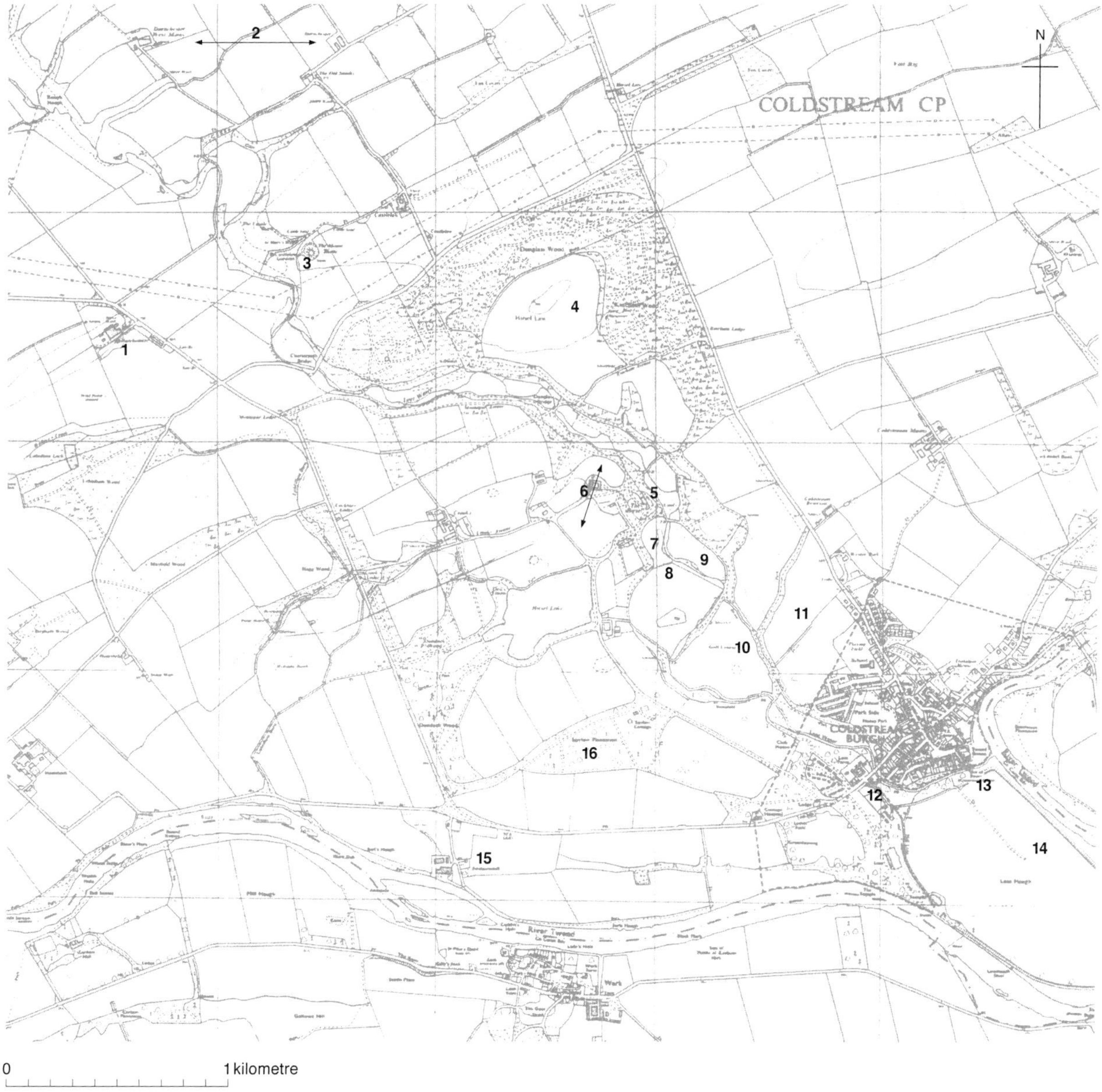

1 Hatchednize
2 Darnchester
3 Castlelaw
4 Hirsel Law
5 The Hirsel House
6 Old Countess Croft
7 Dial Knowe, archaeological site
8 Low Fields (Rondes)
9 Low Meadow
10 Mill Field, possibly part of Coldstream Acres
11 Coldstream Acres
12 Leet Mill, site of
13 Coldstream Priory, site of
14 ?*Braidhayhe*
15 Fireburn Farm
16 ?*Hyndislaw*

FIGURE 2.2
The Hirsel estate and its named elements (after Cramp and Douglas-Home 1980, fig 1)

xxiv), but bare of growing timber, which seems to have been largely cleared before historic times. This picture is borne out by the excavations which provide abundant evidence, from the earliest levels onwards, for cereal crops (especially oats, see Chapter 10), as well as evidence for the marshy areas from which the region derived its name, and, in the earlier archaeological contexts, of heather from the higher ground. It seems likely that, here as elsewhere, sheep raising became more intensive in the medieval period with the consequent pressure for extra pasture on the other habitats, and indeed disputes about the rights to pasture sheep occur in the Hirsel documentation (see below, and for a wider account of these problems, see Hamilton 2010, 151–157, 167).

2.2 THE HISTORICAL EVIDENCE FOR THE ESTATE, AND THE CHURCH AND CHURCHYARD

Rosemary Cramp

The River Tweed has, since at least the early 11th century, determined the line of the much disputed

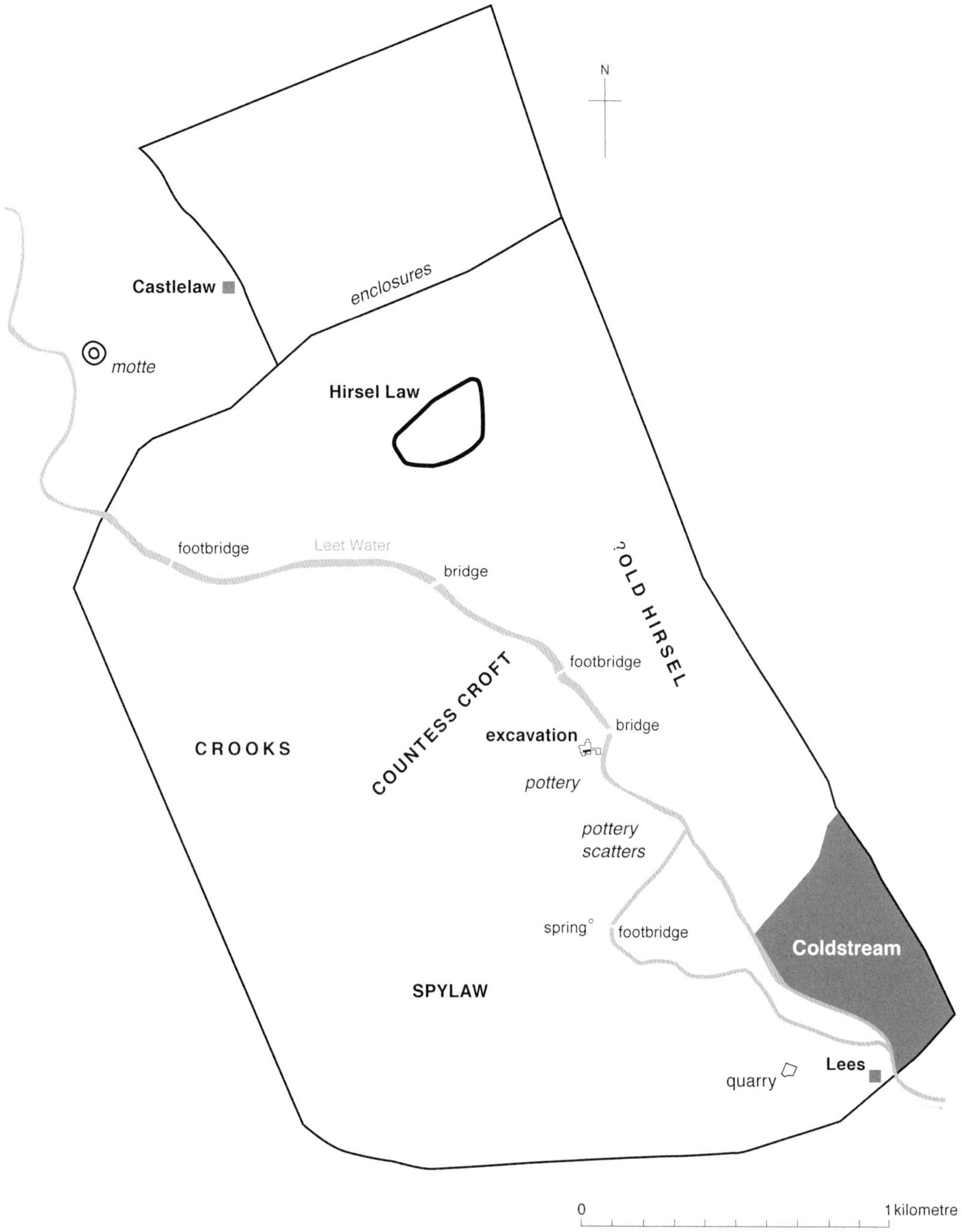

FIGURE 2.3
Sketch of the estate showing possible location of Old Hirsel, other sites mentioned in the early documents, and the archaeological evidence

border between England and Scotland (Barrow 2003, 119–125), but in earlier periods it appears that the region between the Tyne and the Forth 'formed a cultural and, more often than not, a political unity: first as the tribal territory of the Votadini; afterwards as the province of Bernicia' (Barrow 2003, 120), so that the Forth rather than the Tweed was the inter-tribal boundary. The low-lying, easily worked lands of the Merse have been attractive to settlement from prehistoric times onwards, but intensive cultivation over millennia has destroyed much of the archaeology of the area, whilst providing a rich harvest of crop marks, as for example circular enclosures around Dunglass Wood at The Hirsel (NT 845 W), or the 'fort' at Hatchetnize (Figures 1.5, 2.2 and 2.3) or further afield the Whitmuirhaugh early medieval settlement (St Joseph 1982).

Coldstream, the modern parish in which The Hirsel is located (Figure 2.4), is the main fording point of the Tweed on the east, although in the Roman period the major route crossing was Dere Street further west, leading to the fort of *Trimontium*/Newstead (McNeill and MacQueen

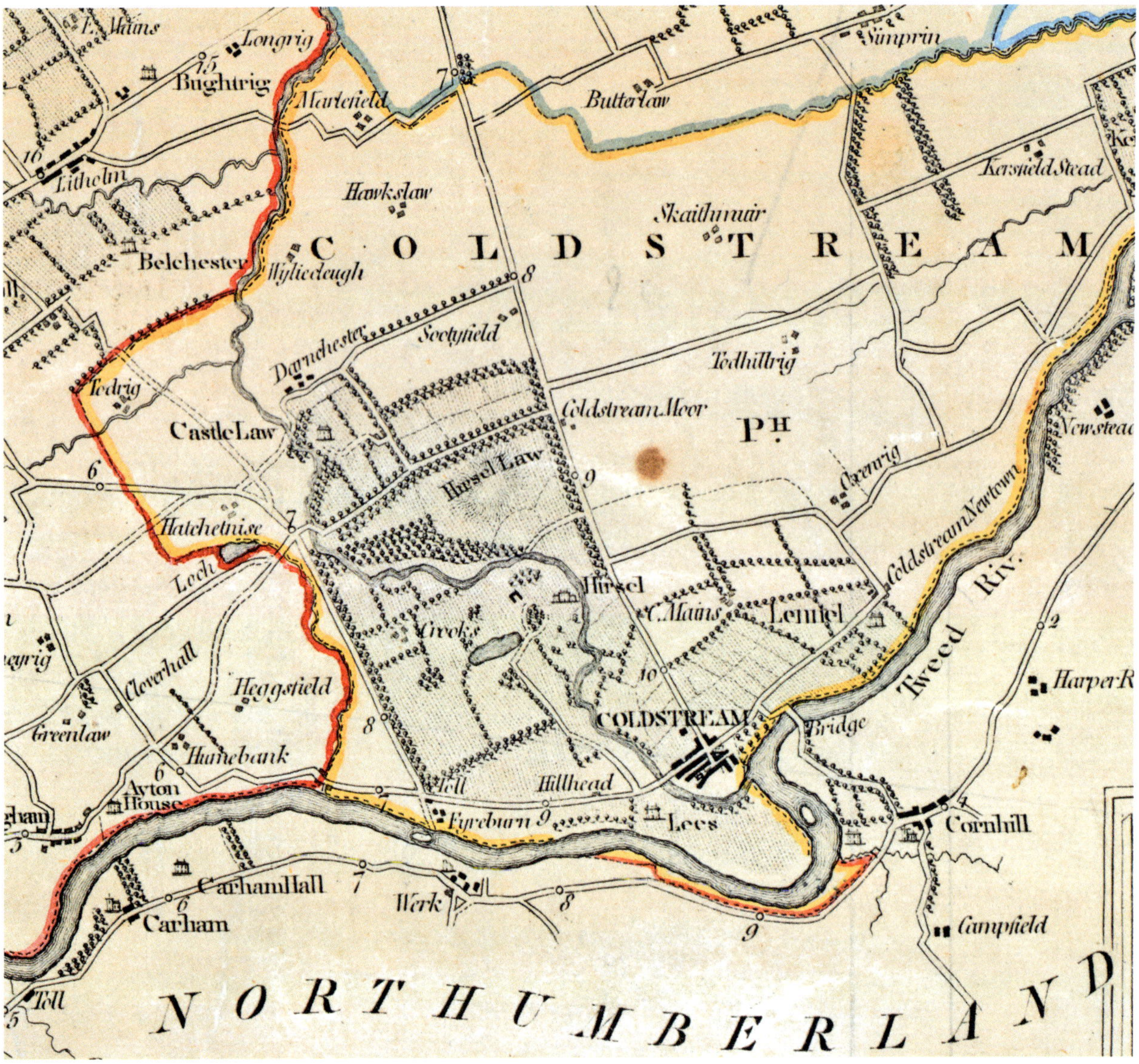

FIGURE 2.4
John Blackadder 1797, 'Berwickshire' (detail) © National Library of Scotland

1996, 38–44). This, the most northerly of the forts which survived the collapse of the Antonine Wall, seems to have been abandoned in the late 2nd century, but before then must have exercised considerable influence in the area, and the many native sites which were occupied in the nearby region (which would have included The Hirsel) have produced a scattering of Roman finds (McNeill and MacQueen, 1996, 45; see Chapter 16 below). From the 3rd to the 7th centuries the area seems to have reverted to governance from local tribal centres, probably as part of the hegemony of the Votadini, whose territory later formed part of the Anglo-British province of Bernicia, which plausibly had a southern limit along the River Tees (Barrow 2003, 135).

In the sub-Roman period, the border area seems to have been Brittonic speaking with little trace of Pictish influence (McNeill and MacQueen 1996, 51), although the Picts were, by the 4th century, a force which constantly threatened north Britain and their presence in the area of the estate is attested by the Pictish chains, seven out of the ten now surviving being found in the modern Borders region, and of these three were found in Berwickshire, one of them, from Greenlaw, being very near to The Hirsel (Elliott 1872, 18; J A Smith 1881). Unfortunately none of them was found in a good archaeological context, although the sites where they were found could merit further investigation, and their very association with the Picts has been questioned (A C Thomas 1995, 5–6) despite a more widely held view that they are distinctively Pictish. Modern research has favoured a view that dress ornaments are not necessarily an ethnic indicator, and these chains could seem to be more of a status symbol, in the tradition of the torques which distinguished some Celtic rulers. Moreover their use has a limited temporal and locational currency and may be seen as one of several manifestations of the way in which the peoples of North Britain created new identities in the 5th to 7th centuries.

A recent suggestion by Collins postulates that within the northern frontier zone there was a transformation of the soldierly garrisons at the Roman forts into local war bands whose leaders could operate like indigenous tribal chiefs (Collins 2011). A further complexity in the ethnic mixture in the Border area is the presence of Germanic speaking groups which became apparent in the sub-Roman period.

It has been suggested that '...it is possible also that there was Anglo-British contact beginning in late and sub-Roman times leading to widespread Anglo-British or Anglo-Pictish coexistence, either as isolated mercenaries or through settlement by Old English speaking communities with the permission of the local Britons or Picts' (Proudfoot and Aliaga-Kelly 1996, 11).

More recently the evidence for early acculturation between the Britons and Anglo-Saxons has been further discussed by Waddington in relation to settlements sites around Milfield, Northumberland (Passmore and Waddington 2012), and the recent work of Mark Wood on place-names has revealed a complex pattern of coexistence. In North Northumbria and the Borders, for example, there seems to be some form of Anglian-Brittonic interaction, whereas the Milfield and Till basins seem to have been Brittonic-controlled territory in the 6th and 7th centuries. In the Tweed basin there are contrasting patterns of evidence: 'One interpretation may be that a territory or territories centred on the mid-Tweed basin was either established or taken over at an early date by the Angles but a different process was involved in the coastal and lower valley territory, with possible Brittonic continuity and only a limited Anglian presence until the late seventh or eighth century' (Wood 2011, 65).

Certainly, however, by the 6th century Angles had settled on the coastal fringes of North Britain, with a major centre at Bamburgh, and had penetrated inland to sites such as Yeavering or Milfield where settlements of this period have been identified by aerial photography and partially excavated (Hope-Taylor 1977; Johnson and Waddington 2009, 155–174; O'Brien, 2011). There is however a lack of contemporary excavated settlements of this period to the north of the Tweed, although the cropmark site at Whitmuirhaugh near Sprouston (Roxburghshire) is of a closely similar form to that of Milfield/*Maelmin* (see Smith 1992), and the area of the lower and middle Tweed valley, together with the whole eastern area south of the Forth, contains a dense distribution of Anglian settlement names, with the Merse specially defined as a focus (Smith 1990, fig 7.1; McNeill and MacQueen 1996, 61). The period from the late 7th to early 9th century, when the area was part of the Anglian kingdom of Northumbria, has left an indelible mark on the settlement pattern, especially in relation to the place-names, but recently the few stray finds such as the Anglo-Saxon figure decorated plaque from Ayton (Blackwell 2007) have been augmented by other discoveries of metalwork (Campbell 2009, 257–259, fig 11.2). In the earliest post-Roman phase however, it is not clear how often Anglian centres of power and their estates represent a takeover of an earlier native settlement pattern, but in the Merse, as Smith has illustrated, there is an abiding Anglian influence in the area, with the Roman road of Dere Street providing the western boundary, and the coast the eastern.

The nature and organisation of the Christian church in the region up to this period is problematic. If there was an organised church in the Roman period which continued into the 5th century, there would have had to be some presence of bishops to fulfil the functions of ordination and confirmation, but although the inscription on the Peebles stone (Thomas 1971, 16–18) could imply the presence of bishops, it has not been possible to define the boundaries for any diocese in northern Britain, and it seems probable that the bishops were peripatetic, attached to native tribes and their kingdoms, rather than to a diocese based on a single major centre (Thomas 1981, 267–270). The diocese could then be the political unit and such a political unit has been suggested for the upper Tweed region (Forsyth 2005, 120–121). The 'Eccles' names (derived from vulgar Latin *ecclesia*) could imply, as Barrow suggested, a British Christian centre in the region, embracing a large *parochia*, as well as being the centre of an old shire (Barrow 1973, 30; 2003, 23 and map 3). The Hirsel would have been in that case contained in the orbit of Eccles, but what one should expect to discover physically in such dependencies is uncertain, since cist burials, which used to be considered indicators of Christian practice and of a sub-Roman date, continue in sporadic use much later (see Chapter 6).

No traces of churches from this period, other than the partially excavated church of Auldhame (Hindmarsh and Melikian 2008), have been found in this area of southern Scotland although the dedications to saints with Celtic names such as St Bathan could imply their presence. There were certainly monasteries by the 7th century, such as Melrose (which became a dependency of Lindisfarne), but there has been no excavation of the main site at Melrose although the perimeter has been explored (Thomas 1971, 35, fig 11). It seems likely within the earlier large territories served by the monasteries that lesser churches were founded, as in England, by local landowners on their estates and there developed a coincidence of parish and manor (Cowan 1995, 1–5), with the estate's lands and tenants supporting the church with tithes (teinds) and it was such proprietary churches that were later appropriated to support the newly founded monasteries of the 11th and 12th centuries (see Chapter 27).

On present evidence it appears that the earliest churches were constructed in wood, both before and after the Northumbrian takeover of the region, as the Whitmuirhaugh cropmark (Smith 1992) or the Ardwall and Whithorn excavations demonstrate (Thomas 1967, 169–172; Hill 1997, 146–153, fig 4.12). The first church at Lindisfarne is recorded as of hewn oak 'in the manner of the Scots' (Bede, *HE* III 25, Plummer 1896, 181), which could imply that there were distinctions in wooden architecture between that of the Scots of Argyll and the Angles, although not necessarily between the Angles and the Britons. In addition, as with the earliest structure at The Hirsel, church buildings could have been formed from dry or earth-bonded stone which were later obliterated by mortared stone structures. So far the evidence is sparse, but the lack of surviving early church structures is not just a phenomenon north of the Tweed but pertains also on the south of the Border in Cumbria and Northumberland (see also Chapter 27).

The extensive territory claimed by Durham as once in the ownership of the church of Lindisfarne would have included The Hirsel. The *Historia de Sancto Cuthberto* 4 (Johnson South 2002) is the only source for the boundaries of the area of this land-holding and although it is a matter of debate as to whether the territory claimed was held by Lindisfarne as early as the lifetime of St Cuthbert, its boundaries are quite specific. The grant included an area of 'land beyond the Tweed from the place where the river Adder rises in the north as far as the place where it flows into the Tweed, and all the land that lies on the east side of the water that is called the Leader as far as the place where it flows into the Tweed towards the south' (Barrow 2003, map 3; Morris 1977; Smith 1990, 7.20; Johnson South 2002, 46–47). In the *Historia* 2, Cuthbert was said to be tending his lord's sheep by the River Leader when he decided to enter the religious life.

The Lindisfarne estates had become debateable land by the 10th century, at a time when Northumbrian power had been weakened by internal wars and Scandinavian incursions and settlements, and when the Picto-Scottish kings had become stronger and more aggressive. The religious community of Lindisfarne with its bishop moved south to Chester-le-Street and then Durham and, from about the 940s, lost control of their lands north of the Tweed. From that time it seems that the area came under the ecclesiastical jurisdiction of the Scottish bishop of St Andrews. But the bishops of Durham did not cease to pursue their claim to lands and religious establishments north of the Tweed and in the Tweed valley, despite the fact that the area was under the political control of the Scots king by the 10th century. Simeon of Durham records that bishop Ealdhun was heart-broken at the defeat of the Northumbrians at the battle of Carham in 1018 (Arnold 1886, 84; Duncan 1976, 21). This is the battle which Barrow in his discussion of the Anglo-Scottish Border says '...put the English of Northumbria on the defensive for a generation or so, south of a Border which fundamentally was already defined' (Barrow 2003, 123).

In fact, the church at Durham did gain land in Coldinghamshire and Berwickshire under Edgar in 1095, and its estates (as derived from a charter of William Rufus, which recorded the estates ceded in Berwickshire to Durham) were west of Berwick between the Whiteadder and the Tweed (Barrow 2003, map 3). These included neighbouring parishes to The Hirsel at Lennel and Birgham. In the later dismemberment of Berwickshire, Birgham and Lennel were acquired by the Dunbars, but we have no record of who held The Hirsel before the foundation of Coldstream Priory.

The estate of The Hirsel and its ownership

The Hirsel estate and its church enter recorded history when they are mentioned as part of the foundation donation for Coldstream Priory by Gospatric, Earl of Dunbar, and his wife Derder *c*1160–1165 or earlier (*Cold. Cart.*, 6, no. 8; 8, no. 11)[1] the grant being confirmed by Bishop Richard of St Andrews in 1166 (*Cold. Cart.*, 46–47). For the powerful lords who were granted lands in southern Scotland in the 12th century, there can hardly have been a cultural divide along a notional border since they held lands on either side of it and were equally at home in the courts of the English and the Scots kings. The Dunbars were also cross-border lords with extensive land holdings in Northumberland (Hamilton 2010, map 5) whilst in Scotland their vast estates stretched from the Tweed to the Whiteadder (an area which was, as noted above, the heartland of the old Lindisfarne holdings), and then in a broad swathe around the fortress of Dunbar from which they eventually were to take their title (Perry 2 000, illus 5; Hamilton 2010, map 4). The Hirsel estate was then at the southern limit of the Earl's territory in Scotland, but not far from the most northerly of his estates in Northumberland (Figure 2.5).

The family was in origin not Norman, but English, descended from the royal house of Wessex and from the ancient house of Bamburgh, which had maintained some independence from both the Scandinavian and West Saxon rulers in the 10th century, but whose members had later taken refuge in Cumbria, an area ruled over by the Scottish kings from 1018 to 1092. The insertion, in the 11th century, of a Brittonic name — Gospatric — amongst the traditional Germanic names of

FIGURE 2.5
Major identifiable lands of the earls of Dunbar in the 12th and 13th centuries in Lothian and the Merse with lands granted to Coldstream Priory (after Hamilton 2010)

the lineage may well have been derived from the Cumbrian connection as indeed likewise the name Dolfin of the lord who was ousted from Carlisle in 1092 by William Rufus. Dolfin was either the son or nephew of the Gospatric (Gospatric I), who had held the earldom of Northumbria, had been deprived of his office by William I (allegedly for treachery), and was granted Dunbar and the lands surrounding it, *c*1072, by the Scottish King Malcolm III. The tangled and often obscure story of the descent of the house of Gospatric has been recently critically reviewed by Elsa Hamilton who has provided a clear and authoritative account of the establishment of the dynasty and the careers of the first three lords of Dunbar: Gospatric I, II, and III (Hamilton 2010, 5–75, table 1). Gospatric II was granted land by both the king of the Scots and Henry I of England, and his lands in Northumberland, as Hamilton points out, significantly straddled the route between Corbridge and Berwick, thus providing a strong control on the borders of both kingdoms (Hamilton 2010, 36–38).

Gospatric II died in 1138–39 and was succeeded by his son Gospatric III, who styled himself Earl of Dunbar, and it was due to his largesse that the convent at Coldstream owed its foundation, supported by lands and incomings from estates around, including The Hirsel (Figure 2.4). Although the Earl endorsed the gift of The Hirsel, it was his wife, the Countess Derder, who donated from the estate *unam carucatam terre de terra de Hirsill, et ecclesiam de eadem villa* ('a ploughgate of land from the land of Hirsel and the church of that vill') (*Cold. Cart.*, nos 8 and 11).

How the Countess with the Irish Gaelic name Deirdriu/Deirdre inherited The Hirsel estate — whether as a family possession or a wedding gift — is unknown, but there is the possibility that the estate could have been part of her own family holdings (Hamilton 2010, 54). Indeed the earls' acquisition of lands in the Merse and to its western reaches is something of a mystery and it can only be surmised whether they were acquired through marriage or a royal grant.

Unfortunately the history of the Countess's family is also a mystery. Thomas Clanchy (pers comm) suggests that her name, that of a heroine in a Gaelic heroic tale, 'is not a name usually given, as far as we can see, to real people', but could fit in 'with a range of names across the linguistic communities in 12th and 13th century Scotland where people seem to have adopted names from literature'. Of course if her family had moved with Gospatric from Cumbria, an area which remained native speaking and with some strong Irish links, an Irish name could be traditional in the family. Her name however does add to the other hints of Irish connections in the Tweed valley which have recently been remarked (Forsyth 2005, 121–122).

In this area of cross-border cultures there is a similar ambiguity in the etymology of the estate name which is variously spelled in the Coldstream Charters as *Herishill(e)*, *Herisehill*, *Hirsell*, as well as elsewhere as *Hershale*. The name has usually been associated with the Middle Scots *hirsale/hirsel*, 'flock of sheep, ground where a flock of sheep were pastured', derived from Old Norse *hirzla*, 'custody or safe keeping'. An Old Norse word could also have a Cumbrian origin, since it was an area heavily settled by the Scandinavians, but Williamson has suggested that the 'flock of sheep' interpretation was a late association with a Scottish word and that the name could be in origin English, incorporating the word 'hill' with a doubtful first element (Williamson 1942, 47). A further suggestion could be that it was an Old English name incorporating the word *here*, 'lord', used in the genitive, and so it could be *hereshill*, 'the lord's hill'. In the light of the importance of Hirsel Law in the history of the estate (discussed at length below) this is an attractive idea, but of course there is plenty of ideal grazing for sheep on the estate pastures and the common later meaning could be possible at an earlier date.

The Hirsel is now in the burgh of Coldstream, but that name is not used in the foundation charter of the priory of Coldstream, where Earl Gospatric granted land *sororibus de Witehou* ('to the sisters of *Witehou*'), and this name, which could mean 'white hill' has not been identified and located, although within the context of the sentence the place would seem to be less likely to refer to their new location than where the sisters had come from. Possible topographical names for religious communities in England which could have connections with the Earl's family have been discussed by Hamilton, but without a conclusive identification (Hamilton 2010, 70–71). Rogers' suggestion that *Witehou* was an earlier name for Coldstream (*Cold. Cart.*, viii) is also inconclusive, although it might have referred to a nearby settlement where the nuns stayed whilst the monastery was being built. But the name 'Coldstream' for the priory makes an appearance soon afterwards in Bishop Richard's confirmation of the donation to the priory (*Cold. Cart.,* 46, Appendix no. 1). It is a simple topographic name and it has been suggested that it might have derived from the Leet or even the Tweed (Williamson 1942, 68). The buildings of the Cistercian house at Coldstream are no longer extant, although the site is marked on early maps and it has left its mark on the place-names in the town such as Abbey Road and Nun's Walk. Recently Michael Hickman has, with the aid of a sketch plan of 'St Mary's Abbey, lands and buildings' dated 1589, been able to locate its elements more closely (Hickman 2010, 31–33).

The series of charters which record the gifts of land from The Hirsel estate to Coldstream Priory, in *Carte Monialium de Caldstrem*, potentially provide much valuable background to the site and estate (Cramp and Douglas-Home 1980, 223–227). The foundation gift of Gospatrick III and his wife Derder has been quoted above and the grant was confirmed by their son Waldeve the fourth Earl (*Cold. Cart.*, 18, no. 26), although by this time The Hirsel had passed to his younger brother, Patrick. The land grant, with the church and its pertinents, was confirmed by Derder's grandsons, Patrick the fifth Earl, and William, Earl Patrick's cousin, who inherited the land from his father Patrick (*Cold. Cart.*, 11, no. 15 and 12, no. 17). So the estate seems to have continued in the junior branch of the family. Elsa Hamilton has noted how, by the late 12th century, the Dunbar earls had become, with the earls of Fife, leading magnates in the Scottish kingdom. Patrick I, with his marriage in 1184 to Ada, natural daughter of William I, became the son in law of the king. Patrick II, his successor, was described on his death in 1248 as the most powerful magnate in Scotland, while Patrick III was the confidant of both Alexander III and Henry III (Hamilton 2010, tables 2 and 3). Their social contacts could then have affected the buildings they caused to be built and patronised. The sites of their main power centres are debateable; some may have been old centres of power at which they maintained a presence in various ways either by secular or ecclesiastical settlements. Eccles was obviously recognised as an important site and the Dunbar connection is underlined by the fact that at least one of the Dunbar earls was buried there: Patrick I was buried at Eccles in 1232 (Hamilton 2010, 172).

Hamilton considers that the flat-topped motte at Castlelaw (Figures 2.2, 2.3, 2.4, 2.6) could have

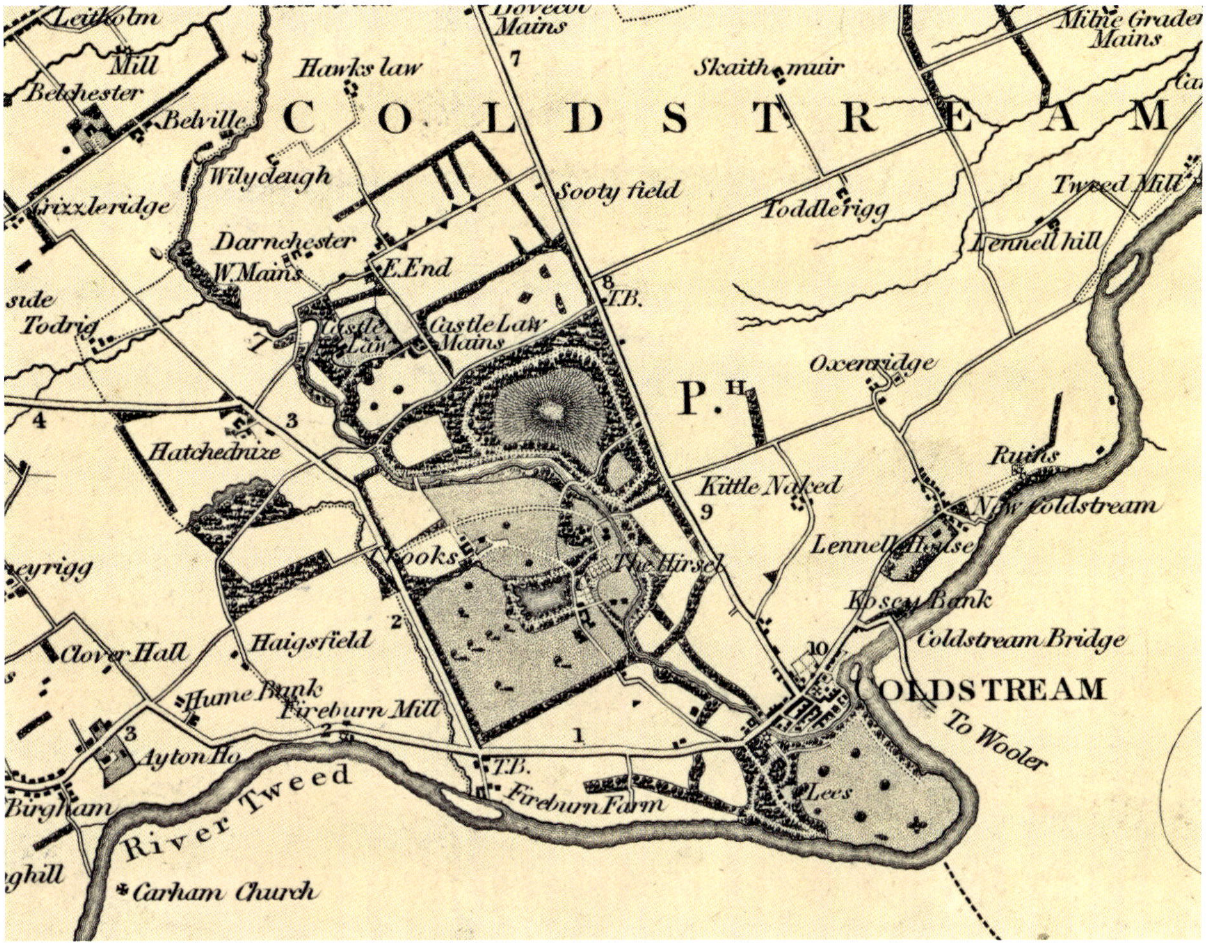

FIGURE 2.6
Christopher Greenwood 1826, right side: The County of Berwick (detail) © National Library of Scotland

been a major centre of Dunbar power, and this may indeed, in the Middle Ages, have been the political centre of the wider grouping of Dunbar lands in the western Merse. The antiquity of the motte before the Middle Ages has, however, not been demonstrated whilst Hirsel Law (the largest enclosed prehistoric site in the region and one which dominates the Tweed Valley at that point) does continue to act as a focus of power, although not necessarily as a settlement. A case can indeed be made that the prehistoric hill top site could have been the foundation centre of the original Hirsel estate, as discussed below. The donation of The Hirsel church with incomings implies that it was a proprietary church with a parochial status and its 'parish' may have been coterminous with the estate (Cowan 1995, 7–9).

The Countess Derder's donation of land was probably not a compact unit and further grants were added which perhaps consolidated the holding. William, Derder's grandson, grants in Charter 18: '...*terram que dicitur Rondes et pratum que vocator Bradspotes in territorio meo de Herissill*' ('land which is called *Rondes* and the meadow which is called *Bradspotes* in my territory of Hirsel) (*Cold. Cart.*, 13). It is possible that *Rondes*, 'a border of land on a river bank', could be what is now known as the Low Field (Figure 2.2; and Cramp and Douglas-Home 1980, 225).

In Charter 24, William confirms his grant adding more names: '...*totam terram quam tenent in feodo meo de Hersill scilicet terram que vocatur Thothhereg et Spechenes et Kaldestreflat*' ('...all the land which they hold in his feu of Hirsel, that is, the land called *Thotheryg* and *Spechenes* and *Kaldestreflat*') (*Cold. Cart.*, 17). These are long lived names which in the 16th century are plausibly mutated into Todrig, a farm still in existence to the north of The Hirsel estate near to Darnchester, Hatchednize and Coldstream flats (Figure 2.2; Cramp and Douglas-Home 1980, 225–226).

Another parcel of land was granted to the nuns by Patrick the fifth Earl in Charter 19: '...*terram illam apud Herssil que iacet iuxta Let ex australi parte pontis sicut eam eisdem perambulavi habendam et tenendam de me et heredibus meiis...*' ('...land at Hirsel which is next to the Leet, south of the bridge as I have perambulated it for them [the nuns] to have and to hold from me and my heirs...' (*Cold. Cart.*, 13–14).

FIGURE 2.7
John Blaeu, and Timothy Pont, 'Blaeu Atlas of Scotland, 1654' (detail)
© National Library of Scotland

In Charter 20, his son Patrick (later the sixth Earl) granted: '....*totam illam terram juxta Let que vocatur Putanyshalwe scilicet de Let ex parte orientali totaliter usque ad terram dictarum monialium*' ('...all that land next to the Leet which is called Putanyshalwe, that is on the east side right up to the land of the said nuns') (*Cold. Cart.*, 14).

An earlier attempt to locate these named areas was only partially successful (Cramp and Douglas-Home 1980, 224–226), and the picture is complicated by the fact that some lands have been subdivided, like the 'Countess Croft' (which may have been the original donation), but it is remarkable that so many names have survived from the Middle Ages and that the estate has remained so intact. Where lands can be identified they form a compact group in the south-east of the estate and are closely associated with the River Leet right up to the priory estate. The Leet indeed remains a clear point of reference in dividing off the nuns' holdings on the east bank from those of other tenants into the 16th and 17th centuries, and possibly in dividing Hirsel from Old Hirsel (Figure 2.3).

The distinction between the territory of Hirsel and of Old Hirsel is found as early as the charters of Earl Patrick II (1232–1248), who granted to Coldstream Priory one carucate of land at *Haldhersehyll*, this being a parcel of land which had been held with heredity rights by 'Walter called the chaplain' but he had forfeited it for defect of service to the Earl (*Cold. Cart.*, 11, no. 16). In Charter 21 (*Cold. Cart.*, 15), Walter of Darnchester donated 12 acres '*in Veteri Herissill*' and that was witnessed by John the Chaplain of Hirsel. This donation was confirmed by Thomas of Darnchester, his son, in Charter 23 (*Cold. Cart.*, 16). Over the centuries, however, the distinction between Hirsel lands and Old Hirsel lands, which seem to have been attached to Hirsel Law, became blurred and a matter for dispute.

The Dunbars forfeited lands to the crown in 1435–1436, and these included lands at Birgham and Hirsel (Hamilton 2003, 131). Their powerful role in the borders was taken over by the Douglases, and by the 15th century this was the most powerful and influential family in the Merse, yet by the middle of that century the family of Home had strengthened its position and in the aftermath of the crushing of the Douglas power by James II the Homes became the greatest family on the Merse (RCAHMS 1915, 15, xix–xx). In the following century, when Sir Andrew Kerr and Alexander Lord Home held some land at The Hirsel towards the end of the life of Coldstream Priory, an interesting law suit took place in 1566, regarding the proprietorship of lands of Auld Hirsell as well as the rights of the Coldstream convent (Burton 1877, 309–314). The depositions of witnesses in the action revealed something of the later medieval topography of The Hirsel, as well as the confusion in the nomenclature, and the continuing importance of Hirsel Law. The witnesses' testimony was rambling but John Polwart (aged *c*80) claimed that he knew only one hill called Hirsellaw which is east of the water (river) and the said hill where witnesses 'were resarvit' was always called Auld Hirsel. He then added the confusing statement that 'sum men callit ane auld house besyde the Kirksted of Hirsell Auld Hirsell, quhilk Auld Hirsell was sett with all landis of Hirsell that Schir Andrew Kerr now occupies... And sum men callit the samen the Kirkshott' (Reg. Privy Council 1545–1689, 309–310).

This mention of a house by the Kirksted is an interesting testimony to the memory of the church and to a house near to it, evidence for which was revealed by excavation (see Chapter 7). Another witness, John Watson, could not say whether the Hirsell Law was the property of Hirsell or Coldstream (priory) but 'as to the landis of Auld Hirsell, sayis that there is an auld house sted lyand on the west side of the Watter of Leit hard besyde the kirkyard quilk is callit the house of Auld Hirsell' (Reg. Privy Council 1545–1689, 311). He further testified that the grazing for the prioress was on the east side of the river 'forananet the place of Hirsell quhilk is now biggit' (Reg. Privy Council 1545–1689, 312). Another witness also mentions 'Putanishaugh' which lies 'on the eist syd of the Watter foranent the new house of Hirsel' (Reg. Privy Council 1545–1689, 314). This places the original lord's house at Hirsel probably on the site of the present Hirsel House and dates it as shortly before 1566. In later documents there is a reference to a tower which accompanies the lands of Hirsel west of the Leet (*Reg. Mag. Sig.* 1620–1633, no. 186, 1621 and 1624) (Figure 2.7, where such a tower is depicted).

Andrew Home (aged *c*68) testified in the *Register of the Privy Council* that the place where the witnesses were received was known as Blak Hirsell and Auld Hirsell. This was where the Coldstream nuns pastured their sheep on the east side of the Leet. On the west side of the waters of Leet the land was Hirsell and occupied by Sir Andrew Kerr, except certain pieces which pertain to the prioress. Another testified that he had never heard the Law called Hirsellaw but Auld Hirsell, another that the hill was called Black Hirsel because it was overgrown with heather (which sounds like a folk etymology).

In summary then, the original grant and the name of the areas such as Countescroft and Coldstreamflats persisted into the 16th century and the Countescroft until today. There was a distinction between the lands east and west of the River Leet, those on the east attached to Hirsel Law and on the west just to the territory of Hirsel. Up to the Dissolution, the Coldstream nuns maintained their rights to pasture mainly on the east side of the river but also to part of the lands to the west, although as time passed, as the dispute above illustrates, this was not without difficulty.

As late as 1535, the prioress of Coldstream received further land at The Hirsel: a half husbandland with pertinents (Rogers 1879, xxix, Appendix VII, 55). The convent was burnt to the ground by the Earl of Hertford in 1545, and in the subsequent valuation of its assets these are described as paid out of the lands (amongst others) of *Lanaile, Hirsell, Todrig... Kirk of Hirsell* and *Bassinden* (*Cold. Cart.*, xxxiii). In the *Books of Assumption* of the mid-16th century the record of rentals paid to the priory of Coldstream, 'Auldhirsell with uther pertinentis of the same haldin', paid a substantial sum of £20, whilst Hirsel only pays 3 c (chalders) of victuals, but other elements of the original Dunbar donations, such as 'Leis', Hatchnis, Todrig and Dernchester, are now considered separately (Kirk 1995, 186). These holdings are now outside the bounds of the existing Hirsel estate (Figure 2.2). The church at The Hirsel had gone out of use long before the 16th century (see Chapter 5), but the name 'Kirk of Hirsill' is an interesting link with the continuing intermittent use of the kirkyard up to the 17th century, which the excavation of the cemetery has demonstrated, as also with the law suits quoted above.

Lennel has survived as the parish for Coldstream, after the priory disappeared in 1621, and seems, from an unrecorded date, to have included The Hirsel, the ecclesiastical situation being set out in a report signed in the church in 1627: 'as for cheplanries we know none to be within our said parish bot ther hes bein of old neir to the Hirsell ather chappell or kirk quair of ther is onlie restand ane kirk yaird callit Granton kirkyard possessit be the Earle of Home and we know no benefeit belonging thairto' (Robson 1896, 70).

Granton is shown on Robert Gordon's map of *c*1640 (Figure 2.8) alongside the name Hirsell, but it is impossible at the map scale to determine whether this could be in the location of the burial ground excavated at The Hirsel (see Chapter 6). Later maps provide no record of the burial ground, but the distinctive shape of the estate survives, and has survived to the present day, in the ownership of the same family: the Homes. In 1605 George Home was created Earl of Dunbar and in 1611 the family exchanged most, if not all, of their land around Jedburgh for the Kerr land at The Hirsel (Hickman 2010, 22; CDLHS 2010, 209).

2.3 THE TOPOGRAPHY OF THE ESTATE

Rosemary Cramp

The boundaries of the estate have changed little since the earliest maps, for example on Armstrong's map of 1771 (Figure 2.9). It fronts on to the River Tweed with the resources that this provides for

FIGURE 2.8
Robert Gordon (1580–1661), 'A description of the province of the Merche. The Mers' (c1636–1642) (detail) © National Library of Scotland

FIGURE 2.9
Andrew and Mostyn Armstrong, 1771, 'Map of the County of Berwick' (detail) © National Library of Scotland

fishing, transport and milling. The position of a mill adjacent to the old fording place of the Tweed at Fireburn Mill marked on the early modern maps could well have continued from the medieval period. The River Leet bisects the estate and encloses the site of the church and cemetery. It served as a tenancy boundary within the estate (see above *Cold. Cart.*, 13–14, no. 19; 14, no. 20) and it too had its crossing points, one of which mentioned was a bridge (Figure 2.3). The lands stretch from the water meadows around the river through good agricultural land to the higher ground around Hirsel Law, which provided grazing land for sheep, and which was such a contentious issue between the nuns and land holders in the 16th century. It may be significant also that sheep produced such a high percentage of the animal bones in the medieval period (Section 10.2).

Both the high ground, with its heather, and the low marshy ground, with its reeds, provided useful resources which have been traced in the botanical record of the site. In fact, in the grant to the priory by Earl Patrick III (1248–89) of a ploughgate of land at Old Hirsel, the resources of such an estate are well enumerated as moors, marshes, meadows, pastures and mills (*Cold. Cart.*, 11–12, no. 16). It may be significant that there is no mention of woodland, which could have been in short supply, since it is generally considered that there had been a massive clearance of woodland throughout the Merse from prehistoric times (Tipping 2004).

Another resource which is not mentioned in the records but which has emerged from the excavations is the availability of stone. The bed of the River Leet itself probably provided the large rounded stones which formed the construction of the first church, and the stone for the ashlar blocks from which the extended Phase III church was constructed seems to have come from a quarry near to the present golf course on the estate, still accessible at the beginning of the excavation (Figure 2.3).

With a site which largely comprised a church and cemetery, with some traces of domestic buildings in the north of the cemetery, it is not surprising that the botanical samples are not rich (see Chapter 10). Nevertheless, there is good evidence for cereal crops, with a preponderance of oats, although bread wheat, rye and barley were also present. The traces of other food crops, such as peas and beans, could imply habitation nearby that the excavation only narrowly missed. The same may be said for the faunal evidence where the preponderance of finds come from the west of the church (Chapter 10). The phosphate survey also indicated human activity to the west of the site (see Chapter 3) and a significant quantity of medieval pottery was also noted in the ground disturbed by rabbit and mole action in that area. The geophysical surveys also indicated that there could have been occupation to the south as the ground sloped up and then dipped down towards what is now the Homestead area (see Chapter 3). Nevertheless a major focus may well have been, as now, on the elevated ground to the north of the excavated area where early maps showed a tower house (Figure 2.7) and where the present Hirsel House stands, whilst within the larger estate there were other centres, the most eminent of which seems to have been the motte at Castle Law (Figures 1.5, 2.2, 2.3; Hamilton 2010, 113). The small area of the estate which has been excavated can then hardly be expected to provide a full picture of the estate economy, but the additional survey work on the dominant hillfort at Hirsel Law provides a further insight into the topographic importance of the site.

2.4 HIRSEL LAW (NGR: NT 82529 41600)

Arnold Aspinall and Rosemary Cramp

In the surviving documentary and cartographic evidence for the history of the estate, the hill, Hirsel Law, figures as an important landmark dominating the north-east corner of the medieval estate and used as a point of reference in land-holding disputes, as a venue for law suits (see above), for the mustering and disbanding of troops, and for executions (see below). This is a remarkable testimony to the surviving importance of what formally appears be a prehistoric monument and, during the excavation, it was decided that the Law deserved further study.

At the time of the study, Hirsel Law was an unencumbered grass covered hill, situated in the north-east section of The Hirsel estate and about 1km north of Hirsel House (Figure 1.5). At the highest point it is 94m above sea-level, with the land sloping most steeply to the south, but dominant views can be obtained in all directions at the summit. Although this is still today a notable landscape feature, and the RCAHMS has two good aerial photographs (Figure 2.10 and 2.11) which show a roughly D-shaped enclosure, the site had been entirely neglected in the discussion of enclosed settlements in the Borders until the campaign of excavation began in 1979. Since then, as well as the publications associated with The Hirsel excavations (Aspinall 1985), there has been some notice in other publications, the most comprehensive being Kokeza (2008, 151–152; 220), based on Aspinall's 1985 account and plan.

The survey was coordinated by Professor Arnold Aspinall and, as a first stage, utilised a rectified image of the aerial photographs produced by John Haigh of Bradford University (see site archive). In plotting what could be seen in the parch marks in the grass land, the two edges of the ditch were identified, as were the rectangular buildings which cut the ditch on the southern slope. It was, however, felt that electronic survey could provide more precise detail, and it was therefore decided to test

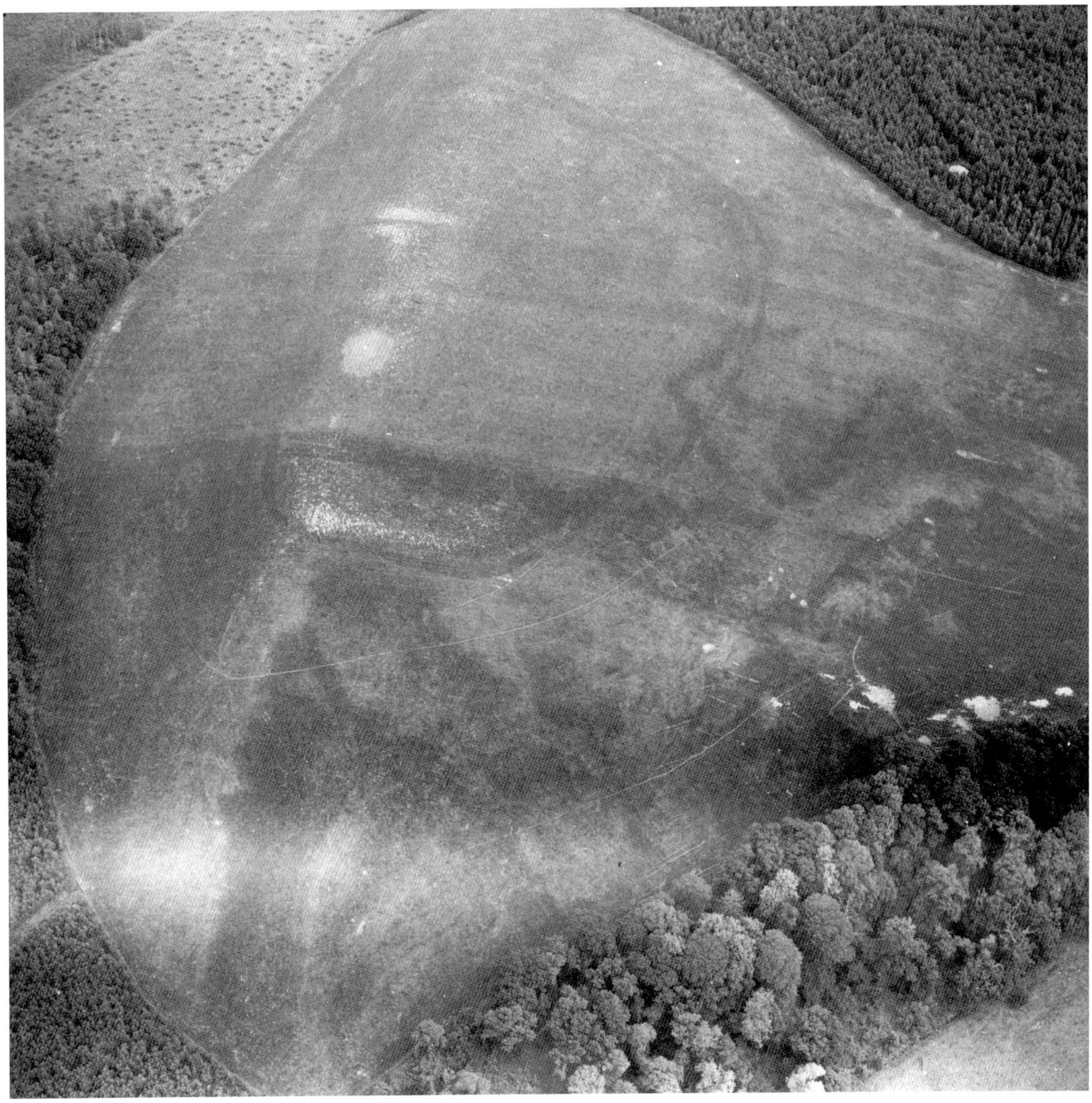

FIGURE 2.10
Hirsel Law aerial view (Berwickshire NT 82 41.1977 BW/1885) © RCAHMS

some features initially by earth resistance methods (Aspinall 1985).

The triangulation pillar was used by Fred Bettess as a basis for laying out reference lines, with a grid one minute west of the National Grid and, in 1982–83, seventeen 20m squares in the vicinity of the assumed enclosure ditch were surveyed at 1m intervals, using Bradphys resistance instruments. This pilot survey confirmed the presence of a single ditch as a low resistance anomaly. After 1983 it was decided that magnetometry afforded a more rapid method of survey and an area covering the majority of the enclosure ditch was completed in 1984. The original 20m square grid layout was used and readings were taken, as before, at 1m intervals, now using a Plessey fluxgate gradiometer.

Further investigation was obviously needed, especially in the southern area of the site where the rectangular and sub-rectangular features were visible on the aerial photograph and, after the Hirsel excavation, Paul Johnson and a team from Glasgow University enlarged the survey in 1994, nearly completing the perimeter and a considerable part of the interior, leaving just over half untouched. All these data have been enhanced and plotted by Arnold Aspinall more recently, with significant results (Figure 2.12). The plan now shows an enclosed eastern entrance, and within the site there is evidence for round structures, one of which is about 25m in diameter with internal features — apparently a large central posthole (Figure 2.13). Interestingly the ditch shows as a low

FIGURE 2.11
Hirsel Law aerial view (Berwickshire NT 82 41.1977 BW/1884) © *RCAHMS*

magnetic anomaly in keeping with its excavation in a volcanic (magnetic) geology. An erratic high intensity anomaly in the west of the interior is consistent with a lightning strike on this geology.

Unfortunately, before the rectangular features visible on the aerial photographs, could be examined, the area was planted with pheasant cover so the detail of that part of the site is unrecorded. In the small area surveyed where they appeared to cut the enclosure, the magnetic survey did not pick them up, and it is possible that the foundations were too shallow to cut into the bedrock and, therefore, magnetically there was no contrast. They are important evidence for a later use of The Law as discussed above, and it is possible in the future that resistance survey in optimum conditions could pick them up.

The picture as it stands now is of an enclosed site covering about 7 hectares (18 acres), and 340+ m E–W and 200m N–S, sited on a volcanic plug (see Figure 2.12). It is in a dominating position overlooking the low-lying land of the river valley with its dense occupation and the easy crossing point of the Tweed. The Hirsel Law site dwarfs other enclosed sites in the region, most of which are multivalate and mostly much smaller, although Humbleton Hill is 3.6 hectares (Oswald *et al* 2006, fig 6.1), but in scale, and indeed shape, the nearest parallel is Yeavering Bell, in Northumberland (Oswald *et al* 2006, 96–100, fig 4.27). Here the perimeter survives as a visible enclosure of stone but there are many other sites in the North British region where hillfort-like enclosures have

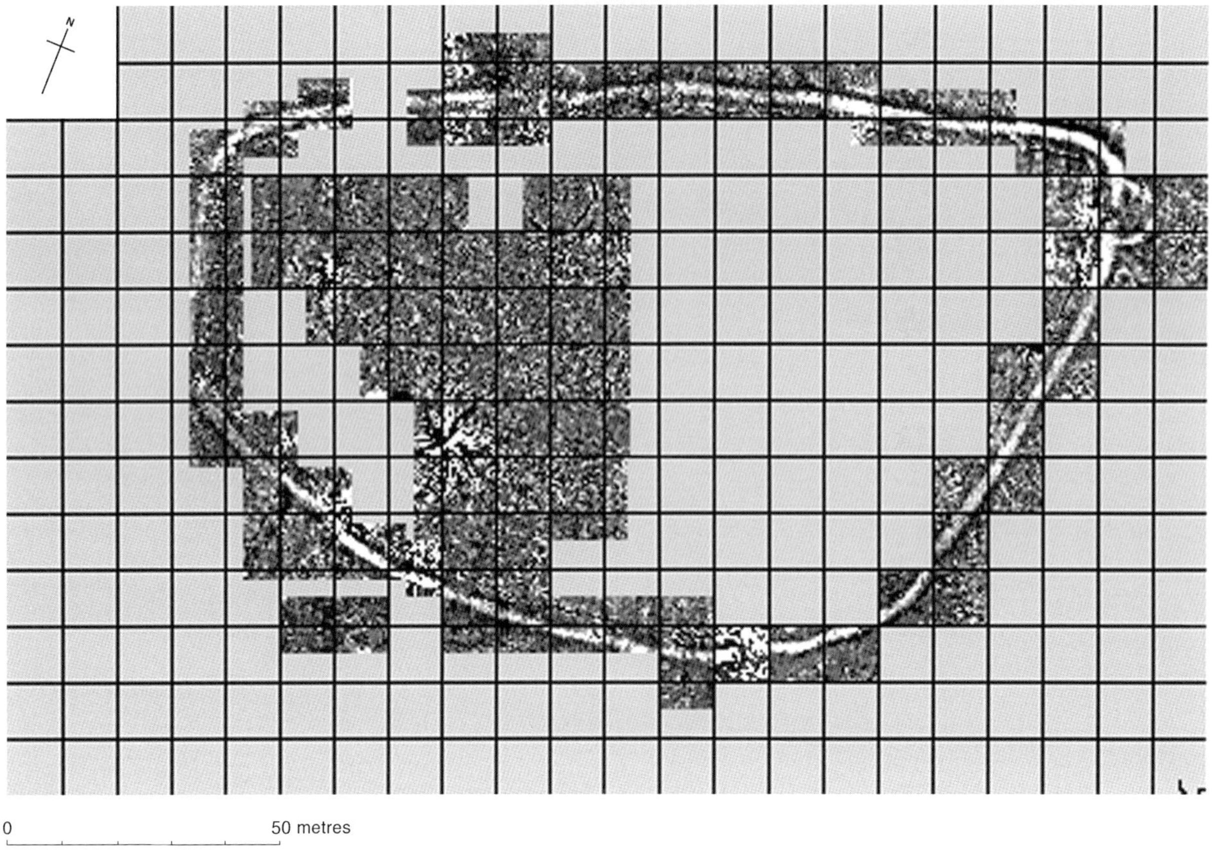

FIGURE 2.12
Hirsel Law magnetic survey

been identified by aerial photography as ditched enclosures (Oswald *et al* 2006, fig 4.28). The inner line visible on the Hirsel survey is interpreted by Aspinall as the magnetic up-cast from the cutting of the ditch, and this could have formed the foundations of a palisade. The lobed ditched entrance on the east is not a feature found in many of the enclosed sites, but there is a possible similar feature at Hayhope Knowe (Piggott 1949, fig 1A; Reynolds 1982) and a similar but much larger feature encloses the entrance at Yeavering Bell. It is also noteworthy that a significant proportion of hillforts, and indeed their circular houses, had their entrances to the east, which could suggest that direction had a symbolic significance (Oswald *et al* 2006, 51). This view is, however, dismissed by Kokeza whose study has shown that although entrances to enclosed sites in Berwickshire and Dumfriesshire were most commonly orientated E and ESE, other orientations exist (Kokeza 2008, fig 93). The enclosed sites in her study area are subdivided in relation to approaches, whether in relation to those closest to water resource, orientated towards the easiest approach, or not dependent on either (Kokeza 2008, 80–81). She tentatively places Hirsel Law in the second category.

Her discussion of Hirsel Law (2008, 151–154) is the fullest publication so far and it is unfortunate that she did not contact those writing up the site for an up-to-date plan, since this shows more detail of the entrance and also the roundhouses in the interior. She concludes: 'Apart from the size and the location of the enclosure, there are no other similarities between other big enclosed sites and Hirsel Law. The position of its rampart shows that it was possible to see inside the enclosure from a distance' (Kokeza 2008, 152). This last interesting point is one which has a bearing on its later use.

Her concluding remarks about the site also need further debate:

> There does seem to be one key difference between the *minor oppida* of SE Scotland, NE England and Hirsel Law. All the other sites show signs of long-term usage and several phases of occupation. It is possible that we are missing a great amount of data from Hirsel Law, as this was never studied properly. But this is, however, unlikely. The geophysical survey and the aerial photographs would show at least some hint of long term usage. Is it possible that we are dealing with an 'unsuccessful' big enclosed site, which was abandoned soon after completion?
>
> (Kokeza 2008, 154).

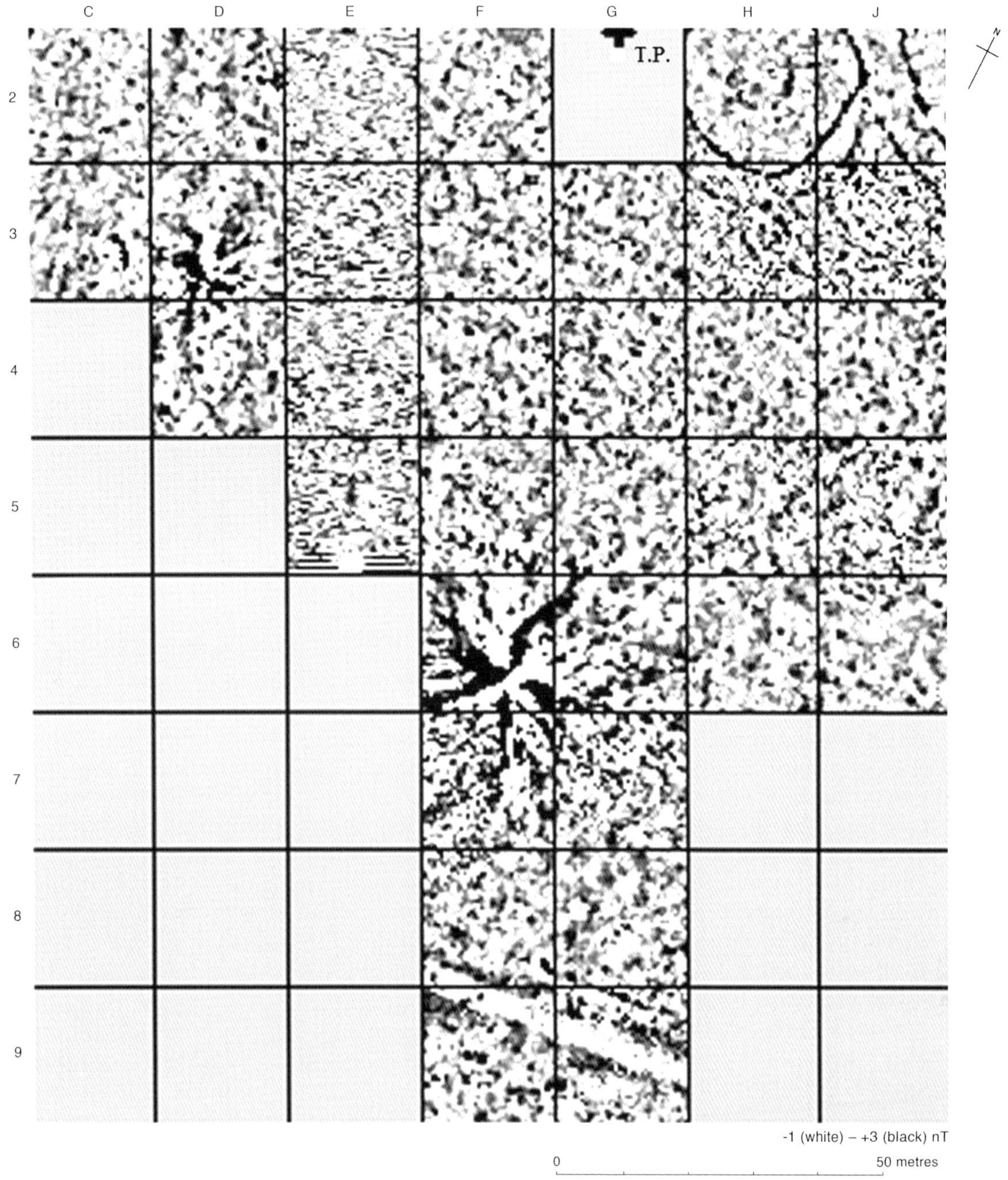

FIGURE 2.13
Detail of magnetic survey of the interior of Hirsel Law

The enclosure however must have been a substantial feature since to the present day it was visible in air photographs even in grassland. The roundhouses indicate that it was occupied in later prehistory, but the really remarkable fact about Hirsel Law is its documented record of use throughout the Middle Ages and into the 17th century (see above).

Without excavation of the enclosure, the roundhouses and the external rectangular features, which appear in the south of the site on the aerial photographs, the history of this site cannot be unravelled. The most easterly rectangular 'building' clearly cuts the enclosure, so at the time of its construction the prehistoric enclosure would have ceased to function as such. Other structures appear to cut each other. Formally, however, these structures are not easy to date, and although the D-ended structure is a type which is commonly assigned to an early post-Roman period, they could, on the whole, be of any date from the Roman period to the 17th century.

Hirsel Law summary

In view of the current debate about the dating of enclosed sites, it is impossible to date this structure on the survey alone, as Macinnes says: 'In the later first millennium BC south of the Forth, a trend towards more strongly defensive sites is well attested'. These forts 'are generally of small size like the palisades which preceded them but a few large sites — the so-called *minor oppida* — are also found like Traprain Law' (Macinnes 1982). Kokeza has taken a firm view that typological sequences of enclosure types 'have now been proved to be flawed' (2008, 4). If then the simple taxonomy of Later Prehistoric enclosed sites can be dismissed, one would need to investigate the interior structures, and the line of up-cast, in the hope of achieving some dating evidence. When considering the published plans of nearby enclosed sites, that of Hayhope Knowe, Roxboroughshire (Piggott 1949) with possible palisade and earthwork and with hut circles in the interior, is not unlike Hirsel Law in form, but that site also needs further investigation.

As stated above, the scale of Hirsel Law most resembles Yeavering Bell which encloses an area of 5.6 hectares (*c*13 acres) and is by far the largest hillfort in its region, but, as Frodsham says, in discussing Yeavering Bell, 'No two hillforts are the same' (Frodsham 2004, 37). Nevertheless the scale of Hirsel Law would suggest that it was an important, even regional, centre in later prehistory, and the site was obviously reoccupied at the time the rectangular structures cut across the enclosure.

Hirsel Law was plausibly also a focal part of the territory which later made up the estate. As David McOmish said: 'Settlements do not develop haphazardly in the landscape' (1999, 120), and this site, which remains a prominent feature in the landscape even today, could have been occupied at the same time as the Hirsel platform by the river, which has yielded Neolithic pottery and possibly linear features. There is also some slight evidence for later prehistoric occupation on the riverside site. The dark sandy loam and gravel with charcoal inclusions which underlies the church as discussed above, has yielded pottery dated by thermoluminescence to 1540 BC±290 = 1830–1250 BC and AD 400±165 = AD 235–565 (see Section 9.3). The excavation has also produced some other fragments of Roman pottery, including Samian, which might link with an occupation on the Law indicated by the rectilinear structures. Unfortunately the layers beneath the church and cemetery have not been excavated extensively enough to reveal the nature of the pre-medieval occupation (see site introduction and prehistoric phasing), and a range of radiocarbon dates from the platform on which the church was constructed have produced mainly 11th–12th century dates (see Chapter 9). In addition, the Aspinall site survey has opened up the possibility that there was another focus of occupation of pre-medieval date higher up the southern slope in the Dial Knowe (see Section 3.2). Nevertheless, The Law would have provided a dominant reminder of the prehistoric heritage and perhaps ancestral claims to the territory surrounding it. It has been a matter of some speculation as to the uses of hillforts during the medieval and later periods but, for this one at least, there is good evidence, as discussed above, for its use in law suits and later evidence for its use as a place where armies were mustered and disbanded, and where executions took place. For example, in August 1640 there was mutiny in England amongst the Scottish soldiers of the Dunfermline Foot and the Fleming's Foot, and after they were marched back to Scotland, according to the Fleming record 'Upon reaching Hirslaw Leslie (the general) had one of the mutineers executed on 25th August at 6pm. Later in the evening the army disbanded' (Furgol 1990, 55). The Dunfermline record has the same date and time for the execution with the additional detail that 'Leslie had one of the mutineers shot at the post' (Furgol 1990, 50). Executions as well as law giving have been noted in recent research on assembly places in medieval Europe (Semple 2004; Pantos 2004), and in Scotland hillforts are seen as places of inauguration (Driscoll 2004), but this little known hillfort could imply that they had a more extensive afterlife.

Hirsel Law, which is totally unexcavated, would repay further study and its date depends at the moment on the layout so far revealed. This, according to current thinking, could be a very wide date bracket indeed. Harding, in his review of later prehistory in south-east Scotland, dismissed the attribution of hillforts to an exclusively Iron Age horizon together with their defensive typology:

> If we accept that earthwork enclosure for a variety of purposes was a feature of insular as well as Continental societies in north-Alpine Europe from the Neolithic onwards, then the settlement evidence at any given period might be expected to include both enclosed and unenclosed or 'open' variants depending upon those factors, social political or economic, which prompted their construction
>
> (Harding 2001, 364).

Within the context of the medieval and post-medieval worlds, however, the interest of Hirsel Law is that it could still be related to land divisions and the focus for military and legal gatherings.

Notes

1 The donations to Coldstream Priory are contained in the *Carte Monialum de Caldstrem* (British Library Harley MS 6670) and were edited for the Grampian Club by Charles Rogers in 1879. Recently these charters have been re-evaluated by Elsa Hamilton, first in a PhD thesis (Hamilton, 2003) and later in a book (Hamilton 2010). I am deeply grateful to Dr Hamilton for allowing me to use her work, which has provided important insight into the background for the early history of The Hirsel site.

3
THE SITE SURVEYS

3.1 INTRODUCTION TO THE SITE
Rosemary Cramp

The co-ordinates for all of the surveys, and for the excavations, were those of the main grid set out on the site by Fred Bettess, together with a very detailed contour survey at 10cm intervals (Figure 1.7).

The field in which the excavations took place (the Dial Knowe or Low Field) to the south of Hirsel House, sloped down to the west to lower lying wetter ground and the path alongside the walled garden of the house (Figures 1.4 and 1.5). On the south the ground rose towards a hilltop with a good view towards the present town of Coldstream, and on the east the ground dropped sharply down to the River Leet in a series of terraces which, before the ploughing, were clearly edged with stones, but still showed in outline on the Bettess contour survey. There is a crossing of the Leet at this point which could be ancient and which is now bridged. The dense plantations of trees along the east bank of the Leet appear, from the early maps (see Figures 2.2 and 2.8) to be largely post-18th century and there had also been recent tree planting in the excavation field which accounted for some of the gaps in the survey.

3.2 MAGNETOMETER AND RESISTIVITY GEOPHYSICAL SURVEY
Arnold Aspinall

The site grid for the survey at Dial Knowe covers an area 100m (west to east) by 200m (north to south) (2.4 hectares) within which 131 square data grids of 10m sides were laid out. These encompassed the area to be covered by excavation together with a swathe to the south to the line of break of slope of the field. The main method of geophysical investigation was that of earth resistance measurement ('resistivity') using the so-called twin-probe technique (Aspinall and Lynam 1970), and the individual data grids were examined at 0.5m intervals, giving 400 data readings per grid. Although in earth resistance measurement a dry region (typically buried walls, rubble or rock) will show as high resistances, and moist ditches, scoops or storage pits will have a low resistance, the contrast between these two extremes is highly dependent on weather conditions immediately before and at the time of survey. There will be little contrast between a stony feature and the earth in very dry conditions; alternatively ditches are unlikely to be detected during a prolonged wet period.

Several teams of Durham University students, with their supervisors, participated in the Hirsel survey using Bradphys earth resistance instruments (Cramp and Douglas-Home 1980, pl 18). The weather was very variable over the three-year period of the survey seasons, including a period of snowfall (Figure 3.1)! It was therefore remarkable that, using the full facility provided by the computer program Geoplot, a reasonably consistent pattern of earth resistance eventually emerged from the diverse data sets (Figure 3.2). Early hand-processing, although pointing the way to areas to be selected for excavation, showed inconsistencies that prevented

FIGURE 3.1
The Hirsel survey in snow in 1978

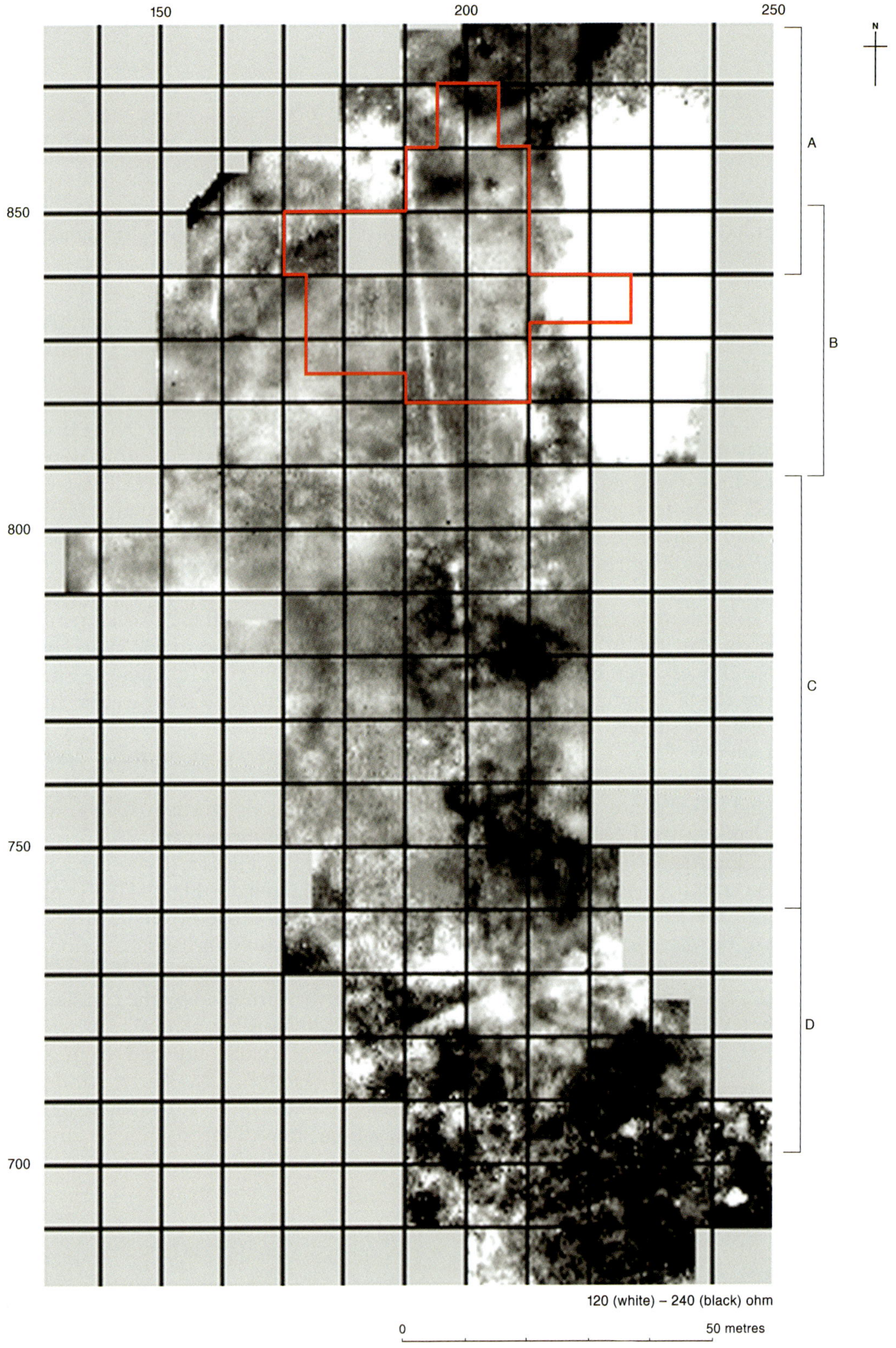

FIGURE 3.2
Extent of resistance survey, with location of excavation trenches marked in red

detailed analysis, but the final images, reinforced by positive evidence from excavation, were highly informative. A limited, supportive magnetometer survey (see below) over the southernmost area of the site was also valuable in the interpretation of some of the earth resistance anomalies.

The survey has been broken down into four areas (Figure 3.2) so that A and B cover the excavations during the period 1979–84, whereas areas C and D were to the south of the excavated area and are, obviously, open to more speculative interpretation. They, however, could form the basis for future programmes at the Dial Knowe. The dominant feature across the whole survey was a sharply defined, linear, low resistance anomaly, seen at its northern end at co-ordinates 190/870 and traversing the site on an approximate southern bearing to 206/705 when it turns slightly westward and leaves the grid at 202/680. Early in the excavation this feature proved to be a shallow trench cut to accommodate a lead-sheathed electrical cable (hence low resistance), probably a buried service line joining the main Hirsel complex with an outlying facility. The clarity of the anomaly, through a widely diverse surface geology, lent confidence as to the reliability of the data as a whole. It should be emphasised, however, that, as used, the twin-probe resistance method has a limited depth sensitivity, usually quoted as up to one metre, although this will obviously depend on the resistivity contrast in the ground.

Area A (co-ordinates 150/880 to 230/840)
(Figure 3.2)

This area takes in the excavations during the 1979–81 period extended to the north by 10m and excluding the church site. It reveals the presence of a low resistance ditch-like anomaly in the north-east corner that encompasses a high resistance anomaly, sharply defined as a bank, at its southern edge. This takes in features C112 and C117 (prehistoric curved strips of compacted gravel) from the 1979 excavation trench D (see Chapter 4). Further to the south, the cemetery perimeter appears as a strong, high resistance, linear anomaly, apparently interrupted by possible occupation (identified as C299 and C301 in the 1980 excavation, see Chapter 7). Unfortunately the data grid to the west has been lost during the prolonged data transfer procedures. West of this, however, a prominent high resistance linear edge, running north-east/south-west, possibly defines a well-drained area to its east. There is no evidence of the 'palisade' trench, seen by the excavators, in this data grid but, interestingly, in those further west and south, a 'beaded' high resistance anomaly extrapolates the palisade line.

Area B (co-ordinates 150/860 to 230/810)
(Figures 3.2 and 3.3)

This study overlaps, to some extent, that of area A so as to establish the continuity of the survey. The greyscale presentation, however, covers a more restricted resistance range to distinguish, in this area of low resistance contrast, possible archaeology revealed by the 1982 excavations. Thus the perimeter of the post-medieval compound (see Chapter 8) appears, in 170/850–190/830, as diffuse, high resistance, linear anomalies with an evident extension to the south-west. There is also

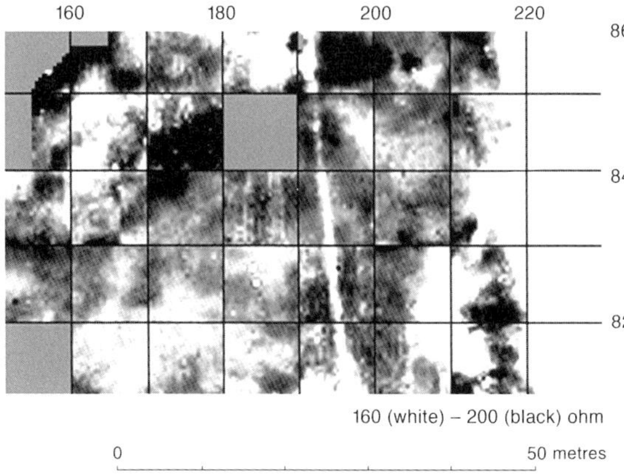

FIGURE 3.3
Resistance survey, Area B

evidence of high resistance (therefore dry) linear anomalies extending to the south-west from grid square 180/850–170/840, thus continuing the edge seen in A (Figure 3.2). Discrete high resistance, linear anomalies can be seen to define the eastern end of the church complex (see Chapter 5), but its presence is lost west of the north/south divider wall along the 200 grid-line. This may be due to the prominent presence of the cable trench, which, further south in 190/830–200/820, also cuts a high resistance anomaly of roughly rectangular shape. The influence of the cable trench on its immediate surroundings may be significant here and elsewhere due to the deposition of the trench fill in its immediate vicinity. The plateau on which the church was built falls away sharply on the north to south line defined roughly by the 215 grid-line, identifiable as a sharp drop in earth resistance to the east. However a noticeable broad high resistance ridge can be seen, starting at 210/830 and running south of the image; this appears to be an outcrop of the plateau.

Area C (co-ordinates 170/810 to 230/740)
(Figures 3.2 and 3.4)

This area, which is south of the excavations, is dominated by two broad, high resistance anomalies through which the cable trench passes and disturbs. An exploratory pit in the southern feature revealed the presence of a shale fill immediately beneath the ground surface which would account for the high resistance. However clear, sharply defined, linear anomalies can be seen alongside and across the cable trench giving the impression of buried wall lines. Again the lines parallel to the trench may well be shale up-cast. Close examination of the area north, east and west of the northern high resistance 'lens' shows faint parallel linear anomalies running in a WSW direction, roughly parallel to the prominent lines through the cable trench, suggesting possible plough lines and, hence, cultivation disturbance. A weak, broad, high resistance anomaly running generally south along grid-line 175 is likely to reflect a change in surface geology to the west of the site.

Area D (co-ordinates 190/740 to 230/700)
(Figures 3.2 and 3.5)

The earth resistance survey of the Dial Knowe was augmented, on a limited scale, by a magnetometer survey with a fluxgate gradiometer at this southern extent of the site. This could reveal ditches and pits with a detrital fill, hearths, kilns and igneous geological rocks. Earth resistance and magnetic methods of survey complement one another well, a ditch dug into sedimentary geology will exhibit low resistance but enhanced magnetism; a kiln will show high resistance and magnetic anomalies. Significantly a ditch cut into an igneous geology will show as a low resistance and a low magnetic anomaly due to the absence of highly magnetic material in the ditch. Up-cast from the ditch will, of course, show high resistance and magnetic anomalies.

Area D shows these phenomena well. At its southern end, below the break of slope and running roughly WSW from 230/730, earth resistance is generally high with striations suggesting terracing. Along a line from 225/735 to 190/720 at the crest of the hill, however, there is a linear low resistance anomaly which is clearly defined along its northern edge and less so to the south. The magnetic survey picks up this line as a low anomaly with a distinctive 'high' along its northern edge — typical of a ditch cut into igneous geology with up-cast to the north. To the south of this ditch the low magnetic values roughly mirror the low resistance variations, suggesting 'scoops' in the geology. Our later magnetometer survey of the Hirsel Law hillfort, to the north of Dial Knowe, clearly demonstrates that this hill is an igneous 'plug' and it would appear that the highest point at Dial Knowe is also a plug, probably with a deeper soil overburden. The significance of this transverse anomaly is unclear. There is no indication of the cable trench in the magnetic survey, suggesting that it is not dug into the igneous bedrock. The anomaly is, therefore, likely to be due to the presence of a ditch cut shallowly (?) into the rock, at the crest of the hill, to accommodate a palisade with protective up-cast to the north.

The area to the south of the 700m line was not, unfortunately, surveyed magnetically so that comparison of anomalies cannot be made. Examination of the resistivity survey reveals, however, the presence of a linear, low resistance feature running WSW from 235/695 suggesting a small ditch, to the south of which are several high resistance anomalies, possibly from enclosures. In the light of recent observations that pottery from the church site includes a number of Roman wares (see Chapter 16), it is tempting to suggest that the south-facing slope contains remains of that period. This, of course, is pure conjecture and awaits magnetic survey and subsequent excavation as do other areas on the site.

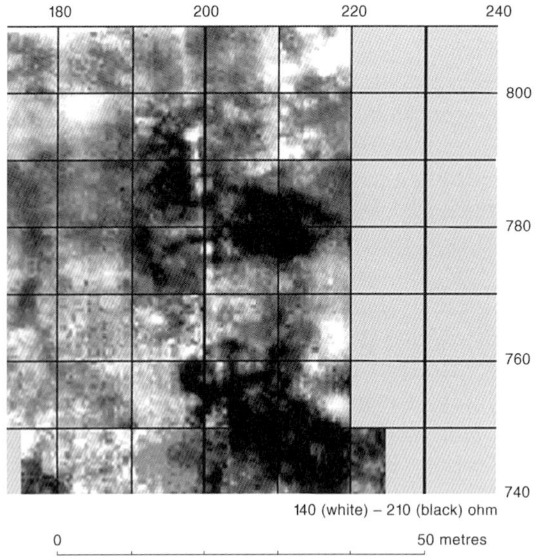

FIGURE 3.4
Resistance survey, Area C

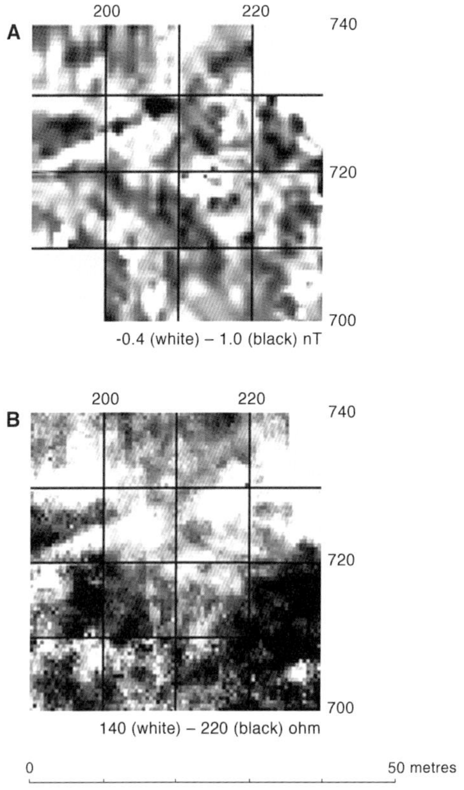

FIGURE 3.5
Area D. A: Magnetometer survey. B: Resistance survey

3.3 THE ARCHAEOLOGICAL SIGNIFICANCE OF THE MAGNETOMETER AND RESISTIVITY SURVEYS

Rosemary Cramp

The magnetometer and resistivity surveys were a fundamental element in the interpretation of the site. The survey before excavation began (Cramp and Douglas-Home 1980, pl 18) provided an indication of a perimeter which, in the light of the ploughed up gravestones, was identified as a possible perimeter for a churchyard. This proved to be the case although it was a more complex entity than it first appeared. Nevertheless, its presence determined the position of the excavation trenches. It is interesting, however, that the church was not visible; its foundations were so deeply buried under stone and earth that it showed as a blank on the plot, with a perimeter which indicated the extent of the rubble covering. Other features which were later excavated, such as the late compound/enclosure on the west or the ephemeral gravel structures in the north, did, however, show on the plot.

Perhaps, though, the most important evidence from these surveys is the evidence for features and structures outside the excavated area. In the extreme north of the site the excavation trenches have only clipped an area of considerable activity and in the light of the Neolithic pottery discovered there this is an area for possible future investigation.

To the south of the site on the slope and summit of the hill there is evidence for considerable activity of which the large ditch which appeared clearly in both the magnetometer and resistance surveys is of obvious importance. Moreover, some of the features could reasonably be interpreted as structures. This area is currently unprotected but deserves preservation or investigation.

3.4 SOIL PHOSPHATE TESTING 1979–1980

Michael Alexander

Background

The use of phosphate surveys is based on two assumptions, the first being that most human activities in and around settlements/buildings result in the addition of phosphates to the soils, derived from the decomposition of organic materials that accumulate in and around settlements as a direct consequence of human activity. The second is that on entering the soil system phosphates are readily immobilised in all soils and thus the enhanced levels of phosphate remain in the soil-plant cycle for prolonged periods (for a detailed discussion of phosphorus in the soil see Larsen 1967). The phosphate levels cannot, however, be used on their own to identify the nature of that activity; further studies, for example resistivity, gravimetric and excavation, are required to identify what the nature of this activity may have been.

The Hirsel survey was conducted following the rapid field method developed by Eidt (1977), with the levels of phosphate detected being graded as follows: 1 (none), 2 (weak), 3 (average), 4 (good), 5 (strong). The grades 4 and 5 are usually accepted as indicative of enhanced phosphate levels and hence may indicate past human activity. As well as being used in rapid surveys, these tests can be used to provide more detailed information of phosphate levels at specific locations, for example in graves or middens.

Purpose

The investigations conducted in 1979 were designed to provide a comprehensive survey of the site so as to identify any locations of anomalously high level of soil phosphate, which might, together with other survey and excavation work, indicate areas of previous human activity. This general survey was followed up in 1980 with more detailed and focussed sampling.

In 1979 the survey was carried out across the site at 5m intervals using the grid already established across the site (Figure 1.7). This covered the area 880/190–210 to the north-east diagonally across to 790/135–160 in the south-west (Figures 3.6 and 3.7). The grid also provided the basis for the more detailed work in 1980 which was focussed on specific areas. Sampling was generally carried out at depths of 0.30m and 0.45m below the ground surface, depths which eliminated any potential phosphate input from recent agricultural activity, but alternative depths were used at specific locations. All results were plotted on grids, colour coded according to the level of phosphate recorded.

Results of the 1979 survey

This survey revealed a number of areas of raised phosphate levels at both 0.30m and 0.45m depths, especially at 0.45m. At 0.30m the raised phosphate levels were concentrated at the south-west end of the church and then in a diagonal trend continuing south-west (Figure 3.6). At 0.45m this trend was reinforced with a more extensive area of raised levels; especially immediately north, west and south of the nave of the church (Figure 3.7). Most of these areas were later to reveal extensive burials. The areas to the south-west of the church were not excavated, thus no definite cause for the enhanced phosphate levels here can be identified. None of the analysed samples contained, however, any obvious mortar, charcoal or bone fragments, thus in the absence of these materials the origin of the enhanced phosphate levels is likely to be general waste from normal human activity.

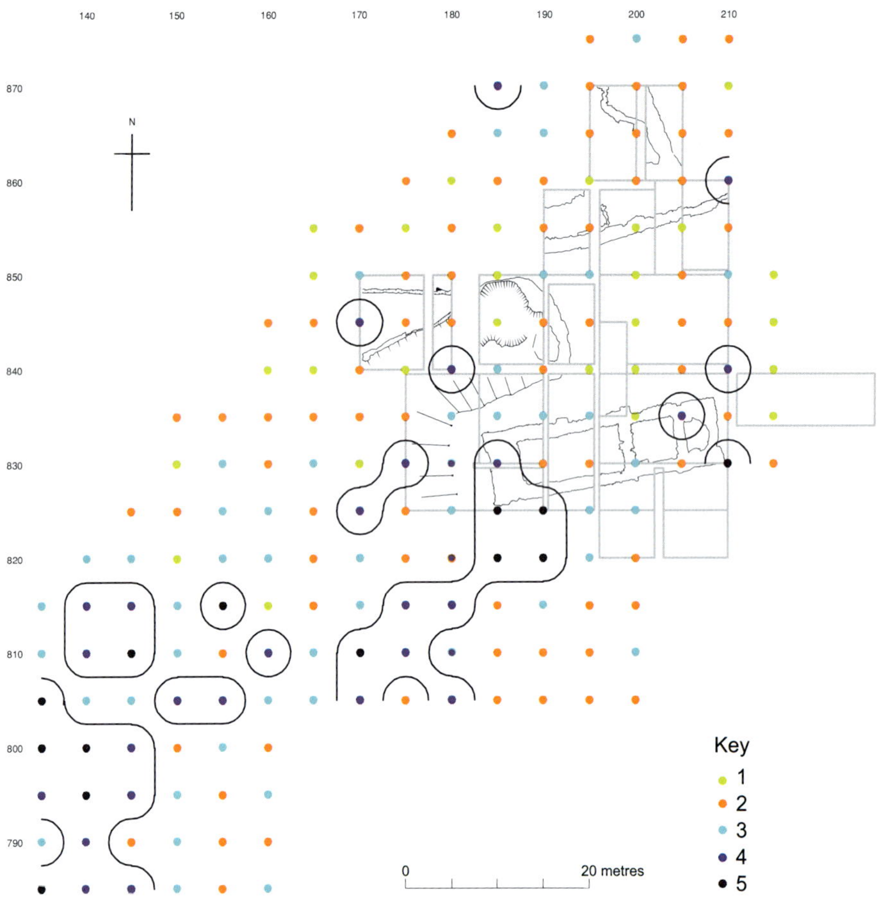

FIGURE 3.6
Results of the 1979 soil phosphate survey at 0.30m

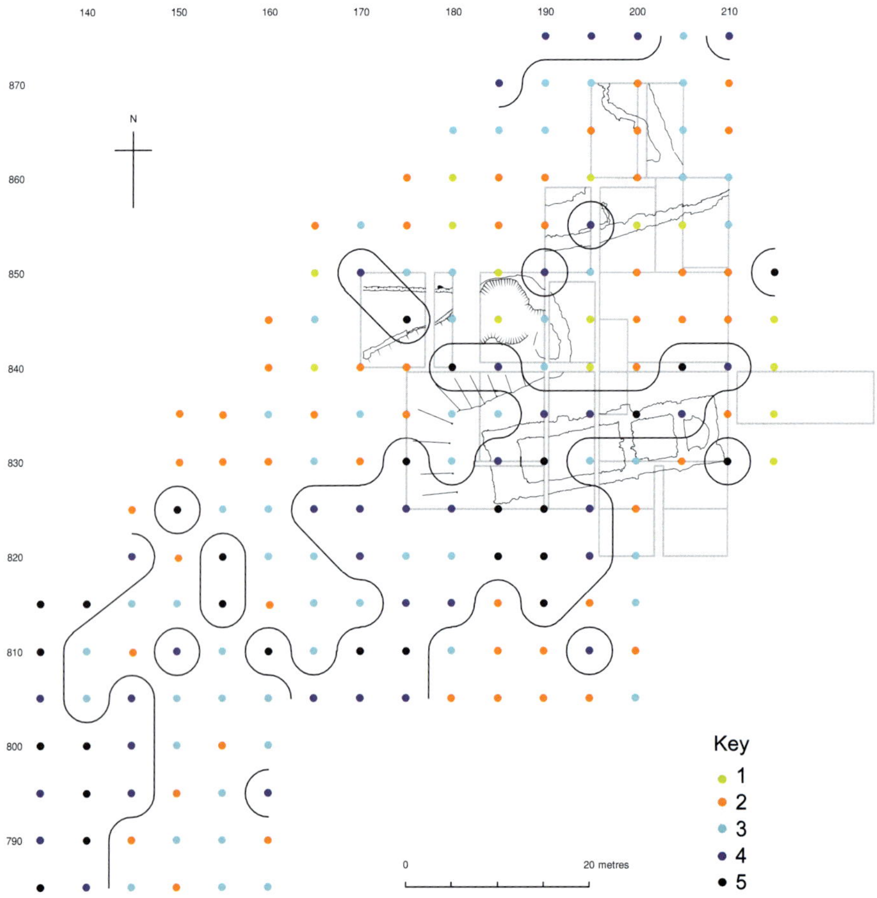

FIGURE 3.7
Results of the 1979 soil phosphate survey at 0.45m

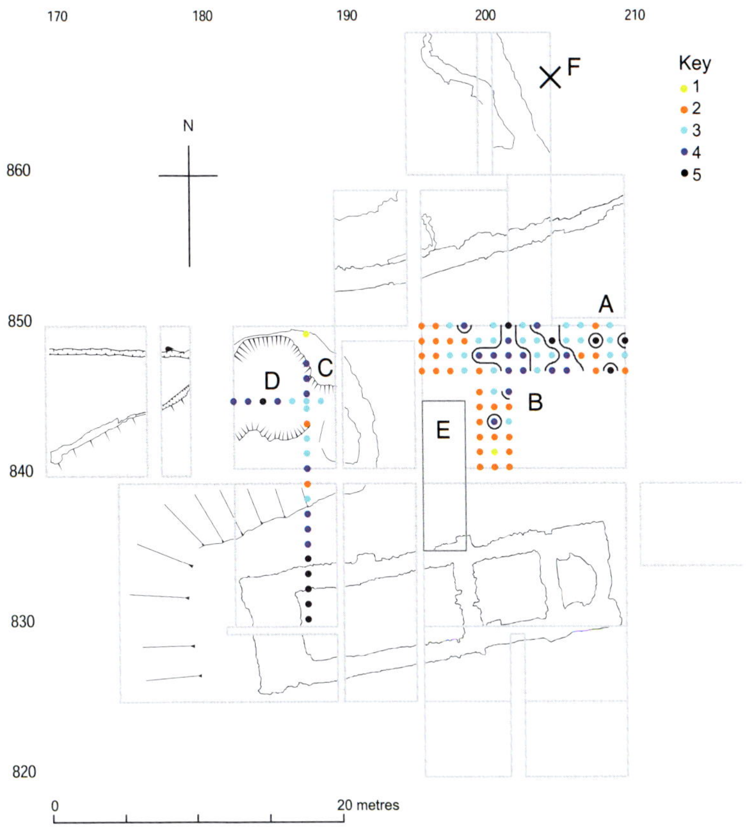

FIGURE 3.8
Results of the 1980 soil phosphate survey of areas A, B, C and D at 0.30m, and locations of E and F

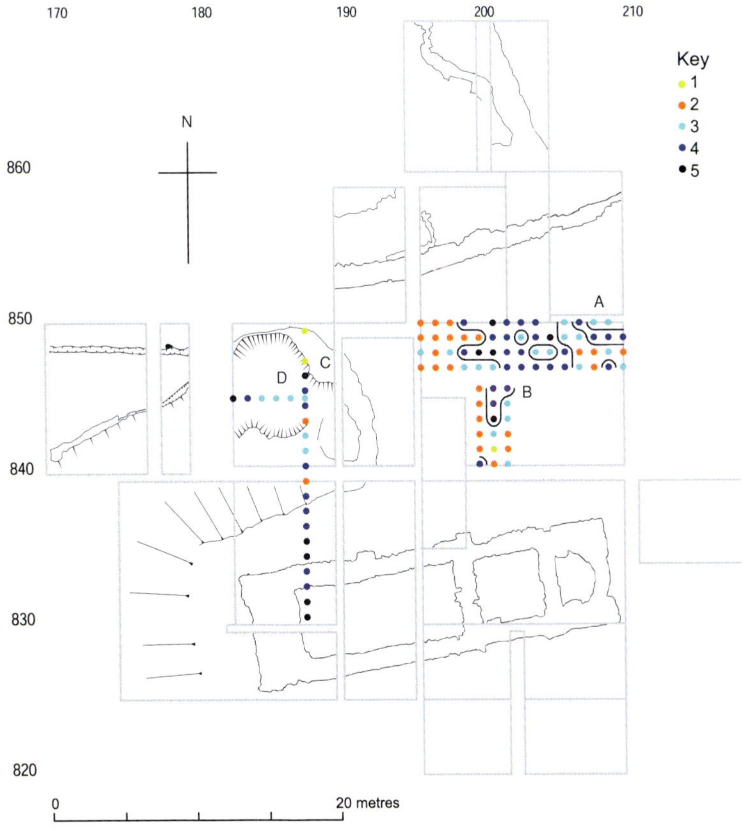

FIGURE 3.9
1980 soil phosphate survey of areas A, B, C and D at 0.45m

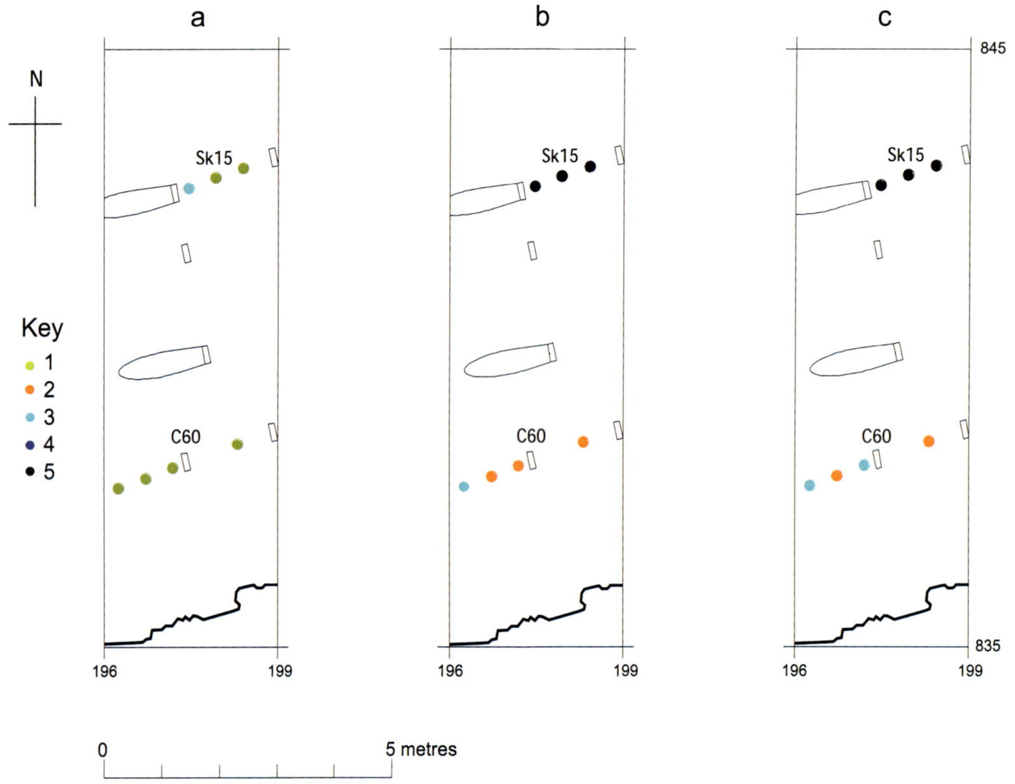

FIGURE 3.10
Soil phosphate sampling of graves in Area E (a. surface; b. 0.30m; c. 0.45m)

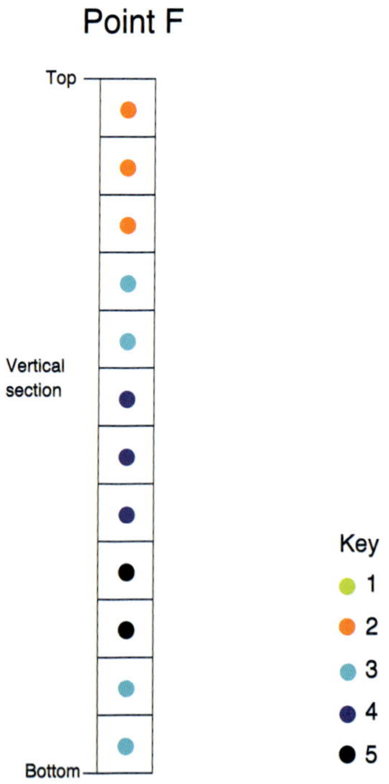

FIGURE 3.11
Samples taken from point F at 10cm intervals down a vertical section

Results of the 1980 survey

Two areas, A (195–210/845–850) and B (200–202/840.5–844.5/), were sampled at 1m spacing, and two lines, C (188/830–850) and D (183–189/845), were also sampled at 1m intervals (Figures 3.8 and 3.9).

Area A showed raised phosphate at both 30cm and 45cm levels, and while no discernible burials were revealed, the areas of high phosphate coincided with bone and charcoal fragments.

Area B was sampled at 0.30m and 0.45m below the level excavated (C503). The 0.45m depth shows the greatest frequency of raised phosphate levels and on excavation, bone fragments were found in areas where high phosphate readings were recorded.

The lines C and D were sampled at 0.30m and 0.45m from ground level in the area north of grid 840, while south of this, line C was sampled from the excavated surface. In the unexcavated sections, there were some raised phosphate sections, especially along line D, the raised levels being explained by mortar in the samples tested. To the south of this, enhanced phosphate levels at both depths were associated with excavated mortar in the church and burials immediately to the north of the church.

Further samples in Area E (196–199/835–845) were focussed on two particular locations between the head stones that demarcated the grave of Sk15 and the stones, including two possible uprights, which formed C60 (Figures 3.8 and 3.10).

The surface samples from the grave of Sk15 showed no enhanced phosphate levels, however both the 0.30m and 0.45m samples showed enhanced levels of phosphate. While initial excavation revealed no trace of skeletal remains, the enhanced phosphate levels would strongly indicate that a body had been present and a few fragments of bones were subsequently recovered.

Around C60, none of the samples from any depth showed any significantly raised level of phosphate. On excavation, no skeletal remains were discovered and the lack of enhanced phosphate levels would suggest that the grave had never been used.

Samples were taken at 10cm depths down a vertical section at the point F (205/866.7; Figures 3.8 and 3.11). The resultant pattern of phosphate values showed significantly raised levels between 0.31m and 0.91m, but excavation revealed no obvious structures, thus the enhanced levels are likely to be related to general human activity, for example general organic waste, middens, or manuring.

3.5 THE ARCHAEOLOGICAL SIGNIFICANCE OF THE PHOSPHATE SURVEY

Rosemary Cramp

The original brief for the phosphate survey was to attempt to gain an impression of where human activity on the site had been concentrated, and to see if the survey could determine the extent of the burial ground, which had been postulated by the disturbed gravestones. After excavation in 1979, when some apparently empty graves were found, it was decided to test individual graves where cuts showed in the surface or there was a stone grave-marker (see Figure 3.10).

The burial ground around the church did provide significant levels of phosphate and the spot checks on the graves seemed to provide definitive answers (see above). The most interesting results, however, were unexpected, and mainly related to areas outside the section of the site which was excavated. As Alexander notes above, the high readings at 0.30m and 0.45m concentrate on the SW of the site, although there are some high readings at the western end of the church and to the NW near to the stone dump. These last could be associated with the last use of the site and the demolition of the church. Alexander also notes, however, that in the north (Figures 3.8 and 3.11, location F) the peak readings were at a considerable depth on the site (between 80 and 90cm), and it was here that excavation was to a greater depth. The area in which the readings were taken was one of the medieval cultivation terraces. In addition, samples were tested in and around the prehistoric pottery from the northernmost trench. These indicated that the area might have had a domestic rather than a funerary use (see Appendix 3).

The most significant grouping to the south-west of the area excavated is not associated with bone or mortar. It is therefore noteworthy that the red-brown soil level, which underlay the west end of the church and the area to the south-west, has been assigned to a pre-ecclesiastical phase which must fit into the long gap between the Roman and the early medieval as defined by the presence of the pottery. In fact, the area to the west and south of the church has yielded the most evidence for domestic activity in the medieval and pre-medieval periods and this combined with the evidence from the resistance survey for activity to the south provides a pointer to useful areas for future investigation.

4

PRE-MEDIEVAL

Rosemary Cramp

4.1 PREHISTORIC

One small sector in the most northerly cutting in the site (195–205/860–870), an area excavated first in 1979 and completed in 1980, produced Neolithic pottery and a possible associated ground surface which had been cut by medieval features; most radically a cultivation terrace (C125 and C131), but there was also other evidence for medieval disturbance in the form of pits and possible ploughing (C122–4, C128; Figure 4.1). A possible plough tip (Fe87) was found in the soil level C128.

Neolithic (Phase 1)

(Figure 4.1)

In the northern sector of the trench, immediately below the disturbed medieval levels (C133), and at times difficult to distinguish from them, was a feature formed by C112, C121, C126, and C152 which consisted of a curved strip of orange sand, gravel and clay with small stake-holes enclosing a truncated deposit of orange/brown soil (C126) which filled a scooped area in the natural gravel (Figures 4.1–4.5). The orange-brown soil contained Neolithic pottery, animal bone, and flint. Two vessels (prehistoric Pots 1 and 2), one inside and one outside the structure, were placed on stones and were covered with stone slabs. Both were originally set in shallow depressions although in the deposit to the west of the structure C112, Pot 2 had been more disturbed and not all of its deposition was excavated (Figures 4.6–4.10). Underneath Pot 1 was a fragment of cinder, but only small patches survived of the surface of the natural sand into which the curving feature and the pots had been set.

The clay and gravel structure had been disturbed by ploughing, but probably continued further south where there was more disturbance, some also apparently from tree or bush roots. When the central baulk was removed in 1980 concentrations of small holes and disturbances in the clay and gravel (C135) were revealed, some of which (C158) could have been an extension of the prehistoric features to the north. But, because of the nature of the natural sands and gravels (which were full of solution holes), and because there seems to have been evidence for roots and pits (plausibly later vegetation) in the gravel covering the early prehistoric feature C112 (Figure 4.1), it was more difficult sometimes to distinguish between genuine wattle or post pipes, and root holes than it had been in the interior of C112 to the north (Figures 4.3 and 4.4).

In the south-west sector of the cutting, an area of pinkish clay and sand with patches of dark soil (C120) overlaid the natural sand (C134) and was possibly once part of a feature, similar to C112. But this seems to have been laid at a higher level and is more disturbed by the medieval activity (layer 133), which could account for the small patches of clay and sandy gravel found here at higher levels. On the other hand the curving line of possible stake-holes, which cut into natural sand and gravels (C132, C135) looks like a genuine structural feature (Figures 4.1 and 4.11). To the east of the baulk most of the early levels had been demolished in medieval cultivation, which at this point was also terraced (C122 and C131), although there were traces of root holes and possible postholes in the surface of the natural gravel within the baulk and just to the east (Figure 4.1).

The geophysical survey demonstrated interesting anomalies to the north of the excavated area which could include structures so far unexplored (see Figure 3.2) and this supposition was also supported by the phosphate survey, which showed high readings just to the north of the excavated area (see Figure 3.7). In this northern area then it appears that Neolithic structures, pits, and deposits were cut into the natural sand and gravel and are the earliest occupation evidence on the site. At some point after that period the evidence points to a scrub and possibly tree growth over the site, until medieval ploughing disturbed some areas and destroyed some levels completely. One strange feature, however, is that the line of the curving structure seems to have been visible quite late in the site sequence (Figure 4.12), and it — as well as the hard-packed cobbles (C121) which outline its edge — yielded four sherds of medieval pottery in the upper levels. This could be contamination by ploughing and it is possible that there was a compact area of cobbles here from the earliest period excavated, but this clear line remains an enigma.

It is probable that the Neolithic occupation not only continued north, as mentioned above, but extended more widely in unexcavated areas

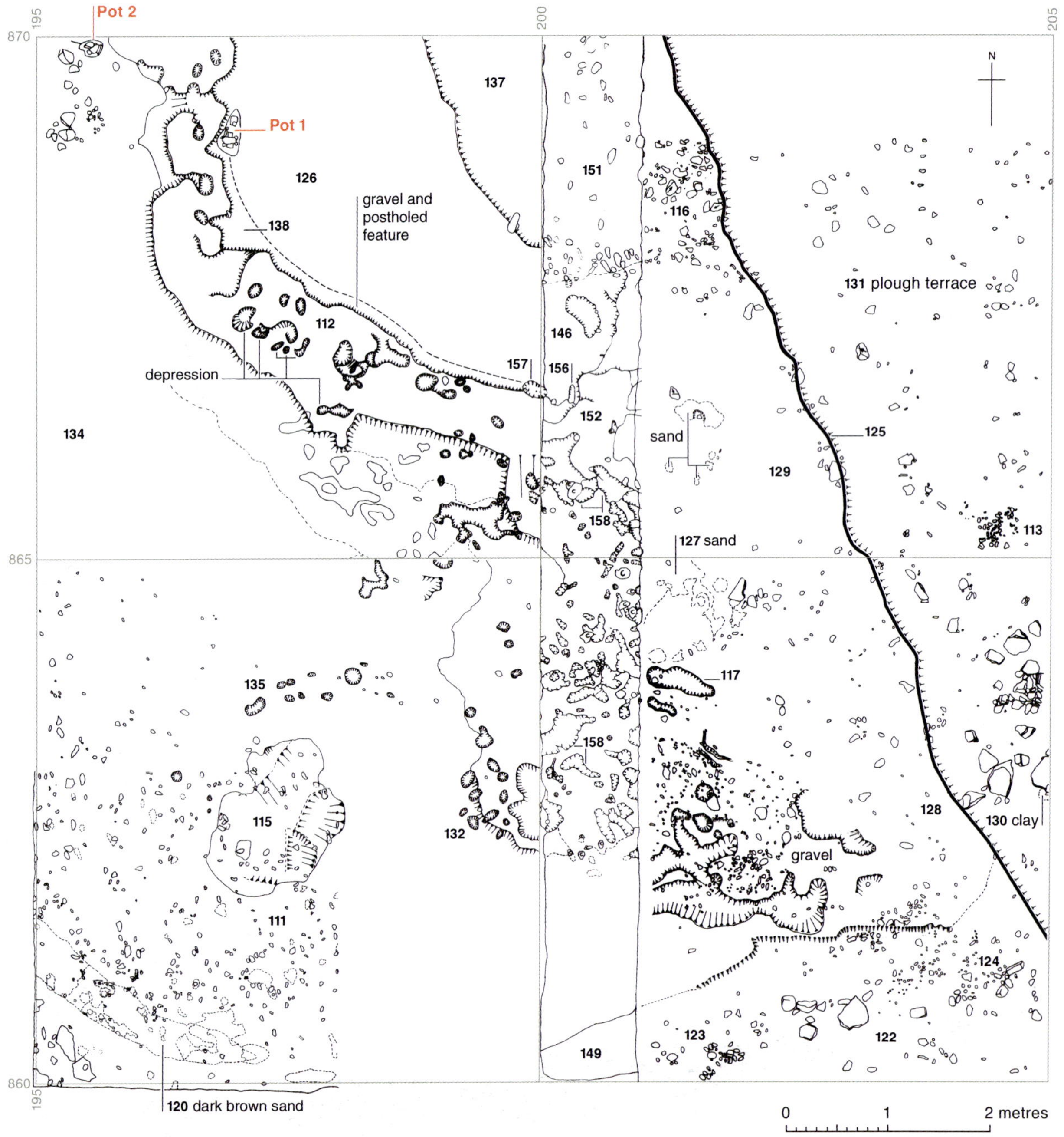

FIGURE 4.1
Plan of northernmost trench showing prehistoric features and location of Pot1 and Pot 2

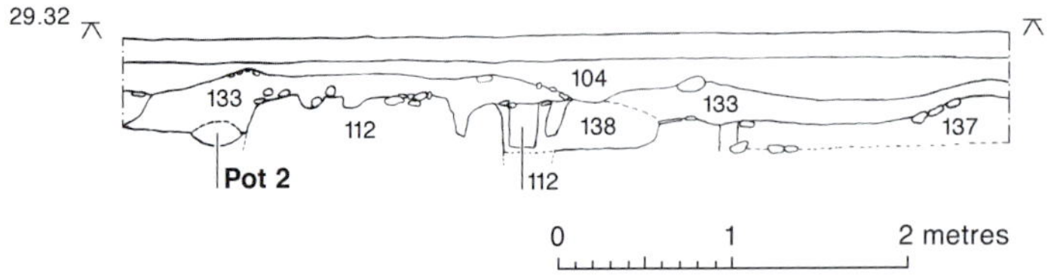

FIGURE 4.2
South-facing section on grid-line 870/195–199, showing position of Pot 2

FIGURE 4.3
Northernmost trench, western section, looking south, towards the end of the excavation and after removal of Pot 1

beneath the cemetery and church platforms, since evidence for earlier settlement was found on the western periphery where the levels beneath the gravel platform on which the church was sited were revealed. Here, Neolithic pottery was recovered from C931, a posthole, and from C851, and later prehistoric pottery from C845, both C851 and C845 being of brown crumbly soil west of the church. There was also a significant distribution of flint from this area (Figure 4.13) although, as Young points out, the flint assemblage is not closely diagnostic of any one period from the Mesolithic to the Bronze Age (see Chapter 23). There was also one fragment of pottery from C635 which has been assigned a Bronze Age date by thermoluminescence dating, and slightly later by the pottery expert (see Chapter 15).

In addition in the area 175–182/836–839.5 there were features in the natural gravel such as the broad shallow gulley C1225, and the holes C1223–1224, C982, C997–999 (Figure 4.14), which could have been natural solution holes, plant holes, or possibly

FIGURE 4.4
View from the north of the site, showing prehistoric features in the west, with Pot 1 removed, and agricultural terrace to the east, with perimeter wall to the south. Note difference of depth of excavation between the two trenches

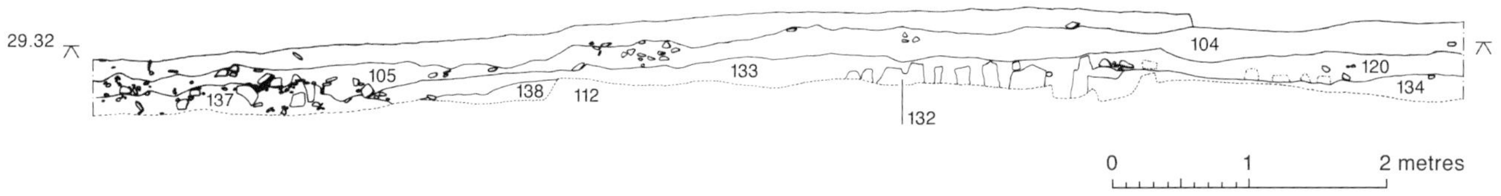

FIGURE 4.5
West-facing section on grid-line 200

stake-holes. Since these are areas around the church and cemetery platform where the pre-medieval deposits were most fully revealed, the distribution may not be meaningful, but the reddish earth and charcoal beneath the nave of the church and cemetery also seems to have a westerly distribution.

4.2 OTHER PRE-MEDIEVAL FEATURES (Figure 4.15)

As mentioned earlier, it has proved difficult to isolate and identify the phases of occupation between the prehistoric and medieval. The evidence is sparse: one sherd from C845 has been assigned a Middle Bronze Age date, and two others Late Bronze Age/Iron Age. The Neolithic pottery is distinctive enough to enable one to define its phase, but there is other pottery from the site of a coarse gritty type which could be later prehistoric or native Romano-British (see Chapter 15) and, as such, could, like the undoubtedly Roman pottery (see Chapter 16), date to early in the first millennium AD or could, as one TL result has indicated, have a late BC date (see Chapter 9).

FIGURE 4.6
Neolithic pottery, Pot 1 (87) in situ

FIGURE 4.7
Relationship between deposits of Neolithic pottery vessels

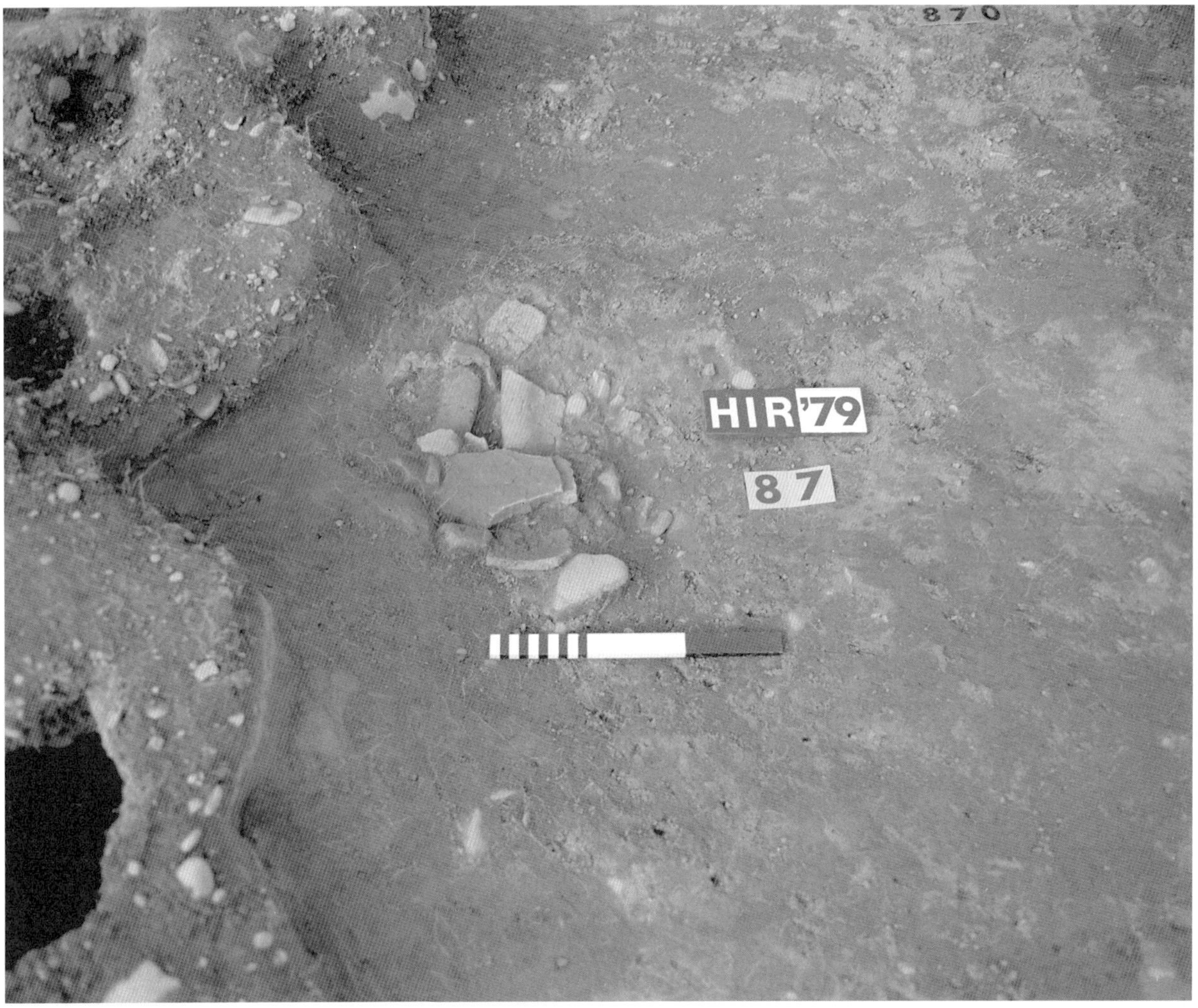

FIGURE 4.8
Detail of Neolithic pottery, Pot 1 (87), in shallow pit covered by stone slab

FIGURE 4.9
Neolithic pottery, Pot 1 (87) in situ, after removal of stone slab

FIGURE 4.10
Neolithic pottery, Pot 2 (88) in situ

FIGURE 4.11
View of northernmost trench looking east, showing Neolithic surface cut by terraces and later pits

There does seem to be a native occupation in the Roman or immediately post-Roman period, but only one radiocarbon date from the carbon in the soil in these lower levels (C899, below the nave floor) provided a date (155 BC–AD 70) which supported the case for occupation of this period. From such limited evidence it is also not easy to decide whether there was a continuing native occupation of the site after the Roman period. Finds such as the glass bangle (see Figure 25.1) and the half quern stone (see Figure 24.9) built into the foundation of the first church could be of Roman Iron Age or Northumbrian date. Nevertheless the reddish carbon flecked soils glimpsed in the western area do provide a tantalising glimpse of earlier occupation.

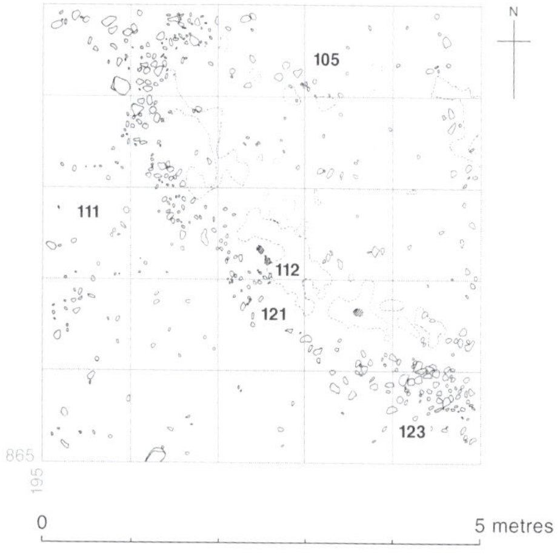

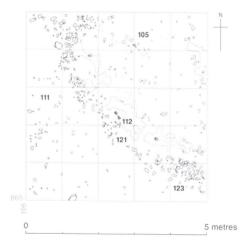

FIGURE 4.12
First emergence of C121 and C112

There are other features, which can only be defined as pre-medieval since they could be of any date earlier than the main occupation of the site when the cemetery and church were in use. One is a linear cut (C1340) running south-east to north-west, discovered and sampled in 1984 at a late stage of the excavation. The cut was V shaped with sharply sloping sides and an irregular base which may have been caused by post impressions (Figures 4.15–4.17). At the top it was 1.30m wide and, where sectioned, was 0.80m deep. Its outline was visible for 2.2m south of the south wall of the chancel. There were two fills in the cut: a central fill of dark brown to greyish sand mixed with humic soil (C1339) and a wider fill for the whole cut (C1342) of dark greyish brown sand which seems to be natural subsoil. This feature was difficult to date. It was cut by the chancel wall and the east wall of the earliest church, and it is not clear what level in the cemetery sand it cut although it underlay the graves of Sk316 and Sk319 which contained only clean sandy fills. In the area within the church, the

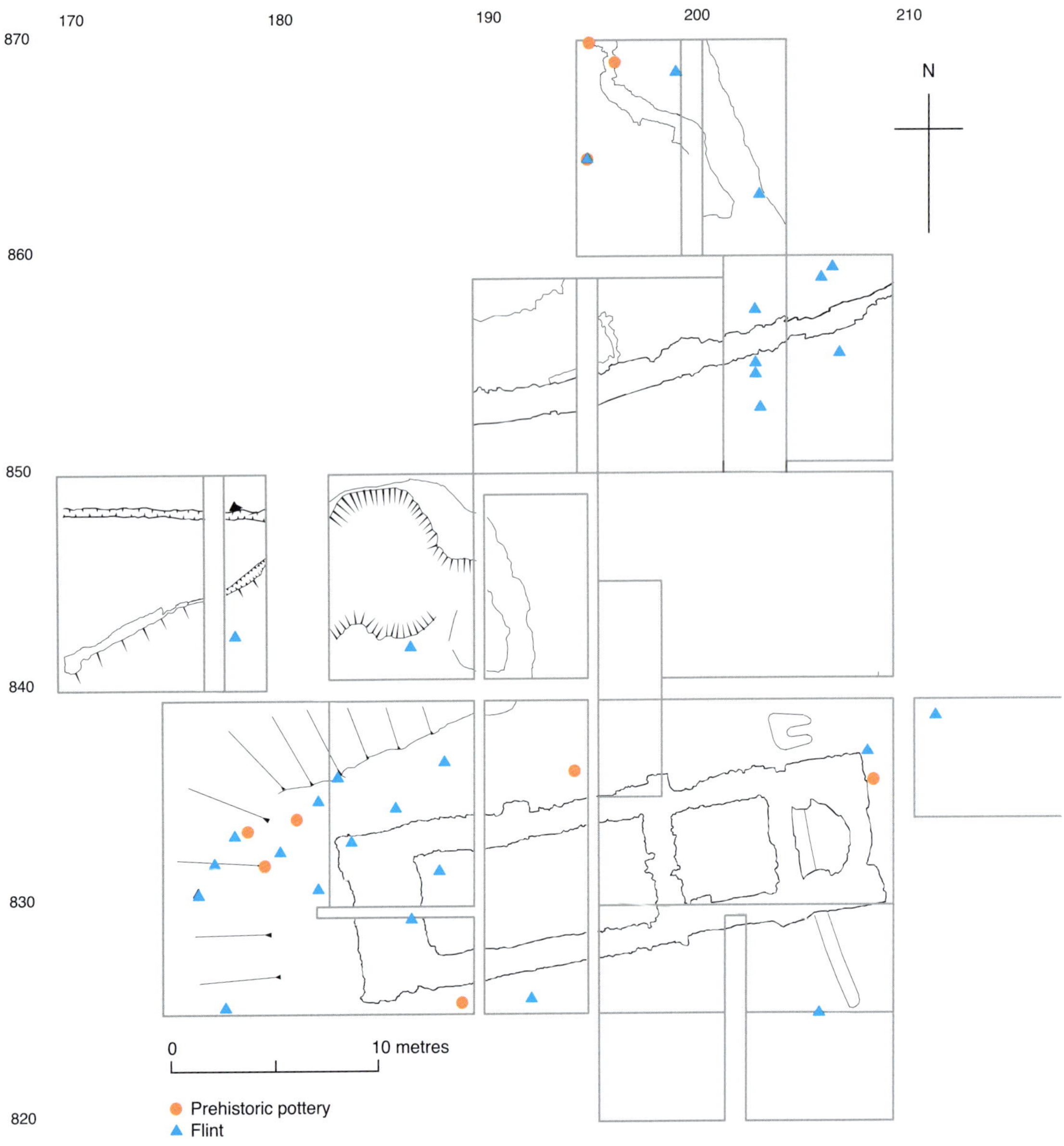

FIGURE 4.13
Site distribution of flints and prehistoric pottery

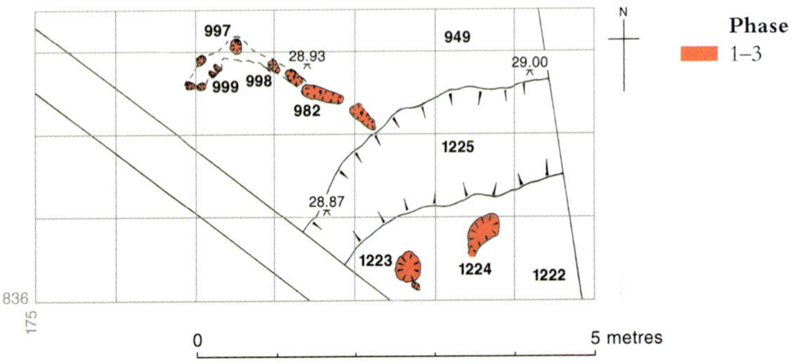

FIGURE 4.14
Gulley C1225 and associated features

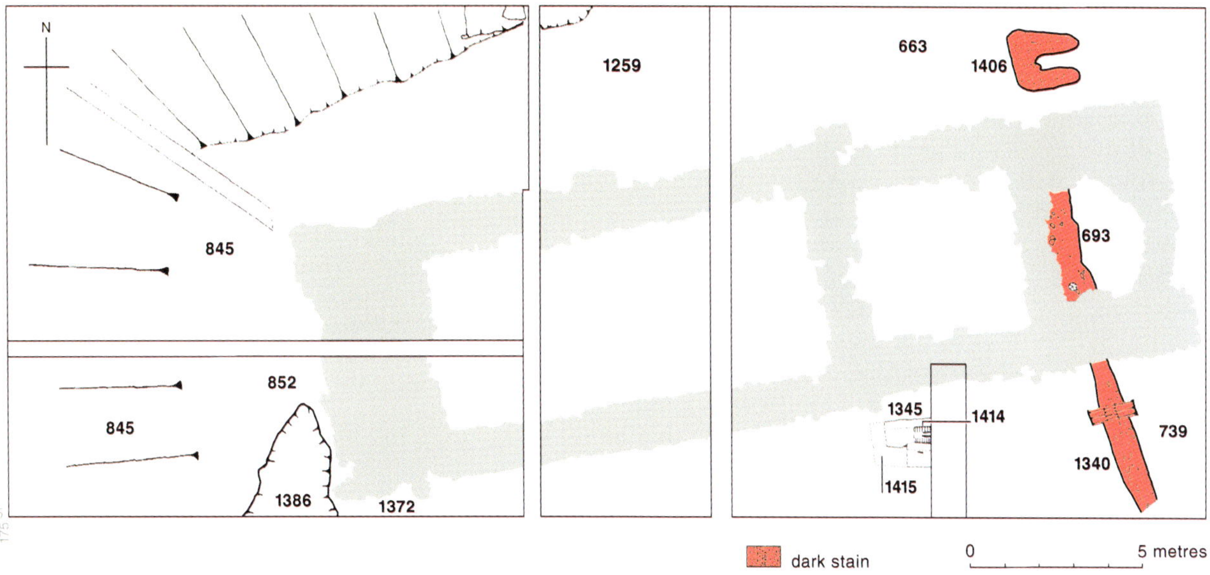

FIGURE 4.15
Features which pre-date the church

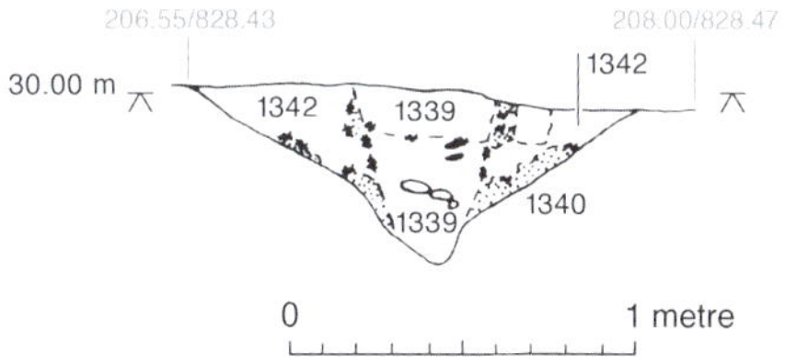

FIGURE 4.16
South-facing section through cut 1340

FIGURE 4.17
Photograph of section through cut 1340

line had been disturbed by the plough and yielded a clay pipe stem and a sherd of Tweed Valley Ware. The dark line was, however, noted early on during the excavation, and was at one stage considered as probable evidence for an earlier timber church. This interpretation has now been rejected.

Further west, to the south of the Phase I church, a small section of a ditch-like feature (C1345) 2m long survived amongst the burials, its fill (C1413) was clean, and this feature was cut by a narrower V-shaped ditch (C1414) filled with a mottled sandy fill (C1415). The length of C1414 was 1.5m, width 0.45m, depth *c*0.50m (Figure 4.18). It is possible that there were burials at a lower level than this, and it is impossible to date the feature save that it was certainly overlain by Sk278 with a sherd of Tweed Valley Ware (type 2.2) in the grave.

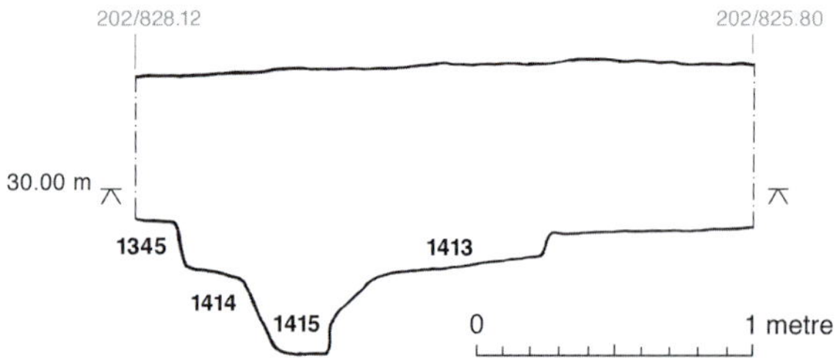

FIGURE 4.18
West-facing profile through C1414

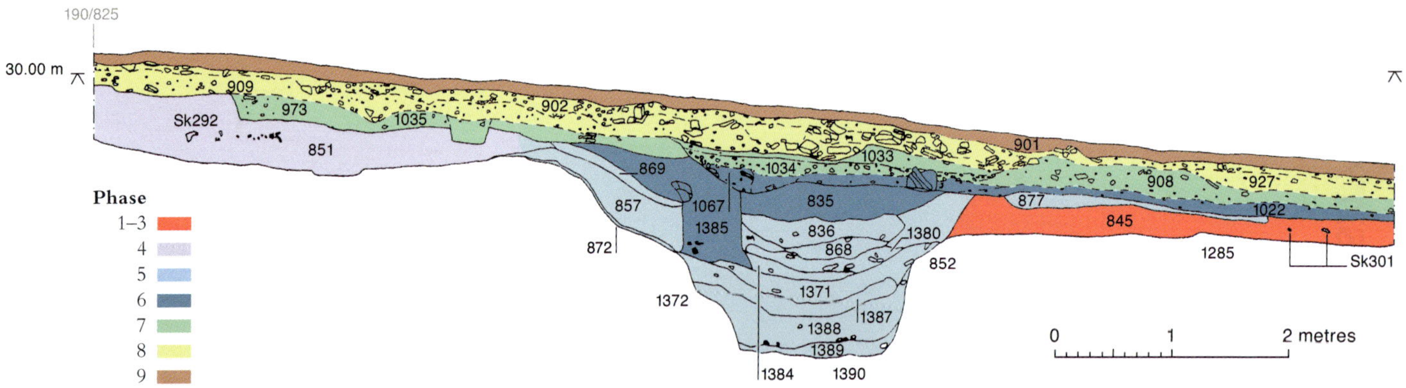

FIGURE 4.19
North-facing section through feature 1386 on grid-line 825

FIGURE 4.20
Grave cuts showing subsidence in top of feature 1386

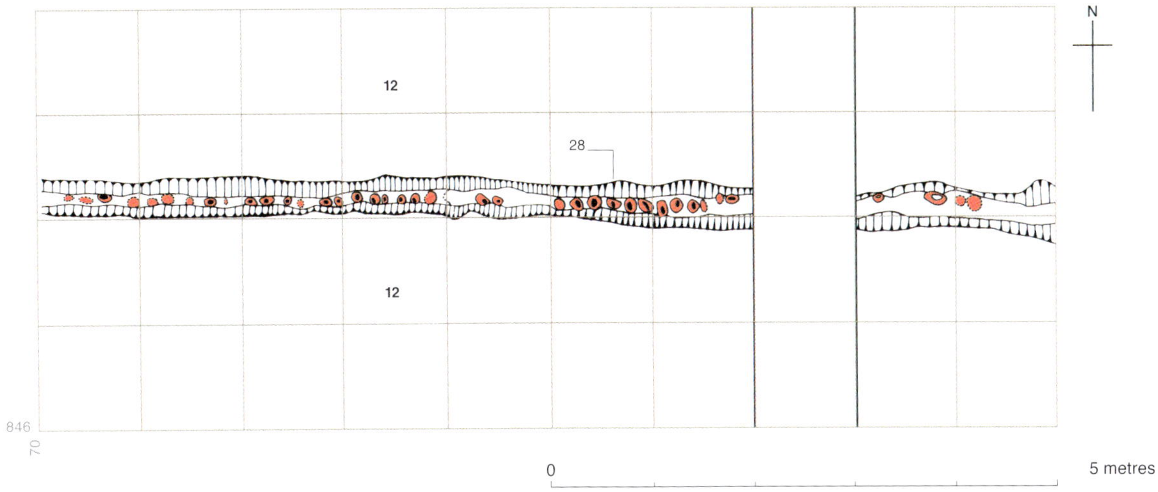

FIGURE 4.21
Palisade trench (C28) to west of site

A much more substantial negative feature, pit or ditch (C1386) at the west end of the church was sectioned, but not fully excavated because of lack of time at the end of the excavation (Figure 4.19). It extended 3.2m into the trench and terminated with a rounded end. This was an elongated pit or part of a ditch which seems to be cut from C1372 (a layer with no finds, but the upper surface C852 produced one fragment of Coarse Gritty Ware possibly 10th–12th century). Further north, the lowest soil level into which the ditch was cut (C1285) was a wet, dark, silty composition which produced one piece of Roman coarse pottery and a possible buckle tongue. The lowest fills of the feature, C1388 and C1389, provided radiocarbon dates ranging from the late 10th to the mid-12th centuries.

The ground over the ditch sank markedly over time and was levelled up by deposits (C868, C836) which included pottery types of Coarse Gritty Ware (type 1.2) and Scottish White Gritty Ware (type 2.1). The line of the ditch was apparent also in a line of graves to the west of the church which dipped into it (Figure 4.20). It then seems to have been levelled up perhaps in the strengthening of the west end of the church (see Chapter 5), and covered with new deposits of cemetery earth (C845/851; Figure 4.19). The uppermost levelling deposit (C835) contained White Gritty Ware and Buff White Ware (type 5.1, 13th–15th century).

4.3 THE PALISADE (C28)
(Figures 4.21–4.23)

This is an enigmatic feature which ran almost due east–west in the most northerly and westerly trench 170–180/840–850. The cut was about 40cm wide, with a deeper cut some 6–7cm wide and 20cm deep (Figure 4.22) and, when the clean sand and grit

FIGURE 4.22
View of palisade trench from the east

FIGURE 4.23
View of section through palisade trench in the process of excavation

fill was excavated, stake-holes were revealed in the base. The stratigraphic relationship of this feature was a matter of debate during the excavation. When first identified it was seen as a band of darker sand and stones cutting the natural sand, and partly overlaid by a cobble bank (C12) which seems to be a natural deposit reshaped in the medieval period. As recorded in the trench book 'removal of C12 then commenced more fully to reveal feature C28'. Later, however, there was some doubt as to whether the feature cut disturbed natural subsoil (C50) which yielded one sherd of White Gritty Ware, or underlay it. However cuts across this area from later ploughing did confuse matters. Despite the coincidence in part with the line of C28 and the gravel bank (C12), the 'palisade' continued further west than the bank. It is possible, however, that in the earliest shaping of the natural gravel which composed C12, the palisade coexisted with it, forming some sort of barrier against the hard surface of the natural gravel in the manner noted in the early prehistoric surface in the north-west of the most northerly trench (see above). The fill of the palisade trench was quite clean throughout and, if it had cut the medieval and later levels above, it is surprising that there is no evidence of this in the fill. The 'dark brown sandy loam' which is its fill is very much like the underlying layers under the church platform. Although efforts were made in 1980 to trace this feature further east, the huge pit and stone dumps of the post-medieval period in that area would have destroyed it.

These negative features which seem to belong to pre-church phases provide only an imperfect picture of what could well be occupation in this field spanning a period from the early prehistoric to medieval, with possible major foci in the areas not excavated. The magnetometer plots (see Section 3.2) show a very large ditch at some distance to the south of the church and cemetery, and this could be of early date but, like the potential structures south of the excavation towards the top of the hill, these features have not been tested by excavation.

5

THE CHURCH: THE EXCAVATED EVIDENCE

Rosemary Cramp

5.1 SEQUENCE AND CIRCUMSTANCES OF EXCAVATION

The church did not show up clearly on the pre-excavation resistance plots, largely perhaps because it had been covered with a dense rubble spread at the end of its life (see below and survey report, Section 3.2). Its location was first established in 1979 in the form of a small patch of the north wall of the nave, which emerged in the south section of the small trench C (Figure 5.1). In 1980 the eastern section, comprising the Phase I church and the east end of the lengthened nave, was revealed. This area was excavated further in 1981, 1982 and 1984. In 1980 the north wall of the church was identified further west and in 1981 the west end of the church was defined, and further excavated in 1982. It was completed in 1984. Also in 1982 and 1984 a central strip of the second nave was excavated, completing the whole plan of the church. Unfortunately the sections which were taken across the church in this piecemeal excavation did not usefully relate the apse and chancel to the nave and so the relationships of the various parts have been determined largely by lateral stratigraphy, and the nature of the stonework.

The extent of the building was defined in the upper levels by a loam and rubble spread which had been deliberately packed over the building line of the robbed walls of the church (Figure 5.2 and Chapter 8). The densely packed rubble covering was bounded on the west by the north–south grid-line 184 and on the east by north–south grid-line 205, so it did not overlap the eastern part of the church, and, as a consequence, the apse was the first element of the church to appear under the general soil and rubble covering of the site (Figure 5.3).

Although this stone covering was only 10 to 20cm below the turf line, the location of the building had been lost to memory, apparently as early as the 17th century (Chapter 2), and so it seems likely that the field remained as grass for most of the period from the 17th to the 20th century.

The 1977 ploughing had caused considerable movement of stone through the rubble covering and, across all of the church, parts of walls were displaced, especially the blocks of flaggy sandstone over the cobble foundations of the early church, although much of the superstructure throughout

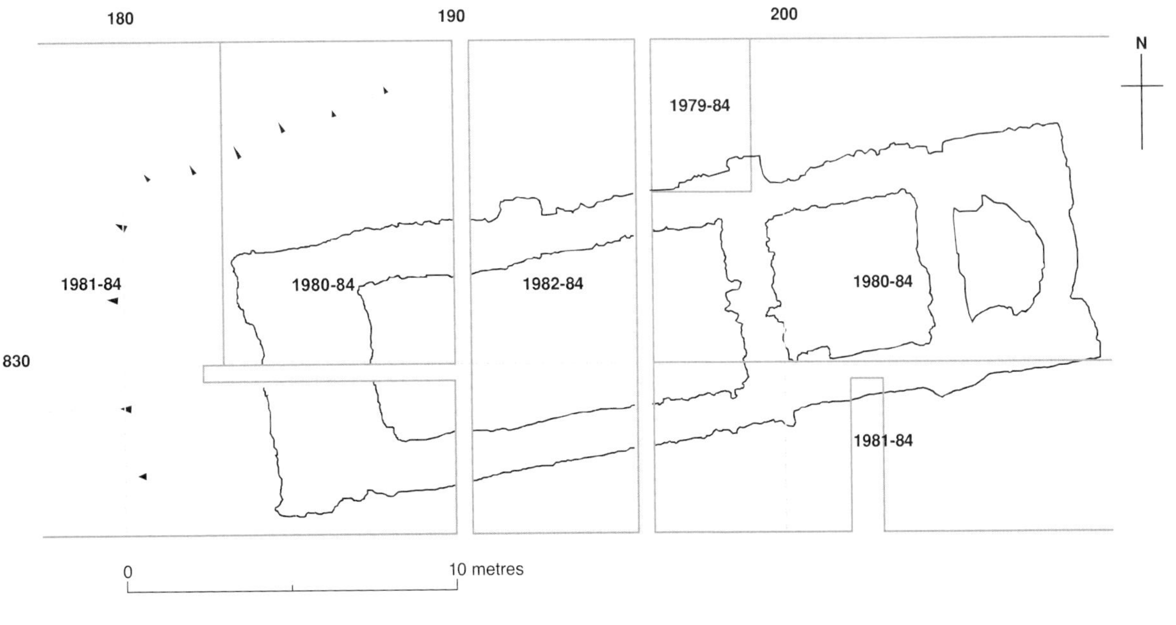

FIGURE 5.1
Sequence of excavation of the church

FIGURE 5.2
View from the north under the topsoil, with the dense covering of stone over the church in the background

had been comprehensively robbed. There was one especially wide plough drag through the north wall (Figure 5.3), which revealed the lower foundations of the building. The reason for such a wide disturbance might be that there was an opening at this point, or because a particularly large stone was dragged through. It was notable also that the south wall of the nave of the Phase III church was more deeply buried than its north wall, but also there seems to have been a greater displacement through the suggested doorways of the later nave (see discussion of the last phase of building use).

Although the robbing trenches were excavated, the surviving foundations of the excavated church were not removed because, at that time, there was the hope that the building could be consolidated and displayed. The interior was sectioned and, from the deeper excavation of the surrounding cemetery, it was clear that the ground sloped away from the church on all sides. The church then was sited on a low eminence, about 18.50m from the enclosure wall to the north, and below the steeply rising ground to the south (see Figure 1.7), the east end was near to the steep terraced slope above the River Leet and, at the west end, the natural gravel dropped away quite sharply. It must have been quite a prominent landscape feature as it was approached from the west or the river crossing on the north-east.

5.2 THE FOUNDATION OF THE CHURCH

It appears that the natural gravel and sand had been levelled and this created a platform which would have supported the church. It is impossible, however, to know from the present excavations whether this platform was already in existence during the pre-medieval occupation of this area. The natural gravel intermixed with sand (the usual subsoil of the site) is, in the church area, different from the pale sands to the north. The gravels and sands cut by this building at the east, such as C1301, were all clean and devoid of finds. At the west end of the nave of the later extended church (see Phase III), however, the level below the floor is characterised by traces of charcoal which in C899 has been radiocarbon dated 155 cal BC to cal AD 70 (SUERC-16084) and the same context produced a flint (F12, Chapter 23), which could imply an earlier occupation in this area as suggested in Chapter 4, whilst in the dark mottled sands at the west of the site there is evidence for domestic occupation, for example C1058

FIGURE 5.3
First appearance of the Phase II apsidal church, east end, showing rebuilt south-east corner and plough drag, possibly through opening

yielded animal bone, fuel ash and three sherds of Coarse Gritty Ware, one of which was dated by thermoluminescence to 810±130 (Dur84TLqi 22-1). A few sherds of Roman pottery also came from these deposits, for example the mottled sand in the north part of the nave (C882) yielded one sherd of Roman coarse ware (see Chapter 16). It is possible, therefore, that the Phase I church was constructed in an unencumbered area, but to the west of it there had been earlier occupation.

5.3 PHASE I: THE SINGLE-CELLED CHURCH (PHASE 4, EM1)

(Figures 5.4–5.9)

This single-celled church in Phase II becomes the nave and in Phase III the chancel (see Figure 5.7).

Structural description

It should be noted that since in most cases the walling is represented by robbed foundations, no measurements are as precise as those which could be obtained from standing walls.

This structure was a single rectangular cell measuring about 4.5 x 4.6m internally. The walls (624, 640, 646, 703; Figure 5.4), about 1.40m wide, with rounded external corners, were constructed of water-worn cobbles set in a V-shaped construction trench *c*0.50m deep, which had been cut through in one place by a U-shaped robber trench (C649) exposing the lowest foundations. The cobbles were larger and more irregular at the base of the trench (C662), but well sorted above ground. Some courses were set at an angle, and throughout they seem to have been earth bonded, although there were traces of mortar on and alongside the interior face. The west wall survived to three courses and, to the north of the central opening, large boulders were set forward on foundations of slanting upright cobbles. These marked a western entrance, about 1.20m wide. At both the north-west and the south-west corners of this primary building the side walls appeared to extend a little beyond the west wall. There were traces of disturbed cobbles at the east end, which could have been similar projections but this is not conclusive, and the cobbles at this point are perhaps best associated with the Phase II church (see below).

The identification of this single-cell structure as the primary building is supported by the fact that the stones which round the corners are continuously bonded and all other walls of the church either butt up to or override the cobbled walls. The apse,

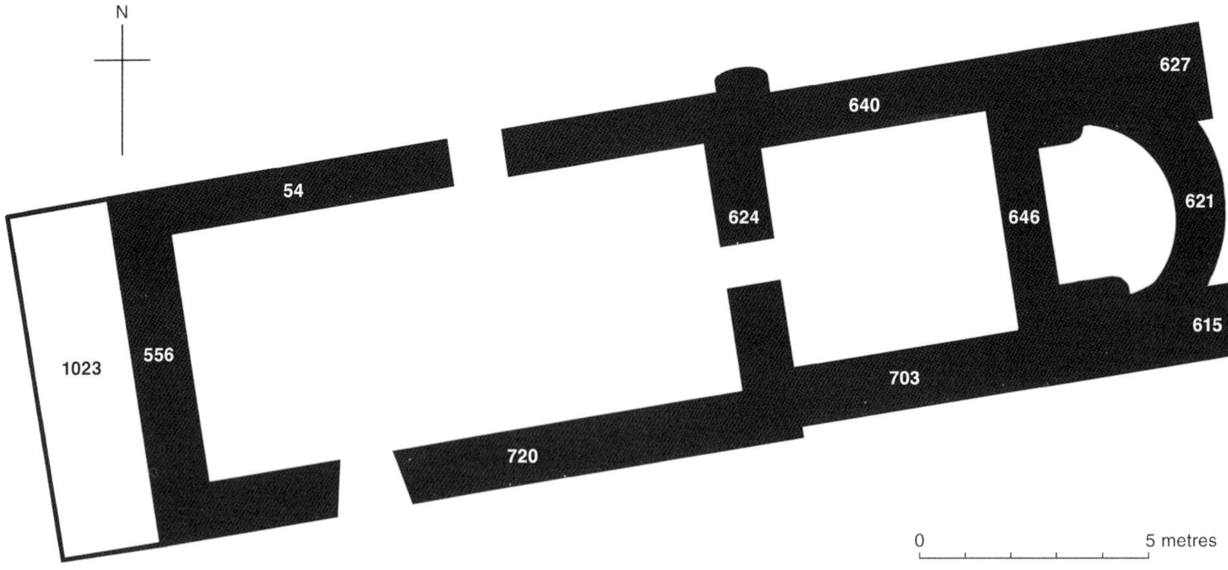

FIGURE 5.4
Site numbering of church walls

which is also constructed of river cobbles, but with a different and better sorted mixture, is butted up to the east wall at foundation level although, particularly on the north side, it is clear that the walls of the Phase I building were patched when the apse was added (Figures 5.10 and 5.11). The foundation trench of the north wall (C640) contained a sherd of Coarse Gritty Ware (type 1.3), currently dated between the 10th and 12th centuries.

Occupation

In the centre of the church the sand (C685) seems to be below the earliest occupation level and there is no trace of a continuous floor for this little building, although the slabs (C1311) at the west end, which appeared to have been laid together with the west wall, may indicate that the floor was once stone paved. The posthole (C1328) in the centre of the west wall may have been associated with the door, probably a door pivot (Figure 5.5). Two other enigmatic features at the east end may have some liturgical significance: a neat circle of small pebbles (C1248) was buried in the sand (C685), and may have been a soakaway, possibly for a pillar piscina or a font tub (Figures 5.5, 5.8 and 5.9), while the curious stain in the centre of the east wall against its western face, which was partially outlined with small pebbles (C1263), may indicate the position of the altar. The stain could be where the dregs of water for washing the celebrant's hands and the altar plate had been disposed of just under the altar, which would normally be in this position (see Parsons 1986; Ó Carragáin 2010, 191).

5.4 PHASE II: THE APSIDAL CHURCH (PHASE 5, EM2)

(Figures 5.10–5.12)

Structural description

The addition of an apse to the east of wall C646 created a church some 8.2m in length internally and 10.7m externally and the apse added about 2.6m of interior space to the east of the old east wall. Its walls cut natural sand and gravel and were constructed in neat well matched cobbles which were earth bonded. The interior seems to have been lime-washed at some stage. Part of the exterior curve of the apse on the south was hidden under subsequent building (Figure 5.10).

In this phase, wall 646, the east wall of the Phase I church, seems to have been partially demolished to create an opening into the apse and the two rounded cobble pads which projected from the north and south walls of the apse could have supported columns on either side of the opening. The position of the altar may have remained the same, or it may have been moved onto the line of the old east wall, to a position marked by a stone with a rectangular socket (C650) (Figure 5.10). This was clearly inserted into the foundations of wall 646, but whether in this phase or the subsequent phase, has proved impossible to determine (Figure 5.7). In either case it blocked the opening, but enabled the priest to officiate from inside the apse facing the congregation, alternatively the altar could have been placed against the apse wall with the priest officiating as before facing east, but more cut off

FIGURE 5.5
Foundations of the Phase I church with stones from later rebuilding shown in grey

FIGURE 5.6
Phase I church viewed from the north

from the congregation. There is no evidence for the foundations of an altar within the apse, the three postholes, C671, C672 and C673 (Figure 5.10) all contained lime wash and so are more likely to have been used in the construction either of this phase of structure or of the next one rather than as marking the altar. It is possible that the addition of the apse added status to the building as discussed in Chapter 27 and may have created a more sophisticated liturgical space.

It is presumed that the door in the west wall continued as the main entrance to the church.

Occupation

It has not proved easy to identify floor surfaces belonging to the Phase II church since, as with the first building, such surfaces had been largely stripped off. A possible vestige of early floor levels was the sandy soil with small angular stones and mortar (C670), which yielded one nail and a shell, but this is plausibly an under floor level and the stone floor postulated for the Phase I church may have continued in use. One cannot therefore distinguish clear cut phases of flooring within the two earliest churches.

The interior area of Phase I and II of the church was, however, markedly clean in comparison with the extended nave; the earlier flooring had been largely removed and later it was apparently subjected to fewer episodes of use. The levels east to west through the church were: apse 29.89m OD, chancel 29.85m OD, nave east end 29.69m OD, west end 29.76m OD, but, since the floor levels were so fugitive, this does not represent very wide differences of level, although it possibly does indicate that the east end floor was higher, marking the most sacred area of the building.

5.5 PHASE III: THE REBUILT AND EXTENDED CHURCH (PHASE 6, MEDIEVAL)

(Figures 5.13 – 5.15)

Structural description

In this phase of use, a western adjunct measuring about 11.5m x 5.0m internally was added to the west wall of the earlier church, thus forming a new nave, whilst the Phase I church became a chancel with the apse to the east. This addition was on the same alignment (roughly 83°) as the earlier church. The walls of the addition, *c*1.40m wide, were constructed of flaggy greenstone blocks, local stone probably from a quarry on the estate (see Chapter 2), and they were tooled with crisp diagonal tooling (see Chapter 12). Some cut blocks were found in the foundation trenches intermixed with cobbles

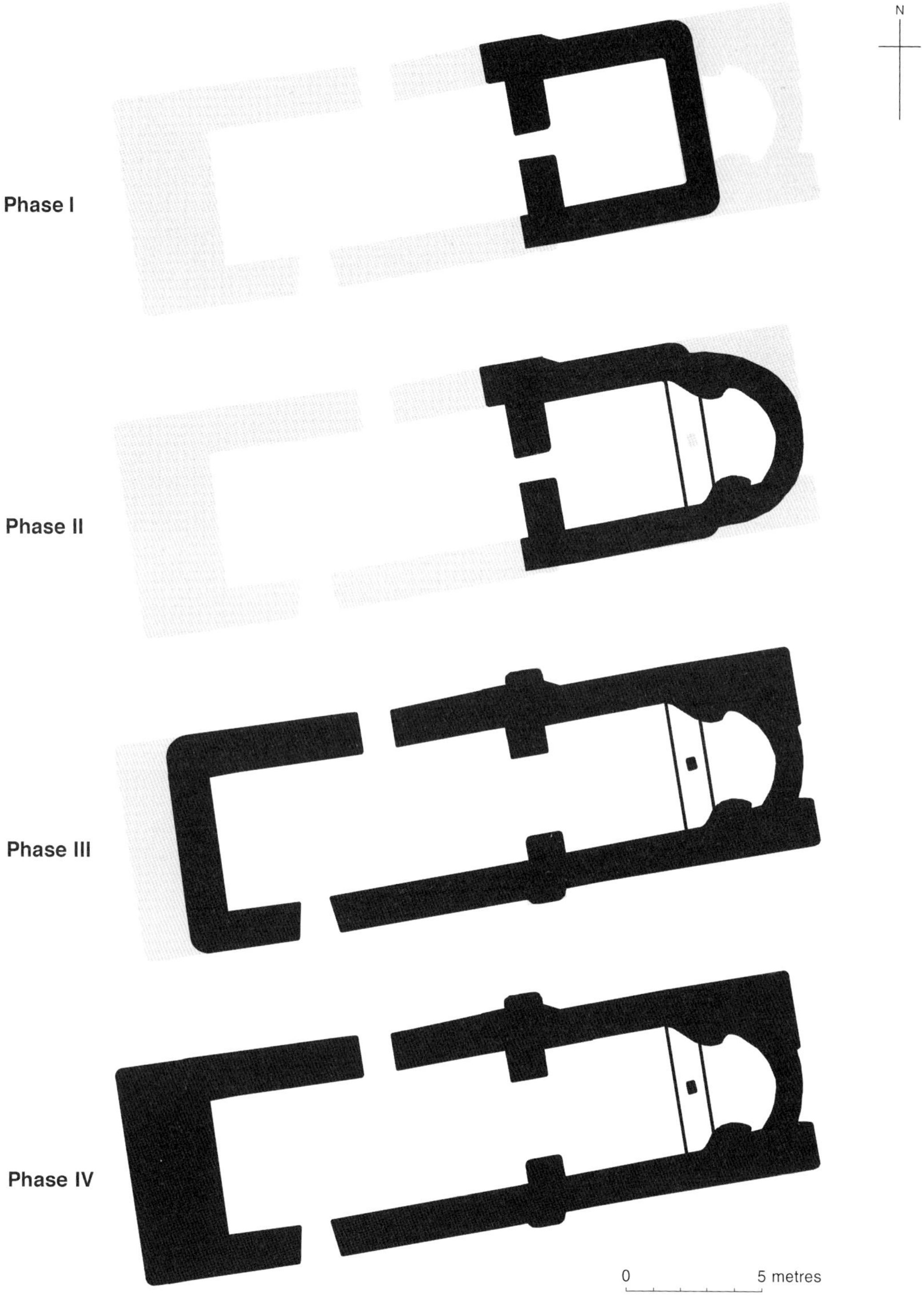

FIGURE 5.7
The four phases of the church's development

which probably derived from the earlier fabric of the church, while at the east end some blocks were still lying alongside the walls and overlying the cobble foundations of the earlier church and the apse at the beginning of the excavation (Figure 5.3). It is clear that, in constructing the larger nave, the earlier church must have been substantially demolished to foundation level or a course above — the north and south walls of the new nave overlapped the original west wall (C624) at each end (Figures 5.4, 5.7, 5.13, 5.14), and were strengthened at the point of junction by larger stones of a quoin-like form (Figure 5.16). The walls 615 and 627 also wrapped round the apse leaving only the curved centre of the original cobbled wall face visible. In fact, except for this feature, the church must have appeared of one new phase, since the cobble foundations of the north and south walls would hardly have been visible above

FIGURE 5.8
Setting of small pebbles, possibly a soakaway, in the north-east corner of the Phase I church (photographed from a balloon)

ground. The ashlar walls were slightly wider than those of the original church and the stones which were laid in straight sided foundation trenches, up to 46cm below floor level, were mortared below floor level with traces of a hard whitish mortar.

The new nave cut natural sands and gravels, for example C1306 and C1307 (Figure 5.15) corresponding with C1131, the lowest cemetery level to the north of the church, which produced one sherd of Late Bronze Age/Iron Age pottery. To the west, the walling of the extended nave was cut into C895, a mortary deposit of red-brown soil, above C899 (Figure 5.17) which as noted above provided radiocarbon date of 155 cal BC to cal AD 70 (SUERC-16084). The original west wall of the extended (Phase III) church (C556; Figure 5.4) cut contexts which would place the beginning of that church considerably later, having been dated 11th–12th century (see radiocarbon dates for C851, C857; Chapter 9). The skeletons in the graves which also cut these contexts (Sk239, Sk247 and Sk338) have been assigned a long date, but their radiocarbon dates centre around the 13th century. These graves are cut by the extended west wall of the nave (Phase IV) (see below). As with the earlier phases of the church, there was no unequivocal evidence that the Phase III church cut any burials (see Chapter 6).

FIGURE 5.9
Detail of setting of small pebbles

In the new construction, the original west door was probably enlarged to provide an arch through to the chancel, and the foundations of wall C624 may have provided a slight step up to the eastern sanctuary. There must have been external entrances into the new nave and there is a break in the north wall at an approximately central point, between north–south gridlines 192 and 194 (Figure 5.15). At this point there is an area of projecting masonry externally and, in the centre of the wall, a patch of mortar which could have supported a threshold. There is a similar dislocation further west in the south wall, which could indicate where a door had been, and outside the building and parallel with the south wall, there were at this point small patches of hard-packed gravel (C1137 and C1138) which could have been paths at a late phase in the existence of the church. One sherd of Tweed Valley Ware (type 3.1) was found in C1137. During excavation it was conjectured that there had also been an opening in the west wall, on the 830 east–west grid-line where there was a substantial pad of mortar but this was blocked later. These openings, however, need not all be of the same date.

The construction of the original west wall of the extended nave was solid and well bonded with the north wall, but it was obviously built on unstable ground since it was so close to the edgc of a slope and to a deep pit/ditch (C1386, described in Chapter 4). This ditch underlay graves at the west end (see Figure 4.19) and the radiocarbon dates for its upper fills indicate an 11th–12th century date, which could relate to the beginning of the cemetery in this area. It seems unlikely that the nave would have been constructed before the ditch/pit was filled in and levelled.

Occupation in the interior of the new nave

Although some patches of stratified deposits remain, it has proved as difficult to provide a coherent interpretation of the sequence of surfaces throughout the nave, as it was for the earlier nave and chancel, not only because there had been disturbances and robbing, but also because there seems to have been such differential use of the structure in the later medieval period, with the central area of the nave (opposite the suggested door openings) having particularly heavy use, so that only vestiges of earlier surfaces survived. The floors here were grounded on a greenish sandy mortar deposit (C1352). Further east the underlying layers are interleaved gravels and sands (C1306, C1307, C1408; Figure 5.15). The lowest floor surfaces survived best at the west end of the nave where the greenish sandy mortar, already mentioned, was lying directly on the red-brown soil which covered the natural gravel (C895, C899) (Figure 5.17). Above this was a white mortar surface (C1068). The mortar floor here is directly above the greenish sands (C1352), supporting the view that this sand is a levelling deposit, and C1068 was the first floor of the extended church (Phase III). Cutting into this surface was the bell casting pit and flue (C898 and C1279).

The bell casting area, in the north-west corner of the nave (Figures 5.15, 5.17–5.20)

The form of the bell-pit and the casting process is discussed separately in more detail (see Chapter 26), but since this is a rare survival for Scotland, it is pertinent here to note briefly that the feature consisted of a circular cavity with an internal lip which measured some 0.80m across the top and 0.48m on the lip, and this was at the same level in the cut as the flue which was about 1m long and tapered from a width of some 0.5m. (The bell when reconstructed was about 0.31m high and 0.40m in rim diameter, which is slightly smaller than the lip, but this would have accommodated bell and mould; see Figures 5.18 and 5.21.) There were two small stake-holes on the outer rim of the circular cut (C1271, C1272) which could be contemporary with its construction, and probably supported a shelter superstructure (Figure 5.19). The rectangular cut for the flue was filled with charcoal and silt (C1363) while the lowest fill of the pit was a yellow-grey and charcoal stained clay (C1283); above that brown crumbly soil (C1284), then a layer of burning and clay (C1278) which, like C1284, contained twigs of heather, heather flowers and weed seeds. Above that were fills which must post-date the casting since they contained fragments of bell mould (Figure 5.20). The whole was covered with layers of red-brown soil (C897 and C881) which contained charcoal with inclusions of copper alloy, twigs, cereal and weed seeds, mortar fragments and sherds of Coarse Gritty Ware (type 1.2) and Scottish White Gritty Ware (type 2.2, 12th–15th century). This fabric was elsewhere dated by thermoluminescence to 1060±110, which could provide a *terminus post quem* for the bell casting of the early 12th century.

The casting could have been contemporary with either the extended nave (Phase III) or the further western extension of the nave (Phase IV), but if the pit to the east (C1348) is part of the same process, as assumed in the technical report (p 307), then it is more likely that it was cast before Phase IV. This pit, which was sited about 1.8m to the east of the casting pit, was roughly circular, about 50cm deep and nearly 1m in diameter (Figure 5.15). It had straight sides and a flattened base and was filled with brown silty soil, charcoal, copper-alloy waste and daub (C1347), and yielded eleven sherds of a large Coarse Gritty Ware jar (type 1.3). This fill seems to be contemporary with the upper fill of the bell-pit (C897), with its evidence for bronze melting and some daub, and it is interpreted as the place where the copper alloy was smelted before being poured into the casting pit. The pottery in its fill is dated to the late 10th to 12th century and the radiocarbon date from charcoal within the fill, cal AD 1015–1185 (SUERC-15892), as well as the patch of burning above the pit C1226b, which

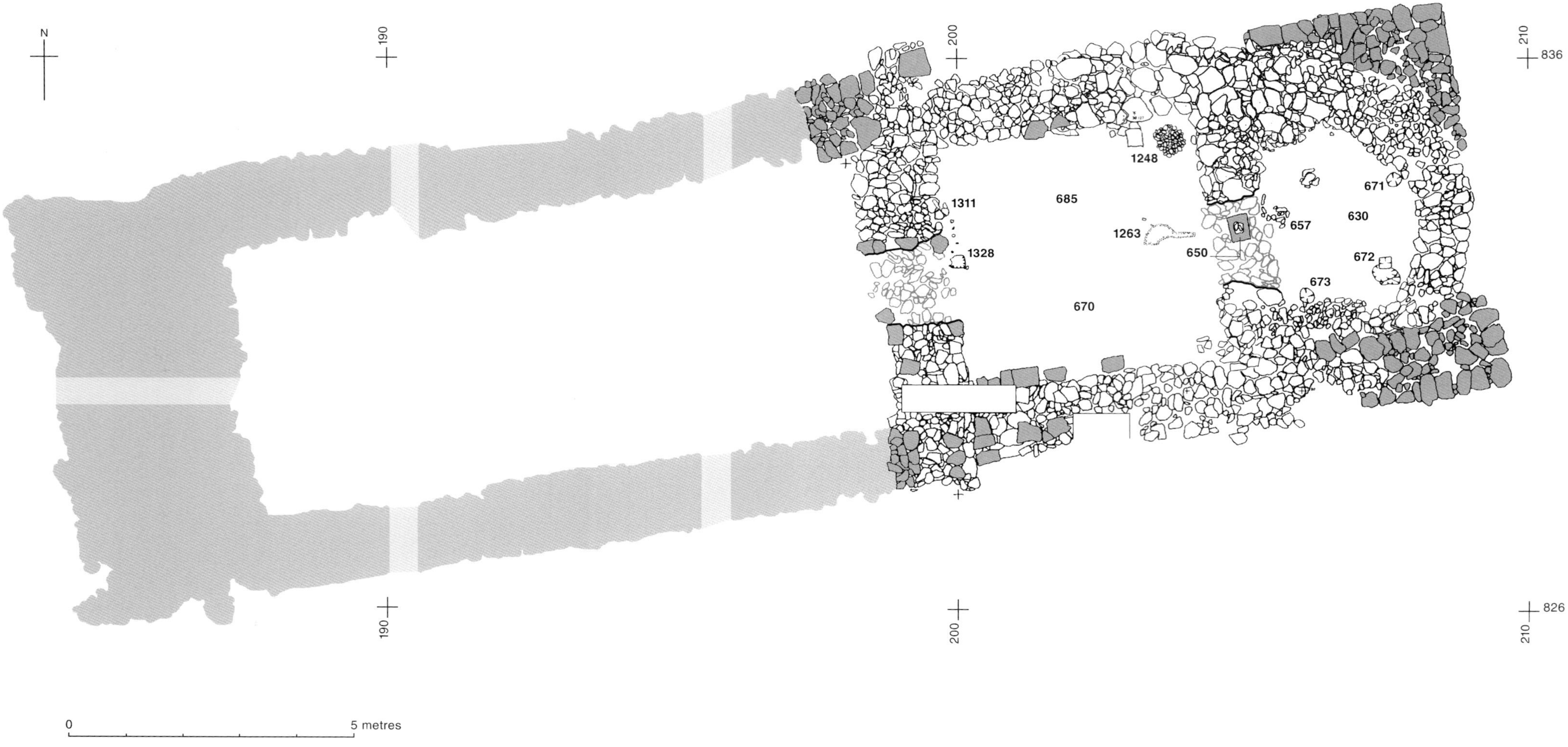

FIGURE 5.10
Foundations of the Phase II apsidal church, with later stonework shown in grey

FIGURE 5.11
The apsidal end of the Phase II church viewed from the east

likewise gave a date AD 1015–1185 (SUERC 15887), further supports the idea that the bell casting occurred quite early in the history of the extended church, and the bell could have hung in both the Phase III and Phase IV churches. Within the Scottish series of medieval bells, the Hirsel bell is notably small, but its dimensions are comparable with those of the lost bell from Ayton (Clouston 1998, 236) and the Hirsel bell has also been compared by Clouston with two bells that have been discovered at Kersmains Farm, Roxburghshire, which date from about 1190 (Clouston 1998, 246) (see Figure 5.21).

Cutting the floor (C1068) is a rectangular cavity (C1072) which seems to be later than the bell casting activity since it cuts through one of the burning areas, but its fill was clean except for traces of mortar, and it remains an enigma. It is only in this small area in the west of the church that substantial floor levels survive (Figures 5.15 and 5.17); here there is a spread of yellow mortar (C1083) above the burning (C1069), and a thin spread of loam (C1063), before a new floor level of green sand was laid (C1036). This floor yielded 32 fragments of a Coulston type Ware jug (type 2.4) and a sherd of Reduced Gritty Ware (type 4.1), seemingly spanning the ecclesiastical life of the building, and it had been cut by many later

FIGURE 5.12
East end of the church showing later walls enclosing the apse on the north and overlapping it on the south

FIGURE 5.13
The excavated church viewed from the east, with section below lowest floor surfaces

FIGURE 5.14
Excavation site 1981 showing the Phase II church, with later floor levels and the east end of the Phase III nave; cemetery to the north, with enclosing wall, Hirsel House in the background

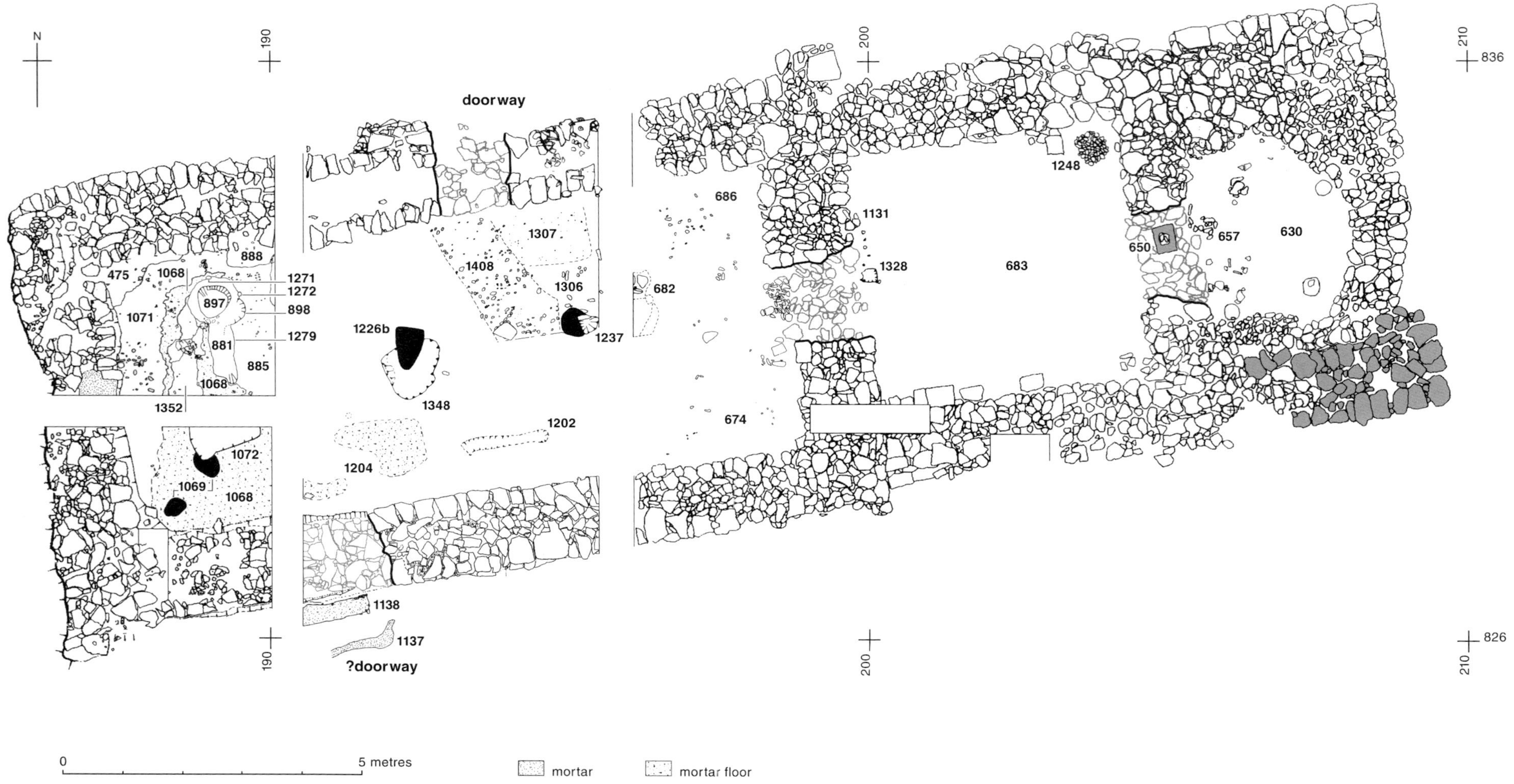

FIGURE 5.15
The Phase III extended church showing vestiges of early floor levels cut by pits for bell casting

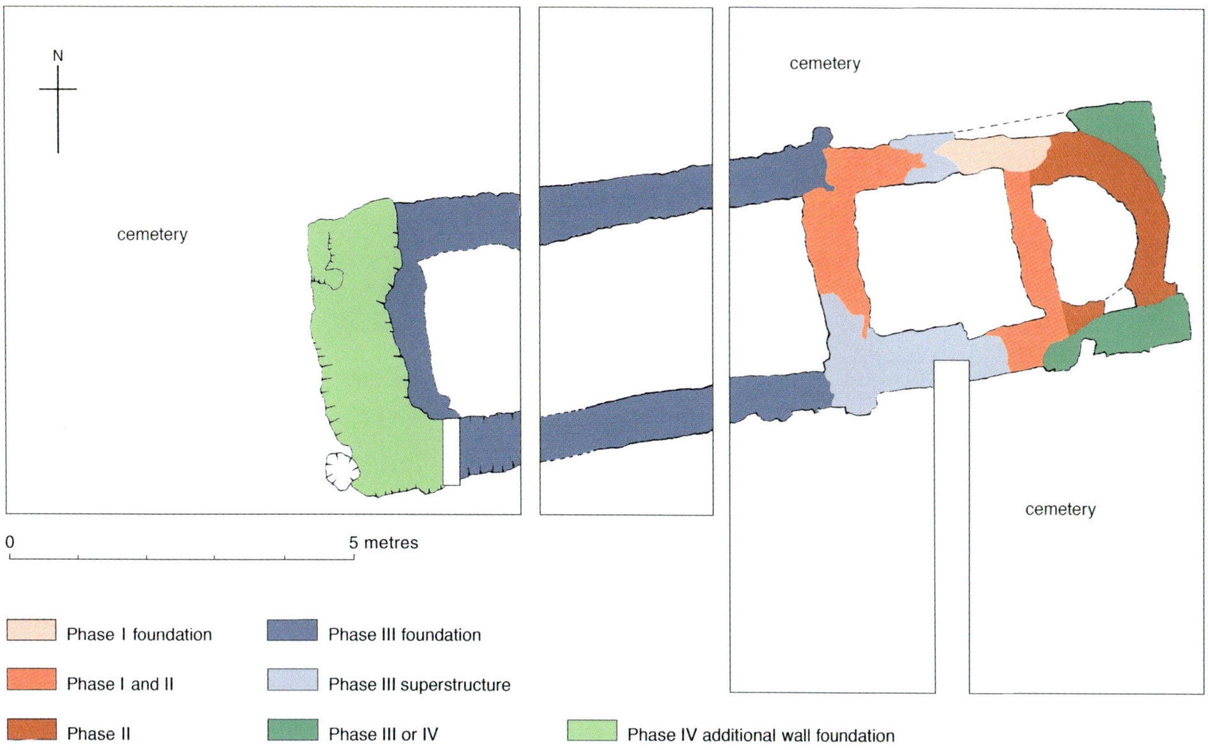

FIGURE 5.16
Plan of church walls showing phases of construction

features, including a cut along the inner face of the west wall 556, exposing C1071 which yielded a sherd of Tweed Valley Ware (type 2.1). It is possible that this cut was to examine the foundations before their strengthening over the soft ground and slope to the west, in Phase IV.

Thin traces of the greenish sandy deposit with a mortary surface were also found further east in the central part of the nave (C1204, C1203), and these directly overlaid a clean reddish brown soil (C1205), but these vestigial worn surfaces may be traces of the floor to the west (C1036), and included some evidence of later occupation in the shape of Scottish White Gritty Ware and Reduced Gritty Ware. There were patches of burning (C1069) above C1068, and, this, like other burnt patches in the nave, such as C1226b, was probably associated with the casting. These sandy mortar floors could have been covered with stone slabs but none survived *in situ*. It seems possible, from the meagre dating evidence which the pottery and radiocarbon dates provide, that the earliest nave floor could have been 12th century in date and that there was not a long gap before its replacement after the bell casting episode.

At the east end of the church, in the chancel, a more disturbed surface of small stones (C683), as well as the spreads of angular stones, could be vestiges of flooring which spanned the life of the church since they included early pottery, but also a sherd of Reduced Gritty Ware (dated 12th to 16th century).

Within the apse a yellowish sandy loam (C630), which overlaid clean natural sand, was the only possible surviving floor surface, and this produced occupation debris including one sherd of Tweed Valley Ware (type 3.1) and a leaf spring from a small padlock, as well as animal bone. These deposits, judging by the pottery, could belong to this phase or to Phase IV of the church.

5.6 PHASE IV: THE STRENGTHENING OF THE WEST WALL

(Figures 5.16 and 5.22)

Structural description

In this phase the west wall was buttressed by an outer wall with a wide foundation (C1023; Figure 5.4), providing a massive double wall *c*3.35m wide, and this cut the cemetery layer (C1058) and a row of burials which must have originally butted up against the west wall (Figures 5.23 and 5.24). One of these, a female burial in a cist (Sk338; Figure 5.25), was dated by radiocarbon to cal AD 1050–1285 (GU-1901) and the one sherd of pottery in the grave (Coarse Gritty Ware, type 1.1) is dated 10th–12th century. There was one sherd of Buff White Ware (type 5.1) and three sherds of Coarse Gritty Ware (types 1.1, 1.2) in

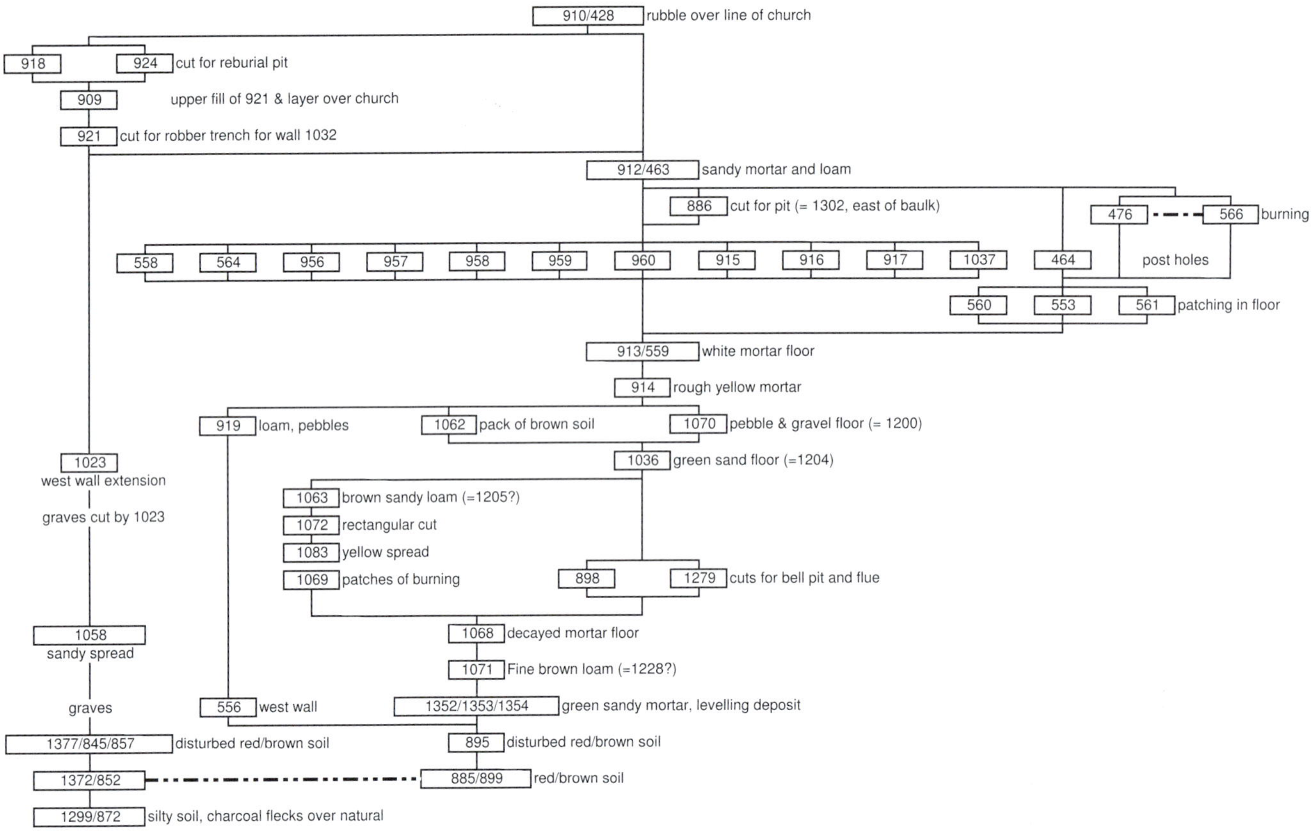

FIGURE 5.17
Matrix of contexts within the west end of the nave of the church

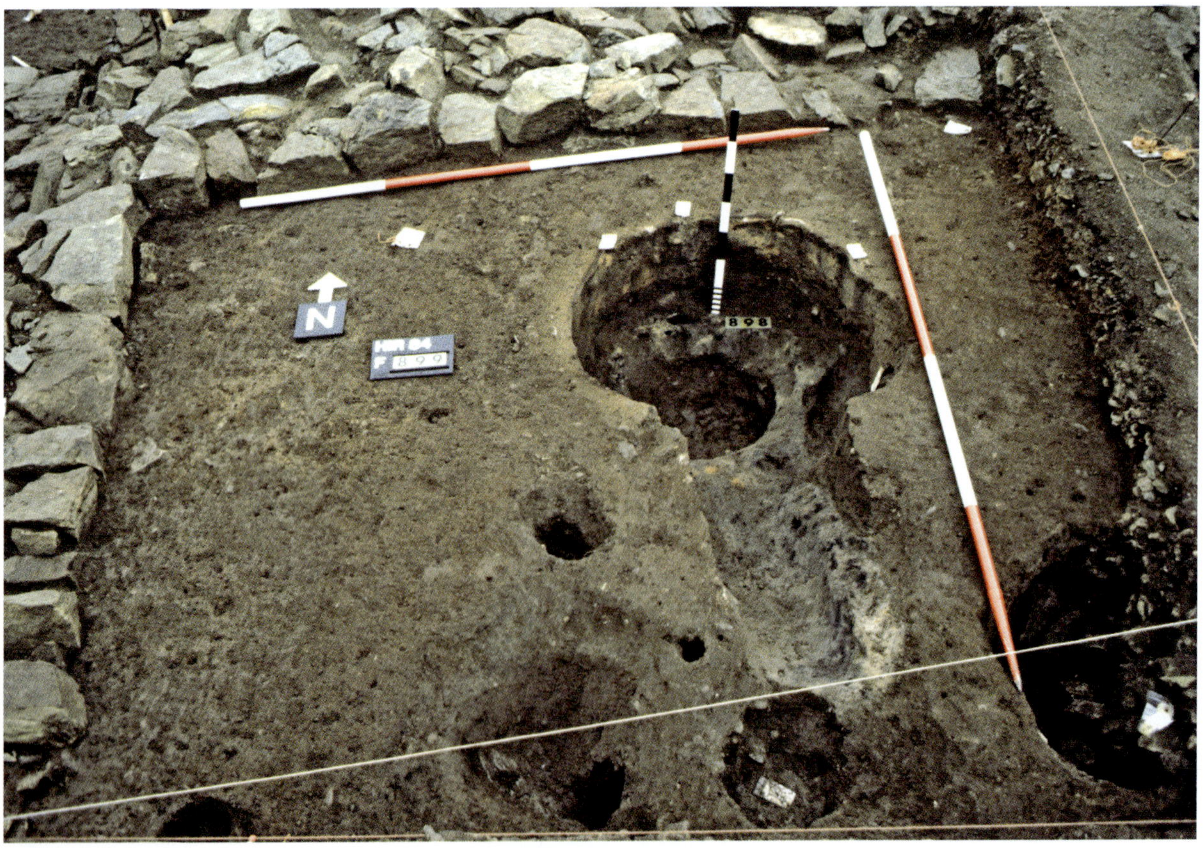

FIGURE 5.18
Detail of casting pit

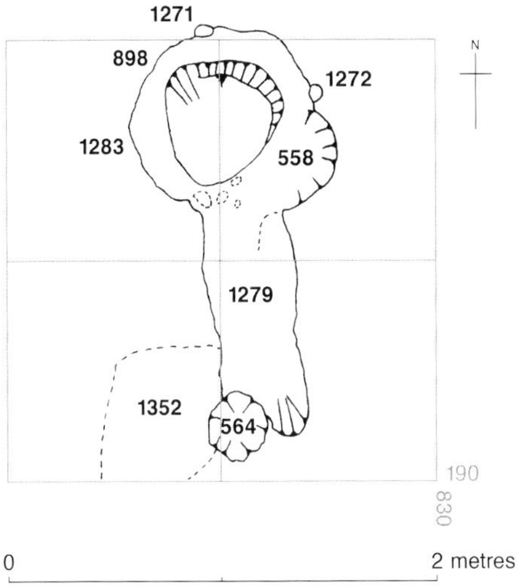

FIGURE 5.19
Drawing of casting pit

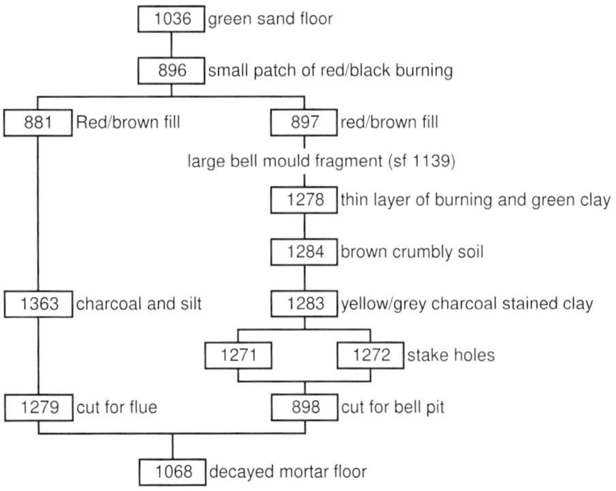

FIGURE 5.20
Matrix of casting pit for bell

what was probably the construction trench for the secondary wall, so there is a likelihood that this adjunct was added during the 13th century. It is possible that an opening in the previous wall was retained but it can hardly have been used as a doorway since this area was used for burial, right up to the church wall, from the earliest to the latest period of cemetery use. There could, however, have been a cavity such as a cupboard or bell-ringing niche in the new west wall since there is a void in the stonework at that point. The reason for the thickening of the west wall could have been purely because of the sinking of the ground over the graves and the pit (C1386; Figure 4.20), but it may have been also to strengthen a bell cote, as mentioned above. Both the original west wall and the thickened wall could have been raised into a simple pierced gable for the bell, and, if the more westerly wall is as late as the 13th century, then it presumably was needed to give further support to the bell turret.

At the east end of the church, the south-east wall buttress against the apse (C615) is of a different construction from the north and it is possible that it has been modified or rebuilt in this phase.

5.7 LATER OCCUPATION IN THE INTERIOR OF THE NAVE OF THE CHURCH, PHASES III AND IV (PHASE 7, LM)

(Figures 5.26–5.28)

The pottery in the foundations of the extended west wall (C1023), as noted above, included Coarse Gritty Ware (types 1.1 and 1.2), and one sherd of Buff White Ware (type 5.1). Unfortunately it is unclear whether some or all of this pottery was deposited in the construction or the robbing

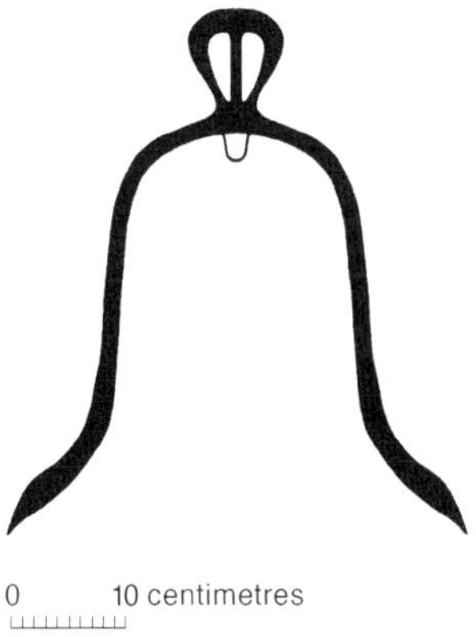

FIGURE 5.21
Reconstruction of the Hirsel bell (by Philip Clogg)

of the west wall. It is clear nevertheless that the original west wall and the north and south walls of the nave had been substantially robbed before the next phase of discernible activity which survives most clearly at the west end of the nave as a rough mortar deposit (C913) (Figures 5.26 and 5.27). This mortar deposit, which had a hard rough whitish surface over a yellowish base, was the latest flooring within the building, but may not have covered the eastern part of the nave.

Further east, in the centre of the nave, the floor had been much worn and patched and it was difficult to relate the vestiges which survived with either the green sand floor (C1036) or the later mortar flooring (C913). The greenish sandy spread (C1204) which produced one sherd of White Gritty Ware may be the same as C1036. Above this in the south part of the nave is a layer of pebble and gravel (C1200) with the same type of pottery (Scottish White Gritty Ware, types 2.2 and 2.3).

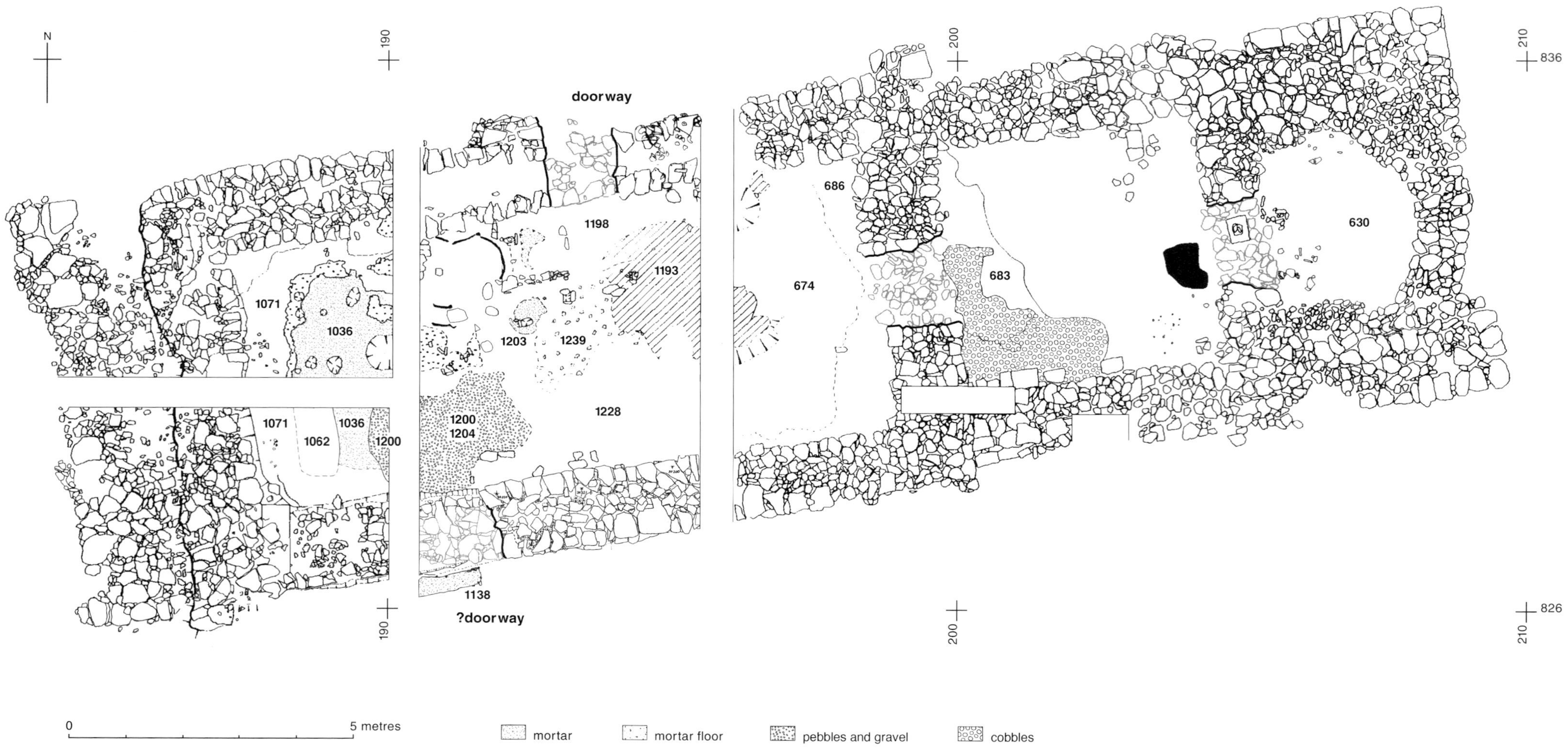

FIGURE 5.22
The church Phase IV, with strengthened west wall and vestiges of medieval floor surfaces

FIGURE 5.23
The cemetery to the west, sloping up to the church, which is robbed, with the late plaster floor (C913)

FIGURE 5.24
Burials cut by the extended west wall of the church

FIGURE 5.25
Cist burial cut by the extended west wall of the church

So it would appear that there was considerable patching and robbing in the nave by around the 14th century.

Many small postholes were either cut into or were set with the mortar flooring (C913). Some (C958, C957, C956, C564, C917, C1037) were roughly aligned north–south and further east, where the mortar spread did not exist, there were diagonal lines of posts (C1175, C1177, C1179, C1197, C1231, C1233, C1235) running east–west (Figures 5.26 and 5.28). Although some seemed to be in alignment, they made no obvious pattern and they need not all have been cut in the same episode. Three at the east end of the nave (C676, C677, C682) were in line and neatly edged with flat stones, as were postholes C1175 and C1179, and these could be distinct from those in the mortar at the west end. An area of trampled clay (C1191, yielding a sherd of Reduced Gritty Ware, type 4.2) could be of this phase, and a remnant of the floor surface into which the posts were set. They seem too small to hold up a roof, but could have supported some temporary stone and timber structures for people and/or animals.

Probably of this same phase, when much of the nave walling had been robbed, is a rough line of stones by the south door, running north–south (C1156), and a line of angular stones (C1157) running parallel to the north wall of the church. The former could be the base of a screen wall, dividing off the central sector of the nave with its north and south doors, whilst C1157 could be the base for a bench or another division. The rough walling (C1156) included architectural stone (Figure 5.29), presumably from the robbed walls of the church, and C1157 included part of a pot, other sherds of which were found in the pit (C1302) which was capped by a hearth (C1227; Figure 5.26). All of these features, like the clay surface and the post lines, contain later medieval pottery (Reduced Gritty Ware) and indicate a phase when the nave of the church at least had been given over to secular use. The finds of animal bone and iron work, including arrowheads, are indications of this type of occupation of the building and the most blatantly secular feature is the pit (C1302), which was filled by straw, vegetation and faecal matter. It also had some cut stone in the fill which supports the view that at least part of the church fabric was already destroyed. This latrine pit need not have been opened for long, as is suggested by the fact that the pottery in its lowest levels joins with sherds from the hearth (C1227) which capped it.

There were other hearths further east, which also seem to belong to this phase (C675, C679). The interior of the chancel is cleaner, but in the centre of the area there was a hearth (C681; Figure 5.30) which, after its use, was covered by a capping of stones (C656) producing a sherd of Scottish White Gritty Ware (Figure 5.31). There was no clear evidence for the type of floor which the hearth scoop cut, although burnt orange sand below it (C685) may be a remnant of a subfloor. This phase then seems to represent a short, and fairly destructive, occupation of the extended nave which seems at that juncture to have been robbed and ruinous, but with the structure still being used with temporary timber shelters for either people or animals.

5.8 THE FINAL PHASES

(Figures 5.32–5.34)

There may have been only a short time span between this secular occupation and the final destruction of the building as demonstrated in the areas of burning which characterise the end of its life. Some of the burning deposits, such as C566 at the west, clearly overlaid the latest mortar floor C913. Others, where earlier floor levels have been worn away to sand and gravel, contained the same type of material as the pits and other features which they covered (see C1135, C1151, C1160, C1159 over a possible floor, C1158, and to the east C623; Figures 5.32 and 5.33).

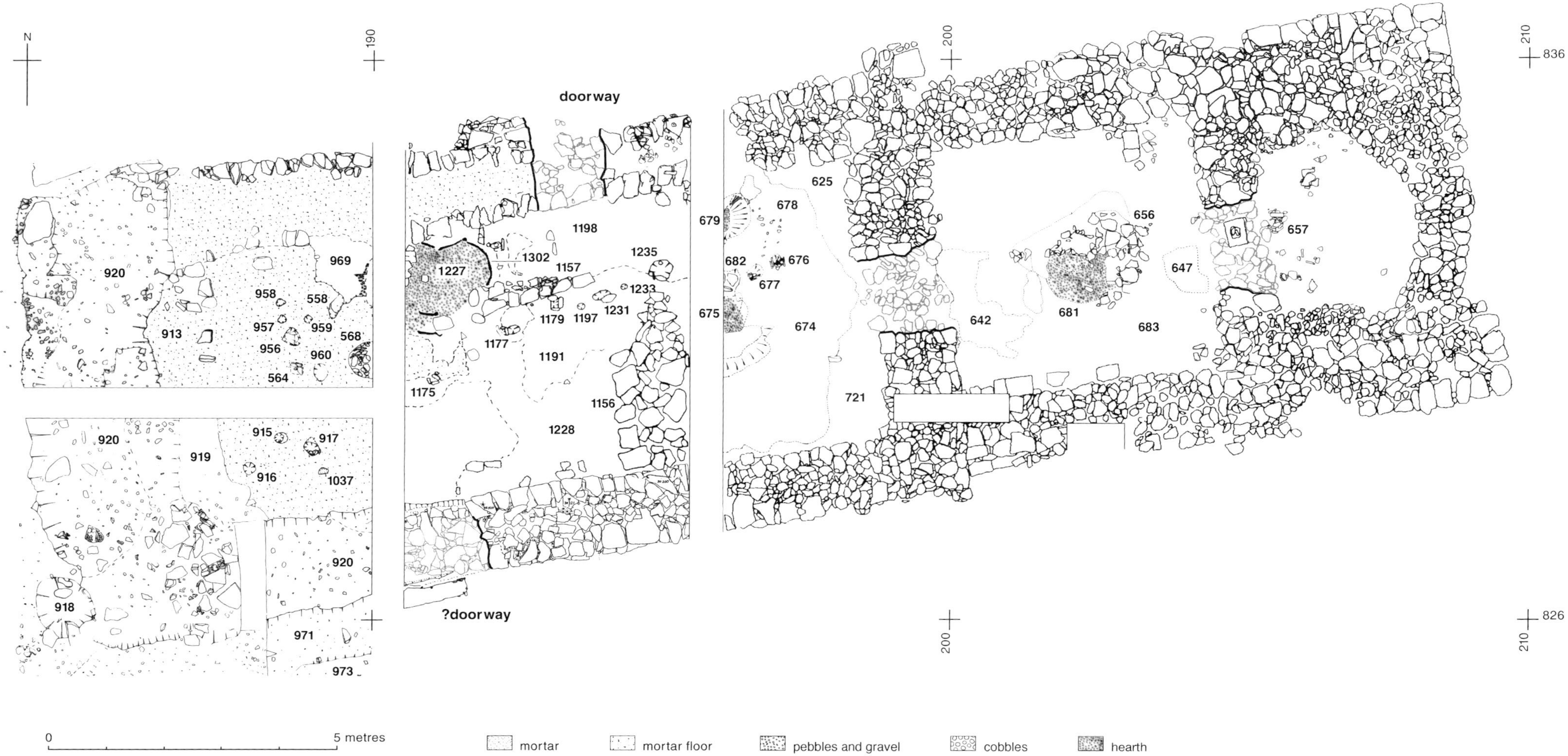

FIGURE 5.26
The latest phases of activity within the church

FIGURE 5.27
The robbed out church with mortar floor spreading over the demolished walls

The destruction

The latest discernible surfaces were overlaid with debris containing a significant number of nails, which may indicate the demolition of wooden structures by fire. The deposits of burnt matter were spread throughout the nave, although they did not extend to the wide west wall, and it would seem that, although this wall was robbed in several phases, the original gable end stood longest. The burnt matter on the floor contained burnt grain as well as metal work and Reduced Gritty Ware (see C1135, C1160, C1159). An area of intense burning at the east end of the nave (C623) was particularly rich in occupation debris, including cereal remains and animal bones, arrowheads and other iron objects, and Reduced Gritty Ware, which is the latest medieval pottery from the site. One sherd from this context provided a TL date of 1475±55 (Dur84TLqi22-3), which could indicate the period of this final destruction (Figure 5.34).

The arrowheads from within the burnt matter were of the same type as had been found in the previous phase of occupation, and may have survived in the building from that phase; likewise there were such notable deposits of grain in the burning that they could have been stored there and burnt *in situ*, implying that the nave had been used as a barn or storage shed. As noted above, the latest and predominant pottery from all of the features and burnt deposits is later medieval Reduced Gritty Ware, with no trace of post-medieval items. This seems therefore to be a short-lived phase, in which what was left of the building was burnt down after a period of use in which grain, and possibly hay and other items, had been stored there and where people who used hunting arrows had encamped. If these had been arrows for warfare then one could have concluded that there was a short occupation, and desecration of the building by the military, since there is plenty of evidence for the depredations of the English army at this time, and this is discussed further in Chapter 27.

It is possible that the first deposit of worked stone to the north-west of the site, and also the building of the enclosure wall to the north (see Chapters 7 and 8), took place before this use of the church, since the occupation, as noted above, spread over the robbed north and south walls. The time scale, however, which could include the destruction of the building, its occupation and final burning, is difficult to determine, but could have been relatively short.

Since the most intense use of the building in the latest and more domestic period seems to be concentrated in the centre of the nave between the postulated north and south doors, in the interim

FIGURE 5.28
Detail of line of stone-packed postholes in the nave (photographed from a balloon)

reports (Cramp 1985) it was suggested that the extended nave existed as a domestic building for a time, and that the chancel and apse went out of use. The west end does not appear, however, to have been a separate domestic structure, although it does seem nevertheless that the east end was more respectfully treated than the nave, despite the occurrence of the single hearth. The eastern part of the church was the first part to emerge under the topsoil in the excavation and there was a significant amount of cut stone lying around (see Figure 5.3) which could imply that the whole of that part of the church remained standing until it was robbed of the cut stone, at a later date than the nave, and this could have been just before it was covered by the last rubble spread. The view that there were several different periods of robbing is supported by the fact that in the extended nave above the burning, there was a layer of a brown sandy loam, which may signify abandonment or another use and, as noted above, there is evidence of some clearance of the building possibly connected with the enclosure wall to the north (see Chapter 7).

Other deposits of sandy loam mixed with mortar and rubble and with late medieval pottery (C1126, C1127; Figure 5.35) accumulated in what seems to be a definite period of abandonment, a view supported by the finds of owl pellets in C463 and C619, which were directly under the rubble mass sealing off the structure (see also Section 10.2). This was crushed down neatly over the lines of the church. The major stone deposit (C421, C1124) to the north-west of the church contained a great deal of cut stone as well as some window glass and bottle glass (see Chapter 8), and it seems to be connected with the obliteration of the walls of the church. Since none of the robbed wall trenches yielded pottery later than medieval, and there is a notable absence of late medieval types in the whole site assemblage, the date of the destruction of the church seems unlikely to have been later than the 14th to 15th century. The actual covering of the church with a dense layer of rubble seems to have occurred at some interval after the robbing of the walls and abandonment, but again the pottery does not include late types, and the sealing off of the church appears to be of a late medieval period. The churchyard was, however, left open for longer (see Chapters 2 and 6) until it, and the church, were covered by another rubble spread directly under the topsoil.

5.9 SUMMARY OF THE ARCHAEOLOGICAL SEQUENCE

The sequence as discussed above could range from about the 10th century to the 13th for the four main phases of construction, with the church abandoned during the late 14th century,

FIGURE 5.29
Head of opening amongst the robbed walling

and with a variety of activity in its ruined frame until around the 15th century. The chronology can be tentatively summarised as follows: the Phase I unicellular church could be, on the basis of the pottery found alongside its north wall, as early as the 10th century or as late as the 11th. The addition of the apse follows, but there is no independent archaeological dating for this, and any suggested must depend on architectural views as to the dating of apses in Scotland, discussed below. The thorough rebuilding of the church in mortared and cut stone must also depend on well dated parallels for its plan, and for the sculptural fragments which could be assumed to be associated with it, but the dating of the pottery in the fills of the bell casting features and the radiocarbon dates from the associated pit are useful since both features cut the first floor of the church and, even if the bell making took place very soon after the construction of the nave, they could indicate a construction date in the mid-12th century. The thickening of the west wall can be tentatively dated to the 13th century by the pottery in its foundation trench and the levels and burials which it cut through. The demise of the church as a consecrated building and its conversion to secular use, based on the artefactual evidence, seems to occur by the end of the 14th century, with subsequent robbing, adaptation and the final obliteration of the building taking place in the early 15th century.

5.10 THE EVIDENCE OF THE ARCHITECTURAL DETAIL AND DECORATIVE ELEMENTS

The carved stones might have helped to refine the archaeological dating of the church sequence, but although there is a number of fragments of carved stone (see stone catalogue, Chapter 12) none are *in situ* and the most substantial were those discovered in the stone dumps in the north-west section of the

FIGURE 5.30
View of the church from the east, showing the hearth in the centre of the chancel

FIGURE 5.31
The latest floor surface in the east end of the church; the hearth is capped with stones

site or those which had been cleared from the field during the ploughing before the excavations began (Cramp and Douglas-Home 1980). One curving fragment, possibly the arch over an aumbry or piscina, was found lying amongst the stone of the rough transverse 'wall' (C1156; Figure 5.29) which was constructed in the last phase of occupation. A few pieces of architectural stone were also found during excavation, forming part of the foundations and the collapsed fabric of the wall to the north of the graveyard (C214/291, C1007). Some carved stones had obviously been dragged by the recent ploughing, such as the fluted column AF2 which was reconstructed from four pieces spread across the site. Others, such as the column fragment and chevron fragment (AF1) in C708 were found in the rubble spread of smashed stone which formed a hard standing in the post-medieval phase. Because of this it is not possible to associate the architectural elements directly with the different parts or phases of the church, but where fragments have diagnostic features, Fawcett has seen them grouped around the later 12th century, and these (with the exception of AF2) are all in the same micaceous sandstone as the walls of the Phase III church. So there is a generation or so difference in the dates indicated by the architectural and archaeological development.

The small square unicellular church of Phase I could have been a very simple structure, with low walls and a roof of turf, or thatched with heather or straw, traces of both being found in the botanical record of the site (Figure 5.36). There were no traces of roof supports at ground level but, as with other clay bonded buildings elsewhere, the roof could have been supported on crucks embedded in the upper part of the walls (Figure 5.37). The only opening is at the west. It is likely that the exterior would have been lime-washed, but no conclusive evidence for this was found during the excavations. Simple rectangular structures such as this are commonplace among early ecclesiastical buildings in western Scotland and The Isle of Man although they are not closely dateable (see Chapter 27).

There is little evidence for the appearance of the interior. The only feature which might have supported a furnishing was the small neat circle of rounded cobbles (C1248) in the north-east corner of the first nave, which appeared below the sandy floor at a late stage of the excavation of that area (Figures 5.5, 5.8 and 5.9). These cobbles could have supported something like a reading desk, or have served as a drain for a pillar piscina or wooden font. The altar would most reasonably have been in the centre of the east wall (see Fawcett 2002,

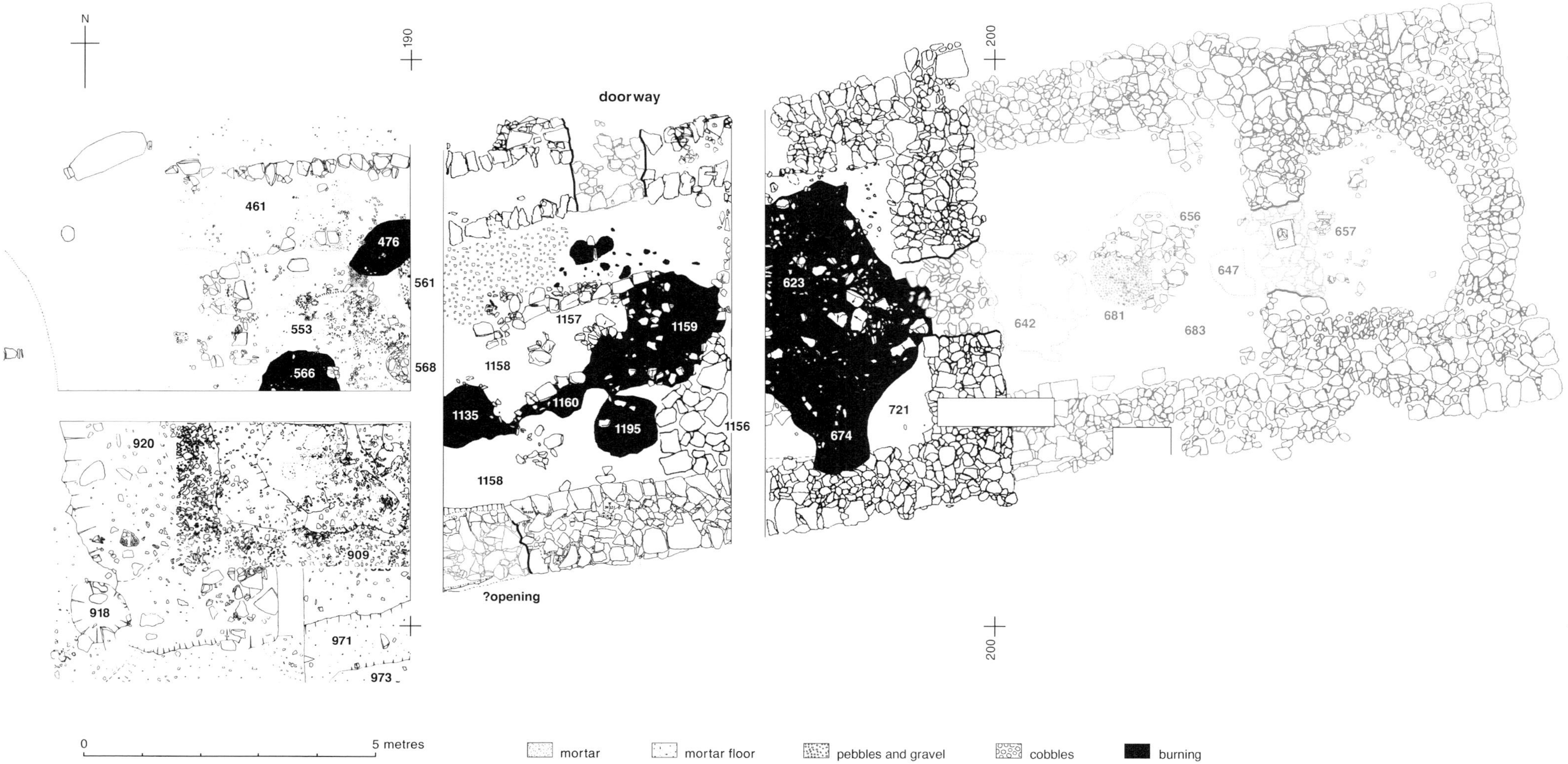

FIGURE 5.32
Plan of the final phase showing burning deposits over the nave of the ruined church

FIGURE 5.33
View of the central and eastern part of the nave, showing burnt deposits

FIGURE 5.34
Detail of burning deposit at the east end of the nave spreading into the robbed south wall

248–251), and the strange 'drip line' marked by small pebbles (C1263) could be evidence for its position (Figure 5.5). If it was moved in Phase II or III, the socketed stone (C650; Figure 5.38) could have been placed there either marking its position, by supporting a cross, or to support a new piscina, since it has been suggested that after an altar was moved, a cavity to support or to serve as a new piscina could have marked the original position of the altar (Anon 1984, 250). Its position is discussed further below and under AF 23. There is no evidence for the form of the openings, but some roughly shaped bars (AF13–17) with tapered ends may have been parts of windows.

The tentative reconstruction is based on this rather limited evidence (Figure 5.36); the position of the western door is certain, the position of any window is conjectural; there might have been a window at the east end to light the altar. The heather roofing and the gable infilled with wattle and daub are suggested as possible features which could have been supported on these cobble walls. The projections from the north-west and south-west corners of the west wall did exist, but in such a fragmentary state that their form is conjectural. The door lintel with an incised cross is not based on evidence from this site.

The addition of the apse in Phase II could be seen as a significant upgrading of the church to imitate

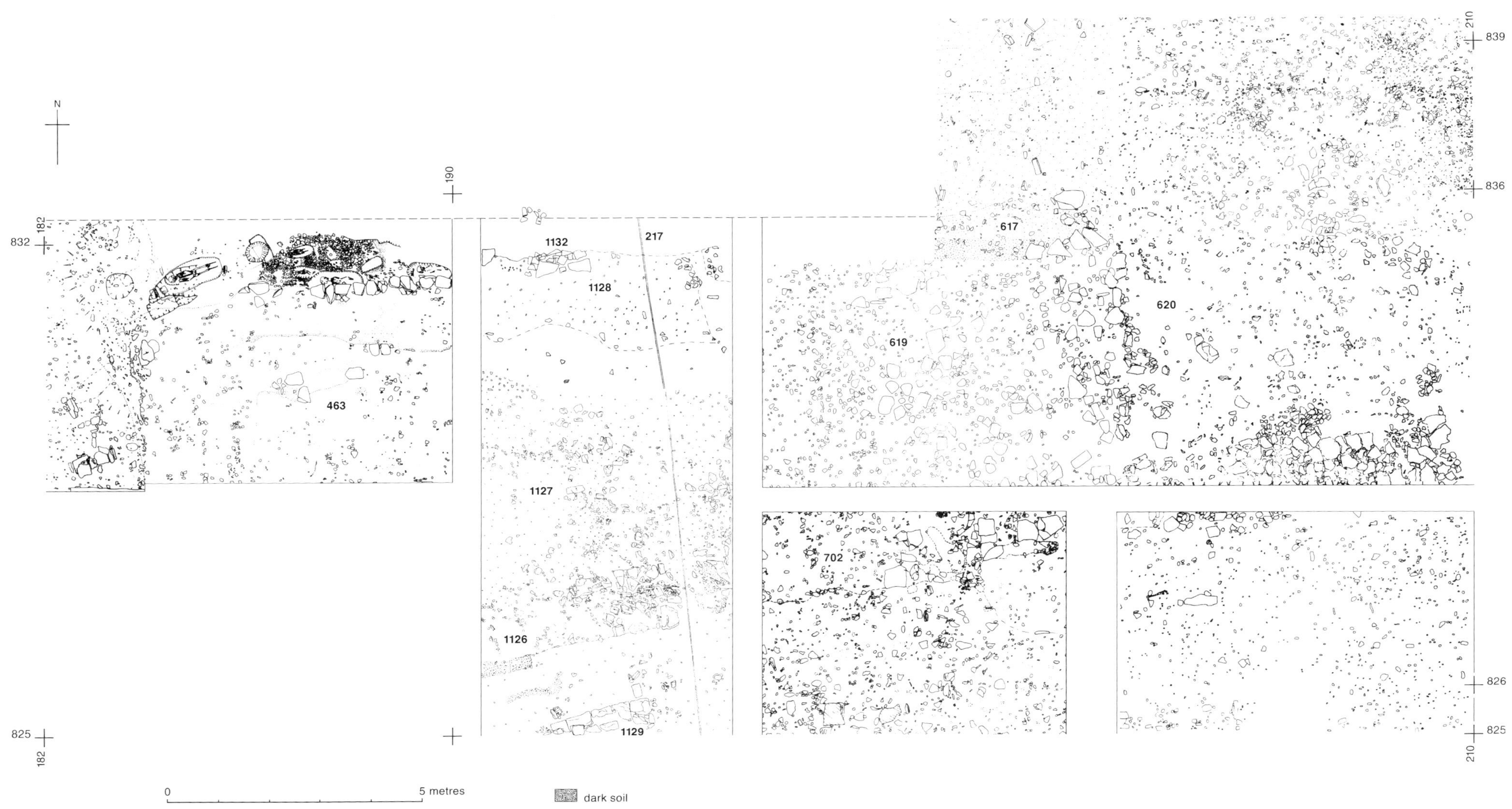

FIGURE 5.35
The church covered by rubble as revealed beneath part of the stone covering

FIGURE 5.36
Hypothetical reconstruction of Phase I church

FIGURE 5.37
Detail of roof construction, Old Yeavering farm building (Northumberland)

new fashions in architecture or developments in liturgy. The main structure need not have changed, but there may have been some elaboration of the fittings such as an aumbry or decoration of the new opening into the apse. Fawcett sees the semi-circular apse as 'one of the architectural elements brought up from England as Scottish patrons sought masons to build the churches required by the new monasteries and parishes, and the new or re-established dioceses' (Fawcett 2002, 25; and Chapter 27).

The cobble foundations are, as noted above, rather smaller and better sorted that those in the first church, but it is still simple building technology and it appears that this apse could have been added to the earlier structure without much disturbance other than breaking through the east wall. It is possible that the two 'pads' on either side of the opening might have supported shafts, and the imposts could have been of the simple block shape as found at the nearby (undated) church of Bunkle (Figure 5.39). There are, amongst the surviving stones, fragments of plain columns, but these could have embellished openings in the later extended church, and two roughly chamfered bases (AF24 and AF25; see Figures 12.25 and 12.26), others were discovered spread over the floor (C629) of the chancel of the Phase III church and could have been the supports for such columns. How the windows were formed is not clear; they could have been formed with simple stone framing

FIGURE 5.38
Detail of the socketed stone (C650) as excavated

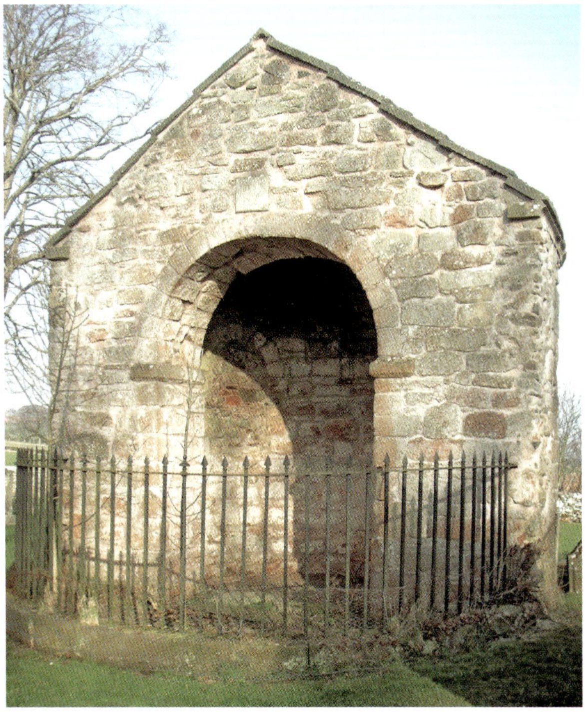

FIGURE 5.39
Bunkle old church, Berwickshire, showing the arch into the sanctuary with simple slab imposts

and the strap hinge (Fe1; Figure 20.1) might have been from a shutter or door, but while this came from the mound of rubble over the west end of the church (C404), it could have belonged to any of its phases, or, like the strengthening for small chests or the padlocks (Chapter 20, Figure 20.1), it could have belonged to furnishings which survived through several phases.

There is, however, one interesting fragment which might have been part of a fitting such as a screen or altar frontal in the Phase I or Phase II church in the shape of a slab carved with incised wavering interlace (AF26; Figure 12.27) which was built into the south wall of the chancel of the Phase III church. This type of interlace is plausibly late 11th to early 12th century in date.

The extension of the church in Phase III was a major operation involving the use of cut and mortared stone, although, as suggested above, the stone could have been derived from a quarry nearby (see Figure 2.3). The slabs on the north and south corners of the junction with the nave, which look like quoins, could, if one followed the suggestions of Potter (2006), be considered as 'stone emplacements' which he considers represent a prolongation of pre-Norman traditions. His list of such churches in Scotland (Potter 2006, 232–233) include others in the Borders which have features in common with The Hirsel, for example

Abbotrule, Ayton, Lamberton and Preston, but such a slight feature does not provide a firm basis for dating.

Most of the carved stone is, as mentioned above, of the same greenish micaceous sandstone with fine diagonal tooling which formed the walls of the extended nave, and indeed some stones are marked with masons' marks (AF6), which could indicate a professional team was used. With the demolition of the earlier churches, and the building of the larger Phase III church in cut and mortared stone, it is easier to consider embellishment and parallels, and it seems clear from the dating of the sculpture that this was the most highly decorated stage in the church's history.

This is a church without aisles, and there is no evidence in the surviving fragments of columns of anything substantial enough to have formed major structural supports. There are fragments with different diameters, some round and some octagonal or semi-octagonal facetted, which could have enriched doorways or other openings, and, like the more elaborate fluted column AF2, have been assigned by Fawcett to the later 12th century. The stone with deep incision (AF1) is a fragment of chevron decoration and is similarly tooled. It was found in the demolition rubble packed over an area south of the nave of the church and may have been part of a decorated opening leading from the nave into the chancel, or part of the south door to the nave. The chevron has been dated by Fawcett to the third quarter of the 12th century. In fact most of the carved fragments have been dated to the later 12th century with the exception of a block with panel and roll found in the revetment at the west of the site which could be later (C946).

There is no unambiguous evidence for the base of an altar in the curve of the apse, but the postholes C671–673, which it is suggested above could have been part of the constructional phase of the mortared building, might alternatively have been connected with the altar as a canopy. The stone socket in the centre of wall C646 was of smooth greenish sandstone, probably from the same quarry as the rest, and this, as suggested above, may have marked the site of the altar, and then a piscina, whilst another explanation is that it served as a depository under the altar for the disposal of consecrated elements, as has been claimed for the pottery vessel in the floor of the church at Raunds (Parsons 1996, figs 11 and 16). The most credible explanation, however, could be that it supported a cross, in the position of a rood screen in a more elaborate church since, although a lectern base has been suggested for a socket stone from Arbroath Abbey in Angus (Fawcett 2002, 248–51, 280, fig 4.47), the position here is more normal for a cross than a lectern.

As far as *in situ* examples are concerned, three socket stones were found associated with Building 6, dated to the Northumbrian Period, at Castle Park, Dunbar, which are tentatively assumed to have been footings for timber-framed walls (Perry 2000, 67, fig 54). More relevant formal parallels are, however, a very similar shaped stone with a single socket (use unknown) in the centre of the chancel wall in the church at Finchale Abbey, County Durham (Figure 5.40), built between the late 12th and 13th century, and a socket stone from the face of a wall in the period 2 structure at Auldhame (East Lothian) which, it has been suggested, supported a cross (Crone *et al* forthcoming). At The Hirsel, the base does not fit the shaft of the stone cross from the site and may, in that case, have supported a wooden cross. The socket stone had been broken and mended at some stage in its life and, when found, the hole was filled with stone chippings so that it may have had various successive functions.

FIGURE 5.40
Finchale Priory, Durham, showing stone with socket adjacent to the wall of the choir

The smashed window mullions in the rubble spreads (C103 and C1005) indicate that there must have been some elaborate windows, although not enough survives to reconstruct their forms. They have been shown in the speculative reconstruction (Figure 5.41) as the most common 12th century forms in the Borders and Northumberland, whilst the window in the rebuilt west wall has been shown with a slightly later form. There was a small quantity of window glass from the site, one

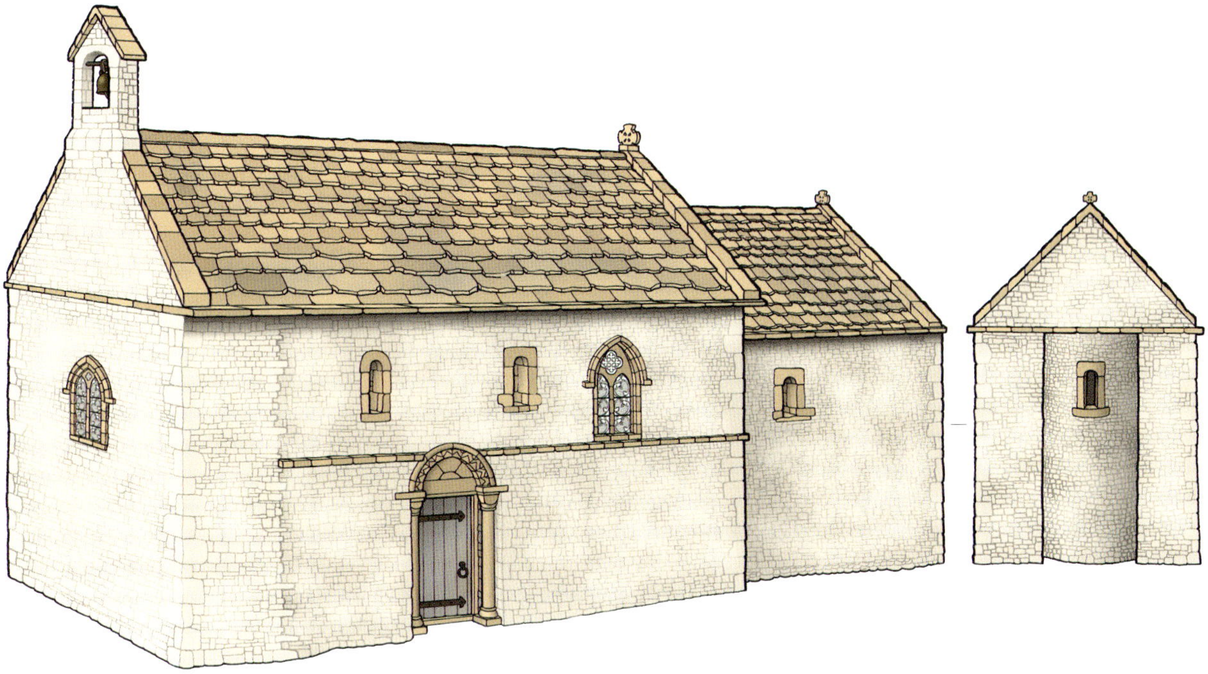

FIGURE 5.41
Hypothetical reconstruction of the Phase IV church, with a separate view of the east end

piece of which was grisaille, painted with a floral and diaper pattern such as has been found at other Scottish sites, such as Coldingham, and dated 13th to 14th century (see Section 12.3, Figure 12.34). This, and a small amount of lead which came from demolition contexts (C708 and C623), indicate that the windows of the extended church were probably conventionally glazed, and to the standard of the surrounding monastic houses. There are no fragments of ceramic floor tiles from the site, but the few nicely finished rectangular and triangular stone tiles which survive in secondary contexts (e.g. C1305), and the traces of mortar floors which could have supported them, imply that the church was paved with stone. It seems probable also that the roof of the extended church was of stone flags since several were found in the rubble dumps surrounding the church, one with a nail hole (SF3; Figure 12.33) and one with a nail still attached (SF2, FeS5).

It has been suggested above that the west wall could have been strengthened because of its instability. Bell turrets became more common on Scottish churches in the 13th century (Fawcett 2002, 70–71), but the dating of the bell-pit could put it earlier, as part of the late 12th century church. There is then a possibility that the use of a bell could have helped to weaken the already unstable west end and it is of interest that the ruined church of Lennel, another Dunbar holding and the parish church of Coldstream (see Chapter 2), also has a 'double' western gable (Figure 5.42). There may have been a strengthening and refurbishment of the west end, before the recorded rededication by David de Bernham, Bishop of St Andrews, on 31 July 1247 (Ferguson 1892, 182; and see Chapter 2). Alternatively his visit may have drawn attention to the need for rebuilding!

FIGURE 5.42
The surviving west wall and south-west quoining of Lennel church

Within the church there is no evidence, such as a drain, which could lead one to suppose that there was a font, and baptisms could have taken place elsewhere, even in the river, although since stone fonts are a late phenomenon in Britain, a wooden tub would not leave much trace (Blair 2010). The church would have been quite impressive when rebuilt in cut stone, with its long nave leading up to a chancel with a cross probably in the centre of wall 646 and the altar within the apse with columns flanking the opening. In fact, it is a church 'of modestly high architectural quality' (Chapter 12, p 185). As Fawcett has remarked: 'Before the twelfth century it seems that the religious needs of the lay folk of Scotland had been rather patchily met by a variety of types of churches. In southern Scotland, and to a lesser extent elsewhere, it is likely that some of these churches were similar to the "minsters" of pre-Conquest England' (Fawcett 1985, 24).

The status of The Hirsel church is not likely to have been of a mother church, which in this area could initially have been Eccles, and later The Hirsel became part of the large parish of Lennel, as discussed above (Chapter 2, p 19) but, from the 7th century onwards, churches are recorded on private estates in North Britain and seem to have become more common from the 10th century. The wider comparative context for The Hirsel church is discussed in Chapter 27.

6
THE CEMETERY

Rosemary Cramp and Belinda Burke

6.1 INTRODUCTION

The extent of the graveyard and its population

Burials were found surrounding the church on all sides (Figures 6.1 and 6.2) and although only a small area was examined to the east, a cutting running east from the cemetery platform through the terracing towards the river revealed a terminus for burial at that point. In the area to the north of the church there was a well defined terminus for the burials, which was first marked with a shallow ditch and then with a drystone wall (see Chapter 7). To the north-west of the church, burial did not extend further than the scarped slope of the natural gravel, but this had been apparently reshaped several times, and since the burial of Sk294 had been truncated by the late enclosure (C946), others may have been lost between it and Sk183 and Sk271 when the scoop filled with rubble and the enclosure were constructed (see Chapter 8). In that case, the curving line of burials to the north-west may be illusory and the line of the scarp as shown on the resistance survey (Figures 3.2 and 3.3) could have been the north-western perimeter. Directly to the west of the church the burials extended down the slope and no terminus was found. Only a small area was examined to the south of the church (between north–south grid-lines 185 and 210), but here burials were closely packed with many super-impositions and inter-cuttings. One area between grid-lines 195 and 200 was left unexcavated after the surface was taken off (because of time constraints), and it is likely also, in the most densely packed area to the south of the church, that not all the burials in the area opened were retrieved. There is indeed every possibility that the burial ground continued for some distance to the south (see perimeter survey, Chapter 3).

In summary then, the area to the north of the church (which was excavated to a depth of over two metres) may have been bottomed for burials, but, with an unknown number of burials remaining unexcavated to the south and west, the total population of the graveyard is not known. This means also that the size of the contributing population cannot be calculated either. Nevertheless, the total of 330+ burials which are discussed in detail in Chapter 11 represents one of the most substantial rural burial communities for this period in southern Scotland, the only comparable group being from Auldhame, where 240 burials were recovered and 66 identified but left *in situ* (see Hindmarch and Melikian 2008, 37–39), while the urban burial ground at St Nicholas' church, Aberdeen (Cameron 2006), where 900+ burials have been excavated, begins around the 12th century but continues up to the 18th century. The articulated remains at The Hirsel represent a minimum of 181 adults (68 males, 17 ?males, 65 females, 23 ?females, 8 unsexed) and 150 children (Figure 6.3). (For a fuller discussion see Chapter 11.) Palaeopathological and anthropological analysis was undertaken initially by Dr David Birkett, who aged and sexed all skeletons up to the 1984 season. After his untimely death the work was taken over by Sue Anderson who reported on all the skeletons save two and who is responsible for the full report which was completed in 1994, and has been used by many students since. It has not been updated, and so lacks the more scientific enquiries, such as stable isotope analysis, which are found in more recent reports. But specific studies, for example of the children's teeth undertaken by Sonia Williams (Williams and Curzon 1986) were innovative at that time, while later, a study of Schmorl's nodes by Janet McNaught developed another aspect in detail from a more limited sample (see Archive). A comparative study of some aspects of the pathology has also been carried out in the new report on the Auldhame remains.

The record and general problems of interpretation

The burials were given numbers in sequence following through the four seasons of excavation and the grave fills were assigned individual context numbers. The individual site records consist of proforma sheets identifying which bones were present and their condition, orientation and body position, type of cut or coffin, grave fill and relationships. Each burial was recorded by a drawing and photograph and this was added to Anderson's palaeopathological record. The skeletal archive is held by National Museums Scotland.

The grey sandy loams and gravels into which the graves were cut did not define the grave cuts very clearly, especially in dry conditions, and, although

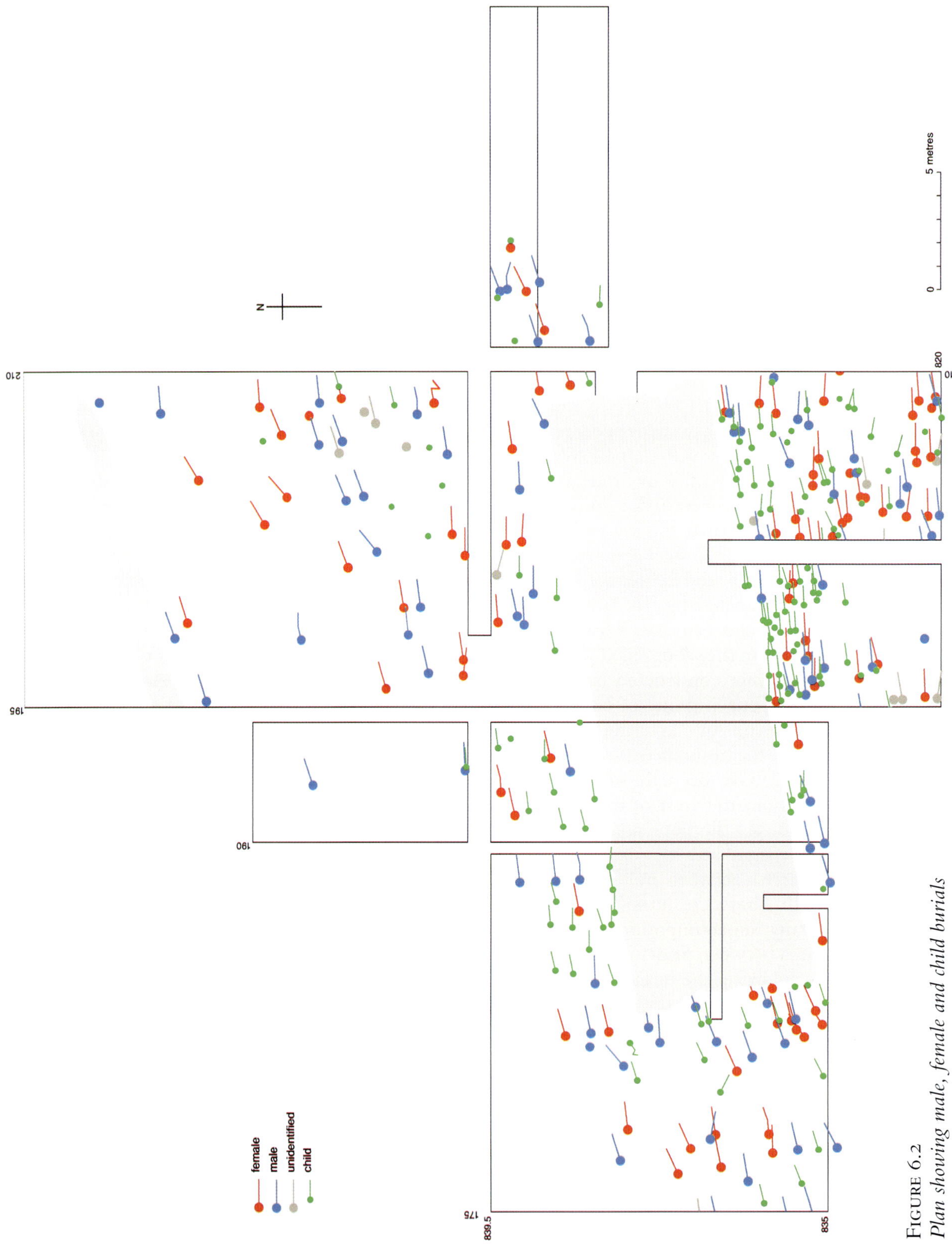

Figure 6.2
Plan showing male, female and child burials

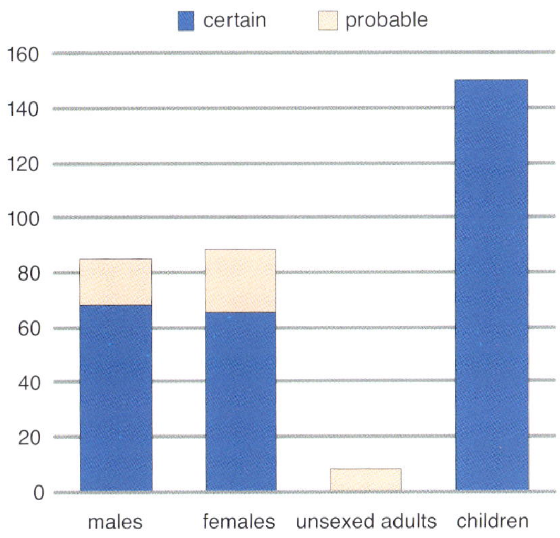

FIGURE 6.3
Relative numbers of male, female and child burials

on the north side of the church some graves were marked by upright stones and on the south by plain recumbent slabs, it was often difficult to link a burial with the marker since very often they did not coincide (see Section 6.9). Another problem, common to the whole site, was the disturbance caused by the recent ploughing and this exacerbated the problems of the inter-cutting of graves as well as often disturbing the level from which the cut had been made. On the whole, bone survival was moderately good, but in a few graves such as those of Sk24, Sk43, Sk48 or Sk52 (Figure 6.4), there was very poor survival, and in a few places, for example C62, no bone had survived, although the head and foot of the cut were well marked (Figure 6.5). In one case to the north of the chancel the phosphate survey indicated an apparently empty grave, although subsequent excavation revealed a body described by the excavator as 'particularly rotted' (Sk15), and in another case, under a spread of stones with two uprights (C60), it seemed unlikely that the grave had contained a body (see Section 3.3).

6.2 GRAVE MORPHOLOGY

With the exception of the few burials in cists, which are discussed below, the majority of the graves were earth dug. Since, as noted above, it was often difficult to define the grave edges, only general rather than statistical comments can be made on the grave shapes and dimensions. Although some graves had well defined shapes, not much wider than the bodies, and showed a tapering form, in many instances it was not possible to discern whether the cuts had rounded or rectangular ends. Often also, because the level from which the graves had been cut was obscure, it was not possible to

FIGURE 6.4
Poor bone survival (Sk48)

FIGURE 6.5
Context 62, a marked, but empty grave

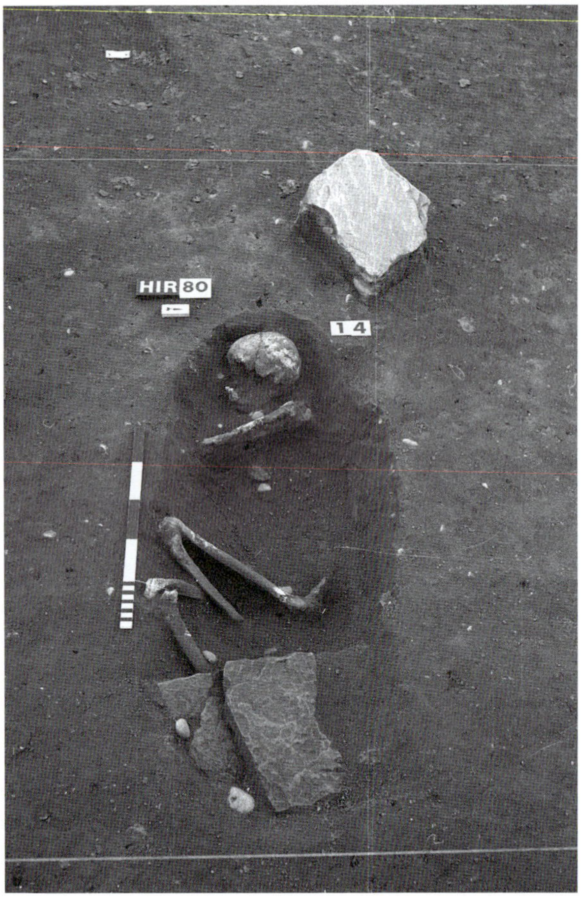

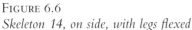

FIGURE 6.6
Skeleton 14, on side, with legs flexed

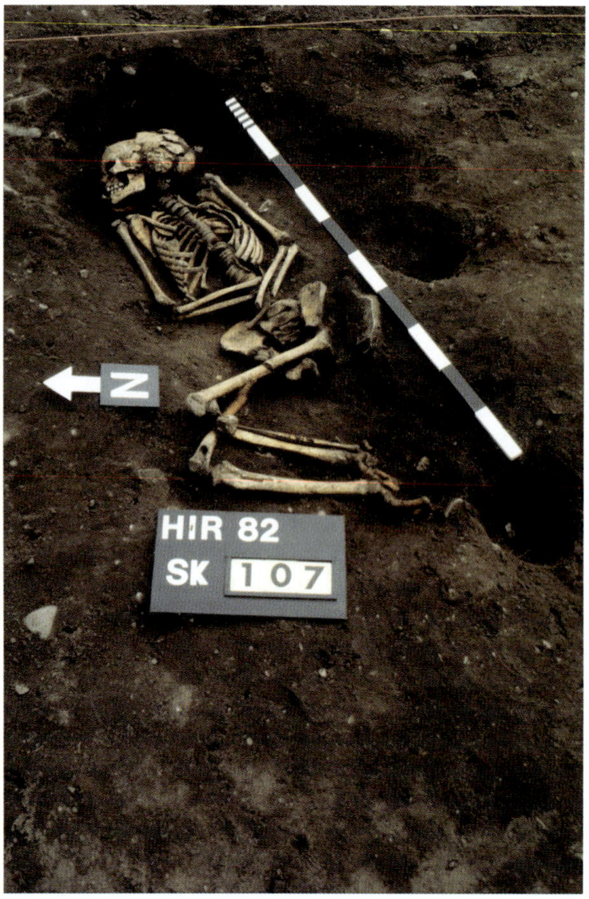

FIGURE 6.7
Skeleton 107, flexed burial orientated with head to the east

determine the depth of graves. Where there were recumbent stone grave-markers, however, grave depths could be measured and these varied from 0.6m for Sk78, or 0.54m for Sk284 through 0.44–0.47m for a number of burials, to the very shallow grave of Sk166, 0.27m. In the area to the north of the church, where markers of head and footstones survived, the depth of one grave (Sk20) was only about 0.25m. This was a child's grave, however, and they tended to be shallow, but in several other cases depths ranging from 0.30m to 0.47m were recorded in that area. There does not therefore seem to be much difference in grave depths in the different groupings whether in place or time.

6.3 BODY POSTURE

All skeletons, with one exception (Sk107), had the head to the west, and where the bodies were undisturbed, the great majority (98%) were supine, with the face upwards, legs straight, and feet near together. There were no prone burials. Skeleton 14, which was flexed, appeared to be on its side, but none were fully turned onto the right side in a tightly fitted position as for example in the Anglo-Saxon monastic cemetery at Wearmouth (Cramp 2005, fig 8.8). Skeleton 95, Sk107, Sk274, Sk310 and Sk320 were supine, but had legs flexed and bent to the right, but of the above mentioned only Sk14 and Sk107 warrant special comment. Skeleton 14 (Figure 6.6) an adult ?female, had the head turned to the right, the bent knees jammed up against the side of the grave cut, and large stones covered the lower legs. Underneath her skull was another skull and this was interpreted during excavation as from an earlier grave. This is probable since Sk14 has been dated by radiocarbon to cal AD 1215–1525 (GU-1488). Skeleton 107, a young person (11–12 years old) who had suffered from spina bifida occulta, also had the head turned on the right cheek and the knees were tightly flexed, while, as noted above, the body was not orientated in the orthodox Christian manner but north-east/south-west with head to the east (Figure 6.7). The significance of these oddly positioned burials is discussed below.

Of the 178 skulls *in situ*, where the positions could be determined, 84 faced straight up, 53 were turned to the left, and 41 were turned to the right, although these distinctions may have been affected by post-mortem movement. The arms were usually close to the sides with either one or both bent, and hands crossed on the pelvis, see Sk110 (Figure 6.8).

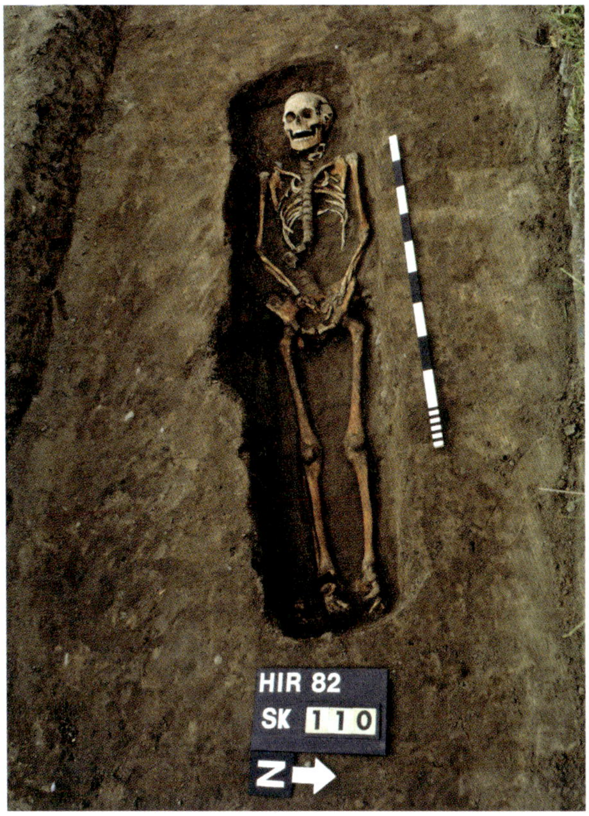

FIGURE 6.8
Skeleton 110, possible coffin burial

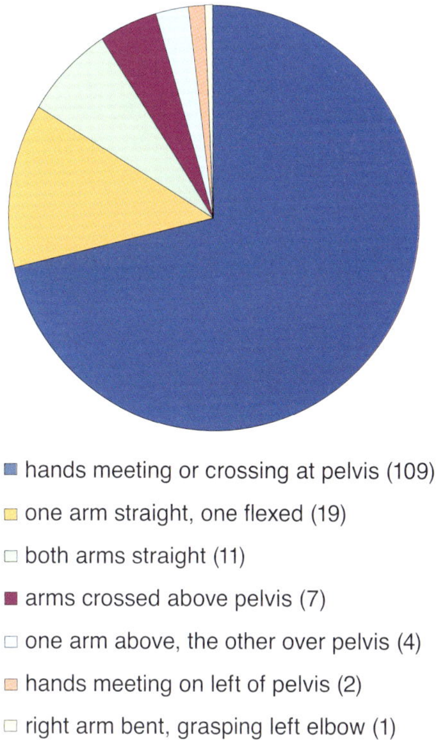

FIGURE 6.9
Pie chart showing arm positions of skeletons

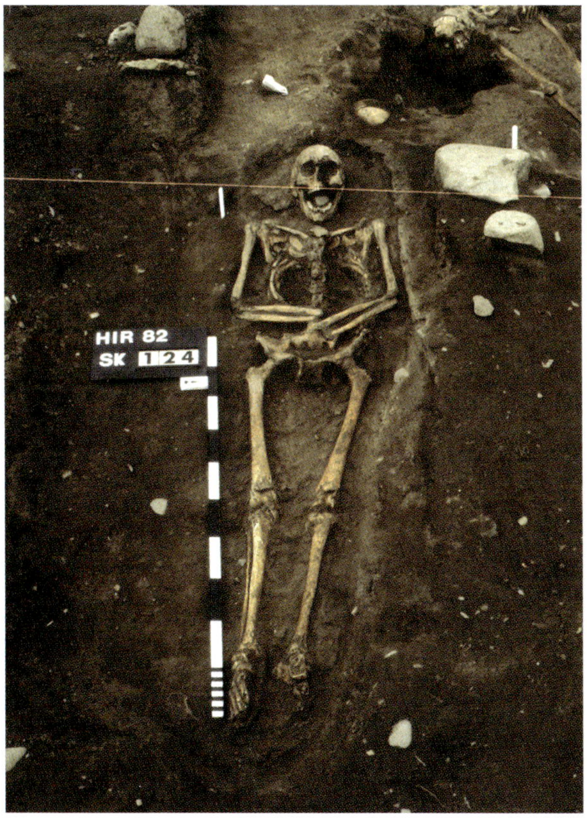

FIGURE 6.10
Skeleton 124, with both arms flexed at the elbow

FIGURE 6.11
Skeleton 44, with hands clasped on the left of the pelvis

Of the 153 articulated skeletons where both arms (but not always complete hands) were present, the majority (121) had both arms flexed at the elbow (Figures 6.9 and 6.10). One (Sk325), in what was possibly a coffined burial, had the right arm bent at a right angle at the elbow and grasping the left elbow and the left hand over the pelvis. In two instances (Sk44 and Sk121), the hands met on the left of the pelvis (Figure 6.11), and the position of Sk170 was unusual with the right arm angled out straight and the left arm flexed.

There is then a considerable conformity in the positioning of these burials, and where there are differences the positions may be specifically personal, for example Sk71 and Sk72 were parallel with each other and Sk71 had its head turned to the north and Sk72's head was turned to the south so that they faced each other, and this could signify some close relationship. There seems, moreover, to have been no sex or age difference relating to the body positions.

6.4 ORIENTATION

The alignment of all skeletons was recorded by compass (Figure 6.12), they were photographed with an accurate north pointer, and all were drawn, but very precise orientation has not been possible

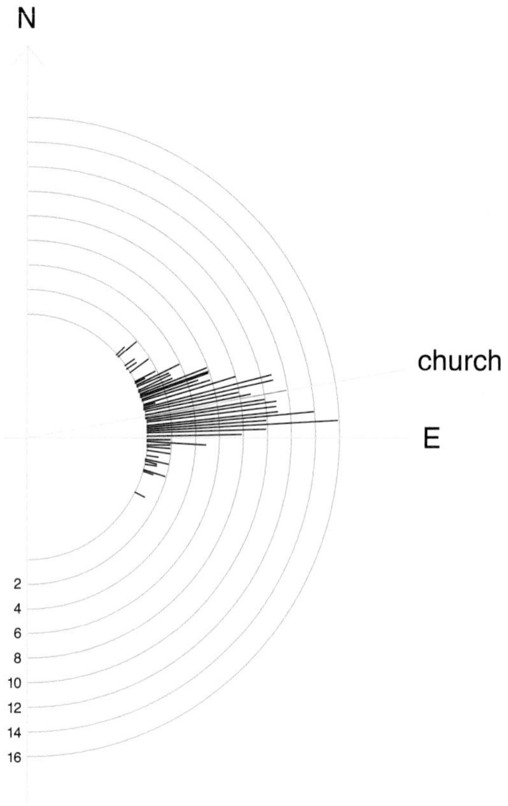

FIGURE 6.12
Burial orientation

FIGURE 6.13
Possible orientation marker in cemetery

to work out for the whole burial population, although broad groupings did emerge, the data in Figure 6.12 being based on site drawings. With the exception of a group to the north-east of the church, which were orientated south-west/north-east, most of the burials were approximately aligned on the church, although the orientation of those on the extreme north and west had been affected by the topography of the enclosure, which has turned them somewhat, for example Sk3, Sk30 and Sk294, where the orientation varies between around 71° and 80°. Nearer to the north wall of the first church, there is a group comprising Sk44, Sk45, Sk66, Sk94, Sk96, Sk106, Sk259, Sk323–325 and Sk357, which are more truly east–west, and immediately to the south of the church burials are more regularly disposed about 81°–90°. In fact, the majority of burials clustered between 80°–90°, but it would seem that some of the earliest burials (see chronology below) were closer to an east–west alignment than was the extended church, which was orientated *c*80°. Nevertheless, since these burials were scattered throughout the burial ground and Phases I and III of the church were on a truer alignment, this does not seem enough of a difference to deduce that the cemetery preceded a church on the site. It is here of interest to note that feature C511, a pile of corroded sandstone with two lines of stones meeting at a right angle, could have been an orientation marker (Figures 6.13 and 6.14) although it must be said that this would not have given a very precise orientation, and would scarcely have been needed with the church nearby. It might, however, have been a temporary guide for a grave digger.

To the north of the early nave, nearer to the boundary, the burials are more widely spaced and more random in orientation, with a small group of four (Sk12, Sk24, Sk25 and Sk89) markedly different in orientation; all are fragmentary, as are others in this area, but these are aligned south-west/north-east and some were marked by stones characteristic of this area (Figure 6.15). A rough dating for this group as later medieval is based on the position of Sk89. This grave cuts into the domestic spread of that area (C299) and there was a considerable quantity of pottery from that occupation level, the earliest being Tweed Valley Ware (type 2.1) and the latest Reduced Gritty Ware (type 4.2). This seems to indicate a Phase 7, Late Medieval date.

Where the children were not closely associated with the walls of the church they could be more randomly orientated than the adults, for example Sk161 and Sk168 to the south, which lie in the middle of a rather empty area while Sk70, Sk79 and Sk80 seem to be focussed on the adult Sk84 below them. This could mean, however, that they were of the same family (see below). In summary, although most of the children were disposed with what seems special care, a few were given casual treatment, and since these are often late in the sequence it could be that some children, possibly the unbaptised, continued to be buried here after the adult population had moved to a graveyard elsewhere.

6.5 CEMETERY ORGANISATION

It is difficult to determine whether the burials were grouped into family plots or into rows which could have been chronologically developed, both systems seem to occur and anyway are not mutually exclusive. There appears to be a certain amount of organisation into strings running east–west, to the north and south of the church and in some areas, particularly on the north side of the church, and often in what seem to be the later phases of burials, there is some appearance of north–south rows. To the west, north of the extended nave, there are short rows, such as Sk294, Sk109, Sk205, Sk223 and Sk247; Sk111, Sk224, Sk222 and Sk20; Sk27, Sk246 and Sk241. There is very little inter-cutting north of the church and this may signify less pressure on space in that area, either because it was a less desirable location, or because it was initially used for another purpose, and so was filled up later. It is unfortunate that the evidence from the radiocarbon dating (see below and Chapter 9) provides no clear picture of the development of the cemetery, but Sk3 in the north of the site has been dated as early as any in the cemetery, and it seems more plausible that this area was assigned to different family or social groups since the area is also distinguished by upright stone markers, found *in situ* (Figures 6.15 and 6.16). If one considers the cranial indices (see Chapter 11), it is indeed possible that some of the burials on the north are earlier, although it could be that their head shapes were an indication of a different genetic grouping, rather than a chronological feature.

At the west end of the extended nave, there seems to be an inner zone of burials which closely follow the alignment of the church and were possibly grouped in clusters, which could signify family plots (see below). On the south side, where burials were densely packed with a great deal of inter-cutting, there were some possible lines parallel to the church, and some evidence for family plots, but it is difficult to determine patterning.

Anderson (p 167) identified three possible family groups based on the combination of traits and spatial characteristics (see Figure.6.14). The first, which was on the north of the church, has been mentioned above when the conformity of orientation in this group was discussed. The second group was buried to the south-west corner of the church and consisted of Sk225(F), Sk232(M?), Sk239(F), Sk240(M?), Sk293(F), Sk314(F?), Sk321(M), Sk336(F) and Sk338(F).

FIGURE 6.15
Grave markers north of the church

A few children, Sk179, Sk248 and Sk249, could also belong to this group. The kinship of this group may also be emphasised by the superimposition of Sk239 on Sk240 and the fact that Sk293 is cut by the child burial Sk248. The two earliest burials in the group are Sk240 and Sk336, the latter having a coin in the grave dated 1165–1214, and these are below Sk239 which had a radiocarbon date of cal AD 1215–1330 (GU-1718), while Sk293 has later medieval pottery in the grave. Anderson notes that this group showed little respect for existing graves, perhaps suggesting a smaller burial plot, although this could also mean that there was an important focal burial here, and the predominance of females in the group is also noteworthy. The third group was in the south-eastern extension of the cemetery and consisted of Sk174(F), Sk186(F), Sk199(M), Sk200(F), Sk209(F). Here again there are several super-impositions: Sk186 and Sk200 seem to be the earlier burials and the grave fill for Sk187, which is superimposed on Sk186, yielded Tweed Valley Ware pottery (type 2.2), and was dated by thermoluminescence to 1060±110. Anderson is at pains to note though that the evidence for family units is not unassailable.

It is possible also that groups which share the same congenital anomalies such as spina bifida occulta and which were grouped together in the

FIGURE 6.16
Head and foot stones in situ to north of the church

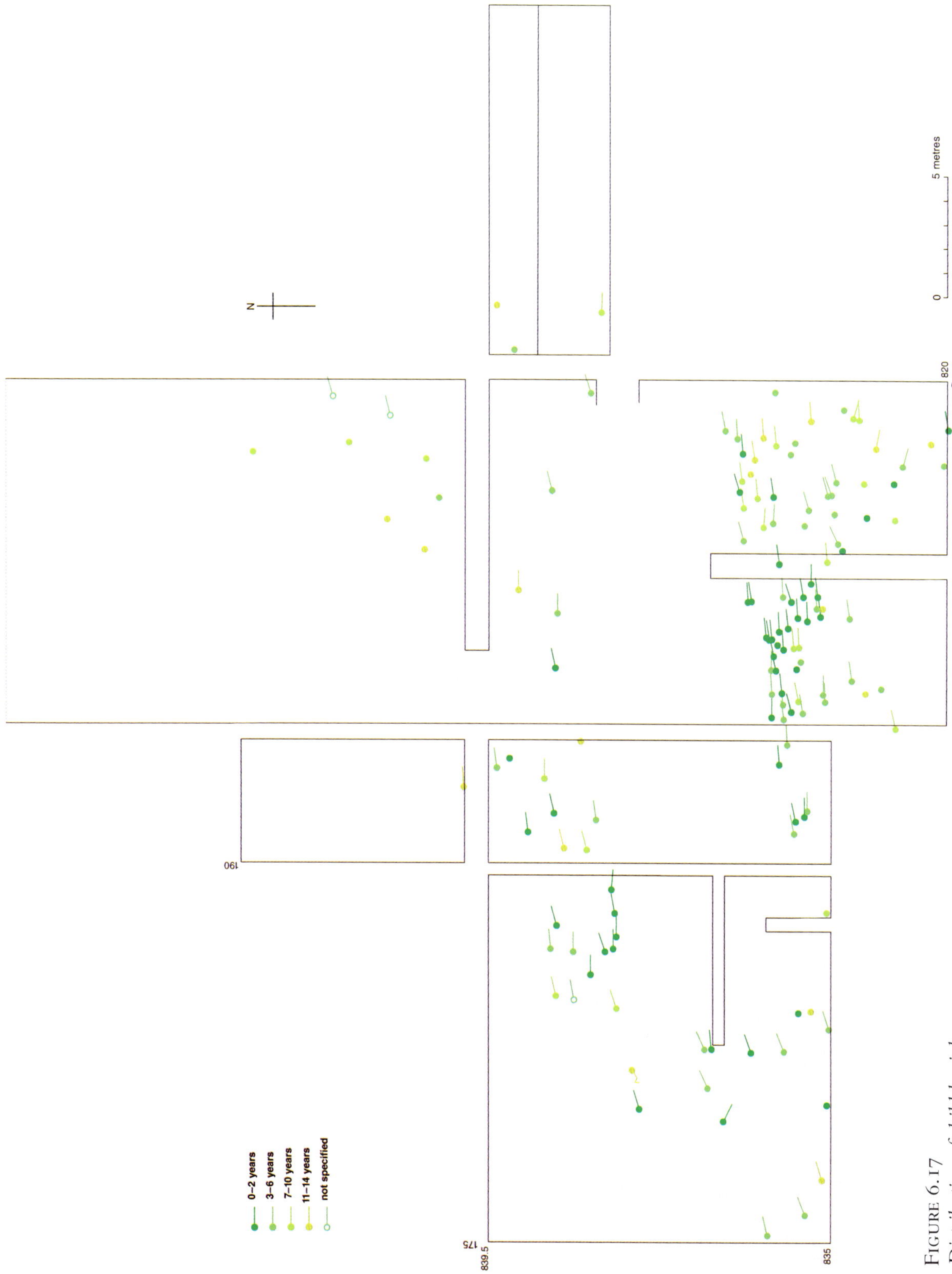

FIGURE 6.17
Distribution of child burials

FIGURE 6.18
Infant burials (Sk9, Sk19 and Sk18) along north wall of the Phase III nave

burial ground, for example to the north-west corner of the church, Sk205(F), Sk107(C), Sk223(M) and Sk20(C), were all one family. There were also what seem to have been communal burials, for example Sk151 and Sk155 were two children in the same grave and it is possible that when several people were buried in the same grave they may have been related: Anderson makes a case for Sk306 and Sk308, and also notes that the males and females in the cemetery were of the same physical type, implying that this burial ground was used by a fairly closed community.

6.6 DISTRIBUTION BY SEX AND AGE

It seems clear that there were no specific divisions by sex in the placing of the bodies, but rather, as suggested above, that they were often in family groups. There is, however, as already noted, a marked distribution of young children close to the church, and in one area 195/200 it appears as if they are closely associated with individual women (Figures 6.2 and 6.17). It has been suggested for some burial grounds elsewhere that women were segregated or more carelessly buried than men, but there seems no such evidence for this practice at The Hirsel. Indeed one of the most elaborate burials (Sk338), in a cist at the west end of the church, was of a female, as was the burial of Sk336, which included a coin and a quartz pebble. The special care given to child and infant burials is reflected not only in the fact that their graves were often carefully marked, or that they were buried in neatly constructed cists (see Figure 6.22) but

FIGURE 6.19
Skeleton 310, child covered with large stones

FIGURE 6.20
Skeleton 20, child's burial in large grave cut

that they occupied the specially privileged position close to the walls of the church in the 'eaves-drip' (Figures 6.17 and 6.18). It is also noteworthy that six out of the nine graves in which quartz pebbles were found in the graves were those of infants and children and only one of the others was that of a mature adult. The burial of Sk310 (Figure 6.19) to the north of the church is an interesting one since the grave was covered by several large stones as well as an upright grave-marker and the child (of about 8 years) buried within was accompanied by a quartz pebble and an animal tooth, but the fill also included a sherd of Tweed Valley Ware (type 2.2) so this type of deposition could have continued for some time. In contrast with the evidence for care in child burial, for Sk20 (Figure 6.20) a large grave had been marked out, but only a small body interred. Skeleton 86 is also exceptional in that a pit had been dug and the child thrown in carelessly with the legs resting on the side of the pit.

To the north of the extended nave there was a cluster of new born infants, with others aged 2–10 years ranged at a slightly greater distance from the walls of the nave and chancel (Figure 6.17). To the south there was a much larger number of child burials, with the youngest packed in very close to the church, Sk53 overlay Sk253 and may be late while Sk117 and Sk253 (Figures 6.21 and 6.22) were in or by well constructed cists and there were two other cists for small children, also alongside the chancel wall.

The child burials at the west end of the church were more dispersed, although Sk248 and Sk249 were cut by the extended west end and so may have been close up to the original west wall of the nave. There are also several very young individuals amongst the apparent rows of adults at the west end of the church (Figure 6.2).

In summary, it would seem that in the early phase children could be buried in family groups as Sk248, Sk249, Sk179, or the group of children rather randomly orientated in the south-east of the excavated area. In a later phase, however, they were clustered by the church walls, with a particularly dense area of child burial to the south of the chancel of the church and to the north of the nave. It is possible that there may have been phases of high infant mortality which could account for some of the depositions, but the care exercised is notable. Their care in life may have been less benign. Between 1982 and 1986 Sonia Williams and M E J Curzon studied 21 of the child skeletons

FIGURE 6.21
Cist (C723) to the south of the church, with newborn infant Sk117 and Sk118

FIGURE 6.22
Cists (C758 and C759) by south wall of church

FIGURE 6.23
Infant teeth showing evidence of severe hypoplasia

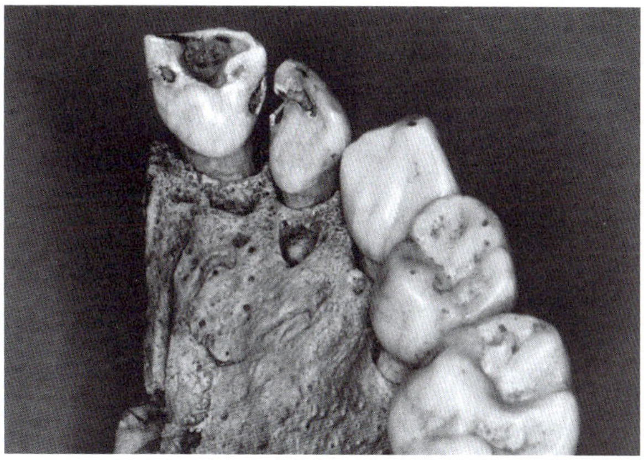

FIGURE 6.24
Infant teeth with caries

under the age of 6 (see Archive report 28.08.85 and Williams and Curzon 1986), and found some evidence for severe hypoplasia suggesting stress from birth and in early infancy (Figure 6.23), but also dental erosion/caries on the palatal surfaces of the maxilliary primary incisors which could suggest feeding methods with a feeding device containing cariogenic foods such as pap, oatmeal, honey and milk with bread (Figure 6.24).

6.7 DISPOSITION AND CHRONOLOGY

There are odd empty spaces in the cemetery, for instance to the north-east of the church surrounding the child Sk6, Sk8 and Sk103, but this could have been because of poor preservation of bone in this area. Elsewhere there could have been movement of burials, as was clear in a deposit of about 12 individuals in a pit (C924) to the south-west of the church (Figure 6.25). These seem to have been re-interred after the church wall had been robbed in that area. A puzzling disposition in the extreme south-east of the excavated area is the child burial Sk161 which, as mentioned above, seems strangely isolated in the middle of a group of adults, but this is an area which may not have been bottomed.

Within the broader picture, to the west and north of the nave, there is more evidence for north–south rows as well as west–east, and certainly the burials appear to be more spaced and organised there, but, although this is an area which seems to fill up late in the sequence, this organisation may not be a chronological feature, but just easier to identify because there are fewer burials.

Despite the evidence for inter-cutting and superimposition, it has proved difficult to organise the burials into broad chronological phases throughout the site, rather than discrete sequences (see also Section 6.12 below). As noted above, there was a number of super-impositions

FIGURE 6.25
Rebuiral of 12+ individuals (see Chapter 11) in pit (C924), deposited after the destruction of the west wall of the church

particularly south of the church which provide a relative sequence of burial and may indeed indicate family burial plots: Sk77 lay directly over Sk117 and Sk118; Sk82 partly overlaid Sk120 and Sk114, and Sk213 partly overlaid Sk212. Some double burials appear to be contemporary, such as Sk112 and Sk113, Sk117 and Sk118 (Figure 6.21), or Sk138 and Sk137 where the head of Sk137 lay directly on the feet of Sk138 (Figure 6.26), while Sk151 and Sk155, although superimposed, are orientated differently and could have been buried with some interval in between (Figure 6.27). In one sequence an adult, Sk153, cut the grave of Sk220, which is over Sk230, and a group of children aligned with Sk220 (Sk182, Sk211, Sk212, Sk213, Sk116, Sk120, Sk117 and Sk118) may be chronologically linked,

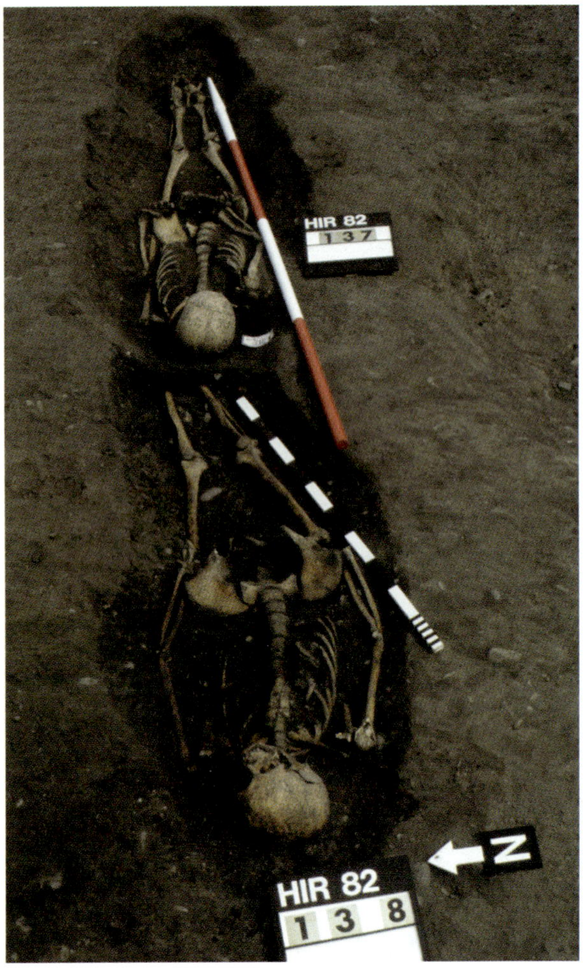

FIGURE 6.26
Skeletons 137 and 138 in linear arrangement

while Sk82, Sk83, Sk77 and Sk53 could be later since they are superimposed on other children.

To the south of the church there are also many instances where earlier burials had been disturbed and dispersed by later graves, but occasionally care had been taken to replace the earlier bones, for example Sk248 and Sk249 had been disturbed and re-interred.

6.8 GRAVE FORMS AND BURIAL MODES

With the exception of an adult stone cist to the west (Figure 6.28), a possible one for a child to the north of the church (Figure 6.29) and the small stone cists for the newborn to the south of the church (Figure 6.22), all of the graves were earth cut, many with rounded ends and a slightly tapering form with a width of about 1m or less, usually only about as wide as the body. There were no clear remnants of elaborate metal coffin fittings as in earlier chest burials elsewhere in north Britain (Hill 1997, 412–415), and at Wearmouth (Cramp 2006, 291–303), although the clasp Fe25 and brackets Fe11–13, one of which (Fe11) was found in cemetery earth, might be part of coffin fittings. The six nails with the burial Sk121, and five with Sk9 are probably better evidence for coffins. Two nails were found in the graves of Sk192 and Sk270 and single broad-headed nails, found in the graves of Sk58, Sk82, Sk203 and Sk286, could also be from coffins, especially since wood staining was identified in the grave of Sk203. Most of these items were to the south of the church, but all

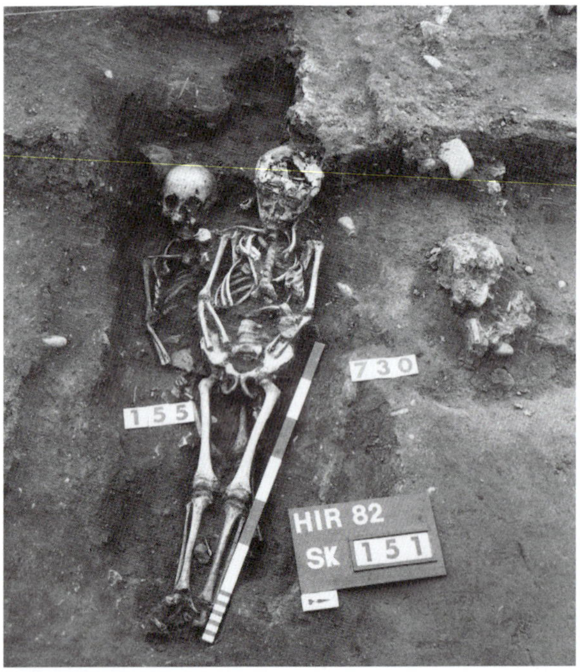

FIGURE 6.27
Skeletons 151 and 155

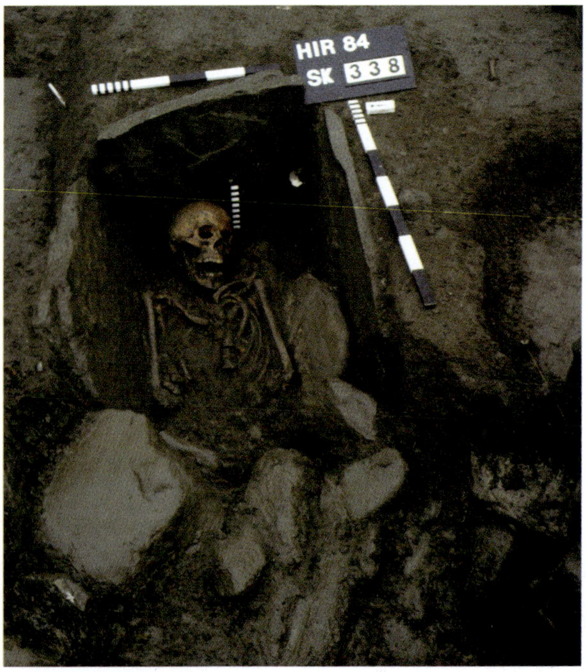

FIGURE 6.28
Skeleton 338 in cist (C1293)

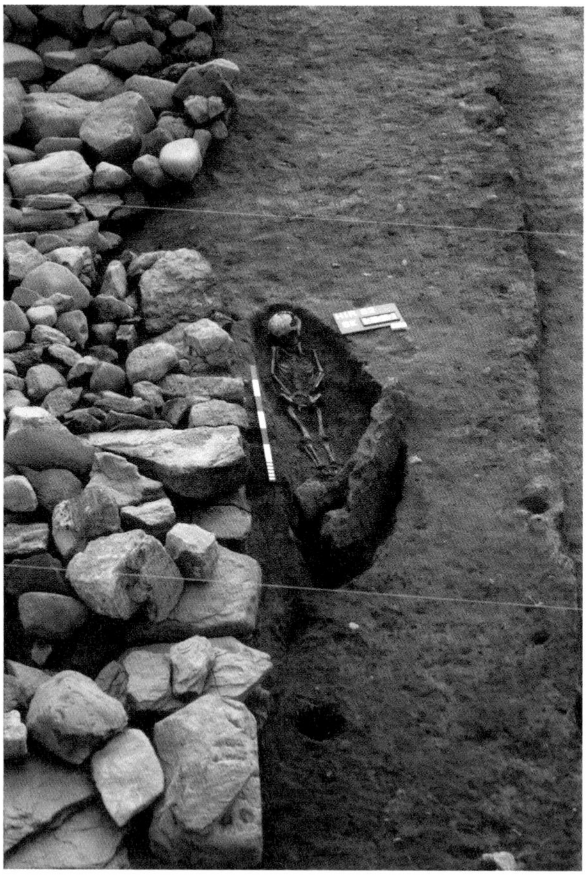

FIGURE 6.29
Skeleton 252 to north of the church, possible cist burial

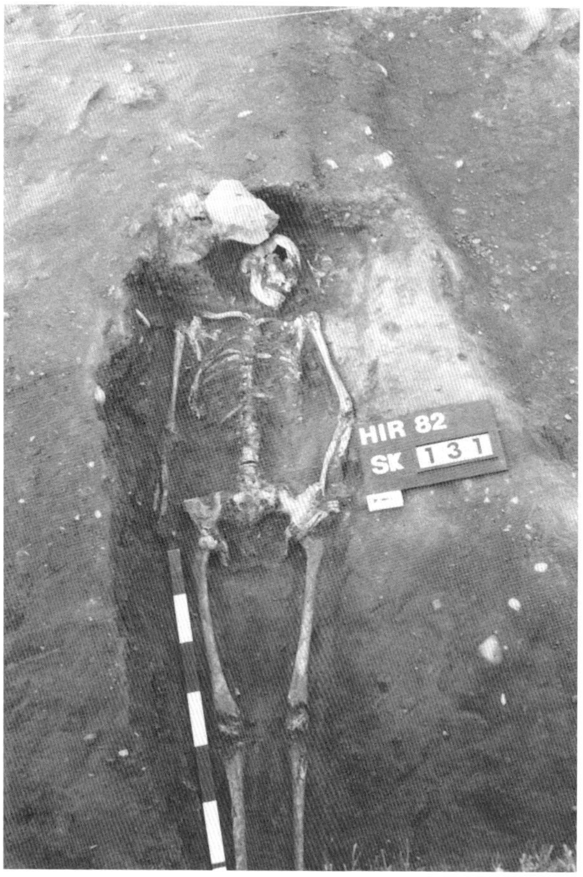

FIGURE 6.30
Skeleton 131 in a relaxed position

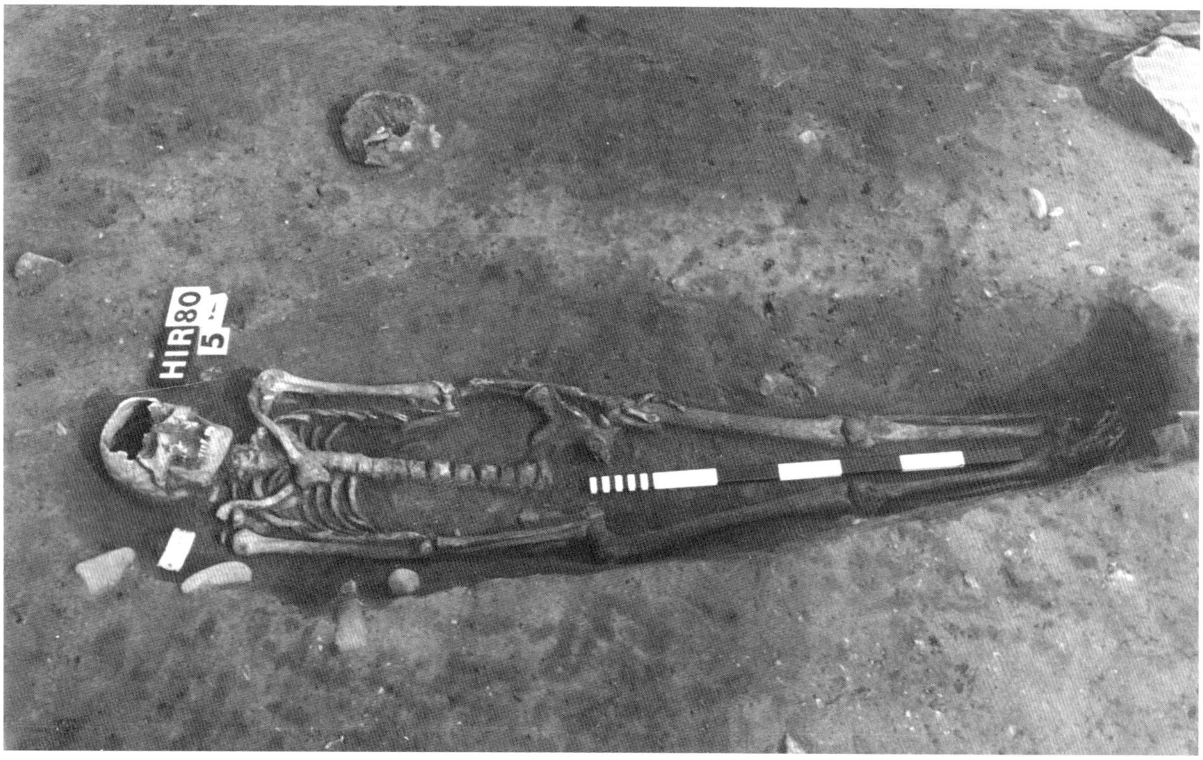

FIGURE 6.31
Skeleton 5, possible shrouded burial

of them could have been random deposits (see Section 12.5).

In some cases, however, coffined burial without nailing is evident, for example in the female burial Sk110 immediately to the north of the chancel, where wood samples survived in the grave and the toes of the skeleton were turned up as if the body had been fitted into too short a space. There were traces of wood and dark staining under the bodies of the female Sk30, in the north, and Sk215 in the extreme south of the excavation. Traces of rust were noted in the grave of another child (Sk280). The relaxed position of Sk174, also a female, could indicate a coffin burial, and a few others, such as Sk131, were in a similarly relaxed position (Figure 6.30), but since uncarbonised wood only rarely survived in the site soil conditions, there was only a limited indication of such containers (see above). Mostly the position of the bodies could indicate that they were shrouded (Figure 6.31), and since only one copper-alloy pin has been found (at the top of the grave fill of Sk20), and one needle was found in a grave (Sk1) it seems reasonable to suppose that the bodies were sewn into the shrouds and then placed in the dug grave as was normal practice in medieval burials (James and Yeoman 2008, 33). On the occasions where the bodies had been surrounded or directly covered with stones (see below) it seems probable that they were placed straight into the dug grave without a container.

6.9 MARKING OF GRAVES

Throughout the cemetery there is a variety of grave-markers and covers (Figures 6.14 and 6.32). As already noted, some children are interred in short cists and many child burials are marked, usually by a head or footstone, and in one case (Sk20) by a post. There may indeed have been more post markers than were recognised since a possible posthole was recorded for Sk1. On the north side of the church, small upright head or foot stones still survived *in situ* (Figures 6.15 and 6.16), but they were not always a guide to an exact burial location, and indeed some seemed to be alongside burials (Figure 6.33). An upright stone was, for example, found between the two burials Sk101 and Sk102, while Sk44 and the underlying Sk64 both retained footstones. Over the whole site many possible stone markers were recorded, some clearly in relation to burials, but others may have defined family burial plots. There were, however, no inscriptions on stones and the more elaborate monuments such as the cross, the cross-marked stones, and tooled grave covers were not found *in situ* (see Chapter 13).

Sometimes there seems to have been a combination of flat slabs and head or footstones as for example the child's grave, Sk9, which had both markers. One area south of the nave (196–203/820–825) was heavily covered with stones as if there had been a disturbed cairn (C708 and C715; Figures 6.14, 6.34 and 6.35). Amongst the stones were flat slabs bounded by upright stone ends (C711) and a large (broken) slab (C712). These covered the graves of Sk98 and Sk78 (Figure 6.35). To the east, a line of flat slabs (C726) covered the much-decayed Sk166 while to the south a slab (C725) partially covered the degraded Sk185 which had possibly disturbed another body (Sk266). Skeletons 197–199 were covered with closely packed stones (C706). Since these 'cairns' contained rubbish as well as rubble and were just under the surface, it is possible that they covered burials which post-date the use of the church. Immediately to the north, in the area 196–202/825–830, this stony area and its graves covered a group of burials which were especially closely packed, and marked by a line of headstones, while to the south there seems to have been an enclosure of stones, but in the south-east corner of the trench, the cemetery earth was probably not bottomed. This southern area is, then, one of dense burial with many fragmentary skeletons, and no doubt stone markers have also been disturbed. The south of the church alongside the early nave could well have been a desirable place for burial if one can compare the site with medieval burial grounds elsewhere (Gilmour and Stocker 1986, 15), but not a wide enough area to the south or against the east end has been excavated for a reliable picture to emerge, nor can any one area be linked with the more elaborate covers or crosses which were discovered in the ploughing of the site.

The rectangle of flat, well laid stones (C1129; Figure 6.14), parallel to the south wall and near to the presumed south door of the nave, was originally thought of as a grave cover, but the two children, Sk280 (whose grave yielded a sherd of Tweed Valley Ware, type 2.1) and Sk285, respected its edge and so did another child and the old male, Sk288, who lay below them (Figure 6.36). Nevertheless, underneath the stones there were some disturbed human bones, so these stones may have marked earlier burials. It is possible also that this feature may be what Gilchrist has called a marker plinth (Gilchrist and Sloane 2005, 189, fig 136), in which case it might have supported one of the well-carved stone grave covers in this prestigious place near to the south door of the nave. A group of burials seem to form a north–south line here (Sk34, Sk235, Sk307, Sk308), and these could have been buried alongside a path to the entrance.

6.10 STONE INCLUSIONS AND ARRANGEMENTS IN THE GRAVES

Many of the graves had stones in the fill, and given the nature of the moraine subsoil, it was sometimes

Sk	Sex	Grave markers						Stone arrangements in grave			
		Head	Foot	Horizontal	Cist	Pebbles delimiting	Posthole	Around head	Under body	Over body	Pebbles
1	M			X			X			X	
2	C		X	X							
3	M	X									
4	0	X	X								
6	C								X		
9	C	X	X	X							
10	C	X									
11	C		X								
14	F?									X	
16	C	X									
20	C	X	X				X				
23	U					X				X	
24	F		X?							X	
25	F?	X?				X					
37	M?	X									X
38	F	X									
44	F	X	X?								
45	F	X									X
47	M?	X?									
48	M	X	?								
57	M					X					
62	M	X	X								
64	F	X	X?								X
66	F										X
67	C			X							
69	M										X
70	C	X									
71	M		X							X	
73a	C		X?								
77	C	X	?								
78a	C			X						X	
82	C		X								
84	M?	X?									
92	M?	X									
93	M	X									Q
94	F	X	X?								
95	?	X	X								
98	C				X						
101	F?	X	?								
102	M	X?									
107	C					X					
108	M	X?									
109	M					X					
110	F?			X							
111	C					X					
113	C										Q
114	C										X
116	C										X
117	C	X?									
122	C								X		X
123	M?									X	
124	M							X			X
126	C	X	X?								
127	C										X

Sk	Sex	Grave markers						Stone arrangements in grave			
		Head	Foot	Horizontal	Cist	Pebbles delimiting	Posthole	Around head	Under body	Over body	Pebbles
128	C					X					X
129	C							X			F
130	C									X	
131	F							X			
132	C										X
136	C								X		X
147	F					X					
159	C			X							
160	F?	X?									
163	C	X?									
166	C		X	X							
170	M?										X
171	M										X
181a	C	X?									
185	F			X				X			X
197	F							X			
200	F	X?	X?								
202	M			X?							
205	F?										X
219	M					X					
220	C	X?									
226	F									X	
230	C	X?									
237	F	X?									
252	C				X?						FQ
253	C				X						
254	C									X	
261	C	X?									
271	M										X
274	C									X	
276	M								X		
277	C								X		Q
280	C	X	X								F
281	F			X							
282	M							X			
284	C			X							
285	C	X	X								
288	M										Q
289	F					X					
302	F									X	
304	F?					X					
310	C	X								X	Q
314	F?			X?							
316	C									X	
317	F?							X			
320	C										Q
322	C										Q
323	M									X	
324	C	X?									
331	F							X			
333	M							X			
336	F										Q
338	F				X						

FIGURE 6.32
Table of grave markers and stone arrangements in graves

FIGURE 6.33
Skeleton 23, with grave markers

difficult to decide whether their presence was an intentional inclusion or not. Fragments of flint and quartz pebbles were found most frequently in the children's graves, although one young woman (Sk336) was buried with five quartz pebbles, and this, like the stone cists, may be the survival of an earlier fashion. Sometimes the quantity or the arrangement of ordinary pebbles and cobbles in the graves did appear intentional: the children's Sk114 and Sk122 were lying on a layer of pebbles, and there was a significant number of pebbles in other graves, while sometimes pebbles delimited the grave cut (Sk128) (see Figure 6.32).

Other graves had stone arrangements which seemed to be placed to support and protect the body, for example Sk1 had stones packed over the knees and thighs (Figure 6.37). To the south, Sk123 had stones around the head and shoulders; with Sk160 the head is flanked by stones, and Sk282 had a large flat stone packed by the side of the head (Figure 6.38). These were all male, while Sk185 and Sk317, both female, had stone pillows (Figure 6.39); an old male, Sk276, had a large stone under the neck, a young adult, Sk277, had stones under the ribs; to the west, the grave of female Sk289 had a number of large flat stones in the fill, particularly around the legs and along the south edge of grave. The grave of Sk310, buried on her side and with flexed knees, had stones placed over her body;

FIGURE 6.34
1981 aerial view showing 'cairn-like' spread of stones (C708, C715) to the south of the church

FIGURE 6.35
Detail of C708 and C715, with slabs C711 and C712, which covered Sk78 and Sk98

FIGURE 6.36
Skeleton 288, placed alongside stone feature C1129

FIGURE 6.37
Skeleton 1, with stones packed over knees and thighs

FIGURE 6.38
Skeleton 282, with stone by the side of the skull

FIGURE 6.39
Skeleton 317 was found with feet removed

the head of the female Sk331 rested between two large stones or 'ear muffs' (Figure 6.40), as did that of an old male (Sk333), who had 'ear muffs' on either side of his skull (Figure 6.41). Both of these skeletons seem to have been buried in natural sand, and could be early in the sequence. To the north of the church, the grave of Sk64 contained some cobbles packed round the body, the head was supported on a stone pillow, and a footstone was firmly associated with the burial. In one curious

FIGURE 6.40
Skeleton 331, with stone 'ear muffs'

FIGURE 6.41
Skeleton 333, with stone 'ear muffs'

case a female Sk317 had been carefully buried with a stone pillow, but had missing feet (Figure 6.39). Here it is possible that they had been removed by later digging, but this was not evident from the grave definition at the time of excavation. It is noteworthy that most of those with stone features in their graves were adults, but they do not seem to belong to a particular grouping of burials, nor is there a difference between the sexes.

6.11 TRAUMA AND HEALTH

This subject is more fully discussed in Chapter 11. The five burials which have evidence for head wounds could belong to fighting men. These were Sk265 and Sk153 to the south of the church, Sk192 to the west, and Sk1 and Sk323 to the north. Skeleton 1 had a well healed cut at the front of the skull and a cut from the back which seems to have been sustained at the time of death; both were identified as sword cuts. All were males in the prime of life. The prick spur found near to Sk13 and Sk15 (see Section 20.9, FeSp3 from C503) could, like the sword cut, indicate a person of some status, and since this was on the north side of the church, and another spur (FeSp2) was found in the disturbed burial earth near to it, this could imply a prestigious area of burial. The west end of the church also seems to have had a group of burials which could imply fighting men. There was another prick spur (FeSp1) found in the burial earth, and two males, Sk104 and Sk108, had anomalies of the right shoulder which Anderson suggested could indicate the persistent use of the longbow (Chapter 11) but, as she says, other occupations could potentially have the same effect. Skeleton 22, to the north of the church, had an iron tool (Fe66) apparently embedded in the body which may also have been the cause of death, although it could have been intrusive in the grave. The enigmatic iron object between the teeth of Sk42 (Figures 6.42 and 6.43), also buried to the north of the church, could have been inserted post-mortem, but in both of these cases violence is a possibility. Other traumatic conditions which left traces on the bones, notably in the form of breaks, are discussed in Chapter 11, where it is concluded that this is a population with a relatively poor diet, although lacking in much serious disease, with patterns of physical stress consistent with a rural community making its living from the land. At the time of the report only very broad phasing of the cemetery was available to Anderson and so it has not been possible to see whether there was a change in health through time or in relation to special positions of burial. The Williams and Curzon reports on the children (see above) were, of course, concerned with those who did not survive into adult life and so the evidence for severe hypoplasia (Figure 6.23), suggesting chronic disease or malnutrition, was not surprising. The caries in the incisors, suggestive of artificial infant feeding conditions, was at the time of the report an early example of this practice (Figure 6.24).

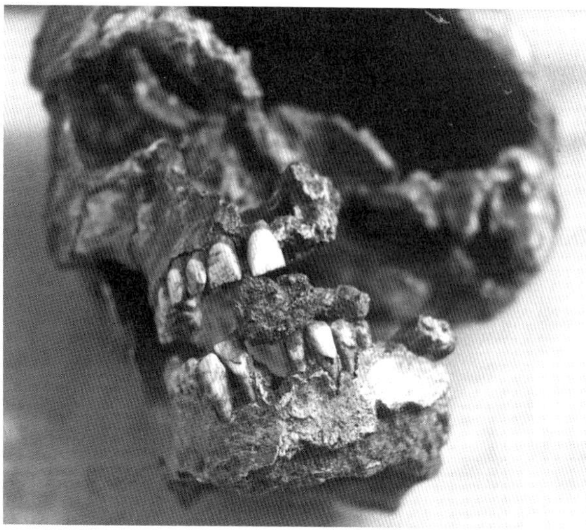

FIGURE 6.42
Skull of Sk42, with iron object in jaw

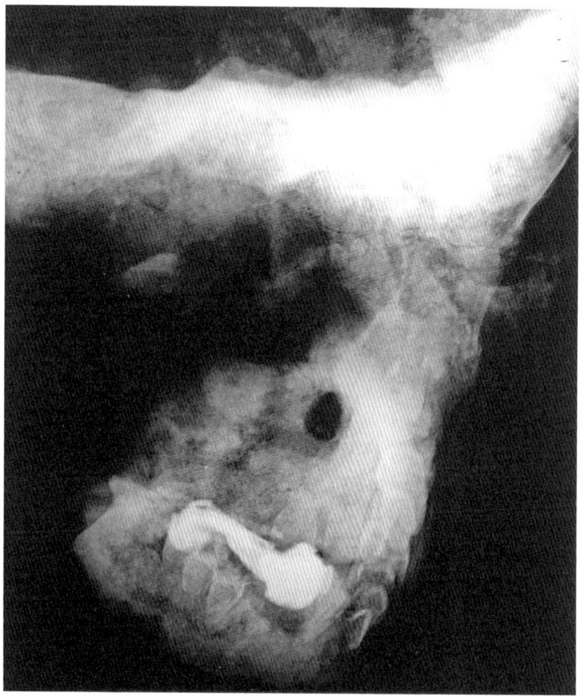

FIGURE 6.43
X-ray of skull of Sk42 showing the iron object between the teeth

6.12 PHASING AND DATING

It is not easy to date and phase any complex cemetery with the type of inter-cutting and plough disturbance encountered at The Hirsel, and with the knowledge that the entire burial population has not been revealed. The following factors have been taken into account. The radiocarbon dating of the individual skeletons and the dating of material in the graves, such as coins and pottery, which give a *terminus post quem*, can help to define groups with the same orientation. The relationships to the churches and other features could give relative dating for adjacent graves, and the dating of the layers through which graves were cut, where they can be established, could provide a *terminus post quem*. It has not been possible to link these layers north and south of the church and obviously the upper layers of the densely buried area to the south and west of the church were often difficult to establish, but the relative stratigraphy of the burials, and the formal characteristics of the interments, can also help with phasing.

To consider the dating of individual burials first: at The Hirsel, the dating for both the church and burials has relied heavily on a limited number of radiocarbon and thermoluminescence dates, combined with a certain amount of documentary evidence (see below).

As far as the radiocarbon dated burials are concerned (Figures 6.44 and 6.45; and see Figure 9.3), the dates are too few and not precise enough to indicate that one area was primary for burial. The earliest dated, Sk3 in the extreme north of the burial area, could be at the earliest mid- to late 11th century, but the cist burial to the west is only a generation later and most graves cluster in the period 12th to 14th century with the crouched burial Sk14 being one of the latest. The summary of the data provided for radiocarbon dating is that the cemetery is unlikely to have started before the mid-12th century and to have gone out of general use before 1450. There were, however, odd graves which were later as mentioned above.

Not all finds in graves were deliberately placed, but coins probably were. The female burial Sk336 to the south-west of the church had a folded coin of William I the Lion beneath the chin (Nu1, circulation date 1175–1195). The coin was perhaps placed originally in the mouth and there were also five quartz pebbles in the grave. Skeleton 56, which was part of a disturbed group of bones to the south of the chancel, had two coins (Nu2, James VI, 1588) in a bag in the grave, and, in the light of the documentary evidence (see above Section 2.1), this was probably one of the latest graves. Both sets of coins were considered to be fairly new and the significance of such inclusions in graves is discussed below.

The scientific and coin dates are, however, too few and too unrepresentative to provide a meaningful burial sequence, and as far as relative dates are concerned the situation is not much more helpful. Several burials overlaid the ditch/pit (C1345) at the south-west end of the site (see Figure 4.20) and contexts in the base of this feature yielded radiocarbon dates of cal AD 1010–1180 (SUERC-15889) and cal AD 995–1165 (SUERC-15890), thus providing a *terminus post quem*. There are no radiocarbon dates for the lowest level of burials cut into clean sand at the south of the site, which could possibly be earlier, and, although one could assume that the earliest burials would be closely associated with the church, it is not uncommon in the early medieval period to find small dispersed groups of burials which are not adjacent to churches (Hadley 2002, 214). The widely dispersed burials on the extreme north of the burial area could have been such a group and there is plenty of unexcavated ground to the south which could have included other groups.

Nevertheless, using only the excavated evidence, there were no burials demonstrably earlier than the early phases of the church (which have been considered as *c* late 10th to 11th century for Phase I, and *c*1100 for Phase II); no burials were clearly cut by the church walls of Phases I–III and no burials were discovered in the interior of the Phase I–III church, although the extended west end of the church cut through several graves, including the cist containing Sk338.

The fill of the graves sometimes included material which could randomly derive from the layers through which they had been dug, and the pottery found in graves can be accounted for in this way (Figure 6.46). The date range assigned to most types of Scottish medieval pottery is very wide, as is mentioned at the beginning of the report, and this means that although quite a large number of burials had pottery in their grave fills, it is not much help in dating either the graves or the layers they cut. Nevertheless, it is useful in identifying late layers and graves and there is a broad distinction in the layers between those which contain the later pottery groups 3–5 and those with earlier Gritty Wares (groups 1 and 2). The burials with early or with late pottery are scattered throughout the burial ground, and the burials yielding large quantities of structural debris and other late artefacts, such as glass bottle fragments, indicate that burial was continued after the church had been destroyed. It is noteworthy, however, that no burials are cut into the abandoned church.

Stratigraphic sequences

To the north of the church two main cemetery layers were identified under the disturbed topsoil: at the lowest level, burials are cut into a compact mottled sandy soil which seems to be the top of the natural. Those nearest to the early church (Phases I and II) such as Sk325, Sk96 and Sk97 are cut into

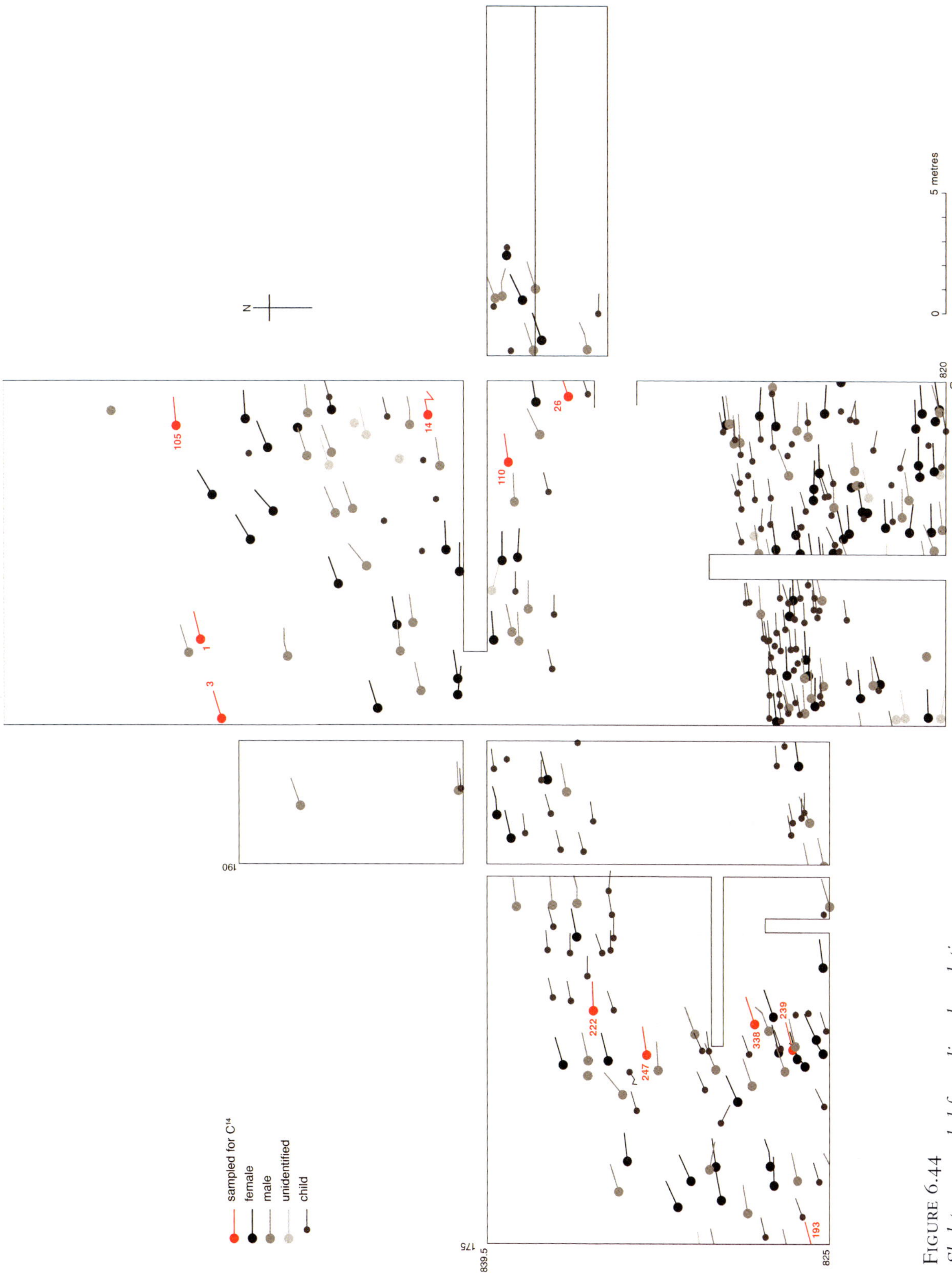

FIGURE 6.44
Skeletons sampled for radiocarbon dating

Skeleton number	Co-ordinates	Laboratory Code	Calibrated date using IntCal09 with probability
Sk1	200/852	GU-1309	1155–1400 (95.4%)
Sk3	197/851	GU-1310	1035–1280 (95.4 %)
Sk14	209/842	GU-1488	1215–1525 (93.3%) 1575–1585 (0.3%) 1590–1625 (1.8%)
Sk26	210/836	GU-1487	885–1495 (95.2%) 1600–1615 (0.2%)
Sk105	209/853	GU-1720	1025–1325 (87.3%) 1345–1395 (8.1%)
Sk110	207/839	GU-1721	1025–1260 (95.4%)
Sk193	176/826	GU-1716	1275–1515 (94.1%) 1600–1620 (1.3%)
Sk222	184/835	GU-1719	1260–1455 (95.4 %)
Sk239	184.827	GU-178	1215–1330 (68.3%) 1340–1400 (27.1%)
Sk247	183/833	GU-1717	1040–1105 (7.1%) 1115–1410 (88.3%)
Sk338	184/828	GU-1901	1050–1085 (4.1%) 1125–1140 (0.9%) 1150–1285 (90.4%)

Figure 6.45
Radiocarbon dates for skeletons, simplified from Figure 9.1

Pottery group	Skeleton numbers
Roman	145
Group 1 (late 10th–12th century)	86, 105, 299/300, 311, 329, 335, 338
Group 2 (12th–early 15th century)	11, 27, 33, 46, 64, 68, 74, 77, 79, 81, 89, 90, 93, 99, 104, 119, 121, 122, 124, 130, 134, 138, 143, 144, 149, 151, 153, 155, 158, 159, 162, 173, 174, 187, 189, 201, 209, 212, 215, 219, 221, 222, 223, 228, 243, 245, 246, 265, 276, 278, 280, 289, 310, 312, 328
Group 3, 4 and 5 (late 12th–16th century)	1, 9, 26, 40, 51, 57, 58, 78, 83, 98, 129, 133, 136, 148, 181, 191, 203, 213, 224, 225, 232, 270, 272, 279, 286, 288, 293, 303, 309, 314, 321

Figure 6.46
Table of pottery types found in graves. Where more than one type of pottery is present in a grave, the skeleton is listed under the latest group

a dark sand (C663) and are oriented east–west with head stones. Further north a similar layer (C522) is cut by burials angled more south-east/north-west. Over them C503, a light brown sandy soil, is cut by Sk7 and Sk15 with pottery groups 1 and 2 in the graves and a more disturbed C504, with later medieval pottery, which is cut by a group, Sk24, Sk25, Sk12, Sk37, Sk62, Sk5, etc. These filled in an area of previously domestic occupation (see Chapter 7) and here there is not a great deal of inter-cutting.

Some cemetery levels to the north-west of the Phase III nave seem to be early, but have been disturbed by later activities such as stone dumping. Most of the burials here seem to be medieval, with Sk222 (with the scallop shell), Sk281, Sk244 and Sk247 earlier, and another group, cutting layers C456, C908 and C955, being later. These later burials include the group suffering from spina bifida occulta (Sk20, Sk107, Sk205, Sk223) (Figure 6.14). At a subsequent, post-medieval, date, a group of infants, Sk9, Sk18 and Sk19, were inserted along the wall line, and the randomly orientated Sk17, Sk11, and Sk21 also cut a post-medieval surface.

The layers to the west of the church are complex and interleaved, and the burials, particularly near to the church walls, are often intercut. The earliest group here seems to be those cut by the extended west wall of the church, and Sk336 and Sk321 from the postulated family group which cut a layer (C1067) overlying the ditch by the south-west corner. The orientation of the graves to the west seems to have been dictated by the slope into which they were dug. There are no stone grave-markers in this area but they are regularly spaced except where they are overlaid by later burials such as Sk225, Sk232, Sk249 and Sk284 cut from a late medieval layer (C1082). Two burials in this area are post-medieval: Sk87 cuts C927, and Sk88a cuts C911, both layers yielding 17th-century coins.

The area to the south of the church was that of densest burial and has the greatest potential for future investigation. A few burials in the north-east sector of the trench such as Sk121 and Sk203 had Tweed Valley Ware (type 2.1) in the graves and were more truly oriented; they could belong to a late medieval period. Further west a group cut from the lower cemetery surface, such as Sk299, Sk300, Sk304, Sk305 and Sk308, was orientated on the nave and represent an earlier level of burials which had not been disturbed by the later graves. As one moves further south from the church in the south-east section of the excavation to an area which was excavated to natural, a picture emerges of the medieval burial area in which the earliest internments are those with no finds in the grave fill, and which cut the dark brown charcoal-flecked soil above natural, such as Sk172, Sk188, Sk200 and Sk201. Above this group are others, also well orientated, but with Tweed Valley Ware (types 2.1 and 2.2) in the fill, such as Sk174, Sk187, Sk186 and Sk209. Further west, a double burial, Sk299 and Sk300, which yielded a sherd of Samian Ware near to the body and a sherd of Coarse Gritty Ware (type 1.2) in the fill, could also be early.

A very significant majority of child burials occurs in the upper level of the cemetery in this area. Of the 54 undisturbed burials recorded as cutting layer C710 (the upper cemetery surface),

31 were children, while in the layer below (C739) there were only 4 children out of a total of 31, and in the north-west corner of this area, the upper level was cut by the graves of 34 children and 7 adults while below this C791 and C1269 (natural) were cut by the graves of 5 adults and 4 children. Unfortunately, however, it was more often than not impossible to recognise grave cuts in this area, and children's graves are in general shallower than adults. The carefully constructed cists such as C758 which were close to the south wall of the chancel (see Figures 6.21 and 6.22) appear to be earlier than the other child burials south of the chancel but the intense use of the site into the post-medieval period seems to have displaced and disturbed the earliest burials, as is apparent in the disturbed bones which are found in burial fills.

Further west the large spread of 'cairn-like' stones (C715; Figures 6.34 and 6.35) included a significant quantity of personal rubbish and what seems to be demolished buildings debris, and some personal effects, such as possible fittings from a belt (a buckle and mounts, Fe41–45, and a small whetstone pierced for suspension, SH2) as well as an arrowhead (FeA11); and into this spread, graves with covers had been inserted (Sk98, Sk78 and Sk166, all children). Others lay under the cairn, including another group of child burials (Sk114, Sk211–213, Sk220, Sk230, Sk233 and Sk255) which cut C714, the upper layer of the cemetery surface, and these seem to be aligned on a row of possible headstones running north to the church. In this area, therefore, as to the north of the nave, the latest phase seems to be mainly child burial, but a few burials which are not orientated on the church could be later, including Sk56 which was accompanied by 16th-century coins.

In summary, how the cemetery developed is unclear: there are early burials on the north, including the narrow-headed people that Anderson noted (Chapter 11, pp 165–166), but on the other hand, there are late burials also and, judging by the density of burial in the south, this appears to have been the preferred space. It should be noted, though, that Sk1, which was to the north, showed the clearest evidence of sword wounds on the site and, if these had been acquired in battle, this could have been a high status grave, possibly belonging to the family who, it has been assumed, lived to the north in the area now occupied by Hirsel House (see Chapter 2). In that case, these may have been buried near to where they entered the cemetery, or could have been part of the small family group which has been identified north of the chancel (the earliest part of the church complex). On the other hand, there is another family group at the west end of the church which includes the cist burial, and the burial with a 12th-century coin, which could be equally early, and of equal status, and in addition there is the lowest level of burials to the south of the chancel. It is possible then that from the beginning of the churchyard there were distinct family plots, and that these became blurred later as burial presumably moved to the parish church of Lennel.

The wider issues that this cemetery raises and the parallels which can be seen with other sites are discussed further in Chapter 27.

7
THE PERIMETER
Rosemary Cramp

7.1 INTRODUCTION

The perimeter slope of the raised ground, composed of sand and gravel moraine, was clearly defined in the resistivity survey (see Figure 3.2) but excavation revealed that it had been reshaped on the north, west and east, probably over a very long period of time, and this, together with the ploughing which had deeply disturbed the site in places, made sequencing difficult. The initial resistance survey showed a clear line of high resistance running roughly east to west in the north of the site (Figures 3.2 and 3.3) and since this suggested a cemetery perimeter, the area was tested for this supposition in the first season. It is true that no burials were found to the north of the ragged stone walling which this feature turned out to be, but there is some doubt that its primary purpose was to serve as the cemetery perimeter. It proved to be a complex structure and was certainly a construction of several phases, which was preceded by a ditch, and which cut through earlier occupation in that area (see below). This area was excavated in 1979, 1980 and 1981, but because of the complexity of the church and cemetery to the south, and the necessity to complete these in the available time, the area between grids 195 and 210, immediately north and south of the wall was not taken down to natural (Figure 7.1).

7.2 DOMESTIC ACTIVITY ON THE NORTHERN PERIMETER

Phase ?1–2

This was an area of considerable inter-cutting activity in which it was difficult to separate out the phases. In only one small area was the level reached which produced the prehistoric pottery and stake-holes, in the area to the north in 1979–1980 (Figure 1.9). In the north-west section of the cutting 190–202/850–60, a series of stake-holes (collectively C274) were the lowest feature cut into the sand (C264), which was the disturbed surface of the natural sand C272 (Figures 7.2 and 7.3). The tips of the stakes were pointed and several were equally spaced on the same axis, indicating a possible structure here. There were, however, three sherds of medieval pottery in some fills of the stake-holes, namely Tweed Valley Ware (types 2.1 and 2.2) and one sherd of Coarse Gritty Ware (type 1.1), the earliest medieval pottery in the region. Since the stake-holes were truncated and this is a level cut into by medieval activity above, these sherds could have been intrusive. Dividing these stake-holes from four postholes to the north was a shallow gulley (C271) about 20cm in width, with one sherd of Tweed Valley Ware cooking pot in the fill. These features seem to predate other domestic activity in the area north of the wall. The four postholes (C282) cut a deposit in the north-west bounded by grid-lines 190–5/857–9 (C270), described as loamy brown soil overlying pinkish orange silty clay. Their fills were clean but the clay deposit (C270) contained two sherds of Tweed Valley Ware (type 2.2) and one sherd of Tweed Valley Red Ware (type 3.1) and is seemingly a truncated occupation level. Although the two areas were not joined in the excavation, it is possible that this was part of the clay deposit as found further north in 1979, where the medieval deposits were grounded directly onto the prehistoric levels. The clay 'floor' could have been related to the timber structures mentioned above, or part of the flooring of the structure (C250) discussed more fully below, of which only the south and east walls (C205 and C236) survived (Figures 7.4 and 7.5).

7.3 DOMESTIC STRUCTURES

Phases 4–6

A very large quantity of medieval pottery was derived from this area of the site, with a preponderance of Tweed Valley Ware (type 2.1) and, when considered with the distribution of other finds, it points to medieval occupation of a domestic nature, which seems to be contained in two areas to the north and south of the cemetery perimeter (Figure 7.6).

The partial structure to the north-west (C250) (Figures 7.4–7.6) is defined by walls 236 and 205, and seems to have been an external drystone hut built against the slope, and later partially overlaid, and destroyed by wall 214 (Figure 7.7). Part of the south wall and a rounded eastern corner of the building were several courses high, and there was a major posthole (C244) containing a wooden stump packed with stones and two sherds of Tweed Valley Ware at the east end. This may have been a support

FIGURE 7.1
View from the north towards the northern perimeter wall (C291), showing the difference in level excavated between the trenches to the north and south of grid-line 860

for the end gable. The dark interior deposits were rich in artefacts (especially C240); there was a great deal of Tweed Valley Ware, and a little Reduced Gritty Ware, an 'industrial vessel' (possibly an aludel), some tweezers (CA18 from C240) and a padlock (Fe28). There was further evidence for domestic activity in the level above, disturbed by the plough (C207): a key from a barrel padlock (Fe39), a tool (Fe84), two horseshoe fragments (Fe104 and Fe105), part of a loom weight, and a further horseshoe fragment (Fe99) from C234, associated with wall 214, whilst in addition, a nine men's morris board (OS1) was reused in a later posthole.

There was a second area of apparently domestic occupation towards the east, within the area around 201–7/851–6 south of the perimeter wall (C259). This was bounded by the possible remains of wall footings to the south (C301) and manifested by patches of rubble and paving within dark brown silt which could be a disturbed floor level (see C294 and C300; Figure 7.6). There was a number of domestic objects in the brown silty soils as well as animal bone and a large amount of pottery (the date of which could centre on the 13th century). The artefacts included a pierced hone (SH1), two knife blades (Fe49 from C296, Fe51 from C289)

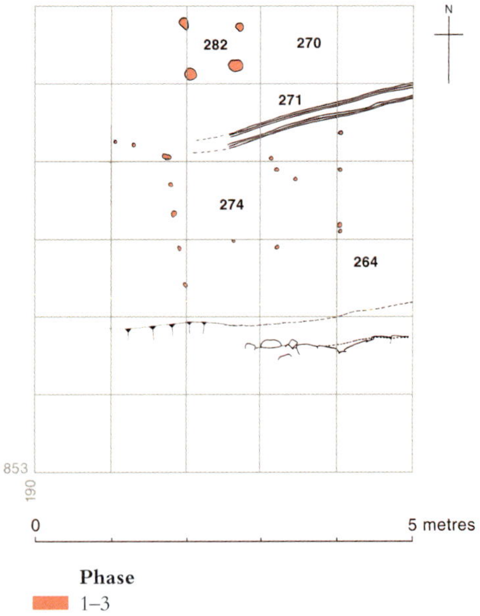

FIGURE 7.2
Earliest features, stake-holes 274 and postholes 282, with associated features

FIGURE 7.3
Posts and stakes cutting natural sand, viewed from the north

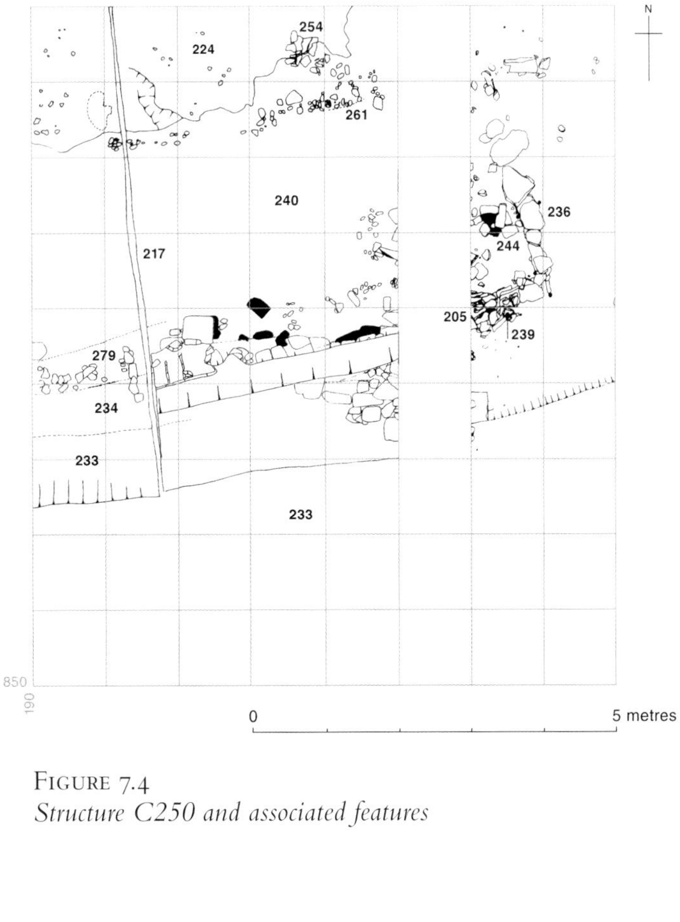

FIGURE 7.4
Structure C250 and associated features

FIGURE 7.5
Structure C250 viewed from the north

and a bone knife handle (WB1 from C299), a decorated rumbler bell (CA26 from C294), three lace tags (CA12–14), and a target arrow (FeA18). This domestic occupation seems to have predated the perimeter wall and a layer above (C1003), which also extended north of the wall, seems to have contained some residual material such as the lace tags (CA12–14), medieval pottery and glass, and a medieval horseshoe (Fe101).

The animal bones in this area distinguished it from elsewhere on the site by a preponderance of cattle consumption, rather than sheep, and in addition marine molluscs are only found in this area of the site, all of which are pointers to a life style of some substance. Horse remains were also more abundant in this area than elsewhere and it is also here where we find the only site evidence for a cat. Reconstructing a domestic building related to these finds is, however, more problematic. Although there were some patches of stones such as C301 and C1007 (Figure 7.6), which could have been the residue of cleared drystone walls, the form of the building was not recoverable. There were fragments of mortar and window glass in the deposits, but drystone or clay-bonded walls resting on the surface of the ground or on stone pads are a possible architectural form which could have characterised this building. There is mention in the 16th-century documentary sources of there having been an old house beside or beneath the 'kirksted' (p 21), which could have been in this area, but could alternatively have been further west on the site.

This domestic activity was earlier than the wall (C291), which cut the layers with the domestic artefacts mentioned above, but it is less easy to decide whether the structure to the north-west was of the same phase or not. The difficulty of attempting to retrieve a chronological sequence from these fugitive structures is that the same pottery types occur on the floor of the putative house to the south-east and the drystone structure to the north-west, with a majority of Tweed Valley Ware and a few sherds of Reduced Gritty Ware (types 4.1 and 4.2). On the whole it would seem that these two domestic areas were contemporary and perhaps complementary. The finds indicate a higher status use for the eastern area and that, perhaps, the western structure was an outhouse.

7.4 THE RETAINING WALL

This wall 214, 245 and 291 (as labelled west to east when excavated) was obviously a feature of several phases and, although initially considered to be the cemetery wall, it could have been constructed to enclose a field to the north when the fields/terraces were developed (see below). The wall only survived as a solid structure from the eastern

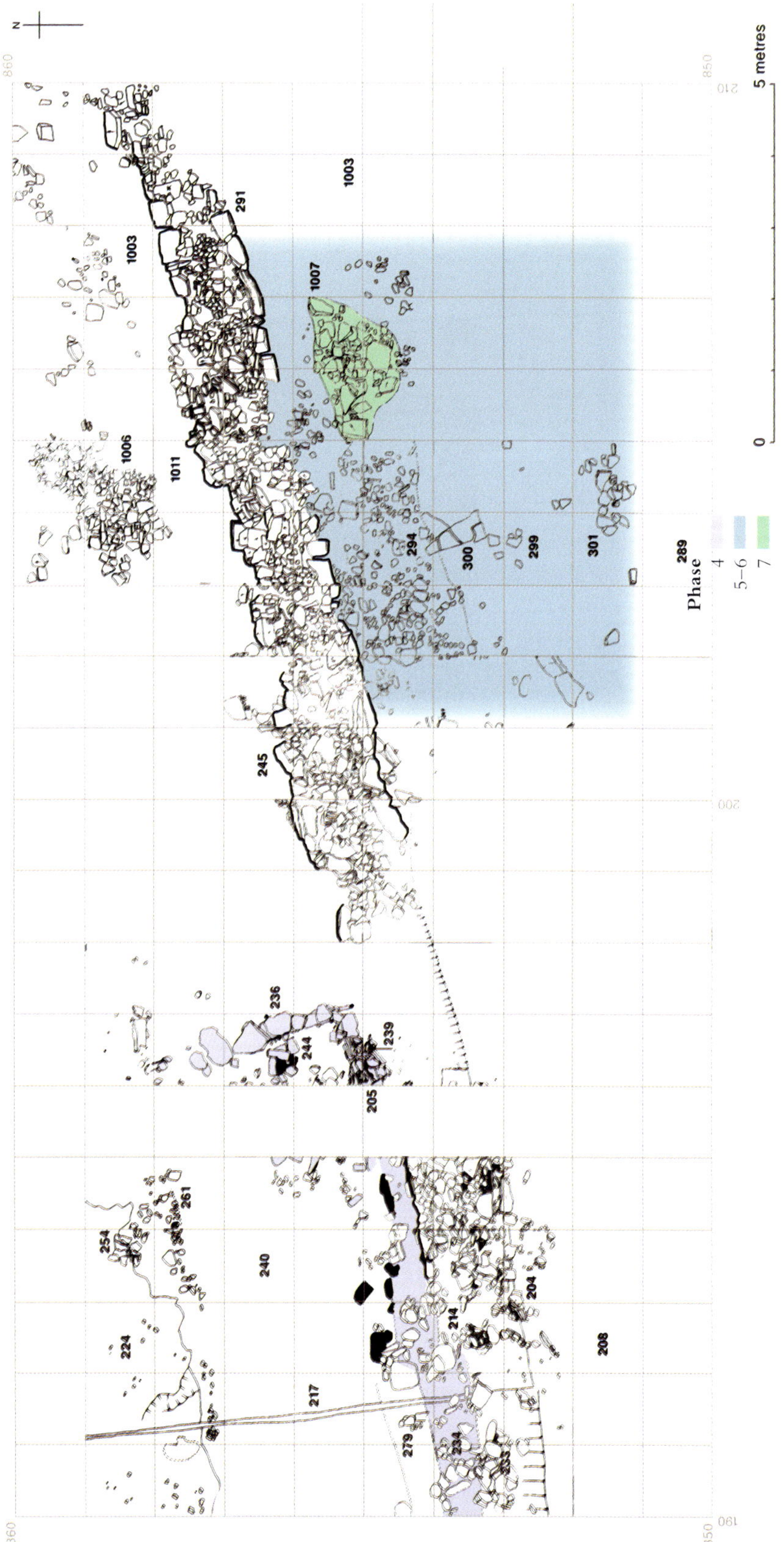

FIGURE 7.6
Composite wall 214/245/291, with structures north and south

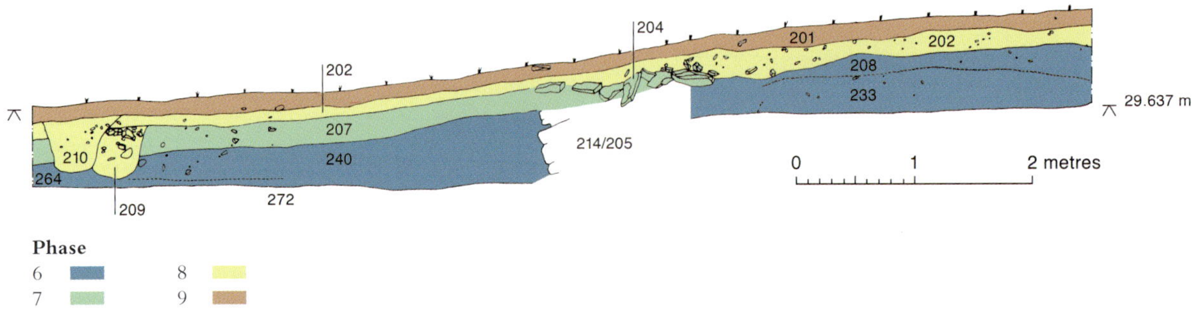

FIGURE 7.7
West facing section on grid-line 195/850-859

limit of its excavation to the area just to the east of the 'hut', which could mean that it was cleared at this point to make the hut walls, but it appears to overlie them (see Figure 7.4 and 7.6), and the gap in the wall beside the eastern wall of the hut seems to be deliberate (Figure 7.5). Its construction cuts the fills within the building (C240; see Figure 7.7) so a more credible explanation is that part of the hut was standing when the wall was built and the gap alongside it may have been caused by plough drag of stones. The walling throughout was a bizarre mixture of cut and uncut stones and also included architectural fragments such as sections of column, which most plausibly derive from a ruined church.

FIGURE 7.8
Structure 250, viewed from the north below floor level, showing the construction trench or gulley to the west

The building sequence

Where the stonework petered out alongside the telephone cable (C217), on the western side of the trench, there were two shelving cuts into the soft sandy soil which could have been robbed out construction trenches for the wall and the building (Figures 7.8 and 7.9) or part of an earlier perimeter trench for the cemetery. Certainly, judging by the resistivity survey, an area of high resistance similar to the walling imprint continues westwards, but at a different angle from the perimeter slope for the cemetery edge on the west and east. It therefore seems more likely that the 'shelf' was used for the construction of the wall and that it may in places have coincided with the edge of the cemetery perimeter. The pottery from the construction trench line was little different from the pottery within the stones of the wall and the layer (C207) which contained the collapse of the wall, although in the last mentioned there was one sherd of Tin Glazed White Earthenware as well as some bottle glass and a clay pipe, which could have been plough disturbance. The great bulk of the pottery in all of this area is Tweed Valley Ware, and it would seem that both pottery and stonework could have been gathered up together from demolished buildings on the site — including the church.

The wall to the east of the hut C250 was a more solid structure (Figure 7.10). It was given the

FIGURE 7.9
Evidence for gulley C234 predating stone wall C214

FIGURE 7.10
Wall 291 in process of excavation, with the fragment of a column in the background

general number 291, and was cut into a mottled sandy deposit (C1011) which yielded mainly Tweed Valley Ware with one fragment of Reduced Gritty Ware (type 4.2). This pottery combined with possible horse-harness (Fe95, C1005) and animal bone confirms the earlier domestic occupation in this area. It seems, as noted above, that the wall cut through occupation which extended to the north of the wall, since, lying between the deep level of sand C1003 and C1011 was a layer of flat slabs (C1006) covered with charcoal and cinders and a considerable amount of pottery (types 2.1–5.1) (Figures 7.6 and 7.11). This was interpreted as a path during excavation but could have been part of a yard, or even an outbuilding floor. The wall (C291) opposite this paving seems to have been rebuilt with a blocking which is of a different form from the orthostats with rubble and mortar fill, which is the main construction of the wall on either side (Figures 7.11 and 7.12). It is therefore possible that the paved area C1006 was a feature which was initially retained when the wall was first built as well as being relevant to the occupation before the wall construction, and that later the entrance was blocked. Alternatively the enclosure wall, which is clearly reshaped in this area, with a large dump of cut stone (C1007) lying to the south, could have started life as a house wall with a northern opening and then been rebuilt

FIGURE 7.11
Wall with facing surviving to the east of the blocked opening, with stone 'paving' (C1006) to the north

as a field wall. This wall had been constructed on a ledge or break of slope; further west and within the rubble fill there was animal bone and White Gritty Ware. The orthostats to the north had collapsed, spreading the rubble fill, but the wall line remained clearly visible under the topsoil (Figures 7.13 and 7.14).

To the north of the wall was another enigmatic structure C288 (Figures 7.15 and 7.16) which overlaid the flat slabs (C1006) and was also directly

FIGURE 7.12
Possible blocked entrance through wall to the east of structure C250

FIGURE 7.13
Detail of wall C291 viewed from the west, showing demolition and possible blocked entrance

opposite the blocked opening in the wall. It was, however, set at a different angle, and composed of a facing of well-cut stone blocks with neat right-angled corners on the east and west. Although there was not a point where C288 touched or cut the wall (C291), at the west end it rested on the deposit of collapsed walling C1005, and so is a clearly later feature than the wall. It extended 4.4m E–W and 1.8m N–S, and when first excavated appeared to have a socket-like rectangle in the centre which was filled with soil and pebbles (C295) and there were postholes against the east and west faces: C247, C249 and C297 (Figure 7.15). Its function is obscure — possible interpretations are the support for a step leading to the cemetery from the north or the support for a monument. It appears to have gone out of use by the 16th century, and to have been covered by one of the areas of cobbling (C287) which survived in discontinuous patches in this northern area of the site (Figure 7.16).

The wall C214/291 in its various stages of construction and reconstruction could have begun around the 14th century (Tweed Valley Ware was found in the construction trench C279 and C234) but went out of use in the later medieval period, since none of the pottery in the destruction levels (C204 and C205) is post-medieval.

The sequence in this northern area is postulated as follows: a church and cemetery coexisted with a domestic building or buildings in the north-east of the site, which, from the evidence of the associated finds, was of quite high status occupation. The presumed floor area is respected by burials, but it could be seen as within the churchyard perimeter, and since there are chaplains of The Hirsel mentioned in the 12th- and 13th-century documents, but not later (see Chapter 2), this might have been the chaplain's house. It was destroyed and its stonework reused around the 14th century.

The cemetery was first enclosed with a simple slope or gulley of a type which survives on the west of the site, then a retaining wall at the north, in part on the same alignment as the gulley, was constructed with stones from earlier buildings. The line of the wall in this area closely parallels the line of the extended church so that it was probably constructed while some vestige of that structure was still visible. This walling need not, however, have been primarily a cemetery enclosure, but could have

FIGURE 7.14
Surface of the demolished wall C291

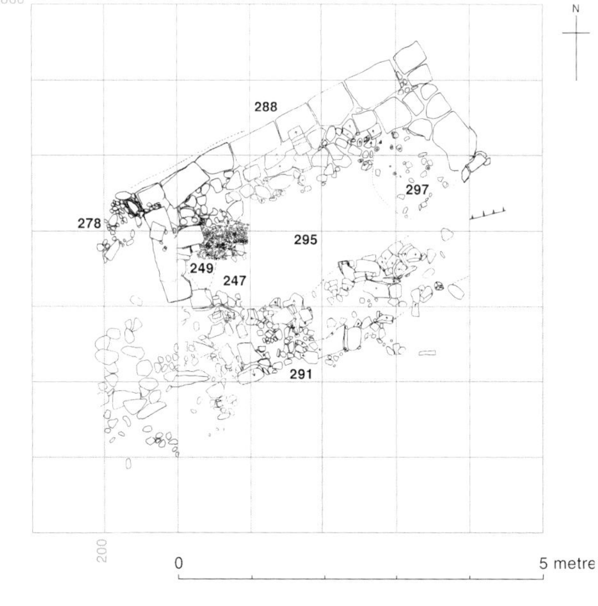

FIGURE 7.15
Structure C288

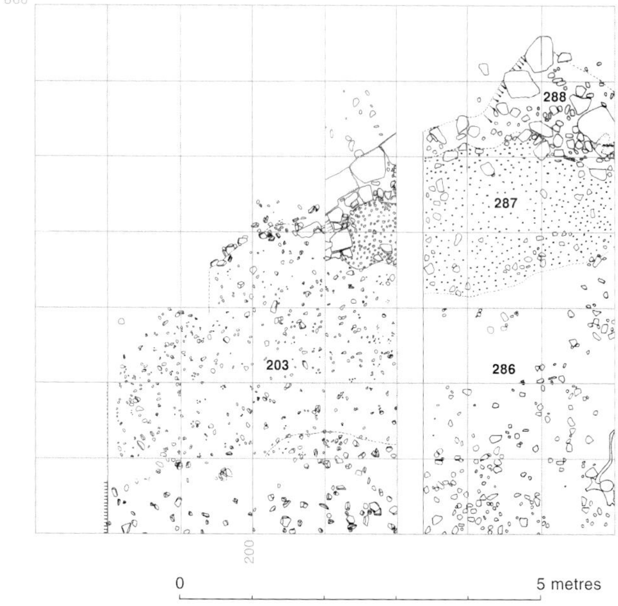

FIGURE 7.16
Demolition and patch of cobbling C287

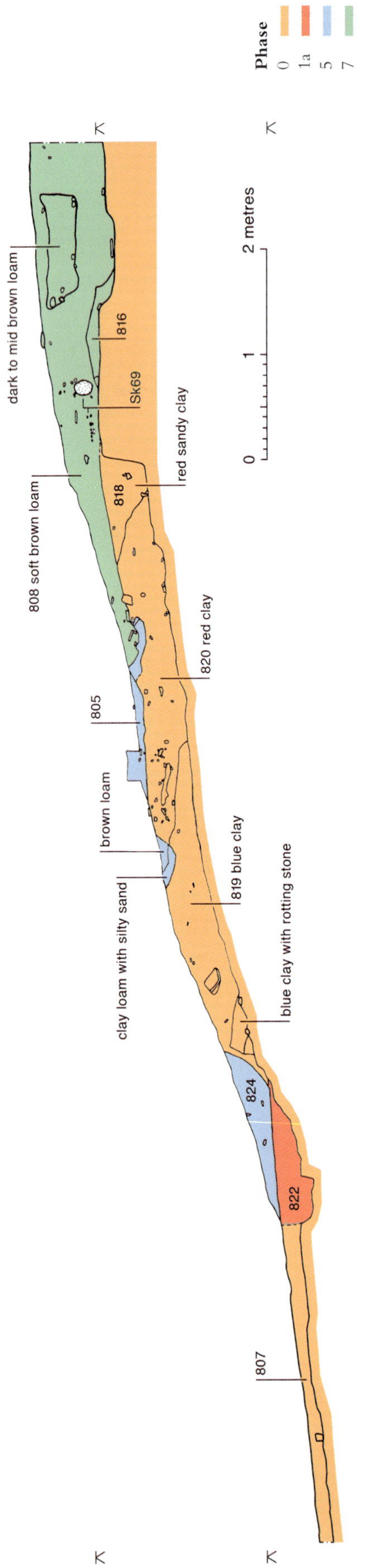

FIGURE 7.17
North-facing section through terrace on grid-line 837.5

FIGURE 7.18
View of section through the terrace from the north

been constructed to separate off the cemetery from agricultural activity, including a terraced field to the north since there is no trace of walling on the west or east of the site. The collapsed rubble of this wall (C204 and C205) contained only medieval pottery, however, and the wall seems to have gone out of use by the time the whole area of the church and churchyard was covered over in the 17th century.

7.5 THE PERIMETER TO THE EAST

On the east of the site there was a steep slope to the River Leet on which there were remains of terraces (see Figure 1.7), which had apparently been clearer in outline before the latest ploughing (Caroline Douglas-Home pers comm). In 1981 a narrow trench was cut into the slope in an attempt to date these terraces and to see if there was a discernible cemetery perimeter. The lower deposits on the slope were of heavy clays and because of the time limits the main trench was sectioned (Figures 7.17 and 7.18). There had been soil creep on the slope and disturbance caused by ploughing, but the general sequence was clear. The natural was blue clay (C819), overlaid in part by bands of red clay (C820 and C807). The deposit (C807) at the base of the slope was devoid of finds, but contained some hill-wash and angular rubble which could have fallen from higher up the slope. Cut into the clays at the base of the slope was an intrusion (C822) filled with clean mixed clay. This seemed to be a tree or bush disturbance and could be pre-medieval in date.

A probable medieval boundary in this area is a ditch at the break of slope (C824) which cut C819 and, covering its western edge, there was a spread of stones and pebbles disturbed by the plough (Figure 7.19). There was one sherd of Tweed Valley Ware (type 2.2) in its fill as well as some animal bone and shell, and a piece of clay pipe stem which could be intrusive. The pottery and food waste could have derived from the area of domestic occupation on the platform above. The ditch fill was covered by soft sandy loam (C803) which contained a mixture of finds from medieval pottery to a cartridge case and can be seen as hill wash. Towards the top of the slope there were layers of soft brown sandy loam (C804, C805) and an upper level (C808) of sandy soil containing pottery which spanned the medieval period. Into this layer Sk49, Sk50, Sk67, Sk68 and Sk69 were cut. The grave of Sk85 was cut into a lower deposit of sandy soil but the graves of Sk73–75 cut the red mottled clay C818 and are considered the earliest (Figure 7.20). The graves do not extend to the boundary ditch, C824, but stop

FIGURE 7.19
View of the terrace from the south showing spread of stones (C824)

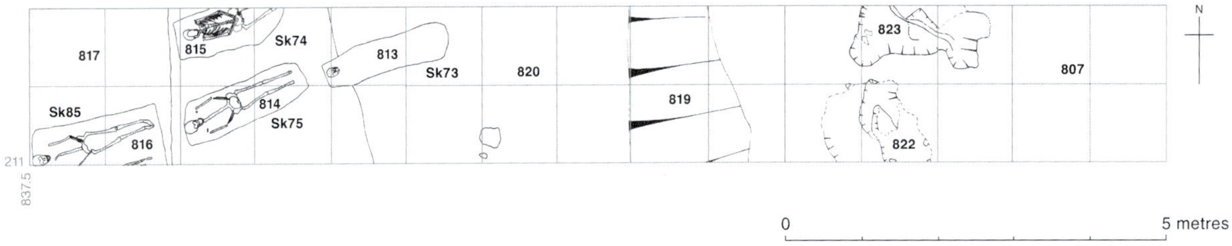

FIGURE 7.20
Plan of the northern half of terrace trench showing lowest level of burials

around the 216 grid-line (see Figures 6.1 and 7.20). It is possible that there was some more substantial line of boundary for the medieval burial ground such as a line of stones and pebbles (C802) which has been ploughed away, but as on the north side, and apparently also on the west, the earliest line of demarcation seems to be a cut in the slope.

8

LATER OCCUPATION OF THE SITE

Rosemary Cramp and Belinda Burke

8.1 INTRODUCTION

The church was, as described above, demolished piecemeal before the final clearance and sealing with a mound of stones (Figures 8.1 and 8.2). What is less clear is where the stone was reused or deposited, other than in the walling north of the churchyard. In Chapter 2, it was noted in a lawsuit of 1566 there is mention of 'ane auld house besyde the Kirksted of Hirsell' (p 19), and in the same document mention is made of the new house of Hirsel, so there could have been domestic buildings nearby which reused the stone. In the north-west of the excavated area of the site (170–195/835–850) the modern ploughing revealed a particularly stony area and here rubble had been used to create hard core surfaces (Figure 8.3) in one place overlying an enclosure. The first evidence for this feature was found in the 1979 excavation in the westernmost trench of the site, where it was seen as a cobble bank (C6) with a stone revetment (Figure 8.4). When the area to the east of this trench was excavated in 1980, the encircling ditch filled with stones (C1124) was not very clear and had been more disturbed, but its line was clearly demarcated in 1982 (Figures 8.5, 8.6 and 8.7).

8.2 OCCUPATION IN THE NORTH-WEST AREA OF THE SITE

The sequence of activities seems to be as follows. A large hollow scoop was cut into clean natural sands, with a trampled layer in its base (C570) that contained no finds (Figure 8.5). An enclosure formed from a curving stone-filled ditch then cut the edge of the scoop, most clearly visible to the east as a densely packed band of stones (C1124), about 0.8m deep and 1.3m wide (Figures 8.1, 8.5, 8.7 and 8.8). To the north, the area was badly disturbed by the modern ploughing, but there appears nevertheless to be a gap in the enclosure, indicating a possible entrance, before the re-appearance of the stones just east of the section on north–south grid-line 183, apparently continuing further west in a line of stones (C4) delimiting a bank of cobbles (C6). To the south, there is also much later disturbance in the form of pits and postholes, but running parallel to this line of stones, although not extending so far west, is a stone-filled gulley (C946), with an overlying layer of cobbles (C1032). Some stones in the surrounding enclosure are worked, and finds associated with them include clear window glass, a few fragments of bottle glass which may be residual from the layers above, and pottery which is medieval, with one sherd of Lead Glazed Red Earthenware from C1124. This context also contained human bone, indicating that the feature had disturbed graves in cutting the cemetery level (C1123); Sk294 was disturbed by the stone-filled gulley (C946), and the grave of Sk27 was directly alongside the line of stones to the south.

The hollow scoop was filled with deposits of rubble and sandy loam, with a large curving tip of rubble (C451) following the southern edge of the scoop (Figure 8.9). This contained one fragment of window glass, one fragment of bottle glass and sherds of medieval pottery, with other contexts in the fill (C450, C452) containing slag and ash, suggesting industrial activity. This was overlain by compacted surfaces (C410, C421; Figures 8.2, 8.10), with similar surfaces overlying the gulley and cobbles to the south (C413 and C911) and, to the west (C906). Immediately underlying C410, there was a large circular area of sand, slag and ash (C450), which contained medieval and 16th/17th century pottery, bottle glass, clay pipe, and a stone hone/pounder (CT13). Various postholes and other cavities were observed, but some proved difficult to define. A line of postholes (C929–938) runs roughly parallel to the line of the compound in the south-west corner (Figures 8.5 and 8.11). They are difficult to date, being devoid of finds, but they cut the later medieval cemetery level (C908) and C937 overlies the grave of Sk107.

In the south-east corner of the feature, cut by the southern section of the trench, there was a pit or soakaway (C966) which was filled with stones, animal bone, 40 fragments of pale green window glass and some large stones in the upper fill (C967; Figure 8.10). This cut the ditch fill and a hard surface of pebbles (C413) which included a sherd of post-medieval pottery. Context 911 contained an arrowhead (FeA15), numerous glass bottles of 17th–18th century type, late 17th century clay pipe, food waste and a coin of Charles I, dated 1642–50 (Nu4). (Another coin of Charles I was found in pebbly soil to the south.) All of these later hard surfaces were disturbed by small hollows and by the plough, but they do seem to constitute working areas which had utilised stone before the field was grassed over.

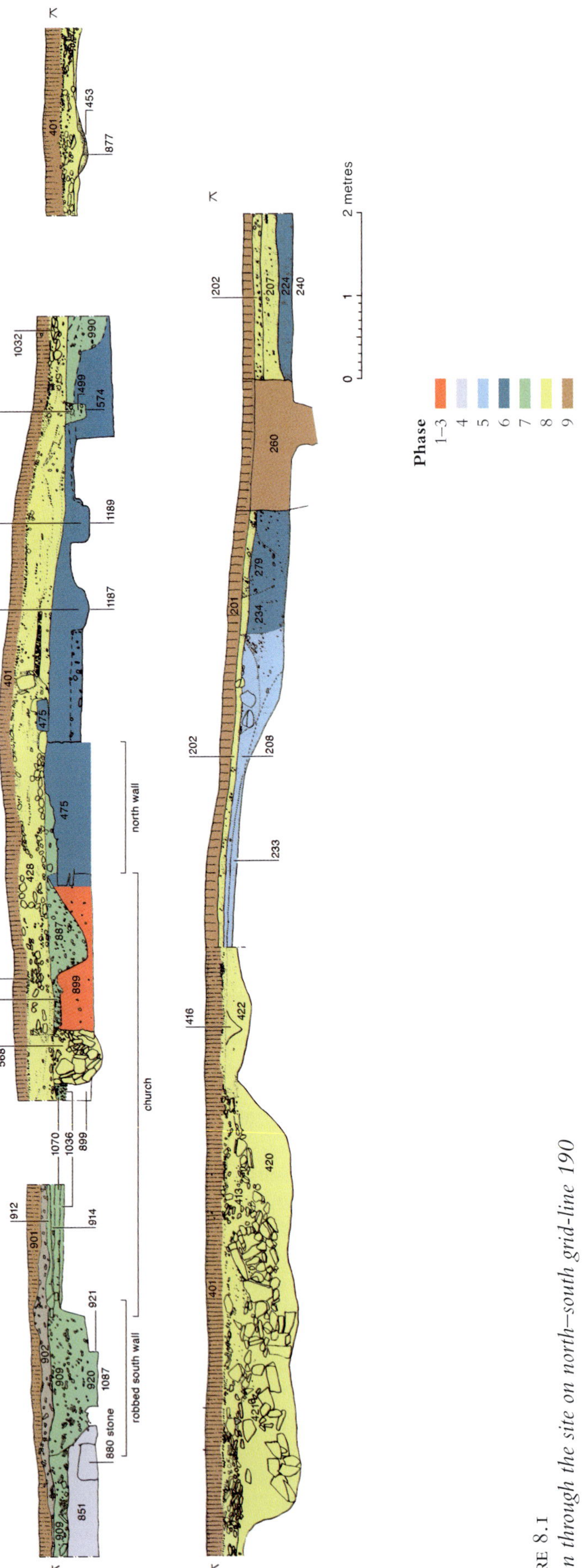

FIGURE 8.1
Section through the site on north–south grid-line 190

FIGURE 8.2
View from the north showing stone surfaces and pits, with the mound of stones over the church (sectioned) in the background

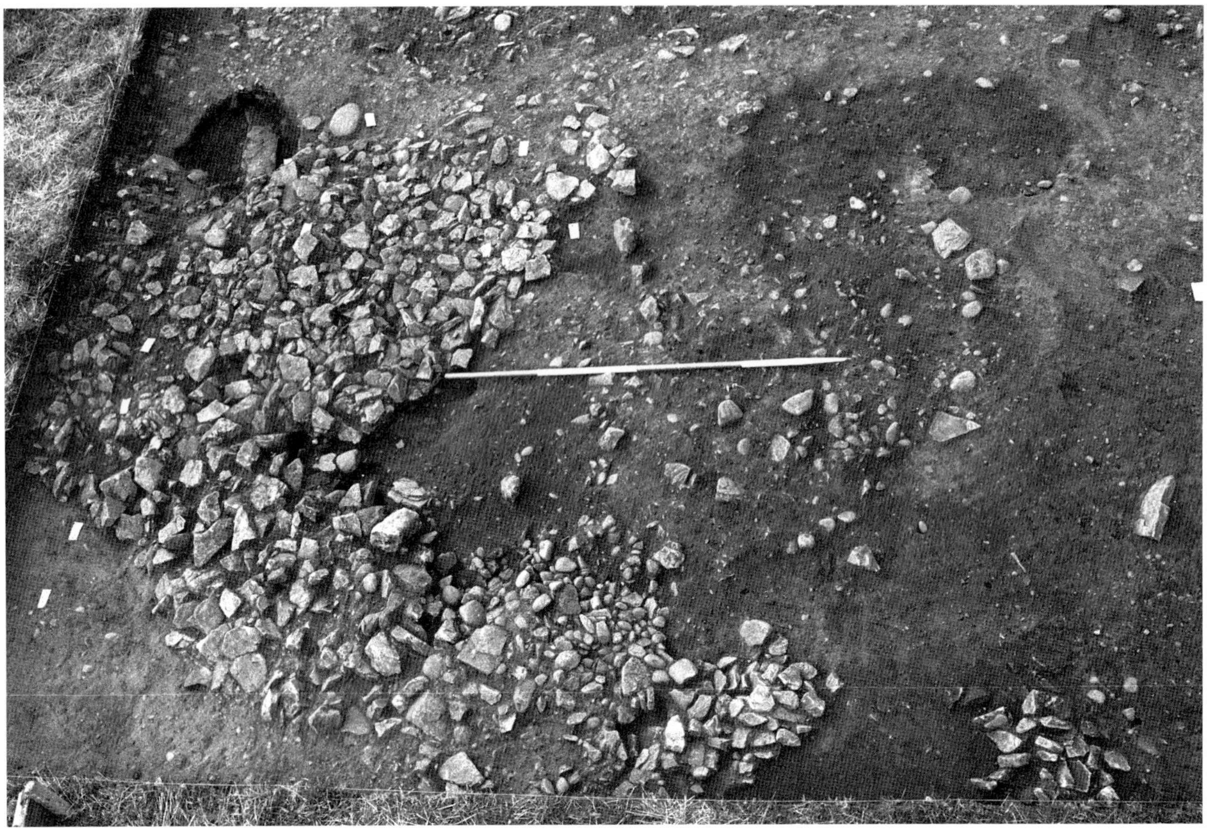

FIGURE 8.3
Detail of stone surface (C448) cut by other features

FIGURE 8.4
Cobble bank (C6) in westernmost trench

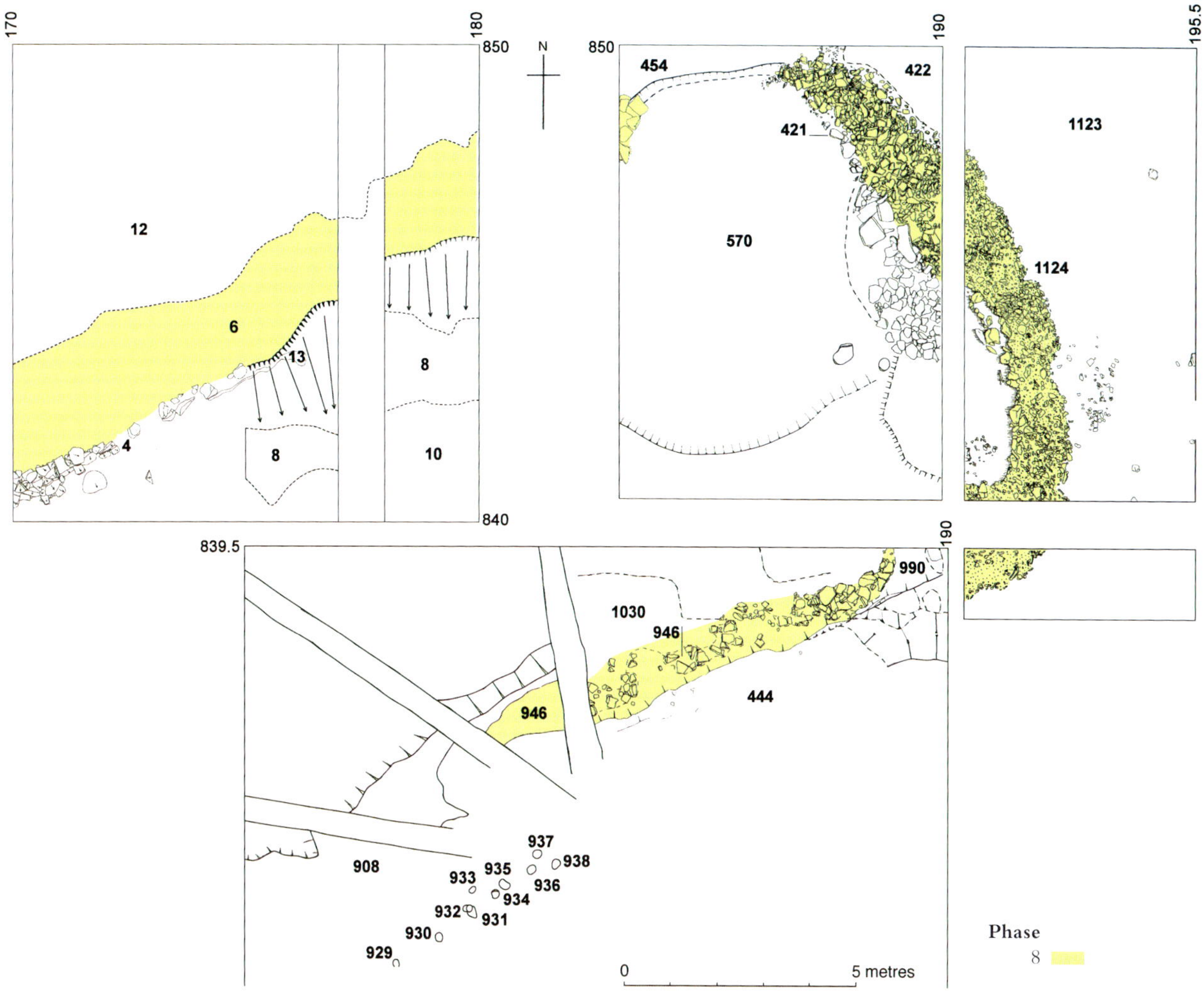

FIGURE 8.5
Plan of the late compound

The composition of these surfaces is very similar to the uppermost surface of the mound of building debris (C403, C404) overlying the west end of the church immediately to the south (Figures 8.2 and 8.10). This consisted of fragments of dressed stone, mortar and slate, and small slab-like stones, approximately 10cm square and 6cm thick, which suggests that they were the offcuts of larger stones, possibly flooring. The mound contained a fragment of bottle glass, Lead Glazed Red Earthenware, 17th century clay pipe, an 18th century bow corkscrew (Fe110), and a large quantity of medieval material, presumably residual. Further rubble deposits underlying the dump and extending over the whole of the area around the west end of the church (C428 and C909; Figure 8.10) also contained some post-medieval material, but the layers immediately covering the church (Figure 5.35) contained exclusively medieval finds, which implies that the mound represents later activity on the site, unrelated to the demolition of the church, although much of the material may have originated from that building.

Similar surfaces were detected outside the cemetery perimeter (Figure 8.10). In the northernmost trench there were areas of densely packed cobbles (C104, C106), which overlay dark brown sandy soil (C105). All contained post-medieval pottery including 17th–18th century porcelain (Figure 17.10, no. 90), clay pipe stems dated mid to late 17th century, and a coin of James VI (1623–1625) (Nu3). Four postholes set in a square (C107–110) were cut into these layers. There was a large quantity of ash and cinder embedded in the surface. Architectural fragments (including part of the column AF2) came from this area, perhaps dragged by the plough. C105 contained two honestones (CT11 and CT12) and smithing slag.

Further west, in trench B (1979), four large, irregular post pits (C209, C212, C213 and C215) were cut into C207, which contained window and bottle glass, clay pipe (17th to early 18th century), cinder and fuel ash, including two fragments of a possible furnace base, and a stone tool of unknown function (CT28).

FIGURE 8.6
First appearance of the stone feature (C1124)

A further surface of cobbles (C287) was packed into the structure (C288) to the north of the perimeter wall (Figure 7.16). Finds included bottle glass and fuel ash.

8.3 DISCUSSION

The function of the stone-filled ditch is open to debate. It is substantial and encloses an area about 9.6m by 11.5m. The lowest level of stones in the ditch includes some large pieces of cut stone which could be clearance from the church or other buildings.

Above them are smaller fragments of cut stone and where the stones are tightly packed and neatly laid they may have formed the hard base of an earthen wall, but this could not have been very substantial, and could have been nothing more than a wind break. Nevertheless, the breaking up of stones into small neat fragments and their careful setting must have been to some purpose.

The distributions of bottles and clay pipes, as well as of some stone tools, are localised in this area and the enclosure could have been used as a building compound for workmen for a new building, utilising stone from the ruins. It is possible though that not all the stone was directly derived from the church. If the church is assumed

FIGURE 8.7
The band of stones (C1124) delimiting the compound to the east, with Sk183 in the foreground

FIGURE 8.8
Section through the south-west corner of the compound, viewed from the north, on grid-line 840.5

FIGURE 8.9
Deposit of rubble and sandy loam (C451)

to have gone out of use in the late 14th century, there is no dateable evidence of activity on the site until the appearance of coins of 1588 associated with the random burial Sk56, apart from one sherd of Langerwehe Stoneware (dated 14th to early 16th century) and one sherd of imported pottery (late 15th to 16th century), both from topsoil contexts in the northern part of the site. Other finds indicate new activity on the site in the 17th and 18th centuries: four coins, some metalwork items including an elaborate shoe buckle (CA4), a small assemblage of post-medieval pottery and glass bottles (with a distribution concentrated in the layers overlying the 'compound'). The assemblage of bottles from C2 and C8 included several large fragments of 'onion' or 'bladder' type wine bottles dating to around 1680–1740 and also 'squat cylindrical' wine bottles of the 18th century (Hugh Wilmott pers comm). While many of the fragments of clay pipe stem may indicate casual losses, the 17th century bowls come from areas where later activity is evident: CP1 from topsoil overlying C2 which yielded CP2–4; CP8 from C928, a layer in the southern part of the ditch surrounding the 'compound', and CP5–7 from the area of the NW perimeter wall.

This activity then seems to centre on the later 17th century and the window glass, which was thin and a cloudy green as opposed to the opaque painted glass from the church, could have come from the 'old house' mentioned above, or the 16th-

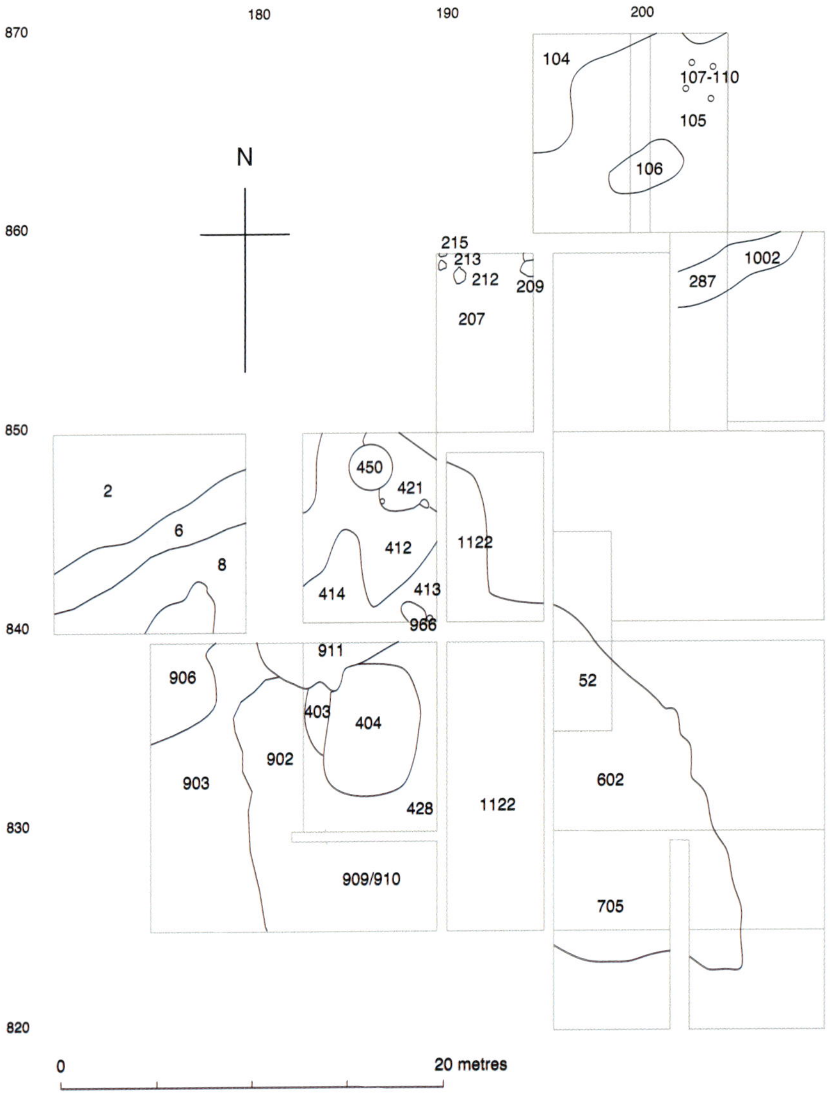

Figure 8.10
Plan of late layers and features

Figure 8.11
Line of postholes (C929–938)

century Hirsel House, since the earliest phases of the present house are considered to be 17th century (RCAHMS 1915, 55, no. 102), and a rebuilding at this period would fit with the evidence from the 'compound' which was formed from reused stone, as well as the other patches of hard surfaces formed from small stone cuttings. This seems a more likely explanation than the one originally considered, and which is still a possibility, namely that this is evidence for military occupation. There is extensive documentary evidence for the importance of Coldstream in the defence of the line of the Tweed during the wars between England and Scotland in the 17th century. Since Hirsel Law was a place where armies mustered (see Chapter 2), the area near to the church and adjacent to the priory overlooking the river crossing of the Leet would have provided a good camping site, and it may be relevant that General Monk camped at Coldstream in 1659. The casual cutting into the cemetery might indicate a military use rather than one which could have included local workers, although by that time the cemetery had largely gone out of use. The coinage, the bottles and pipes could equally indicate workforces of builders or of the military, but there is no artefactual evidence for anything distinctively military. The definitive answer as to the nature of this secular activity or sequence of activities and its duration remains, therefore, uncertain.

9

DATING EVIDENCE

9.1 RADIOCARBON DATING

Andrew Millard

Twenty-three samples from the excavations at The Hirsel have been submitted for radiocarbon dating, of which 21 have yielded dates (Figure 9.1). Human bone samples were analysed in the 1980s at the Glasgow University Radiocarbon Laboratory (GU) and more recently charcoal samples were analysed at the Scottish Universities Environmental Research Centre (SUERC). Calibrations have been made in OxCal 4.1 (Bronk Ramsey 2009) using the IntCal09 calibration curve (Reimer *et al* 2009) and results rounded out to the nearest five years.

Stable isotope measurements ($\delta^{13}C$) were made on all samples except GU-1309 and GU-1310 (Gordon Cook pers comm). For these human bone samples a $\delta^{13}C$ value of –20‰ was assumed in computing the date, and this is justified in the light of the average $\delta^{13}C$ from all other human bone samples of –20.6‰.

To summarise other evidence for dating: cross-marked grave-slabs from the site indicate the potential for early medieval use, but it is possible that such stones continued in use throughout the Middle Ages (see Chapter 13). Skeleton 336 has a *terminus post quem* given by a coin of William I the Lion dated around 1180 (Chapter 14, Nu1). There is mention of a church at The Hirsel in a charter of 1165/66 and there is also a record of its rededication in 1246 (Cramp 1985). However, the location of the church was lost before 1627, though the churchyard still seems to have been known (Chapter 2).

The human bone samples directly date the use of the cemetery, and as a large number of graves were excavated, they probably represent the range of use. A Bayesian chronological model with deposition of some charcoal (SUERC-15888, -15886, -15889, -15890) followed by the cemetery with a single phase of use (Figures 9.2 and 9.3) estimates that the cemetery started within the period *cal AD 1140–1275* (with 95.4% probability), with the probability that the start was *after 1165* being 87%. The end of use of the cemetery is estimated to be within *cal AD 1265–1450* (with 95.4% probability). The radiocarbon dates on human bone are relatively imprecise, so the duration of use can only be estimated to be between 0 and 270 years (95.4% probability). That the cemetery had gone out of use before 1450 is consistent with the record that the site of the church was unknown and the cemetery had gone out of use by 1627 (Robson 1896, 70). The radiocarbon dates are not sufficiently precise to confirm for certain whether it was in use before 1166, but they do suggest odds of about 7:1 against use starting before that date, and there is no evidence from the radiocarbon dates for use in the 11th century or earlier.

9.2 THERMOLUMINESCENCE DATING OF POTTERY

Ian K Bailiff

The application of thermoluminescence (TL) techniques to the dating of pottery from The Hirsel was performed initially in 1980 and a further set of samples was tested in 1984. The differentiation of the pottery on the basis of form or fabric had proved problematic and the purpose of the work was to evaluate the potential of TL dating to aid an understanding of the chronological range of the sites and generic fabric types. In addition to sherds selected from the large body of excavated medieval pottery, two sherds of prehistoric fabric were tested. Although nearly 30 years has elapsed since this work was completed, the procedures applied then can still be considered to have been robust and subsequent developments in the procedures have not invalidated them. In fact, elements of the procedures developed during the original project work were subsequently adopted in the currently used optically stimulated luminescence (OSL) procedures. A full scientific report is available in the archive; this account of the work is based on the experimental report originally produced in 1984 and the opportunity has been taken to refer to more recent research that is relevant to the original experimental work.

Eleven samples recovered from the 1979–1982 excavation seasons at The Hirsel were submitted for dating (Figure 9.4). The samples were tested using procedures based on the high temperature quartz inclusion and quartz pre-dose techniques (Aitken 1985; Bailiff 1991). Each TL date (Figure 9.5) is given with two error terms (Bailiff 2007); the first error term, σ_A, is a type A standard uncertainty obtained by an analysis of repeated observations, and the second error term, σ_B, is a type B standard uncertainty based on an assessment of uncertainty associated with all the quantities

Reference	Description	Laboratory code	Radiocarbon age (BP)	Reported error	Final error[a]	$\delta^{13}C$ (‰)	Calibrated date using IntCal09 at 95.4% probability
Sk1	Human bone from a grave pit in sand	GU-1309	740	70	110	-20 **b**	1155–1400
Sk3	Human bone from a grave pit in sandy soil	GU-1310	840	70	110	-20 **b**	1035–1280
Sk14	Human bone from crouched burial from area E from cemetery on an alignment different from that of structures of medieval period	GU-1488	585	60	110	-20.9	1215–1525 (93.3%), 1575–1585 (0.3%), 1590–1625 (1.8%)
Sk26	Human bone from an extended burial from area E from cemetery on an alignment different from that of structure of medieval period	GU-1487	750	125	175	-21.1	885–1495 (95.2%), 1600–1615 (0.2%)
Sk74	Human bone from an extended burial	GU-1714	Failed to yield sufficient carbon for measurement				
Sk89	Human bone from part of cemetery	GU-1713	Failed to yield sufficient carbon for measurement				
Sk105	Human bone from burial in NE part of cemetery	GU-1720	780	100	100	-19.9	1025–1325 (87.3%), 1345–1395 (8.1%)
Sk110	Human bone from an extended burial. One of a group of burials aligned on the N wall of the church	GU-1721	880	65	65	-22.0	1025–1260
Sk193	Human bone from a burial in the SW corner of the cemetery	GU-1716	540	85	85	-20.0	1275–1515 (94.1%), 1600–1620 (1.3%)
Sk222	Human bone from an extended burial associated with significant group and with perforated shell in grave	GU-1719	595	85	85	-20.1	1260–1455
Sk239	Human bone from one of a group of skeletons directly aligned with W end of the church	GU-1718	705	55	55	-22.1	1215–1330 (68.3%), 1340–1400 (27.1%)
Sk247	Human bone from an extended burial	GU-1717	745	100	100	-21.6	1040–1105 (7.1%), 1115–1410 (88.3%)
Sk338	Human bone W of church, cist burial	GU-1901	810		50	-18.1	1050–1085 (4.1%), 1125–1140 (0.9%), 1150–1285 (90.4%)
C678	Early layer in N of nave (Roman pot TL 400±320, no other pot)	SUERC-15891	670		40	-25.1	1265–1330 (51.4%), 1340–1400 (44.0%)
C851	Charcoal associated with Neolithic pot (and 4 medieval sherds)	SUERC-15888	950		40	-25.8	1015–1185
C857	Reddish soil cut by graves and wall of church	SUERC-15886	975		40	-26.8	990–1160
C899	Red-brown soil into which nave was cut/levels within nave	SUERC-16084	2015		35	-25.6	155–140 BC (0.5%), 115 BC–AD 70 (94.8%)
C1226b	Patch of burning in nave, possible bronze-working	SUERC-15887	940		40	-26.4	1015–1185
C1347	Fill of bronze-working pit 1348 in nave	SUERC-15892	950		40	-26.5	1015–1185
C1388	Lowest levels of pit 1385, W end of church	SUERC-15889	955		40	-22.6	995–1005 (0.3%), 1010–1180 (95.1%)
C1389	Lowest levels of pit 1385, W end of church	SUERC-15890	965		40	-24.3	995–1165
C1413	Fills of 1345, early feature S of church	SUERC-15881	935		40	-26.8	1020–1190 (94.7%), 1200–1210 (0.7%)
C1415	Fills of cut 1414	SUERC-15882	905		40	-22.9	1030–1215

a Errors on GU dates up to GU-1500 have been adjusted according to the recommendation of Dr M Stenhouse, as reported in Ashmore *et al* (2000, 45)
b Assumed value (Gordon Cook pers comm)

FIGURE 9.1
Table of radiocarbon dates

```
Options()
{
 Resolution=1;
 Cubic=TRUE;
 RawData=FALSE;
 UseF14C=FALSE;
 BCAD=TRUE;
 PlusMinus=FALSE;
 Intercept=FALSE;
 Floruit=FALSE;
 SD2=TRUE;
 SD3=FALSE;
 ConvergenceData=FALSE;
 UniformSpanPrior=TRUE;
 kIterations=100;
};
Plot()
{
 Sequence("Hirsel")
 {
  Phase("Pre-cemetery")
  {
   R_Date("SUERC-15888", 950, 40);
   R_Date("SUERC-15886", 975, 40);
   R_Date("SUERC-15889", 955, 40);
   R_Date("SUERC-15890", 965, 40);
  };
  Boundary("Start cemetery");
  Phase("Cemetery")
  {
   R_Date("GU-1309", 740, 70);
   R_Date("GU-1310", 840, 70);
   R_Date("GU-1716", 540, 85);
   R_Date("GU-1717", 745, 100);
   R_Date("GU-1718", 705, 55);
   R_Date("GU-1719", 595, 85);
   R_Date("GU-1720", 780, 100);
   R_Date("GU-1721", 880, 65);
   R_Date("GU-1487", 750, 175);
   R_Date("GU-1488", 585, 110);
   R_Date("GU-1901", 810, 50);
   Interval("Cemetery duration");
  };
  Boundary("End cemetery");
 };
};
```

FIGURE 9.2
OxCal Model

employed in the calculation of the age, including those of type A, and is equivalent to the overall error described by Aitken (1985). Expressions for both terms were derived from an analysis of the propagation of errors when calculating the age using measured and calculated values, and hitherto this approach has been generally considered to be sufficiently robust. Unless stated otherwise, all the uncertainties discussed in this paper are given as $\pm 1\sigma$ (that is, at the 68% level of confidence).

9.3 TL DATING: AN ARCHAEOLOGICAL COMMENTARY

Rosemary Cramp

The sherds submitted to the Durham TL laboratory for dating were chosen, during and immediately after the excavation, by Susan Mills, mainly to answer problems concerning fabric types rather than to help with the context dating. The very broad dates assigned to Scottish medieval pottery types proved of little help in separating out phases of site activity within the comparatively limited life of the church and cemetery. When the pottery was first assessed it was assumed that the pottery from this Borders region could share many of the characteristics of the pottery from northern Northumbria and Cumbria. The picture was that the regions were largely aceramic until the 10th century, and throughout the area there is a lack of kiln sites in comparison with the area south of the Tees. From the 12th century onwards there are long lived local pottery types and a steadily growing trade in more exotic types from southern Britain and the continent especially in coastal areas, although these are not represented at The Hirsel. The medieval pottery from Scotland has been subjected to further research since the excavation, and this is considered in Valerie Dean's report (Chapter 17), but the picture is not substantially altered.

The Neolithic pottery TL dated to 3300±435 BC confirms the dating of the type from sites elsewhere (see Chapter 15) and was the first clear indication of occupation of that early date on the site. The very fragile sherd from C635, which has been assigned a TL date of 1540±290 BC, was initially the only indication of Bronze Age activity on the site, but more sherds have now been assigned to this period (Chapter 15). Its context, sandy loam and charcoal, is the soil level which overlies the natural gravels and underlies the church. The worn sherd from C678, which was suggested by Mills as possibly Roman, has been confirmed in the TL dating AD 400±165 as being Roman or sub-Roman. Although it is a type not so far recognised, there is other Roman pottery from the site (see Section 16.2), as well as a glass bracelet and vessel glass, which could support a Roman date also for this sherd, although a sub-

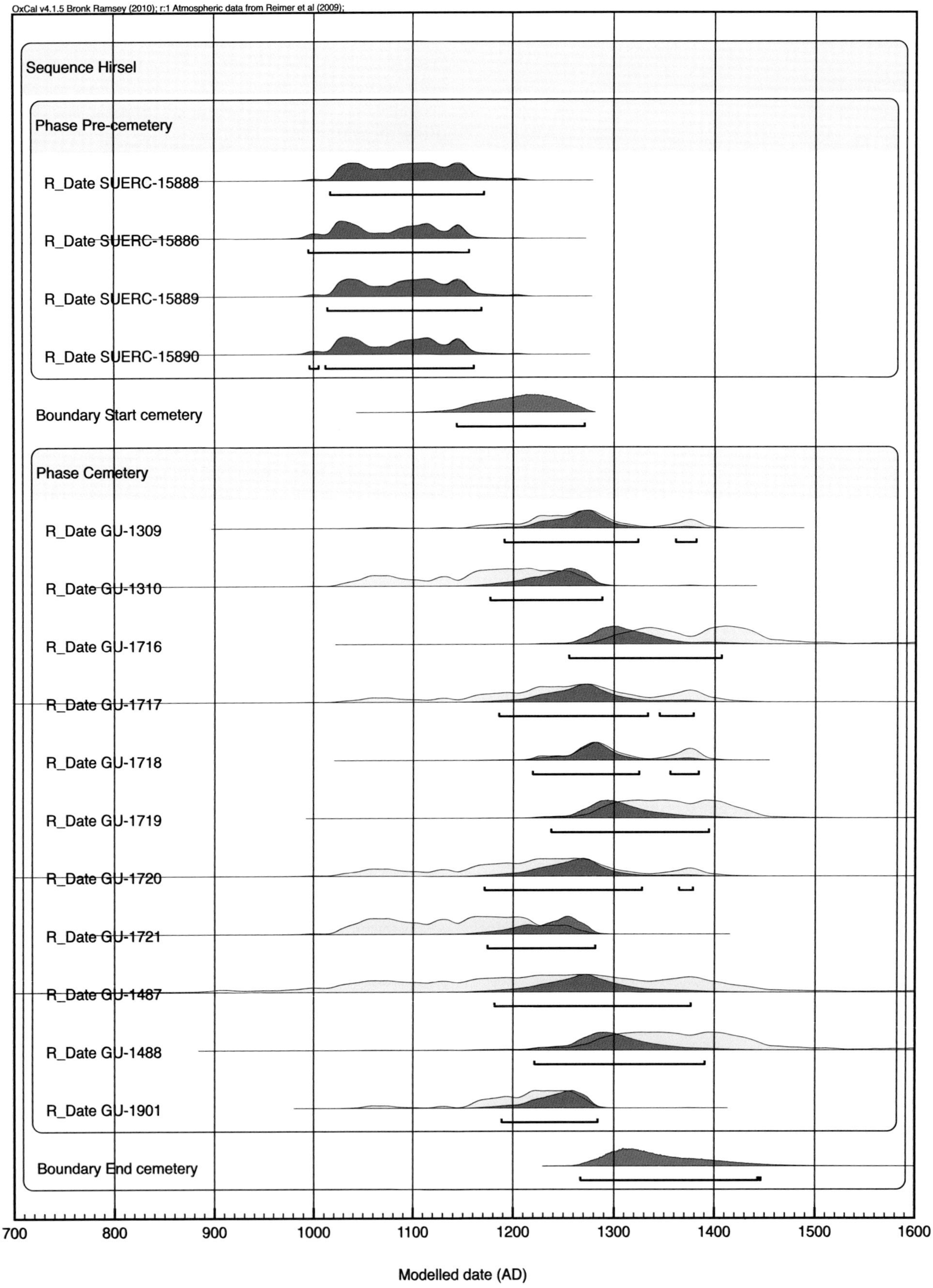

FIGURE 9.3
OxCal Model results

Lab. reference	Finds reference	Context	Fabric
Dur80TLqi 1-0	HIR 79 EX sf88	C132 Disturbed prehistoric level	Prehistoric Pot 2 (Early Neolithic)
Dur80Tlqi 1-1	HIR 82 AA 1 sf380	C635 Disturbed early layer	Prehistoric Pot 10 (Bronze Age/Iron Age)
Dur80TLqi 1-2	HIR 82 BN sf426	C729 Grave fill for Sk136	2.1, E19 Tweed Valley Ware (12th–early 15th century)
Dur80TLqi 1-3	HIR 82 GA sf730	C1091 Grave fill for Sk222	1.2, D13 Coarse Gritty Ware (late 10th–12th century)
Dur80TLqi 1-4	HIR 82 FR sf664	C739 Grave fill for Sk187	2.2, E12 Tweed Valley Ware (12th–early 15th century)
Dur80TLqi 1-5	HIR 82 FA sf744	C745 Grave fill for Sk174	4.1, F11 Reduced Gritty Ware (late 12th–16th century)
Dur80TLqi 1-6	HIR 82 JK sf882	C678 Sand in nave	Hard oxidised ware, unidentified (see Chapter 16)
Dur84TLqi 22-1	HIR 82 HN	C1058 Cemetery surface in the west	1.2, D3 Coarse Gritty Ware (late 10th–12th century)
Dur84TLqi 22-3	HIR 82 ET sf842	C623 Area of burning in nave	4.2, F7 Reduced Gritty Ware (late 12th–16th century)

FIGURE 9.4
Table of TL samples (for fabric identification and dating see Chapter 17)

Lab. reference	Context	TL date	$\pm\sigma_A$	$\pm\sigma_B$
Dur80TLqi 1-0	C132 Disturbed prehistoric level	3300 BC	±320	±435
Dur80Tlqi 1-1	C635 Disturbed early layer	1540 BC	±210	±290
Dur80TLqi 1-2	C729 Grave fill for Sk136	AD 1180	±115	±120
Dur80TLqi 1-3	C1091 Grave fill for Sk222	AD 1170	±70	±90
Dur80TLqi 1-4	C739 Grave fill for Sk187	AD 1060	±100	±110
Dur80TLqi 1-5	C745 Grave fill for Sk174	AD 1100	±80	±95
Dur80TLqi 1-6	C678 Sand in nave	AD 400	±135	±165
Dur84TLqi 22-1	C1058 Cemetery surface in the west	AD 810	±110	±130
Dur84TLqi 22-3	C623 Area of burning in nave	AD 1475	±45	±55

FIGURE 9.5
Table of TL dates

Roman context is also possible. There is little pre-Norman evidence from the site, although the Phase I church could be as early as the 10th century. The Coarse Gritty Wares from the site are often found in early contexts, as was the sherd from C1058 dated by TL to AD 810±130. As Dean has noted, some examples of this type may be compared with Northumbrian late pre-Conquest types and this sherd is a case in point. This type of fabric could have been long lived, but an early 9th century date is interesting. The most common pottery on the site — the Tweed Valley White Wares — also apparently had a long span of life, but where sherds such as qi 1–4, which came from a grave cutting the earliest cemetery surface, appeared in an early context, a date of AD 1060±110 is plausible. Another sherd of the same type from the grave fill C1091 in another area of the site yielded a date of AD 1170±90. This seems to have been residual or derived from the level through which the grave was cut, since the dating of Sk222 gave a radiocarbon range of 1260–1455.

The medieval Coarse Gritty Ware types 1.3 and 1.4 indicate a similarity in date to such white wares in northern England: late 11th–end of the 12th century. The 2.1 type often occurs with the Coarse Gritty type 1.2 and these seem to represent the earliest intensive occupation on the site, which could be associated with the building of the church. The dating of the Reduced Gritty Wares from C623 has confirmed the distinctions seen by the specialists in the pottery of this type, but has focussed the date range more narrowly towards the later medieval period.

The TL dates for the pottery from the site, although limited in number, have proved very useful and have supported the radiocarbon dates in defining the span of occupation at this site. The Neolithic pottery dating has since been refined by archaeological specialists (Chapter 15), but in the light of the difficulties in precise dating of medieval fabrics in Scotland the TL dates have been of substantial value.

10
ENVIRONMENTAL EVIDENCE

10.1 ANALYSIS OF CARBONISED PLANT REMAINS

Jacqui P Huntley

Carbonised plant remains were present in all of the 65 samples received for analysis, with about half of the samples containing more than 300 fragments. Four cereal crops were represented: oats, wheat, barley and rye. Of these, oats were the most abundant in all of the samples, the proportion of the other three cereals varying considerably. Two species of cultivated oat were present. Most of the wheat was bread wheat although an unidentifiable brittle rachis wheat was also very occasionally present. Barley was mainly of the hulled variety and, from the proportion of twisted to straight embryos, was mostly 6-row barley. Other crops grown included peas and broad beans, and flax seeds were also present in a few samples. Lentils were recorded in one sample and have to represent an imported food. The 'weed' taxa were abundant and varied in most of the samples and were mainly representative of plants from arable fields and disturbed and waste ground. Plants of wet, muddy areas, pasture and meadow, and hedgerows were also represented. The data were analysed with two multivariate methods and both divided the samples into two groups, one mainly from inside and one mainly from outside the structure. The former were subsequently divided into two:

— a) a group containing large amounts of seeds of traditional arable weeds seen as representing the main processing and storage of the grain from crops grown at the site and

— b) a group containing many seeds of waste and abandoned ground taxa, and these are seen as representing the vegetation of the site immediately following the fire which destroyed it.

The samples from outside the structure represent the general vegetation in the vicinity at the time of their deposition and although they do form groups these are not as ecologically distinct as those groups of samples from inside the structure.

Introduction

Preliminary analyses of exploratory samples were made by van der Veen (1982). These revealed that there were large amounts of well preserved carbonised plant material over much of the archaeological site known as The Hirsel. Intensive sampling of the site was therefore carried out from 1982 in order to allow detailed identification and quantification of these remains. Samples of varying size were collected from various localities and stratigraphic positions within the site. The samples were dried and then floated, with the flots sieved through a 500 micron mesh. Forty five such flots were analysed by the author in 1984–85 (Huntley 1984) with a further two in 1985. Eighteen samples were floated during this period but were not analysed until 2007 when they were completed by the author. This report combines all samples from the main phases of excavation, and excludes the exploratory samples.

Laboratory procedure

The flots were examined at magnifications of x50 using a Wild M3 stereomicroscope and all carbonised fruits, seeds and other potentially identifiable plant remains were removed. Carbonised items were identified by comparison with modern reference material belonging to the author. In a few instances, the flots were so rich that only proportions of them were analysed. In these cases, the data presented have been calculated to represent the whole flot. For comparative purposes percentage data have been calculated based upon the totals of these counts as it was not possible to calculate concentrations per unit volume of sediment in all cases.

Non-carbonised but well preserved fruits and seeds were present in some samples but were not included in the analysis. They are unlikely to have been contemporary with the carbonised material because non-carbonised material does not generally survive for long periods in aerobic deposits. Two samples produced mineral replaced material which is, however, considered most likely contemporary with deposition.

Taxonomy

Nomenclature follows Clapham *et al* (1962). Where remains were identified with a modern family, genus or species, then they take the name of that taxon. In some cases, remains could be assigned to any one of a small number of species. These are referred to using 'species-types' rather than leaving the identification at the genus level. This practice provides the most precise possible identification and

thus makes more ecologically relevant information potentially available. The species included in each species-type used are as follows:
—*Rumex obtusifolius*-type – *Rumex obtusifolius, R. crispus* or *R. longifolius*
—*Vicia cracca*-type – *Vicia cracca* or *V. hirsuta*
—*V. tetrasperma*-type – *V. tetrasperma* or *V. sativa ssp. angustifolia*
—*Lathyrus pratensis*-type – *Lathyrus pratensis* or *L. montanus*
—*Ranunculus repens*-type – *Ranunculus repens, R. acris* or *R. bulbosus.*

Cereal grains were identified as far as possible by, predominately, their shape although cell patterns were used for bread wheat (*Triticum aestivum*). Grains were only included in the counts when the embryo was present although abundance of fragmentary grains was noted on the sample record cards.

Results

Sixty-five flots, representing 54 different contexts, have been analysed. Where contexts were represented by two or more samples, each the data from these have been amalgamated. On-site instructions had called for two bucketsful of material to be collected if possible at each sampling point; the whole of whatever volume was collected was then floated and sieved. In many instances, however, no definite written record is available to confirm that the on-site instructions had been carried out. All of the contexts contained carbonised plant remains although one sample (one of four from C1150) consisted of very coarse gravel which could not have floated; it is considered most likely to have been the flotation residue and offered in error for analysis. The numbers of plant remains varied widely from only 11 up to 15,904 items per original volume of sediment floated (Figure 10.1).

If it is assumed that two buckets of sediment had been collected, then more than half of the samples had concentrations of less than six seeds/litre thus interpretation needs to be cautious.

One hundred and seventeen taxa were recorded; a taxon being any one particular kind of plant remain irrespective of the taxonomic level to which it was possible to identify it. Of these, 85 taxa related to 'weeds' in the broadest sense, 8 were cereal grain types and 13 associated chaff fragments. The remainder include other probable economic taxa, trees/shrubs or seaweed.

Figure 10.2 shows the remains split into the three broad categories of weeds, cereal grains and chaff (other economic, tree/shrub, etc omitted) plotted as a triangular ordination both with, then without *Avena* awns in the calculations. The average values are 73% cereal grains, 12% chaff and 15% weeds, although much of the chaff is represented by large numbers of Avena awn fragments which are almost certainly somewhat misleading for interpretation of crop husbandry patterns. Excluding these awns, the proportions are 80% cereal grains, 4% chaff and 16% weeds.

Such plots are commonly produced for late prehistoric/Romano-British sites, such as Thorpe

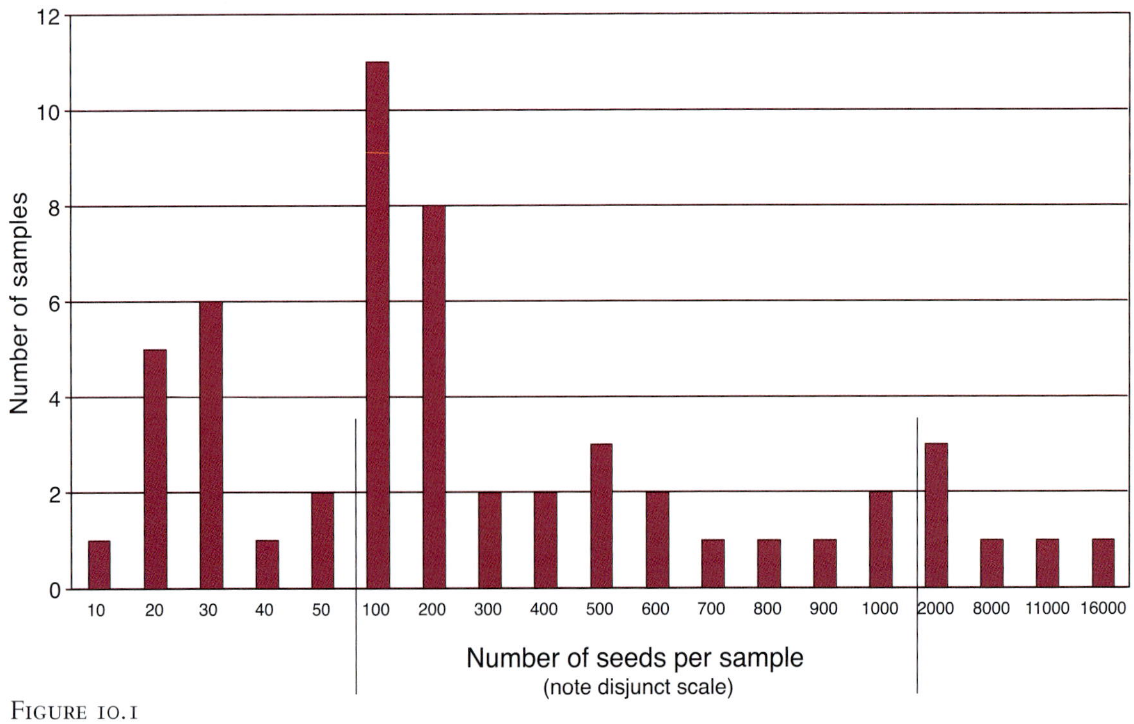

FIGURE 10.1
Concentration of seeds/context

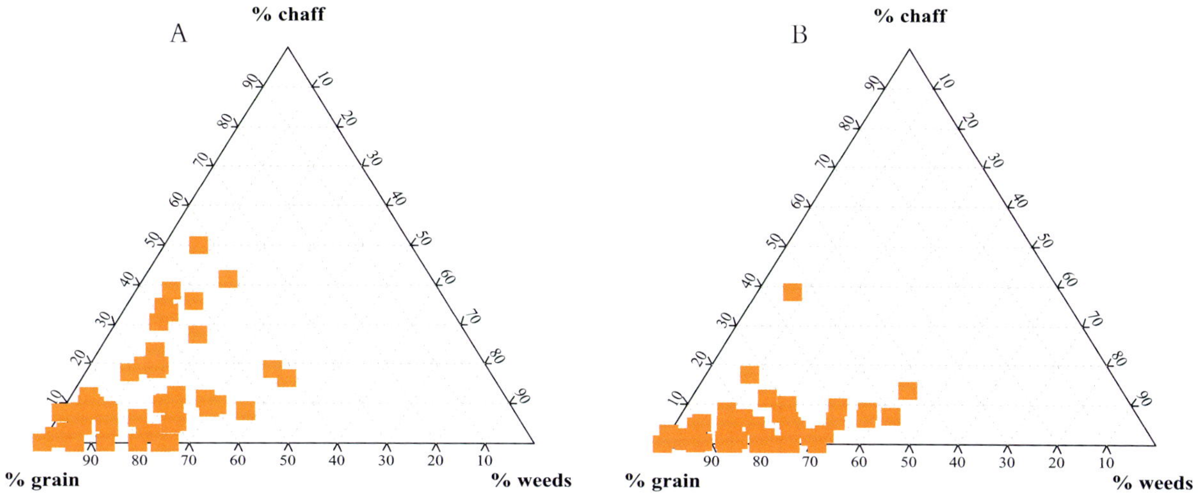

FIGURE 10.2
Triangular ordination of total seeds from grain, chaff and weed taxa. A: plot all fragments, B: plot excluding Avena awns

Thewles (van der Veen 1987) and Quarry Farm (Huntley 2008) and are used to discuss the stages of crop processing that are represented. For these earlier periods, however, spelt wheat was the most common wheat and this is a glume wheat that needs more processing, by parching, than the free-threshing bread wheat dominant at The Hirsel. As parching involves heat (fire), spelt chaff is thus more likely to survive in carbonised assemblages. Once threshed, the bread wheat straw, remaining largely intact, will have other uses and thus not remain with the grain; more importantly it does not need the extra parching thus is less likely to be accidentally preserved at such a stage. The plot does indicate that most of the remains are the grains themselves, probably suggesting largely processed material being deposited. A small cluster of samples does have rather more chaff remains and will be discussed further below.

Looking at dominant species perhaps, by inference, dominant crops, there are only 39 contexts that contain more than 50 grains each: wheat, rye, barley, oats and indeterminate. The indeterminable (%CI) category averages more than 48% but is highly variable, ranging from 88% in C1058 to zero in C1227 and C897. The modal value of 55.6% shows a more or less well distributed pattern between these extreme values.

Figure 10.3 presents the percentages calculated from identified grains only and shows that oats are the most abundant determinable grain in the majority of the samples; the other three grain types (wheat, rye and barley) have varying relative proportions in different samples. C1025 and C1058 are dominated by bread wheat grains and C1276 has moderate amounts of hulled barley. A group of samples from 1123 to 1224 have moderate numbers of rye grains in them.

In terms of specific chaff recovered, sixteen contexts produced more than 50 chaff fragments. Oat chaff was the most frequently found although, as noted above, this was mostly awn fragments. Nonetheless, floret bases clearly from both the cultivated *Avena sativa/A. strigosa* and the wild *A. fatua* have been recovered. Oat chaff in general was most abundant in C1195. Excluding the oat, awns lead to only seven contexts having more than 50 items (Figure 10.4). Culm nodes were almost always the most abundant remain in any context, C1244 being the exception. This strongly suggests that straw was present in quantity at the site. Rye rachis fragments (nodes and internodes) were also common throughout the contexts and abundant in C693 and C1125 although totals in these two did not reach the 50 limit. Bread wheat nodes were abundant in C1223 (again less than 50 items in total) and, interestingly, brittle rachis wheat internodes were recorded too although only in low numbers. These have to have derived from a glume wheat such as spelt or emmer.

Non-cereal food plants

Although cereals were by far the most common food taxa represented, they were not the only ones. Four other species were probably representative of food too, namely: *Lens culinaris* (lentils), *Pisum sativum* (peas), *Vicia faba* (Celtic or broad beans) and *Linum usitatissimum* (flax or linseed). The first three are all legumes with the lentil not being native and almost certainly representing an import to the region. Both the peas and beans could well have been grown locally. Flax/linseed was also quite likely to have been local. It is not possible to say whether it was evidence for fibre or oil production. None was abundant.

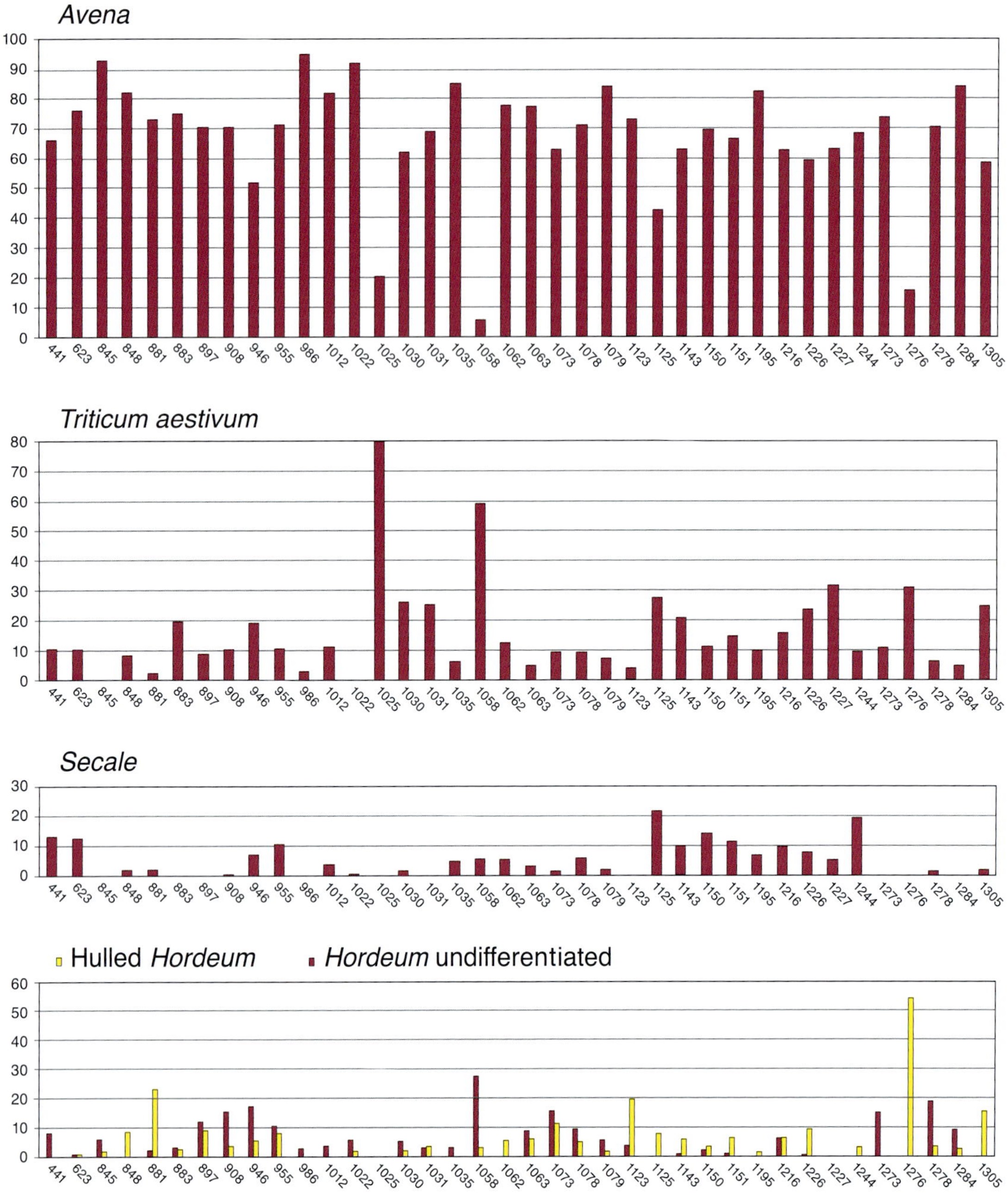

FIGURE 10.3
Cereal grain percentages of total identified grains (contexts with >50 identified grains)

	C623	C1143	C1151	C1195	C1226	C1227	C1244
Total minus awns	960.00	71.00	73.00	1652.00	1105.00	199.00	96.00
Avena fatua floret base		1.41		0.97	0.72		
Avena sativa floret base		2.82	1.37	9.69	4.52	5.53	1.04
Avena sativa/strigosa floret base		4.23		25.18	7.60		
Avena strigosa floret base					0.72		
Culm node	50.00	40.85	41.10	38.74	47.06	34.17	17.71
Hordeum 6-row rachis	1.67	1.41	1.37			1.51	
Hordeum rachis	3.33	12.68	6.85		3.08	1.51	
Secale rachis	40.00	26.76	34.25	21.31	7.06	15.08	65.63
Triticum aestivum internode	1.67		1.37		1.45	8.04	
Triticum aestivum node	3.33	8.45	12.33	3.87	23.89	33.67	13.54
Triticum brittle rachis		1.41	1.37	0.24	3.89	0.50	2.08

FIGURE 10.4
Percentage of types of cereal chaff remains, contexts with more than 50 fragments of chaff excluding Avena awns

Multivariate analysis

In order to draw out patterns that might be interpretable in archaeological terms, some mathematical analyses were undertaken. At the time that this report was written it was the first occasion upon which multivariate methods had been applied to archaeological material although such methods have since become a more routine practice for some assemblages. Two broad approaches were used: classification and ordination.

Classification

This kind of analysis defines groups of contexts or samples which have similar assemblages of taxa. The method used was divisive, that is, all samples were initially considered as one group which was then split into two groups on the basis of some criterion of similarity; the two groups then in turn being further split in two and so on until either the number of groups equals the number of samples or the groups formed each consist of no more than a predetermined maximum number of samples. Classification may use so-called 'indicator species' to split the samples, each split being made according to the presence or absence of one or more of these indicator species. TWINSPAN (Two-way Indicator Species Analysis), the method used here, uses groups of indicator species rather than single indicators and hence produces a more reliable analysis, based upon more of the information contained in the data (Hill 1979b).

Ordination

Ordination methods extract major axes of variation from the data; these axes being those corresponding to the primary patterns or structure in the data. Sample positions along these axes are determined by the taxa content of the samples. The ordination method used on these data was DECORANA (Detrended Correspondence Analysis), a particularly powerful technique with numerous mathematical advantages over other ordination methods (Hill 1979a).

Although the data have as many spatial dimensions as variables (the 117 taxa in this case) it is impossible to visualise these; we can only easily visualise up to three dimensions. Ordination provides us with the principal axes of the data and so allows the main patterns therein to be graphically displayed by plotting samples in the plane of the first and second ordination axes, the first and third, and so on. Only the first four ordination axes are considered since these normally contain most of the useful information.

The results of the classification are presented in Figure 10.5 and of the ordination in Figure 10.6. Both methods of analysis grouped the samples in a similar way, both indicating clearly that they fall into two major groups. The first group consists mostly of samples from within the church and the second mostly of samples from outside the church. The detailed results of the two analyses are detailed below.

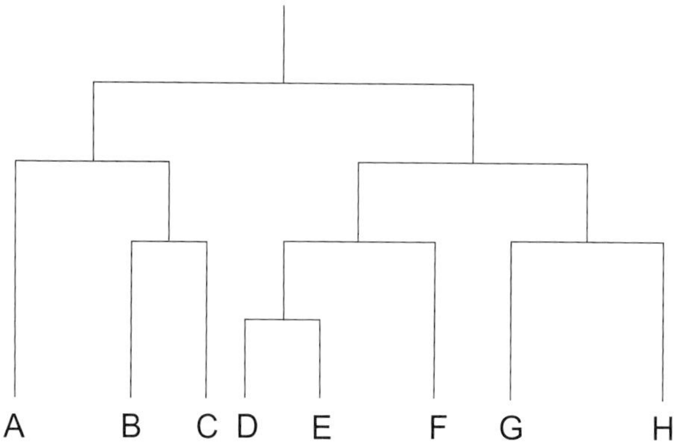

FIGURE 10.5
TWINSPAN groups of samples

Classification results

TWINSPAN allows the user to control the taxa used as potential indicator species. In the present case all taxa were allowed but less weighting given to the rare taxa. The resulting dendrogram (Figure 10.5) can be likened to a mobile in that the samples can pivot around a node. There are no 'right' positions for these samples; simply a mathematically derived order and they should thus be used as an aid to interpretation only.

Typically, the first division separates the richer samples from those with fewer remains and this, whilst not especially helpful for the archaeological situation, is almost always the case. With the aid of these analyses the following groups of samples are recognised (Figure 10.6):

— **Group A** (C623, C1195, C1151, C1226b and C1227) (Appendix 1). This group is characterised by rich assemblages of cereal grains and chaff as well as a good variety of weed and other seeds. The dominant taxa are bread wheat and oat grains but culm nodes, rye chaff and grain, grass seeds and sheep's sorrel seeds are also abundant. Although indeterminate cereal grains are abundant in four contexts they are absent in C1227 – this might reflect a simple recording difference such as not being counted as it seems unlikely that none is present. However, C1227 is also somewhat different from the others within this group in that it contains no stinking mayweed (*Anthemis cotula*), no hulled barley (*Hordeum*) nor a series of other weedy taxa that are, otherwise, constants within this group. Its assemblage is overwhelmingly

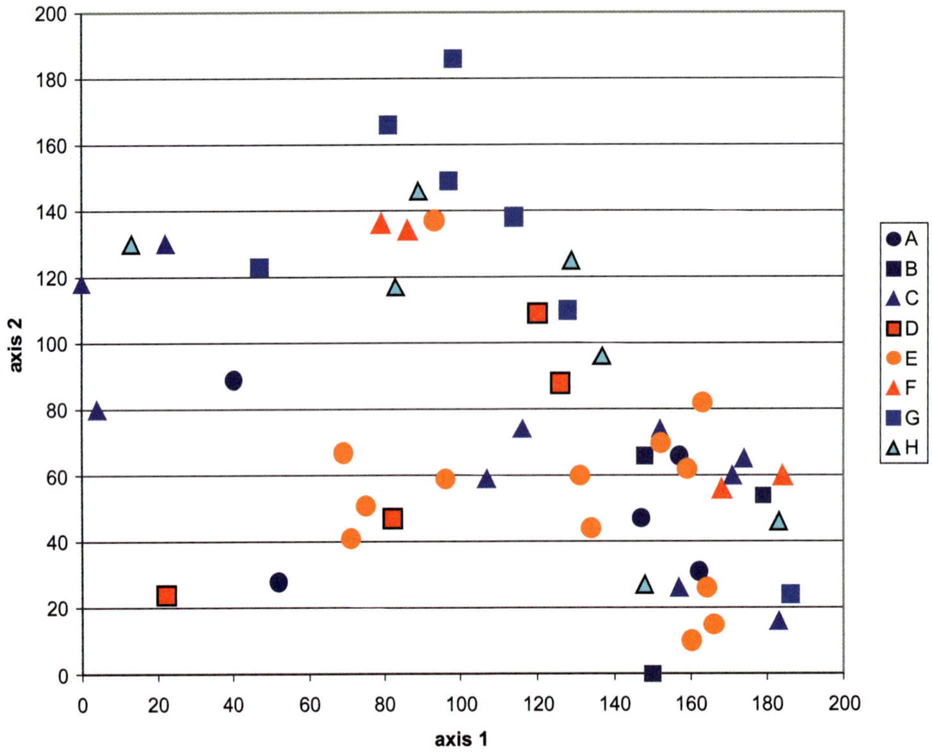

FIGURE 10.6
Ordination results for axes 1 and 2, with samples coded according to their classification groups

dominated by oat and bread wheat grains perhaps suggesting that it derives from cleaned grain with little associated debris and that it was deposited and sealed quite quickly leading to very well preserved material. Archaeologically these contexts all relate to burning in the nave of the church, although C1226b is considered to belong to an earlier phase. C1227 is a hearth over pit C1302. These all indicate intense use or processing of cereals within the building at some time.

— **Group B** (C1125, C1143 and C1150). Similar to Group A but lacking high values of chaff or weed seeds. Preservation is generally less good as is suggested by the higher quantities of indeterminate cereal grains compared with identified oat, bread wheat and rye grains. The contexts date to the late medieval or early post-medieval period and hence are later than those of Group A; the deposits, although again within the nave, relate to tumble of walls and rubble. There has to be some consideration as to whether charred plant material from the earlier period has become mixed in with the rubble.

— **Group C** (C908, C946, C955, C1022, C1035, C1058, C1062, C1063, C1073, C1078 and C1079). This group is dominated by indeterminate cereals and oat grains and awns with lesser quantities of bread wheat and barley grains. The group could be subdivided with six contexts (C1035, C1078, C1062, C1022, C908 and C946) being characterised by more small legumes and five (C1079, C1073, C1058, C955 and C1063) by more grass caryopses (Gramineae undiff.), ribwort plantain (*Plantago lanceolata*) and indeterminate oat chaff (*Avena* sp floret bases). This also ties somewhat with the archaeology with many of the six contexts being associated with the nave, being either inside or just outside. The group of five contexts comprise pit fills or soils associated, or probably associated, with cemetery earths. Interestingly, the middle fill of pit C1072 falls into the first group, but the other two fills fall into the second.

— **Group D** (C441, C739, C740 and C1027). This is a generally taxa- and seed-poor group with indeterminate cereal and oat grains constant but in rather low numbers. Oat awns were moderately abundant in C441 and grass caryopses scattered throughout. Archaeologically the samples are from gravel and pebbly layers outside the buildings but from varied time periods.

— **Group E** (C568, C982, C986, C1012, C1013, C1025, C1030, C1031, C1071, C1123, C1131, C1273 and C1284). This is another group with rather sparse seeds: indeterminate cereal, oats and bread wheat are the constants. The constant, although low numbers, of bread wheat distinguish it from Group D. There are, however, quite moderate numbers of other taxa present. Archaeologically this is a mixed group with samples associated with graves, grave fills themselves, pit fills, general layers and at least one (C1071) from within the building. In many respects this group clearly demonstrates the 'mobile' effect of the analysis' dendrogram in that it is more similar to Groups A, B and C than is D.

— **Group F** (C848, C1244, C1260 and C1305). The group is characterised by constant but low numbers of oats, indeterminate cereals and bread wheat grain with small legumes and a small, but constant, amount of rye grain. Rye chaff is particularly abundant in C1244. Weedy taxa are generally not well represented. They are found either to the west of the church or in post-ecclesiastical contexts associated with the church.

— **Group G** (C881, C883, C897,C948, C1216, C1278 and C1403). As with Group D, this one had constant indeterminate cereals and oat grains but with barley and wheat grains moderately common. Whilst weeds and chaff are not that common generally, sedge nutlets, redshanks and fat hen are constant in a sub-group of C881, C897 and C1278. The contexts primarily relate to deposits within or associated with the early medieval cemetery.

— **Group H** (C761, C836, C845, C984, C1276, C1341 and C1349). This is an extremely taxa-poor group with indeterminate cereals and oat grains in common but little else present.

Ordination results

Figure 10.6 shows a plot of axis 1 versus axis 2 produced by DECORANA using all of the data. These produced the best spread, that is, most variation within the dataset, whereas axis 3 (not presented) tended to have a few samples at each extreme and the majority bunched together near the centre and axis 4 (not presented) had, primarily, one sample rather isolated from the rest. Figure 10.5 shows a reasonable separation of the various TWINSPAN groups (A–H) but with a certain amount of overlap demonstrating that the assemblages are not unique to any group.

Habitat analysis

Although each sample has, so far, been treated as an individual, it is important to realise that it may represent several different kinds of vegetation. It is, indeed, very unlikely that samples from outside the church would represent only one type of vegetation. It is just possible that those samples from inside the structure, if they are from pure grain deposits, do so although, even here, contamination by, for example, grassland plants prior to deposition, is possible.

Each taxon has, therefore, been assigned various habitat characteristics such as arable weed, grassland plant, plant growing in wet/dry soils, of acid soils, etc, the details of which are presented in the archive report. Some of the taxa were not included, for example, legume >4mm diameter since it could, and probably did, represent more than one species and thus was impractical to assign them to one particular habitat. Some plants have been assigned to several habitats, for example, *Rumex acetosella*, which can be an arable weed or a grassland plant on sandy soils. Data about the habitat preferences of these taxa were taken from Clapham *et al* (1962) and, where available, from the Biological Flora of the British Isles.

The taxa were then grouped together and classified on the basis of European phytosociological units (Runge 1973; Shimwell 1971; Silverside 1977), nothing, at the time of writing the original report, being available for Britain alone. This is not totally satisfactory because of the relative oceanicity of Britain compared with the rest of Europe. However, the more recent volumes detailing the plant communities of Britain (Rodwell 2000) only describe open communities of a more ruderal nature and not classical arable weed communities since these are largely absent from Britain today as a result of decades of intensive agricultural practices. The groupings as originally presented in the archive report are therefore retained rather than trying to discuss habitats present at The Hirsel against two classifications. Habitats represented at The Hirsel can be broadly classified in this way as being representative of seven Classes, one of which may be divided into two Orders. It must be noted that all of the groups have other character species as well and that are not recorded from The Hirsel assemblage.

— 1. *Bidentetea tripartiti Tx. Lohn. Prsg.50*
Nitrophilous weed communities in places subject to periodic flooding, such as the sides of streams and rivers, edges of cattle ponds, etc. They can also develop in hollows in fields which have been lying fallow for several years or in the furrows in pasture. The characteristic species represented in the current dataset are *Atriplex spp., Chenopodium glaucum, C. rubrum* and, the often dominant species, *Polygonum hydropiper.*

— 2. *Stellarietea mediae (Br.-Bl.31)Tx. Lohn. et Prsg.50*
These are communities of arable fields and disturbed ground. The Class is an amalgamation of two Classes: the Chenopodietea (Br.-Bl.51), vegetation of disturbed ground, root crops and pioneer vegetation of ruderal sites, and the Secalinetea (Br.-Bl.51), of thermophilous weed communities

of cereals and flax. Many of the constant species of these two classes are the same and many character species of the former also occur in summer cereals. Two Orders are considered here, broadly corresponding to the original two Classes:

a) Chenopodietalia albi Tx. et Lohn.50. These are the nitrophilous communities of root crops and, occasionally, summer cereals. Their character species include *Polygonum persicaria, Chrysanthemum segetum, Brassica rapa, Spergula arvensis, Raphanus raphanistrum* and *Chenopodium album*. Other common species include *Rumex acetosella, Erysimum cheiranthoides, Polygonum lapathifolium, P. aviculare, P.convolvulus, Centaurea cyanus* and *Scleranthus annuus*.

b) Centauretalia cyani R.Tx.,Lohn et Prsg.50. The vegetation of cereal crops and broad beans is placed in this order. The species are generally thermophilous and relatively sparse in northern Europe today, being most prevalent in the Mediterranean and southern Europe. The character species are *Matricaria recutita, Scleranthus annuus, Avena fatua, Anthemis cotula, Agrostemma githago, Centaurea cyanus, Papaver* spp. and *Sinapis arvensis*.

— 3. *Plantaginetea majoris Tx. et Prsg.50*
Communities of trampled tracks, gateways and farmyards are included here. The community may also develop in arable fields where the soil has become very compacted. The main species are: *Plantago major, Polygonum aviculare* and *Matricaria matricarioides. Veronica serpyllifolia* also frequently occurs in the less trampled parts of the community.

— 4. *Artemisietea vulgaris Lohn., Prsg., Tx.50*
These are the communities of generally disturbed ground such as the edges of quarries, farmyards (not trampled), muckheaps, etc. The character species are: *Chenopodium bonus-henricus, Rumex obtusifolius, Urtica dioica* and *Conium maculatum*. High nutrients are indicated by their presence and many of the taxa are perennials.

— 5. *Molinio-Arrhenatheretea Tx.37*
This Class includes pastures, hay meadows and generally modified and disturbed grasslands on a variety of soils but avoiding the extremes of acidity and basicity. Roadside verges, hedgebanks and grassy edges of fields would also be included in this Class. Character species include *Trifolium* spp., *Lathyrus pratensis, Anthriscus sylvestris, Ranunculus repens, Plantago lanceolata, Prunella vulgaris, Rumex acetosa, Galium verum* and *Centaurea nigra*.

— 6. *Festuco-Brometea Br.-Bl. et Tx.43*
These are calcareous grasslands of all types, whether they are grazed or not, on limestone or chalk. They are characterised by the presence of *Pimpinella saxifraga, Plantago media, Linum catharticum, Campanula rotundifolia* and *Hypochoeris radicata*.

— 7. *Trifolio-Geranietea Th. Muller 61*
This Class represents rich calcareous grasslands at the edge of scrub. Its most common species are *Centaurea nigra, Lathyrus pratensis, Vicia cracca, Galium mollugo, G. verum* and *Corylus avellana*.

In order to see whether or not the sample groups A–H are ecologically distinct, the proportions of each of the above ecological groups present in each of these sample groups have been calculated (Figure 10.7). This assumes that the present-day classification and ecological tolerances of the taxa are the same as those during medieval times. Although this is considered to hold true for most plants, there is a notable exception in the case of *Vicia* spp., the vetches and tares. Today they are plants of grassland and waysides whereas 400 years ago it was said that '... it is the worst wede that is except the tare' (John FitzHerbert, Boke of Husbandry; quoted in Salisbury 1961). Tare is the grass *Lolium temulentum*. Although tare, or darnel, was not recorded from The Hirsel contexts, it was abundant in contexts associated with a grain drying kiln in Durham dating from the medieval period.

Figure 10.7 indicates that, on the whole, the sample groups are quite uniform with respect to the ecological groups amongst the taxa. This suggests that their 'catchment' areas and the activities carried out therein were also rather uniform. Only groups A, B and C show any evidence of trampled communities (Class 3) whereas E, G and H lack the calcareous influence (Class 6), G and H also lacking the grassy, scrubland edge (Class 7). The slightly more nitrophilous communities (Class 2a) common in root crops are most abundant in sample groups E–H although still frequent in A–D. Meadow-pasture-wayside grassland (Class 5) is abundant throughout the sample groups but less so in E; waste ground (Class 4) vegetation is common in B, absent in H and sparsely represented elsewhere. It is only when we look at the abundance of the remains that it becomes obvious that there were, for example, many more arable weeds found inside the church structure than outside.

Cereal analysis

Oats

Oats *(Avena* spp.) grains were present in all of the samples containing carbonised material. It is generally accepted as impossible to identify the grains alone to the specific level although it is possible to identify floret bases further on the shape of their basal scar at the point of attachment to the pedicel and on the angle and length of a stalk at the base of the floret. The distinctive horseshoe-shaped base of *Avena fatua* (the wild oat) was present in several samples and quite characteristic of Group C. The narrow and shortly stalked base of *Avena*

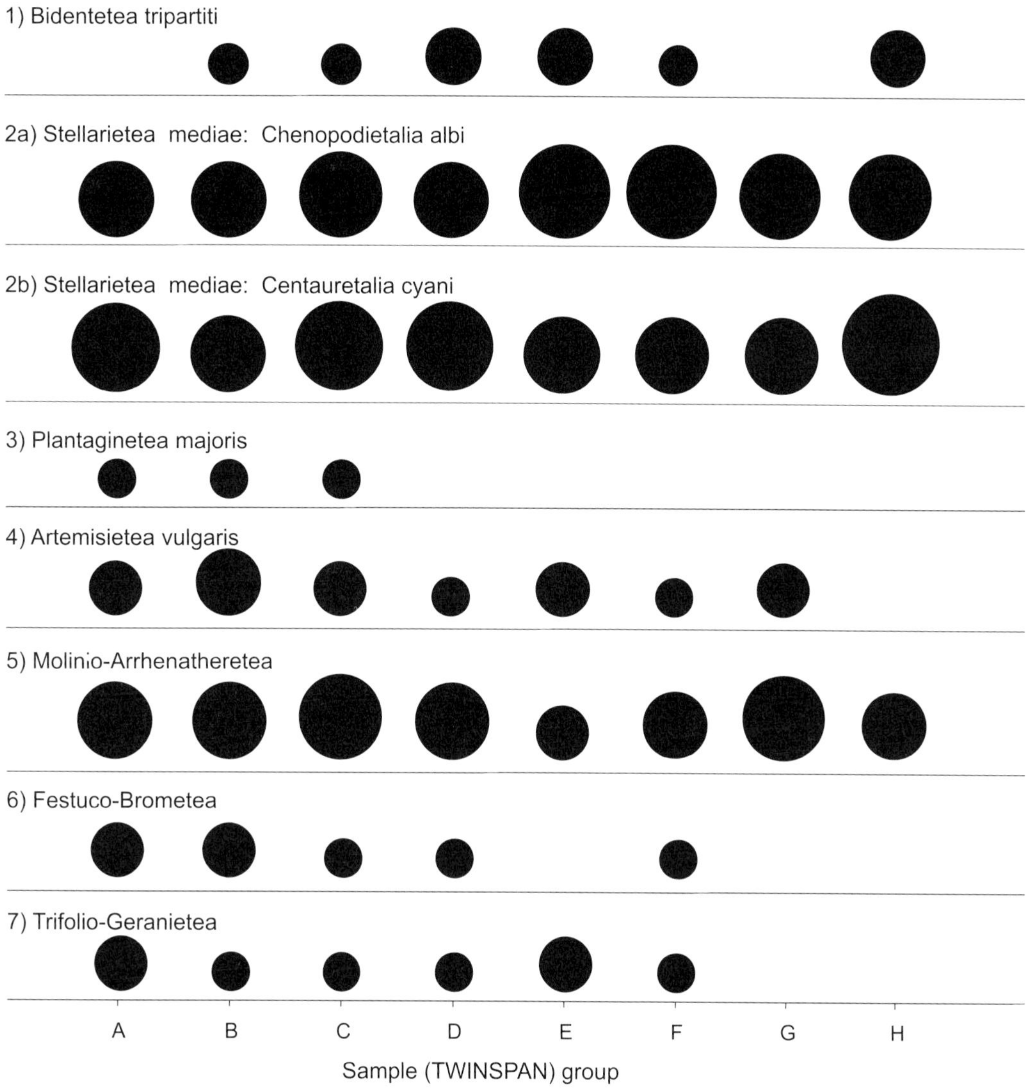

FIGURE 10.7
Bubble plot of habitats

strigosa (the bristle oat) was only present in three samples, one in each of C1226b, C1012 and C908, whereas the broader, non-stalked bases of *Avena sativa* were scattered throughout the samples, most commonly in Groups A, B and C. Many bases were fractured to such an extent that they were left as *Avena sativa/strigosa*.

Fragments of spirally twisted awn which could be attributed to *Avena* sp. or to *Arrhenatherum elatius* (the false oat grass)/*Helictotrichon* species, were present in all but a few samples, often with values exceeding 200. Although it cannot definitely be known to which of these species they belonged, it is considered most likely that they were *Avena* awns in view of the fact that *Arrhenatherum* tubers were only present in two samples, one of which, C1216, had no awn fragments and very very few other large (>4mm) Gramineae caryopses were recovered at all.

Today oats are grown predominantly on the poorer and sandier soils of Britain and tend to be most common in the north. *Avena fatua* is more widespread and is still a troublesome weed in some parts of the country. Oats are used for both human food and animal fodder although documentary evidence suggests that they were more commonly used for food in the past (Collins 1975).

Rye

Rye (*Secale cereale*) is typically planted on light sandy soils and, in Britain, is mainly grown in East Anglia today. It is a more continental species than the other cereals; that is, it is hardier in tolerating low winter temperatures. It is also more tolerant of acid soils.

Only one species of *Secale* is cultivated and it has rather wheat-like grains but with a distinctive pointed embryo and triangular cross-section. The seed coat becomes distinctly and characteristically glossy when carbonised. The grains are especially characteristic of Groups A, B, C and F.

The rachis fragments often have a small ridge running down their edges and tend to be more or less rectangular in section. There is a small bulbous nose at the junction of two adjacent segments but the edge of it is not well defined as it is in barley. The bristles/hairs along the edges of the internodes and especially at the nodes tend to preserve extremely well. Groups A and C were the only ones which had a considerable number of rye rachis fragments, with group F having a few but in most of its samples.

Wheat

Wheat was common throughout the samples and most of the grains belonged to the more rounded form of *Triticum aestivum* (bread wheat), sometimes known as *T. aestivo-compactum*. Rachis fragments of bread wheat were also scattered throughout the samples, most abundantly in Groups A, B and C. The fragments consisted of rachis segments showing the pair of folds characteristic of hexaploid wheats and so-called floret bases with the scars showing the original position of the grains.

In Group A there were numerous *Triticum* rachis segments that showed clean breaks along their upper edges. These have been attributed to a brittle rachis wheat, that is, one in which the head breaks into pieces on threshing, such as emmer, spelt, or einkorn. However, no other rachis fragments nor grain were clearly attributable to anything other than bread wheat.

Wheat grows best on a deep, moist but well-drained soil.

Barley

Barley (*Hordeum* spp.), like wheat, is common in most of the samples. Of the better preserved grains, most were of the hulled variety although the odd naked grain was present in Groups A–E. Where possible the grains were also scored for 'straight' or 'twisted' embryos in order to determine whether 6-row or 2-row barley was being grown. No single sample had enough grains for this purpose and therefore the results from all of the samples were amalgamated, giving a total of 65 twisted and 47 straight grains. Since 2-row barley produces only straight grains and 6-row barley 2 twisted to 1 straight grain the observed ratio of 0.58 (47/65) straight to twisted indicates that the majority of the barley found at The Hirsel was probably 6-row, although a small proportion could have possibly been 2-row.

Barley rachis segments were generally rather sparse and fragmentary, the distinct and definitive bulbous 'nose' where two segments joined, being the main fragment. Three of these were of *Hordeum vulgare*, the 6-row barley, the others were indistinct. Only nine of these fragments were complete thus allowing length and breadth to be measured and these showed that at least some of the barley was of the rather dense-eared form (length <2mm between nodes).

Barley grows well on light soils but is intolerant of high soil acidity. It grows successfully further north than, for example, wheat because it has a shorter growing season, around 2 months from germination to harvesting (spring-sown crops).

Other potential crops

Pisum sativum (the pea)

Peas occur in a few samples with eighteen found in C1227, nine in C1022 and six in C1125. The taxon 'legume >4mm diameter' also occurs in Groups A and B and may be attributable to *Pisum* although the characteristic, almost circular, hilum is absent.

Peas require a calcareous soil but not necessarily organically rich since, like all legumes, they fix their own nitrogen. They require a cool and moist climate for best cropping.

Vicia faba (broad bean, horse bean)

One seed of *Vicia faba* was found in sample C1143. Beans prefer a heavy clay soil which, nonetheless, is reasonably well drained. *Vicia sativa* (common vetch) and *Vicia cracca* (tufted vetch) are no longer considered as sources of human food in the 20th century, although the former is used as animal fodder in Asia. Hegi (1924) claims that seeds of *Vicia sativa* ssp. *obovata* are occasionally used for human consumption.

Other legumes were present which consisted only of single cotyledons or were very worn, the shape and size of the hilum hence being indistinguishable. These appeared to fall into two size classes, namely '<2mm diameter' and '2–4mm diameter' and so were recorded as such. It is now considered that these two classes could usefully be combined into 'legumes <4mm diameter' because these differences cannot be allocated to any taxon or group of taxa consistently in fresh material.

All legumes less than 4mm diameter, including those put only into size classes and those identified to taxa such as *Vicia sativa* and *V. cracca*-type are scattered throughout the samples, especially in Groups A, B, C, E and F.

Linum usitatissimum (flax)

Seeds of flax occurred sparsely in a few samples. They were all more than 3.5mm long indicating that it was the cultivated flax that was present. The considerably smaller and somewhat different shaped seeds of *Linum catharticum*, the purging flax, were also present in sample C1216. This is a native plant of limestone grassland. Cultivated flax grows best in a moist climate on rich and well-drained soils, rather like those required by wheat. It may be grown for its fibre or oily, protein-rich seeds from which linseed oil may be extracted.

Chenopodiaceae (goosefoot, orache)

The genus *Chenopodium* (Goosefoot) was commonly used as a source of food in earlier times: *Chenopodium bonus-henricus* (Good King Henry) for salad greens and *Chenopodium album* (fat hen) for its seeds. The latter and Chenopodiaceae (undiff.) are common in most of the samples.

Atriplex spp. (Orache) were also used as salad greens and are present in a few samples. The family is, however, more typically found as weeds on well-manured plots, fields and gardens. Given their relative abundance amongst the cereals in this assemblage they may well reflect mostly weeds rather than deliberately grown crops.

Cruciferae (cabbages, mustards etc)

Various members of the Cruciferae (such as *Sinapis arvensis*, *S.* cf. *alba*, *Brassica rapa*, *B. nigra*, *Raphanus raphanistrum*, and *Erysimum cheiranthoides*) occur sporadically through the samples. *Sinapis alba* is grown for leaves as a salad crop and the familiar yellow mustard is produced from its seeds. *Brassica rapa* is the turnip, the modern form of which is considered to have been introduced to Britain in the 17th century. *B. nigra*, the black mustard, has long been grown for its seeds which yield black mustard and also an oil which is used medicinally.

Polygonaceae (docks and knotweeds)

Polygonum spp. have a high starch content in their seeds and, since these seeds are produced in vast numbers, they may have proved attractive as a source of food. The closely related buckwheat, *Fagopyrum esculentum*, is still used in cakes and bread making, particularly in America.

Rumex acetosa (sorrel)

Rumex acetosa has leaves with a sharp and tangy taste which are used in salads. They were considered to be indispensable by King Henry VIII. The seeds of this species are scattered through the samples.

Discussion

Of the 54 contexts which contained carbonised plant remains, about half had fewer than 300 remains. The remaining and richer samples were mostly either from within the structure or else to the west of it (principally Groups A, B and C with E due mainly to its larger number of samples each of which having several unique taxa thus total number of taxa in E being quite high) (Figure 10.8). Sample C1022, to the south-west, was also rich. Although the remains found in the samples can reflect the immediately surrounding vegetation, this should not be as obvious from samples from within the church, and, indeed, there are fewer remains of disturbed ground taxa within the structure than there are cereals and arable weeds.

Statistically the samples with fewer remains are likely to give a less accurate picture of what was going on at the site than those samples with considerably more remains (van der Veen and Fieller 1981). These generally poorer samples are, however, found typically at the edges of the site. Two of them (C1131 and C568) are from inside the structure but are possibly from a different level and, hence, time. The results from these sparser samples are considered to reflect the vegetation present in the immediate vicinity, such as the disturbed and nitrophilous grasslands often found around a farm yard, etc but they are of less value in indicating what, if any, cultural activities were present. Looking at the stratigraphic layers from which the samples came, at least some of these poor ones were from the period prior to the main agricultural period at The Hirsel.

Two groups (TWINSPAN Groups A and B) of samples may be distinguished from inside the structure, one of which (A) is from the intensely burnt layer and the other (B) from a slightly higher and later level. A is considered representative of the farming activity immediately prior to the fire which destroyed the site. B, with more waste ground species and considerably higher proportions of indeterminable cereal grains, is considered to comprise partly vegetation developing on the site after the main fire but probably mostly incorporation of Group A material during demolition either as a deliberate act or simply the building decaying naturally after the fire. Although owl pellets were absent from any of the contexts analysed here, there was evidence of them in the last phases of the church building which would lend credence to an undisturbed, derelict place. If it does represent vegetation developing after the fire, there has to be a mechanism by which the plant remains were burnt and this could simply reflect casual and occasional occupation.

The seed assemblages of samples especially from Group A are considered to comprise crops being grown, processed and stored at The Hirsel. Being clean grain it could, of course, have been imported from further afield; however, chaff of all four species of cereal is present and this, especially the culm or basal straw nodes, most likely indicates that all four cereals were grown locally. A small number of per-mineralised seeds were recovered from two samples within Group F. Both of these were fills in pit C1302 and it seems clear that the pit was in receipt of some faecal material. In addition

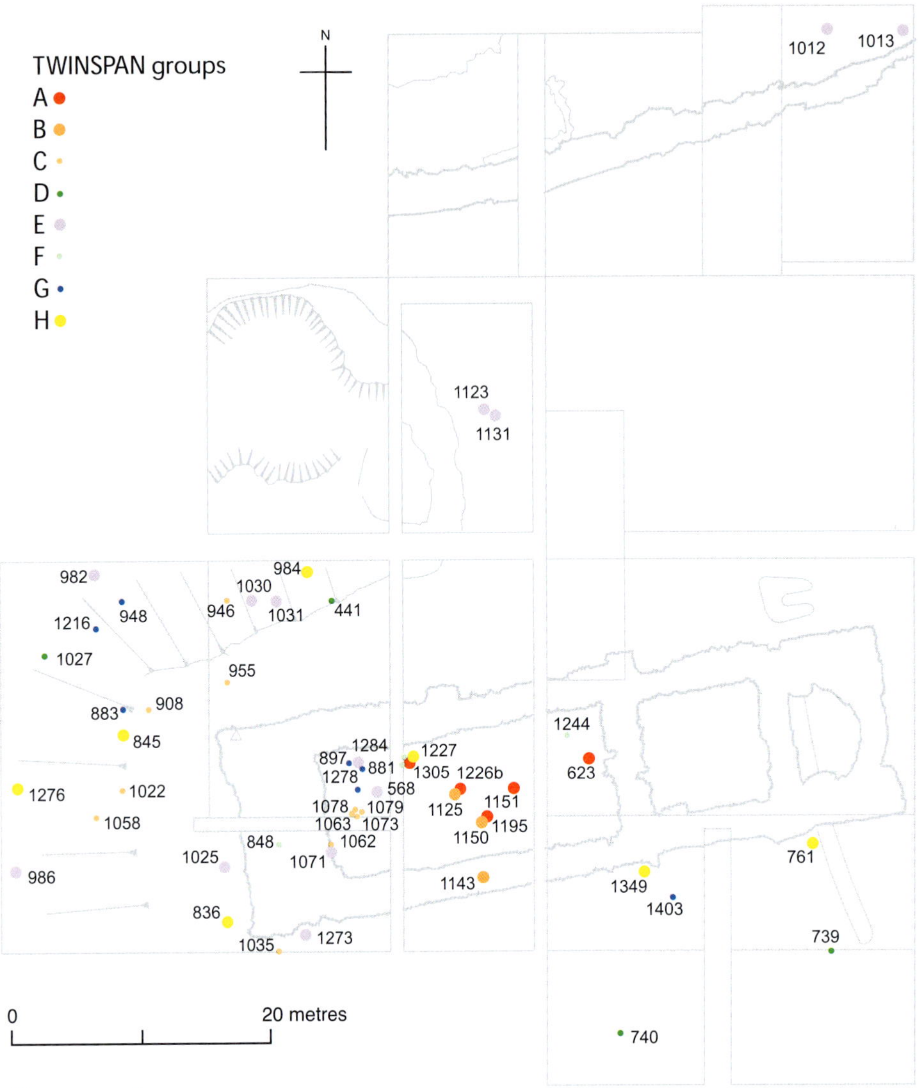

FIGURE 10.8
Location plan of the samples

to the mineralised seeds, a distorted fish vertebra was recovered; the somewhat flattened and twisted shape is characteristic of having passed through a digestive tract.

Fragments of heather wood and occasional flowers and twigs were recorded in quite a few samples, mostly from within the building. It seems possible that these reflect heather thatching although they might, of course, be the remains of flooring/bedding material during occupation or even debris from kindling.

The remains indicate that the cereal crops grown at The Hirsel were predominantly oats although wheat, barley and rye are all commonly present. A brittle rachis wheat, not further identifiable, also seems to have been grown. These may not all represent crops grown in a single year but such resolution is unlikely to be achievable in the archaeobotanical record. Peas, Celtic bean and large legume fragments are also present but not in quantity; it is considered that they probably would have been grown at the site but were not being stored inside the church structure at the time of the fire. As noted above, their survival as charred remains is rather more opportunistic than that of cereals. Although present in Groups A, E and F, all of the samples containing these crops were within or very close to the building.

Six-row barley, *Hordeum vulgare*, seems to have been the most abundant barley although the ratio of straight:twisted grains suggests that it is possible that a small amount of 2-row barley (*H. distichon*) was also grown. It is often said that the change from 6-row to 2-row occurred during the Middle Ages although well dated assemblages from this period remain rare; today most barley grown in Britain is 2-row.

Two cultivated species of oats were grown (*Avena sativa* and *A. strigosa*). From the relatively few floret bases it is not possible to say how much of each was present, although it is likely that there was more *A. strigosa* than *A. sativa* given the abundance of awn fragments. Today *A. strigosa* is cultivated in the islands of west and north

Scotland, Ireland and upland Wales where the conditions are less favourable for the growth of *A. sativa* (Hubbard 1968).

Flax, although present, is very sparsely represented and may just be the remains of a few plants grown some time before. There is no good evidence that it was a contemporary crop at The Hirsel although most settlements during the medieval period would have had plots of flax in order to produce their own fibre and, from that, linen.

Further information about farming practice can be gained by looking at the weed and chaff taxa. It is generally accepted that the cereal fields of the past contained a wide variety of weeds, often in vast quantities, and indeed many fields were still in such a state at the beginning of the 20th century before the widespread use of inorganic fertiliser and herbicides. It is therefore not surprising that large numbers of carbonised weed seeds are present in the samples from The Hirsel. In the few samples with <10% weeds their absence could be real, although other interpretations are possible. It may mean that the grain was harvested later and after most weed seeds had been shed, that each ear of grain was cut separately as stated by van Zeist (1970) — this seems extremely unlikely because of the extra work involved — or, most likely, that the grain was cleaner in these contexts. This itself might mean that the contexts were buried more rapidly with no further contamination or mixing being possible.

It is interesting to note that a few of the more common present-day arable weeds are absent or very rare in the samples, for example, *Papaver* spp. (the poppies) and *Viola arvensis* (field violet). The latter, along with *Anagallis arvensis* (scarlet pimpernel) both have larger seeds but are very low growing and so could have been left behind if the cereals had been cut 10–15cm above the ground. This would not account for absence of the taller growing poppies however.

Most of the arable weeds present are annuals. It is generally considered that the introduction of the mouldboard plough during medieval times allowed deeper and more thorough cultivation and that led to the disappearance of many of the biennial and perennial weeds, such as *Verbascum* spp. (mulleins), some *Cirsium* spp. (thistles), etc, which were associated with earlier cultivation methods. Since very few of the arable weeds represented by seeds at The Hirsel are biennials or perennials, this does suggest mouldboard rather than ard cultivation. One exception should be noted; *Anthemis cotula,* which is a biennial or short-lived perennial, appears to survive under mouldboard cultivation. It, however, behaves like an annual in that it flowers in its first season of growth and produces many seeds before the cereal is cut. It also commonly shows autumnal re-growth and a second flush of flowering and fruiting in September–October.

Jones (1980) states that, from sites so far studied, *Galium aparine* (goose grass) is confined to autumn-sown crops. Its fruits appear sporadically at The Hirsel, and here, at least, it is considered just as likely to have been growing in any disturbed, nitrogen-rich ground such as near old muck heaps, abandoned middens, etc, especially as it occurs in Group A, those samples considered to be from the time of the destruction by fire.

By looking at the chaff fragments it has been possible, in some cases, to gain insight into the crop husbandry practices at the time of charring (Dennell 1974; 1976; Hillman 1983). At The Hirsel, Group B samples are from a thin, severely burnt stratigraphic layer which represents an apparently catastrophic event and the material preserved should thus represent a relatively short time interval, a few years at most. This should, in turn, mean that fewer practices are represented than might be the case in a layer that had formed over many years.

Inferring past farming practices from carbonised plant remains requires appropriate ethnographic models based upon modern data. Their use, like the use of modern data relating to ecological preferences of taxa, makes one basic assumption, namely, that present-day analogues can be found for the past. Current ethnographic models tend to be based on data obtained from the Middle East and southern Europe where traditional farming methods still prevail but which are areas geographically remote from British archaeological sites. The specific species grown are also different. More appropriate models could be constructed if more information about traditional farming methods in Britain, or at least adjacent north-west Europe was available, since there are, and will have been in the past, considerable differences between Britain and the Middle East. Such information is rarely available although, for example, 6-row barley is still grown for human consumption in Orkney and is still cut by hand and dried in the traditional way on a few farms on the more isolated islands.

The following general stages and methods of processing crops have been identified, particularly by Hillman (1981):

Sowing and cultivation
Reaping
Threshing
Winnowing
Coarse sieve
Fine sieve
(Drying)
Storage, main grain with little 'debris'.

In the present study the samples of Group A are the most likely to represent stored grain. Given the amounts of chaff and weed remains present, however, it is considered that there are too many of these 'impurities' for the samples to represent only fully processed grain. By implication, therefore, the church structure is unlikely to have been just a grain store.

Before attempting to compare the Group A samples with Hillman's seven categories of processing products several relevant facts must be noted:

— Large numbers of awn fragments and small seeds, such as those of *Legousia hybrida*, are present. These would have been mostly removed at the winnowing stage.

— Culm nodes and rachis segments, particularly those of rye and some of which are up to 1cm long, are also present in quantity. They would normally have been broken up as the ears were threshed and removed at the coarse-sieving stage.

— Weed seeds are present in quantity. They would have been removed either by fine sieving when the grain remained on the sieve, or they would have been picked out by hand if they were of the same proportions as the grain.

— The oceanic climate of northern Britain means that threshing and winnowing tended to be carried out indoors, often utilising a pair of doors on opposite sides of the building to provide necessary draughts. These can still be seen in many crofts in the north of Scotland and are characteristic of many barns on post-medieval farms throughout the lowlands of England. Occasionally sites of this type are excavated and produce charred plant assemblages as, for example, at 9th century Whithorn (Huntley 1997). Debris from the various stages would, therefore, be deposited in a mixture. It would thus not be surprising if the debris from the various processing stages was indistinct, several of these stages having being carried out in the same area.

It is very difficult, if not impossible, to assign Group A to any one stage of processing. The samples seem to fit best with material just prior to the first sieving stage, although the large numbers of awns present should have been removed at the previous stage of winnowing. The absence of coarse straw fragments and capitulae or heads of weeds support this view since these would have been broken up at threshing and partially removed at raking prior to winnowing. All the samples of this group come from the central area of the church and it would have been interesting to have undertaken detailed spatial sampling from that stratigraphic layer. In this way, areas of processing or storage might have been isolated.

The samples outside the church structure with abundant remains have, on the whole, considerably fewer chaff fragments and are considered to represent the general farming activity of the site rather than one particular process. It may well be that the deposits are generally less well preserved and may have been moved around or trampled to a greater extent prior to burial. Group D samples are richer in chaff fragments than the other groups, except B, and they are mainly just to the west of the building with one sample (C1022) to the south. Some of the Group D samples are from the later medieval period, as are Group B samples and they both perhaps represent disposal of processing waste just outside the processing floors.

In conclusion, it is considered most likely that the samples in Group A represent cereal crops that had perhaps been raked into heaps in the building after threshing. Thorough winnowing is unlikely to have taken place in view of the presence of large numbers of *Avena* awn fragments. The samples certainly do not represent stored grain alone because of the large amounts of weed seeds and chaff fragments present, but they may consist of mixtures of stored grain with intermediate processing products. There are suggestions from later deposits that processing debris was present just outside the building — whether this reflects continuing activity or reworking of material contemporary with Group A samples remains unclear.

In terms of comparative sites, it is disappointing that even 25 years since excavation there are very few. Hoddom in Dumfriesshire is the nearest (Lowe 2006) where charred plant remains were recovered in abundance and analysed from at least two periods of drying kilns (Holden 2006). As at The Hirsel all four major genera were recovered with oats overwhelmingly dominant. In the case of Hoddom, these were considered to be largely bristle oat, *Avena strigosa*, from the floret bases and the strongly twisted awns that were both abundant. Awns were also prevalent at The Hirsel and bristle oat may, therefore, have been common here too despite the relatively few floret bases recovered. Some of the contexts at Hoddom were drying kilns thus, not surprisingly, most of the remains were grain. A few contexts containing mostly wheat did produce large numbers of seeds of weedy taxa and these were classed into habitats very similar to those at The Hirsel. Unfortunately no data tables are presented in the main text so no further comparisons may be made. Suffice it to say that there are apparently many parallels between the two sites in terms of crops being grown and nature of local soils.

10.2 THE ANIMAL BONES

Louisa J Gidney

The archive report on the animal bones (Gidney 1986) was written in 1986. Since then further work has been done on the phasing, which has necessitated some recalculations. The animal bones have been returned to National Museums Scotland.

For this report, the deposits producing animal bones have been divided into six period groups. It can be seen from Figure 10.9 that the pre- and post-medieval groups are very small and therefore

	Pre-medieval	Early medieval	Medieval	Late medieval	Early post-medieval	Post-medieval
Cattle	6	22	109	39	47	1
Sheep/goat	2	11	150	143	155	4
Sheep			1	2	1	
Pig		4	46	31	23	
Horse	1	4	31	4	9	
Dog	3	1	5	7	4	
Cat			1	1		
Roe deer			1			
Hare				1		
Rabbit			2		1	
Stoat					1	
Weasel				2	1	
Large ungulate		4	14	10	8	
Small ungulate		2	16	21	25	1
Domestic fowl		1	4	4	6	
Goose			7	4	2	
Duck				1		
Partridge				1		
Quail				1		
Woodcock			1			
Starling			11			
Small passerine			1		1	
Kestrel			2		2	
Rook/crow					2	
Total	**12**	**49**	**402**	**272**	**288**	**6**

FIGURE 10.9
Fragment counts for the species present

will not be included in most analyses. The early medieval group is also small and has been combined with the medieval for some comparisons. Likewise the late medieval and early post-medieval groups have been considered together.

Methods of recording

The assemblage was catalogued using a computer based system (Jones *et al* nd). Bones were identified to species where possible, using the Department of Archaeology, Biological Laboratory reference collection. For the archive report (Gidney 1986) all fragments were counted. For this study, only identified fragments with zones or teeth were counted for the common domestic farm animals. All fragments of all other species present were included. The zones used are those defined by Rackham (1978) and are listed in the archive. In brief, a zone is a single diagnostic feature on an element and is only recorded if at least half of the feature is present. This procedure reduces the over-recording of heavily fragmented bones and gives a truer indication of the relative abundance of the species exploited for food.

Rib and vertebrae fragments were assigned to the categories of large or small ungulate. Only proximal ribs with the epiphysial end, or vertebrae with a zone, were counted. The large ungulate category will be considered with cattle for some analyses and small ungulate with sheep/goat.

For the relative frequency figures, the numbers of atlas and axis vertebrae have been doubled and the numbers of first phalanges reduced to equate them with the paired elements (Appendix 2).

Preservation

The collection was in general greatly fragmented and poorly preserved. Some of the fragmentation may have been accelerated by grave digging and the 20th-century ploughing of the site. A total of 2170 fragments of mammal bone were recorded for the archive, of which only 1029 fragments (47%) were identifiable to species. Counting only the identified fragments with zones from the common domestic food species, and bones from the domestic companion animals reduces this portion of the assemblage to 967 fragments.

It can be seen from Figure 10.10 that loose teeth contribute a high proportion, varying between a fifth and a third, of the identified fragments of cattle, sheep and pig, with the exception of the late medieval group. Teeth are extremely robust and survive after the surrounding bone has decayed. The decline in the numbers of loose teeth in the late medieval group suggests less residuality and more undisturbed contemporaneous deposition of faunal refuse in these contexts. The proportion of loose teeth is a further indication of the preservational bias affecting this assemblage and the inherent problems of interpretation.

		Early medieval	Medieval	Late medieval	Early post-medieval
Cattle	No. identified	22	109	39	47
	No. loose teeth	4	33	2	14
	% loose teeth	18%	30%	5%	29%
Sheep/Goat	No. identified	11	151	145	156
	No. loose teeth	4	45	27	35
	% loose teeth	36%	29%	18%	22%
Pig	No. identified	4	46	31	23
	No. loose teeth	1	15	1	5
	% loose teeth	25%	32%	3%	21%

FIGURE 10.10
Loose teeth as a percentage of identified fragments

Distribution of fragments

The number of loose teeth and bones subjected to sub-aerial weathering prior to final deposition indicates that many bones were not in a fresh state before final incorporation into the archaeological deposits. Many finds of animal bones may, therefore, be residual in the deposits in which they were found. The exclusion of fragments without zones for this study should reduce the effect of residual material on the analyses.

Some chronological patterning in the disposal of faunal waste is, even so, apparent in Figure 10.11. The pre-medieval deposits with bones were confined to the west cemetery area. In the early medieval group, bone deposition was also concentrated in the west cemetery area but there was also low density dispersal of fragments into all areas excavated apart from the north-west area. In the medieval group, the volume of bone and dispersal across the excavated areas increases dramatically. All areas produced bone but finds were scanty only in the north-west area and north of the perimeter. In contrast, the bulk of the late medieval faunal remains is concentrated in the church and western cemetery with small numbers of fragments also found in the north-west area. This may reflect the supposed location of a late medieval settlement to the west of the site. The early post-medieval animal bones were widely distributed with concentrations in the areas of the former church, north and west cemetery and absent only from the south cemetery. The concentration of faunal remains in the vicinity of the church in the medieval and early post-medieval groups indicates ongoing secular use of the site.

Unfortunately many of the deposits interpreted as containing finds associated with the late medieval occupation were not well stratified and therefore the animal bones were not retained for analysis. The late medieval and early post-medieval groups are, therefore, not necessarily fully representative of the faunal remains originally deposited.

In the post-medieval phase the ruined building also appears to have been used as an owl roost, from the quantity of small animal bones found during excavation which were thought to derive from owl pellets. Samples were taken of these deposits and the bones sorted. No laboratory identifications were made, however, and the bones no longer appear to be extant. One skull from one pellet was identified on site as *microtus agrestis*, and other bones as frog, vole and shrew, by a visiting biologist (Fred Holliday pers comm).

Species

The relative proportions of cattle to sheep/goat and pig fragments are given in Figure 10.12. The sample size for the early medieval group is very small and indicates 2:1 cattle:sheep bones. Since cattle bones are more robust than those of sheep, this probably indicates comparative preservation rather than economic importance. The medieval group shows an increase in the proportion of sheep to cattle remains. It is unclear if this represents a genuine economic shift or merely an improvement in the survival of the more fragile sheep bones. However similar proportions have been recorded from medieval deposits with good faunal preservation in Leicester (Gidney 1991, 23). The late medieval and early post-medieval groups show identical trends with a predominance of sheep remains compared to those of cattle. Such a high proportion of sheep is unusual, even on contemporary sites with good preservation. Given the rural location of The Hirsel, it would appear that the produce of the local flocks was consumed on site. Pig remains occur at a consistently low level in all periods.

Although the sample size is very small, the species proportions derived from most frequent zone counts in Figure 10.13 suggest that, while the smaller species may be somewhat under-represented in Figure 10.12, the general proportions of identifiable fragments per species deposited remain in the same order of abundance. The very low numbers of individual elements with zones for this analysis emphasises the poor quality of the assemblage and reduces the efficacy of this technique.

		Church	North cemetery	South cemetery	West cemetery	NW area	NE perimeter	North of perimeter
Pre-medieval	Cattle				6			
	Sheep/goat				2			
	Horse				1			
	Dog				3			
Early medieval	Cattle	5		2	13		1	1
	Sheep/goat	3		3	4		1	
	Pig		1		3			
	Horse			3	1			
	Dog				1			
	L. ungulate	2			2			
	S. ungulate				2			
Medieval	Cattle	3	13	27	27	6	32	1
	Sheep/goat	26	22	35	44		23	1
	Pig	19	7	3	12	2	3	
	Horse	1	3	2	7	2	16	
	Dog		1	1	3			
	Cattle		1					
	Rabbit		1	1				
	Roe Deer			1				
	Weasel		1		1			
	L. ungulate	2	3	1	5	1	2	
	S. ungulate		2	1	12		1	
Late medieval	Cattle	17			19	3		
	Sheep/goat	69			69	7		
	Pig	19			9	3		
	Horse	3			1			
	Dog	4			3			
	Cat				1			
	Hare	1						
	L. ungulate	3			7			
	S. ungulate	10			10	1		
Early post-medieval	Cattle	7	12		10	1	16	1
	Sheep/goat	44	42		57	4	4	5
	Pig	10	4		6	1		2
	Horse				1	3	4	1
	Dog	2	1		1			
	Rabbit				1			
	Weasel	1						
	Stoat				1			
	L. ungulate	5			3			
	S. ungulate	14	4		7			

FIGURE 10.11
Species fragment distributions by area

	Early medieval		Medieval		Late medieval		Early post-medieval	
	no.	%	no.	%	no.	%	no.	%
Cattle and large ungulate	26	60	123	36	49	20	55	23
Sheep/goat and small ungulate	13	30	172	50	161	66	164	67
Pig	4	10	46	13	31	13	23	10
Total	**43**		**352**		**230**		**242**	

FIGURE 10.12
Relative proportions of the domestic species from fragment counts

	Early medieval		Medieval		Late medieval		Early post-medieval	
	no.	%	no.	%	no.	%	no.	%
Cattle	Jaw 1		Humerus 6		Skull 8		Centroquartal	
	2	40	5	26	3	14	3	16
Sheep/goat	Innominate 3		Tibia 7		Tibia 7		Tibia 7	
	2	40	11	57	12	57	13	68
Pig	Phalanx 2		Scapula 3		Humerus 6		Scapula 3	
	1	20	3	16	6	28	3	16
Total	**5**		**19**		**21**		**19**	

FIGURE 10.13
Relative proportions of the domestic species from most frequent zone counts

The low numbers of bones from wild species suggest that hunting was not an activity contributing significantly to the accumulation of faunal debris. Given the presence of remains from infant calf, lambs and piglets suggesting deposition of faunal refuse in spring, an absence of game hunted in winter is perhaps merely negative evidence for such seasonal activity on site.

Cattle

The numbers of individual skeletal elements of cattle present in each period are extremely low. For Figures 10.14 and 10.15, the relative frequency of the skeletal elements identified is presented as a percentage of the most numerous element. The early medieval and medieval groups have most parts of the body represented with little differentiation between fore and hind quarter. The missing elements are generally more fragile bones which may not have survived. The late medieval and early post-medieval groups have surprisingly poor representation of the fore limb. The presence of head, fore and hind feet bones together with the hind limb bones may suggest the original presence of hides with the head and feet attached and either preferential consumption of the hind leg or boning out of the hind limbs for the marrow bones with the meat being consumed elsewhere. Preservation is less likely to be the sole factor influencing skeletal representation in the later groups.

Only one jaw was found with a tooth row from which a Mandible Wear Stage (MWS) could be calculated (after Grant 1982). This was from the early medieval group and was from a calf with the first molar coming into wear, probably aged about six months at death. The general tooth wear in Figure 10.16 indicates even representation of juvenile/immature to adult animals in the early medieval group. Permanent teeth in full wear predominate in the medieval group but some teeth from younger animals are present. The late medieval group has no later erupting permanent teeth present. The early post-medieval group suggests the slaughter of more juvenile and immature than mature adult animals.

The information on the age at slaughter from epiphysial fusion in Figure 10.17 is very scanty. Unfused ends are infrequent and are of the later fusing bones only in the medieval phases. This suggests that unfused bones of immature animals may not have survived. Some unfused ends are present in the early post-medieval group, indicating at least one animal that was killed at less than four years old. Juvenile animals in this phase appear to be under-represented by the epiphysial evidence compared to the tooth evidence.

Very few cattle bones were sufficiently intact for measurements to be taken. These were principally phalanges and carpals. The sample sizes were too small for any interpretation of the metrical data. There were two complete metacarpals from the medieval group from which withers heights of 0.99m and 1.14m were estimated. These fall within the range normally found on medieval sites.

Sheep/goat

The number of sheep/goat fragments from the early medieval group was very low and this is reflected in the very restricted suite of skeletal elements in Figure 10.18. The much larger medieval group in Figure 10.18 has all parts of the body represented, indicating utilisation of whole carcases in the vicinity. The pattern is strongly affected by preservational factors with peak representation of the densest bones such as distal tibia and humerus. The late medieval and early post-medieval groups in Figure 10.19 again show representation of all parts of the body. There is more even representation of bones from the forelimb than was seen for the earlier groups. This could in part reflect a generally better state of preservation in the later material. A change in the human utilisation of the sheep carcase may also be indicated as a similar trend has been observed for contemporary deposits in Leicester (Gidney 1992, 5), Newcastle Blackfriars (Gidney 1987) and York (Terry O'Connor pers comm).

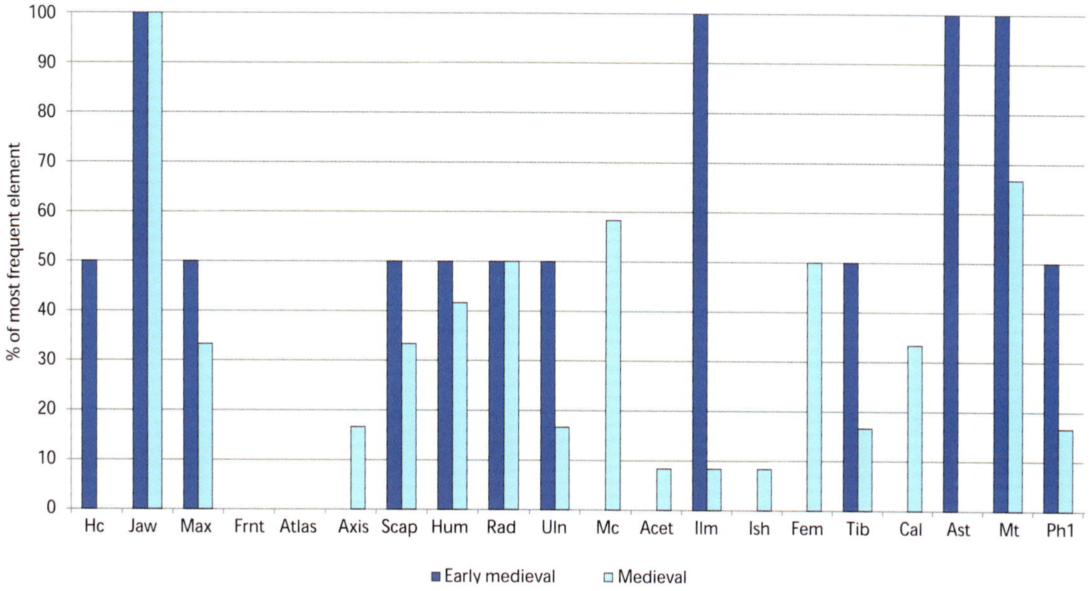

FIGURE 10.14
Cattle fragments, early medieval/medieval

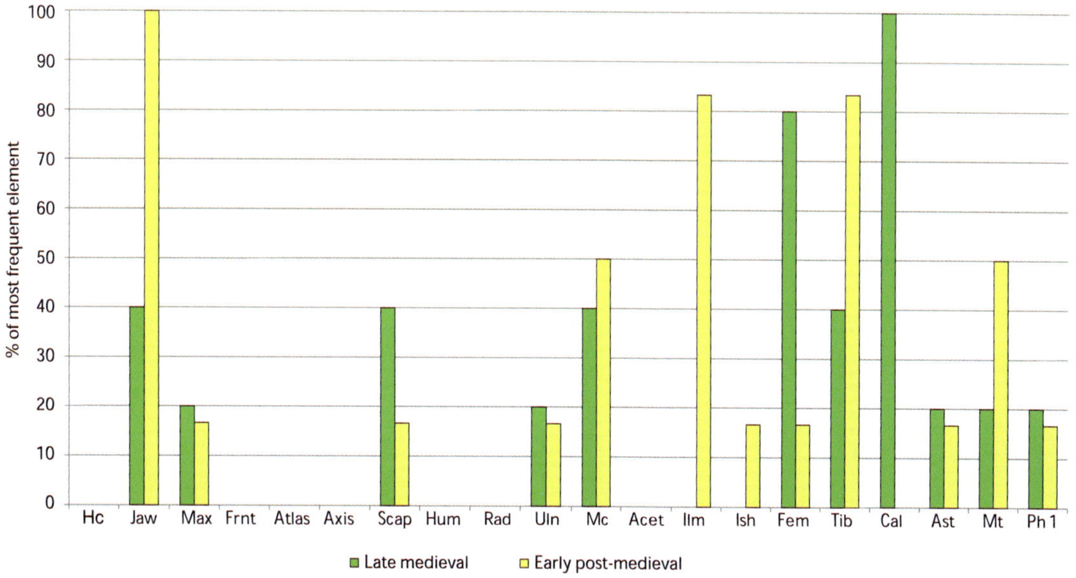

FIGURE 10.15
Cattle fragments, late medieval/early post-medieval

The total absence of horn cores in Figures 10.18 and 10.19 is interesting. The high proportions of lower jaws indicate utilisation of the heads on site. The late medieval group produced two skull fragments, one with a small horn bud rather than core and one polled. The early post-medieval group produced one skull fragment which had had the horn core chopped off. It would seem that horns were removed from those sheep heads that carried them and were traded off the site rather than worked in the vicinity.

Only eight jaws from all periods combined had intact tooth rows for MWS to be calculated. Three were from first-year animals with the first molar coming into wear; one was probably a yearling animal with the second molar coming into wear; two were second-year animals with the third molar coming into wear; one was from a mature animal with all permanent teeth in full attrition and one was from an aged animal with severe tooth wear. No jaws from infant lambs were found in any period.

		Early medieval			Medieval			Late medieval			Early post-medieval		
		U	S/W	H/W	U	S/W	H/W	U	S/W	H/W	U	S/W	H/W
Cattle													
Molar 1	5–6m		1	2			11			3		1	4
Molar 2	15–18m						5			1		1	2
Premolar 2	24–30m	2					2				1		
Premolar 3	18–30m	1			4		3				2		1
Molar 3	24–30m						9					1	1
Premolar 4	28–36m	1		2	3		4				3		
Sheep/goat													
Molar 1	3–5m		1	3			22			19		1	15
Molar 2	9–12m		1			11	9		6	3		3	4
Premolar 2	21–24m	1			1		2	1	1		1		
Premolar 3	21–24m	1			1		6	2	1	1	2		3
Molar 3	18–24m		1			4	9		6	4		5	14
Premolar 4	21–24m	2			5		11	2	2	6	2	1	5
Pig													
Molar 1	4–6m					1	3		1			2	1
Molar 2	7–13m					1							
Premolar 2	12–16m		1			2					1		
Premolar 3	12–16m		1	1	1	2					1		
Premolar 4	12–16m		1	1		1	1	1			1		
Molar 3	17–22m							1		1			

FIGURE 10.16
Teeth in approximate order of eruption. Ages after Silver (1969)
(m = months, U = Unerupted/deciduous, S/W = Slight wear, H/W = Heavy wear)

	Early medieval			Medieval			Late medieval			Early post-medieval		
	Fused	Just fused	Unfused	Fused	Just fused	Unfused	Fused	Just fused	Unfused	Fused	Just fused	Unfused
by 18 months												
Scap tub												
Acet symph												
Prox rad				3								
Dist hum				3								
Prox Ph 2	1			3			2			2		
Prox Ph 1	1			4			3			1		1
by 2–3 years												
Dist tib										2		1
Dist mc				3						1		
Dist mt	1			2						1		
by 3.5–4 years												
Prox cal				1		1	1		1			1
Prox fem				1					1			
Dist rad				3								
Prox hum												
Prox tib							1					
Dist fem						1						
P&D uln	1			1								
by >5 years												
Ant vert ep				5		3			1			2
Post vert ep			1	2	2	4			1			1

FIGURE 10.17
Cattle epiphyses in approximate order of fusion. Ages of fusion after Silver (1969)

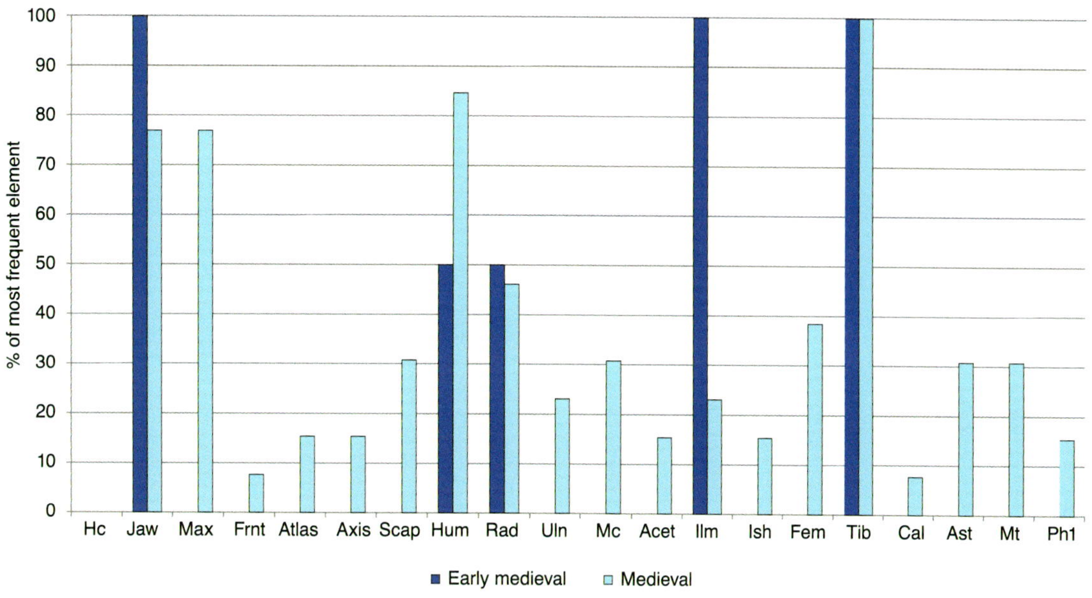

FIGURE 10.18
Sheep/goat fragments, early medieval/medieval

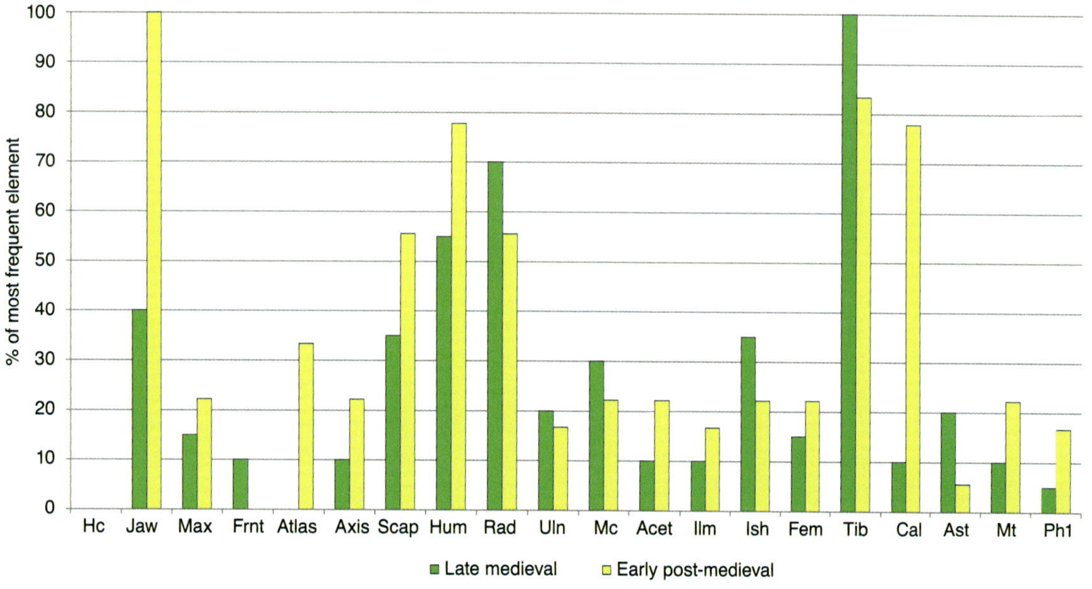

FIGURE 10.19
Sheep/goat fragments, late medieval/early post-medieval

The general stages of tooth wear in Figure 10.16 indicate the presence mostly of first to second-year animals in the early medieval group. In the medieval group the permanent molars with only slight wear indicate a substantial cull of yearling animals with perhaps an equal proportion surviving to full dental maturity, over two years old. The teeth in the late medieval group also suggest a preferential cull of probably second-year animals with permanent teeth coming into wear. In the early post-medieval group, the proportion of permanent teeth in full wear is greater suggesting fewer animals were killed before about two years old.

The epiphysial evidence in Figure 10.20 for the age structure of the cull population has been restricted by poor survival of bone compared to teeth. In the early medieval group there was only one bone with unfused epiphyses. The medieval group has twice as many fused as unfused ends. The unfused ends in the first two age groups complement the teeth in suggesting a cull of second-year animals. Half of the vertebrae are fused and are, therefore, from animals that survived to full skeletal maturity. The late medieval and early post-medieval groups exhibit continuity of the pattern observed for the medieval group.

	Early medieval			Medieval			Late medieval			Early post-medieval		
	Fused	Just fused	Unfused	Fused	Just fused	Unfused	Fused	Just fused	Unfused	Fused	Just fused	Unfused
by 1 year												
Dist hum				4			4		1	5		2
Prox rad				1		1	5			1		
Scap tub							1			3		1
Acet symph				2			1			1		
by 1–2 years												
Prox Ph 2				2	1		1			2		
Prox Ph 1				3	1	1	7	1	1	3	1	2
Dist tib					4	1	5		1	3		
Dist mc							2					1
Dist mt							1			1		
by 2.5–3.5 years												
Prox fem										1		3
Prox cal					1		1			1		2
Dist fem					2		1		1	1	1	
Prox tib							1		2	1		
Dist rad						2			1	2		
Prox hum					2				3	1		4
P&D uln						1	1			1		1
by >5 years												
Ant vert ep			1	5		4	1	2	5	2		5
Post vert ep			1	6	1	3	2		6	3		7

FIGURE 10.20
Sheep/goat epiphyses in approximate order of fusion. Ages of fusion after Silver (1969)

Despite the absence of the more robust jaws, fifteen bones from infant lambs were found, principally in the late medieval and early post-medieval groups. Some lacked epiphysial ends and therefore do not appear in Figure 10.20. These fragile bones are fortunate to have survived in a generally hostile burial environment and are likely to be greatly under-represented. Such baby lambs have been considered a delicacy in the recent past (Spry 1956, 553). Alternatively they may represent natural mortalities at lambing time which may have been skinned. The skin of a dead lamb was traditionally put on an orphan lamb to persuade the ewe to adopt it. Lambskins were also valuable and widely traded (Veale 1966, 5 and 216–217). If the skins were traded to the tawyer with the heads in, the absence of jaws to complement the post-cranial elements could be explained.

More sheep than cattle bones were measurable but most were tarsals and phalanges. The samples of seven distal humeri and eleven distal tibiae did not show any clear differences between the medieval, late medieval and early post-medieval stock. Four complete bones were found from which withers heights of 0.50–0.54m were estimated. One example at 0.50m was from the medieval group. Three examples at 0.50–0.54m were from the post-medieval group.

Pig

Pig remains were far less numerous than those of cattle and sheep. For this reason the early medieval/medieval and late medieval/early post-medieval groups have been combined for Figure 10.21. The pattern of skeletal representation for both groups is similar and appears to be a product of preservational factors rather than human selection.

A single jaw from the early post-medieval group had an intact tooth row with MWS 8, a first-year animal with molar 1 coming into wear. The numbers of pig teeth in Figure 10.16 are low, the largest sample being from the medieval group. The teeth suggest that the majority of animals were killed by or in their second year. The epiphysial evidence in Figure 10.22 also indicates that the lifespan of the pigs was very short. Four bones from the medieval group (C459, C629, C638 and C1148) and one from the early post-medieval (C1150) were from very young piglets. These were rather too small to have been eaten as sucking pig and suggest that pigs were breeding in the vicinity. Like the lamb bones, these piglet bones indicate superior preservation, or lack of disturbance, in some deposits.

Only one pig bone was measurable.

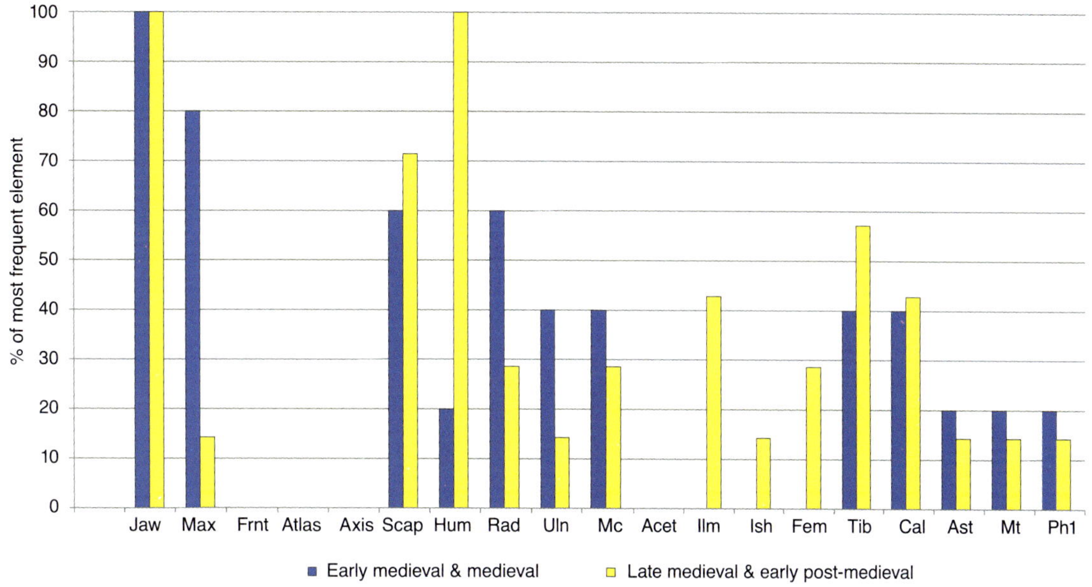

FIGURE 10.21
Pig fragments

	Early medieval			Medieval			Late medieval			Early post-medieval		
	Fused	Just fused	Unfused	Fused	Just fused	Unfused	Fused	Just fused	Unfused	Fused	Just fused	Unfused
by 1 year												
Acet symph												1
Scap tub				1								
Prox rad				2		1	1		1			
Dist hum						1	1	1				1
Prox Ph 2	1											
by 1–2 years												
Prox Ph 1							2		2			
Dist mc							2					1
Dist tib				1			1					
Dist mt							1		1			
Prox cal							3		1			1
by 2.5–3.5 years												
P&D uln												
Prox tib							1		1			
Prox hum							1		1			1
Dist rad							2		1			
P&D fem												
by >5 years												
Ant vert ep							1		1			
Post vert ep							1		1			

FIGURE 10.22
Pig epiphyses in approximate order of fusion. Ages of fusion after Silver (1969)

Horse

Horse bones were found in all but the tiny post-medieval group. The proportion of horse bones in the pre-medieval to medieval groups is level at 7–8% of the identified fragments in Figure 10.9. This comparatively high proportion suggests disposal of non-domestic waste. Only one horse bone was measurable for an estimate of withers height. This was from the medieval group and gave an estimated height of 1.29m which represents a pony of about 13 hands. The proportion of horse bones drops to 1% in the late medieval and 3% in the early post-medieval groups, which have a large component of domestic detritus. The horse bones appear to be widely distributed in Figure 10.11, with only a suggestion of a concentration in the NE perimeter area in the medieval group. There was no evidence for the consumption of horses, nor for *in situ* burial of carcases. Over 40% of the horse remains were loose teeth. It seems most probable that the majority of bones derive from carcases disposed of away from habitation areas, which subsequently decomposed and were scavenged leading to distribution of skeletal elements across the site and reworking within the sequence of deposits before final burial.

Dog

Dog bones are not as numerous as those of horse but were also found in all groups except the post-medieval. Most bones in all periods were found in the west cemetery area with a wider spread for the medieval and post-medieval groups. All the bones found had fused epiphysial ends. No long bones or skull fragments were sufficiently intact to be measured for estimates of either shoulder height or facial characteristics. Like the horse bones, there was no evidence for consumption of dog nor for *in situ* burials. Some 30% of the dog remains were loose teeth. The dog bones may have entered the archaeological record in the same way proposed for the horse bones.

Cat

Single examples of cat bones were found in the medieval and late medieval groups. Both were found in the cemetery in areas attracting human food debris. Domestic cat bones are frequently found in later medieval urban deposits (Gidney 1991). Alternatively these could derive from wild cats procured for their skins, cat skin being valued for garments (Veale 1966, 3–5).

Roe deer

Only one roe deer bone was found in the medieval group, deposited in the south cemetery. It was a radius which is a meat-bearing bone. The absence of further bones suggests venison was not readily available.

Hare

A single hare bone was found in the early post-medieval group. It was found in the eastern end of the church. While other small bones interpreted as owl pellets were found in the same context, it is possibly more likely to derive from human food debris than to be such a natural mortality. The hare is too large to be hunted by the indigenous owls or kestrels that would appear to have been using the ruin as a roost.

Rabbit

Two rabbit bones were found in the medieval group and one in the early post-medieval group. These do not appear to be modern contaminants. Lever (1977, 65–66) suggests that rabbits were introduced to Britain in the 12th century but did not become widespread until the mid-13th century. Rabbit meat remained a rare and highly prized foodstuff due to the difficulties of rearing them in the inhospitable British climate (Bailey 1988, 1–2).

The scarcity of bones of deer, hare and rabbit may suggest that they represent the remains of occasional festive dining, or a low success rate at hunting or poaching. Alternatively, human use of the site may have been concentrated early in the year, when the young calf, lamb and piglet bones would have been deposited. Hunting is an activity later in the year, after harvest.

Stoat

Stoat was represented by a single bone from the early post-medieval group. This was found in the west cemetery area. It seems most probable that this represents a natural mortality on the site.

Weasel

Two weasel bones were found in the late medieval group and one in the early post-medieval. The former were found in the north and west cemetery and the latter in the east end of the church. Like the stoat, these bones seem most likely to derive from natural mortalities.

Both mustelids would have been attracted by the voids in the derelict ruin as cover to hunt small mammals. They could also have fallen victim to the owls, or other birds of prey, also using the derelict building from which to hunt.

Birds

(Identified by Dr E Allison)

Bird bones were concentrated in the medieval to early post-medieval groups. Domestic fowl and goose bones were found in all three groups with a similar overall frequency. There was some variation in the size of the goose bones but all fell within the known range of domestic geese. The late medieval group produced one duck bone comparable with mallard, one partridge and one quail bone. The partridge is still a widespread game bird. Quail are thought to have been commonly found into the 15th century but had become scarce by the 17th century (Reid-Henry and Harrison 1988, 94). A single woodcock bone was found in the medieval group. Like the partridge, the woodcock is still widely distributed and prized for the table. The collection of starling bones in the medieval group represents a large part of one bird which appears to have been a natural mortality. The small passerine bone from the medieval group was thought by Dr Allison to be comparable with lark. The bird had been eaten as there were knife marks on both proximal and distal ends. Kestrel bones were found in both the medieval and early post-medieval groups and rook/crow in the latter group. These bones seem most likely to derive from natural mortalities. Such resident kestrels may have deposited some of the accumulations of small mammal bones.

Fish

(Identified by R Nicholson)

The Hirsel excavations yielded very few fish bones, from only two contexts. One of these was medieval and one early post-medieval. All of the bones were from large cod, but the elements recovered (fin rays and one branchiostegal ray) do not allow further estimation of the size of the fish represented.

Summary

Excavations at the Hirsel produced small groups of identifiable fragments associated with phases of domestic use of the church. Bone preservation was generally not good and there were indications that many fragments had been redeposited.

The majority of the bones appear to be domestic food waste and derive from cattle, sheep and pig. Other species present indicate very limited use of game animals and birds for food. Other wild species most probably indicate natural mortalities on the site.

Sheep bones are most abundant from the medieval group onwards. A preference for prime mutton animals, generally less than three years old is indicated. Whole carcases appear to have been utilised on site with preservational factors accounting for low representation of the more delicate bones. Horns appear to have been detached and removed from the site. It is particularly interesting that patterns of utilisation noticed on urban consumer sites are also apparent on this rural site. This may indicate a consumer rather than producer role for the Hirsel which may be linked in part to the domestic use of the former church.

The presence of bones from very young calf, lambs and piglets suggests some seasonality in deposition of faunal refuse early in the year. The abundant small mammal bones suggesting roosting activity by birds of prey, such as the kestrel represented on the site, may indicate less human activity later in the year, allowing wildlife to use the site.

11
HUMAN SKELETAL REMAINS

Sue Anderson

11.1 INTRODUCTION

Three hundred and thirty burials were recovered from the cemetery site at The Hirsel. Of these, 325 were analysed by the present author and two were reported on by Dr David Birkett. There was also a large quantity of disarticulated bone, and little could be done with this other than to record its presence.

Method

Measurements were taken using the methods described by Brothwell (1981), and a few from Bass (1971) and Krogman (1978). Sexing and ageing techniques follow Brothwell, and the Workshop of European Anthropologists (1980). Stature was estimated according to the regression formulae of Trotter and Gleser (Trotter 1970). All systematically scored non-metric traits are listed in Brothwell, and grades of cribra orbitalia and osteoarthritis can also be found there. Pathological conditions were identified with the aid of Ortner and Putschar (1981).

Comparative material

Comparisons are made with the Anglo-Saxon/medieval monastic sites of Jarrow and Wearmouth (Anderson *et al* 2006), and the two York churchyards of St Helen-on-the-Walls (Dawes 1980) and St Andrew, Fishergate (Stroud 1993). Jarrow and Wearmouth have been chosen because they represent a contrast (being monastic sites) and also because they have been studied by the present writer. The two sites in York have been used because, like The Hirsel, they are medieval churchyards which have been excavated almost in their entirety.

Number of individuals

Of the 325 burials, 23 contained the remains of more than one individual, and one interment, Sk46, was a mass burial or 'bone dump'. The estimated minimum number of individuals for this site was approximately 331.

Condition

The bones were generally in fair condition, although the whole spectrum of preservation from very poor to very good was represented in this population. Unfortunately a number of skeletons from the early years of the excavation had not been washed, and this had not contributed to their preservation. Most of these, unless they were in good condition to begin with, had deteriorated badly, and in many cases the outer layer of the bone had become separated from the main part. Consequently they were of minimal use for pathological study.

11.2 DEMOGRAPHIC ANALYSIS

Juveniles

Of the 331 individuals from The Hirsel, 150 (45.3%) were juveniles under the age of 18 years. This is a high proportion in comparison with other groups. At Jarrow, in the Anglo-Saxon period the percentage of children was also high (42.9%), but it dropped in the medieval period (39.2%), whereas at Wearmouth the proportion was much lower (35.5%). In York, at Fishergate only 22.4% of skeletons were children, and at St Helen-on-the-Walls the figure was 30.5%. The two sites which would seem to be most comparable with The Hirsel, that is, the two medieval churchyards in York, have low proportions of children. One possible reason for this could be the amount of disturbance which occurred in these urban cemeteries, both during their periods of use and during later development. This is probably not the case at The Hirsel, although the disarticulated material contained the remains of at least 13 extra children and fragments of many more individuals. The figures here may be a fairly accurate representation of child mortality in the parish during the use of the churchyard, although the apparent clustering of child burials around the church building may have produced an artificially high proportion because the outer edges of the churchyard, where more adult burials might be expected, were not excavated.

The estimated average age at death (calculated from the medians of age ranges) for the 142 child skeletons which could be aged was 5.1 years. Broadly similar means were found at the two north-eastern sites. The average age at death of the children at Wearmouth was 4.2 years, at Jarrow in the Anglo-Saxon period it was nearer 7 years and in the medieval group it was 5.5 years. Figures were not available for the York cemeteries.

Age	No.	%
0–2	52	35.9
2–6	48	33.1
6–10	26	17.9
10–14	15	10.3
14–18	4	2.8

FIGURE 11.1
Table showing distribution of age at death

The distribution of age at death is shown in Figure 11.1. Over two-thirds of juvenile deaths occurred before the age of 6 years, with the greatest mortality occurring in the 0–2 year age group, 50% of which died before reaching around the 6 months of age. A similar pattern was found at Wearmouth. At Jarrow, approximately half the aged children died before the age of 6 years, but the proportion in the 0–2 year age group was much smaller in the later period. At St Helen-on-the-Walls, the group with highest mortality was found to be the 6–10 year olds, whilst at Fishergate, over half the early period children died before the age of 5 but the later period deaths were spread more evenly between the ages of 0–15 years. In general, later sites seem to have proportionately fewer infant burials, although this may be a result of preservation bias. The fact that the pattern at The Hirsel is most comparable with earlier groups could suggest that a different life-style was practised there in comparison with contemporary groups further south.

Adults

Of the 181 adults buried at The Hirsel, 85 were male (of which 17 were?male), 88 were female (23?female) and 8 were unsexable. This population was difficult to sex owing to a large number of skeletons with female pelvises but with skulls which appeared male. Because of this, there may have been a bias towards sexing as female when the evidence of the pelvis was less certain, although if the skull alone was available it is possible that some female skeletons were attributed to the male sex.

A male:female ratio of almost 1:1 is usual in a normal population, and would be the expected result at a site like The Hirsel. Monastic sites tend to show a bias towards men. At Wearmouth the sex ratio was 1.4:1 in favour of men, and at Jarrow it was similar (1.3:1). Fishergate produced the same result as Wearmouth for the early period there, but in the later period the churchyard was used by a priory and the male:female ratio changed to 3.2:1. There was a slight reversal of the pattern at St Helen's, where the ratio was 0.9:1. In general, The Hirsel would seem to represent a fairly normal secular group in terms of its adult sex distribution.

Since current methods of ageing adult skeletons are known to be inaccurate, no attempt has been made to calculate a mean age at death for this population. A possible distribution of age at death for each sex is recorded in Figure 11.2.

This suggests that the women were in general dying at a younger age than the men, and this is a fairly normal finding in medieval and earlier populations. However, there may be a number of factors which influence such a result. If age is estimated from molar attrition, for example, it is possible that there was a difference between the food eaten by men and women, and this could be reflected in the amount of wear. If the women were eating softer food than the men, their teeth would not be as worn as those of men of the same age. This is probably unlikely, since it seems reasonable to assume that bread, which was one of the major contributors to molar attrition, was eaten in similar quantities by both sexes.

Similar adult mortality patterns were found at Wearmouth, Anglo-Saxon Jarrow and St Helen-on-the-Walls, although the sex difference was less marked at Anglo-Saxon Jarrow. The figures for Fishergate and medieval Jarrow show a reverse trend, with proportionately more men than women in the youngest age groups. It may be that they represent the beginnings of a change towards modern British demographic patterns.

11.3 METRICAL AND MORPHOLOGICAL ANALYSIS

Measurements for individual skeletons, and means of each measurement, are recorded in tables in the archive.

Stature

The means and ranges of estimated heights (in metres) at The Hirsel and other sites are recorded

Age group	Suggested age range	Male		Female		M + F + ?	
		No.	%	No.	%	No.	%
Young	17–25	9	11.1	17	20.5	26	15.5
Young / Middle-aged	25–35	23	28.4	30	36.1	54	32.1
Middle-aged / Old	35–45	34	42.0	25	30.1	61	36.3
Old	45+	15	18.5	11	13.3	27	16.1

FIGURE 11.2
Table showing distribution of age of death for each sex

Site	Male			Female		
	No.	Mean	Range	No.	Mean	Range
The Hirsel	61	1.680	1.552–1.772	58	1.586	1.470–1.697
Jarrow (Sax)	19	1.710	1.609–1.844	12	1.591	1.488–1.666
Jarrow (Med)	33	1.710	1.580–1.862	39	1.597	1.522–1.680
Monkwearmouth	42	1.719	1.519–1.884	19	1.595	1.459–1.692
St Helen's, York	240	1.693	–	268	1.574	–
Fishergate, York	205	1.715	1.55–1.90	73	1.585	1.45–1.70

FIGURE 11.3
Table showing the means and ranges of estimated heights (in metres) at The Hirsel compared with other sites

Index	Type	Male		Female		Total	
		No.	%	No.	%	No.	%
Cranial (length/breadth)	Dolichocranial	4	14.3	7	21.2	11	17.5
	Mesocranial	15	53.6	16	48.5	31	49.2
	Brachycranial	8	28.6	9	27.3	18	28.6
	Hyperbrachycranial	1	3.6	1	3.0	3	4.8
Height/length	Chamaecranial	5	22.7	13	54.2	18	37.5
	Orthocranial	14	63.6	10	41.7	25	52.1
	Hypsicranial	3	13.6	1	4.2	5	10.4
Height/breadth	Tapeinocranial	13	65.0	17	73.9	32	71.1
	Metriocranial	7	35.0	6	26.1	13	28.9
	Acrocranial	0	–	0	–	0	–
Upper facial	Euryen	2	20.0	1	14.3	3	16.7
	Mesen	5	50.0	2	28.6	8	44.4
	Lepten	3	30.0	4	57.1	7	38.9
Nasal	Leptorrhine	8	42.1	6	35.3	14	38.9
	Mesorrhine	5	26.3	3	17.6	8	22.2
	Chamaerrhine	6	31.5	8	47.1	14	38.9

FIGURE 11.4
Table showing cranial indices

Site	Male			Female		
	No.	Mean	Range	No.	Mean	Range
The Hirsel	29	78.9	73.9–88.2	33	78.2	71.8–86.0
Jarrow (Sax)	5	75.3	70.4–79.8	3	74.3	70.6–77.0
Jarrow (Med)	7	75.7	72.2–82.4	5	76.4	74.3–77.9
Monkwearmouth	6	69.8	65.8–72.8	8	72.7	66.6–79.9
St Helen's, York	158	79.4	–	184	81.1	–
Fishergate, Early	8	75.9	72.5–80.7	9	76.4	71.9–82.7
Fishergate, Late	49	81.1	73.2–92.1	13	79.6	73.6–89.0

FIGURE 11.5
Table showing comparison of cranial indices from The Hirsel with those from other sites

in Figure 11.3. Mean stature of the males from The Hirsel was slightly less than the figures from other sites, although the females showed little difference and were actually slightly taller than the York women. However, the difference between the largest male mean (Wearmouth) and the mean at The Hirsel is only 4.2cm (1.6"), which is within normal limits for contemporary groups.

Cranial indices

Cranial measurements were taken from 90 adult and six juvenile skulls, in varying quantity. Of the adult skulls, 62 were complete enough for the calculation of one or more cranial index. The distributions of these are recorded in Figure 11.4 (the total includes two sub-adults).

From this it can be seen that the males and females at The Hirsel were in general of similar physical type. The indices suggest that they had broad, rounded, low heads with narrow faces and noses, and this impression is confirmed by a visual inspection of most of the skulls.

The simplest comparison of these data with other sites involves the use of means and ranges of the cranial index (Figure 11.5).

The broad, low heads of The Hirsel group are similar to other medieval populations. In general,

Cranial type	Area of churchyard		
	North	South	West
Dolichocranial (<74.9)	2	6	1
Narrow Mesocranial (<77.4)	4	7	3
Broad Mesocranial (>77.5)	4	7	5
Brachycranial (>80.0)	2	10	7

FIGURE 11.6
Table showing cranial index types by area

Trait	Male			Female			M + F + ?		
	No.	+	%	No.	+	%	No.	+	%
Metopism	58	3	5.2	65	3	4.6	127	7	5.5
Parietal foramen	56	41	71.9	66	45	68.2	127	89	70.1
Coronal wormians	54	4	7.4	59	5	8.5	117	9	7.7
Sagittal wormians	53	4	7.5	59	6	10.2	116	11	9.5
Lambdoid wormians	56	25	44.6	59	38	64.4	121	67	55.4
Epipteric bone	36	2	5.6	40	9	22.5	77	11	14.3
Parietal notch bone	41	0	–	41	3	7.3	85	3	3.5
Inca bone	53	2	3.8	63	2	3.2	121	5	4.1
Asterionic bone	41	3	7.3	50	4	8.0	94	8	8.5
Torus palatinus	43	12	27.9	56	14	25.0	101	26	25.7
Tori maxillares	48	7	14.6	57	7	12.3	107	14	13.1
Tori mandibulares	52	1	1.9	62	0	–	118	1	0.9
Torus auditivus	59	0	–	65	1	1.5	129	1	0.8
Double hypoglossal canal	34	12	35.3	39	7	17.9	75	19	25.3
Post-condylar canal	34	7	20.6	39	10	25.6	75	17	22.7
Septal aperture (humerus)	51	0	–	56	5	8.9	111	5	4.5
Third trochanter (femur)	52	6	11.5	58	10	17.2	113	16	14.2
Atlas double facet	38	7	18.4	35	4	11.4	73	11	15.1
Acetabular crease (pelvis)	45	5	11.1	51	8	15.7	97	13	13.4

FIGURE 11.7
Table showing non-metric traits

later sites have higher means, reflecting the general trend from narrow to broad skulls which appears to have taken place throughout Europe at about this time. It has been suggested that changes in the cranial index may be related to climate change (Beals *et al* 1983). At Fishergate, the change seemed to be due more to a decrease in length than to an increase in width. The same was true of the Jarrow females, but the opposite was the case for the males. The Hirsel skeletons have not been divided by phase, but plotting the cranial index types on the site plan produces the results in Figure 11.6.

This suggests that there are slightly more broad-headed people (index >77.5) to the south and west of the church than to the north, which could suggest a shift in use of the churchyard from north to south. The results are, however, far from conclusive. It was noted that one possible family group, identified from non-metric traits (see below), at the south-west corner of the church, consisted of four overlying burials, the earliest of which was brachycranial, followed by a broad mesocranial, a narrow mesocranial, and finally a dolichocranial. Clearly this 'family' shows that there were exceptions to the general trend.

Non-metric traits

Non-metric traits are genetic anomalies found in various bones of the skeleton, but most frequently looked for in the cranium. They are scored on a present/absent basis, since they are generally too small for measurement. The percentages of each trait found (out of the number of individuals in which that area of the skeleton was available) are shown in Figure 11.7. Note that bilateral traits have been scored by individual rather than by side.

Although there is a slight difference between males and females, in general this does not appear to be very large. The difference was tested using the chi-square statistic (Perizonius 1979; Green *et al* 1979) and only three of the 19 traits were found to be significantly different at the 5% level, but none at the 1% level. The three significant traits were the parietal notch bone, double hypoglossal canal, and septal aperture of the humerus. The last is often found to be more common in females and may be related to robusticity, although this does not preclude a genetic origin. Other noticeable (but not significant) differences are in the epipteric bone in more females than males and the atlas double facet in more males than females. The females tended to have more extra-sutural bones than the males.

No comparison was possible between sites because of the different methods used and the variety of traits scored by other workers.

Non-metric traits have often been used to establish the presence of family groups within a burial population. If one or more of the rarer traits are noted in individuals buried close together, there is a fair chance that some relationship between the two existed. At the Hirsel, only three males were found to have retained the metopic suture into adulthood. Two of these individuals (Sk306 and Sk308) were buried next to each other on the south side of the church, and at similar levels.

Three possible family groups were identified based on their combinations of traits and their spatial distribution. The first was to the north of the church and consisted of eight burials (Sk44, Sk65, Sk93, Sk94, Sk96, Sk323, Sk325, Sk327) which respected each other but seemed to be clustered together on a similar alignment. Three other burials in this general area could not be scored for traits (Sk66, Sk95, Sk324). Three of the skeletons have sagittal wormian bones, three have coronal wormian bones and five have lambdoid wormian bones. Other traits include post-condylar canal (3), torus palatinus (2), double hypoglossal canal (2) and epipteric bones (2).

The second group has already been mentioned above, in connection with cranial index types. It is a group of nine individuals (Sk225, Sk232, Sk239, Sk240, Sk293, Sk314, Sk321, Sk336, Sk338) buried at the south-west corner of the church. A few un-assessable children (Sk179, Sk248, Sk249) may also belong. This group shows little respect for graves, perhaps suggesting a smaller family burial plot than was available to Group 1. Eight individuals had lambdoid wormian bones, and other extra-sutural bones, double hypoglossal canal and post-condylar canal each occurred in three individuals.

The third group is at the south-eastern extreme of the excavated area and is not so clearly defined. There seemed to be a fairly high concentration of torus palatinus in this area, and all five of the individuals (Sk174, Sk186, Sk199, Sk200, Sk209) identified as part of Group 3 had this trait. The graves are all on the same alignment, though not particularly clustered. Other un-assessable individuals (Sk187, Sk201 and Sk261) may belong. The other traits included four post-condylar canals.

These 'family' groups may be valid, but they should not be regarded as certainties. There could be up to 350 years between the first and last burials on this site, which suggests an average of one burial per year from the skeletons available for study. It is reasonable to assume that family plots were used in the past, but it is less reasonable to assume that these can be easily identified.

11.4 DENTAL ANALYSIS

There were 50 male maxillae, 55 male mandibles, 69 female maxillae and 68 female mandibles. These represented 56 males and 71 females.

Of the 3,872 possible positions, 398 were either uncertain or destroyed. This left 3,474 tooth positions which could be studied. 458 (13.2%) teeth had been lost post-mortem, 239 (6.9%) ante-mortem, and 96 (2.8%) were unerupted (or congenitally absent). This left a total of 2,681 teeth present in the jaw.

Of the children, 108 had surviving dental remains, although many of these were small infants in whom the teeth were just forming at the time of death. In addition, 34 juvenile dentitions were studied by Williams and Curzon (1985; 1986), some of which were not seen by the present writer and are not included in the above total.

Ante-mortem tooth loss

Ante-mortem loss of one or more teeth was present in 32 males and 34 females, 57.1% and 47.9% respectively, 52.0% overall (Figure 11.8). The table shows that tooth loss was greater in the mandible than in the maxilla, and in males than in females. A similar pattern was found at Wearmouth and Jarrow, although in the Wearmouth females and the Jarrow males percentage loss was slightly higher in the maxilla than the mandible. Information concerning sex differences is not available for St Helen-on-the-Walls, but in the total population slightly more mandibles than maxillae were affected. At Fishergate, women were affected most by ante-mortem loss, and the figures for their mandibles were greater than for their maxillae. The male maxillae had slightly more ante-mortem loss than their mandibles. Chi-squared tests showed a significant difference between the sexes at The Hirsel, medieval Jarrow and the earlier period at Fishergate.

The combined figure for both sexes and jaws is a fairly average one for the period. At Wearmouth the figure was 7.8%, at Anglo-Saxon Jarrow 4.2% and medieval Jarrow 9.5%. At Fishergate, the figure for the early period was 3.2% and for the

Sex	Jaw	Places	Lost	%
Male	Maxilla	693	46	6.6
	Mandible	787	74	9.4
Female	Maxilla	961	50	5.2
	Mandible	1033	69	6.7
Both	Maxilla	1654	96	5.8
	Mandible	1820	143	7.9
Both	Both	3474	239	6.9

FIGURE 11.8
Table showing ante-mortem tooth loss

later 11.4%. The greatest prevalence was found at St Helen-on-the-Walls, with 17.5%. In general, the trend from this and other studies suggests that ante-mortem tooth loss increased from the Anglo-Saxon to the medieval period.

The greatest tooth loss occurred in the molar areas of the jaws (74.4%), followed by the premolars (18.1%), the incisors (7.1%) and the canines (0.4%). The same pattern was seen at Wearmouth, medieval Jarrow and Fishergate, but at Anglo-Saxon Jarrow no incisors were affected. Figures 11.9–11.12 show the distribution of lesions per tooth in the maxillae and mandibles of both men and women at The Hirsel (although not by side). From these it can be seen that in general the first molar showed the greatest loss, although in male mandibles slightly more second molars were affected.

Caries

One or more carious teeth were found in 12 males (21.4%) of which 10 had only one lesion and 2 had two lesions, and 21 females (29.6%) of whom 14 had one and 7 had two lesions (Figure 11.13).

The overall rate of caries at The Hirsel was low in comparison with other medieval groups, and was closer to the figures found at Wearmouth (1.0%) and Anglo-Saxon Jarrow (1.0%). Medieval Jarrow was slightly higher (4.4%), St Helen-on-the-Walls had 6.1%, and the figures for Fishergate were 4.3% in the early period and 12.1% in the later. Generally the trend is one of increase in caries from the Anglo-Saxon to later periods. The low percentage at The Hirsel may be related to the smaller number of old individuals at this site in comparison with the others, or it may be due to the relatively low status of the site and the population.

Unlike ante-mortem loss, caries was slightly more prevalent in the maxilla than the mandible. The two may be related if caries was the cause of much of the tooth loss seen here, since it may have affected the lower teeth earlier and caused them to be shed earlier in life. The differences between areas of jaw, however, were not statistically significant.

Men and women were affected to a similar degree, as was the case at Wearmouth and Anglo-Saxon Jarrow. At medieval Jarrow and Fishergate, the women were affected more than the men, although the difference was only statistically significant at Fishergate. As was the case with tooth loss, the majority of carious lesions were found in the molar area of the jaw. Percentage distributions for each tooth in the maxillae and mandibles of males and females are shown in Figures 11.9–11.12.

Juveniles were also scored for caries, although only those with at least one erupted tooth were included, a total of 82. Of these, 9 (11.0%) were

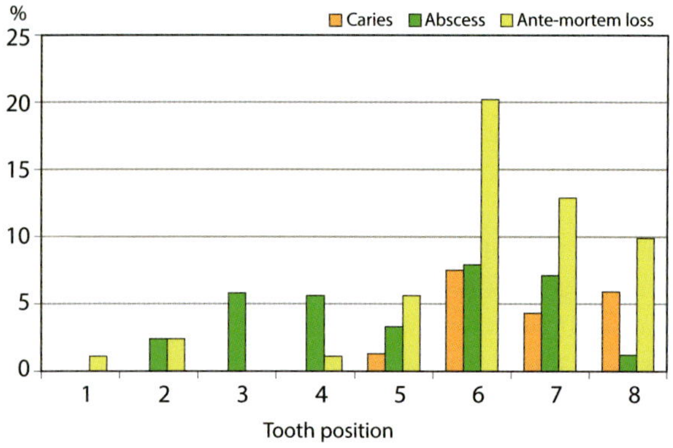

FIGURE 11.9
Tooth position, male maxilla

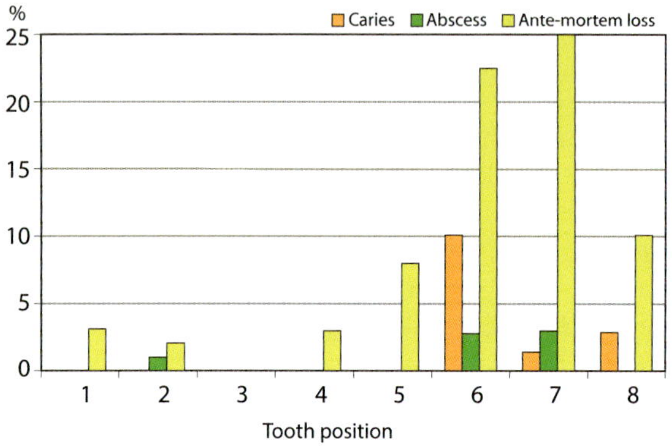

FIGURE 11.10
Tooth position, male mandible

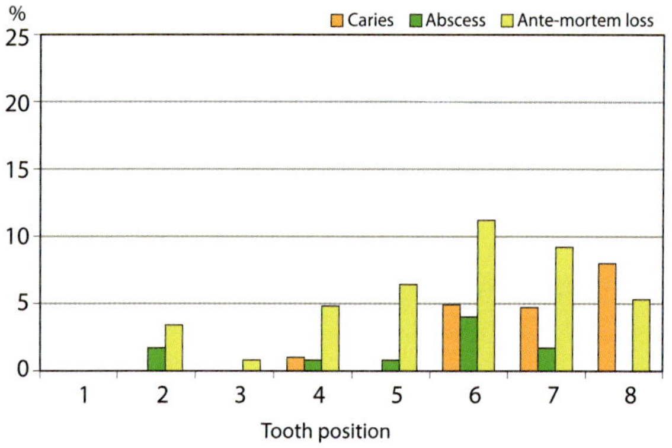

FIGURE 11.11
Tooth position, female maxilla

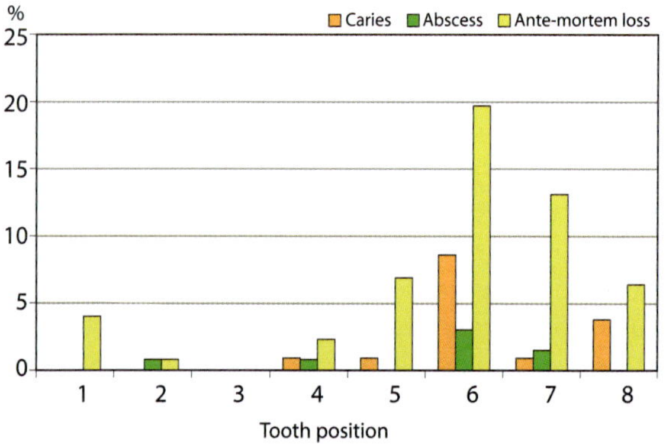

FIGURE 11.12
Tooth position, female mandible

found to have carious lesions, the majority of which were in the deciduous molars. Williams and Curzon (1985; 1986) found that 11 of the 34 children which they saw had carious teeth, of which 4 had permanent teeth with lesions.

Periodontal disease

Twelve men (21.4%) and 15 women (21.1%) had periodontal abscesses. Of the 12 men, 4 had one abscess, 3 had two, 3 had three, 1 had four and 1 had more than five. Twelve women had one abscess, 2 had two, 1 one had four. Abscesses were found in various positions in the jaws (Figure 11.14).

The male maxillae were most affected by abscesses, and overall there was a significant difference between maxillae and mandibles. In common with the other dental pathologies, abscesses affected the molar teeth to the largest extent (Figures 11.9–11.12). Overall the percentage of abscesses was very low. In the case of periodontal disease, there does not appear to be any correlation with time. At Wearmouth the overall figure was 2.2%, whilst at Jarrow in both periods it was 1.1%. A slight increase was seen at Fishergate from 1.9% in the early period to 4.5% in the later, but at St Helen-on-the-Walls the figure was only 1.2%.

Sex	Jaw	Teeth	Carious	%
Male	Maxilla	542	12	2.2
	Mandible	588	10	1.7
Female	Maxilla	756	17	2.2
	Mandible	795	15	1.9
Both	Maxilla	1298	29	2.2
	Mandible	1383	25	1.8
Both	Both	2681	54	2.0

FIGURE 11.13
Table showing dental caries

Sex	Jaw	Places	Abscess	%
Male	Maxilla	693	28	4.0
	Mandible	787	7	0.9
Female	Maxilla	961	11	1.1
	Mandible	1033	8	0.8
Both	Maxilla	1654	39	2.4
	Mandible	1820	15	0.8
Both	Both	3474	54	0.2

FIGURE 11.14
Table showing periodontal abscesses

General dental pathology

Figures 11.15–11.16 show the percentages of lesions per tooth in male and female maxillae and mandibles, as discussed above. As well as being related to the area of the jaw, the number of lesions also correlates with age. At The Hirsel, there is a clear increase of pathology in the older age groups, which is particularly noticeable in the case of ante-mortem loss. The effect of this, in inter-site comparison, is to increase the overall percentages of each type of lesion in populations with relatively large proportions of old people. Only 18.5% of the adult population at The Hirsel fall into the 'Old' category, whereas at Wearmouth and Jarrow the figure is around 40%. At Fishergate, the figures are also high (although they are not directly comparable because different age groups were used), but at St Helen-on-the-Walls the percentage is only slightly higher than The Hirsel (23%). If this were the only element involved, then the prevalence of dental disease should be similar at St Helen's and The Hirsel

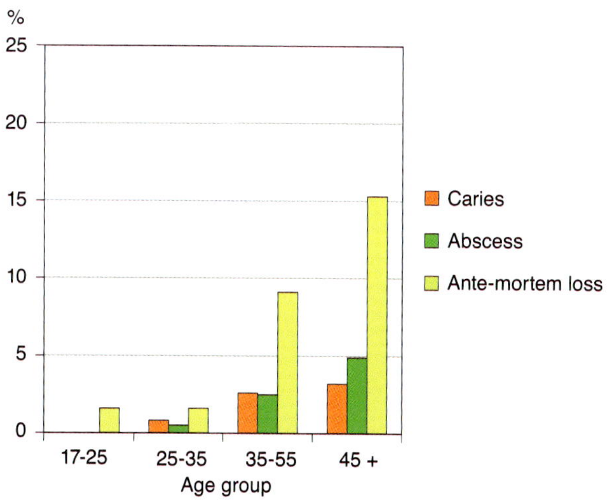

FIGURE 11.15
Age group 1

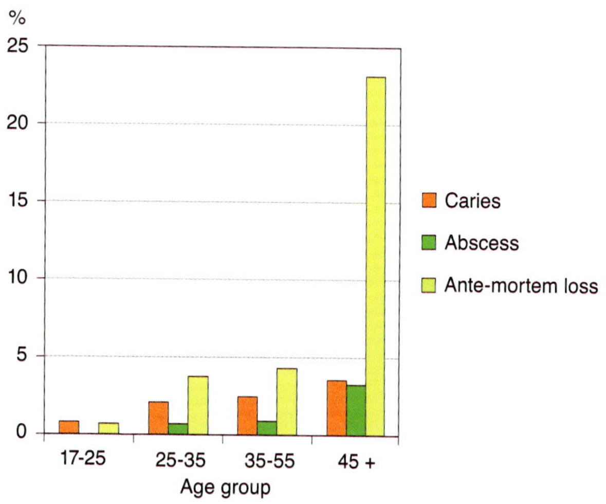

FIGURE 11.16
Age group 2

and markedly different at the other sites. This is not the case, and there are clearly other factors which need to be identified. One of these is probably the time period, since later groups presumably had greater access to cariogenic foodstuffs, and status would also be a consideration here.

Unerupted/congenitally absent teeth

The overall frequency of 'unerupted' teeth at The Hirsel was 2.8%. Other sites have produced similar figures. At Wearmouth it was 1.8%, Anglo-Saxon Jarrow 3.9%, medieval Jarrow 2.6%, and St Helen's 2.9%. The third molars were the most common teeth to have remained unerupted or to be congenitally absent, and the frequency for these was 19.6% at The Hirsel. As proportions of third molar positions, 13.3% of males and 24.4% of females lacked third molars, and this difference was significant in a chi-squared test. A few other teeth were unerupted or congenitally absent. One female individual lacked one premolar from each quadrant of her dentition. Three individuals lacked one or more canines, and two lacked an incisor. One female lacked the right mandibular second and third molars.

Calculus and hypoplasia

Dental calculus, or tartar, was scored on a four-point scale (Brothwell 1981) in all skeletons excavated in 1980–82, and enamel hypoplasia was scored using a similar method (Figures 11.17 and 11.18).

There is very little difference in calculus amounts between the sexes, although the women seem to have had slightly heavier deposits than the men. Children generally were not affected to any great degree, as would be expected. The percentages of people with calculus at medieval Jarrow and St Helen's are roughly similar to these, but in the Anglo-Saxon period fewer people were affected, perhaps reflecting a change in eating habits.

With regard to enamel hypoplasia (Figure 11.18), the majority of individuals had very slight lesions, largely consisting of shallow ridging on one or more permanent teeth. The males were affected to a slightly greater extent and a higher degree than the females, although the children exhibited the most gross lesions. It is possible that the worst examples of this condition are consistent with long periods of illness in childhood, which makes it less likely that the affected individuals would reach maturity.

Calculus amount	**Male** No.	%	**Female** No.	%	**Unsexed** No.	%	**Child** No.	%
None	17	37.8	22	40.0	3	75.0	57	78.1
Slight	19	42.2	18	32.7	0	–	14	19.2
Medium	8	17.8	11	20.0	1	25.0	2	2.7
Heavy	1	2.2	4	7.3	0	–	0	–
Total	**45**		**55**		**4**		**73**	

FIGURE 11.17
Table showing dental calculus

Hypoplasia amount	**Male** No.	%	**Female** No.	%	**Unsexed** No.	%	**Child** No.	%
None	14	31.1	20	37.0	2	50.0	9	11.8
Slight	26	57.8	32	59.3	2	50.0	60	78.9
Medium	5	11.1	2	3.7	0	–	7	9.2
Gross	0	–	0	–	0	–	2	2.6
Total	**45**		**54**		**4**		**76**	

FIGURE 11.18
Table showing enamel hypoplasia

11.5 PATHOLOGY

The pathological study of this series of skeletons was originally undertaken by Dr David Birkett. Unfortunately, since his death, it has not been possible to find his notes and the whole group has been re-evaluated by the present writer. Only a very short space of time could be allowed for this study and therefore some aspects of the study are less complete than they would normally have been. In particular, it has not been possible to record the presence or absence of each bone and joint, so prevalence of some diseases could not be calculated. Also, it was not possible to assess every rib for fractures, or every hand and foot bone for arthritic change.

Congenital anomalies

A number of congenital malformations of the skeleton were found in this group, the majority of which affected the spine.

Spina bifida occulta affected the S1 sacral segment in eight individuals, the S4–5 in two, and the complete sacrum in seven people. This made a total of 17 (8 males, 5 females and 4 children) out of 109 assessable sacra (15.6%). In one case of full spina bifida occulta, the L5 vertebra was also affected (but the arch was not detached). Some of these individuals were grouped together in the cemetery, notably Sk205, Sk107, Sk223 and Sk20 at the north-west corner of the church.

Detached neural arch (spondylolysis) was noted in six individuals, all male and all in the L5 vertebra, with a prevalence of 4.8% (6/126). No spatial groupings were found. One example (Sk325) was affected on the left side only. Another (Sk292) was unusual in that the arch had become displaced to rest against the arch of the L4 above, causing eburnation, lipping, flattening of both spinous processes, and the formation of a large exostosis on the right L5 at the point where the arch should have joined the body. This example,

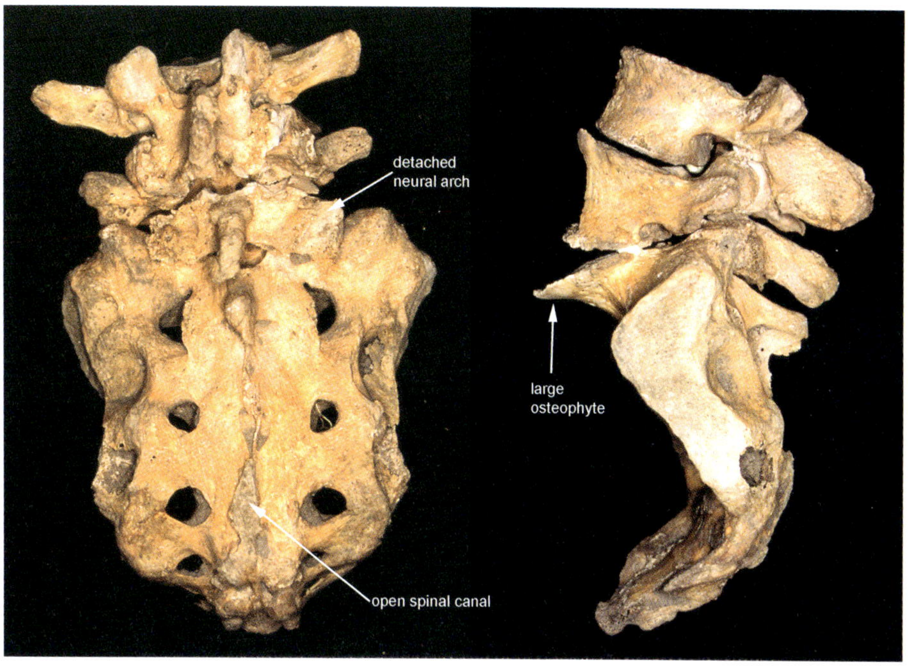

FIGURE 11.19
Posterior and side views of the L4–5 and sacrum of Sk292, showing spina bifida occulta, detached neural arch and spondylolisthesis

may also have had slight gliding of the vertebral body to the anterior (spondylolisthesis), causing large osteophytes on the left side of the L5 and the first sacral segment (Figure 11.19).

Sacralisation of the L5 vertebra was found in four individuals (3 male, 1 female), in every case affecting the left side only. Again, no spatial groupings occurred, but three of the four were buried south of the church.

Sterno-manubrial fusion had occurred in three individuals (2 male, 1 female), although one of these was affected with ankylosing spondylitis (see below) and the fusion could be a result of this disease.

Other potentially congenital anomalies included a possible epicondylar process, found on one left humerus (Sk5, male), a bifid mid-rib (anterior end, Sk210, female), and an asymmetrical cranial base (Sk240, female). See 'Miscellaneous lesions' below for other less certain anomalies.

Arthropathies and degenerative disease

Spinal osteophytosis was noted in the vertebrae of 62 out of 97 adults (63.9%), made up of 35 out of 48 males (72.9%) and 27 out of 49 females (55.1%). The thoracic region was affected to the greatest extent, with 27 men and 20 women having osteophytes in this region. In the lumbar region, 20 men and 16 women were affected, whilst in the cervical region only 5 men and 2 women had osteophytes.

Osteoarthritic change occurred in the spines of 23 out of 89 assessable adults (25.8%), 13 out of 46 being male (28.3%) and 10 out of 43 female (23.8%). The cervical vertebrae were the worst affected, with lesions occurring in the vertebral bodies of ten men and five women and facets of two men and two women. In the other areas of the spine, facets were more affected than bodies. Five women had lesions of the thoracic facets and four men and a woman were affected in the lumbar vertebral facets. Only one woman and two men had lesions of the thoracic vertebral bodies, and one male lumbar vertebral body was affected. In the majority of cases the lesions were of Grade II severity, Grade III occurring only in cervical vertebral bodies and facets, and some lumbar facets.

Figure 11.20 shows the general regions affected by osteophytosis and osteoarthritis in the rest of the skeleton. Unfortunately it was not possible to calculate prevalences due to the short time available for this study. From the raw figures, it appears that men were generally affected to a greater extent than women. Lesions occurred mostly in the hips and shoulders of men, and the pelvic area and knees of women, perhaps reflecting differences in daily tasks. In general, the results from this basic analysis suggest a similar pattern to that found at contemporary sites, with men being affected more than women, and with a sexual difference in the areas of the skeleton where lesions occurred.

Region	Osteophytosis		Osteoarthritis	
	Male	Female	Male	Female
Shoulders	6	1	6	1
Elbows	7	1	3	0
Wrists	6	2	0	0
Sacro-iliac	7	0	1	4
Pubic symphysis	0	1	0	2
Hips	14	5	5	6
Knees	5	2	0	2
Ankles	5	1	0	0

FIGURE 11.20
Regions affected by osteophytosis and osteoarthritis

Figures for spinal pathology are also comparable with other sites.

A few other degenerative pathologies were observed. Diffuse idiopathic skeletal hyperostosis was not found in this population but its spinal form, ankylosing hyperostosis, was noted in three individuals. In one female it occurred on the T11–12, a male had large lips of bone on the T9–11, and another man was affected in the L3–4. In every case it affected the right side of the spine only, and no ankylosis had occurred.

Osteoporosis had occurred in the skeletons of five women. A lesion on the skull of one male (Sk72) could be interpreted as osteoporosis of the skull, although it was not bilateral and may have been traumatic in origin. One male (Sk177) had osteoporotic leg bones, possibly as a result of immobilisation due to gross osteoarthritis of both hips (Figure 11.21).

Another man showed signs of osteoporosis, possibly also linked to lack of movement, since his spine was almost completely rigid due to ankylosing spondylitis (Figure 11.22). This case is a classic example of the disease, with fusion of the sacro-iliac joints and ankylosis of the complete thoracic and lumbar spine, including the costovertebral joints. In the lumbar vertebrae only the lateral edges of the vertebral bodies are joined, but the spinous processes have become a solid mass extending up to the T10 vertebra. The spine is kyphotic (bent forward) around the T8–9 area. The sterno-manubrial joint is also fused. This disease is an inflammatory arthritis of unknown cause, which works progressively up the spine from the pelvis, bringing increasing immobility as the joints are fused. It occurs mainly in men and usually begins at a relatively early age (around 30). This man had, however, survived into old age.

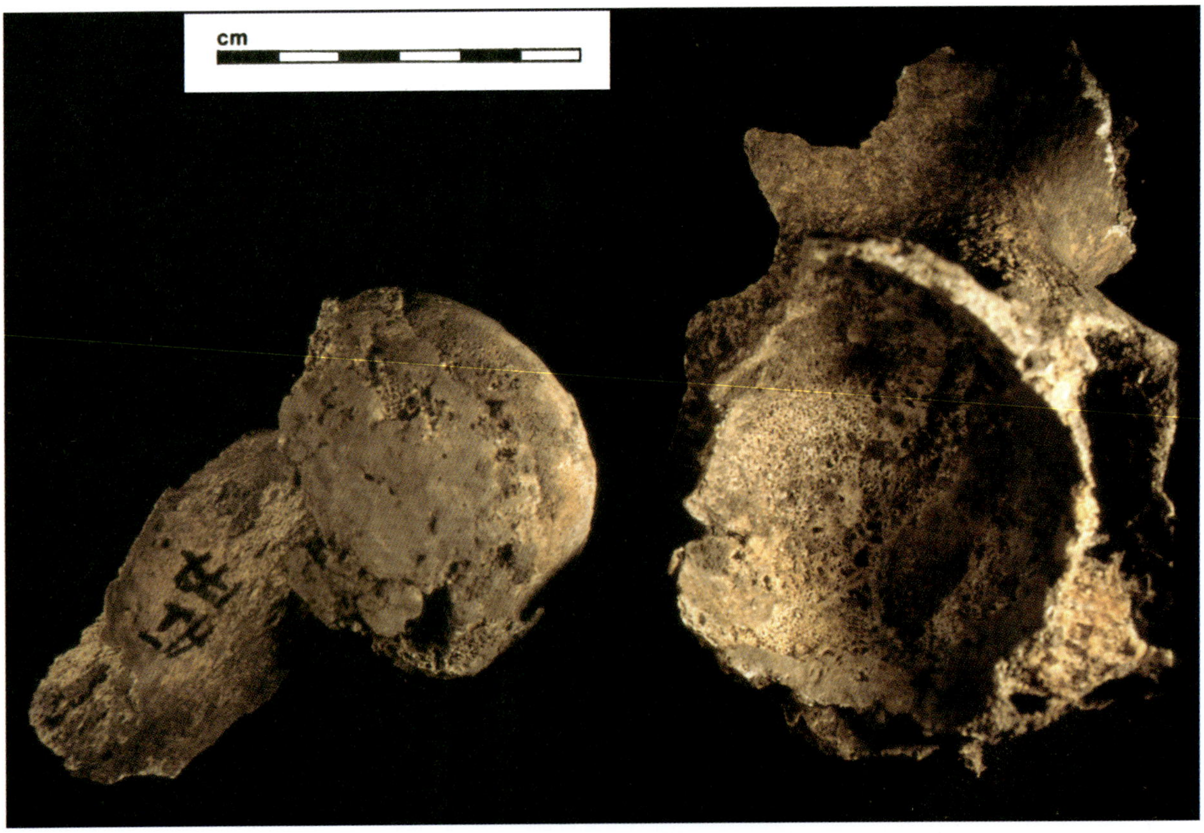

FIGURE 11.21
Osteoarthritis of the left hip joint of Sk177, showing enlargement of the acetabulum to accommodate the new bone growth around the femoral head

General spinal pathology

Schmorl's nodes are depressions in the superior and inferior surfaces of the vertebral body which are caused by rupture of the intervertebral disc. They are related to physical stress, occur almost exclusively in the thoracic and lumbar regions of the spine, and are often found in young adults. At The Hirsel, 36 out of 49 men (73.5%), 27 out of 54 women (50.0%) and one unsexed adult were affected, a total of 64 out of 104 individuals (61.0%). The mid-lower thoracic region was the most commonly involved and a number of cases were quite severe. Similar sex-related differences are found at other sites which, when coupled with the pattern of degenerative spinal disease, suggest differing roles for men and women in Anglo-Saxon and medieval society.

Other less common spinal pathologies were found. The L5 of Sk184 (female, 35–45) was wedged to the left, and the S1 was wedged to the right, so that there was no scoliosis. The L4–5 vertebrae of Sk30 (female, 35–45) were fused together at the bodies and the facets, possibly a congenital or developmental anomaly, since there was no evidence for trauma or infection. The L5 of Sk44 (female, 35–45) was ankylosed to the sacrum, with rounded bone at the anterior, but no fusion of the arches. The cause of this is unknown, but it may be related to trauma. Ankylosing hyperostosis of the T11–12 was noted in this skeleton, so the ankylosis could have occurred simply due to a degenerative change in the intervertebral disc.

Metabolic disorders

Cribra orbitalia, or pitting in the roof of the eye socket, has been associated with iron deficiency anaemia. It occurred in 4 out of 51 men (7.8%), 7 out of 61 women (11.5%), and 22 out of 66 children (33.3%) at The Hirsel (Figure 11.23). These figures are higher than those found at Jarrow and Wearmouth, but considerably lower than those from Fishergate.

The majority of lesions (15 right, 22 left) were of the mildest porotic form, with very few cribriotic (2 right, 4 left) and trabecular (1 right, 2 left) lesions. Thirteen individuals had lesions in both orbits, one had lesions only in the right and four only in the left, eleven individuals had lesions in the left orbit but were not assessable in the right, and four had lesions in the right orbit but were not assessable in the left. This may account for the apparent bias towards lesions in the left orbit.

Porotic hyperostosis, or pitting of the external cranial vault, was not found in its classic form at this site, but some cases of porotic new bone growth on the crania of children were observed. Eight out of 94 juvenile skulls (8.5%) were affected in this way, ranging from pitting over the parietals and occipital

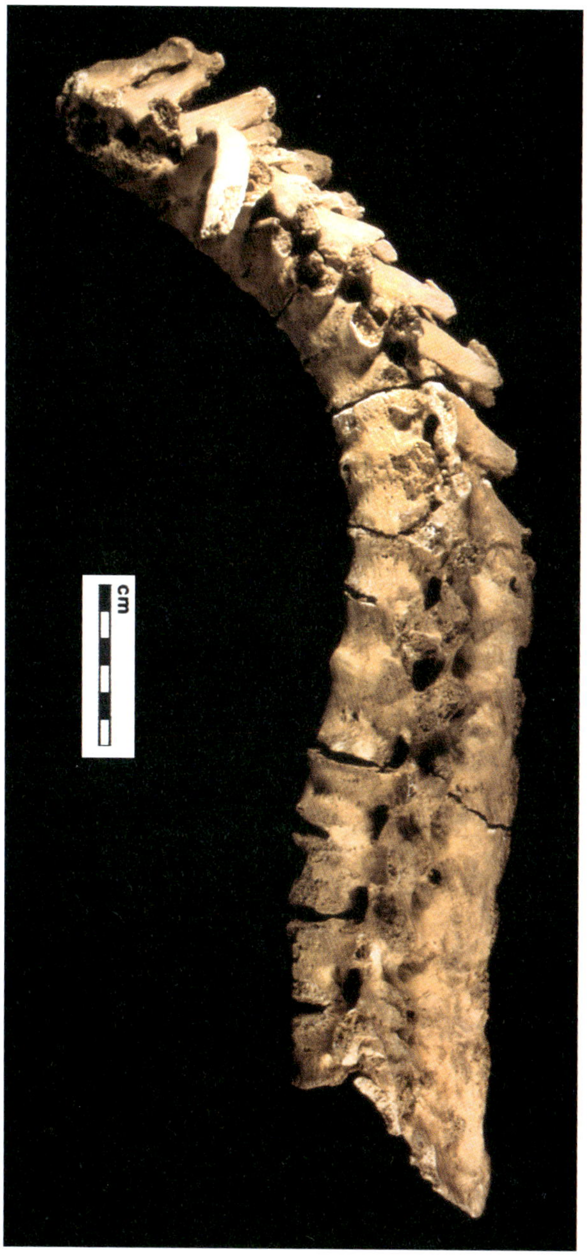

FIGURE 11.22
The spine of Sk199, showing almost complete fusion due to ankylosing spondylitis

Orbit	Male No.	Male %	Female No.	Female %	Child No.	Child %
Right	3/46	6.5	5/56	8.9	10/47	21.3
Left	4/46	8.6	4/53	7.5	20/54	37.0

FIGURE 11.23
Distribution of cribia orbitalia

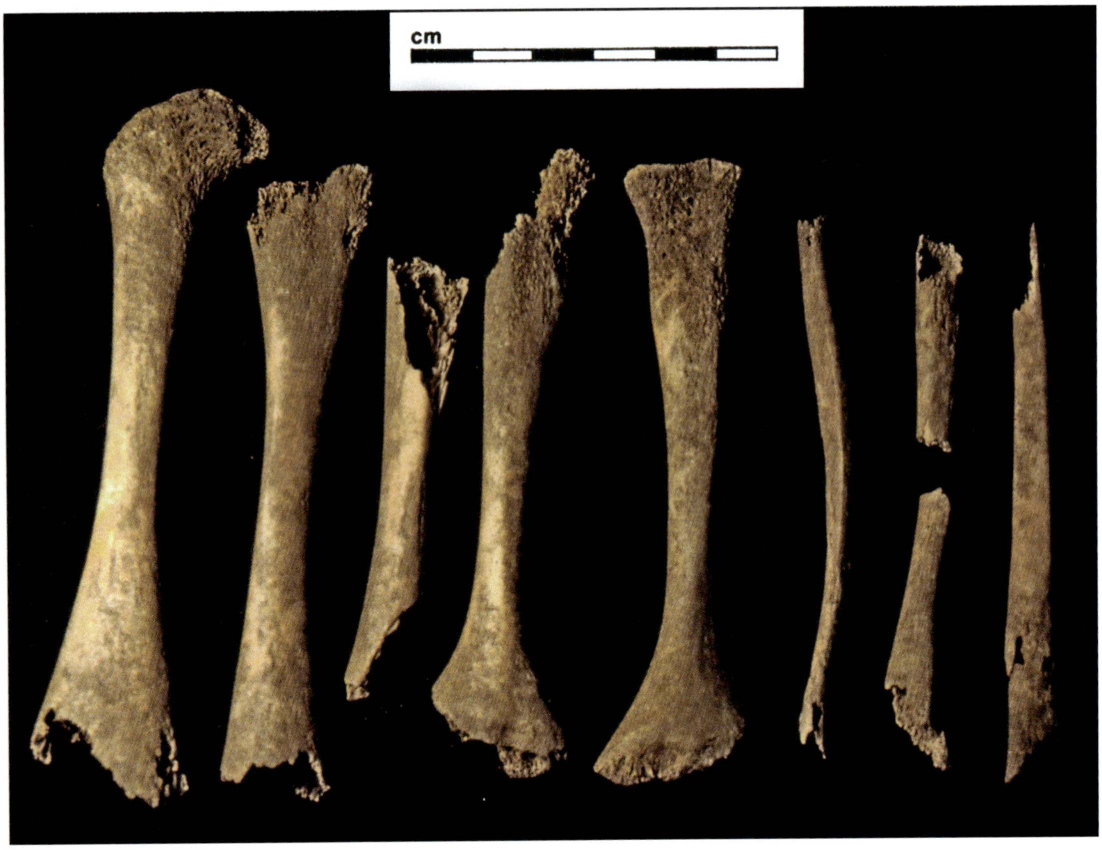

FIGURE 11.24
The surviving long bones of Sk29 (12–18 months) showing enlargement of the shafts and some bending, possibly due to rickets

to thickening and porous bone formation. In addition, pitting and 'lumpiness', sometimes with striation, was noted on a number of adult skulls, and this could be interpreted as 'healed' porotic hyperostosis (although in some cases it may be the result of an inflammatory disease of the scalp). Eleven of 54 men (20.4%), 4 of 65 women (6.2%) and 1 of seven unsexed individuals were affected.

The skeletons of 48 children showed signs of porous new bone growth over one or more bones. In most cases this could be attributed to normal growth, but in some the distal femora appeared flared and there was slight bending of the tibiae or widening of the shaft of the bone. In at least 17 of these children the changes were felt to be more than just the normal process of bone growth, although the majority of these could not be attributed to any particular disease. The following individuals seemed to have the greatest evidence for pathological change:

— Sk9: 12–18 months. All bones showed some degree of porosity, but the tibiae and femora were worst affected. The tibiae had porous new bone growth along shafts, especially laterally. The distal halves of both femora were enlarged and curved anteriorly with porous new bone and flaring.

— Sk18: *c*12 months. The right tibia appeared to be slightly enlarged on the medial surface at the distal end and there were slight periosteal deposits on the posterior surface of the shaft. Bilateral flaring of both distal femora. Small spurs of bone had formed in the proximal quarter of both humeri.

— Sk29: 12–18 months. All the bones had enlarged medullary cavities, especially the proximal end of the left femur, proximal and distal ends of both tibiae, and proximal ends of both humeri (Figure 11.24). The left femur appeared bowed anteriorly just distal to the head. The large spaces in the cancellous bone suggested fast growth or resorption of bone. The anterior of some ribs were also abnormally thickened. Skull unfortunately not available.

— Sk119: Newborn–3 months. All the long bones were thickened and roughened along the shafts, suggesting periostitis caused by an infection (although the changes could be due to erosion). A thin layer of fibre bone had formed in both orbits, but the rest of the skull did not appear to be affected.

— Sk133: *c*18 months. Very slight pitting of both orbits, and the skull appeared thickened and striated especially on parietals. Both tibiae were bent in the proximal halves to the lateral with fibrous

FIGURE 11.25
The long bones of Sk211 (18–24 months) showing new bone growth periosteally and widening of the ends, possibly due to scurvy or another deficiency disease

new bone in layers on the lateral side. The distal ends of both radii appeared flared. A fragment of distal femur showed slight pitting and striation and may also have been flared. There may also have been new bone growth in layers on the ectocranial surface of the skull.

— Sk211: 18–24 months. All the bones (except the right radius) were diseased (Figure 11.25). There was new woven bone growth on the surface of the shafts and widening of the metaphyses. The enamel on the upper right deciduous canine was not properly formed, and the unerupted adult incisors were slightly deformed. Porotic cribra of the left orbit. There was growth of porous new bone and fibre bone ecto- and endocranially, and some fragments of skull appeared thickened in the inner and outer tables.

— Sk229: *c*30 months. The posterior shafts of both femora were thickened, and the anterior of both humeri were also affected. There appeared to be some periosteal graining and thickening of cortical bone. The tibiae were also affected.

— Sk235: *c*2–3 years. Both femora were in poor condition, but showed thickening of the cortex or 'bone within bone' appearance, with some bowing. The skull was thickened between the plates. There was no cribra orbitalia. The ribs and fragments of other long bones were also affected, with graining of the periosteum.

Some of these changes are consistent with iron deficiency anaemia, rickets (particularly Sk9 and Sk29) and possibly scurvy (Sk211?). Some may simply be due to an infection, or possibly even normal growth. Given the high infant and young child mortality at this site, however, it is not unreasonable to suggest that poor nutrition was one of the major factors involved in many of these premature deaths. Unfortunately the evidence from the bone is difficult to interpret.

Circulatory disturbances

Osteochondritis dissecans is generally the most common form of circulatory disturbance found in archaeological populations. The disease involves the joints, is associated with physical stress particularly in young males, and takes the form of a small pitted erosion. It may heal spontaneously, or the piece of bone which has been lost may remain in the joint space and cause great pain. The most common area of occurrence is in the knee joint (femoral condyles) but no example of this was found at The Hirsel. The majority of lesions in this group occurred in the ankle joints. Four individuals (2 male, 2 female) had lesions in the talo-calcaneal joints, two males had pits in the talo-tibial joints, and one male left navicular facet for the talus was affected. The proximal articulations of one male proximal hallucial phalanx and one male first metatarsal were also affected, although these lesions are not considered to be true osteochondritis. The only other lesions were found in the scapular glenoids of three individuals (2 female, 1 male), although these pits are more likely to be developmental defects.

Anterior epiphyseal dysplasia occurred in five individuals. Three males were affected in thoracic vertebrae (Sk87, T11–12; Sk108, T9; Sk325, T6–7, T9, and T11), and two females in lumbar vertebrae (Sk174, L4; Sk190, L1). In all cases these erosive lesions were in the superior margin of the vertebra, except those of Sk325 in which the T11 was affected both superiorly and inferiorly and the other three vertebrae had lesions of the inferior borders.

Infectious diseases

Periostitis is the most frequently occurring inflammatory response in most archaeological groups. Its cause is generally unknown, but it is usually recorded as a non-specific infection. At The Hirsel, 15 males, 7 females and 2 children showed evidence for periostitis of the lower legs. In the adults, this varied from minor pitting and graining of the outer layers of bone to thickening and a lumpy appearance. None of these cases could be described as 'gross'. The two children had very thick layers of porous new bone growth on the tibiae, which may have been due to an infection. One of the children (Sk151) had very curved tibiae, but the interosseous lines were straight so the cause was not rickets. In one male and one child the lesions were also present on the lower parts of the femora.

Three individuals had lesions which could be interpreted as osteomyelitis. A child aged 6–7 years (Sk156) had an enlarged proximal right tibia with a large ?cloaca medially and porous new bone growth on the proximal half of the shaft. Unfortunately the area was broken and the distal femur was missing, so the diagnosis remains uncertain.

Another child (Sk310) aged around 8 years had very thick deposits of porous new bone growth in layers on the shaft of the left humerus, the lateral left clavicle, and rounded deposits of new bone on the thickened scapula (Figure 11.26). Unfortunately the humerus was in very poor condition, so the cause of these inflammatory changes could not be identified. An infection such as osteitis or osteomyelitis seems likely, however. Other porous new bone, particularly on the leg bones, could be related but may be the result of normal bone growth.

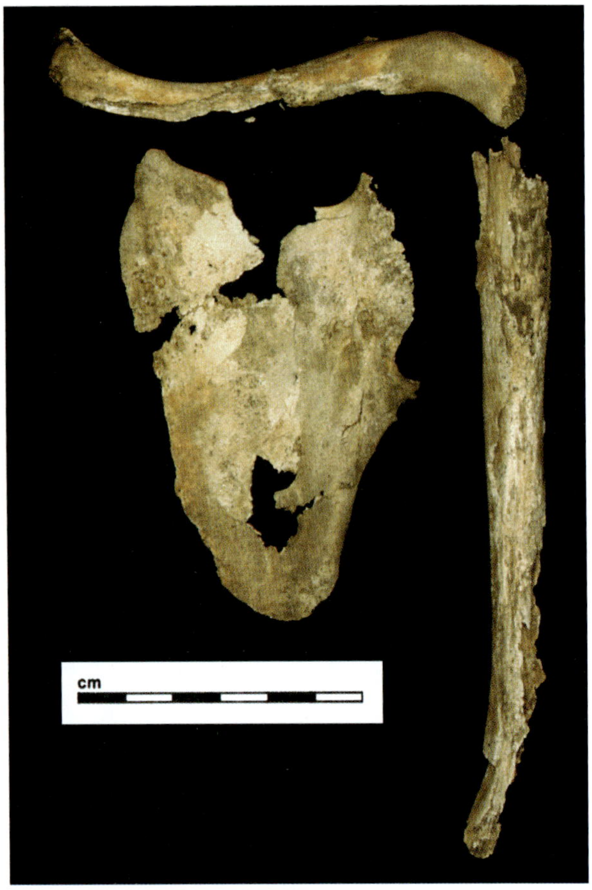

FIGURE 11.26
New bone formation on the left shoulder and humerus of Sk310 (c8 years), possibly due to osteomyelitis

An old man (Sk198) had slight flattening and ?destruction of the left humerus head with a possible cloaca behind a U-shaped depression in the superior edge of the joint. Again, the bone was in very poor condition, but the appearance of the fragment suggests possible trauma followed by an infection.

A possible case of tuberculosis was identified in the fragmentary remains of one adult female (Sk281). A destructive process affected the T7–11 vertebrae. The T7 had large sequestra especially on the left side tunnelling into the centre of the body (Figure 11.27). The T8 body had a slightly lumpy appearance with pock-marks which would presumably have developed into sequestra. Only the upper part of the body of T9 survived but there is evidence of a large sequestrum. The body of the T10 was completely lost, but evidence from the arch suggested that this may have occurred in vivo. The upper zygapophyseal facets were partially fused to the T9 lower facets at an angle which suggested collapse of the T10 body and probable fusion with the T9. The left area of attachment of the arch to the body showed no signs of post-mortem breakage, only reactive pitting and bone

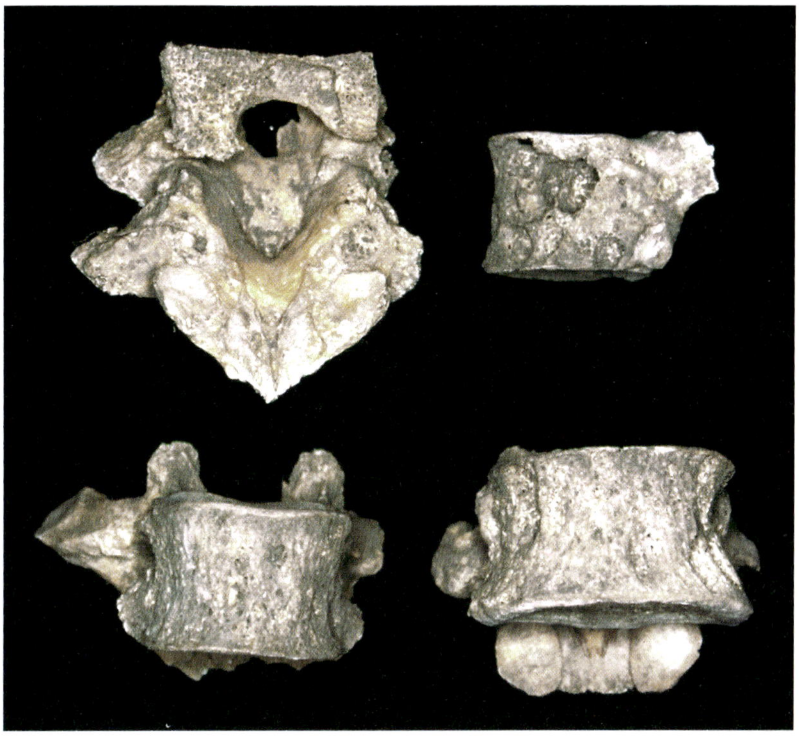

FIGURE 11.27
Four thoracic vertebrae of Sk281 showing sequestra probably caused by tuberculosis

growth, suggesting that it was resorbed in life. The T11 was similar to, but more involved than, the T8, with at least three pock-marks on the left, one on the anterior and one on the right. There was a probable kyphosis (gibbus) on the T10. The most likely cause for these lesions is tuberculosis, although osteomyelitis or actinomycosis cannot be entirely ruled out.

Very few skeletons were assessable for maxillary sinusitis, because when the sinus area was present it was either still attached to the skull or full of soil. In many burials it had been lost completely. Evidence for the condition was found in two men, seven women and three children, and consisted of thickening, pitting and new woven bone formation. In one male it was probably related to the draining of an abscess. The other cases, particularly the women and children, may be related to dust and smoke inhalation which would be common in the typical medieval house.

A few other individuals had lesions which may be the result of infections. A middle-aged female (Sk240) had an enlarged incisive foramen of the palate (the individual also had a crush fracture of the T7–8 vertebrae, although this was not felt to be the result of an infection). A child (Sk256) aged around 12–13 had very slight pitting on the right nasal floor. A number of individuals were found to have pitting of the palate, but generally it was related to the presence of an abscess and where this was not the case the cause may well have been gingivitis. One of these was an old man (Sk329) who also had signs of inflammation on the bodies of his T11–L2 vertebrae, particularly around the Schmorl's nodes. This may have been caused by osteoarthritis, but it did not have the usual appearance of this disease. The presence of lumpy reactive bone growth may suggest an infection, although probably not tuberculosis.

Trauma

The most common form of traumatic injury was the presence of one or more exostoses, found in the bones of nine men and eight women. The majority of these occurred in the legs or feet and were related to torn muscles, tendons and ligaments. One of the most common areas was the ankle, reflecting the probability that sprained ankles were a common occurrence. Tendons and muscles connected with the knee area were also affected in a number of individuals. Injuries of this type were probably the result of walking over rough or slippery ground in poor footwear.

Fractures were found in the bones of 18 individuals. The majority of these were stress fractures of the ankle bones, particularly the posterior edge of the talus. A number of individuals

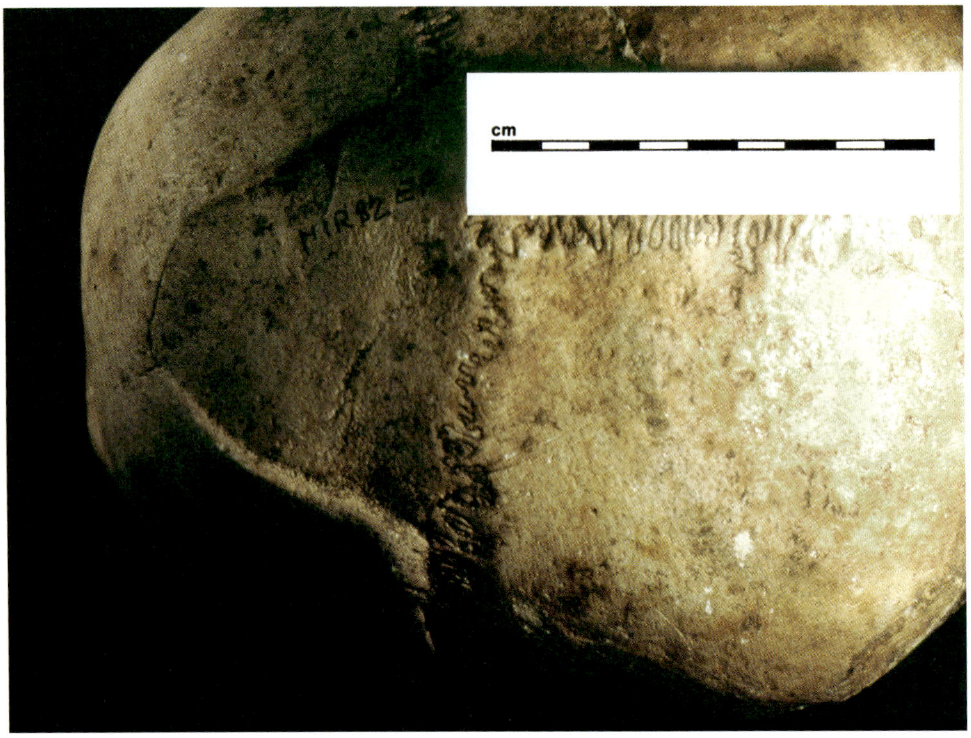

FIGURE 11.28
The frontal bone of Sk192, showing a healed cut across the glabella

in this group had a small lip of bone at the back of the large inferior facet of the talus, presumably a normal variation. In four women this area was fractured either partially or completely, and in one of these individuals both tali had semi-circular lesions reminiscent of aseptic necrosis in the affected area. One man (Sk84) showed signs of pressure or trauma on the superior edges of the calcaneal facets for the cuboids, with reactive growth and destruction and a possible fracture line on the left. Similar changes were seen in the feet of another man (Sk301) at the tarsal–metatarsal joints. The right foot was worst affected, with gross new bone formation and pitting of the joints, especially the MT2-cuneiform joint. There was eburnation of the proximal MT4, and a possible fracture line ran diagonally across the proximal facets of MT3–4. In the left foot the MT3-cuneiform joint had osteophytic growth, eburnation of the facets and some destruction of the cuneiform facet. A stress fracture line was also observed in the lateral-superior part of the right patella facet of a male (Sk288), and another was seen at the point of fusion of the ilium and pubis in the right acetabulum of Sk265, extending some 2cm into the socket. All these injuries could have a similar cause to the exostoses mentioned above, although the damaged foot bones seen in one man may have been the result of crushing by a heavy object or trampling by a horse.

Other more conventional fractures were found in the forearms of two men (right and left radius) and two women (right ulnae). All were well healed with little callus, and only one right radius was distorted. Such injuries can be the result of direct violence, where the arm is held up to defend the head, but they can equally be the result of an accident.

Two males had fractured ribs. Sk306 had breaks in at least five right ribs (?5th–9th) in the lateral posterior area, all well healed with angular callus and some misalignment. Two left ribs (?8th–9th) were affected in Sk303, both well healed with rounded callus. This individual also had gross arthritic change to the left elbow joint (radius and ulna) which may have been secondary to trauma, possibly in the left humerus which was not present.

Evidence for head wounds was found in five male skulls. A slight depressed fracture of the skull was present on the central part of the left parietal of Sk265, extending around 20 by 7mm. Sk153 had a circular area of pitted new bone, 35mm in diameter, on the superior part of the frontal which was suggestive of inflammation following trauma.

The largest head wound was sustained by Sk192, and consisted of a depression on the frontal bone with straight edges on three sides (Figure 11.28). It was 69mm wide along the coronal suture, narrowing to 24mm wide in mid-frontal. A split or cut ran down the left side of the skull just posterior to the coronal suture, and showed evidence of healing. This individual also had two ankylosed cervical vertebral bodies (C6–7) and a detached neural arch of the fifth lumbar vertebra. These lesions could be

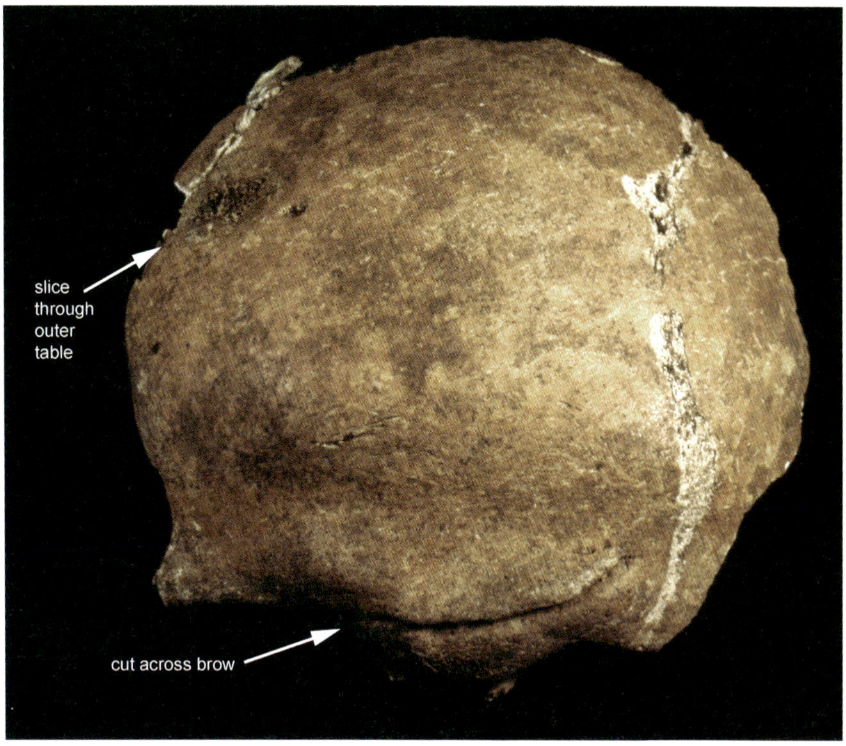

FIGURE 11.29
The skull of Sk1, showing a healed cut across the brow ridges and an unhealed slice

congenital, but they are also consistent with trauma and may have occurred at the same time as the skull fracture. The fracture was healed but had left an indentation on the top of the head. It may have been the result of direct violence, but could equally have been due to an accidental blow from a heavy object.

Sk1 had a well healed cut on the frontal area of the skull running transversely above the root of the nose and left orbit (Figure 11.29). The deep part of the cut seemed to communicate with the frontal sinus. This would seem to be an old sword cut which did not penetrate through to the inner table of the skull and so was unlikely to have caused permanent damage, apart from the danger of osteomyelitis complicating frontal sinusitis during upper respiratory infection. In addition, there was a cut diagonally across the skull at the back of the crown of the head travelling down to the left. The cut had a sharp edge at the top but was broken off at the margins. It appeared fresh and suggested a sword cut sustained at the time of death, although it did not affect the inner table of the skull and was therefore unlikely to be fatal unless the force of the blow induced internal bleeding. This blow would probably have been struck from behind and to the left with the man upright or possibly delivered when lying prone on the ground having been felled from a previous blow. The impression given by these wounds is that they were not sustained with the full force of the sword and may have occurred while wearing some form of protective headgear, such as a leather helmet. This skeleton also had a circular erosive lesion 20mm across on the right parietal. There was no reaction around it and it may be a wound received near or at the time of death, possibly a glancing blow by a sharp blade. Once more it only involved the superficial part of the skull (notes by Dr D A Birkett).

The fifth skull wound was unfortunately not available for study as it had been removed from the collection at some point. It consisted of a healed lesion on the frontal bone with a circular area of new bone covering a visible cut (Sk323).

A crush fracture of two thoracic vertebrae (T7–8) with subsequent ankylosis of the bodies and spines of four vertebrae (T6–9) and kyphosis was found in the spine of an adult female (Sk240; Figure 11.30). There was no evidence for an infection in the bones, and lesions found in the lower zygapophyseal facets of other vertebrae suggested that there was a downward force acting on the whole spine.

Other possible trauma was seen in the left humerus head of Sk198 (mentioned above in connection with an infection), and in a disarticulated distal femur from Sk46 which appeared to have been crushed laterally causing one condyle to be forced down in relation to the other.

One example of a dislocation was found in an adult male (Sk97). The right hip socket was greatly reduced in size and was triangular in shape with rounded thick new bone forming the borders

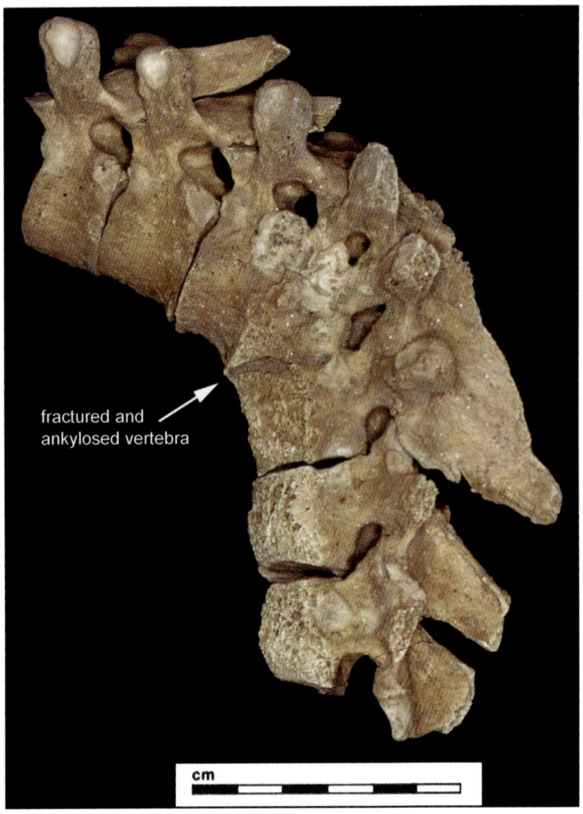

FIGURE 11.30
Ankylosis of the thoracic spine with kyphosis in Sk240, probably the result of trauma

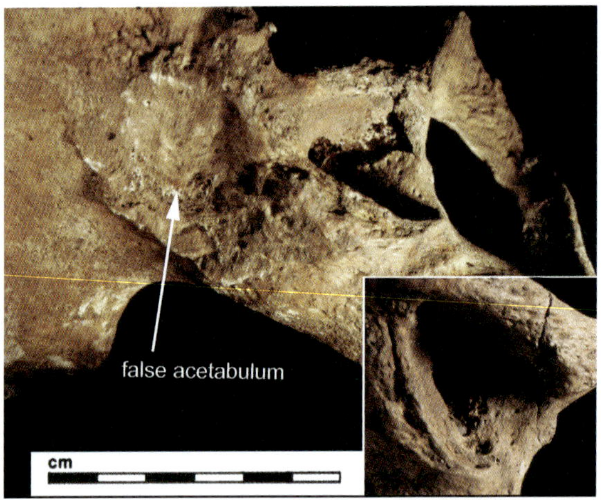

FIGURE 11.31
Partially closed acetabulum of Sk97 (inset), with false acetabulum on the rear of the ilium, due to unreduced hip dislocation

(Figure 11.31). A false acetabulum had formed on the lower part of the ilium and there were large lips of new bone either side of this. Unfortunately the femur was not available for study, but the right tibia and fibula were noticeably less robust than those on the left, perhaps indicating that there was wasting of the right leg due to lack of use.

Neoplasms

Osteomata occurred on the skulls of three females and two males. These benign tumours take the form of bony warts and are most commonly found on the frontal and parietal regions of the cranial vault. All were small, the largest example being 9mm in diameter, and three individuals were affected on the frontal bone, two on the left parietal.

The proximal tibia is a common site for another benign neoplasm, the osteochondroma. This small exostosis forms before the epiphysis unites with the main part of the bone in the late teens. Examples were found on the proximal left tibiae of three males and the proximal right tibia of one female. The latter took the unusual form of a button-shaped growth. The largest example (15mm long) was seen in the area of the proximal tibio-fibular joint of a male aged 35–45 (Sk222), and a depression had formed in the head of the fibula to accommodate it. However this example at least may be a normal variant known as a 'tug' lesion (metaphyseal fibrous defect).

One other possible tumour was found on the medial surface of the left femur of an adult female (Sk194) at the distal third of shaft, and measured 43mm long by 11mm wide. It was probably a form of benign osteoma.

Miscellaneous lesions

A number of lesions do not fit easily into the categories discussed above.

An elderly woman (Sk64) showed bilateral coxa vara (the femoral heads were lower than the greater trochanters). This may be congenital, or can be the result of abnormal strain in diseases such as rickets or osteoporosis. In this case, as the anomaly is bilateral and was probably the cause of Grade II osteoarthritis of the lower part of the acetabulum, it is likely that the condition was congenital.

Evidence for genu valgum (knock-knee) was found in at least two individuals. Again this may be congenital or a strain-induced deformity in rickets and osteoporosis. A female (Sk147) showed proximal bending of both tibiae to the lateral and a very small patch of eburnation had formed on the left lateral tibial and femoral condyles. However the main change which had occurred as a result of this was in the ankle joints. Both tali were slightly rotated towards the medial and had flatter medial facets than normal, the left being more affected than the right. Presumably the changes occurred whilst the bones were still forming. This compensation in the ankle may have caused a degree of flat-footedness. Pitting in both ankle joints suggested inflammation of the synovium/joint capsule, and may well have developed into osteoarthritis later in life. The thickened patches of bone on the inferior parts of both femoral heads and the lipping of both acetabuli at the inferior part may also be related to a slightly abnormal gait. A male (Sk153) showed similar changes, although only the right leg was available for study. Both also had grained tibia shafts. Bilateral proximal bending of the tibiae was observed in at least five other individuals at this site (three males, one female, one child), but none showed the other changes noted above. The cause of this is unknown. It may be due to rickets, but with so many cases a congenital origin cannot be ruled out.

One other skeleton (Sk176, sub-adult male) showed bilateral curvature of the tibiae, but in this case the bending appeared to have occurred in the distal part of the shaft. This would probably also result in an abnormal gait, flat-footedness and genu valgum.

An adult male (Sk76) had generally very well muscled, large and robust bones, some with exostoses (particularly in the lower legs). The humeri had very large insertions for the pectoralis major and latissimus dorsi muscles, so presumably the upper arms were heavily muscled. However, both humeri are disproportionately short in relation to the femora. In comparison with another male (Sk104) with the same femoral length, the right humerus of Sk76 is 30mm shorter and the right radius 17mm shorter. The cause of this is unknown, but it may be related to muscular development.

A disease which commonly affects middle-aged (post-menopausal) women was seen in Sk243 (female, 35–45+). This was a thickening of the internal surface of the frontal bone, a condition known as hyperostosis frontalis interna.

The left acetabulum of an adult male (Sk265) was lipped on the dorsal part of the rim, and there was a large roughened area (36 by 16mm) superior to the socket at the insertion of the rectus femoris. This may represent a partial dislocation or other trauma, particularly as a stress fracture was noted in the right acetabulum, but could also be the result of an infection.

The left sacro-iliac joint of an old man (Sk271) was probably ankylosed, although the joint was in poor condition and the sacrum was not present. The right sacro-iliac joint was too poor for assessment. There was certainly no fusion of the vertebrae, so this is probably not the result of ankylosing spondylitis. The most likely cause would seem to be trauma, or possibly proliferation of bone in old age.

An anomaly at the head of the left second metacarpal of another old male (Sk84) took the form of an extra spur of rounded bone on the dorso-lateral side. This could be a congenital anomaly, perhaps related to polydactyly (extra fingers).

A small oval hole (8 by 6mm) in the centre of the left temporal of an 18-month old child (Sk118) had rounded edges and may have been present in life. Presumably this was simply a developmental defect or congenital anomaly.

A number of children were aged differently from their teeth and long bone sizes, but in two individuals this difference was pronounced. The teeth of Sk140 suggested an age of 10–11 years, but the bone lengths suggested only 7–9 years. The third molars of Sk277 were almost completely erupted, but the long bone lengths and stage of epiphyseal fusion suggested an age of around 14 years. There was no possibility of either skeleton being mixed with another individual. The discrepancies may be the result of poor nutrition, but in the case of Sk277 there may be some other reason. The skull has some of the characteristics of the 'mongoloid' skull described by Brothwell (1960), specifically that it is large and round, flat at front and back, and has the largest cranial index (88.8) of any skull in this group. However, such a diagnosis is far from certain on such tentative evidence.

Two males (Sk104 and Sk108) had an anomaly of the scapula known as Os acromiale, in which the acromial epiphysis remains unfused. In both cases it occurred only in the right shoulder, and lipping or arthritic change was present on the new joint. One (Sk108) had osteophytosis of the right shoulder joint. This developmental defect was found to occur frequently in the skeletons from the *Mary Rose*, and Stirland (1986) has suggested an occupational cause, such as persistent use of the longbow. Other occupations requiring similar actions of the right shoulder could potentially have the same effect.

One other fairly common anomaly, which today is found in about 20% of the adult population (Cotta 1980), was found in an adult male (Sk292). This was a calcaneal spur of the left calcaneus and was caused by the pull of the foot muscles, in particular those related to the flattening of the longitudinal arch. It is unlikely to have caused any pain.

Two skeletons had ankylosed bones which were not available for study by the present writer. These were the left tibia and fibula of an adult male (Sk219) and the pubic symphyses of another male (Sk321). Such ankylosis could be the result of an infection, but was most likely caused by trauma.

11.6 SUMMARY AND DISCUSSION

The 331 individuals buried at The Hirsel presumably represent a large proportion of the original number of burials at the site. As such, they are an important group in the archaeology of the Scottish Borders, where few comparable cemeteries have been excavated to date.

The 325 burials which were submitted for analysis were thought to represent a minimum of 331 individuals. These consisted of 181 adults (68 males, 17 ?males, 65 females, 23 ?females and 8 unsexed) and 150 children. The disarticulated remains contained at least 13 extra children, and probably also increased the number of adults, although many of the small fragments could well have belonged to articulated burials.

The proportion of adults to children at this site is very high in comparison with others. The large numbers of infants and young children are also unusual. There may be a bias due to the area excavated since many of the children were clustered around the church building, but this cannot be the only factor involved. The possibility of infections and deficiency disorders has been discussed, and this may be the cause of the apparent high infant mortality in this population. Whether the deaths were spread evenly over the whole period of use of the churchyard or whether they represent a few bad years is impossible to tell.

The male to female ratio of almost 1:1 suggests that this group represents a normal population. However, juvenile skeletons cannot be included in this ratio and adult sexing was sometimes difficult, so conclusions based on percentages of the sexes at the site can only be tentative.

In terms of distribution of age at death in both adults and children, The Hirsel was found to be more comparable with Anglo-Saxon groups than medieval, possibly reflecting its rural location and relatively low status. Other factors, however, such as the greater disturbance of urban medieval churchyards, must also be considered.

Metrical and morphological analysis suggested that the people of The Hirsel were generally slightly shorter and more gracile than their contemporaries further south, and this was the impression given from a visual inspection of their long bones. Their cranial indices placed them squarely in the medieval period, and their broad low heads fit well into the pattern emerging across Europe at this time. Obviously there were exceptions, with some individuals having narrow heads or robust or stocky bones, but the majority were of a similar physical type. Analysis by phase was not practical owing to the reduced sample size.

The study of non-metric traits in this group has allowed for the identification of four potential family groups, in areas to the north, south-west, central south, and south-east of the church. Only one of these could be anything more than a vague possibility, namely the presence of two metopic individuals buried side-by-side close to the south wall of the church. In general terms, there was nothing particularly unusual in the frequencies of non-metric traits in this group, and there was no real difference between males and females.

Dental disease was found to be related to sex, age and area of the dentition. Generally, older individuals were the worst affected, and the molars were the most commonly involved teeth. As there were more old men than old women at this site, it is perhaps not surprising that dental disease was slightly greater in men than in women. Ante-mortem loss and abscesses occurred at a similar rate to other contemporary groups, but caries was found in fewer individuals at The Hirsel, possibly reflecting a low status rural economy with little access to cariogenic foodstuffs. Unerupted teeth were significantly more common in women than men, but overall rates were comparable with other sites. Tartar was found to occur at similar frequencies in the medieval groups, and enamel hypoplasia affected children more than adults in all groups.

A number of congenital anomalies was found in this group, the majority of which affected the spine. Spina bifida occulta was particularly common, and spatial analysis of the trait suggested some possible family groupings. Other congenital anomalies did not produce spatial groups.

Degenerative disease was found most commonly in the spine, as is normal in most archaeological populations. Osteophytes (and Schmorl's nodes) were more common in the lower spine, whilst arthritis was most frequent in the neck. It was not possible to work out prevalences, but from the raw data there was an apparent sexual difference in the areas of the skeleton affected by osteoarthritis and other stress-related diseases. Similar patterns have been noted at other sites, in particular the frequencies of degenerative disease in the knees of women and the shoulders of men. These findings suggest differences in the use of joints by men and women, and could reflect occupational stress.

The most interesting arthropathy in this group was a classic example of ankylosing spondylitis which affected the pelvis, spine, and rib cage of an old man.

Diseases which have an accepted correlation with iron deficiency anaemia were not particularly common in this group in comparison with urban populations from York, although they were more prevalent at The Hirsel than at the two north-eastern monastic sites. However, changes in some juvenile skeletons suggested the presence of metabolic disorders such as rickets and possibly scurvy in this population, and the high infant mortality could be a result of poor nutrition generally (even if infections were the actual cause of death in many cases). Although work has been done on anaemia and its effect on the skeleton, the information available on other nutritional disorders is sparse. It is particularly difficult to be certain of 'normality' in a juvenile skeleton, because the very fact that the child has died suggests that something abnormal has occurred. Certainly in comparison with other groups studied by the present writer, the juvenile skeletons of The Hirsel exhibit a high degree of porous new bone growth, which may or may not be 'normal' in this group.

Unlike other contemporary groups, periostitis was not common at The Hirsel. As the condition is non-specific and its aetiology is generally unknown, the reasons for this difference are difficult to speculate upon. Some cases of possible osteomyelitis were found, particularly in the shoulder of one child and the knee of another. In both cases the bones were in poor condition.

Only one specific infection was observed, this being a tuberculous spine in the skeleton of a woman. Unfortunately the most diagnostic part had been damaged post-mortem, but the remaining vertebrae showed lesions consistent with the suggested diagnosis.

Physical trauma was widespread in this group, although for the most part the lesions were not very serious. A number of people had torn ligaments/tendons or damaged bones in the knee, foot or ankle regions, which is consistent with poor footwear and walking on rough ground. Aseptic necroses were also common in the ankle.

Four people had 'parry' fractures of one of the forearm bones and two men had fractured ribs. Head wounds were found in five male skulls, of which at least two were probably inflicted by weapons. A crush fracture in the spine of a woman was probably not the result of an infection, and could have been caused by a fall. A unilateral hip dislocation in one man probably resulted in the wasting of the right leg due to lack of use.

Benign neoplasms occurred in a number of skeletons, and were either osteomata on the skull, or osteochondromata on the tibiae, apart from one unidentified neoplasm (?osteoma) on the femoral shaft of a woman.

Miscellaneous lesions included abnormal gaits due to coxa vara and genu valgum, one case of hyperostosis frontalis interna, and evidence for possible occupational stress in two men with Os acromiale.

The evidence from these skeletons can be used to paint a picture of the daily life of some of the medieval people of The Hirsel. Assuming that the burials are spread evenly through time, the general pattern suggests a low life expectancy in comparison with contemporary urban and monastic groups, a high probability of death in childhood, and a fairly hard life for those who survived into adulthood. Nutrition may have been relatively poor for the period, although a lack of carbohydrates probably prevented tooth decay for the majority of people. Infections and cancers of the bone were not common, but this may in fact suggest a less healthy population in which people died before the lesions spread to the skeleton. Tuberculosis was present, but there was no evidence for other serious illnesses such as leprosy or syphilis. Patterns of physical stress are consistent with a rural community making its living from the land, with their fair share of accidents and some degree of violence. Some of the men may have been soldiers, and their survival of some large head wounds perhaps suggests the use of helmets. Evidence from two skeletons suggests the possibility that they were employed as bowmen. The presence of a scallop shell in one grave has been interpreted as the burial of a pilgrim, but the skeleton itself is unremarkable and average in physique. Some diseases found in this group were probably crippling, notably the two women with bent backs from tuberculosis and vertebral crush fracture, a man with grossly arthritic hips, and another man with one dislocated and virtually useless hip. In these cases there must have been some degree of care to enable the individuals to continue living.

Although post-mortem changes in the soil, graveyard disturbance and degree of bias in the excavation are all factors which have to be taken into consideration, the major differences between the people of The Hirsel and those of Jarrow, Wearmouth and York can largely be related to differences in status, life-style, physical appearance and resistance to osseous diseases.

12
STRUCTURAL MATERIALS

12.1 STRUCTURAL AND ARCHITECTURAL STONE

Richard Fawcett and Rosemary Cramp

The comprehensive robbing and destruction of the church, which followed a partial destruction and reuse of the building, meant that no architectural details were found *in situ* and those which survived in secondary positions were usually broken into small fragments. In the catalogue, the individual entries are initialled according to author.

Assuming that all of the worked architectural stones found during excavation at The Hirsel originated at the church rather than at an adjacent residence of the church's patron, they suggest that the church in its final state was a building of modestly high architectural quality. It must be stressed that the stones are too few and too fragmentary for certainty, but a number of them point to the possibility of a phase of activity around the later years of the 12th century that resulted in a building with decorative emphasis on a number of architectural features. The evidence would be consistent with a view that, as was most usual, those emphasised features included the principal doorway into the church, possibly the chancel arch, and a window. (RF)

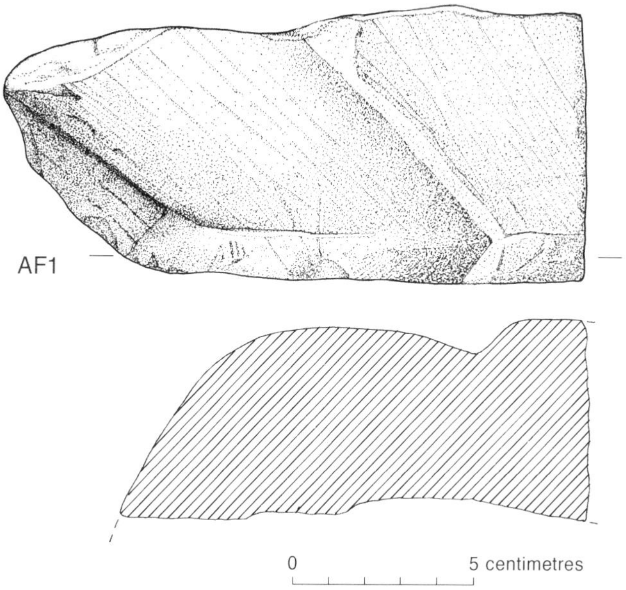

FIGURE 12.1
Chevron fragment, AF1

AF1 (Figure 12.1)
A fragment of chevron-decorated stone probably from an arch. Fine micaceous sandstone.
It is unweathered, with fine diagonal tooling and the setting out lines are still visible. Two dressed faces, the others broken. What survives is part of the blocked corner and the springing roll. This piece is the only evidence surviving at The Hirsel for the presence of a decorated opening with basic chevron ornament.

Chevron decoration became common in Scotland from around the 1120s, at the time of the revival of the Church under Alexander I and David I, when there was a more widespread introduction of architectural ideas from south of the Border. In earlier examples, such as the nave doorways at Dunfermline Abbey (Fife) and the south nave doorway at Holyrood Abbey (Edinburgh), both of which were started in about 1128, the chevron is generally of relatively shallow depth, and consists of sequences of multiple nested V-shapes wrapped around arch orders in which a sub-square profile clearly remains in evidence. At a later date, probably around the third quarter of the 12th century, the lines of chevron tend to become more individually defined, being expressed as three-quarter roll mouldings, either carved singly, as in the south doorway at Chirnside church (Berwickshire) (Figure 12.2), and in the chancel arch of Gullane church (East Lothian), or in complex interlocking patterns, as in the south-west nave doorway of Jedburgh Abbey (Roxburghshire) or the re-set doorway of Lamington church (Lanarkshire). The fragment from The Hirsel is too small to permit firm conclusions, though on balance the high relief of the chevron, and the way it is set at the junction of two parallel planes, suggests that it is of the later type, and that it therefore dates from around the third quarter of the 12th century.

The most common location for such decoration is on the arches, and to a lesser extent the jambs, of doorways and chancel arches; but in the most richly decorated churches it might also be applied to other elements, including windows, as at Dalmeny (West Lothian). In a church of the scale of The Hirsel it is perhaps most likely to be from the principal entrance. Insufficient survives to determine if it formed part of a jamb or part of an arch voussoir, though the latter is more common and therefore perhaps more likely. (RF)
Found in a spread of broken stone in the cemetery south of the church, which yielded other fragments of carved stone as well as 14th–15th century pottery.
155mm x 80mm x 73mm.
Third quarter of 12th century.
C708, Phase: 7 LM, Findspot: 201.89/724.32.

FIGURE 12.2
Chirnside doorway (Berwickshire), showing comparable chevrons

AF2 (Figures 12.3 and 12.4)
Four adjoining pieces of a slender columnar shaft.
Pale yellow micaceous sandstone.
Towards what can probably be referred to as the front, the stones are of semi-octagonal profile, into the angles of which narrow rolls are recessed. Towards the rear they are of tapering profile, into which rebates are cut. The stone is worked with diagonal tooling towards the rear, but towards the front it has a smoother finish, which may be the result of weathering, but could have been because it had been given a polished finish.

The rebate on each side of the rear was evidently designed to accommodate a symmetrical pair of associated elements, the most likely candidates for those elements being frames for glazing, shutters or door leaves. So far as the last of those possibilities is concerned, while a stone of this kind could certainly have functioned as the *trumeau* of a large doorway, such double doorways are usually only to be found at churches of the largest scale, and it is unlikely that a church of the size of that at The Hirsel would have had such a doorway. On balance, therefore, the stone appears more likely to have formed part of a mullion set on the external plane of a glazed or shuttered window of two or more lights, with the tapered flanks to the rear corresponding to the outer part of the splayed embrasure of the window rear-arch.

Since there are few precise analogies for such a feature, it is very difficult to suggest a date for it. However, if parallels may be drawn with works of larger scale, there was a taste for octagonal profiles with rolls sunk into the angles around the later years of the 12th century. Responds of this form, for example, are to be seen in two closely related buildings: the south transept arcade of Arbroath Abbey (Angus) and the choir of Hexham Priory (Northumberland), and there is a pier of this type in the north nave arcade of Brechin Cathedral (Angus). None of these is closely datable, though they can all be placed around the later 12th century, and, in the absence of more precise comparative material, a similar date could be tentatively advanced for the stones from The Hirsel.

It is possible, however, that partial analogies might also be sought in some of the earlier windows in the choir aisles of Glasgow Cathedral, where work was started around the 1240s. Some of the plate-traceried windows there have relatively heavy mullions with rolls at the angles that show some similarities with what is to be seen in the stones from The Hirsel, though at Glasgow the rolls rise proud of the surface. The Glasgow examples are perhaps of greater interest for confirming that heavy mullions decorated with rolls are to be found elsewhere than for indicating a likely date range, and on balance a date around the last decades of the 12th century appears preferable for stones from The Hirsel. (RF)

Although this piece has been compared with a similar shaft now set as the central section of a mid-wall shaft in the Late Saxon tower of Morland church in Cumbria (Bailey and Cramp 1988, 167–168 and illus 644–647) the position of the Cumbrian shaft is not primary, and it could have been set there to make up the shaft at any time after the church was built, nevertheless this shaft could have served as the mid-shaft of a similar double opening.

Found in C101 and C102 (topsoil), and two pieces from the plough pre-excavation (Cramp and Douglas-Home 1980, 228–229, fig 2 and pl 17). All fragments are marked by the drag of the plough, and the pieces discovered in the excavation were in the most northerly trench about 20m from the church.
Total H 929mm. Diam 170>140mm.
Third quarter of 12th century (RF).
C101, C102, u/s topsoil, Area: 195–205/860–870.

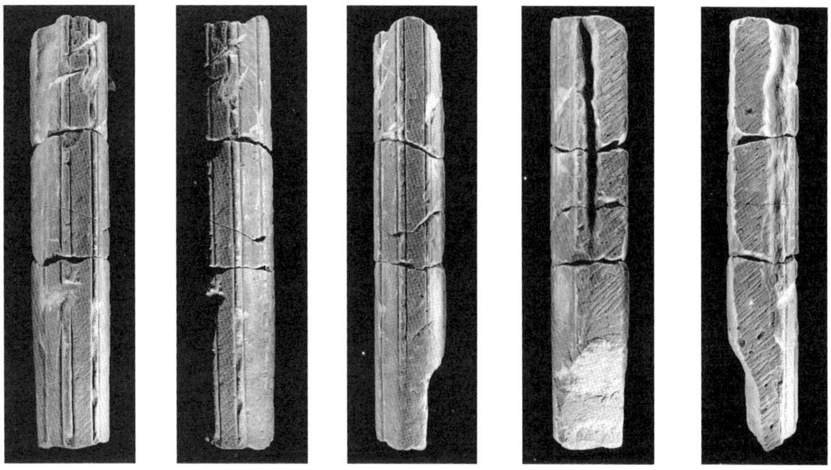

AF2 a b c d e

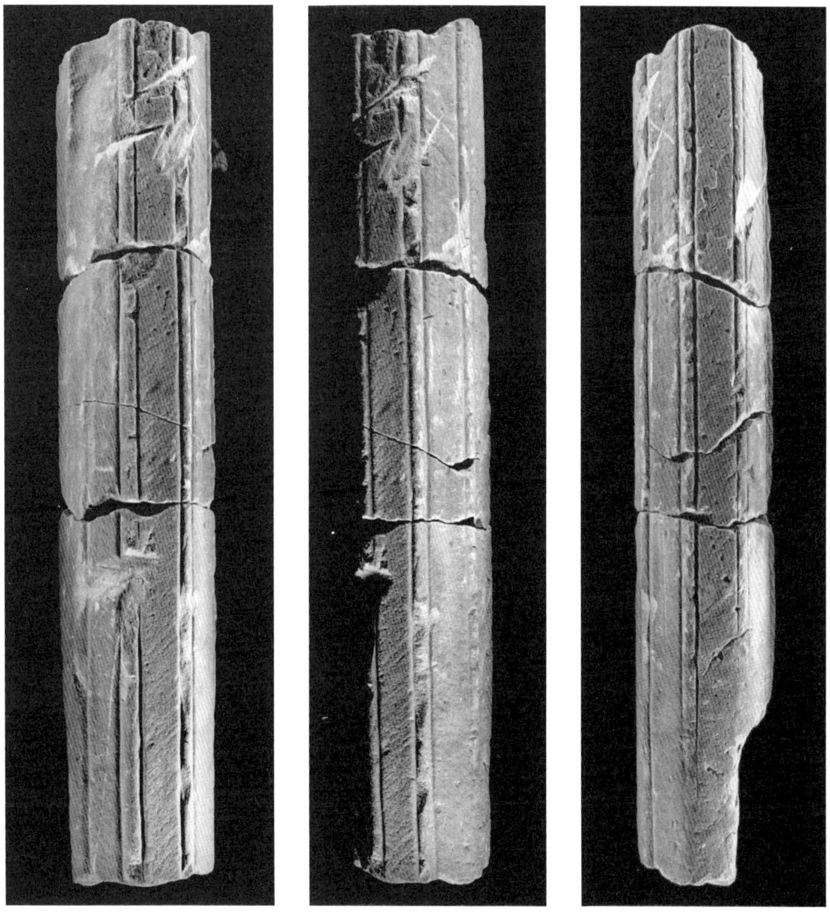

AF2 a b c

FIGURE 12.3
Columnar shaft, all faces, AF2

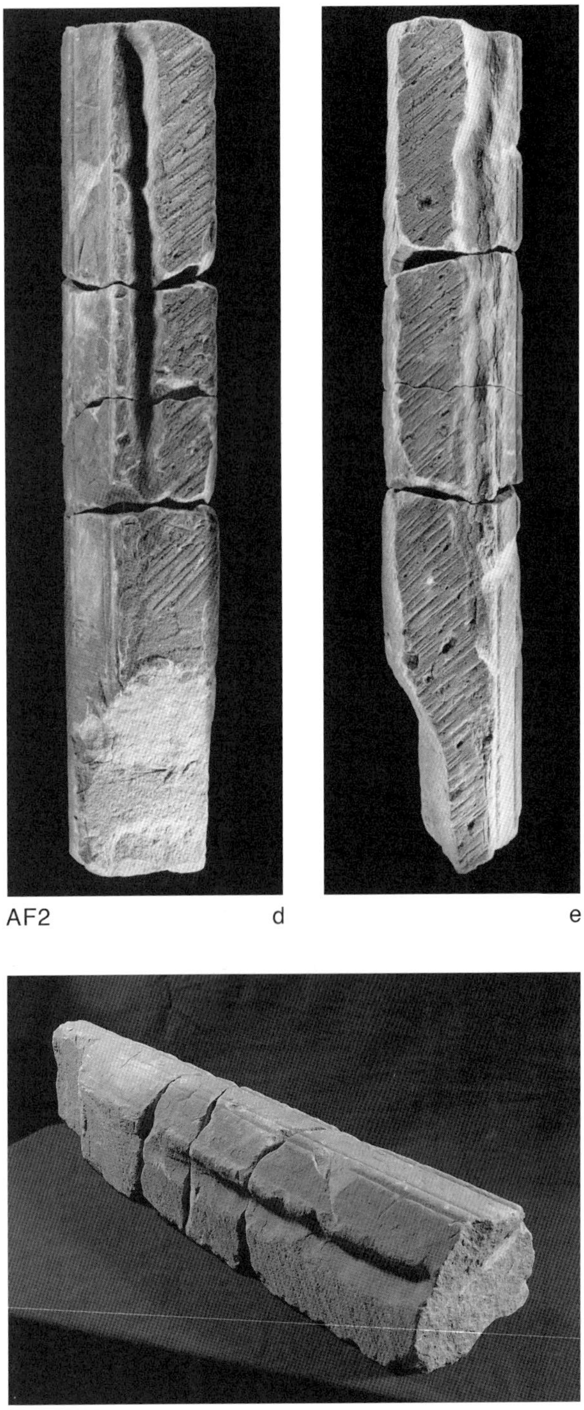

FIGURE 12.4
Columnar shaft, faces d and e and profile, AF2

AF3 (Figure 12.5)
Architectural feature, part of a larger formation; probably reused.
Micaceous sandstone.
A diagonally tooled broken fragment with a roll sunk into the angle between two diagonally set faces, and with possible traces of lime render.

One possible interpretation is that this stone formed part of a stone of octagonal or semi-octagonal profile with sunk rolls at the angles. If that were the case, the same point could be made as was made for AF2, that this might be a reflection of a late

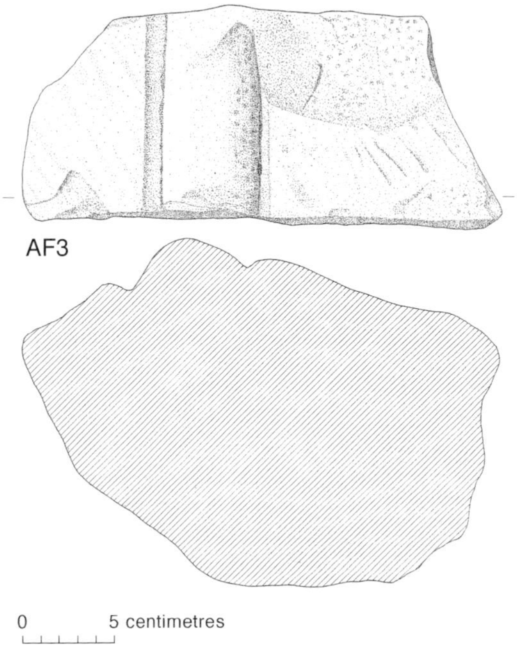

FIGURE 12.5
Curved fragment with panels divided by a roll moulding, AF3

12th century taste for responds and piers of basically octagonal profiles, but with rolls sunk into the angles. In discussing AF2 attention was drawn to other examples of this approach.

Nevertheless, there could be no certainty that this fragment did originate as part of a stone of octagonal or semi-octagonal profile. Alternative possibilities are that it was either part of a larger moulding formation, or that it was designed as an edge roll to an opening with its flanks at an oblique angle to the wall face, such as a window or doorway rear-arch. The similarity however of the tooling to that on the less polished parts of AF2, together with the formal similarities evident in the choice of a sunk angle roll may make a date around the third quarter of the 12th century more likely than any other. (RF)
Discovered in clearance deposit.
250mm x 140mm x 110mm.
?Late 12th century.
C421, Phase: 8 EPM, Area: 188–90/842–50.

AF4 (Figure 12.6)
Architectural block with sunken roll moulding between two chamfers.
Fine-grained sandstone.
Possibly re-cut on either side of the moulding. It could be an order in an arch or part of a vertical jamb (Eric Cambridge pers comm). (This fragment was originally mistakenly published as a grave-marker; Cramp and Douglas-Home 1980, 228, no. 6.)
445mm x 400mm x 235mm.
?12th century.
Unstratified; found by the plough before excavation.

AF5 (Figure 12.7)
Irregular fragment with three diagonally set worked faces, and one worked bed.
Fine-grained micaceous sandstone.
The worked faces have parallel diagonal tooling. The tooling

AF4

FIGURE 12.6
Fragment with sunken roll, AF4

AF6

FIGURE 12.8
Fragment with chamfered faces, one incised with a cross, AF6

AF5

FIGURE 12.7
Section of an octagonal feature, AF5

AF7

FIGURE 12.9
Irregular fragment with two chamfered faces, AF7

being similar to that on AF1 could point to a similar date, although there is no basis for certainty on such limited evidence.

In the absence of any indicator as to the full profile of the stone when complete, there must be doubt about its intended function. If it had once formed part of an octagonal or semi-octagonal feature, it could have belonged to a small pier or respond, for example. But the scale of the diagonal face possibly suggests that it is more likely to have been part of the chamfered edge to a wall opening, such as the inner order of the jambs of a doorway or the reveal of a window, with the latter perhaps being more plausible. (RF)
Found in the rubble of the late compound.
140 mm x 100mm x 55mm.
?Third quarter of 12th century.
C421, Phase: 8 EPM, Area: 188–90/842–50.

AF6 (Figure 12.8)
Fragment with three diagonally set worked faces.
Greyish sandstone.
The surfaces are chipped and very worn, but there is an incised cross which could be a mason's mark on one face. Fragment of a larger respond or chamfered off jamb. (RF)
Found on the western part of site, with broken stone, and 17th-century pottery.
285mm x 220 mm x 105mm.
12th century.
C3 (stony deposit), Phase: 8 EPM, Area: 176–7/840–842.

AF7 (Figure 12.9)
Irregular fragment probably re-cut. Two diagonally set worked faces with diagonal tooling.
Grey micaceous sandstone.

AF8

FIGURE 12.10
Wedge of shaft, AF8

The piece is too fragmentary to suggest a use, but the stone and the tooling are similar to the other pieces above.
Found in the post-medieval stone edging of the compound.
210mm x 110mm x 110mm.
?12th century.
C946, Phase: 8 EPM, Area: 178–82/836–9.

AF8 (Figure 12.10)
Wedge of shaft possibly cut for reuse or to fit an angle. The curved face is finely tooled, one flat face with rough tooling, and mortar on the other flat face. (RF)
Grey micaceous sandstone.
Found in C421, as above (AF5).
140mm x 110mm x 100mm.
?12th century.
C421, Phase: 8 EPM, 188–90/842–50.

AF9 (Figure 12.11)
Curved fragment, either cut for reuse or to fit an angle. Fine tooling on the curved and one flat face, and cruder tooling on the angled and the other flat face. (RF)
Grey micaceous sandstone.
Found in C421, as above (AF5).
90mm x 145mm x 90mm.
?12th century.
C421, Phase: 8 EPM, Area: 188–90/842–50.

AF9

FIGURE 12.11
Curved fragment, possibly cut to fit an angle, AF9

AF10 a

b

FIGURE 12.12
Irregular fragment of a shaft, AF10

AF10 (Figure 12.12)
A broken fragment with a curved face displaying predominantly vertical tooling, and with part of a worked bed.
Grey micaceous sandstone.
This appears to have formed part of a small non-engaged shaft, and its most likely function is presumably that of an *en-délit* nook-shaft. As such, it is most likely to be from a doorway, but could possibly be from a window or chancel arch. (RF)
Found in C421, as above (AF5).
105mm x 160mm x 70mm.
?12th century.
C421, Phase: 8 EPM, Area: 188–90/842–50.

AF11

FIGURE 12.13
Curved fragment possibly part of a shaft, AF11

AF12

FIGURE 12.14
Irregularly shaped fragment of a shaft, AF12

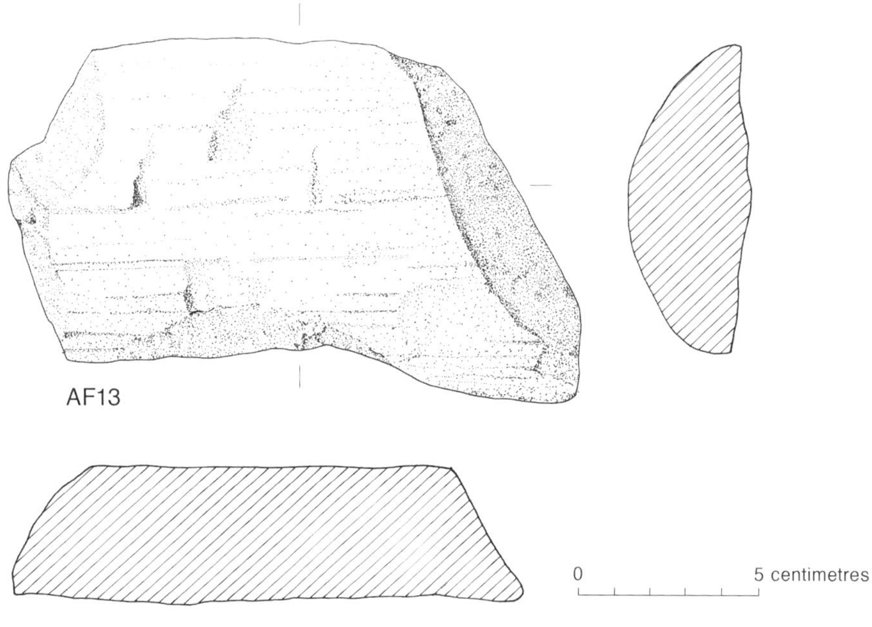

FIGURE 12.15
Fragment of moulding, AF13

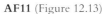

AF11 (Figure 12.13)
Curved fragment with vertical and diagonal tooling on one face. Possibly part of a shaft.
Grey micaceous sandstone.
Found in a deposit of demolition rubble south of the church and cut by late graves.
190mm x 140mm x 80mm.
?12th century.
C708, Phase: 7 LM, Findspot: 198.71/826.62.

AF12 (Figure 12.14)
Irregularly shaped fragment with one curving face of shaft. Base or top smoothed and tooled with fine vertical tooling, and a possible mason's mark.
Sandstone.
This is a more substantial piece than the shafts AF10–12 above and could be from a doorway. (RC)
Reused in wall C288, the northern enclosure wall of the cemetery.
260mm x195mm x 115mm.
?12th century.
C288, Phase: 7 LM, Findspot: 204.5/859.

AF13 (Figure 12.15)
Fragment of moulding.
Grey sandstone.
Irregular fragment with distinct vertical tooling. One end of this piece is flat and the other rounded, but despite its battered and worn surface the tooling is fine and professional.

It is impossible to say from what survives what was the original form and it is possible, as with other fragments found on the site periphery, that it was not associated with the church. (RC)
Found in the cemetery soil to the west of the site.
L 140mm. Diam 80mm. Th 30<35mm.
?12th–14th century (RC).
C1022, Phase: 6 Med, 179–181/825–7.

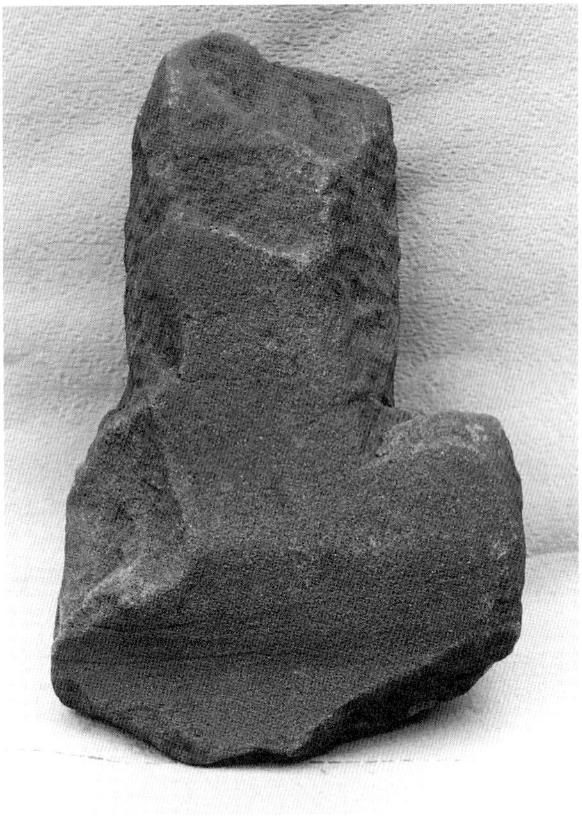

FIGURE 12.16
Irregular T-shaped fragment possibly of a window opening, AF14

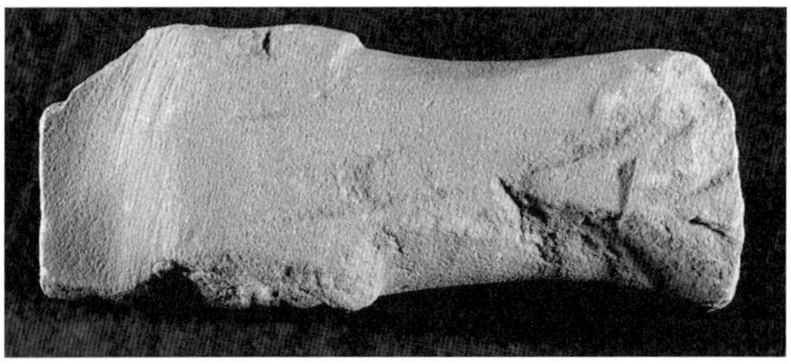

FIGURE 12.17
Irregular bar with junctions for cross pieces, AF15

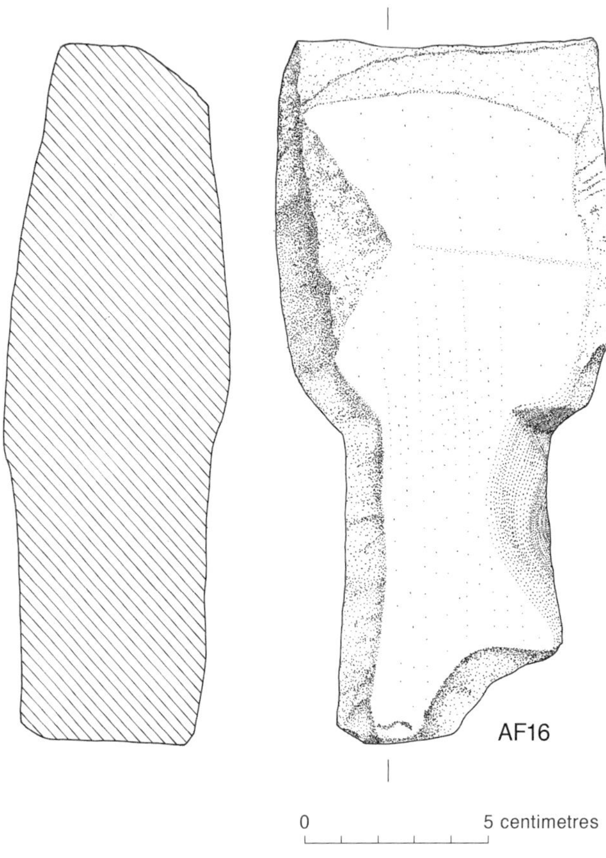

FIGURE 12.18
Irregularly shaped bar, possibly part of a frame, AF16

AF14 (Figure 12.16)
Irregular T-shaped fragment broken at every termination. A tapering bar, roughly chipped into shape, with two faces flattened and smoothed, and developing into a right-angled cross piece.
Fine sandstone.
This piece is tooled in a quite different way from the main architectural stonework and what is presumably the front and back of the piece is smoothed by abrasion (cf. AF15 and AF16). It could have been derived from an early phase of the church, or a domestic building sited to the north of the church. Its function is uncertain but could have been part of the frame of a simple window opening which would not have been glazed but closed by a shutter. (RC)
Found in the topsoil to the north of the church.
150mm x 100mm x 50mm.
?10th–16th century.
C103, topsoil, Area: 203–4/862–3.

AF15 (Figure 12.17)
Irregular and fragmentary bar.
Fine sandstone.
The piece is smoothly polished, tapered at one end, and waisted in the middle. Like AF15 and AF17 it could be part of a window frame. (RC)
C103, as above, AF15.
200mm x 80mm x 50mm.
?10th–16th century.
C103, topsoil, Area: 203–4/862–3.

AF16 (Figure 12.18)
Part of a ?frame with a block base developing into a bar. The stone is badly worn and broken on four faces. Both broad faces are flat with a smooth surface and no evidence of diagonal tooling (cf. AF15 and AF16).
Fine-grained sandstone.
These crudely shaped pieces may be earlier than architectural details from the extended church, although none are stratified in an early context, and since all have been found in the north of the site it seems plausible that they were from a domestic building in that area. (RC)
Found in a spread of densely packed cobbles.
55mm x 50mm x 45mm.
?10th–16th century.
C1005, Phase: 7 LM, Findspot: 209.3/858.2.

FIGURE 12.19
Part of a roughly tooled rounded bar, AF17

AF17 (Figure 12.19)
Part of a small rounded shaft broken at both ends. It has been roughly shaped into an oval with hammer blows and deep irregular chiselling.
Grey sandstone.
The finish of this stone is quite unlike the professional chiselling of most of the worked stone. It is small enough to be a window mullion, and compare the possible window bars, AF14 and AF16. It is possible that like them it could belong to a building other than the church, or one of the earlier church phases. Alternatively it could be an unfinished piece. (RC)
Found in a disturbed level with 18th-century pottery at the west of the churchyard.
L 150mm. Diam 45mm and 52mm.
?10th–16th century.
C928, Phase: 8 EPM, Area: 175–86/833–40.

AF18 (Figure 12.20)
Possibly part of an arch which has been re-cut; the lower curve being later (Eric Cambridge pers comm).
Sandstone.
Found in disturbed ground level, ?17th century.
120mm x 100mm x 110mm.
?13th century.
C455, Phase: 8 EPM, Area: 184–6/843–7.

AF19 (Figure 12.21)
Curved opening ?window or aumbry.
Fine-grained sandstone, not micaceous.
The rounded shape is carved from a single block with a rectangular cross section, one face is smoothly dressed, the opposite face is wider and left rough. There is one complete dowel hole and the remains of another at the broken tapering end and there is mortar coating across the curving top, where it was probably inset into a wall.

The stone type and the dressing are different from other architectural features. The holes could have held a closure bar and this head would frame a small opening. This could have been similar to the type of window still existing in the ruined churches of Bunkle and Simprim (Berwickshire) (see Figure 27.1), alternatively it might be the head of an aumbry. (RC)

This piece was reused as part of a rough line of stones (C1156) butted up to the south wall of the nave and belonging to its last phase of use (Figure 5.29).
330mm x 90>75mm x 85>65mm.
12th century (RC).
C1156, Phase: 7 LM, Findspot: 194.90/830.55.

AF20 (Figure 12.22)
Fragment of window?
Yellowish sandstone.
100mm x 75mm x 40mm.
C105, Phase: 8 EPM, Area: 2034/8623.

AF21 (not illustrated)
Fragment of window.
Sandstone.
Found in topsoil to the north-west of the church.
152mm x 100mm x 54mm.
C1, topsoil, Area: 174–5/842–5.

FIGURE 12.20
Fragment possibly of an arch recut, AF18

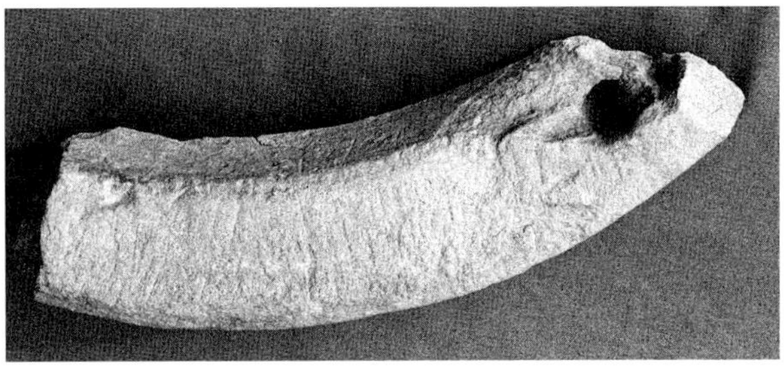

AF19

FIGURE 12.21
Part of a frame for an opening, with holes for bars, AF19

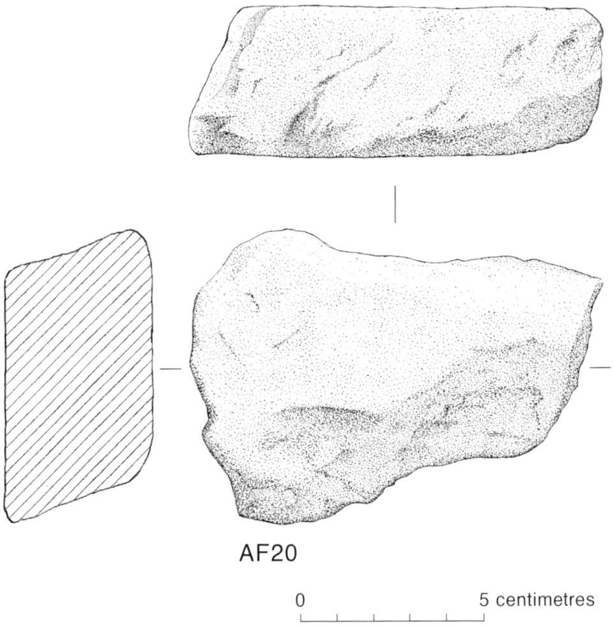

FIGURE 12.22
Fragment possibly of a window bar, AF20

AF22 (Figure 12.23)
Block fragment with one roughly finished panel bordered by a narrow roll and with a smoothly finished surface developing into a curve. Possibly a window jamb with a groove for glass.
Fine micaceous sandstone.
Found in the band of stones delimiting the post-medieval compound.
Maximum 250mm x 110mm x 84mm.
13th century or later (Eric Cambridge pers comm).
C946, Phase: 8 EPM, 178-82/836-9.

AF23 (Figure 12.24)
Rectangular, slightly tapering stone, broken and mended in antiquity. Its surface is smoothly polished and in the centre is an irregularly worked oblong hole with sides which taper inwards.
Grey fine-grained micaceous sandstone.

Stones with socket holes do not immediately declare their function and can be found in various forms and in multiple groupings, and so they are not a 'class' of object, but for comparison need to be of similar form and found in similar positions in relation to structures. In Scotland, socket stones have been found in a number of contexts. At Arbroath Abbey (Angus), a tall socket stone with tapering sides is set on the central axis of the presbytery. There is a pair of sockets in a related location to that at Arbroath at St Andrews Cathedral (Fife). In that case they are cut into the steps in front of the site of the late medieval altar, where they are set on an east–west alignment.

One possible use for sockets in such a position could have been to accommodate a lectern. In the greater churches, however, it was more usual to have a pair of lecterns in the presbytery area, one for the Gospels and the other for the Epistles, and possibly a third lectern between the stalls in the choir, so that it is not clear what purpose a single lectern could have served. An alternative possibility could be that such sockets were to accommodate a Paschal candle.

Socket stones that were presumably associated with liturgical furnishing have also been found during excavation at Linlithgow Carmelite Friary (West Lothian). There a pair that was found behind the high altar was almost certainly for the support of the reredos. (RF)

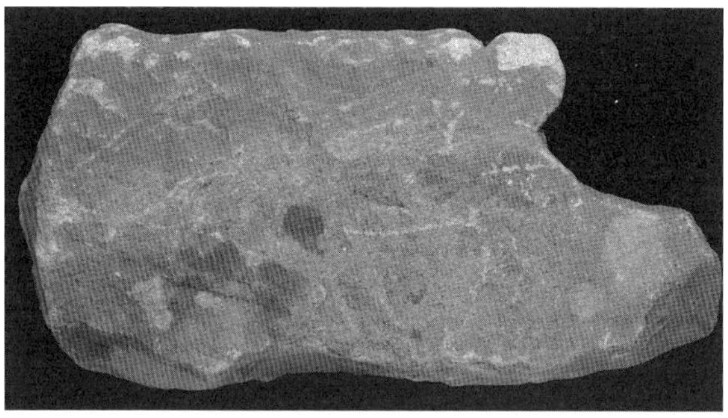

AF22

FIGURE 12.23
Block fragment possibly of a window jamb, AF22

Other occurrences of these socketed stones are mentioned in the discussion of the church (Chapter 5) where it is suggested that the comparison of the liturgical fittings of major monastic or cathedral churches may not be applicable to a simple parish church like The Hirsel, and this single stone may have marked the position of the altar, or, if the altar were set back in the apse, it might have held a lectern or, more likely, a cross. It is probably useful to distinguish between those stones in which the socket had a base and those where the stone was pierced right through. An example of the former type which has been re-cut from a block was found in the churchyard at Wharram (North Yorkshire) where it has been interpreted as for holding a wooden cross as a possible grave-marker (Stocker 2007, 293–294, pls 119–120). Whatever the original function of the socketed stone from The Hirsel, it seems to have been put out of use when the hole was filled with slivers of stone. This could have taken place when the building ceased to function as a church. (RC)
The stone had been inserted into the foundations of wall C646, the sleeper wall on the chord of the added apse of the church, previously the east wall of the first church (see Figures 5.7, 5.10 and 5.38). (RC)
L 480>465mm; W 340mm; Th 120mm; Hole L 200mm; W 160mm.
Probably 12th century.
C646, Phase 5 EM2, Area: 204–5/832–3.

AF24 (Figure 12.25)
Two worked faces with chamfered edges and two broken, possible base or plinth.
Sandstone.

AF23 a

b

FIGURE 12.24
Rectangular socket stone, possibly to support a cross, AF23

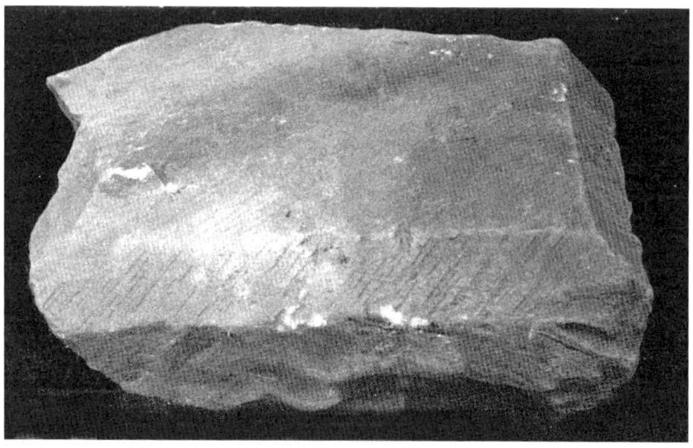

AF24

FIGURE 12.25
Fragment with two chamfered faces possibly a base or plinth, AF24

The tooling on this piece is similar to the diagonal tooling on some of the diagnostic architectural pieces and like AF25 could belong to the extended church. (RC)
Discovered in cemetery surface to the south of church, in a medieval level.
200mm x 160mm x 90mm.
C716, Phase: 6 Med, Area: 196–8/820–2.

FIGURE 12.26
Block, very worn, with one chamfered edge, AF25

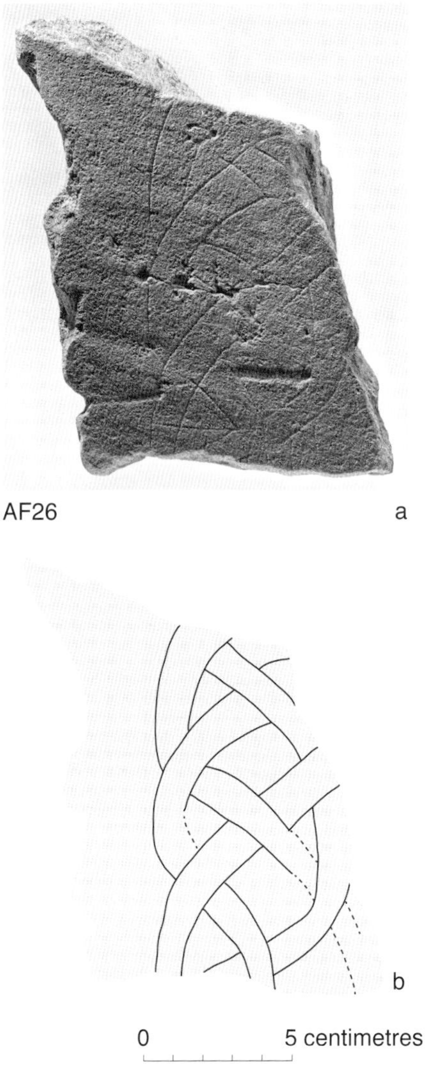

FIGURE 12.27
Fragment of a slab incised with interlace, possibly part of a church furnishing, AF26

AF25 (Figure 12.26)
Two tooled edges, one chamfered, all surfaces very worn.
Sandstone.
Possible base or plinth probably reused as a grave-marker, found associated with Sk67.
L 320mm; W 220mm; Th 130mm.
C808, Phase: 7 LM, Area: 211–15/839.

Nine further chamfered stones are recorded: three from a spread of angular stones, possibly a disturbed floor, in Nave 1 (C629), one from a floor level in the west end of the church (C461), one fragment lining one of the postholes in the nave (C682), three from cemetery levels to the south and west, and one from the stone dump (C421).

Only one of these stones was found in what may be a primary context, that in C461, but this is the abandonment layer in the church. The others had either been reused in roughly laid floors or possibly as grave-markers in the cemetery. They could possibly have functioned originally as the bases of openings or more continuous plinths. (RC)

AF26 (Figure 12.27)
Fragment with interlace, possibly part of the fitments of the church.
Fine micaceous sandstone.
Fragment broken on all edges and some damage with what could be tools. The only dressed face is incised with an interlaced design. The pattern is not geometric and the strands are of varying widths, but it can be reconstructed into a four strand pattern (Figure 12.27b), although it has the tentativeness of a trial piece. Such simple non-geometric plaits occur, usually in a more competent form, on the narrow faces of late crosses in Scotland such as St Andrews 14 (Allen 1903, no. LXXIII, 359), although the broad strands and open spaces between the intersections are remotely paralleled in the crudely carved left side of the cross Abernethy 5 (Allen 1903, fig 326b).

The position of the find is ambiguous. It was found amongst a scatter of tooled stones from the rebuilt chancel

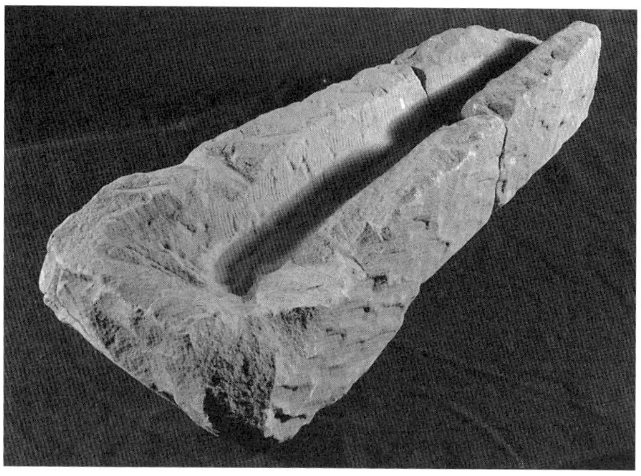

AF27

FIGURE 12.28
Part of a gutter or drain, AF27

AF28

FIGURE 12.29
Socket stone for a door pivot, AF28

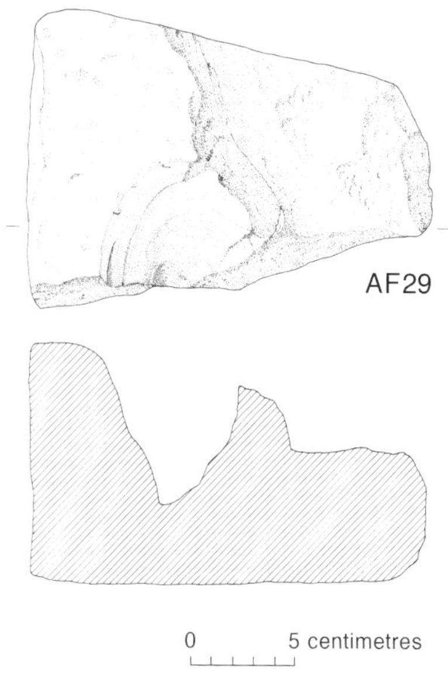

FIGURE 12.30
Well shaped sandstone slab with a pivot hole, AF29

south wall, and could have been used as part of the walling of the 12th-century church, although it was discovered with later medieval pottery in what seems to be a robbing deposit. The carving could be placed between the 10th and 12th century, and may have originated with the first church, but, if it is assigned to the earlier part of the date bracket, it is of interest because so few pre-Norman carved sculptures have been found in this region, and although the sites at Legerwood and Mertoun have produced sculptured fragments with interlace, it is not of this type (Ferguson 1899, 26, pl III, fig 1; RCAHMS 1915, 125, no. 239; 148, no. 259). This piece is, however, not part of a cross shaft and may have been intended as an altar frontal, although in the church no base for a stone altar was found and altars of the date of this stone could have been of wood (Ó Carragáin 2010, 188).
Maximum: 145mm x 105mm x 56mm.
10th–12th century.
C703, Phase: 5 EM2, Findspot: 198.85/829.90.

AF27 (Figure 12.28)
Part of a guttering or drain, broken into two sections.
Coarse micaceous sandstone.
The block is oblong and tapers towards one end, with a central grooved channel and outflow at the narrow end. The underside of this end is chamfered. This piece is tooled in a different manner from the other stones; the sides seem to be dressed with a claw hammer or very broad chisel, the interior with a fine claw chisel.

This piece was found by the plough and could be of any date between the 12th and 16th centuries. (RC)
L 635mm; W 210>95mm; Th 125>110mm, interior border of channel 45mm, interior depth 45mm.

AF28 (Figure 12.29)
Fine sandstone slab, now broken into two pieces, with a flat smooth base and broken upper surface with a turned U-shaped socket.

This door pivot could have been redeposited from the church or domestic buildings to the north of the church. It is, however, finely worked and should be from a building of some status.

From a cindery surface in the north of the site, 17th–18th century in date but containing artefacts ranging from the 13th to 17th centuries. (RC)
270mm x 175>130mm x 110mm. Hole Diam: 65; Depth 35mm.
?Medieval.
C105, Phase: 8 EPM, Findspot: 203/866.

AF29 (Figure 12.30)
Sandstone slab dressed on three faces but broken on two sides and with the upper face with pivot-hole damaged.
From a clearance deposit to the north of the church containing medieval pottery, window glass and cames. This piece is likely to have come from the church and to have been a pivot for one of its doors.
180mm x 130mm x 105mm.
Medieval.
C984, Phase: 7/8 LM/EPM, Findspot: 180/836.

AF30 (not illustrated)
Dressed stone, triangular, with a possible mason's mark on the main dressed face, composed of two sets of parallel lines at right angles to each other, forming a box-like pattern.
355mm x 270mm x 100mm.
?Medieval.
C1260, Phase: 7 LM, Area: 190.3–192/830–833.

a

b

FIGURE 12.31
Dressed stone block

a

b

FIGURE 12.32
Dressed stone, typical of walling of Phase III church

Many dressed stones with characteristic diagonal tooling which were complete building blocks were found in the clearance deposits to the north of the church, and also in the spread of stones (C708) to the south. These were neatly cut (Figures 12.31 and 12.32), not cut to regular dimensions, but they would have a rough conformity, for example items from C421: 320mm x 223mm x 170mm; 300mm x 290mm x 200mm; 400mm x 290mm x 140mm; 420mm x 300mm x 280mm.

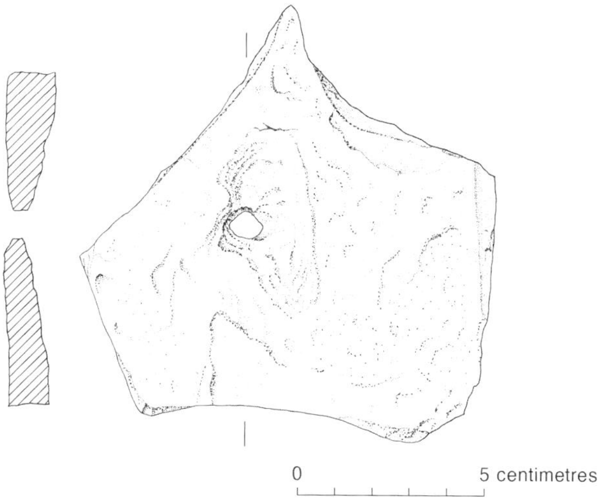

FIGURE 12.33
Sandstone roof tile probably from the church, SF3

12.2 STONE ROOF FLAGS
Rosemary Cramp

A dozen fragments of stone roof flags were found in the clearance deposits of the site, but two were found inside the church after it had been robbed, but was still in some form of use. One of them, SF2, still preserved its nail.

SF1 (not illustrated)
Sandstone, flat on one face.
Found in a destruction level inside the church.
L 120mm; W 70mm; Th 10mm.
C1148, Phase: 7 LM, Area: 193–195.5/828–830.

SF2 (not illustrated)
Sandstone, burnt, with iron ?nail attached (see below, FeS5)
From the hearth in the top of pit C1302.
L 104mm; W 96mm; Th 13mm.
C1227, Phase 7 LM, Findspot: 190.93/832.50.

SF3 (Figure 12.33)
Sandstone, with nail hole (Diam 8mm).
From the revetment surrounding the late compound.
L 110mm; W 105mm; Th 12mm.
C946, Phase: 8 EPM, Findspot: 184.67/837.66.

12.3 MEDIEVAL WINDOW GLASS
Pamela Graves and Rosemary Cramp

Only a small quantity of early window glass was found, but this was clearly associated with the church. The pattern on GlW1 was identified by Pamela Graves as belonging to a type of early- to mid-13th century grisaille glass found elsewhere in the diocese of St Andrews, the nearest being Coldingham Priory and Dunfermline Abbey (Graves 1994, figs 2 and 3). The quality of the church at The Hirsel is emphasised by the fact that the other sites were important abbeys, cathedrals or castle churches.

Fragments of medieval window glass were found in uncontaminated medieval contexts in the mortar floor at the west end of the nave of the church (GlW3) and in a grave just outside the walls (GlW1). GlW4 and GlW5 were associated with the robber trench of the south wall, which implies that this glass was *in situ* when the wall was robbed. All of these fragments were weathered and opaque and of high potash metal. The medieval fragments clustered around the western end of the church and it seems probable that when the nave was enlarged in the third phase of church construction, the windows were then glazed. No window glass was found at the east end of the church, which might indicate that in the earliest phases the windows were not glazed. With so few fragments one cannot be dogmatic, but one medieval fragment was found near to the cemetery perimeter to the north where it has been postulated that there was a dwelling in the medieval period.

A significant quantity of plain window glass was recovered from the post-medieval to modern contexts, which is not reported on here, but is listed in the archive.

GlW1 (Figure 12.34)
Three joining fragments of 13th-century grisaille window glass, painted red/brown, with a trefoil in relief on a cross-hatched ground. Traces of burning, two cut edges, one straight and one curved. Corner fragment, one edge grozed and lead stained. Found in a late grave (Sk286), cut into the destruction level to the south of the nave.
L 53mm; W 35mm; Th 3mm.
L 32mm; W 17mm; Th 3mm.
L 27mm; W 25mm; Th 3.5mm.
C784, Phase: 6 Med, Findspot: 194.90/826.49.

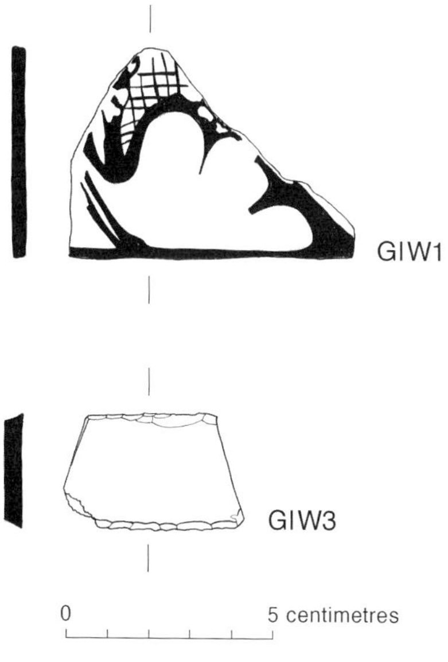

FIGURE 12.34
Fragment of grisaille window glass, GlW1; fragment of opaque medieval window glass, GlW3

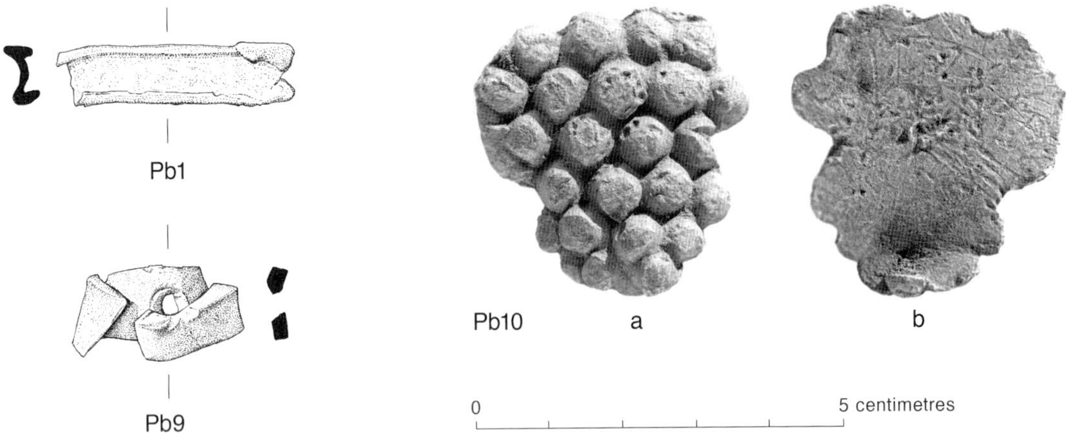

FIGURE 12.35
Section of H-shaped window came, Pb1; folded strip with two pierced holes, possibly a binding, Pb9; fragment of decorative appliqué with pellets or berries, Pb10

GlW2 (not illustrated)
One piece of medieval window glass, opaque, greenish, with black corrosion products. Found with building debris in enclosure wall to north; 14th-century deposit (different from the rest).
From area of 'house' north of churchyard.
L 24mm; W 22mm; Th 3mm.
C289, Phase: 6 Med, Area: 202–205/854–856.

GlW3 (Figure 12.34)
One piece of medieval window glass. Polished surface, shiny, black, opaque. Two coarsely grozed edges and two cut straight edges, forming a trapezoid shape.
From the mortar floor of the church.
L 43mm; W 25mm; Th 4mm.
C559, Phase: 7 LM, Findspot: 188.2/831.

GlW4 (not illustrated)
Two small featureless fragments of opaque window glass, medieval. Found in a baulk overlying the robber trench of the south wall of the church.
L 15mm; W 8mm; Th 2mm.
L 11mm; W 10mm; Th 2mm.
C014, u/s, Area: 187.75–188.25/824.8–827.6.

GlW5 (not illustrated)
One fragment of degraded and crystalline medieval window glass. One side polished, the other with corrosion products, traces of a curling stem. Corner piece, grozed on two sides. 12th–13th century (no later than early 14th). Found in the robber trench of the south-west corner of the south wall of the church.
L 44mm; W 27mm; Th 4mm.
C909, Phase: 7 LM, Area: 184–90/825–34.

12.4 LEAD
Rosemary Cramp

There is a small amount of lead from the site. Pb7 could indicate that there had been some leading on the roof of the nave such as flashing for the ridge, but there is not sufficient evidence to deduce that in any phase the church had been roofed with lead. There is clear evidence for leaded windows, particularly from the nave (see Pb2–4) but the one H-shaped came (Pb1) came from an area south of the nave in a deposit which could signify the rebuilding of the Phase I and II churches or a possible replacement of windows. Pb9 and Pb10, which were found in late contexts, are not structural, but their function is uncertain.

There were three lumps of melted lead (not catalogued) found in the secular occupation levels of the ruined church or in the final burning (C568, C623, C961), which could indicate that recycling of the material had taken place.

Pb1 (Figure 12.35)
Section of window came of H-shaped section, broken at the junction with another piece. This was found in a deposit of rubble to the south of the nave.
L 33mm; W 7mm; Th 1mm.
C708; Phase: 7 LM; 196.14/827.42.

Pb2 (not illustrated)
Fragment of window came, with central ridge, from a late medieval area of destruction in the nave.
L 35mm; W 10mm; Th 3mm.
C984; Phase: 7–8 LM–EPM; 180/836.

Pb3 (not illustrated)
Strip of folded window came, with central ridge, from clearance deposit in western ditch.
L 83mm; W 9mm; Th 3mm.
C928; Phase: 8 EPM; 175–186/830.

Pb4 (not illustrated)
Twisted fragment, possibly melted window came, from burning area in the western nave.
L 40mm; W 9mm; Th 2mm.
C623; Phase: 7 LM; 196.76/832.20.

Pb5 (not illustrated)
Fragment, possibly of window came.
L 23mm; W 8mm; Th 4mm.
C105; Phase: 8 EPM; 201–2/860–1.

Pb6 (not illustrated)
Folded scrap, possibly of roof lead. Found in the northern sector of the site, in an early medieval context.
L 22mm; W 14mm; Th 2mm.
C128; Phase: 5? EM2; 203.35/861.71.

Pb7 (not illustrated)
Folded strip, possibly an offcut, evidence for lead roofing? Found in a cesspit in the church.
L 34mm; W 20mm; Th 1mm.
C1305; Phase: 7 LM; 191.45/831.70.

Pb8 (not illustrated)
Strip, squared at one end, tapering at the other, function unknown. Found in the earlier floor level of the nave.
L 49mm; W 9mm; Th 3mm.
C1063; Phase: 6 Med; 188.80/829.20.

Pb9 (Figure 12.35)
Folded strip with two small holes. Possible binding. Found in a spread of gravel and pebbles.
L 23mm; W 9mm; Th 6mm.
C704; Phase: 8 EPM; 205.96/828.13.

Pb10 (Figure 12.35)
Fragment of decorative appliqué ornament. Pelleted design. Found in topsoil.
L 40mm; W 40mm; Th 4mm.
C3; Phase: 8 EPM; 177.70/840.28.

12.5 BUILDING IRONWORK

Belinda Burke

The majority of the extensive collection of iron artefacts is discussed in Chapter 20. This section summarises the collection of nails, hooks, staples and clench bolts found on the site, and predominantly in the area of the church. While some of these elements may well have been associated with furniture, or possibly coffins, it may be assumed that most were structural. The hinge pivot (FeS15) may also reasonably be considered to have been part of the church structure, being found amongst building debris in the eastern end of the extended nave.

Nails

(Figures 12.36 and 12.37)

A total of 1148 nails was recovered from the site (although most of those from the 1979–82 seasons are now missing). All were measured and listed, some were drawn and further observations have been made on the basis of X-rays. A full list of nails by context exists in the archive.

The largest concentration of nails was in the area of the extended nave, particularly in levels associated with the final secular phases of the building. Probably most of the nails related to timber structures within the church, particularly the roof, but they could also have been from furniture, either present in the church, or used as firewood. A total of 80 nails came from the layers in the pit C1302, including 29 nails from the hearth that sealed it (C1227), while C623, a layer characterised by intense burning, yielded 108. Other nails might have come from coffins; six nails were found associated Sk121, and five with Sk9; Sk192 and Sk270 each had two nails associated with them and single nails were found with Sk58 and Sk82 (Figure 12.37: 5), Sk286 and Sk203 (Figure 12.37: 19), which also appeared to have a stain indicating the presence of a coffin in the grave. As seen from the illustrated examples, nails found with skeletons were of varying form. It is probable that in some cases the nails were accidentally redeposited when the graves were dug, as were other finds, for example potsherds. A group of nails found together within a cemetery layer (Figure 12.37: 6–10) included a probable horseshoe nail.

Where nail heads survive, the vast majority are flat, and not very regular in shape, varying from roughly circular to sub-rectangular, lozenge or trapezium shaped. The shanks are generally square or rectangular in section, some tapering to a sharp point, while others are more blunt-ended, although often the full length of the nail may not survive. Some nails have burred heads where they have been struck with a hammer, rather than a flat head deliberately formed with an anvil or nailing iron (Figure 12.37: 19–20; Ottaway 1992, 608–611; Coghlan 1977, 69–71). One nail (Figure 12.37: 18), from a posthole in the nave, has a 'figure-of-eight' shaped head, with two curved projections, paralleled by type G from Canal Street in Perth (Ford and Walsh 1987, Ill 72), and type 10 from Ludgershall Castle, which McNeill sees as being split and hammered out in two halves (McNeill 2000, 229, 232). He interprets this as a type used to secure horizontal shelving or vertical panelling, alongside his headless type 15 for securing floor boards, postulating that these types replaced earlier T-shaped headed nails from the first half of the 13th century, signalling an increase in mass production methods.

Two loose nails were identified as types found associated with horseshoes. One 'fiddle-key' with a D-shaped head (from unstratified C013c to the west of the site), and a nail with a 'sub-fiddle-key' head (Figure 12.37: 10), of a type seen at Whithorn as a forerunner or variant of D-shaped fiddle-key nails (Nicholson 1997a, 408); see also an example from the Thames foreshore at Queenhithe, found with a type 3 horseshoe (Clark 2004, 117, no. 148). One nail with a T-shaped head was found in a horseshoe (see Figure 20.10, Fe97).

Illus	Description	Measurements (mm) L	WS	WH	Context
1	Lozenge-shaped head, square-sectioned shank, tapering to a point	37	4	14	C622, over line of cross wall of apse, Med
2	Flat head, fragmentary, shank of rectangular section, tapering to a point	44	7	20	C428, rubble over church, EPM
3	Slightly domed head, square-sectioned shank, squared end	40	8	18	C428, found with Fe2, EPM
4	Flat rectangular head, shank of square sectioned, tapering to a point	50	7	16	C52, rubble spread from wall C54, cemetery north of the church, L Med
5	Oval head, incomplete, square-sectioned shank, broken, coffin nail?	14	5	20	Associated with Sk82, Med
6	Rectangular flat head, shank with lozenge-shaped section, tapering	65	5	17	C707, patch of compact pebbles and stones in cemetery south of the church, LM
7	Flat square head, rivet or bump where attached to shank, which is rectangular in section, tapering	39	8	16	C707, as above
8	Flat rectangular head, short rectangular shank, tapering	24	5	16	C707, as above
9	Flat squarish head, shank of rectangular section, broken	25	8	22	C707, as above
10	Sub-fiddle type, for horseshoe?	30	4	13	C707, as above
11	Irregular lozenge-shaped head, shank with irregular lozenge-shaped section	50	8	22	C705, layer of rubble in cemetery, cf C707, LM
12	Irregular-shaped flat head, rectangular-sectioned shank, tapering, possibly incomplete	30	4	16	C1004, rubble spread north of the perimeter wall, Med
13	Irregular head, damaged, rectangular-sectioned shank, bent, possibly incomplete	50	6	22	C240, possible cultivation level, north of the perimeter wall, Med
14	Irregular head, square-sectioned shank, tapering to a point	54	5	17	C1001, rubble spread over area north of the perimeter wall, EPM
15	Small irregular head, square-sectioned shank, tapering to a point	85	5	9	C220, layer south of the perimeter wall, Med
16	Small rectangular head, slender square-sectioned shank tapering to a point	108	6	14	C623, area of intense burning in Nave 2, LM
17	Flat square head, long slender rectangular-sectioned shank, curled around on itself at tip	95	5	15	C629, Floor surface, Nave 1, Med
18	Figure-of-eight shaped head, square-sectioned shank, tapering to a point	53	5	11	C1178, fill of posthole in extended nave, LM
19	Burred head, rectangular shank, tapering to squared tip	63	8	9	C739, associated with Sk203, Med
20	Burred head, shaft of rectangular section, becoming thinner towards point	34	7	11	C1159, area of concentrated burning in Nave 2, LM
21	Burred head, bent at right angle, tapering to a point	57	6		C907, rubble over west end of church, EPM
22	Shank with square section, bent at right angle	50	4		C705 (see above, 11)
23	Square-section shank bent at a right angle with tip tapering to a point, head missing	50	4		C1158 possible floor level in Nave 2, Med

L = length WS = width of shank WH = width of head

FIGURE 12.36
Table of illustrated nails

The strap hinge (Fe1) had two nails with angular cuboid heads, a third similar nail being found nearby (Fe2). No other nails of this type were found on the site.

Inevitably many nails are bent, but some are deliberately clenched. One example (Figure 12.37: 17) has a long slender shank curved around to form a loop at the tip. Other nails are bent in a right angle (Figure 12.37: 21–23), where they would have been driven through layers of wood and clenched, performing a similar function to clench bolts (see below). Nails were also clenched in shoe making, using a cobbler's foot (Salaman 1986, 106). One example from C1332 (not illustrated) has a sub-rectangular head, its shank bent at a right angle, with the tip curved inwards. The measurement between the head and the bend indicates that it would have passed through a piece or pieces of wood with a thickness of some 50 mm. Other bent nails are headless.

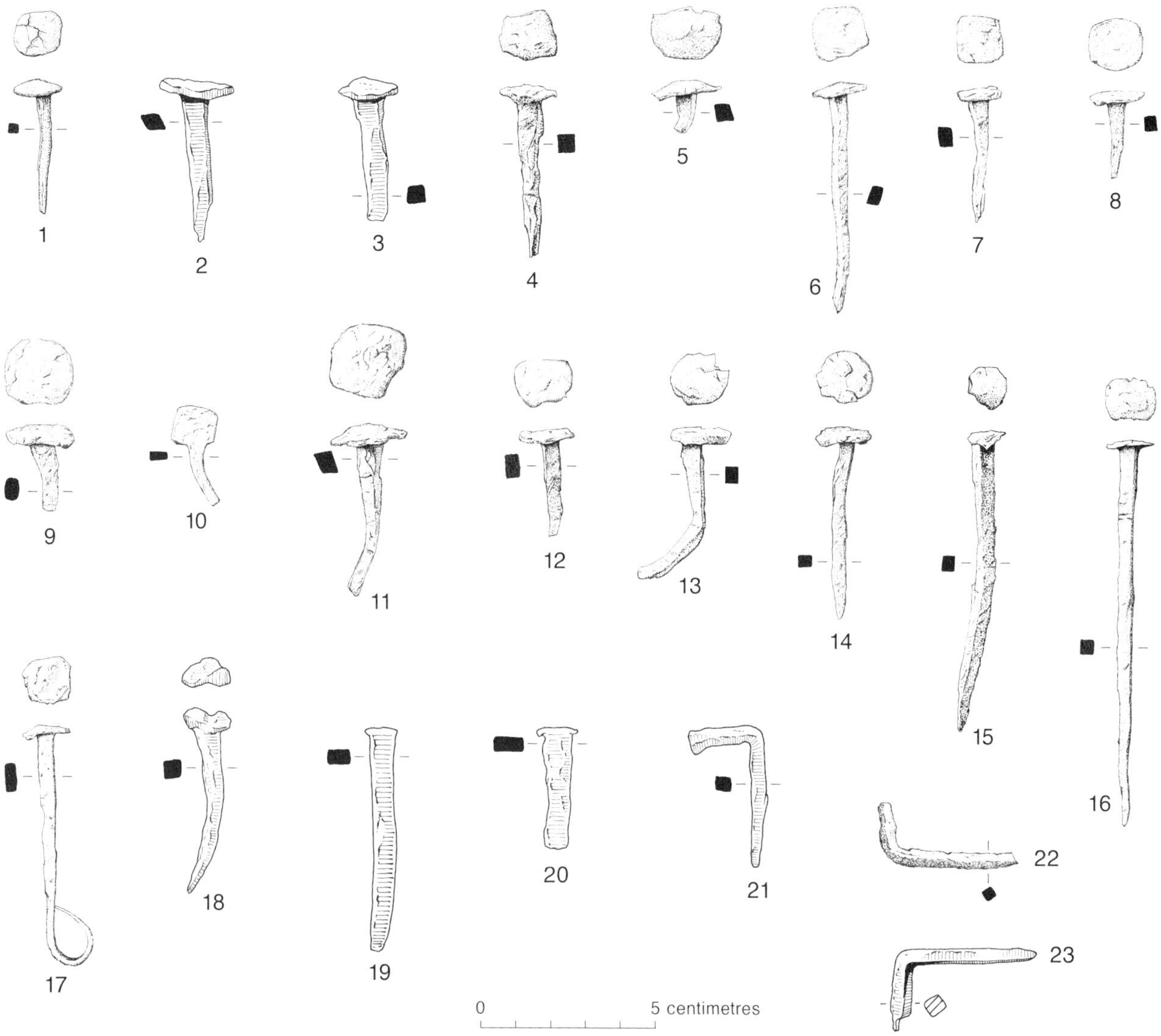

FIGURE 12.37
Structural iron, specimens of nail types

Clench bolt and rove

FeS1 (not illustrated)
Iron clench bolt, with flat circular head, rectangular shank and rectangular rove. Clench bolts were used in ship building, but also occur in other contexts, and are often found on doors (Ottaway 1992, 617–618). This example was found in the lower fill of pit C1302 in the nave of the church in a layer that included building rubble in its matrix, as well as several nails and other metalwork.
L 55mm; W (head) 27mm; W (shank) 7mm; L (rove) 24mm; W (rove) 18mm; distance between rove and nail head 35mm.
C1305, Phase: 7 LM, Findspot: 191.44/831.92.

FeS2 (not illustrated)
Rove fragment. Found in a floor surface in the chancel/first nave area of the church.
L 24mm; W 18mm; Th 4mm.
C629, Phase: 6 Med, Findspot: 202.31/834.06.

Hooks

Two small hooks were identified, in the layers over the church. Their function is uncertain, but they could have secured roofing flags, as could some of the right angle bent nails. The remains of an iron nail or spike (FeS5) are attached to a roofing flag from the hearth in the nave (C1227), which supports the theory that the roof of the nave was of stone flags, attached with iron fittings rather than wooden pegs or sheep bones.

FeS3 (Figure 12.38)
Square-section iron bar with right angle bend.
Total L 70mm; W 5mm; Th 4mm.
C456, Phase: 6 Med, Area: 183–5/835–7.

FeS4 (not illustrated)
Right-angled metal bar, rectangular section; the longer arm

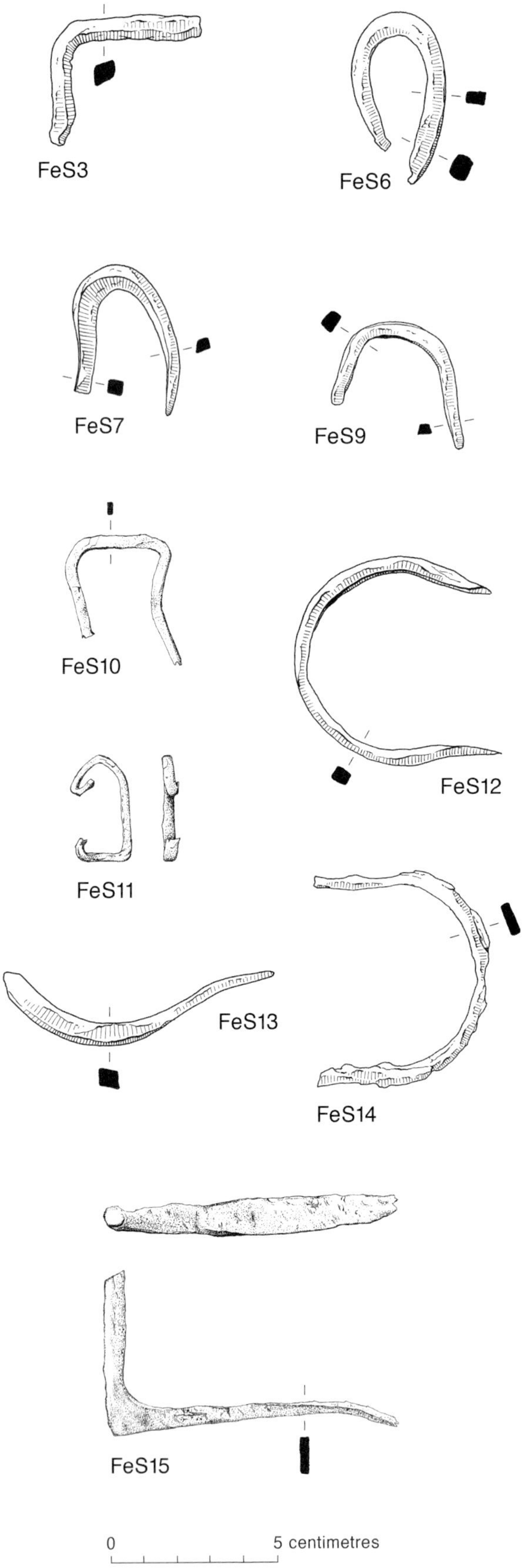

FIGURE 12.38
Structural iron, staples and hinge pivot

(67mm) ends in a point, the shorter (25mm) is blunt. Angle iron or latch? Found in the rubble pack over the line of the church.
L 92mm; Th 5mm.
C1122, Phase: 8 EPM, Area: 190–195.5/826–8.

FeS5 (not illustrated)
Corroded iron ?nail attached to a burnt roofing flag fragment.
L 48mm; Th 10mm.
Roof flag: 121mm x 78mmm; Th 14mm.
C1227, Phase: 7 LM, Findspot: 190.93/832.50.

Staples

Nine staples were identified from the site in total, of which three have been classified as post-medieval (see below). All except one (FeS8) have a rectangular or sub-rectangular section. FeS6–10 could have been used as fastenings with chains or hasps and padlocks, or they could have held rings or handles for doors or chests (Goodall 1990c, 328–329), whereas FeS11, a more delicate object with clenched terminals, may have held together two pieces of wood.

The three largest examples (FeS12–14) form a distinct group, and their size suggests that they were attached to a structure, possibly used as rings for tethering animals. These were found in late contexts in the area of the compound to the north-west of the church and are probably post-medieval.

FeS6 (Figure 12.38)
U-shaped staple, the tips pointing inwards, rectangular profile. One terminal is missing, the other is wedge shaped, tapering towards the tip. Found in a rubbish pit to the north of the site.
L 50mm; W 30>15mm; Th 7>4mm.
C1012, Phase: 6 Med, Area: 206.89–207.11/858.72–860.

FeS7 (Figure 12.38)
U-shaped staple with rectangular section. One terminal is flattened to a point, the other is broken off. Found in cemetery earth to the west of the church.
L 47mm; W 32mm; Th 6mm; total length straightened out 90mm.
C1022, Phase: 6 Med, Findspot: 180.52/832.49.

FeS8 (not illustrated)
U-shaped staple with rounded cross section. The arms are parallel and the terminals taper to sharp points. Found in the lower fill of the pit in the extended nave.
L 50mm; W 19mm; Th 4mm; total length straightened out 105mm.
C1305, Phase: 7 LM, Findspot: 191.45/831.70.

FeS9 (Figure 12.38)
U-shaped staple with flattened head, rectangular section. One terminal tapers, the other is possibly incomplete. Found in cemetery earth associated with Sk121.
L 75mm; W 5mm; Th 5mm.
C710, Phase: 6 Med, Findspot: 203.721/827.88.

FeS10 (Figure 12.38)
Rectangular/flat-headed staple with rectangular section. Found in cemetery earth.
L 40mm; W 32mm; Th 4mm.
C504, Phase: 7 LM (disturbed), Area: 204–6/846–8.

FeS11 (Figure 12.38)
Staple, with inturned ends, similar in form to an example from Wintringham (I H Goodall 1981, fig 56.4) and Winchester, where comparable examples come from contexts dated 10th–13th centuries (Goodall 1990c, 335), the ends may have been turned inwards to clamp together two pieces of wood. See also CA21.
L 32mm; W 17mm; Th 3mm.
C428, Phase: 8 EPM, Area: 186–8/837–9.

FeS12 (Figure 12.38)
Round headed staple with rectangular section, terminals flattened.
L 65mm; W 60mm; Th 5mm.
C901, Topsoil, Area: 175–182.5/837–839.5.

FeS13 (Figure 12.38)
One arm of a round headed staple similar to FeS17, with rectangular section and a tapering terminal.
L 87mm; W 7mm; Th 10>4mm.
C901, topsoil, Area: 175–182.5/837–839.5.

FeS14 (Figure 12.38)
Round headed staple with flattened rectangular section and tapering terminals.
L 62mm; W 50mm; Th 9>3mm; total length straightened out 130mm.
C903, Phase: 8 EPM, Findspot: 179.48/834.5.

Hinge pivot

FeS15 (Figure 12.38)
Hinge pivot, the guide arm has circular section. The angle between the guide arm and the shank is flattened in the vertical plane, while the shank itself is flattened horizontally and slightly downturned, suggesting that it was set into masonry. It could have supported a small door or window shutter (Goodall 1990c, 330). Found in an area of rubble in the eastern end of the extended nave.
L 125mm; W 12>5mm; Th 6>1mm.
C638, Phase: 7 LM, Findspot: 196.92/831.05.

13

FUNERARY MONUMENTS

Rosemary Cramp and Derek Craig

The Hirsel cemetery yielded what may be the full range of types of grave-markers in use in rural churchyards from the early medieval to early modern period. None were of a very high standard or workmanship, but perhaps the most remarkable survival was the area of the simple unshaped stones marking graves or grave plots north of the church (see Figures 6.15 and 6.16). The more elaborate grave furniture was unfortunately not found *in situ*. The coffin (FM1) may not have come from this site, nor the huge slab with a small incised cross (FM2), since both had been reused in later contexts. The cross shaft and head (FM6 and FM7), which were not connected, were recovered in 1977 from the stone dump after the field had been ploughed. No obvious setting was found for a cross base in the churchyard, and the socket stone inside the church which may have held a cross (see AF21) is the wrong size for the base of the cross shaft, so this may indeed have stood in the cemetery marking a primary grave. The shape of the only cross-head (see discussion below) seems to be 11th–12th century in date if compared with monuments elsewhere. It is suggested that it might be a finial cross for a church gable, rather than the top of a cross shaft, but it has been left with this group.

The upright grave-markers FM3 and FM4 are potentially the earliest of the recovered stones, but such plain slabs, with simple incised crosses, seem to have a long history. As noted in a previous publication (Cramp and Douglas-Home 1980, 229) rough slabs such as FM3 are found in North Britain, Ireland and Wales from the 5th century onwards, although the terminal date for such production is not known, and crosses in circles can occur as late as the 11th century. Single linear crosses on small slabs were considered by Thomas as 'primary grave-markers' (Thomas 1967, 152–153, fig 37 and pl 17B), but more recently, in discussing the West Highland grave-slabs, Ian Fisher has noted in relation to simple linear incised crosses, that they are 'widely distributed occurring in about a quarter of the carved stones in the area, sometimes in combination with other cross types, and on the walls of caves', and further notes that although a 7th–9th century date is often suggested, such simple crosses are carved on grave-markers at many periods (Fisher 2001, 12), a view reiterated in relation to a cross-marked stone from St Ninian's Isle (Fisher 2011, 122 and fig 4.23). The broad faces of FM4 are more carefully finished than FM3, particularly below the cross where the stone was presumably once buried in the ground. The cross is also delicately carved and the terminal points have the same geometric precision as the centring of the circles on the recumbent slab (FM5). A parallel form of the cross is found on a slab from the old burial ground of Eileach an Naoimh, Inner Hebrides (Allen 1903, fig 421).

Plain flat grave covers such as FM5 are rare in Scotland, and are not very common in England either, since as grave covers they are most commonly carved with a central cross from about the 10th century onwards. Plain tapering covers have been found in St Mark's cemetery in Lincoln, where they have been dated to around the mid-10th to 13th centuries (Gilmour and Stocker 1986, fig 57), and there are a few (undated) from Cumbria, as at St James, Ormside (Ryder 2005, 41.8), Furness Abbey (Ryder 2005, 191.10) or Gosforth (Ryder 2005, 81.3). Compass-drawn circles on slabs have been found in contexts at the monastic site at Whithorn (Hill 1997, fig 10.108), although not necessarily as grave covers or markers. For a detailed discussion of the Whithorn pieces and their affinities, see Craig (1997, 439–441). The large cover (FM5) from The Hirsel is very unweathered and may indeed have been inside the building although, as noted elsewhere, no burials were located in the church, and there is just the possibility that this was a seat and not a grave cover. Other plain flat grave covers, more roughly shaped, were found in a 'cairn' covering Sk78 and Sk98 (Figure 6.34) to the south of the church, and many broken fragments of flat grave covers were recorded, mostly south of the church, while to the north of the church, cobbles and more rounded stones served as grave-markers for head and foot stones (see Figure 6.1). These and the stones of the cists are listed in archive.

FM1 (Figure 13.1)
Sandstone coffin/sarcophagus with head indent, angular shoulders and central drain-hole.

The stone is very abraded and shows signs of reuse in the sloping cuts on each side of the rim. Their function is obscure.

The *New Statistical Account* states that 'stone coffins have been found in different parts of the parish (Coldstream) and likewise great quantities of human bones, particularly in the grounds of Hirsel' (Goldie 1841, 207). By that date it seems to have been located outside the south-east corner of the walled garden and presumably was discovered not far from there (Cramp and Douglas-Home 1980, 227).

The lack of precision as to where this stone coffin was found could mean that it was originally buried in the priory, the cemetery of which would have been not far from the site, and another coffin with a similar angular head indent (Figure 13.2), which is now built into a the stable wall of Hope Park, Coldstream, may also have come from the priory (Hickman 2010, 37–38). Monolithic stone coffins usually contain an important burial, whether lay or clerical, and similar sarcophagi with angular shoulders were found in the cemetery at Jedburgh, although there the sides were formed from several pieces rather than being monolithic as here (Lewis and Ewart 1995, illus 92). As noted above in Section 2.2, it is uncertain whether any of the Dunbar earls were buried at The Hirsel site, though the church and land still remained as part of the Dunbar estate even when its rights were transferred to the priory (Hamilton 2010, 79–81) but, if the sarcophagus came from this burial ground, it might have been for the interment of one of the parsons, who also, from documentary evidence, could have been family members (Hamilton 2010, 143).

The interior of the coffin measures 193cm in length at the rim and 183cm at the base, and tapers from 47cm wide at the shoulders to 25cm at the foot. It is 26cm deep, except at the foot, which is chamfered. The head indent is 26cm long and varies in width between a maximum of 26cm and 20cm at the opening. The drain-hole, 100cm from the head end, is 3cm in diameter. The flat rim of the coffin is about 7cm wide, except at the ends, where it is 85mm.

External measurements: L 208cm; W 63>39cm; Th 31>29cm.

12th–13th century.

Original location unknown.

FM2 (Figure 13.3)

Grave cover or marker of micaceous sandstone.

A large oblong slab, with a small linear cross incised in the upper part of one face.

Original location unknown. Found built into the west wall at Crook's House, a mile from the site (Caroline Douglas-Home pers comm).

The slab has been roughly shaped, but its surface today is rough and irregular.

This large rough slab has no diagnostic features. It could be medieval or later.

The cross is 41cm from the broader end, and measures 7cm x 6.5cm.

L 189cm; W 95>93cm; Th 14>10cm.

Probably medieval.

FIGURE 13.1
Stone coffin found on the estate, FM1

FIGURE 13.2
Stone coffin now at Hope Park, Coldstream

FM3 (Figure 13.4)
Upright grave-marker of grey-green micaceous sandstone. Original position unknown, found before excavation in the stone dump.
The stone tapers slightly, and only the broad faces are worked.

Face A is decorated only with a linear cross, 17.3cm x 17.8cm. It is well centred in the slab (4cm from top, 4.5cm from either side) and has been carefully and deeply cut with a chisel.

Face B has suffered considerable damage from the ploughing. It has been roughly dressed back to leave a deep boss (Diam *c*4.5cm; Depth 0.8cm), which has been centrally placed on the upper portion of the stone. Superimposed on it is a deeply cut linear cross (9cm x 8.5cm), the lower arm of which projects beyond the circle of the boss.

The cutting of the linear cross on face A is deep and confident unlike roughly scratched crosses at, for example, Portmahomack (Carver 2008, ill 5.2). The cross on the raised boss can be paralleled in Northumberland at Warkworth (Cramp 1984b, 230, illus 1282 and 1284), and is also found incised on flat surfaces at Warden and Corbridge in Northumberland (Cramp 1984b, illus 1287 and 1337). These monuments have been dated as probably 11th century.
H 42.5cm; W 34>26.7cm; Th 8.3>6.3cm.
?11th century.
Reference: Cramp and Douglas-Home 1980, 227, no. 1, pl 13a–b.

FM2 a

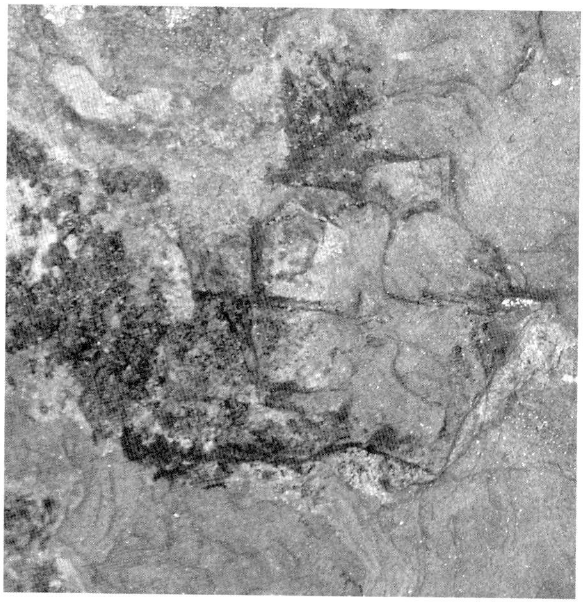

b

FIGURE 13.3
Grave cover with detail of small incised cross, FM2

FM3 a b

FIGURE 13.4
Upright grave marker, FM3: (a) Face A, with deeply incised cross; (b) Face B, with cross on boss

FM4 (Figure 13.5)
Upright grave-marker of fine-grained grey sandstone.
Found before excavation in the stone dump.

The stone is roughly shaped, with a rounded top and slightly tapering (chisel-cut) sides, but the broad faces are smoothly finished, in particular below the linear cross. Only one face is carved. Carefully centred on the upper portion of the slab (7cm from top and sides) is a fine linear cross, 19.6cm high by 18.4cm wide. It is lightly cut but with deeply punched dot terminals on three of the cross-arms. The base of the slab is much damaged by the plough, perhaps indicating that it was broken off from an upright position.

Although the form of the cross with its distinctive dot terminals such as are found at Eileach an Naoimh might indicate an early date, and this is a more carefully produced monument than FM3 where there is no evidence for the use of a chisel, one cannot be precise in dating this piece.
H 79cm; W 37.7>32.5cm; Th 11.5>11cm.
?11th–12th century.
Reference: Cramp and Douglas-Home 1980, 227, no. 2, pl 13c.

FIGURE 13.5
Upright grave marker with linear cross with dot terminals, FM4

FM5 (Figure 13.6)
Tapering recumbent slab of fine pinkish-grey sandstone, broken into three sections.
Found before excavation in the stone dump.

The upper face is very smoothly dressed; the lower face is roughly finished. The edges are chamfered, with clear diagonal chisel marks surviving. On the upper face are five compass-drawn circles. Three of these have intersecting arcs

FM5 a b

FIGURE 13.6
Recumbent slab with chamfered sides and compass-drawn circles and intersecting arcs on upper face, FM5

forming crosses with expanded arms. The arcs in the circle nearest the foot of the stone (Diam 8.3cm) are extended outside the circle and join to form ellipses. The cross adjacent to this on the other side of the break is enclosed within a double circumference (Diam 8.2cm and 9cm). The other cross on this central fragment has arcs extending outside the circle but not joining (Diam 12cm). The two circles placed asymmetrically in the upper part of the slab are very worn. One has two arcs forming a single arm within the circle (Diam 8.2cm), the other appears to be plain (Diam 8.2cm). All five circles have central compass point depressions. The surface of the slab is very heavily marked by plough drag.

As noted above, such plain slabs have been found in early medieval cemeteries in England but have not been assigned very precise dates from 11th–13th century. In Scotland, such a slab with a head or foot stone exists at St Blane's church Kingarth, Bute (Fisher 2001, 76, *B* 15). Compass-drawn circles on monuments especially to form crosses of arcs have a long history in the British Isles from the 7th century onwards and recent finds such as those from Inchmarnock are seen as this date, on the other hand the shape of the slab and its chamfered edges would put this monument later.

L 184cm; W 39>32.5cm; Th 16cm; Width of chamfer 4>3.5cm.
11th–12th century.
Reference: Cramp and Douglas-Home 1980, 227–228, no. 3, pl 14a.

FM6 (Figure 13.7)
Cross shaft of fine pinkish-grey sandstone.
Found before excavation in the stone dump.

The upper portion has been broken in antiquity, and there is considerable damage from recent ploughing. The broad faces are dressed very smoothly, but their chamfered edges (30mm wide) and the narrow faces have fine diagonal chisel marks. On one narrow face there is a long groove running approximately parallel to the edge, which seems to have been made with a tool. In the top of the shaft is a deep dowel hole, 9cm deep and 3cm in diameter, which must have supported a head.

Plain shafts with no edge mouldings and chamfered edges are in Northumbria of post-Norman date as, for example, at Blanchland (Vallance 1920, pl 44) or Kirkhaugh in Northumberland (Cramp 1984b, 243). This shaft could be of a similar date.

L 119.5cm; W 30.5>23cm; Th 16.5>14.5cm.
11th–12th century.
Reference: Cramp and Douglas-Home 1980, 228, no. 4, pl 15.

FIGURE 13.7
Plain cross shaft broken at the top with socket dowel for head, FM6

FM7 (Figure 13.8)
Upper portion of a ring headed cross, pinkish-grey sandstone.
Found before excavation in the stone dump.

The piece is the most weathered of all the stones in the (1977) group. The arms of the cross are wedge shaped, tapering into a small, flat, rounded centre. The ring has been formed by roughly chiselling into the block from each broad face.

When found and in previous publication, this head was assumed to be the terminal of a cross shaft possibly of FM6, although even then it was questioned whether it might more fittingly have been part of a head or footstone (Cramp and Douglas-Home 1980, 230). Such grave-markers exist in some numbers in Scotland (Fisher 2001, illus p. 76). Normally, however, such grave-markers are disc-headed with the ring unpierced as are those from Northumberland with similar shapes of cross (Cramp 1984b, pls 234, 236–237) some of which may have been terminals for grave-markers others may have been finials for church roofs. There is nothing which is an exact parallel for the Hirsel head and in view of the form of the break and the piercings it is suggested that another possible use for this piece could have been as the terminal for a roof ridge presumably for the church.

H 24cm; W 38cm; Th 15cm; Diam of ring 12.5cm; Upper arm L 16.5cm (from centre)
?11th–12th century.
Reference: Cramp and Douglas-Home 1980, 228, no. 5, pl 14b.

FM7 a

b

c

FIGURE 13.8
Upper portion of a ring headed cross which could be the terminal for a cross or the terminal of a roof ridge, FM7

14

COINS

Marion M Archibald

All the coins are Scottish and most are worn and corroded. Many counterfeits of the smaller, base-metal, 17th-century denominations were common and widely current alongside the official issues, and are identified by their irregular style and light weight. The condition of the present coins makes it difficult to distinguish these characteristics, but the coins of Nu2 are probably counterfeits. It should be noted that the Scottish issues of Charles I were continued after his death.

Nu1 (Figure 14.1)
William I, the Lion, 1165–1214.
Penny, Second Coinage, class 1.
The coin is bent double and so only the obverse is visible.
Obv: (+) LE(RE(IWIL(AM (in most cases only the bases of the letters are visible). Crowned bust to left; in front, cross-pattée sceptre. Pellet in annulet behind head.
Wt 1.43g (22.0gr) (uncleaned).

No die-identity has been found, but among coins of the pattée sceptre group, obverses with LE before REI are confined to the Perth mint. It is therefore probable that this coin is also from the Perth mint and was struck by Fobalt, the only moneyer known to have worked there at this time. Without a die-identity. however, it is impossible to be certain.

The date of the start of the Second Coinage is not known. Within it, the change from a pattée to a pommée sceptre is associated with the introduction of the latter in the English Short-Cross coinage in 1180. Although the Scottish mints need not have followed suit immediately, the pattée sceptre phase may be dated in round terms around 1175–1180 with a possible extension of a year or two at either end. Coins of this group remained in circulation until the introduction of the Scottish Short-Cross in 1195.
C1365 (with Sk336), Phase: 5 EM2, findspot: 182.50/825.30.

Nu2 (Figure 14.1)
James VI.
Two coins stuck together, obverse of one and reverse of the other visible, found in a 'bag' of textile and leather, associated with Sk56.
Twopences (hardheads), Second Issue, November 1588, probably counterfeits.
Wt 1.86g (relatively little wear, but corroded and textile adhering).
Reference: cf Stewart 1967, pl xv, 200.

The style of the lion on the reverse looks irregular and the two pellets indicating the denomination are sited above the top of its tail rather than beside the lower loop as on official coins. The weight is low for two coins even after making allowances for the condition.
C713, Phase: 8 EPM, Findspot: 205.64/823.30.

Nu3 (Figure 14.1)
James VI.
Twopence (hardhead) of Second Issue, 1623–1625.
Wt 1.30g.
C104, Phase: 8 EPM, Findspot: 203.83/866.84.
Reference: Stewart 1967, pl xvi, 217.

Nu4 (Figure 14.1)
Charles I.
Twopence (turner), Third Issue, date illegible, but issued 1642, 1644 and 1650 *(sic)*.
Wt 2.08g.
C911, Phase: 8 EPM, Findspot: 182.60/838.55.
Reference: Stewart 1967, pl xviii, 239.

Nu5 (not illustrated)
Charles I.
Twopence (turner), Third Issue, date and initial mark illegible, but issued 1642, 1644 and 1650 *(sic)*.
Wt 1.54g.
C927, Phase: 8 EPM, Findspot: 176.90/830.45.

Nu6 (Figure 14.1)
Charles II.
Sixpence (bawbee) of Second Issue, date illegible, but struck 1677, 1678 and 1679.
Wt 6.81g.
C701, topsoil, Area: 196–210/820–2.
Reference: Stewart 1967, pl xviii, 244.

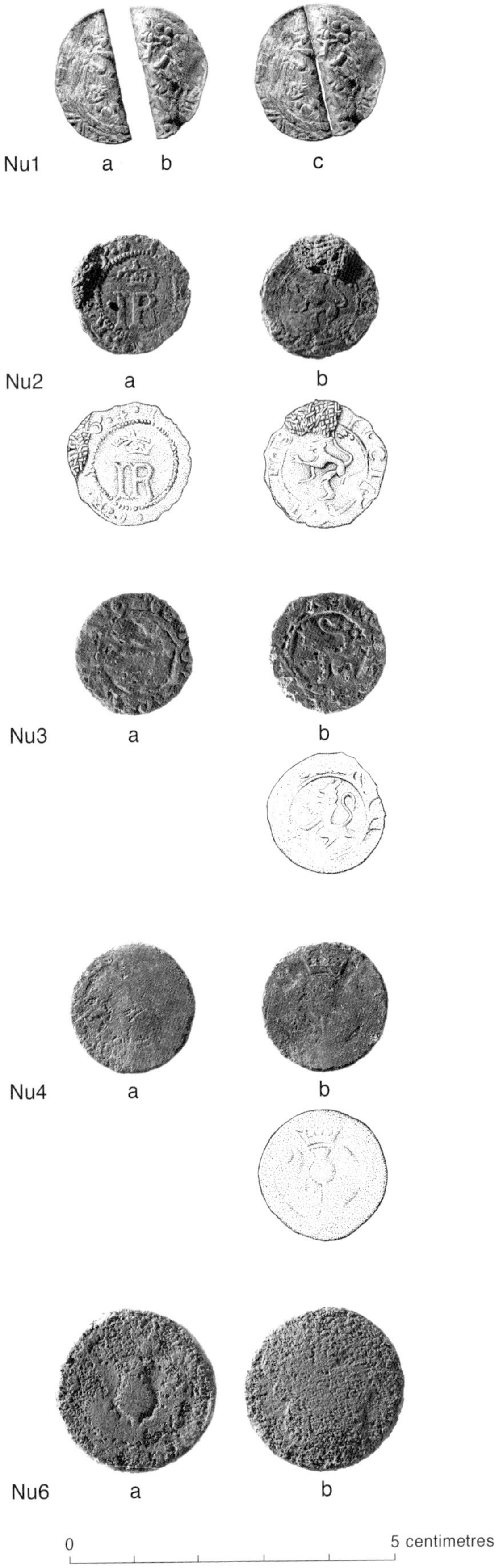

FIGURE 14.1
Coins from the excavated site

15

PREHISTORIC POTTERY

Alison Sheridan

The small assemblage of prehistoric pottery consists of substantial parts of two Early Neolithic pots (Pots 1–2), together with eight sherds from a further eight pots, of which four (Pots 3–6) are of Early Neolithic date and four (Pots 7–10) are most likely to be of Middle to Late Bronze Age date. The pottery had previously been catalogued, and the catalogue numbers stuck on the sherds, but this report supersedes that; a concordance list, giving the new Pot Numbers, along with all the previously available labels and contextual information relating to the sherds, has been lodged in the site archive.

Individual sherds (and samples of soil found adjacent to them) have undergone various kinds of analysis, namely thermoluminescence (TL) dating (Pots 2 and 10), phosphate analysis (of soil adjacent to Pots 1 and 2, and of a sherd and sample of organic encrustation from Pot 2) and, most recently, lipid analysis (Pots 1 and 2). The results of these analyses are summarised below; the full reports on the TL dating and the lipid analysis are presented in Appendices 3 and 4.

The pottery will be described and discussed according to period.

15.1 EARLY NEOLITHIC POTTERY

Description

Pot 1 (Figure 15.1)
Sherds (several refitted, plus some 25 loose) amounting to just over half of a large carinated bowl, with an estimated rim diameter of 290–300mm, an estimated carination diameter of *c*285mm, and an estimated height of *c*146mm. The overall weight of the constituent pieces is 480g. The bowl has a fairly thick, bulbous rim, a short, upright, concave neck and a medium-depth rounded belly; the junction between the neck and belly is marked by a sharp carination. Wall thickness ranges from 6.1mm just above the carination to *c*11mm at the belly. The surfaces had been carefully smoothed, and either coated with a thin slip or wet-smoothed to create a thin surface 'skin'. Parts of the surface had then been polished to a low sheen, probably using a round-ended pebble or similar tool, creating a decorative fluted effect. (Note that the application of consolidant during the pot's conservation has enhanced the sheen, and also darkened the surface and hardened the sherds. The original state of the pot is clear from the unconsolidated sherds.) This fluting extends over the top of the rim, as radial marks, and down into the interior of the neck, where it forms two rows. There are hints that it also extended down the neck on the exterior, but these marks are shallow and obscured by other, horizontal marks which could have been made by rubbing the surface with a bunch of grass. There are also shallow and diffuse fluting lines below the carination, running down the belly in slightly diagonal lines. Other evidence relating to the pot's construction consist of gentle facets on the outer edge and lower side of the rim, suggesting the use of a spatulate object to shape it, and further slight faceting of the interior, which might relate to scraping. To judge from the unconsolidated

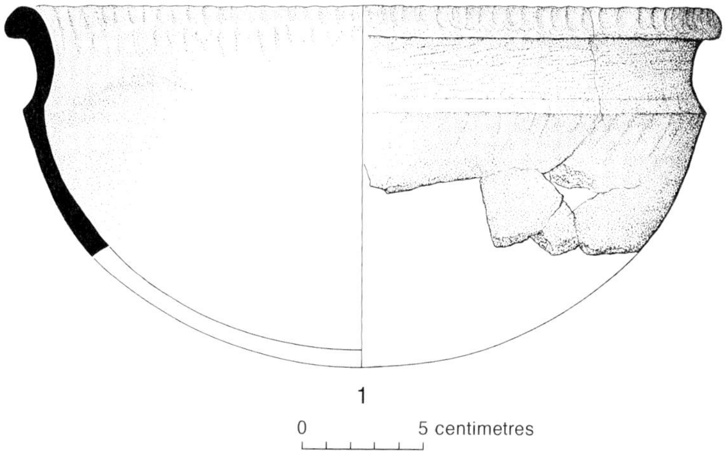

FIGURE 15.1
Neolithic pottery, Pot 1

sherds from this pot, the original colour of the exterior ranges from a light brown at the bottom of the belly to a dark, in places slightly reddish brown, and black-brown (especially around the neck). The core is dark grey in parts and bright red-brown towards the exterior and interior. The interior is a rich reddish-brown and black-brown on the upper part of the body, with a blackish patch further down the belly that may be a firing cloud. One detached belly sherd has a tiny patch of black organic encrustation, and a further patch of thin encrustation is present on the exterior just below the carination, suggesting the pot's use for cooking. Inclusions in the fabric vary in stone type, angularity and density, and are likely to represent both material present naturally in the clay and crushed stone deliberately added as a filler. Over much of the pot they comprise small fragments (<3mm x 2mm) of a dull, black-brown stone (occurring as sub-angular and rounded inclusions) together with mica platelets and angular and sub-angular fragments of a speckled, white and black stone, at a relatively low density of 3%. However, the density of these inclusions rises to 7–10% at one part of the pot (extending from the neck to the belly), making the pot gritty at this point, and one of the inclusions is as large as 7mm x 5mm.

The fracture surfaces are not heavily abraded, and this is in line with the probability (see below) that the pot had been deposited whole and upright, and had subsequently been broken *in situ* (and was then disturbed by ploughing).

Phosphate analysis of three samples of soil associated with this pot (one from within the spread of sherds and two outside the spread) was undertaken by Michael Alexander in 1980 in response to the suggestion (unfounded) that this and Pot 2 had been used as cinerary urns. The results showed that the phosphate levels are no higher than normal background levels (see Appendix 3).

Lipid analysis of two unconsolidated sherds, one from the upper belly of this pot, was undertaken between 2009 and 2012 by Dr Lucy Cramp in Bristol University; this focussed on lipids that had been absorbed into the body of the pot, and which would be invisible (see Appendix 4 for details of the analytical method and results.) Both sherds were found to contain significant concentrations of lipid, thereby confirming that the pot had indeed been used for cooking. In common with other pots that had been used to boil foodstuffs, the sherd from the upper belly was found to have the highest concentration; this is because lipids tend to be wicked up through the vessel wall and also float on the surface of the liquid, which often lies around the area where the belly meets the neck. The origin of the lipids was found to be ruminant carcass fat (from cattle, sheep or goats), and the distinctive distribution of mid-chain ketones (C_{31}–C_{35}) indicated that this animal fat had been heated to over 300°C.

C126, Phase: 1 Neolithic (disturbed), Findspots: 196.90/869.16; 197.18/869.09; 197.20/868.97.

Pot 2 (Figure 15.2)
Around 70 sherds, many conjoined, amounting to around two-thirds of a globular, round-based, thin-walled pot, with an estimated rim diameter of around 220mm, an estimated maximum diameter of 260mm and an estimated height of 180mm; the overall weight is some 400g. The rim is thick, with a rounded top, slightly expanded to the interior of the pot, and hooked on its exterior: it had been rolled outwards, thereby creating the hook. Wall thickness ranges from 5mm to 6.9mm. The surface had been wet-smoothed or slipped, and there are many smoothing facets visible on the exterior and interior. As with Pot 1, its colour, surface appearance and hardness have all been affected by the application of

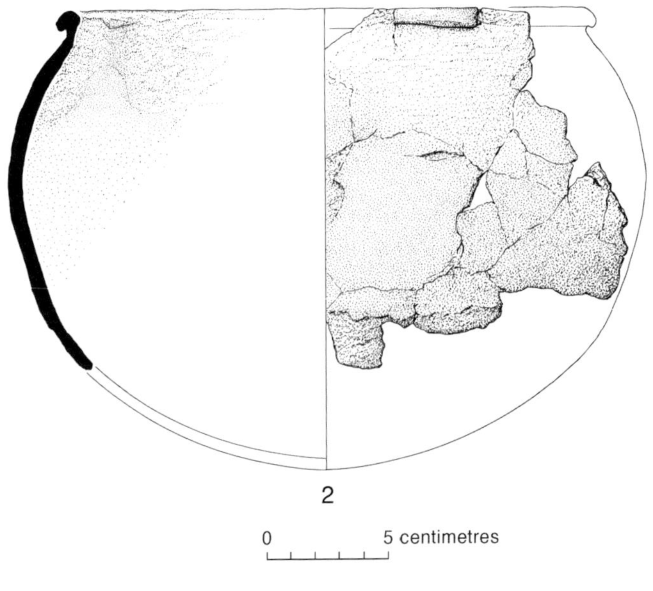

FIGURE 15.2
Neolithic pottery, Pot 2

consolidant, and all the sherds have been so treated, and so it is impossible to tell to what extent the (now-shiny) surface had originally been polished. The exterior colour (which will have been darkened by the consolidant) is black-brown over the upper part of the pot and medium to dark brown over the lower belly; the core is dark grey-brown; and the interior is black at the belly and medium-brown towards the rim. There are tiny patches of very thin black organic residue on the exterior, just below the rim and on the lower belly, and on the belly in the interior; these, and the pot's exterior colour, suggest its use as a cooking pot (see also below). The fabric, now hard from the consolidant, is laminar and contains very sparse lithic inclusions, at a density of 3% or less; these comprise sub-angular fragments of a dull brown stone, up to 6.5mm x 4mm in size, along with angular speckled fragments, and rounded black grains; most match the inclusions seen in Pot 1. The paucity of inclusions is probably responsible for the loss of several spalls from the interior and exterior, including a large spall from the lower belly; this spalling could have happened during the pot's firing. The edge of that spall scar is abraded, indicating that the pot had indeed been used in this condition. The fracture surfaces of the sherds are not heavily abraded, suggesting that the pot had broken *in situ*.

Phosphate analysis of soil adjacent to the sherd spread, of a crushed sherd, and of the black encrustation from its interior, all produced elevated phosphate readings, especially so from the sherd and encrustation. Michael Alexander concluded that these results, rather than indicating the former presence of cremated remains (of which no trace had been found, and which could be expected to have survive, had there been any), instead suggested the pot's use for cooking: 'It could well be that the use of such a pot for cooking over a period of time could impregnate the pot with phosphorus from the items being cooked' (Appendix 3).

Further confirmation that the pot had indeed been a cooking pot was obtained by Lucy Cramp's lipid analysis of a sherd from this pot (Appendix 3). The analysis revealed the presence of ruminant dairy fat (e.g. from milk or butter), in contrast to the ruminant carcass fat that had been found in Pot 1. In addition, there were hints of the former presence of plant material, in the form of degraded waxes.

A sherd from this pot was subjected to TL dating in the 1980s, in order to obtain a general impression of its antiquity (and, in particular, to check whether it could be of early prehistoric age). The result, of 3300±435 BC (at σ_B), served to confirm that it was indeed early prehistoric although, given what we now know about the chronology of this pottery type, it is clear that the date is neither accurate nor sufficiently precise to be of further use (see below).

C132, Phase: 1 Neolithic (disturbed), Findspot: 199.55/869.88

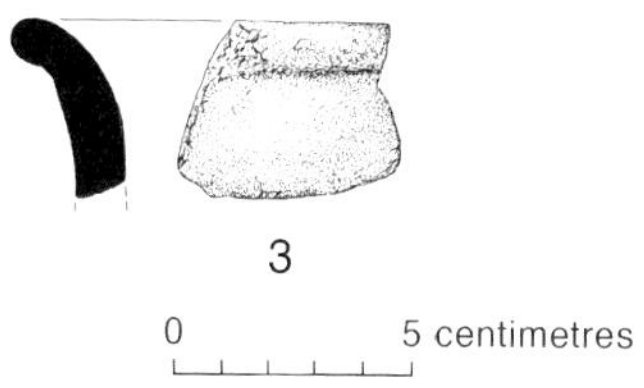

FIGURE 15.3
Neolithic rim, Pot 3

Pot 3 (Figure 15.3)
This pot is represented by a single rim-and-neck sherd, which will almost certainly have come from a carinated bowl. The rim is rounded and gently out-turned, and the neck is fairly straight and would have been either vertical or slightly everted. The sherd is too small to offer a reliable estimate of the pot's rim diameter, but this is likely to have been in the region of 290–310mm, and thus comparable with that of Pot 1. Wall thickness, at the neck, is around 11.5mm; the sherd's weight is 29g. The surfaces had been smoothed (probably wet-smoothed) and there are broad, horizontal facets made by a spatulate tool on the exterior; the exterior is slightly uneven and cracked, and matte. The interior had been polished to a low to medium sheen, and there is a slight ripple-polish effect on the top of the rim. The exterior and core are a mottled dark grey-brown and mid-brown; the interior is black. There are no signs of organic encrustation. Lithic inclusions comprise angular and sub-angular fragments of light grey and creamy-coloured stone, and also fragments of the speckled stone as seen in Pots 1 and 2; the largest inclusion is 4mm x 4.5mm (but most are considerably smaller) and the density is *c*5%, giving the sherd a gritty texture. The fabric is hard. The fracture surfaces are moderately abraded.

C111, Phase: 6 Med, Area: 195–6/864–5.

Pot 4 (not illustrated)
This pot is represented by a large sherd (weighing 90g) from a large, fairly thick-walled, medium- to deep-bellied, carinated or S-profiled bowl; if the former, the carination is barely perceptible. The diameter at this point is estimated at around 300mm, so the pot will have been of comparable girth to Pots 1 and 3. Wall thickness varies from 9.5mm at the belly to 14mm above the 'carination'. The sherd has been consolidated. The surfaces had been smoothed, probably wet-smoothed, and left matte. The exterior is medium-brown with a black firing cloud; the core and interior are black. There are no traces of organic encrustation. Inclusions are sparse (3%) and comprise angular fragments of a hard, light grey crystalline stone, up to 7mm x 5.5mm. The fracture surfaces are slightly abraded.

C112, Phase: 1 Neolithic (disturbed), Findspot: 197.23/869.68.

Pot 5 (not illustrated)
This is represented by a single, small, very thin-walled (4.5–4.7mm), belly sherd, of fine fabric; it weighs just 1.6g. It is too small to estimate the original size of the pot. The surfaces had been carefully smoothed (probably wet-smoothed) and polished to a medium sheen. The colour is black-brown throughout and there are no signs of organic encrustation. Inclusions are sparse (< 3%) and comprise sub-angular grains of quartz, up to 3mm x 2mm in size. The fracture surfaces are slightly abraded.

C851, Phase: 4? EM1, Findspot: 189.40/825.55.

Pot 6 (not illustrated)
This is also represented by a single belly sherd from a thin-walled (6.2–6.8 mm), fine pot, too small to allow the pot's size to be estimated; it weighs 5.2g. The surfaces had been carefully smoothed (probably wet-smoothed) and the exterior had been burnished to a low sheen, with burnishing facets clearly visible. The exterior is black-brown, reddish immediately below the surface; the core is pink-brown, and the interior is pink- and grey-brown. There are no signs of organic encrustation. Inclusions are of the same kinds of stone as seen in Pots 1–3, comprising angular fragments of the speckled stone, and angular and sub-angular fragments of a creamy (and variegated) stone and of a light grey stone; the maximum size is 4.5mm x 3mm, and the density around 3–5%. The fracture surfaces are slightly abraded.

C931, Phase: 6 Med, Findspot: 179.80/831.95.

Discussion of the Early Neolithic pottery

Before considering its cultural affiliations and date, the spatial and contextual distribution of the Early Neolithic pottery needs to be considered. The remains of Pots 1–4 come from the northern part of the excavated area, while the sherds from Pots 5 and 6 are from the southern area, in the vicinity of the church (with Pot 6 being found in a small posthole); a concentration of worked flint had been found in the same area and may be related. Later activities had disturbed and truncated all the contexts in which this pottery was found. It appears, however, that Pots 1, 2 and 4 were associated with a curvilinear, lightly constructed, probably wattle-and-daub built structure (C112), with Pot 2 being found immediately outside, Pot 1 immediately inside, and Pot 4 among the remains of the wall (C112). Both Pots 1 and 2 seem to have been deposited in hollows, with flat stones placed immediately below and above, as if to protect them. To judge from the orientation of the sherds when discovered, Pot 1 had been upright (Figures 4.6–4.8), Pot 2 probably not (Figure 4.9). Both may well have been complete when deposited, with subsequent disturbance (by ploughing) dragging some sherds of Pot 1 further into the interior of the structure; Pot 2 had been more extensively disturbed, and not all of the area around it was excavated (Section 4.1, **p 0000**). The hollows in which Pots 1 and 2 were found do not appear to have been hearths or midden pits. Pot 3 was found a few metres to the south-west of the C112 structure and may have been associated with another, stake-built structure. All the finds of the Early Neolithic pottery are likely to represent settlement activity, with that at the northern end extending beyond the excavated area to the north. The fact that the Neolithic structure/s are lightly built and curvilinear reminds us that a range of habitation structures would have been used, not just the better-known post/post-and-plank-built rectangular houses as seen elsewhere (Sheridan 2007); indeed, Clive Waddington has defined a whole class of ephemeral Early Neolithic structures in Northumberland that feature a triangular arrangement of postholes, as found, for example, in Lanton Quarry (Waddington *et al* 2011, 292–294).

This pottery is instantly recognisable as belonging to the Early Neolithic Carinated Bowl (henceforth 'CB') tradition, one of the two ceramic traditions brought to Scotland (and elsewhere in Britain) by immigrant farmers as part of the Neolithisation process (Sheridan 2007; 2010). The origin of the CB tradition lies in northern France, probably the Nord-Pas de Calais region, and CB pottery can be characterised as one of a range of regional traditions that represent a fusion and re-casting of the Chassey and early Michelsberg traditions (Sheridan 2007). It is found over much of Britain and Ireland and arrived at some point between 4000 and 3800 BC; opinions differ as to whether we are dealing with a diaspora-like spread from northern France (Sheridan 2010) or an initial arrival in south-east England and spread therefrom (Whittle *et al* 2011), but that debate is not of relevance here. Its overall currency in Britain and Ireland, in one form or another, extends to around the middle of the 4th millennium BC (see Waddington *et al* 2011, table 8, for dates relating to its use in north-east England; and Whittle *et al* 2011, Chapter 14, for an overall model; but see also Sheridan 2012 for a critique of the latter).

The question to be addressed here is whether the Hirsel pottery belongs to the earliest manifestation of this 'CB' tradition — which this author has elsewhere (e.g. Sheridan 2007) described as 'traditional CB' pottery — or to a slightly developed form, so-called 'modified' (or 'developed') CB. As explained elsewhere (Sheridan 2007), it is possible to trace the process of 'style drift', whereby the original CB canon, as brought from the Continent, became modified over the generations. This evolution was to some extent technical as well as stylistic, with a trend towards slightly thicker-walled, slightly coarser pots being seen in some areas, along with variation in the carinated and uncarinated vessel shapes. This process of drift took place at different rates, in different ways, in different areas, thereby leading to regional differentiation. In north-east Scotland it occurred rapidly, as can be seen by comparing the CB assemblages from two neighbouring and near-contemporary large houses (or 'halls') at Crathes and Balbridie, Aberdeenshire (Sheridan 2007; 2009). Here it appears that the process of style drift began within a very few generations of the initial appearance of 'the Neolithic' (see Whittle *et al* 2011, fig 14.155, for a model of the dates from Crathes and Balbridie).

The trajectory of ceramic development in north-east England and south-east Scotland is becoming clearer, thanks to discoveries from developer-funded excavations (e.g. at Eweford and Pencraig Hill, East Lothian, found during upgrading of the A1, and through quarrying in the Milfield Basin of Northumberland; MacGregor and McLellan 2008; Waddington 2009a; Waddington *et al* 2011. Note also that a substantial assemblage of CB pottery has recently been excavated by Roger Miket and Ben Edwards at Threefords North, in the Milfield Basin; Roger Miket pers comm). A major debt is owed to Clive Waddington, who has recently synthesised the available dating and ceramic evidence for north-east England (Waddington *et al* 2011, 287; cf Millson *et al* 2012). His Bayesian modelling for all the available radiocarbon dates relating to the use of CB pottery in this region (where the tradition is well represented, and relatively well dated) suggests an overall currency starting *3985–3840 cal BC* (modelled date, at 68% probability; *4065–3840 cal BC* at 95% probability) and ending *3680–3630 cal BC* (68% probability; *3710–3620 cal BC* at 95% probability).

As a result of all this work, we are now able to suggest where and when, in the trajectory of CB pottery development between the Tyne and the Forth, the Hirsel assemblage lies. Essentially, the trend here appears to be towards thicker-walled and less fine-textured vessels, with less carefully finished surfaces than in traditional CB assemblages; lugs also appear in some assemblages.

In south-east Scotland, the process can be discerned by comparing the traditional CB pottery and the modified CB pottery found at Eweford West, East Lothian, in different contexts (Sheridan 2008a; MacGregor and McLellan 2008, figs 2.5, 2.10 and 2.17). Radiocarbon dates suggest that the two assemblages are separated by up to two centuries — perhaps as short an interval as one to three generations (and see Whittle *et al* 2011, figs 14.161 and 14.164 for Bayesian-modelled versions of the dates); the modified CB pottery is associated with a date of 3660–3510 cal BC at 95.4% probability (SUERC-5297, 4800±35 BP, hazel charcoal). The traditional CB pottery is markedly thinner and finer than the modified CB vessels, and the latter have heavier rims.

In north-east England, the process of 'style drift' to 'modified CB' pottery is exemplified by the assemblage from Lanton Quarry, Northumberland, which includes carinated bowls with heavy rims (at least one embellished by fluting); one with a prominent, cordon-like carination; one with a strap lug; and one with along applied lug on its carination (Waddington 2009a). One of the small, ephemeral structures at this settlement (building 7) in which such pottery was found produced a date of 3620–3350 cal BC (at 95.4% probability: Beta-231340, 4640±40 BP, charred hazelnut shell); another (building 8), is dated, again from charred hazelnut shell, to 3650–3520 cal BC at 95.4% probability (SUERC-31575), and here the pottery was found in the same midden pit as the hazelnut shell (Waddington *et al* 2011, fig 8). As with the Eweford West pottery, this assemblage can be compared with others that are closer to (or belong to) the 'traditional CB' canon, as at Cheviot Quarry North (Johnson and Waddington 2008, illus 10), Thirlings (Miket *et al* 2008, illus 21–24), Threefords North, and Yeavering (Hope-Taylor 1977, figs 119, 123.1–7 and 9).

With the Hirsel assemblage, on the one hand, there are elements of the assemblage that are characteristic of the earliest, traditional CB pottery, and which are present virtually throughout the large area of its distribution. These are the almost imperceptible carination of Pot 4, the thinness and fineness of Pots 5 and 6, and the fluting on Pot 1. *Comparanda* among 'traditional CB' assemblages include vessel V2 from Pencraig Hill long barrow, East Lothian, with its fingertip fluting on the rim and interior of the neck (MacGregor and McLellan 2008, fig 2.24; Sheridan 2008b). However, Hirsel Pot 1 is thicker-walled than many of the traditional CB carinated bowls, and its irregular distribution of inclusions is inconsistent with traditional CB potting practice. Furthermore, Pot 2 is more globular than most traditional CB uncarinated pots, and its slight irregularity in shape and surface is also slightly atypical. Therefore, in the author's opinion, the Hirsel assemblage probably does not belong to the earliest part of the CB pottery currency and should probably be regarded as an early kind of 'modified CB', with a probable date in the late 38th or 37th century BC. The aforementioned TL date of 3300±320 BC (at σ_A)/±435 BC (at σ_B), obtained from Pot 2, is not precise enough and can be discounted.

15.2 POTTERY OF PROBABLE BRONZE AGE DATE

Each of the pots in question is represented by a single, small, undecorated sherd (plus two fragments in the case of Pot 10), of which the largest (Pot 8) measures only 55 x 28mm.

Pot 7 (Figure 15.4)
Rim-and-neck sherd of gritty fabric, burnt; weight 19.5g. The rim is upright and rounded, and below it, on the outside, the wall slopes out to a gentle, moulded carination, thereby forming a shallow neck around 23mm broad. If, as seems likely, the base had been flat, the wall would have risen from it near-vertically. Wall thickness ranges from 9mm (at the neck) to 12mm (at the carination). The sherd is too small to allow a reliable estimate of rim diameter, but it may well have been around 190mm; as for vessel shape, if — as suspected — this had been from a flat-based pot, it may have been bucket-shaped, with near-vertical walls. Although the surfaces had been smoothed, several lithic inclusions protrude. The exterior is a red and light brown colour; the core, buff and pale grey; and the interior, buff-brown and light grey. Small patches of a black encrustation on the exterior may well be natural precipitated manganese from the surrounding sediment, rather than organic residue. Inclusions comprise sub-angular and rounded fragments, up to 4.5mm x 3mm in size, of a hard, dark brown, basalt-like stone and of a fine-grained, light grey stone; the density is *c*5%. The fabric is fairly soft; this, and the sherd's colour, indicate that it had been burnt (e.g. by lying around in a hearth). The fracture surfaces are slightly abraded.

C845, Phase: 3–4 Pre-Med (disturbed), Findspot: 179.04/833.50.

Pot 8 (Figure 15.4)
Sherd from the bottom of the wall of a small, flat-based pot with an estimated base diameter of around 120mm and wall thickness of 9mm; weight 16g. Part of the wall-base junction is present, showing that the wall would have risen near-vertically and that the junction, on the interior, was a continuous curve. The surfaces had been carefully smoothed, and may have been coated with a thin slip (or else had been wet-smoothed) and the exterior polished to a low sheen. There are horizontal smoothing marks on the interior. The exterior is black and dark brown; the core, blackish; and the interior, black and dark grey-brown. There is black organic encrustation on the interior at the base-wall junction, plus traces of encrustation on the exterior, suggesting the pot's use for cooking. Lithic inclusions are very hard to see, but there are tiny, shiny fragments of a whitish mineral (possibly feldspar or quartz) and tiny rounded particles of a hard, dark brown stone; the density of inclusions cannot be estimated. The fabric is hard and the fracture surfaces slightly abraded.

C1131, Phase: 2 LP, Findspot: 194.83/836.22.

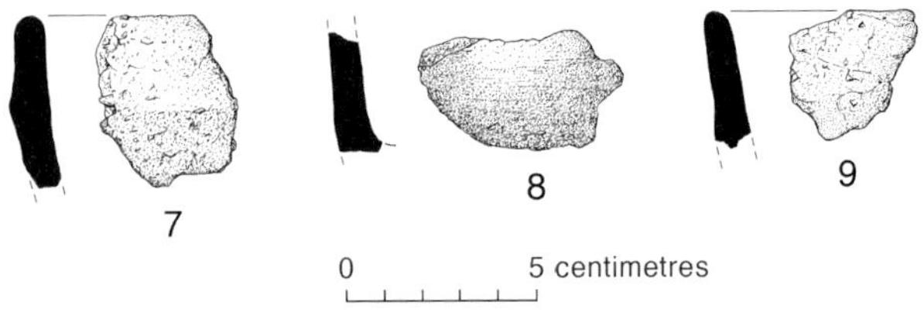

FIGURE 15.4
Pottery of probable Bronze Age date, Pots 7, 8 and 9

Pot 9 (Figure 15.4)
Rim-and-neck sherd from a pot with a hard, gritty fabric and very uneven surfaces; weight 12g; maximum thickness 10mm. The rim is rounded and the wall of the vessel may have splayed very slightly. The sherd is too small to allow a reliable estimate of rim diameter but it could have been around 170mm, and thus comparable to the girth of Pot 7. Despite their unevenness, the surfaces had been either wet-smoothed or slipped. The exterior is black-brown, the core and interior black; there are tiny patches of black organic encrustation on the exterior. Lithic inclusions are fairly abundant (15–20% density) and range up to 8mm x 9mm; they consist of sub-angular fragments of a speckly, grey-cream-dark brown crystalline stone; sub-angular fragments of a soft, light grey stone and a harder, blackish stone; and angular fragments of a fine-grained grey stone. The fracture surfaces are slightly abraded.

C845, Phase: 3–4 Pre-Med (disturbed), Findspot: 181.39/834.06.

Pot 10 (not illustrated)
Single body sherd that had been subjected to TL dating, plus two fragments. Thickness: 11.5mm; weight 3.7g. The exterior is uneven, the interior smooth. The exterior is orange, the core and interior black. The fabric is fairly soft, and inclusions comprise sub-angular fragments (up to 6mm x 4.5mm) of a creamy-grey stone, a light grey stone, and quartz at a density of *c*5%. There is moderate abrasion to the edge and part of the exterior surface of the sherd.

The sherd had been subjected to thermo-luminescence dating, returning a result of 1540±290 BC (at σ_B). See below for a comment on this date.

C635, Phase: 6 Med, Findspot: 209.05/835.84.

Discussion of the Bronze Age pottery

These four sherds were all found in the southern part of the excavated area, in the vicinity of the church. The area had been severely disturbed by subsequent activity — Pot 7, for example, was found mixed with Roman and medieval pottery — and so very little can be said about the original context of its use, other than that it had probably been domestic. The small size, and paucity, of the sherds makes it difficult to be precise about their date; an earlier examination of the pottery (by Val Dean) had suggested that they could be of Roman Iron Age date, contemporary with the occupation phase radiocarbon dated to 115 cal BC–cal AD 70 (SUERC-16084) (p 37). The TL date for Pot 10 would seem to indicate a Bronze Age (or very earliest Iron Age) date but, like all TL dates for pottery, its standard deviation is so wide that it is of limited chronological value. From a typological point of view, the pottery could indeed date from any time from the Middle Bronze Age to the early first millennium AD: undecorated, flat-based, cylindrical and bucket-shaped pots are typical of the later prehistoric pottery in north-east England and south-east Scotland (and indeed further afield), many being grouped within the unsatisfactory and inaccurate (but persistent) category of 'flat-rimmed wares' (for a discussion of which, see Halliday 1988). *Comparanda* can be found across Northumberland (Waddington 2009b, 222; Passmore and Waddington 2012) and in south-east Scotland (e.g. at Knowes Farm and Foster Law, East Lothian; MacSween 2009); a useful discussion of this pottery, within a late 1st millennium BC context, is to be found in Ann MacSween's report on pottery from the Traprain Law Environs Project (MacSween 2009, 121–123).

16
THE ROMAN POTTERY

16.1 PREFACE
Rosemary Cramp

The distribution of Roman sherds from the site, many of which are abraded and worn, when combined with the evidence from the glass fragments (Section 25.1) support the supposition of a Roman presence in the vicinity of the site.

One group came from the lowest levels of cemetery earth south of the church (RP1, RP3, RP13). One other sherd (RP11), dated by thermoluminescence to the Roman period, came from the sand below the nave floor. Others, RP2, RP5, RP6, RP8 and RP9, came from the west of the church where pre-church levels were investigated and where there was a significant grouping of prehistoric pottery. The fragments which came from the cemetery area to the north of the church, RP4 and RP7, were from disturbed and redeposited contexts.

It would appear from the overall distribution that the fragments came from the levels underlying the church and cemetery.

16.2 THE ROMAN POTTERY
Paul Bidwell

Eighteen sherds were selected in the preliminary post-excavation sorting as certainly or possibly of Roman date. Of these, two sherds could be medieval (RP9–10) and four sherds are not identifiable (RP11–14).

Samian Ware

RP1 (not illustrated)
Samian Dr. 37, South Gaulish, late 1st century, fragment with truncated ovolo and beaded row below, other details not recognisable.
Found in grave fill, south cemetery, with type 1.1 pottery
C1251, Phase: 4? EM1, Findspot: 199.53/826.19.

RP2 (not illustrated)
Samian, not seen, type not identifiable.
C845, Phase: 3–4 Pre-Med (disturbed), Findspot: 180.50/832.23.

RP3 (not illustrated)
Tiny abraded sherd, possibly Samian Ware.
C791, Phase: 6 Med, Findspot: 198.91/825.90.

Flagons

RP4 (not illustrated)
Fragment of strap handle and flagon body, buff, slightly gritty fabric with grey core, thin grey-brown wash, late 1st/2nd century.
C145, Phase: 8 EPM, Area: 200–1/860–1.

RP5 (not illustrated)
Base of flagon neck, finer fabric than RP4, but also with thin, dark wash, vertical smoothing on neck.
C903, Phase: 8 EPM, Area: 175–82.5/825–39.5.

Neither sherd is closely datable, but flagons in oxidised ware are common on Roman military sites until the later 2nd century.

Grey wares

Three sherds (RP6–8) were in sandy grey fabrics typical of later 1st to 3rd century types. In addition, RP9–10 were in a hard, slightly gritty, light grey fabric which could be Roman, though the profile of the rim does not suggest any readily identifiable Roman type. The vessel is more likely to be of medieval date.

RP6 (not illustrated)
Sandy micaceous grey ware, closed form, fabric typical of late 1st/early 2nd century.
C1285, Phase: 3? R, Findspot: 178.25/827.76.

RP7 (not illustrated)
Grey ware, slightly sandy, date probably as RP6.
C111, Phase: 6 Med, Area: 195–200/860–866.

RP8 (not illustrated)
Base sherd, coarse, sandy grey ware, late 1st/2nd century.
C1122, Phase: 8 EPM, Area: 190.50–195.50/834–836.

RP9 (Figure 16.1)
Rim in slightly gritty, hard grey ware; RP10 is a larger fragment of the same rim. Roman(?).
C557, Phase: 7 LM, Findspot: 188.8/830.9.

RP10 (not illustrated)
See RP9.
C1122, Phase: 8 EPM, Area: 190.50–195.50/834–836.

Other miscellaneous vessels

RP11 (Figure 16.1)
Base sherd probably from closed form, hard oxidised ware, few visible inclusions, not identified but has been sliced for TL dating (AD 400±165).
C678, Phase: 4? EM1, Area: 196–9/832–4.

RP12 (not illustrated)
Tiny sherd, badly affected by soil conditions, not identified.
C740, Phase: 4 EMed1, Findspot: 200.9/820.13.

RP13 (Figure 16.1)
Tiny rim fragment, oxidised ware, possibly Roman.
C710, Phase: 6 Med, Findspot: 203.78/825.95.

RP14 (Figure 16.1)
Fine, sandy, oxidised ware, pinkish with darker external wash, possibly Roman.
C501, topsoil, Area: 196–210/840–50.

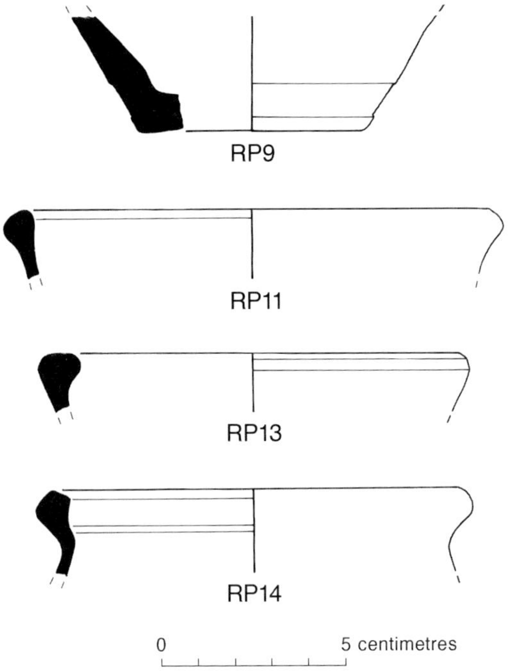

FIGURE 16.1
Roman pottery

The significance of the Roman pottery

Native sites produce very small amounts of Roman pottery, and the total number of sherds from The Hirsel, if they came from such a site, would seem very high, especially as they would represent a peripheral scatter from a focus of occupation outside the excavated area. Finds of local traditional or 'native' ware might also be expected. A connection with the Roman army seems much more likely. One sherd (RP1) is datable to the late 1st century, and the others would certainly fit within the period of military occupation in this part of the Borders, which lasted until shortly after *c*180, when the fort at Newstead was finally abandoned. The Tweed valley provides a direct route from Newstead, 30km (19 miles) west of The Hirsel, to the coast at Tweedmouth, 20km (13 miles) to the east. The importance of this route, including its extension west of Newstead, is demonstrated by the large number of camps along its line; those nearest to The Hirsel are at Carham, East Learmouth and Norham (Welfare and Swan 1995, 82, 95–96, 118). Some more permanent post for the supervision of this route, perhaps a fortlet, was perhaps sited near The Hirsel and could have been the source of the Roman pottery.

17

MEDIEVAL CERAMICS

Valerie E Dean and Susan Mills

17.1 INTRODUCTION

The excavations produced an interesting assemblage of 5,150 sherds of medieval and later pottery (40.26 kg) from some 370 contexts. This report concentrates on the medieval pottery, with brief descriptions being given to post-medieval and later material.

Analysis of the assemblage and establishment of the type series was undertaken initially by Susan Mills, and continued by Valerie Dean. Detailed fabric descriptions are based on the method outlined by Orton *et al* (1993). Colour descriptions and classifications are taken from the *Munsell Soil Color Charts* (Munsell 1975). The work was carried out by visual examination, using a binocular microscope at x20 where appropriate. Without thin sectioning and geological analysis, detailed identification of inclusions was not practicable. Differentiation between natural inclusions in the clay matrix and added temper has not been made.

The pottery has been divided into ten major groups on the basis of fabric analysis. The fabrics have been arranged in sub-groups within the ten categories, which may range from the 10th to the 20th century.

There are no complete or near complete profiles, due to the fragmentation, abrasion or small size of most of the sherds. This has made classification of vessel types difficult and the identification of many sherds extremely tentative. Determination of glaze coverage was not possible. All vessels are wheel-made unless otherwise stated.

Quantification is given by sherd numbers and weights in each group (Figures 17.1–17.4). Figures for vessel numbers are unlikely to be meaningful, for reasons given above; these are based on rim counts, where present, otherwise on estimates. Weights and sherd numbers may give a better idea of the relative quantities. Associated sherds have been grouped, but mostly they are not physical joins; at the time they were judged to be from the same vessel.

It has proved difficult to establish any clear phasing in the pottery assemblage that may correlate with the site phasing as, at the time of writing, this had not been finalised. The detailed quantification by context is available in the site archive.

Fabric groups	Sherds no.	Sherds %	Weight (g) no.	Weight (g) %	MV
1	179	3.48	1340	3.33	18
2	2820	54.76	20435	50.76	278
3	661	12.83	3565	8.85	63
4	1287	24.99	12875	31.98	57
5	74	1.44	215	0.53	4
6	7	0.14	40	0.10	3
7	107	2.08	1625	4.04	32
8	3	0.06	105	0.26	3
9	10	0.19	50	0.12	7
10	2	0.04	10	0.02	1
Total	**5150**	**100.00**	**40260**	**100.00**	**466**

FIGURE 17.1
Pottery quantification by fabric group (MV: minimum number of vessels)

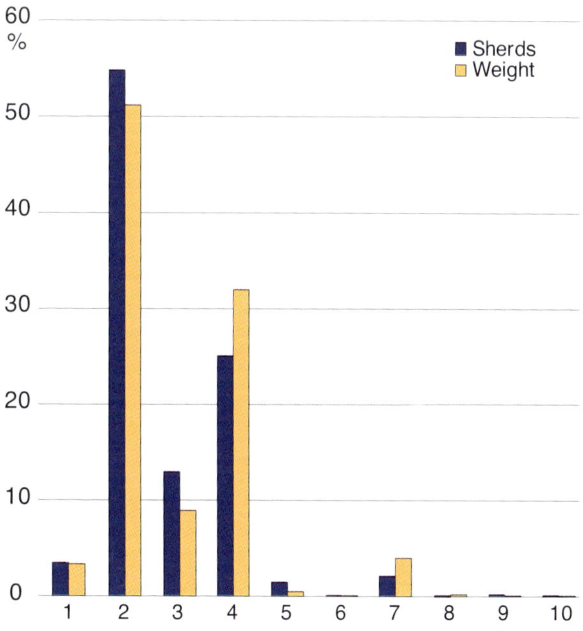

FIGURE 17.2
Bar chart showing fabric group percentages

The bulk of the material is probably Scottish, of local manufacture but, given the proximity of the Border, the presence of unidentified English material is likely. Wherever possible, sources or parallels are given.

The pottery covered by this report is currently in the care of National Museums Scotland (NMS).

17.2 FABRIC GROUPS: GENERAL DESCRIPTION

Group 1: Coarse Gritty Ware

Generally hand-made fabrics, with a chunky appearance and tempered with coarse, poorly sorted inclusions. These rarely show through the surfaces, which are usually smoothed or wiped, giving an effect of fine sandpaper. Sometimes the surfaces are slightly burnished. Firing is variable, usually producing thick, blurred margins. Surfaces vary from light brown to black, with a grey core. Unglazed, except for the occasional spot, probably accidental. The simple rim forms are usually everted, and flattened or bevelled.

Fabrics 1.1 and 1.2 are similar in rim form and appearance to Canterbury ware Groups I to III (Frere 1954, 128–138) (NMS reference collection) which, although the inclusions vary, have a date range from early 11th to mid-12th centuries. They also seem broadly similar to rim types of periods I and II from Durham city, dated from late 10th to mid-12th centuries (Addis 1979, 39–47). Fabric 1.3 resembles Kelso Abbey type 6 (Cox *et al* 1984, 394). A little similar material has been found at Ayr (NMS reference collection).

Such vessels seem to be more usual in north-east England than Scotland during the 10th to 12th centuries, although they do occur at Jedburgh Abbey where they were found to pre-date the white gritty wares. Sherds recovered from an early drain at Kelso bear similarities to this ware. An assemblage of medieval pottery from the late Iron Age site at Hayknowes Farm, Annan (Gregory 2001, 29–46), may also fit this category. Comprising largely of cooking pots with slightly everted rims and flat bases, this assemblage is considered possibly to predate the local availability of the white gritty wares which appeared around the mid-12th century (Hall 2001, 130–132); since publication of the site report, however, associated deposits yielded calibrated radiocarbon dates of the AD 980–1185 and AD 1020–1260 (Haggarty *et al* 2011, 7).

Geological evidence has suggested that some of the Jedburgh material may be of local or Northumbrian origin and that some is similar to material from a kiln of possible 12th-century date at Newcastle (Haggarty and Will 1995, 99).

Fabric sub-group	Sherds no.	Sherds %	Weight (g) no.	Weight (g) %	MV
1.1	72	1.40	525	1.30	5
1.2	78	1.51	515	1.28	10
1.3	29	0.56	300	0.75	3
2.1	1920	37.28	14015	34.81	187
2.2	589	11.44	4250	10.56	62
2.3	104	2.02	800	1.99	5
2.4	203	3.94	1100	2.73	20
2.5	3	0.06	250	0.62	3
2.6	1	0.02	20	0.05	1
3.1	630	12.23	3330	8.27	58
3.2	1	0.02	10	0.02	1
3.3	21	0.41	175	0.43	3
3.4	9	0.17	50	0.12	1
4.1	505	9.81	6600	16.39	28
4.2	782	15.18	6275	15.59	29
5.1	74	1.44	215	0.53	4
6.1	5	0.10	25	0.06	1
6.2	1	0.02	5	0.01	1
6.3	1	0.02	10	0.02	1
7.1	76	1.48	1400	3.48	19
7.2	30	0.58	175	0.43	12
7.3	1	0.02	50	0.12	1
8.1	1	0.02	5	0.01	1
8.2	2	0.04	100	0.25	2
9.1	10	0.19	50	0.12	7
10.1	2	0.04	10	0.02	1
Total	**5150**	**100.00**	**40260**	**100.00**	**466**

FIGURE 17.3
Pottery quantification by fabric sub-group (MV: minimum number of vessels)

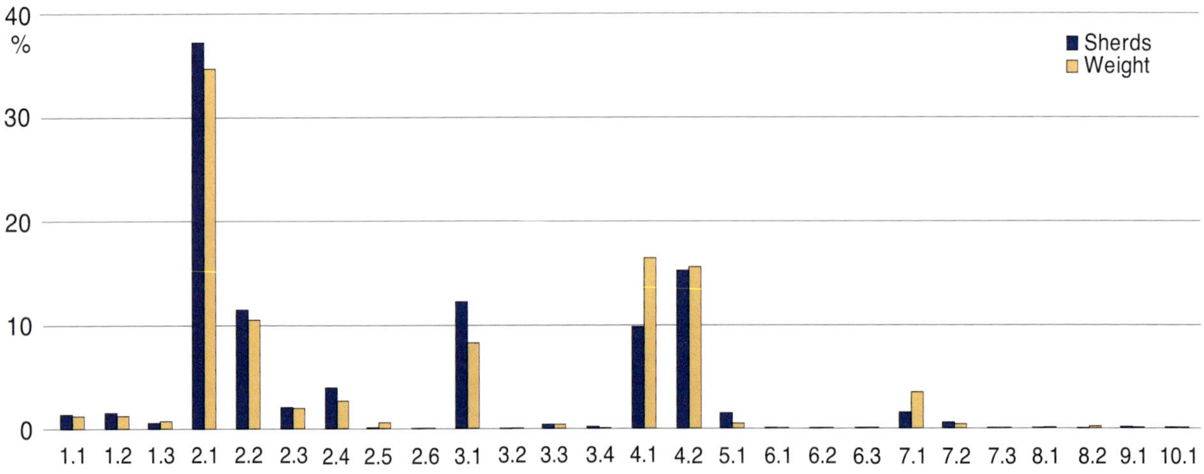

FIGURE 17.4
Bar chart showing fabric sub-group percentages

These fabrics are uncommon in Scotland and, although there may well be an as yet unidentified Borders pottery industry, it is possible that it is coming from production sites south of the border (George Haggarty pers comm). Early results of the Scottish Redware Project (Chenery *et al* 2001) show that these fabrics have distinct identities.

Group 2: Scottish White Gritty Ware

Wheel-made vessels, with wide variations in the considerable inclusions which frequently protrude through the surfaces to give an orange peel effect. They are of an overall white to light buff colour. A small number of sherds are glazed, either splashed or dipped. Pronounced finger-rilling is a feature, and occasional vessels have cordoned shoulders. Stabbed, grooved or applied decoration is minimal, and is confined to fabrics 2.3 and 2.4.

It seems probable that these white gritty wares, like other cooking pots, had a short shelf life, since they were subjected to much wear and tear and it would be difficult to clean food residues from the interiors. The rate at which they were disposed of, however, could be modified by how affluent a site was, and how near to a production centre. In this context it is interesting that cooking pots outnumbered other vessel types in the same manner at the affluent abbeys in the region, such as Dundrennan, Jedburgh, Kelso or Melrose, as they did at The Hirsel.

Most of the white gritty wares, which comprise half the assemblage, are probably of local, Tweed valley origin (fabrics 2.1 and 2.2), and strongly resemble fabrics (types 5 and 1 respectively) and vessel forms from the mid- to late 12th-century pit group at Kelso Abbey (Cox *et al* 1984, 381–397). However, these in turn have a degree of similarity with material from the kiln site at Colstoun (Brooks 1980; Hall 2007), also noted by Bown (1985, 54–59), both in fabric and form; it is therefore possible that the assemblage includes some material from Colstoun. Due to the variety of local clays, considerable variations occur in Colstoun fabrics; no attempt has been made here (fabric 2.4) to differentiate between them. Unfortunately, Colstoun material is difficult to date with any degree of accuracy, but white gritty fabrics span the period from the 12th to the early 15th centuries. Similar rim forms, but in a red gritty fabric, occur in the Carlisle area from the 12th to early 13th centuries (Catherine M Brooks pers comm).

Scottish White Gritty Ware has also been found at a medieval lead-mining site at Sillerholes, West Linton, Peeblesshire, in association with leather footwear of 12th–13th centuries (Dean forthcoming b; Thomas forthcoming). A large assemblage was recovered from excavations on the Isle of May, Fife, where sherds were found in contexts dating from Period II, 12th to 16th centuries (Will and Haggarty 2008, 136–138). It has also been found on sites as far apart as Ayr (Franklin and Hall 2012), Finlaggan, Islay (Dean forthcoming a) and Elgin (Hall 1998a; 1998b). However, Colstoun is the only kiln site positively identified to date, although others are suspected in Lothian, Borders and Fife (Jones *et al* 2003, 44–48).

It has been commented that straight-sided 12th-century vessels from such sites as Berwick, Hawick and The Hirsel were likely to have shared a common geological parentage with material from Kelso and Jedburgh Abbeys (Cox 1984, 4). Although the recent Scottish White Gritty Ware Project has indicated that this pottery was being produced in several areas of Scotland, further work requires to be done (Jones *et al* 2003, 81).

Group 3: Redware

Wheel-made vessels, oxidised to a light red colour, sometimes very pale. It is generally a fine-grained fabric, but can also contain quite coarse grit. Pale buff slip occurs on some vessel interiors. It also appears on exteriors, sometimes underlying the occasional glaze, as at Perth (MacAskill 1987, 91). Generally undecorated, apart from occasional brown strips. The range of rim forms echoes that of Group 2.

Most of the fabrics are probably local, possibly Kelso Abbey type 4 (Cox *et al* 1984, 393), but other unsourced fabrics are present.

Redwares seem to have appeared in the mid-13th century, a little later than white gritty wares. They occur widely across Scotland, with each burgh perhaps having its own variation (Hall 1996), e.g. Aberdeen (Murray 1982, 122–123), Perth (MacAskill 1987, 89–101). Kilns at Rattray, Aberdeenshire, produced redwares from the 13th to the early 15th centuries (Murray 1993). This orange-brown fabric initially contained quantities of quartz but, as firing methods improved and metal was being increasingly used for cooking pots, the gritting became less important. An olive-green glaze was often used. Stenhouse kilns, near Falkirk, were making jugs and storage vessels in a fine red fabric from the late 15th century into the 16th century (Hall and Hunter 2001), although excavations in 2007 suggest that pottery production may have commenced at a slightly earlier period (Hall 2009).

A geochemical study by Scottish ceramicists to evaluate the possibility of accurately fingerprinting redware sherds has shown very promising results in the provenancing of the clay sources. Using inductively coupled plasma-mass spectometry (ICP-MS), it has been possible to identify with considerable accuracy the geographical region of the sherds' origin (Haggarty *et al* 2011).

Group 4: Reduced Gritty Ware

Wheel-made vessels in a moderately gritty fabric, mostly completely reduced to dark grey with thin, sharp margins where oxidised surfaces are present; some vessels are partially reduced. Due to the fragmentary nature of the assemblage, it is difficult to determine the extent of reduction. Shiny, even, dipped glaze frequently occurs. A wide range of decoration is present, including stabbed, impressed and applied forms. Vessels are principally jugs, but bowls, dishes and pipkins also occur.

These may be partially or completely reduced local versions of earlier East of Scotland fabrics, including Colstoun. Although reduced wares were widespread in Scotland, kiln sites, apart from Rattray, are unknown; the material from the Throsk kiln site is of a different tradition and a later date.

A partially reduced jug containing a coin hoard, currently dated to no later than 1322 (Dean 1996; 2007, 452), was recently discovered at Ednam, near Kelso; the fabric strongly resembles that of fabric 4.2. This may be the earliest secure date for this type of fabric in the Kelso area, although a similar fabric was found in the previously mentioned Kelso Abbey pit group (Kelso type 3).

Partially reduced vessels were predominant in the Carlisle area from the late 12th to 14th centuries, with the fully reduced vessels succeeding them and continuing until as late as the early 17th century. Both partially and fully reduced wares occur at Bothwell Castle, and this material was originally dated to the 13th and 14th centuries, no later material being identified (Cruden 1952). However, later research showed that 'the pottair of Bothuile' was supplying wares to the castle in the early 16th century, and it has been suggested that the above earlier forms had continued in production until the later date (Cruden 1956, 68). At Fast Castle, Berwickshire, they were found in association with imported wares of the late 15th to early 16th centuries (Haggarty and Jennings 1992), but occurred throughout the deposits which have been dated from 1450 to 1650 (Dean and Robertson 2001). Partially reduced wares have also been found at Eyemouth Fort in deposits dating from 1547 to 1559 (Franklin 1997), confirming that this tradition continued well into the 16th century. Interestingly, both Fast Castle and Eyemouth Fort were on Home land.

Group 5: Buff/White Ware

Wheel-made vessels, oxidised to an overall buff colour and generally of a fine grained fabric, occasionally extremely fine. Any glaze is smooth and shiny. Sherds are mostly tiny, and vessel identification is extremely tentative.

Copying of Yorkshire types is possible, and a scrap of applied strip decoration is similar to that on Scarborough ware jugs of the 13th century (Farmer 1979). A date of 13th to 14th or 15th centuries seems likely.

Group 6: Imported wares

Imported material is conspicuous by its absence, with sherds of only three vessels being identified in this group. Fabric 6.1 is a piece of Frechen-type stoneware Bartmann jug whose decoration may be the Amsterdam coat-of-arms (Hurst *et al* 1986, pl 44, centre); this can be dated to 1625–1650. Fabric 6.2 is a fragment of Langerwehe-type stoneware of 14th to early 16th century date; it is not sufficiently diagnostic to be identified among the types defined by Hurst (Hurst 1977). Fabric 6.3 is a fine, white, north French ware, perhaps Beauvais, of late 15th to 16th centuries.

Group 7: Post-medieval earthenware

A wide group, comprising red earthenware, including slipware, and tin-glazed white earthenware. Fabric 7.1, coarse red earthenware/slipware, could be expected from the 17th to early 19th centuries. Fabric 7.2, tin-glazed white earthenware, is likely to be of the late 18th and 19th centuries. Fabric 7.3 is of the same tradition as material from the kiln site at Throsk, Stirlingshire (Caldwell and Dean 1992), of 17th to early 18th century date. A coin hoard from Wooden, Kelso, was found in a cooking pot of similar type with the latest coins being dated to 1641–1643 (Bateson 1991). A large jug from Grangemouth was found to contain a coin hoard dating from 1625 to 1675 (Dean 2007, 452).

Group 8: Stoneware/Proto-stoneware

This group includes a sherd of white, salt-glazed stoneware (fabric 8.1), which was being produced in the mid to late 18th century at locations such as Prestonpans, East Lothian (Cruickshank 1982, 5–6). Fabric 8.2 comprises sherds which may be over-fired. A jug handle of proto-stoneware is perhaps in imitation of Rhenish fabrics of the 15th to 16th centuries. Another sherd may be a distorted waster or possibly part of a small triangular crucible, although there are no signs of any internal residues which might be expected.

Group 9: Porcelain

A heterogeneous group including sherds from three vessels of probable Chinese origin, dating to the 17th or 18th centuries.

Group 10: Other ware

An unidentified fabric, oxidised with a reduced core, patchy light yellowish brown glaze and stabbed or combed decoration. A 13th to 14th century date would seem appropriate for the forms.

17.3 FABRIC SUB-GROUPS: DETAILED DESCRIPTION

Group 1: Coarse Gritty Ware

Sub-group 1.1

D1 Hard, hand-made pottery, 3–7mm thick, with a hackly, laminated texture and rough fracture. Variably fired, with a 'sandwich' effect in section of up to five layers. Surfaces vary from brown (7.5YR 5/4) to strong brown (7.5YR 5/6) with a grey core (5YR 5/1). The micaceous fabric contains 15% inclusions, of moderate quantities of poorly sorted, coarse quartz and shell, a little coarse rock and has some straw impressions; there are considerable variations. It is unglazed and there is a hint of surface smoothing. Exterior surfaces are very sooted.

Forms: jars/cooking pots, with everted rims and flat or convex bases.

Figure 17.5: 1, 2.

D5 Hard, hand-made pottery, 4–8mm thick, with a hackly texture and rough fracture. Usually completely oxidised, with thick, blurred margins. The exterior surface is reddish brown (5YR 5/3–5/4) and the interior varies from reddish yellow (5YR 6/6) to light brown (7.5R 6/4) with a light grey core (5YR 6/1). The micaceous fabric's 10% inclusions are generally coarse to very coarse, comprising moderate amounts of quartz and poorly sorted haematite, and sparse rock. Occasionally grains show through the surfaces. A spot of brown glaze was noticed among the otherwise unglazed sherds. There is some exterior sooting.

Forms: jars/cooking pots, one with a rolled rim, with flat or convex bases.

Figure 17.5: 3.

D6 Moderately hard, hand-made pottery, 4–9mm thick, with an irregular texture and rough fracture. Generally oxidised, with a reduced core and thick, blurred margins. Surfaces vary from reddish yellow (5YR 7/6) to pink (7.5YR 7/4) with a grey to light grey core (7.5YR N5/–N6/). The 10–15% inclusions comprise abundant, very poorly sorted coarse quartz, moderate very coarse rock, sparse very coarse haematite, and a moderate amount of mica. Unglazed. There is some external sooting.

Forms: Jars/cooking pots/jugs, with one everted and one thumbed club rim, and flat or convex bases.

Figure 17.5: 4.

Sub-group 1.2

D2 Hard, hand-made pottery, 4–5mm thick, with an irregular texture and rough fracture. Probably completely reduced, but too sooted to be sure. Dark brown (7.5YR 4/2) to very dark grey (2.5Y N3/). Up to 20% inclusions of coarse, poorly sorted quartz, with sparse coarse haematite and rock, and a moderate amount of mica. Slight burnishing on external surface.

Forms: jars/cooking pots, with flat or convex bases.

D3 A coarser version of D2. Moderately hard, hand-made pottery with an irregular, laminated texture and very rough fracture. Variably fired, with vague, blurred margins. The outer surface is brown (7.5YR 5/2–5/4), the interior is grey to greyish-brown (10YR 5/1–5/2) and the core is dark grey to grey (10YR 4/1–5/1). The abundant, coarse quartz inclusions are mostly white, with occasional coarse grains of haematite and rock with some fine mica. Occasional sherds are burnished, and all are unglazed, apart from an occasional accidental spot. Many sherds are sooted, and most are abraded. This fabric has been TL dated to AD 810±130.

Forms: jars/cooking pots, one with a rolled and lid-seated rim, with flat or convex bases.

D4 Hand-made pottery, 3–6mm thick, with an irregular, laminated texture and rough fracture; some cracks are noticeable in the surfaces. Mostly oxidised, with a reduced core and thick, blurred margins. Surfaces are reddish brown (2.5YR 4/4–5/4 to 5YR 5/4), and may be slightly burnished. It is micaceous, and has about 15% inclusions, of abundant, poorly sorted, coarse quartz, with sparse, very coarse rock and haematite. Unglazed. Most sherds are abraded.

Forms: Jars/cooking pots, some small, with everted, occasionally bevelled, rims and convex bases.

Figure 17.5: 5.

D13 Hard, competently thrown pottery, 3–9mm thick, with a fine texture. Surface feel is smooth and the fracture slightly rough. It is almost completely oxidised. The exterior is light brown (7.5YR 6/4), the interior varies from yellowish red (5YR 5/6) to brown (7.5YR 5/2) and the core is brown (7.5YR 5/2). The 10% inclusions contain a moderate amount of poorly sorted medium quartz, mostly white, and sparse, coarse haematite and rock, with a little mica. Unglazed. Practically all the sherds are sooted. This fabric has been TL dated to AD 1170±90.

Forms: Jars/cooking pots, with rolled, everted or bevelled rims and flat or convex bases.

Figure 17.5: 6, 7.

D16 Three sherds of a hard, hand-made fabric, 5–6mm thick, with a hackly, laminated texture and rough fracture. It is partially reduced, with thin margins. Surfaces vary from pinkish grey to pink (7.5YR 6/2–7/4) with a grey core (7.5YR N4/). It has about 15% inclusions of abundant coarse quartz and rock, with occasional large grains, sparse coarse haematite and a moderate amount of medium mica. It is unglazed, and one sherd is burnished. Sooting is evident.

Forms: jars/cooking pots.

Sub-group 1.3

D7 Moderately hard, hand-made pottery, 4–7mm thick, with irregular, laminated texture, pimply surfaces and a rough fracture. Some knife trimming is evident at the base. Firing is very variable, and sherds are mostly oxidised with a reduced core. Margins can be thick and blurred or thin and sharp. External surfaces vary from reddish brown (2.5YR 5/4–5YR 5/3) to pink (7.5YR 7/4) and very pale brown (10YR 8/4). Interiors range from reddish yellow (5YR 7/6) to pink (7.5YR 7/4) and very pale brown (10YR 8/4). Cores are grey to dark grey (2.5YR N5/–5R 4/1). The fabric has up to 20% inclusions of very poorly sorted, very coarse rock and quartz, some grains of which are white, as well as sparse, poorly sorted mica. Unglazed, apart from a few specks on one base.

Forms: jars/cooking pots, some large, with everted or bevelled rims and flat bases. One cooking pot has straight sides and a flat base.

Figure 17.5: 8.

Group 2: Scottish White Gritty Ware

Sub-group 2.1: Tweed Valley Ware

D10 Hard, sometimes quite finely made pottery, 3–8mm thick, with a fine texture. Surfaces are slightly pimply, and it has a slightly rough fracture. Sherds are mostly oxidised with a thin, reduced core and thick, blurred margins. The outer surfaces vary from brown to light brown (7.5YR 5/2–6/4), the interior is reddish yellow (7.5YR 6/6–7/6) and the core is light grey (10YR 6/1). The 10% inclusions are moderate, poorly sorted coarse quartz, with a little very coarse rock, up to 3mm, and a very little mica. On the shoulder of one sherd is a little splashed, very dark, greyish brown glaze (10YR 3/2), and some sherds are sooted.

Forms: Jars/cooking pots, jug? One everted rim, flat bases.

Figure 17.5: 9.

E2 Finely made, thin-walled pottery, 3–5mm thick, with a rough texture and fracture. The exterior is pink (7.5YR 7/4) to very pale brown (10YR 8/3), with a similar core. Internally, it varies from light brown (7.5YR 6/4) through light grey (10YR 7/1) to very pale brown (10YR 8/3). The 10–15% inclusions are as in E11, but finer and fewer. There is some splashed or dipped glaze on shoulder sherds, varying from olive brown to light yellowish brown (2.5Y 4/4–6/4). Many sherds are tiny and abraded.

Forms: jars, cooking pots and jugs, some small, with flat bases.

E4 A hard, coarse fabric with a rough texture and break. More iron-rich than E11, externally it is light reddish brown to pink (5YR 6/4-7/3) and internally it varies from pinkish grey (7.5YR 6/2) to light grey (10YR 7/1). Most sherds have reduced interiors, and a few are oxidised with a thin, grey core (10YR 5/1). The 15% inclusions are as in E11, but a little finer. The olive (5Y 5/3) to light yellowish brown (10YR 6/4) splashed glaze is sparse and abraded, and occurs on rims, shoulders and handles. Many sherds are abraded.

Forms: jars/cooking pots, with convex bases. Jugs with strap handles (some grooved) and flat bases. One bowl with everted rim.

E8 Well-made, fine, thin-walled pottery, 3–6mm thick, with a lightly rough feel and sharp fracture. Firing is variable, and some sherds are almost completely reduced. Margins can be sharp and up to one-third of the total thickness. Exteriors are reddish yellow (5YR 6/6) to pink (7.5YR 7/4–8/4), interiors reddish yellow (5YR 7/6) to pinkish grey and grey (7.5YR 7/2–N5/) and the core grey (5YR 6/1–7.5YR N5/). The 5–10% inclusions in the fine paste consist of very coarse, poorly sorted quartz and rock, a very little haematite and a moderate amount of mica. The abraded, patchy glaze appears to be splashed, and varies from yellowish brown (10YR 5/4) to greyish brown (2.5Y 5/2). Vessels are quite large and thin-walled with finger rilling, and some are sooted.

Forms: jars/cooking pots, sometimes straight-sided, with everted, club or lid-seated rims, and flat or convex bases. Jugs with upright or club rims, flat or convex bases, and one vessel with a grooved strap handle.

E11 Well-made vessels, 3–10mm thick, in a hard, rough-textured fabric with a rough fracture. Mostly completely oxidised, surfaces vary from pinkish white (7.5YR 8/2) to white (10YR 8/2). Where cores and interiors are reduced, these are grey (7.5YR N5/–10YR 5/1). Inclusions comprise up to 15%, and are predominantly brownish-grey, coarse quartz and rock, haematite and a little mica. The grains are sometimes visible on the surfaces. Splashed glazing occasionally occurs on jug shoulders and on vessel interiors. Colours vary widely, from brownish yellow (10YR 6/8) to greyish brown (2.5Y 5/2) and olive (5Y 5/3). Some vessels have knife trimming at the base. Many vessels have extensive sooting.

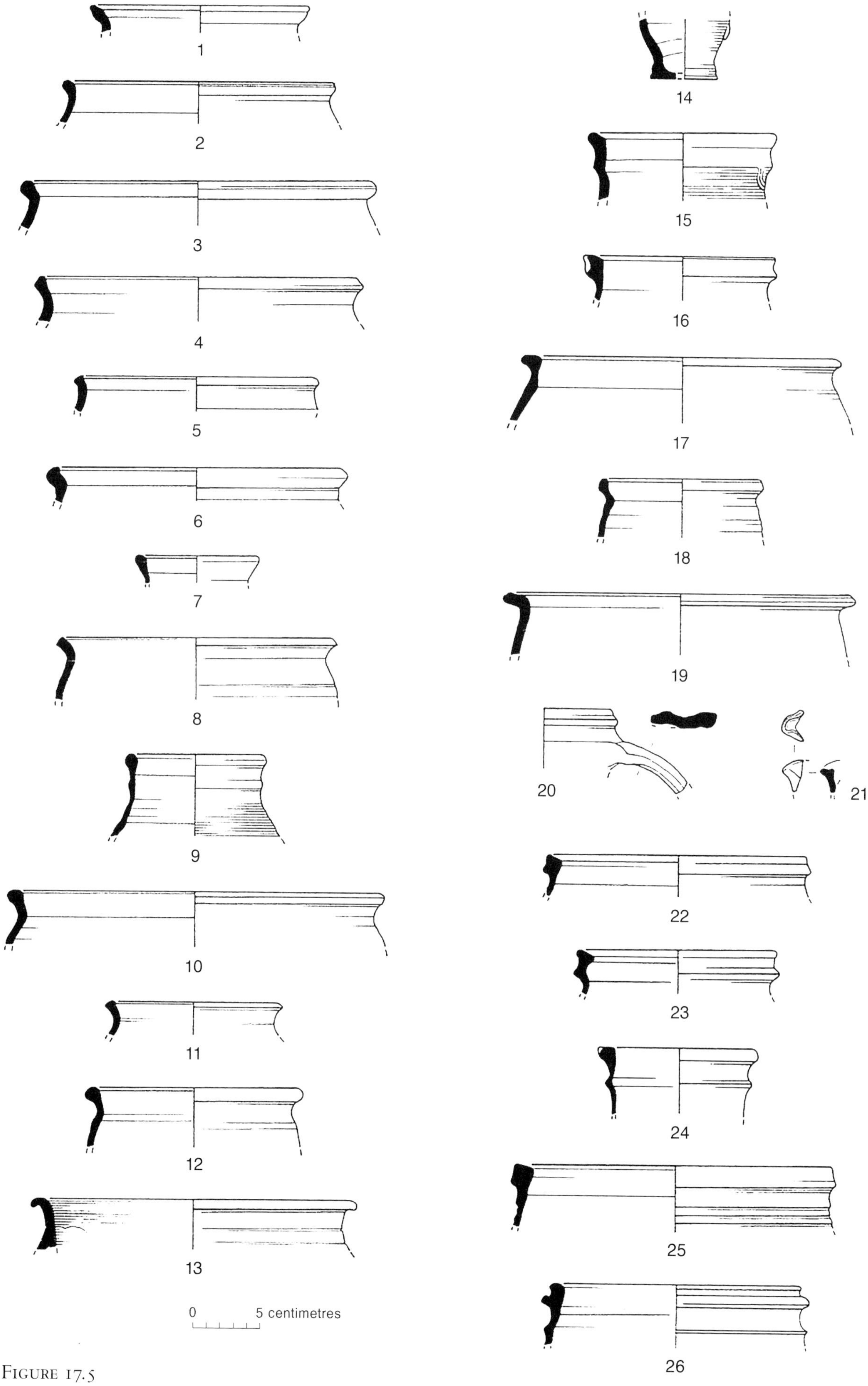

FIGURE 17.5
Medieval pottery types 1.1, 1.2, 1.3 and 2.1

Forms: mostly straight-sided cooking pots and jars, often with distinctive rilling, and rolled, club, everted/flanged, inturned or lid-seated rims. There are occasional horizontal grooves. Bases are slightly convex, and one has a foot-ring. Jugs have rolled, everted club or triangular rims, flat or convex bases and strap handles, some grooved. One bowl/jar has a triangular rim.

Figure 17.5: 10–12.

E13 A hard fabric, generally coarsely made, 4–10mm thick, with an irregular texture and rough break. This variant of E11 is mostly partially reduced with oxidised surfaces; margins can be quite sharp. Exteriors are pink (5YR 7/3) or pinkish grey (7.5YR 7/2), interiors are pink (5YR 7/3–8/4) or dark grey (7.5YR N4/) if reduced. Cores are grey (5YR 5/1–7.5 YR N5/). The 15% inclusions are as in fabric E11, and grains are often visible on pitted surfaces. Any glaze is mostly splashed, and is patchy and dull. It occurs occasionally on cooking pot interiors, and is light yellowish brown (10YR 6/4–2.5Y 6/4) to light olive brown (2.5Y 5/4). Some sherds are very abraded.

Forms: Mostly jugs, some small, with rolled, everted, club, thumbed or upright rims with pulled spouts, flat or convex bases; handles are rod or strap, some grooved or incised. Jars/cooking pots have rolled, everted, upright or club rims, some lid-seated, and flat, convex or occasionally concave bases. There is a bowl/jar with an everted rim.

Figure 17.5: 13–16.

E14 A hard, fine-textured fabric, 3–8mm thick, with a smooth feel and slightly rough fracture. It is usually partly reduced, with thin, sharp margins. Exteriors are light brown to pink (7.5YR 6/4–7/4), and interiors are brown to pinkish grey (7.5YR 5/2–7/2) with a grey core (7.5YR N5/–10 YR 5/1). There are about 15% inclusions, principally of well-sorted, fine quartz with a little very coarse rock and haematite and a little mica. There is a little splashed glazing, patchy and abraded, in greyish brown or olive yellow (2.5Y 5/2 or 6/2). Some sherds are sooted, and most are abraded.

Forms: mostly jugs, one with an upright rim, with flat or convex bases, and one with a strap handle.

E15 More finely potted than E11, this is a hard fabric, 3–7mm thick, with an irregular texture but smooth surfaces and a slightly rough fracture. It is either completely oxidised or has a reduced interior. Very occasionally it is not fully oxidised and has a thin, reduced grey core (10YR 6/1) and blurred margins. Surfaces vary from pink (5YR 7/3) to light brown or pinkish grey (7.5YR 6/4–7/2). The 10% inclusions are as in E11, but finer with more mica. The fabric is slightly more iron-rich. The glaze, dipped and possibly splashed, is abraded and patchy, with a hint of iron globules, and is light olive brown (2.5Y 5/4) or olive (5Y 5/4). It is usually external, but occasionally internal. There is some knife or wire trimming at the base. Many sherds are sooted, and a lot are abraded.

Forms: mostly jars/cooking pots, with rolled, everted or triangular rims and flat or convex bases. Some vessels have horizontal grooves around the shoulder. One jug has a grooved strap handle and a convex base; others have everted, upright or club rims, strap handles, some grooved, and flat or convex bases. There is a possible bowl.

E19 A hard fabric, 4–8mm thick, with irregular texture and slightly rough feel and break. It is more iron-rich than E11, and is almost completely reduced; where surfaces are oxidised, margins are thin and sharp. The exterior varies from pink (7.5YR 7/4–8/4) to very pale brown (10YR 2/3). The interior is pink (7.5YR 8/4) or white (10YR 8/2) where oxidised; where reduced, it is grey (7.5YR N5/–10 YR 5/1). The 5% inclusions are as in E11 but a little finer, and surfaces are slightly pimply with occasional grains visible. There is a little patchy, splashed glaze in olive (5Y 5/4). There is some knife trimming at the base, and one base shows stacking marks. This fabric has a TL date of AD 1180±120.

Forms: mostly jugs, with flat or convex bases. One strap handle. A few jars/cooking pots with rolled or triangular rims and flat or convex bases. One sherd has 2–3 lines of horizontal ribbing on the shoulder.

Figure 17.5: 17.

E21 A very hard fabric, 3–6mm thick, with irregular/laminated texture, slightly rough surfaces and sharp fracture. Usually completely oxidised, exterior surfaces are brown (7.5YR 5/4) to very pale brown (10YR 7/3), interiors are brown (7.5YR 5/4) to very pale brown (10YR 8/3). Generally, it has a more yellow appearance than E11. The 10–15% inclusions are as in E27, but occasional lumps of rock up to 10mm diameter are evident. Only one sherd showed glaze, perhaps burnt, in very dark grey (5YR 3/1), and another had a thin slip, in very pale brown (10YR 8/3). Pronounced external wheel-marks were noted, and some sooting.

Forms: jars/cooking pots, one with an everted, lid-seated rim. Jugs, one with a club rim.

E22 One sherd in a very hard fabric, 5mm thick, of irregular texture and harsh feel, with a rough fracture. Almost completely reduced, it has a thin pink inner surface (7.5YR 7/4) and a grey core (10YR 6/1). It has some 20% poorly sorted, coarse, sub-angular quartz and rock inclusions, very sparse medium haematite and a hint of mica. It has a smooth, shiny, external glaze in olive (5Y 5/6).

Forms: possible jug.

E24 Two sherds of a hard fabric, 4–5mm thick, with irregular texture and rough feel and break. Oxidised, colour varies from light brownish grey (10YR 6/2) externally to pink (5 YR7/3) elsewhere. Inclusions are 15–20%, comprising poorly sorted coarse quartz, a little coarse haematite and flecks of mica. No glaze was evident. Sooting was noted.

Forms: jars/cooking pots.

E25 A hard fabric, 3–10mm thick, of irregular texture and slightly rough feel and fracture. Reduced version of E11. Exterior varies from brown (7.5YR 5/2) to dark grey (2.5Y N4/), and interior from grey and dark grey (7.5YR N5/–N4/) to white (10YR 8/2). The 10–15% inclusions are as in E11. Surfaces show some possible burnishing, and many are sooted. Slight finger-rilling is evident both inside and out.

Forms: jars/cooking pots, some small, with rolled, everted/lid-seated, upright and club rims and flat or convex bases.

Figure 17.5: 18.

E27 A hard fabric, 3–8mm thick, with irregular, laminated texture, and rough feel and fracture. Most sherds are completely oxidised, but some are partly reduced with a diffused core. Overall, it is more yellow than E11. Exterior surfaces are reddish yellow (7.5YR 7/6), light brown (7.5YR 6/4) and yellow (10YR 7/6), and inner surfaces are reddish yellow (7.5YR 7/6) to very pale brown (10YR 7/3). Any core is light brown (7.5YR 6/4) to grey (10YR 5/1). The 10–15% inclusions are as in E11, but with very occasional medium to very coarse rock grains. The paste is a streaky cream/yellow. It was not possible to determine the coverage of the very occasional glaze, whose colour varied from light olive brown (2.5Y 5/4) to olive (5Y 4/4–5/4). Some horizontal lines and wheel-marks were noted on the vessel shoulders, and there is a little knife trimming at the bases. Many sherds are sooted.

Forms: mostly jars/cooking pots, some small, with rolled, everted, flanged, upright/inturned, bifid, club/lid-seated or thumbed rims and flat, convex, concave or thumbed bases. Jugs with rolled, everted, upright, inturned, triangular, club/thumbed rims, and slightly concave bases. One jug has an upright/inturned rim and strap handle, while another has an everted rim and pulled spout. A bridge spout is present. There is a bowl with an everted rim.

Figure 17.5: 19–26.

Sub-group 2.2: Tweed Valley Ware

E3 Well-fired pottery, 4–7mm thick, with a slightly gritty texture and a clean fracture. It is more iron-rich than E12. The outer surface is light reddish brown (5YR 6/3) to reddish yellow (7.5YR 6/6), the interior is pink (7.5YR 7/4) to greyish brown (10YR 5/2). Most vessels have reduced interiors, but some are oxidised with a thin grey (10YR 6/1) core; they are rarely completely oxidised. The 10–15% inclusions are as in E12. There is some knife trimming on the lower body and base. Splashed glazing occurs on some jug shoulders; this is greyish brown to light olive brown (2.5Y 5/2–5/4). One sherd seems to have had poorly applied glaze which has left a thin, dirty white coating. Very few sherds are sooted.

Forms: jars/cooking pots, some small, with rolled rims and flat or convex bases. Jugs, one with a club rim, concave and convex bases, one grooved strap handle. There are occasional horizontal grooves on body sherds.

E10 Well-made, often fine pottery, 3–7mm thick, with an irregular texture and slightly rough feel and fracture. Generally oxidised, the outer surfaces are yellow to very pale brown (10YR 7/6–8/3), the interior varies from grey to white and very pale brown (10YR 6/1–8/2–8/3) with a grey core (10YR 5/1). The 5–10% inclusions are a moderate amount of poorly sorted quartz, with a very little haematite and mica. Splashed glazing is found on exteriors, and a glossy, possibly dipped, glaze on interiors. Colours vary from light yellowish brown and pale yellow (2.5Y 6/4–8/4) to a rich green. A reddish yellow slip (7.5YR 6/6) was noted on the interior of one sherd. There is some knife trimming at the base. Vessels with glazed interiors appear to be cooking pots, as they all have external sooting.

Forms: jars/cooking pots with one rolled rim and one upright/flanged/lid-seated rim, probably straight sided, and with flat or convex bases. Jugs, one with a strap handle. One bowl? A horizontal cordon is evident on some sherds.

Figure 17.6: 27, 29.

E12 This hard, smooth white ware varies from finely turned vessels to large, crude ones. Sherds are 3–8mm thick, with irregular texture and a slightly rough fracture. It is mostly oxidised, although some vessels are partly reduced. Outer surfaces are pinkish grey (7.5YR 7/2) to white (10YR 8/2) and very pale brown (10YR 7/3). Interiors are pinkish white (7/5YR 8/2) to white (10YR 8/2) or, where reduced, grey to light grey (10YR 6/1–7/1). The 5–10% inclusions comprise a moderate amount of poorly sorted, medium sized, grey-brown quartz, a little haematite and specks of mica. Some vessels have patchy splashed glaze of light yellowish brown (10YR 6/4–2.5Y 6/4), sometimes with bright copper green flecks. There is some knife or wire trimming at the base. Many vessels are sooted. This fabric has been TL dated to AD 1060±110.

Forms: mainly straight-sided and globular jars/cooking pots of varying size, with bifid, inturned, club/thumbed, rolled, everted, lid-seated and triangular rims, and flat or convex bases. Jugs with rolled or club rims, flat or convex bases, rod handles and strap handles, some grooved. Some vessels have horizontal ribbing on the shoulders.

Figure 17.6: 28, 30–35.

E23 Very hard fabric, 3–7mm thick, with a fine texture, smooth feel and very slightly rough break. Completely reduced, the exterior is greyish brown to brown (10YR 5/2–5/3), the interior is dark grey (10YR 4/1) or light brownish grey (10YR 6/2). The 10% inclusions are mostly of quite well sorted, medium quartz, with a little very coarse haematite and a little mica. It is unglazed. Some knife trimming at the base is evident, and most sherds are sooted. Many sherds are abraded.

Forms: jars/cooking pots with club rims and flat or convex bases.

Sub-group 2.3

F8 Well-thrown, very hard fabric, 3–8mm thick, with a fine texture and slightly rough feel and fracture. Can be partly or wholly reduced, with exteriors being pink (7.5YR 7/4) to very pale brown (10YR 8/4), interiors pink (7.5YR 7/4) to light grey (10YR 7/2) and a light grey core (10YR 7/2). The inclusions, 10–15% of the fabric, are well-sorted, fine to medium grey-buff quartz, giving a very even texture. Glaze is dipped, usually even and shiny, and over most of the vessel. It ranges from light yellowish brown (2.5Y 6/4) to olive (5Y 5/6) and has some copper and iron streaks. Vessels are glazed on the exterior, with the exception of cooking pots which have an interior coating. Some sooting is present. Often similar to Colstoun ware, but inclusions lack the haematite grains.

Forms: mostly jugs, some small, with everted/flanged/lid-seated, upright, triangular and rolled (one with a pulled spout) rims, ribbed and incised rod handles and strap handles. Jars/cooking pots, one with a folded strap handle. Decoration varies, and the following have been noted: horizontal bands of narrow grooves; stabbed or impressed 'herring bone' designs; applied vertical strips of grey slip or a very dark purple/brown substance.

Figure 17.6: 36–41.

Sub-group 2.4: Colstoun-type Ware

F9/F27 A medium to hard fabric, 4–8mm thick, of a fine texture. The feel varies from smooth to slightly rough, and the fracture is a little rough. Vessels can be either almost completely reduced or nearly completely oxidised. Margins are generally quite thin and sharp. Exteriors vary widely, from red (2.5YR 5/6) to pink (5YR 7/4 to 7.5YR 7/4–8/4) and very pale brown (10YR 7/4–8/3). Interiors run from red (2.5YR 5/6) to pink (5YR 7/4) and very pale brown (10YR 7/3–8/3). Cores are also very varied, from dark grey (2.5YR N4/) and grey (5YR 5/1) to red (2.5YR 5/6), pinkish white (7.5YR 8/2) and very pale brown (10YR 8/3). Inclusions range 5–15%, of moderate to abundant fine to medium, occasionally coarse, quartz of various colours, poorly sorted haematite and a moderate amount of mica. Glaze is mainly external, but occasionally inside cooking pots. It is dipped, sometimes splashed, and quite shiny and even. Dipped glaze is red (2.5YR 4/6), light yellowish brown (2.5Y 6/4) or olive (5Y 5/6), whereas the splashed glaze is coppery, sometimes speckled. There is sometimes a thin coating of white (10YR 8/2) slip on either surface. Some vessels are sooted. Many sherds are abraded.

Forms: jars/cooking pots with rolled, everted and club rims, flat or convex bases, one strap handle. Jugs with rolled or everted rims, flat or convex bases, and strap handles, some grooved. Bowls or dishes of various sizes, one large with everted rim. There is a little vertical applied slip decoration. Shoulder cordons and grooves are also present. One locking lid?

Figure 17.6: 42–48.

Sub-group 2.5

E28 A fairly hard, crudely wheel-made fabric, 10–20mm thick, with a hackly texture, fairly smooth feel and rough fracture. Mostly completely oxidised, surfaces vary from pinkish grey (7.5YR 7/2) to pink (7.5YR 8/4) and very pale brown (10YR 8/3), and the cores from pink (7.5YR 8/4) to grey (10YR 6/1) and very pale brown (10YR 8/3). The 15% inclusions contain abundant grey-buff medium to coarse quartz, moderate amounts of fine to coarse haematite, and fine mica. The rim/open base has been knife trimmed to form a bevelled edge. Unglazed. External sooting.

Forms: unidentified heavy industrial vessels, with a rim/open base diameter of 140–160mm. One may be part of an aludel, a vessel used in distilling.

Figure 17.7: 49.

Sub-group 2.6

F30 One sherd of a heavy slab-built? vessel. It is a hard fabric, 12mm thick, with laminated texture and slightly rough feel and fracture. The core is pink (7.5YR 8/4). The 10% inclusions comprise a moderate amount of fine to medium quartz of various colours, and moderate amounts of very poorly sorted haematite and very fine mica. It has a knife-trimmed exterior. The glaze is overall, apart from a 25mm wide diagonal strip on the exterior which shows a blackened surface. The glaze is olive yellow (2.5Y 6/6) and slightly matt externally, but brownish yellow (10YR 6/6) and shiny internally, and is thick and even.

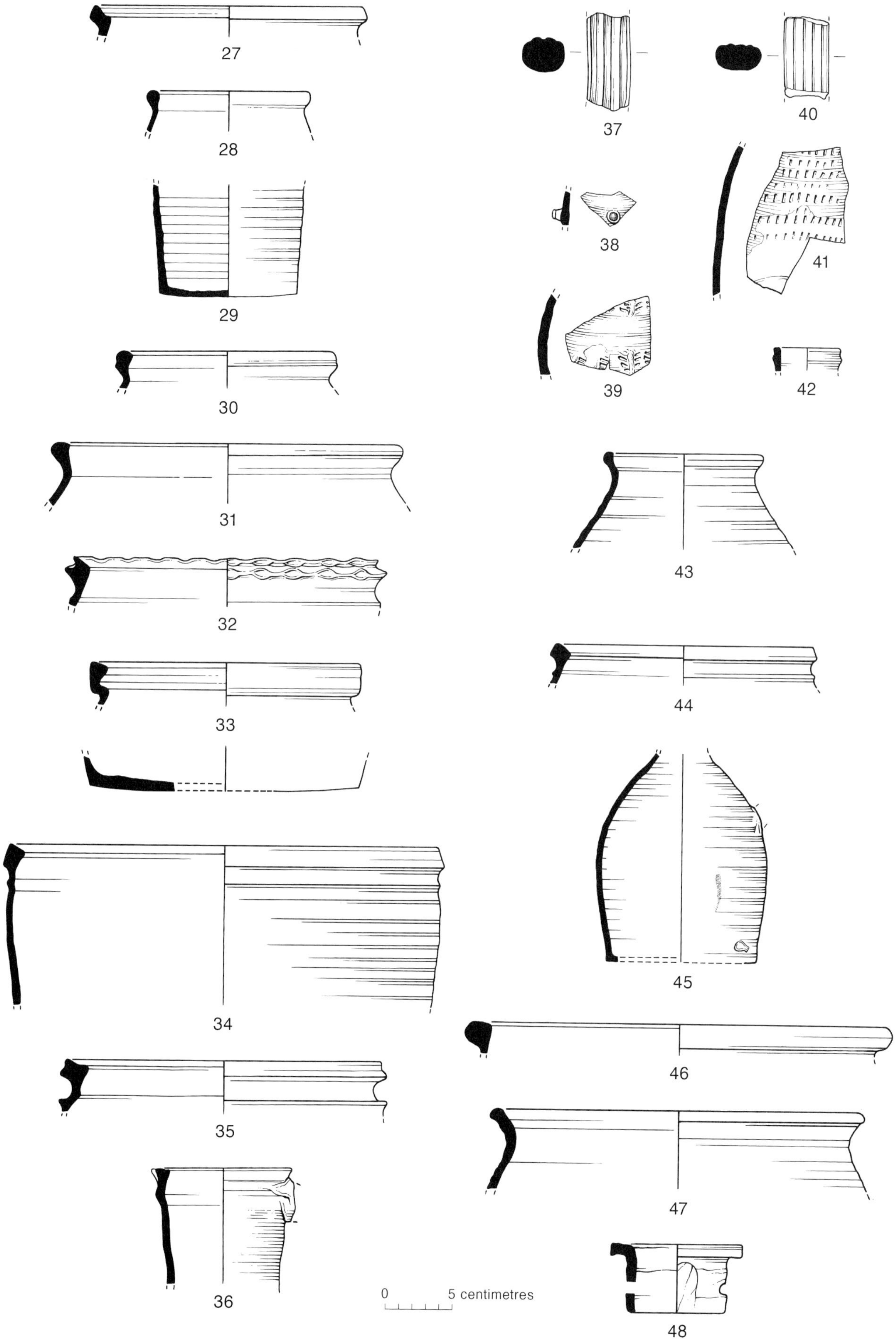

FIGURE 17.6
Medieval pottery types 2.2, 2.3 and 2.4

Forms: wide, shallow vessel, probably a dripping pan.

Figure 17.7: 50.

Group 3: Redware

Sub-group 3.1: Tweed Valley Ware

E1 A fine, hard, iron-rich fabric, 3–10mm thick, with slightly rough surfaces and sharpish fractures. The paste sometimes has cream and pinkish orange streaks. The outer surface varies from light red (2.5YR 6/6) through reddish yellow (5YR 6/4) to pink (7.5YR 7/4). Internally, it is light reddish brown (5YR 7/6) to pink (7.5YR 8/4), sometimes with a grey (7/5YR N5/) core. Usually, it is fully oxidised. The 5% inclusions are medium quartz, a little very coarse haematite and rock, and mica. Glaze is mainly external, but can occur on the inside of cooking pot bases. It can be either splashed or dipped, but is thin and patchy, and varies from light olive brown (2.5Y 5/4) to reddish yellow (10YR 6/8). Some sherds have an internal slip, reddish brown (5YR 5/3) to pinkish grey (7.5YR 7/2). Occasionally it is applied externally, light brown (7.5YR 6/4) to very pale brown (10YR 8/3). Cream slip sometimes underlies the exterior glaze, and can appear as random trails on vessels. There is evidence of some knife trimming at the base. Many sherds are sooted. There are many tiny, abraded sherds.

Forms: jars/cooking pots with rolled or club rims, and flat or convex bases. Jugs with rolled, everted and club rims, and flat or convex bases. One jug has a club rim with pulled spout and a grooved strap handle. A very few sherds have horizontal grooves. Some vessels of each form seem quite small.

Figure 17.7: 51–53.

E5 A hard, fine fabric, 4–7mm thick, with slightly rough surfaces and a clean fracture. The paste sometimes has cream and pinkish orange streaks. It mostly completely oxidised, with surfaces ranging from reddish yellow (5YR 6/6) through light brown to pink (7.5YR 6/4–7/4). The 5% inclusions are as in E1. Too few sherds are glazed to enable definition of the extent or coverage, which seem quite varied. Colour ranges from strong brown (7.5YR 5/6) to brown (10YR 4/3) and olive (5Y 5/4). There is a little knife trimming at the base. Some sherds are sooted. Many sherds are tiny and abraded.

Forms: jars/cooking pots, some small, with rolled, everted, club and lid-seated rims and flat or convex bases. Jugs with everted, upright and club rims, flat or convex bases, and strap handles. There is horizontal ribbing or thin grooves on some shoulder sherds.

Figure 17.7: 55.

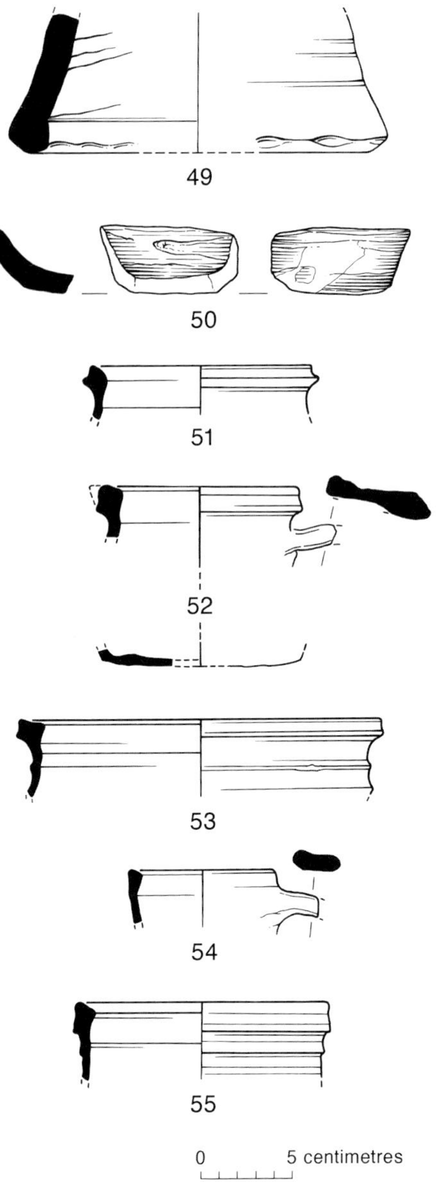

FIGURE 17.7
Medieval pottery types 2.5, 2.6 and 3.1

E18 A hard, finely made fabric, 4–6mm thick, with a smooth texture and clean break. It is more iron-rich than E1, and is usually completely oxidised. Surfaces vary from light red (2.5YR 6/6) to pink (5YR 7/3); any core is grey (2.5YR N5/–N6/). The 10–15% inclusions comprise moderate amounts of medium quartz and haematite, with a little rock and mica. The external glaze is dipped, occasionally splashed, and mostly glossy and smooth. It varies from yellowish red (5YR 4/6) to light olive brown (2.5Y 5/4) and dark greyish brown (2.5Y 4/2). Some thin, cream-coloured runs are evident, perhaps slip, and there is a suggestion of brown strips. Some sherds are sooted.

Forms: mostly jugs, with everted and upright rims and flat bases; there is a strap handle. One jug has an upright rim and pulled spout. Jars/cooking pots with rolled and everted rims, and flat bases. A pipkin?

E20 A hard fabric, 4–6mm thick, with a fine, slightly laminated, texture, smooth feel and clean break. It is very similar to E1, but more finely potted and slightly less iron-rich. It is generally oxidised throughout, but a few sherds have a reduced interior. The exterior is pink (5YR 7/4) to strong brown (7.5YR 5/4) and the interior is pink (5YR 7/3–7/4). The 5% inclusions are as in E1, but a little finer. A little glaze is discernible, both externally and internally; it is yellowish brown (10YR 5/6–6/8). Also noted is an internal smooth, continuous slip in pink (5YR 7/3). Some sooting is evident.

Forms: jugs or cooking pots.

E26 A hard, iron-rich fabric, 3–7mm thick, of irregular texture and slightly rough feel, with a clean fracture. Mostly completely oxidised. Exteriors are red (2.5YR 5/6) to reddish yellow (5YR 6/6), interior surfaces are reddish yellow (5YR 6/6) with occasional reddish grey (5 YR5/2) or reddish yellow (5YR 6/6) cores. The 10% inclusions in this very micaceous fabric comprise a moderate amount of medium quartz, with occasional very coarse grains of haematite, and rock up to 3mm in size. The exterior of one sherd has a little shiny glaze in dark yellowish brown (10YR 4/6) and a hint of a vertical line of dark brown coated slip. Some spots of glaze are visible on the exterior, as is some sooting.

Forms: jars/cooking pots, jugs? A small pipkin? with upright/inturned rim and strap handle.

Figure 17.7: 54.

Sub-group 3.2

F24 One sherd of a finely made vessel in a very hard fabric, *c*5mm thick, with a smooth feel and sharp fracture. It is iron-rich and completely oxidised to light reddish brown (5YR 6/3–6/4). The 5% inclusions are fine to medium well-sorted quartz, very occasional fine haematite, and some very fine mica. It is unglazed.

Forms: jar? with horizontal cordon.

Sub-group 3.3

D12 Crudely wheel-made pottery, 4–8mm thick, with a fine texture. Moderately hard, it has smooth surfaces but a rough fracture. Sherds are mostly completely oxidised, and the fabric varies from red or light red (2.5YR 5/6–6/6) to reddish yellow (5YR 6/6). The 10% inclusions are a moderate amount of coarse, poorly sorted quartz, with sparse coarse haematite and rock, and some flecks of mica. There is some knife trimming at the base of vessels. There is a little splashed, patchy external glaze, light yellowish brown (2.5Y 6/4), on the jug neck with occasional spots on vessel bases. Some thin, abraded pinkish white slip (5YR 8/2) remains on a cooking pot interior.

Forms: jars/cooking pots, jug. Rolled and club rims; flat or convex bases, some thumbed. There is a cordon around a jug neck.

D15 Hand-made pottery, 6–7mm thick, with irregular texture. Moderately hard, it has a smooth surface but a very rough fracture. Due to heavy sooting, it is uncertain if it is completely oxidised. The colour varies from brown to light brown (7.5YR 5/2–6/4). It contains 10% inclusions a moderate quantity of very poorly sorted, very coarse quartz, with grains up to 5mm across, as well as sparse, coarse haematite and rock and fine mica. Unglazed.

Forms: jars/cooking pots

Sub-group 3.4

D14 Hard, competently thrown pottery, 5–7mm thick, with a very fine, slightly hackly, texture. Surfaces are slightly rough, and the fracture is very rough. It is mostly oxidised, with a reduced core and thin to medium margins. The outer surface is reddish yellow (5YR 6/6) to pink (7.5YR 7/4), the interior varies from light red (2/5YR 6/6) and light reddish brown (5YR 6/4) to pink (7.5YR 7/4). The core is dark grey or grey (5YR 4/1 or 7.5YR N6/). The 15% inclusions are a moderate amount of coarse quartz, a little of which is white, some coarse rock and haematite, and mica. Grains can be visible in the surfaces. Unglazed.

Forms: jars/cooking pots, with everted rim and flat or convex bases.

Group 4: Reduced Gritty Ware

Sub-group 4.1

F4 A hard fabric, 3–10mm thick, with an irregular texture and rough feel and fracture. Quite iron-rich, most sherds are completely reduced; where only the interior or core are reduced, margins are sometimes thin and sharp. The exteriors are reddish brown (2.5YR 5/4) to light brown (7.5YR 6/4), the interiors dark grey (7.5YR N4/), light brown (7.5YR 6/4) or grey (10YR 5/1) and cores dark grey to grey (10YR 4/1–5/1). The 10% inclusions comprise medium quartz, some coarse rock and haematite, and mica. Grains are often visible in the very pimply surface. Glaze is mostly dipped, shiny and even; it is mostly on exteriors, but sometimes occurs inside bases, and varies from olive brown to light olive brown (2.5Y 4/45/4). Occasional trails of cream slip appear on body sherds. There is some knife or wire trimming at the base, and some sooting is evident.

Forms: mostly jugs, one with an everted rim and pulled spout, with flat or convex bases and strap handles, some grooved. Occasional jars/cooking pots with flat or convex bases. One sherd has raised brown spots, *c*5–7mm diameter, and another has an impressed scale pattern. One bowl?

Figure 17.8: 56, 57.

F10 Well-thrown, very hard fabric, 5–10mm thick, with a fine texture, smooth feel and sharp fracture. Mostly completely reduced, but where the exterior is oxidised there are thin, sharp margins. Exteriors vary from reddish brown (5YR 5/4) to reddish yellow (5YR 6/6–7.5YR 7/6). The interiors are dark grey (7.5YR N4/) to brown (7.5YR 5/4), and the core is dark grey to grey (7.5YR N4/–N5/). The clay is sometimes poorly mixed, with streaks and blobs of a lighter grey. Inclusions are about 5%, with a moderate amount of medium to very coarse (<7mm) rounded rock, sparse medium quartz, very occasional coarse, sub-round haematite, and a moderate amount of mica. Dipped glaze covers the upper half of jugs' exteriors, and is generally thick, even and shiny. It is olive brown (2.5Y 4/4) to olive (5Y 5/4), and a thin grey skin is sometimes visible below the glaze. Also below the glaze are vertical deep brown streaks, which run in an upwards direction, indicating that these vessels have been inverted in the kiln. Some knife trimming and a little thumbing is evident at vessel bases.

Forms: mostly jugs, with upright rims, flat or convex/thumbed bases and strap handles, some grooved. A band, 90mm deep, of very dark brown spots, *c*7mm diameter, runs around the shoulder of a jug. Horizontal ribbing has also been noted on vessel shoulders, and there is a little applied slip strip decoration. A very few jars/cooking pots, with everted/lid-seated and club? rims, and convex bases.

Figure 17.8: 59–62.

F11 A hard fabric, 4–12mm thick, of irregular texture, rough feel and slightly rough break. It is almost completely reduced, with thin, sharp margins. The exterior is pale brown (10YR 6/3) and the interior varies from light grey (10YR 7/1) to very pale brown (10YR 8/3) with a grey (10YR 5/1) to dark grey (2.5Y N4/) core. Inclusions are 10–15%, and consist of well-sorted, medium, sub-round quartz with mostly white grains, occasionally very coarse, sparse, irregular, fine to medium haematite and sparse mica. The inner surface has an 'orange peel' appearance. Glaze is dipped, mostly thick and glossy, and covers jug exteriors and bowl interiors. Copper and iron streaks and spots are noticeable, and the colour is olive to pale olive (5Y 4/4–6/4). One vessel has a mottled dark reddish brown glaze (2.5YR 2.5/4), possibly accidental. Some sooting is evident. Jugs are more finely made than the bowls, which are thick and coarsely made; some knife trimming at the vessel bases. Sherds of this fabric have been TL dated to AD 1100±95.

Forms: mostly jugs, with upright rims, convex or thumbed bases, and grooved strap handles. Some large bowls/dishes, with upright/thumbed rims and flat bases. Occasional jars/cooking pots, with everted/flanged rims and flat bases. There is occasional decoration of applied brown spots. Three sherds of an unidentified, large, slab-built? vessel of unknown form. It has an applied, thumbed footring; the external glaze also appears on the base and is partially covered with a white, slip-like substance.

Figure 17.8: 63, 64, 66, 67.

F19 A hard fabric, 5–8mm thick, with a fine texture and slightly rough feel and break. It is oxidised and surfaces are pink (5YR 6/4–7/5YR 7/4) with a light grey (5YR 6/1) to grey (10YR 5/1) core. The 10% inclusions are as F9, but finer. Glaze is dipped or splashed, and abraded. It varies from light yellowish brown (2.5Y 6/4) to slightly more coppery than olive (5Y 5/4). Many sherds are abraded.

Forms: jugs of various sizes, with rolled, everted and thumbed/club rims, flat or convex/thumbed bases, strap handles, some grooved. Jars/cooking pots, with rolled, everted/lid-seated and thumbed rims, flat bases, and one extended rod handle. Large bowls? with flat bases.

Figure 17.8: 65.

F20 A medium-hard fabric, 4–8mm thick, with a fine texture, smooth feel and slightly rough break. Apart from some outer surfaces, it is completely reduced to a light brown (7.5YR 6/4) with a very dark grey core (7.5YR N3/). The 5% inclusions are of fine to medium quartz, including white, and some mica. There is a little abraded, dipped glaze in olive (5Y 5/4).

Forms: jugs, with flat or convex/thumbed bases. Jars/cooking pots.

F23 A very hard fabric, 4–8mm thick, of hackly texture, harsh feel and rough fracture. It is partially reduced, with sharp, thin margins. The exterior is brown to pale brown (10YR 5/3–6/3), the interior is pinkish grey to reddish yellow (7.5YR 7/2–7/6) with a grey core (10YR 6/1). Inclusions are 10–15%, of poorly sorted, medium to very coarse quartz, sparse fine to very coarse rock and a little mica. The exterior glaze is dipped and shiny, coloured light yellowish brown (2.5Y 6/4). Some sooting was noted.

Forms: jars/cooking pots, with club rims and flat bases. Jugs, with rolled rims and strap? handles. Decoration comprises very dark purple/brown strips over the glaze with a herringbone pattern of stab marks to either side.

Figure 17.8: 58.

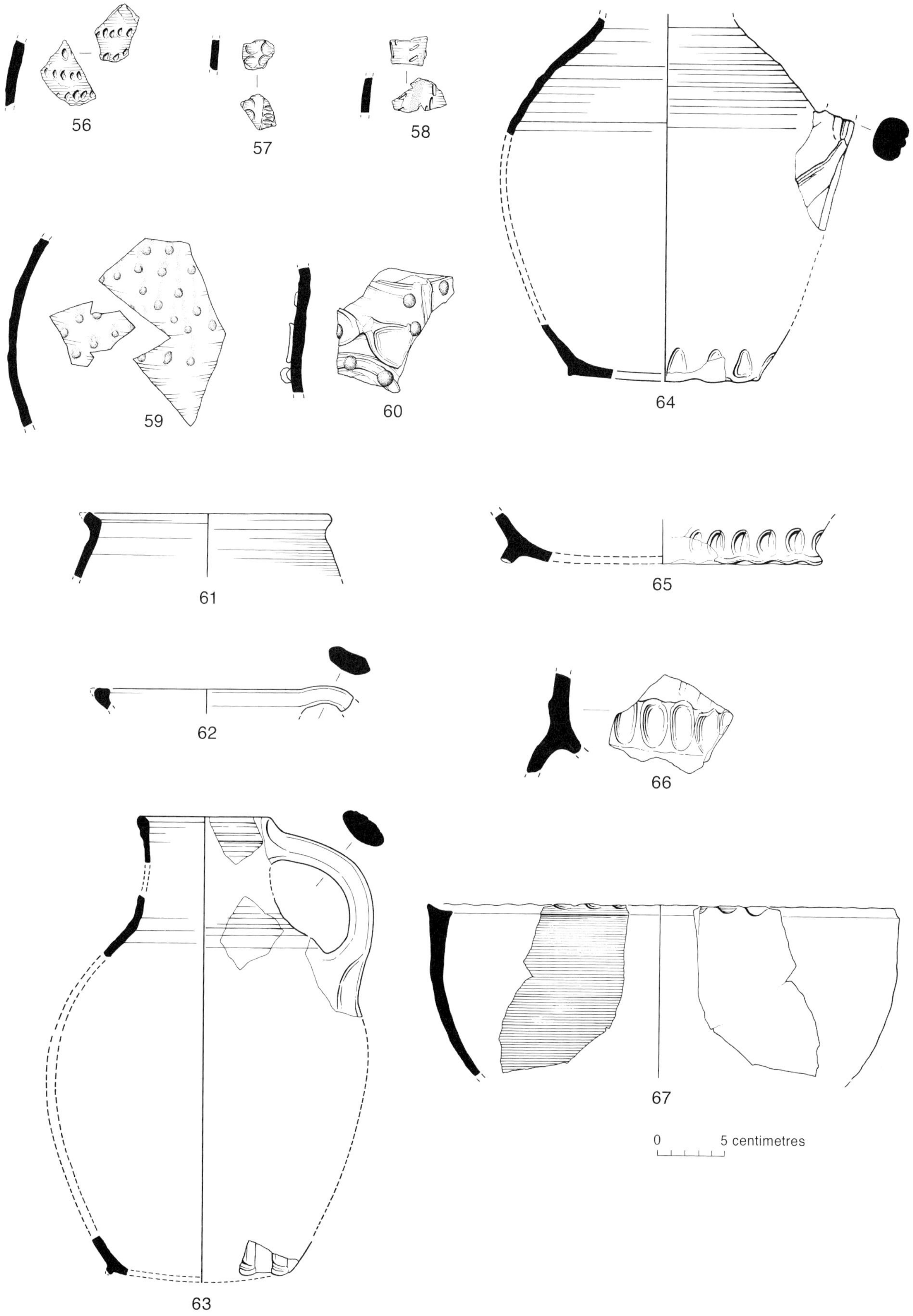

FIGURE 17.8
Medieval pottery type 4.1

F25 A hard fabric, 3–7mm thick, with a fine texture, smooth feel and sharp fracture. It is iron-rich, partially reduced with blurred margins. The exterior is light reddish brown (5YR 6/4), the interior is brown (7.5YR 5/4) to grey (10YR 5/1) and the core is grey (10YR 5/1). Inclusions are 10%, of a well-sorted, fine quartz with occasional very coarse grains and a little mica. There are external runs of glaze, and the lower interior and base of a cooking pot are glazed. It is shiny and patchy, and pale olive (5Y 6/4) in colour.

Forms: jars/cooking pots with flat bases. Jugs. One sherd has a horizontal rib on the shoulder.

Sub-group 4.2

F7 A very hard fabric, 3–10mm thick, with a slightly irregular texture, slightly rough feel and a sharp fracture. Some vessels are finely made, but others are quite coarse. It is partially or completely reduced; where the inside surfaces are oxidised, margins are thin and sharp. Exteriors are reddish brown (2.5YR 5/4), interior surfaces are pinkish grey or light reddish brown (5YR 6/2–6/4) to brown (7.5YR 5/2) with a dark grey core (2.5YR N4/). Inclusions are 5–10% and mainly of medium to coarse quartz, a little poorly sorted haematite and a little mica. The dipped glaze is thick, glossy and evenly covers most of the vessels' exteriors. It is olive brown to light olive brown (2.5Y 4/4–5/4). This fabric has been TL dated to AD 1475±55.

Forms: mostly jugs, some small, with rolled and upright rims, flat or convex bases, and strap handles, some grooved or incised. Occasional cooking pot? Decoration is varied, on jug shoulders, comprising: impressed concentric rings, 10–15mm diameter; stabbed or rouletted squares or triangles, 3mm wide, in horizontal bands; horizontal ribbing; underglaze, vertical lines of slip with accompanying brown spots, 10mm diameter.

Figure 17.9: 68, 69.

F12 Vessels in this hard fabric are both finely and coarsely made. Thickness varies 4–7mm, the texture is irregular with a rough feel and slightly rough, sharp fracture. Most sherds are reduced with oxidised surfaces, sometimes only the exterior. Margins are sharp and thin. The exteriors vary from reddish brown (5YR 5/4) to pink (7.5YR 7/4), the interiors run from pink (7.5YR 7/4) to dark grey (7.5YR N4/) to grey (10YR 6/1), and cores are dark grey to grey (7.5YR N4/–N5/). Inclusions are 5%, of a medium quartz and a little poorly sorted, coarse haematite. Very few sherds are glazed, and include a cooking pot interior. The glaze is abraded, and pale olive (5Y 6/4).

Forms: jars/cooking pots, with flat bases. Jugs, with flat or convex bases, a grooved strap handle. One bowl, with a club rim.

F14 Mostly well-made vessels, but a few are quite crudely thrown. The fabric is hard, 4–7mm thick, of irregular texture and rough feel and fracture. Most sherds are reduced, and some have oxidised surfaces. Margins are sharp and thin. Exteriors are reddish yellow (5YR 6/6) to pinkish grey (7.5YR 6/2), interiors are light reddish brown (5YR 6/4) to dark grey (7.5YR N4/) with a dark grey core (7/5YR N4/). Some very coarse round grey lumps indicate poor clay mixing. Inclusions are about 10%, comprising a moderate amount of medium to coarse sub-round quartz, sparse coarse haematite and abundant mica. The dipped, shiny glaze extends over most of the vessel exteriors, and over some interiors. It is olive (5Y 4/3). There is a little knife trimming.

Forms: mostly jugs, with rolled, everted, upright and inturned rims, flat, convex or thumbed bases, rod and strap handles, some grooved or incised. There is a three-handled jug; another has an upright rim with a pulled spout, and a grooved strap handle. Occasional jar/cooking pot, with everted/flanged rim and flat or convex bases. Two bowls/dishes with flat bases. Decoration comprises: wavy, combed lines; vertical, dark purple/brown underglaze strips; vertical slip strip with dark brown spots on either side; a horizontal cordon around a jug neck.

Figure 17.9: 70–74.

F15 A hard fabric, 4–10mm thick, with an irregular texture and rough feel and fracture. A partly oxidised variant of F14, the exterior surfaces are brown to pink (7.5YR 5/4–7/4), interiors are pink (7.5YR 7/4) or reddish yellow (5YR 6/6 to 7.5YR 7/6) and cores are dark grey to grey (7.5YR N4/–N5/). The 10% inclusions are as in F14 but with occasional very coarse quartz grains up to 4mm in diameter. The external glaze is very varied, being dipped and splashed, shiny and dull. The colour is olive brown (2.5Y 4/4) to olive (5Y 5/3–5/6). Some knife trimming and thumbing is evident at the bases, and one base shows stacking marks. There is a little sooting, and one sherd has a thin, unglazed, burnt patch, 15mm across, of applied clay, probably accidental. Many small, abraded sherds.

Forms: jugs, some small, with rolled, everted and upright rims, pulled and short tubular spouts, flat, thumbed and convex bases, strap handles, some grooved. Jars/cooking pots. One bowl? with everted/flanged rim. Decoration: one sherd is decorated with a strip of five vertical lines, probably made by a comb; one sherd has a band of four horizontal grooves 3mm wide, above a row of closely spaced applied oval slip spots, 8 x 5mm, on the shoulder; another has an impressed concentric rings motif, 10mm in diameter, overlain by a very dark purple/brown substance; and one has a closely spaced stamped grid motif.

Figure 17.9: 75–78.

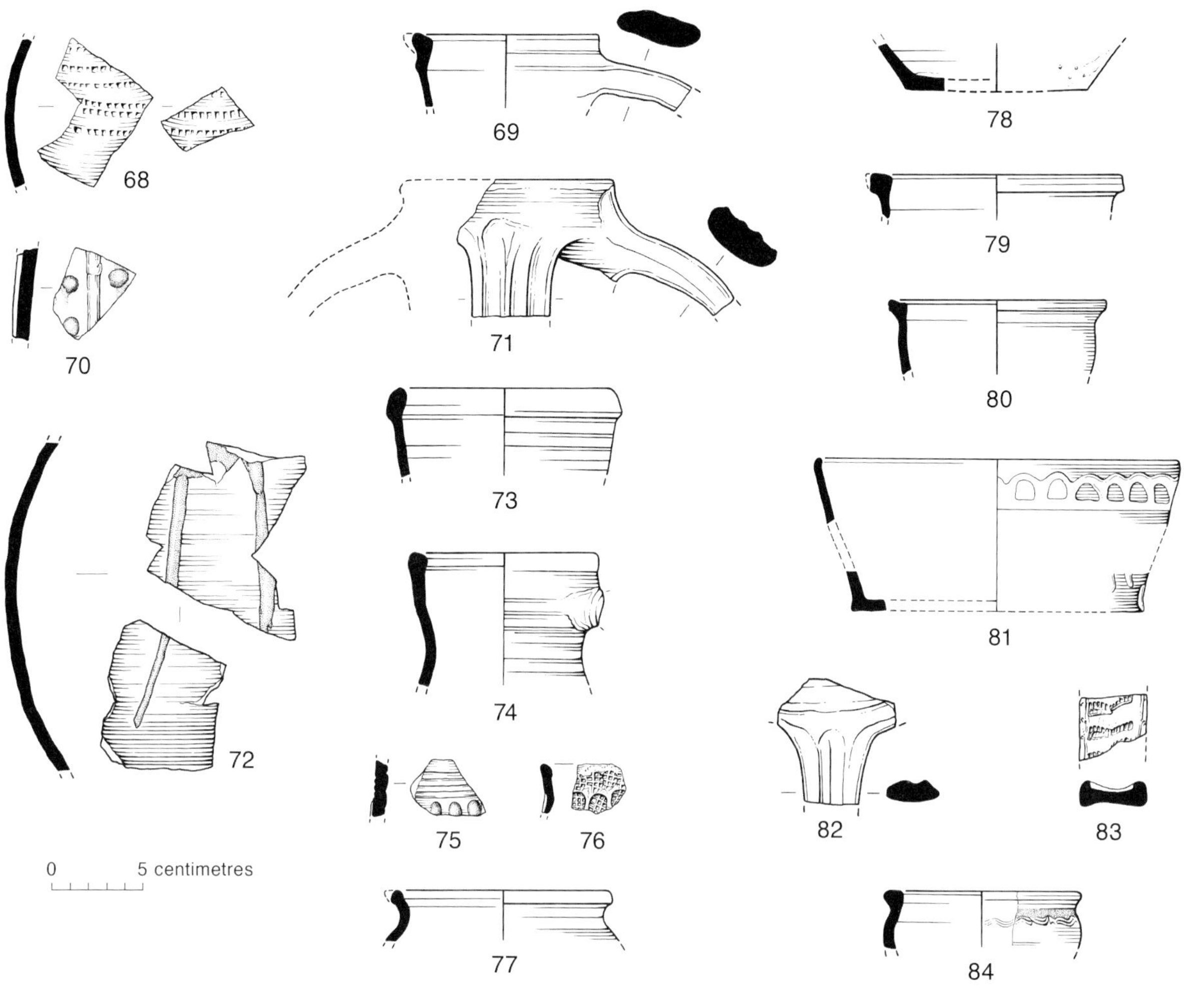

FIGURE 17.9
Medieval pottery types 4.2 and 5.1, and post-medieval type 7.1

F16 A very hard fabric, 3–8mm thick, of irregular texture, rough feel and sharp, slightly rough fracture. It is a more reduced variant of F12, and margins can be very thin and sharp, or thicker and blurred. The exteriors are light brown (7/5YR 6/4), the interiors are light brown (7.5YR 6/4) to pale brown (10YR 6/3) and the core is grey (10YR 5/1). The 5% inclusions are as F12. The dipped glaze appears to cover most of the exteriors. It is shiny, sometimes pitted, and is light olive brown (2.5Y 5/6) to olive (5Y 4/4).

Forms: mostly jugs, with rolled or upright rims, one with a pulled spout, flat or convex bases, and grooved strap handles. Occasional jars/cooking pots. Decoration comprises: a small, clay pellet, 10 x 10mm, on a vessel shoulder; a diagonal, applied slip strip, with notches across its width; vertical, very dark purple/brown strips and spots; some horizontal grooves and ribs, perhaps pronounced wheel-marks, around neck and shoulder areas.

Group 5: Buff/White Ware

Sub-group 5.1

E17 A hard fabric, 3–8mm thick, with a fine texture, smooth feel and clean break. It is completely oxidised and varies from light brown (7.5YR 6/4) to pink (7.5YR 8/4). It has 5% inclusions of fine quartz, medium, sometimes very coarse, haematite, coarse rock and a little mica. The external glaze is mostly dipped and smooth. It is light olive brown (2.5Y 5/4) to light yellowish brown (2.5Y 6/4). Two sherds have a hint of external pink slip (7.5YR 7/4). One sherd is sooted.

Forms: jars/jugs? with upright and club rims, flat base. There is a horizontal cordon on one shoulder sherd.

Figure 17.9: 79.

F1 This fabric varies from medium to very hard, 3–7mm thick, with a smooth texture and feel and a clean break. It is oxidised throughout, and varies from reddish yellow (5 YR 6/6) to pink (5YR 7/4 to 7.5YR 8/4). Inclusions are 5% and comprise well-sorted, fine to medium quartz, medium to coarse haematite and rock, and a little mica. Remnants of flaking, shiny glaze were noted: strong brown (7.5YR 5/6) to a dark coppery olive green (5Y 3/2). Some surfaces appear to have been wiped. There is very little sooting.

Forms: mostly jugs, with an occasional jar/cooking pot, with everted/flanged/lid-seated rims and flat or convex bases. Two sherds have vertical brown strips over the glaze, and there is a tiny fragment of an applied strip decorated with scales bounded by raised lines.

Figure 17.9: 80; 17.10: 86.

Group 6: Imported wares

Sub-group 6.1: Frechen-type stoneware

J9 Five body sherds, 4–7mm thick, of fine-textured stoneware with a fairly smooth surface and a clean break. The inner surface and core are very pale brown (10YR 8/3–8/4). It has a shiny 'tiger' glaze on the exterior. It is reddish yellow (7.5YR 6/6). Most of the interior is covered by a thin, lumpy, yellow slip (approx 10 YR7/6) with a dirty grey appearance.

Forms: Bartmann jug. One sherd bears a segment of a stamped relief, bordered medallion. This shows the crowned head of a sinister supporter (either an eagle or a lion) facing part of a crest in the form of two upright horns with something in between. The curved line at the foot of the sherd is probably the top of the shield. It bears a strong resemblance to a jug bearing the arms of Amsterdam (Hurst *et al* 1986, pl 44 centre).

Figure 17.10: 85.

Sub-group 6.2: Langerwehe-type stoneware

J10 One neck sherd, 4mm thick, of fine-textured, smooth-surfaced stoneware. It has an inner surface of reddish yellow (approx 7.5YR 7/6) with a dirty/grey look, and a core of pinkish grey (7.5YR 6/2). A dulled, weak red (10R 4/2) glaze extends evenly over the exterior, but is patchy on the interior.

Forms: jug. There is very fine rilling on the vessel neck.

Sub-group 6.3: North French ware

J11 One sherd of a very fine white ware, 5mm thick, with a slightly laminated texture and smooth feel. It is hard and has a clean break. The inner surface is white (10YR 8/2) with a very pale brown core (10YR 8/3). The 1–5% inclusions are sparse, fine to very fine, sub-angular haematite and a moderate amount of fine mica. There are no visible quartz inclusions. It has an even, slightly glossy glaze in light yellowish brown (2.5Y 6/4).

Forms: jug?

Group 7: Post-medieval earthenware

Sub-group 7.1

J1 Coarse red earthenware. Heavy, well-made vessels and pantiles in a hard fabric, 5–15mm thick, with an irregular, laminated texture, rough feel and rough fracture. It is iron-rich and completely oxidised. Surfaces vary from light red (2.5YR 6/6) to reddish yellow (5YR 6/6), with a light red core (2.5YR 6/6). The 15% inclusions are abundant, fine to medium, occasionally coarse, multi-coloured sub-round quartz, with moderate amounts of poorly sorted fine to coarse haematite and of fine mica. It is unglazed, apart from a pantile fragment with a dark reddish brown (5YR 8/2) glaze. There is some internal finger-rilling, and knife or wire marks appear on bases. Most sherds are abraded.

Forms: plant or flower pots, with everted rims, flanged and slightly convex bases with a central hole. Pantiles, one glazed.

J2 Lead-glazed red earthenware. Finely made vessels in a very hard fabric, 3–10mm thick, with a smooth texture and clean or slightly rough fracture. Completely oxidised, the iron-rich fabric is red (2.5YR 5/6). The 5–10% inclusions comprise a moderate amount of well-sorted, medium translucent and white sub-round quartz, occasional fairly sorted fine to medium haematite, and poorly sorted medium to coarse rock, and a moderate amount of fine mica. It has an all-over, very shiny, even glaze. It is mainly dark reddish brown (5YR 3/2–3), but also yellowish red (5YR 4/6). Tiny yellow flecks are visible throughout the glaze in most sherds.

Forms: bread crock/bowls, probably flat-based. Mug or cup, with a very slight horizontal cordon.

J3 Lead-glazed slipware. Competently made vessels in a hard fabric, 3–10mm thick, with a fine, sometimes laminated texture, slightly rough feel and slightly rough fracture. Completely oxidised, the iron-rich fabric's outer surface varies from reddish brown (2.5YR 5/4) to pink (5YR 8/3), with a core of light reddish brown (5YR 6/6) to reddish yellow (7.5YR 8/6). There are considerable variations in the 5% inclusions. There is a moderate amount of poor- to well-sorted very fine to coarse haematite, occasional medium to coarse grains of rock and quartz and abundant, fine mica. There are some knife or wire marks on bases. Some sherds have trailed slip decoration, internal and/or external, in pale yellow (2.5YR 8/4) or yellow (2.5YR 8/6), or merely a uniform layer of yellow (10YR 7/8)

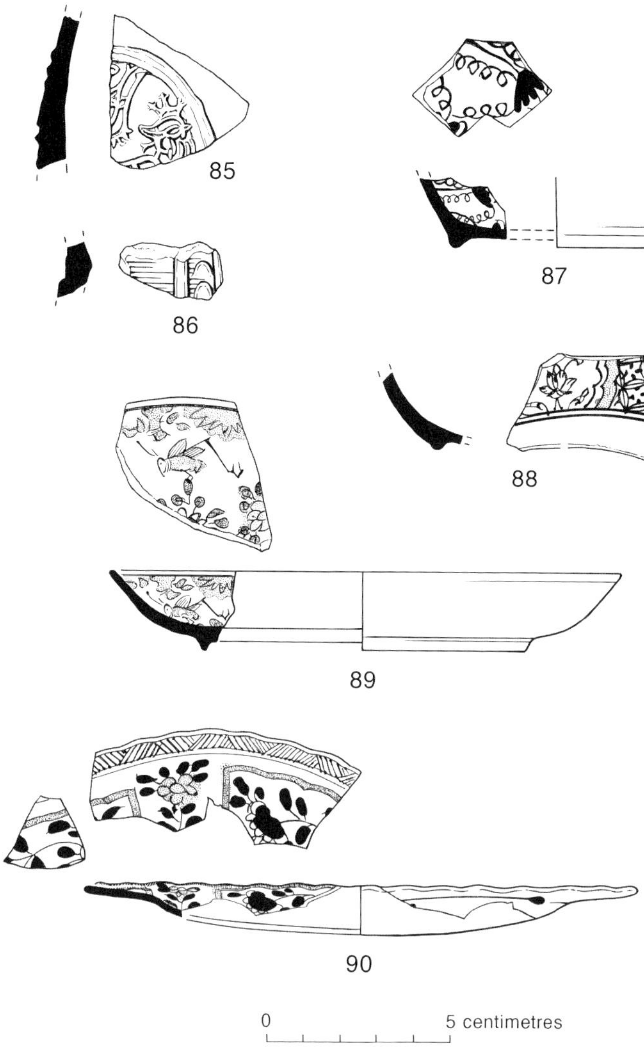

FIGURE 17.10
Medieval pottery types 5.1 and 6.1, and post-medieval types 7.2 and 9.1

underglaze slip. The thick, matt to shiny, flaking glaze can be external and/or internal, and varies from red (2.5YR 5/6) to reddish brown (5YR 4/4) and yellow (10YR 7/6). There is some sooting.

Forms: dishes, with flat, wide, everted rims, and flat bases. Bowls, with everted or upright rims, and flat, slightly splayed bases.

Figure 17.9: 81.

Sub-group 7.2: Tin-glazed white earthenware

J7 An assortment of mostly well-made vessels, 3–8mm thick. The fabric varies from soft to hard with a fine texture, soapy to slightly rough feel and a clean to slightly rough fracture. A white-firing clay, it fires to a very pale brown (10YR 8/3), sometimes with a pink (7.5YR 7/4) core. In some cases, the glaze has completely flaked off. Otherwise, it is thick, shiny and even, generally on both surfaces, and can be white or a very pale blue. A number of sherds are extremely abraded.

Forms: lidded jar, bowls, jugs? Some sherds have blue painted decoration.

Figure 17.10: 87.

Sub-group 7.3: Throsk-type ware

F28 A well-made, very hard fabric, *c*5mm thick, with a fine texture and smooth feel and a very slightly rough break. It is completely oxidised. The exterior red (2.5YR 5/6) with a pink (5YR 7/4) core. The less than 5% inclusions comprise some fine to medium sub-round quartz, medium to coarse rock, medium haematite, and a little mica. There is some even, shiny, dark brown (7.5YR 3/4) glaze on the interior.

Forms: pipkin, with everted rim and extended strap handle.

Figure 17.9: 82.

Group 8: Stoneware

Sub-group 8.1: White salt-glazed stoneware

J4 One sherd of a very finely made, probably moulded, very hard fabric, 3mm thick, with smooth texture and a clean break. It is very pale brown (10YR 8/3) with an overall shiny salt glaze. This is white (10YR 8/1), quite smooth on the exterior but slightly pitted on the interior.

Forms: small jar? The sherd has two parallel, horizontal scores.

Sub-group 8.2: Stoneware/proto-stoneware

J6 Two sherds in a very hard fabric, 4–7mm thick, with irregular texture, slightly rough feel and fracture. A jug handle is almost completely reduced, with reddish brown surfaces (5YR 5/3) and a grey core (5YR 5/1), with thin margins. It has some patchy, shiny olive brown glaze (2.5Y 4/4). The other sherd is completely reduced with very dark grey surfaces and core (10YR 3/1), and has traces of external glaze; its irregular shape suggests an overfired waster. The 10% inclusions are abundant, fairly sorted, medium to coarse sub-round quartz, occasional, very coarse rock and abundant, very fine mica.

Forms: jug, with grooved strap handle. Waster/distorted sherd.

Group 9: Porcelain

Sub-group 9.1

J8 Various sherds of porcelain, 1–8mm thick. Decoration on two sherds has been partially abraded off.

Forms: bowls, saucers/plates? Most have some form of decoration, mostly underglaze blue painted, and may well be Chinese. One sherd has two horizontal, parallel, gilded lines below the rim on the exterior.

Figure 17.10: 88–90.

Group 10: Other ware

Sub-group 10.1

F31 A well-made, hard fabric, *c*6cm thick, with a fine texture and smooth feel and a slightly rough break. It is oxidised with a reduced core, and margins are thick. The exterior is light brown (7.5YR 6/4) with a pinkish grey (7.5YR 6/2) core. The 10–15% inclusions comprise abundant, rounded, fine quartz, with sparse fine to medium haematite and very fine mica. The thin, shiny, patchy glaze is light yellowish brown (2.5Y 6/4).

Forms: jar, jug? Glaze appears on the shoulder (but not the rim) of a jar along with a narrow, horizontal, dark brown strip; underlying this is a narrow band of fine, combed, wavy decoration. A strap handle has a stabbed, herringbone pattern.

Figure 17.9: 83, 84.

Illustrated pottery

1 (Figure 17.5)
Fabric 11, Vessel D1/19. Jar or cooking pot. Rim. Unglazed. Sooted exterior and interior. C1373.

2 (Figure 17.5)
Fabric 1.1, Vessel D1/21. Jar or cooking pot. Rim. Unglazed. Heavily sooted exterior. C1376.

3 (Figure 17.5)
Fabric 1.1, Vessel D5/8. Jar or cooking pot. Rim. Unglazed. C911.

4 (Figure 17.5)
Fabric 1.1, Vessel D6/29. Jar or cooking pot. Rim. Unglazed. ?C605.

5 (Figure 17.5)
Fabric 1.2, Vessel D4/1. Jar or cooking pot. Rim. Unglazed. C452.

6 (Figure 17.5)
Fabric 1.2, Vessel D13/8. Cooking pot. Rim. Unglazed. Heavily sooted exterior. C504.

7 (Figure 17.5)
Fabric 1.2, Vessel D13/5. Small cooking pot. Rim. Unglazed. Heavily sooted exterior. C205.

8 (Figure 17.5)
Fabric 1.3, Vessel D7/19. Cooking pot. Rim. Unglazed. Sooted exterior. C739.

9 (Figure 17.5)
Fabric 2.1, Vessel D10/2. Jar or jug. Rim and shoulder. Flaking patchy external glaze. C12, C240.

10 (Figure 17.5)
Fabric 2.1, Vessel E11/337. Large jar. Rim. Unglazed. C207.

11 (Figure 17.5)
Fabric 2.1, Vessel E11/464. Cooking pot. Rim. Unglazed. Heavily sooted on both surfaces. C1011.

12 (Figure 17.5)
Fabric 2.1, Vessel E11/474. Cooking pot. Rim. Unglazed. Sooted exterior. C289, C294.

13 (Figure 17.5)
Fabric 2.1, Vessel E13/100. Large jar. Rim. Glazed interior. C704.

14 (Figure 17.5)
Fabric 2.1, Vessel E13/101. Small jug. Lower body and base. Patchy external glaze. C708.

15 (Figure 17.5)
Fabric 2.1, Vessel E13/137. Jug. Rim. Patchy external glaze. C290.

16 (Figure 17.5)
Fabric 2.1, Vessel E13/138. Jug. Rim and spout. Unglazed. C289, C294.

17 (Figure 17.5)
Fabric 2.1, Vessel E19/6. Jar. Rim. Unglazed. C442.

18 (Figure 17.5)
Fabric 2.1, Vessel E25/49. Cooking pot. Rim. Unglazed. Heavily sooted exterior. C911.

19 (Figure 17.5)
Fabric 2.1, Vessel E27/48. Cooking pot. Rim. Unglazed. Heavily sooted exterior. C128.

20 (Figure 17.5)
Fabric 2.1, Vessel E27/49. Jug. Rim and part of handle. Traces of degraded external glaze. C1003.

21 (Figure 17.5)
Fabric 2.1, Vessel E27/322. Jug? Spout. Unglazed. C1124.

22 (Figure 17.5)
Fabric 2.1, Vessel E27/102. Jar or cooking pot. Rim. Unglazed. C111.

23 (Figure 17.5)
Fabric 2.1, Vessel E27/186. Cooking pot. Rim. Unglazed. C221.

24 (Figure 17.5)
Fabric 2.1, Vessel E27/202. Jug. Rim. Unglazed. C248.

25 (Figure 17.5)
Fabric 2.1, Vessel E27/335. Jar or cooking pot. Rim. Unglazed. C302.

26 (Figure 17.5)
Fabric 2.1, Vessel E27/337. Jar or cooking pot. Rim. Traces of external slip. C289, C1001, C1005.

27 (Figure 17.6)
Fabric 2.2, Vessel E10/1. Jar or cooking pot. Rim. Unglazed. Slightly sooted exterior. C799.

28 (Figure 17.6)
Fabric 2.2, Vessel E12/75. Cooking pot. Rim. Unglazed. Heavily sooted exterior and interior. C126.

29 (Figure 17.6)
Fabric 2.2, Vessel E10/30. Cooking pot. Lower body and base. Unglazed. Heavily sooted exterior. C131.

30 (Figure 17.6)
Fabric 2.2, Vessel E12/50. Jar or cooking pot. Rim. Unglazed. Heavily sooted exterior. C1003.

31 (Figure 17.6)
Fabric 2.2, Vessel E12/148. Large jar or cooking pot. Rim. Unglazed. C242.

32 (Figure 17.6)
Fabric 2.2, Vessel E12/264. Cooking pot. Rim. Unglazed. Sooted exterior. C427.

33 (Figure 17.6)
Fabric 2.2, Vessel E12/315. Cooking pot. Rim and base. Unglazed. Sooting on base. C1012.

34 (Figure 17.6)
Fabric 2.2, Vessel E12/320. Cooking pot. Rim and shoulder. Unglazed. Sooted exterior. C1109.

35 (Figure 17.6)
Fabric 2.2, Vessel E12/321. Cooking pot. Rim. Unglazed. Sooted exterior. C114.

36 (Figure 17.6)
Fabric 2.3, Vessel F8/9. Jug. Rim and neck, trace of handle. Patchy glaze on neck exterior. C769, C909.

37 (Figure 17.6)
Fabric 2.3, Vessel F8/22. Jug? Handle. Glazed. C1022.

38 (Figure 17.6)
Fabric 2.3, Vessel F8/72. Jug? Shoulder. External glaze. Applied clay pellet. C739.

39 (Figure 17.6)
Fabric 2.3, Vessel F8/76. Jug. Shoulder. External glaze. Stabbed decoration. C145.

40 (Figure 17.6)
Fabric 2.3, Vessel F8/79. Jug? Handle. Glazed. C410.

41 (Figure 17.6)
Fabric 2.3, Vessel F8/80. Jug. Shoulder. Upper portion glazed externally. Rouletted decoration. Unstratified.

42 (Figure 17.6)
Fabric 2.4, Vessel F9/1. Small jar or jug. Rim. External glaze. C963.

43 (Figure 17.6)
Fabric 2.4, Vessel F9/30. Jar or cooking pot. Rim and shoulder. Patchy glaze externally and inside rim. Sooting on both surfaces. C903, C911, C1151.

44 (Figure 17.6)
Fabric 2.4, Vessel F27/5. Jar or cooking pot. Rim. Unglazed. C214.

45 (Figure 17.6)
Fabric 2.4, Vessel F27/101. Small jug. Trace of handle. Even external glaze. C1036.

46 (Figure 17.6)
Fabric 2.4, Vessel F27/48. Large jar? Rim. Unglazed. Slightly sooted exterior. C14.

47 (Figure 17.6)
Fabric 2.4, Vessel F27/104. Large jar or cooking pot. Rim. Unglazed. Heavily sooted exterior. C209.

48 (Figure 17.6)
Fabric 2.4, Vessel F27/105. Locking lid? Trace of glaze on upper surface of flange. C568.

49 (Figure 17.7)
Fabric 2.5, Vessel E28/2. Base of an aludel? Unglazed. Slight sooting on exterior. C240.

50 (Figure 17.7)
Fabric 2.6, Vessel F30/1. Dripping pan? Rim and base. Even all-over glaze except for diagonal strip on exterior which is sooted. C125.

51 (Figure 17.7)
Fabric 3.1, Vessel E1/6. Cooking pot. Rim. Unglazed. Heavily sooted exterior. C428.

52 (Figure 17.7)
Fabric 3.1, Vessel E1/38. Jug? Rim, base and part of handle. Traces of external glaze. C909, C1026.

53 (Figure 17.7)
Fabric 3.1, Vessel E1/110. Jar or cooking pot. Rim. Unglazed. C11.

54 (Figure 17.7)
Fabric 3.1, Vessel E26/13. Small jug. Rim and part of handle. Trace of glaze on handle. C619.

55 (Figure 17.7)
Fabric 3.1, Vessel E5/224. Cooking pot? Rim. Unglazed. Slight sooting on exterior. C710.

56 (Figure 17.8)
Fabric 4.1, Vessel F4/3. Jug? Body sherd. External glaze. Stabbed decoration. C52, C601.

57 (Figure 17.8)
Fabric 4.1, Vessel F4/4. Jug. Body sherd. External glaze. Impressed decoration. C704, C716.

58 (Figure 17.8)
Fabric 4.1, Vessel F23/5. Jug? Body sherd. External glaze with dark brown stripe. Stabbed decoration. C286, C801.

59 (Figure 17.8)
Fabric 4.1, Vessel F10/1. Jug. Shoulder. External glaze with dark brown spots and streaks. C1198, C1260, C1305, C1332.

60 (Figure 17.8)
Fabric 4.1, Vessel F10/3. Jug. Body sherd. External glaze with dark brown spots and applied clay strips and pads. C412.

61 (Figure 17.8)
Fabric 4.1, Vessel F10/48. Jar. Rim. External glaze. C710.

62 (Figure 17.8)
Fabric 4.1, Vessel F10/39. Cooking pot? Rim and part of handle. Traces of external glaze. C707.

63 (Figure 17.8)
Fabric 4.1, Vessel F11/1. Jug. External shiny glaze. C1260, C1305, C1332.

64 (Figure 17.8)
Fabric 4.1, Vessel F11/3. Jug. External glaze, thinning downwards. C1260, C1305, C1332.

65 (Figure 17.8)
Fabric 4.1, Vessel F19/54. Large jug? Base. External glaze. C405, C444.

66 (Figure 17.8)
Fabric 4.1, Vessel F11/7. Large vessel: lid/base/curfew/flanged bowl? Glazed externally and in angle where a white substance adheres to glaze. C452.

67 (Figure 17.8)
Fabric 4.1, Vessel F11/6 . Large bowl. Internal glaze with dark green and brown streaks. Sooted exterior. C295, C1003, C1005, C1007.

68 (Figure 17.9)
Fabric 4.2, Vessel F7/31. Jug. Body sherd. External glaze. Rouletted decoration. C701, C708.

69 (Figure 17.9)
Fabric 4.2, Vessel F7/33. Jug. Rim and part of handle. Patchy external glaze. Slight sooting on interior and exterior. C701, C715.

70 (Figure 17.9)
Fabric 4.2, Vessel F14/97. Jug. Body sherd. External glaze with dark brown spots and applied clay strip. C1151.

71 (Figure 17.9)
Fabric 4.2, Vessel F14/84. Jug. Rim and parts of two handles. External glaze. Both surfaces slightly sooted. C623.

72 (Figure 17.9)
Fabric 4.2, Vessel F14/1. Jug. Body sherds. External glaze with dark brown stripes. C1260.

73 (Figure 17.9)
Fabric 4.2, Vessel F14/18. Jug. Rim. Abraded glaze, externally and inside rim. C1003.

74 (Figure 17.9)
Fabric 4.2, Vessel F14/106. Jug. Rim and trace of handle. External glaze. C444.

75 (Figure 17.9)
Fabric 4.2, Vessel F15/129. Jug. Body sherd. External glaze with abraded dark brown spots. C105.

76 (Figure 17.9)
Fabric 4.2, Vessel F15/143. Jug? Body sherd. External glaze with stamped gridiron decoration. C285.

77 (Figure 17.9)
Fabric 4.2, Vessel F15/2. Jar. Rim. External glaze on top of shoulder. C429, C444.

78 (Figure 17.9)
Fabric 4.2, Vessel F15/142. Cooking pot? Lower body and base. Trace of external glaze. C708.

79 (Figure 17.9)
Fabric 5.1, Vessel E17/14. Jar. Rim. Unglazed. C1126.

80 (Figure 17.9)
Fabric 5.1, Vessel F1/10. Jar. Rim. External glaze runs. C1035.

81 (Figure 17.9)
Fabric 7.1, Vessel J3/1. Bowl. Rim, lower body and base. Both surfaces glazed. Applied slip decoration has flaked off. C452.

82 (Figure 17.9)
Fabric 7.3, Vessel F28/6. Pipkin. Rim and part of handle. Internal glaze. C1121.

83 (Figure 17.9)
Fabric 10.1, Vessel F31/2. Jug? Handle. Glazed. Impressed decoration. C421.

84 (Figure 17.9)
Fabric 10.1, Vessel F31/1. Jar. Rim. External glaze with dark brown glaze over fine combed decoration. C452.

85 (Figure 17.10)
Fabric 6.1, Vessel J9/1. Bartmann jug. Shoulder. External glaze. Applied clay medallion. C106.

86 (Figure 17.10)
Fabric 5.1, Vessel F1/19. Jug? Shoulder. External glaze. Applied clay strip decoration. C710.

87 (Figure 17.10)
Fabric 7.2, Vessel J7/8. Small bowl? Lower body and base. Blue underglaze decoration. C51.

88 (Figure 17.10)
Fabric 9.1, Vessel J8/2. Shallow bowl. Body and base. Blue underglaze decoration. C928.

89 (Figure 17.10)
Fabric 9.1, Vessel J8/1. Wide shallow bowl. Rim and base. Blue underglaze decoration. C928.

90 (Figure 17.10)
Fabric 9.1, Vessel J8/3. Plate. Flat rim. Blue underglaze decoration. C8, C105.

17.4 DISCUSSION

It is interesting to note the almost total lack of imported pottery in this assemblage, with only six imported vessels represented. Wine would have been required at the church, and traces of containers, such as Saintonge jugs, might have been expected. Given The Hirsel's proximity to important burghs and Border towns, and its situation on the road from Berwick to Kelso, it is surprising that more imported wares were not present. It is possible that goods could even have been brought up the River Tweed by small boats, since the Tweed was tidal as far upstream as Norham as late as the mid-19th century. Unfortunately, the imported material is all from topsoil or very late contexts and is thus of little use for dating purposes.

The size of the assemblage seems at odds with the function of the site, in that much more pottery was recovered than might have been expected from what is primarily a church and graveyard. Such vessel forms as can be identified are best characterised as utilitarian in nature, with a lack of more 'exotic' vessels. One curious sherd of a heavy vessel may be the base of an aludel, an open-ended cone-shaped vessel placed between a cucurbit and an alembic in the process of distillation. This, however, may well be explained by the likelihood of the later, secular, use of the site. General Monk, prior to the restoration of Charles II, made Coldstream his headquarters and it not inconceivable that his army might have been camped in The Hirsel grounds, thus accounting for some of the later material.

Many sherds are small and abraded. There are comparatively few joins, and these rarely comprise more than two sherds, suggesting that considerable disturbance of the site had taken place. Ploughing may be one explanation, but the changing use of the site and the lengthy period of activity may also be contributory factors. A large number of sherds has undoubtedly been redeposited and this, together with the complex stratigraphy of the site, makes their interpretation difficult.

The earliest fabrics from sub-groups 1.1 and 1.2 more closely resemble wares from eastern England than from Scotland. They are mainly associated with the church (Phase I, below floor C1068), but pottery from later groups 2 and 3 is also present at this level.

Much of the material, in particular groups 2 and 3, is very similar to pottery recovered from a pit group in the Kelso Abbey excavations, dated to the second or third quarters of the 12th century (Cox *et al* 1984, 395–397). Vessel forms strongly resemble those from Springwood Park, Kelso (Bown 1998). This suggests that 90% of the assemblage, e.g. groups 2, 3 and 4, is of local, Tweed valley, manufacture.

Pottery of group 2 was found within the flue and fill of the bell casting pit in Phase III of the church, whereas sherds of group 4 were first associated with a later, greensand floor/layer, C1036, in Phase IV.

It is becoming apparent that differentiating between clays from different areas of the country is fraught with difficulty, particularly when it is not possible to ascertain whether the inclusions occur naturally or are added as temper. Certainly, the addition of quartz temper would increase the tensile strength of vessels used over heat. Interestingly, the method of clay preparation used at Verwood as late as the 1950s involved wedging the clay on a surface sprinkled with sand (Algar *et al* 1979, 8). If this was the continuation of an earlier tradition, it suggests that the quantity of inclusions within a fabric may be a matter of chance. This is commented on in a project on sourcing white gritty wares. Examination of the fabrics suggested that potters varied the amount of grit in their clays according to the type or part of the vessel under construction (Jones *et al* 2003, 78).

Fabrics of similar types seem to occur at The Hirsel in both reduced and oxidised sherds of varying colours. Here, the larger quantities of white gritty fabric are always in association with red ware and reduced gritty ware, with the sole exception of the fill of pit C1302, which consisted almost exclusively of reduced wares. It has been noted that quantities of reduced gritty vessels were occurring contemporaneously with white gritty vessels on at least two other Scottish sites: Eyemouth town (Crowdy 1986, 50) and Castle Sween (Caldwell and Stewart 1996).

An initial survey suggests that, at The Hirsel, white gritty wares seem to be predominantly jars or cooking pots, whereas the majority of the less gritty reduced wares are jugs. This could suggest that different firing methods are being used to produce vessels for different functions, and would also fit with the hypothesis that temper was added to those vessels being used for cooking purposes.

A recent study of ceramic vessels associated with coin hoards (Dean 2007) shows that their generally accepted periods of use fit with the deposition dates of the hoards. The predominant fabric of 13 vessels containing coins of the late 13th to mid-14th centuries was reduced gritty ware, although a few vessels were of white gritty or red ware. Red ware and reduced gritty ware was also evident in pots containing mid-16th century coins.

A programme of thermoluminescence dating was undertaken at an early stage in the post-excavation work. The resultant dates are given, along with the appropriate fabric descriptions. Unfortunately, the relative lack of large and joining sherds, and the consequent difficulties of reconstruction of rim shapes and vessel forms, makes typological dating of the assemblage problematic.

17.5 CONCLUSION

Although this collection of sherds does not offer an insight into new types of pottery technology or include uncommon imports, it is of importance since it is a large assemblage emanating from a church site. The presence of so few imported vessels could indicate an apparent lack of trading contacts, with vessels instead being acquired from local sources. The volume of local fabrics from The Hirsel, together with material from other Borders sites, suggests the existence of a thriving Tweed valley pottery industry. This assemblage should make an important contribution to further research in this field.

17.6 CERAMIC LOOM-WEIGHT
Rosemary Cramp

CO1 (not illustrated)
Fragment of a ceramic loom-weight in a coarse fabric with oxidised exterior and reduced core, possible inclusions of organic matter. There is a nick to hold the thread on one face. The fragment is too small to reconstruct the form, but since it was discovered in the area of the medieval domestic building on the north-west of the site, in a layer in which the medieval occupation had been disturbed by a plough, it is likely to belong to this period and it sheds further light on the domestic use of that area.
Ring 250mm x 300mm; Th 300mm; exterior diameter of hole *c*250mm.
C207, Phase 8 EPM, Area: 190-202/ 850-859.

18

CLAY TOBACCO PIPES

Lloyd J Edwards

The distribution of clay tobacco pipes represents casual losses over the site, but there are larger concentrations of fragments to the north-west of the church and in the northernmost trench, in areas where there was evidence for post-medieval activity. With the exception of two late 19th–early 20th century fragments, the material can be dated to the 17th and 18th centuries. There is a full listing of clay pipe fragments in the site archive. There are eight bowls of note (CP1–CP8).

CP1 (Figure 18.1)
Complete bowl. I and A in relief on either side of heel. Stem bore 7/64. John Aikens of Glasgow, *c*1700.
C1, topsoil, Area: 170–80/840–50.

CP2 (Figure 18.1)
Bowl with ?turret-type stamp on base of heel. Stem bore 7/64. Mid–late 17th century.
C2, Phase: 8 EPM, Area: 170–80/840–50.

CP3 (Figure 18.1)
Stem fragment with initials I.C. in relief on side of heel. Stem bore 7/64. Possibly James Colquhoun II, *c*1695–1730, of Glasgow.
C2, Phase: 8 EPM, Area: 170–80/840–50.

CP4 (Figure 18.1)
Bowl. Mid–late 17th century. Stem bore 7/64.
C2, Phase: 8 EPM, Area: 170–80/840–50.

CP5 (not illustrated)
Bowl fragment with initials T and B in relief on either side of the heel; Thomas Banks of Edinburgh, *c*1649–61. Stem bore 6/64.
C285, topsoil, Area: 202.4–205/850–859.5.

CP6 (not illustrated)
Bowl fragment with initials T and A in relief on either side of the heel. Stem bore 7/64. Mid–late 17th century.
C1000, topsoil, Area: 202.4–205/850–859.5.

CP7 (Figure 18.1)
Bowl with ?turret-type stamp on base of heel. Mid–late 17th century. Stem bore 7/64.
C1001, Phase: 8 EPM, Area: 205–10/850–8.

CP8 (Figure 18.1)
Bowl with ?initial W on left side of heel. Turret-type stamp on base of heel. Stem bore 6/64. Perhaps William Banks of Edinburgh *c*1622–59.
C928, Phase: 8 EPM, Area: 175–86/833–40.

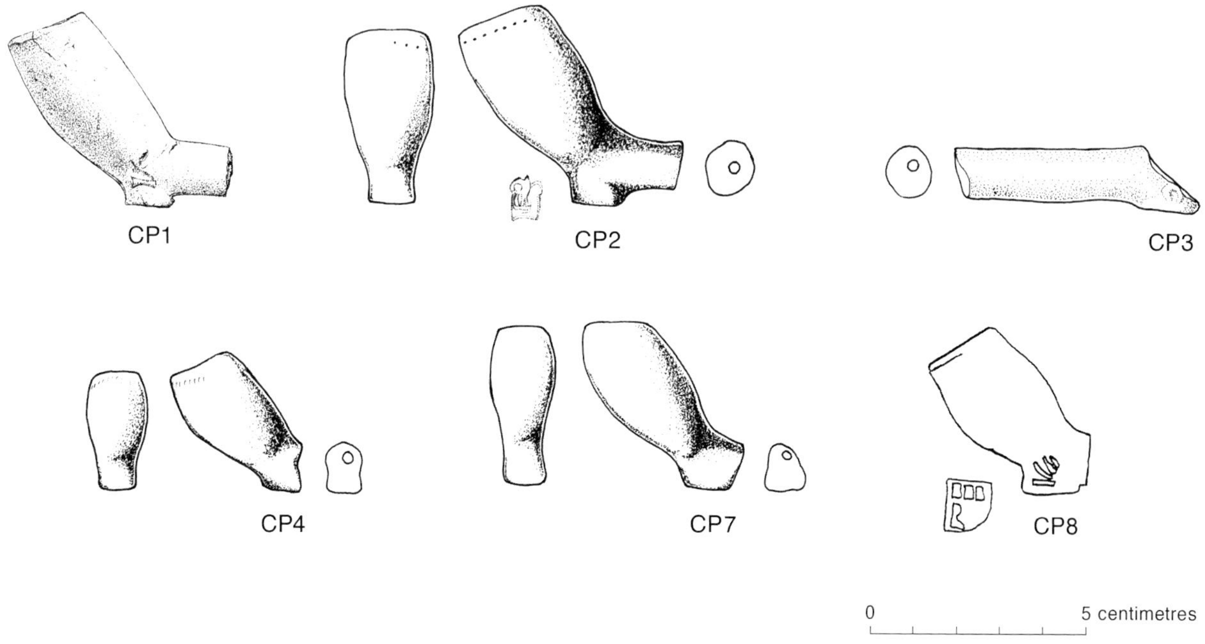

FIGURE 18.1
Clay pipes from the excavated site

19

COPPER ALLOY

Rosemary Cramp and Belinda Burke

There is a small collection of copper alloy from medieval and early post-medieval contexts, but the distribution is interesting; some items were found in clearance deposits or topsoil, most of the personal items have been found either to the west of the church or to the north of the churchyard — areas which have been identified as in domestic occupation. Fragments which are considered bindings, book clasps or mounts were found within the church and the only 'domestic' object is a large needle or awl found with the debris of secular occupation within the nave. The buckle tongue (CA1), chain (CA23) and tweezers (CA19) were found to the west of the site. The lace chapes (except CA10 and CA11), like the rumbler bell (CA26), were found in the area of domestic use in the north-east corner of the churchyard.

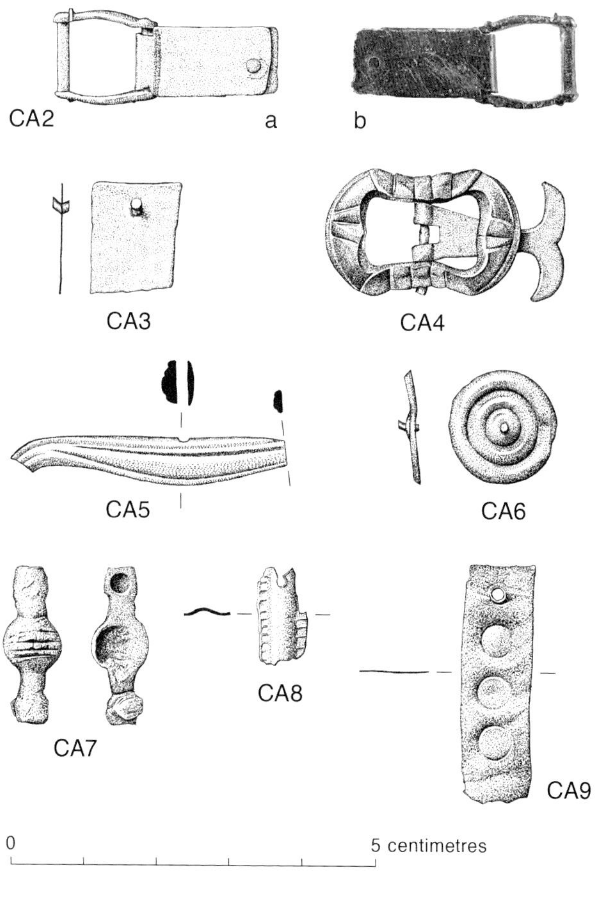

FIGURE 19.1
Buckles and mounts, CA2–9

There is nothing exceptional about this collection, save the richness of the rumbler bell and the complexity of the fine wire chain (CA22).

19.1 BUCKLES AND MOUNTS

CA1 (Not illustrated)
Slightly curved square-sectioned rod with flattened end, possibly a buckle tongue.
From soil into which pit/ditch C1386 was cut.
L 30mm; W 3mm; Th 2mm.
C1285, Phase: 3? Pre-med, Findspot: 179.20/826.96.

CA2 (Figure 19.1)
Frame and plate of a rectangular strap clasp with sub-rectangular loop, finely moulded frame and folded sheet-bronze plate, recessed for the frame, with one rivet. Dateable to the late 13th century to early 15th century (Egan and Pritchard 1991, 116–117, nos 551, 553). It is also very similar to an example from Northampton (Oakley and Webster 1979, 253, Cu26, fig 108). Found at the base of the cut for the late compound to the north-west of the church.
L 31mm; Loop 12mm x 13mm; Width of plate 10mm.
C454, Phase: 8 EPM, Findspot: 186.5/843.4.

CA3 (Figure 19.1)
Fragment of sheet bronze with rivet, possibly one sheet of a rectangular strap plate (see Egan and Pritchard 1991, 226–227, fig 141). 12th to 14th century (Ian Riddler pers comm). Found in a shallow cut to the west of church.
L 15mm; W 12mm; Th 0.5mm.
C457, Phase: 7 LM, Findspot: 183.56/830.00.

CA4 (Figure 19.1)
Double framed buckle with incised ornament and an anchor-shaped tab, tongue missing. Probably a shoe buckle, the elaborate decoration, and hinged shank indicate a post-Restoration date (Egan 2005, 7). A similar frame was found at Ardingley Fulling Mill, dated to the late 17th century (Goodall 1976, 64, fig 9b.52). Found in a deposit at the base of the compound to the north-west of the church.
L 32mm; W 15mm; L of plate 26mm.
Date: late 17th century.
C947, Phase: 8 EPM, Findspot: 182.28/837.01.

CA5 (Figure 19.1)
Tinned bronze fragment of an oblong framed post-medieval buckle, with piercing for a separate spindle, arched profile. Cast, and decorated with curving raised lines. Found in clearance deposit with mid-17th century coins and probably of that date.
L 42mm; W 6mm.
Date: 17th century.
C911, Phase: 8 EPM, Findspot: 184.66/837.56.

CA6 (Figure 19.1)
Circular mount in embossed sheet bronze with central rivet and three concentric raised rings. Such mounts were used as fittings to decorate belts or leather armour; common late medieval form (see Egan and Pritchard 1991, 179, fig 114).
Disturbed medieval surface in area of domestic occupation to north of church.
Diam 14mm.
Date: late 14th century.
C504, Phase: 7 LM (disturbed), Findspot: 204.80/848.76.

CA7 (Figure 19.1)
Bar mount with central and end lobes; the end lobes are riveted and the central lobe is decorated with three incised lines. Solid, cast (rather than stamped). Such mounts have been considered to be harness mounts, but they could have decorated a belt as in depictions of men's waist belts, sword belts, horse harness straps (Egan and Pritchard 1991, 209, 213–214). They are found throughout the medieval period (Egan and Pritchard 1991, 210). Found in the nave of the church with late medieval pottery.
L 21mm; W 8mm; Th 4>2mm.
Date: medieval.
C1194, Phase: 7 LM, Findspot: 191.68/832.22.

CA8 (Figure 19.1)
Fragment of curved mount with milled edges and remains of a rivet hole at one end. Similar to a small rectangular fitting found at Meal Vennel, Perth, in a phase 5 context which also yielded five 13th century coins (Cox 1996, 745, 766, illus 18, 73).
From a medieval deposit in the extended nave of the church.
L 13mm; W 6mm.
Date: medieval.
C128, Phase: 5? EM2, Findspot: 204.99/860.60.

CA9 (Figure 19.1)
Rectangular plate broken at each end, with a rivet hole and three impressed circles. Although it is not certain what this incomplete object is, it resembles pieces which have been identified as strap mounts (Egan and Pritchard 1991, 196–197, ills 123, 1060, 124).
Disturbed medieval ground surface to north of extended nave of the church.
L 31mm; W 9mm.
Date: medieval.
C56, Phase: 6 Med, Findspot: 196.45/836.08.

19.2 LACE TAGS

Lace chapes or tags are a common find in the later medieval period, being used to encase the ends of laces of leather or textile, and reflecting changing trends in fashion from the mid-14th century onwards (Egan and Pritchard 1991, 284). Indeed, paintings and manuscripts which illustrate their uses, for example, for lacing doublet and hose, and bodices, provide an explanation for the large quantities that have been found on archaeological sites (Margeson 1993, 22).

All the tags from the Hirsel are rolled; four (CA12–15) with edge-to-edge seams corresponding with Oakley and Webster's type 1 (Oakley and Webster 1979, 262–263), one with the edges overlapping and tapering at the base (CA13), and three with overlapping edges, corresponding with Margeson's type 3 (Margeson 1993, 22), but none have the inwardly folded edges of the post-medieval type 2 identified at Northampton (Oakley and Webster 1979, 263). All are open both ends, with no evidence of riveting, although in some cases they are probably incomplete. None of them is decorated.

Two (CA10–11, both type 3) were found in the spreads of rubble in the graveyard to the south of the church, which seems to have been redeposited from a domestic structure. CA10 came from the same context that yielded iron belt fittings and a pierced whetstone (Fe41–43, SH2). The rest were concentrated in the northern part of the site, which has been identified as a domestic area, with three (CA12–14) from C1003, a context that yielded a large quantity of medieval pottery and some medieval iron finds, as well as 17th century clay pipe.

CA10 (Figure 19.2)
Rolled lace chape, with overlapping seam.
L 65mm; W 5mm.
Date: medieval.
C715, Phase: 7 LM, Findspot: 198.40/824.40.

CA11 (Figure 19.2)
Rolled and crushed tube of sheet bronze, with slightly overlapping seam. Probably a lace chape, incomplete.
L 42mm; W 7mm.
Date: medieval.
C714, Phase: 6 Med, Findspot: 199.08/825.94.

CA12 (Figure 19.2)
Rolled lace chape with edge-to-edge seam.
L 75mm; W 6>3mm.
Date: medieval.
C1003, Phase: 8 EPM, Area: 205–205.5/850.5–857.

CA13 (Figure 19.2)
Lace chape with overlapping seam, tapering.
L 53mm; W 5>4mm.
Date: medieval.
C1003, Phase: 8 EPM, Area: 207.75–210/858–60.

CA14 (Figure 19.2)
Part of a rolled lace chape with edge-to-edge seam.
L 52mm; W 6>4mm.
Date: medieval.
C1003, Phase: 8 EPM, Area: 205–10/858–60.

CA15 (Figure 19.2)
Part of a lace chape with edge-to-edge seam, one end round, one slightly flattened. Broken at both ends.
L 27mm; W 6mm.
Date: medieval.
C102, topsoil, Area: 195–6/863–4.

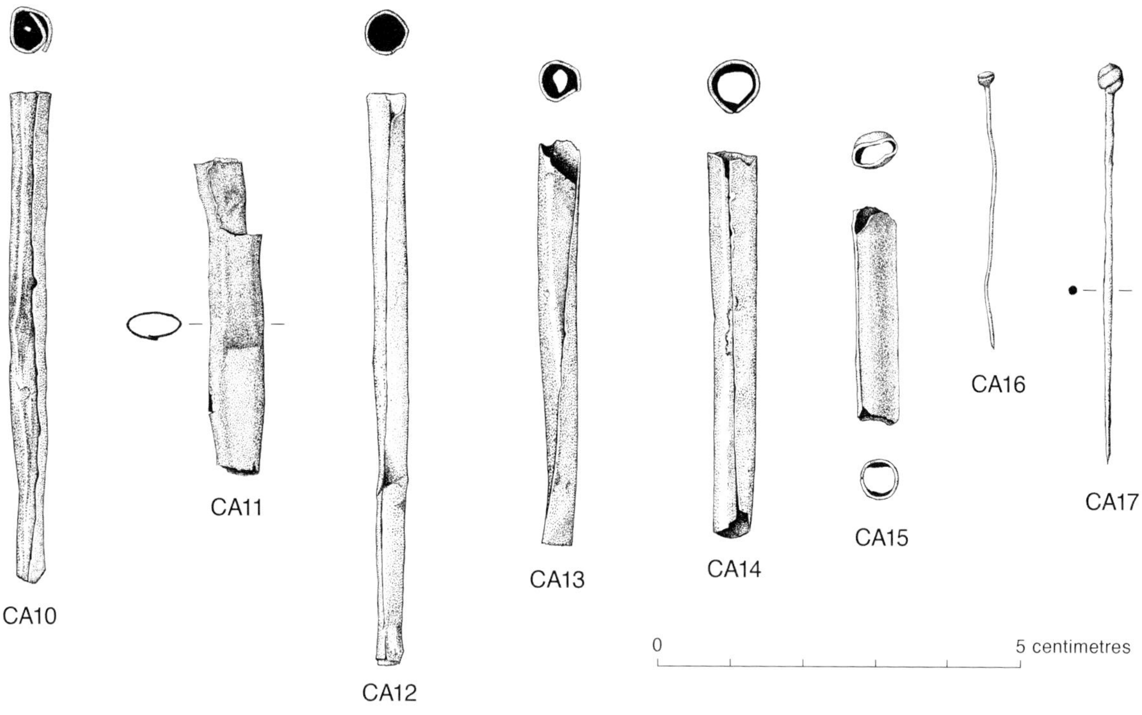

FIGURE 19.2
Lace chapes and pins, CA10–17

19.3 PINS

Two wound wire-headed pins were found on the site. This type first appears in the 13th century, but only becomes common from post-14th century contexts (Caple 1991, 242). While it is not possible to generalise too far from a sample of two pins, Caple (1991, 248) sees pins dating to before 1500 as having mean lengths of 40–50mm, while those from 1500–1630 have mean lengths of 29–35mm. At Castle Park, Dunbar, a significant collection of such pins was recovered from the later medieval and post-medieval phases of the site (Perry 2000, 118–120). At Whithorn, long pins with wire-wrapped heads ranging from 45mm to 60mm in length came from late 14th –15th century contexts (Nicholson and Hill 1997, 361–362). So CA17, being 52mm long, may be an earlier example, while CA16 could be later, although from its context it is not post-medieval.

In London, large numbers of wire pins appear in 14th and 15th century contexts, explained by documentary evidence of pins being used to secure veils, as evident in 15th century paintings (Egan and Pritchard 1991, 297; A R Goodall, 2007, 524, fig 11.2.6).

CA16 (Figure 19.2)
Wire-headed pin, found in the apse of the church, in a late medieval context of occupation.
L 37mm; Diam 1mm, Diam of head: 2mm.
Date: late medieval.
C630, Phase 6 Med, Findspot: 205.60/832.28.

CA17 (Figure 19.2)
Pin with wound wire spherical head. Found in a shallow posthole at the west of the site.
L 52mm; Diam of head 3mm.
Date 14th–15th century.
C430, Phase: 8 EPM, Findspot: 189.3/840.7.

19.4 OTHER ITEMS

CA18 (Figure 19.3)
Tweezers of very simple design, formed from a folded strip of bronze with angled squared-off terminals and loop at the apex (see A R Goodall 1981, 67). Such tweezers are found in Roman and early Saxon contexts as well as medieval, and so are difficult to date, but these seem to belong to the early medieval rather than to the Romano-British activity on the site. Found in the area of domestic occupation to the north of the site.
L 50mm; W 6mm.
Date: medieval.
C240, Phase: 6 Med, Area: 195–6/854–9.

CA19 (Figure 19.3)
Tweezers formed from a folded strip of sheet bronze with widely angled arms, of similar form to CA18, but decorated with crudely incised zig-zag ornament. This is very similar to the pattern on a pair of medieval tweezers from Winchester (Rees *et al* 2008, 237–238, no. 1630).
Found in a medieval context at the west end of the church.
L 60mm; W 6mm.
Date: 12th–13th century.
C1082, Phase: 6 Med, Findspot: 183.75/826.2.

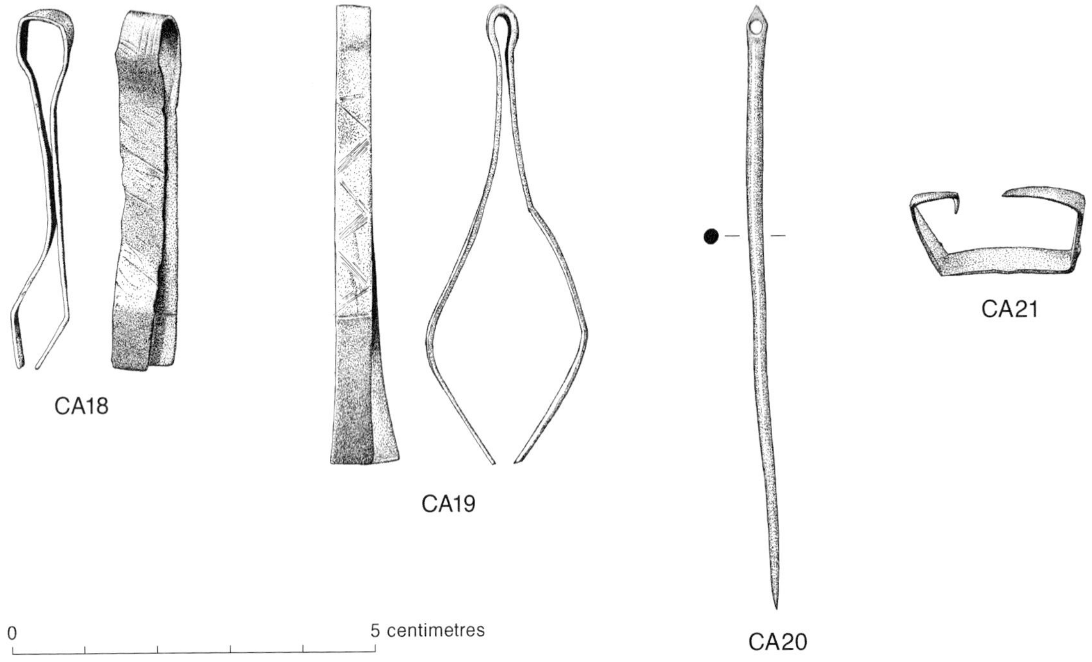

FIGURE 19.3
Tweezers, needle and staple, CA18–21

CA20 (Figure 19.3)
Needle with a round shaft, circular eye and angular head. Similar in form to an example from Meols with a drilled eye and round sectioned point, traits predominant in the late 12th century in London (Egan 2007a, 176, no. 2215, pl 34).
This came from a possible late floor level within the nave of the church.
L 80mm; Diam 2mm.
Date: medieval.
C1158, Phase: 7 LM, Findspot: 193.60/829.16.

CA21 (Figure 19.3)
Strip of bronze with tapered pointed ends, bent round to form a rectangular binding, with one point bent inwards. Possibly a staple or a simple strap guide (Ottaway 1992, 6890), but also paralleled by similar items from Meols, whose function seems less certain (Egan 2007c, 288).
From the grave of Sk180 (an infant) from near the head, and may be intrusive.
50mm x 11mm x 6.5mm.
Date: medieval.
C1162, Phase: 6 Med, Findspot: 194.55/827.26.

CA22 (Figure 19.4)
Chain, constructed from fine woven wires, copper alloy or silver. It is formed from running overhand knots interlinked with external loops. Wire chains such as this may be constructed either with closed loops or in a knitting type with continuous strands (Untracht 1982, 184–191, 228–232). The ends are broken as if the fastenings had been torn off. Wire chains, whether worn as jewellery or for suspension, have a very long history, but this elaborate work would seem to be medieval, and no close parallels have been identified.
Found in the cemetery earth to the south of the church with a considerable amount of disturbed human bone, so it could have come from a grave.
240mm x 2mm.

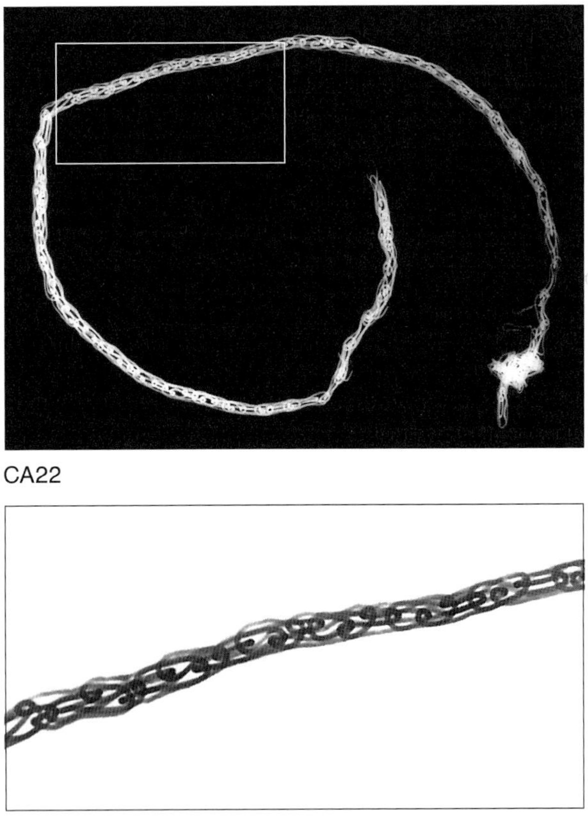

FIGURE 19.4
Elaborately linked chain, CA22

Date: medieval.
C714, Phase: 6 Med, Findspot: 196.76/826.28.

CA23 (Figure 19.5)
Part of a chain, with four flat S-shaped links.
Similar to finds from many sites, including an example from Perth (Cox 1996, 771, illus 20.209).
71mm x 8mm, L of links: 18mm.
Date: 14th–15th century.
C907, Phase: 7 LM, Findspot: 181.65/832.5.

CA24 (Figure 19.5)
Fragment of curved sheet of bronze, with fragments of decayed wood. There is evidence of two keyhole-shaped cuts along the edge, possibly decorative, but the circular openings could have held rivets to secure the sheet to a wooden handle. Part of the binding for the handle of an iron tool? (Ian Riddler pers comm).
From the late secular occupation of the nave, associated with burning.
25mm x 25mm.
Date: medieval.
C623, Phase: 7 LM, Findspot: 198.06/830.81.

CA25 (Figure 19.5)
Fragment of sheet bronze, with scalloped decoration along the edge, roughly incised with vertical lines.
The piece is damaged and incomplete, but it may be identified as a dagger or sword chape, opened out and flattened. There is a dagger chape from Norwich which has incised leaf-like projections along the edge, beneath which is attached an incised metal band reinforcing the top of the chape, and possible evidence of a similar feature may be seen on the Hirsel example in a horizontally worn band 15mm deep. The Norwich chape is thought to be late 14th to 15th century (Margeson and Goodall 1993, 227, no. 1856, fig 175).
From the topsoil to the south of the church.
51mm x 44mm.
Date: late medieval.
C701, topsoil, Area: 196–210/820–829.8.

CA26 (Figure 19.6)
Rumbler bell, oval, with four petal-like tabs cast in one with the loop. Once the iron pea was inserted the tabs were pressed together to hold it. The copper surface has been decorated with incised spirals and leaf scrolls with extensive survival of gilding.

Rumbler bells are a not uncommon find on medieval sites, but this is unusual in material, form and decoration. More common than copper is brass, tin, or pewter, and bells are most often made in two pieces soldered together. Only early examples have been found of this form and they are often decorated, although with less sophistication (Egan and Pritchard 1991, 336–341, fig 221). No close parallels have been found for the Hirsel decoration although the swirls of leaves can be seen on 12th century manuscripts such as The Lambeth Psalter. This is obviously a high status piece, and although bells could decorate the collars of dogs, horse harness, or the jesses of birds of prey, it would seem most likely that this was a dress accessory suspended from a girdle or collar. Pritchard notes that the evidence for bells as dress ornaments is negligible before the late 14th century 'although jesters and acrobats had adopted them earlier as part of their everyday guise (fig 219) and so had pilgrims and priests'(Egan and Pritchard 1991, 336–337). It is interesting that this was found in the area to the north of the site where the priest's house has been postulated.

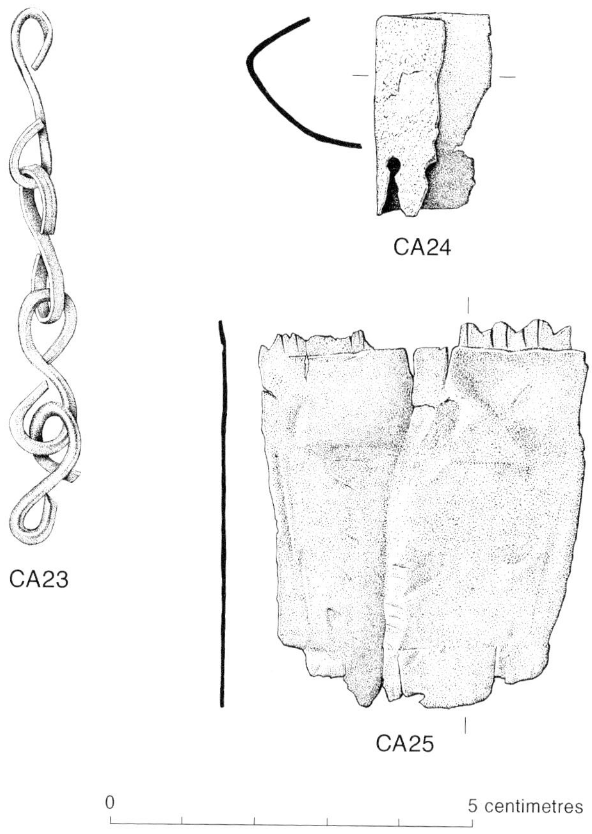

FIGURE 19.5
Part of an S-shaped chain, CA23; curved sheet with keyhole-shaped cuts, CA24; scalloped sheet, probably a dagger or sword chape, CA25

From medieval flooring, but disturbed by the plough and with one sherd of post-medieval pottery.
H 30mm; Diam 25mm.
Date: medieval.
C294, Phase: 6 Med (disturbed), Findspot: 203.2/853.8.

CA27 (Figure 19.6)
Curved strip, slightly eliptical in section, broken at both ends, rivet hole at one end. Difficult to decipher; it could be part of a purse frame or a balance?
From a medieval sand and cobbled surface in the chancel.
53mm x 5>4x4mm.
Date: 12th–14th century.
C683, Phase: 6 Med, Findspot: 201.70/834.32.

CA28 (Figure 19.7)
Two rim fragments of a hand held/pocket sundial, marked XII–V. The larger has a rivet hole under the numeral XII, and the other has an elegantly curved internal tab, similar examples were found at Meols (Egan 2007b, 228, pl 49, no. 3145, although this has Arabic numerals) and Norwich, with Roman numerals stylistically dated to the early 16th century (Margeson 1993, 72, no. 448). The type however continues, and this could be later.
The layer in which it was found yielded 19th century pottery.
35mm x 5mm; 25mm x 5mm.
Date: 18th century?
C803, Phase: 9 LPM, Findspot: 223.8/835.2.

CA29 (not illustrated)
Oval, saucer-shaped boss, with central indent.
This could be the outer casing of a mount.
Found in an early post-medieval context, plough soil.
30mm x 25mm.
Date: medieval?
C8, Phase: 9 LPM, Findspot: 173.42/840.90.

CA30 (not illustrated)
Bent fragment of small rod.
Possibly the shank of a long rivet.
The only find from a patch of burnt, decayed material and small cobbles in the south-east corner of the chancel.
L 15mm; W 2mm.
C647, Phase: 7? LM, Findspot: 204.20/831.04.

CA31 (not illustrated)
Small fragment of copper-alloy sheet.
From a surface cut by graves in the northern part of the cemetery.
12mm x 7mm.
C522, Phase: 6 Med, Findspot: 190/847.

CA32 (not illustrated)
Featureless lump showing patches of tinning. Waste?
From an area of late medieval concentrated burning in the nave.
22mm x 13mm x 12mm.
C1159, Phase: 7 LM, Findspot: 195.20/832.4.

Additionally, numerous copper-alloy fragments were found associated with the bell-casting pit (from C881 and C897), the associated pit in the centre of the extended nave (C1347 and C1226b) and a thin spread of burnt material immediately to the north of the nave, presumably also representing debris from the bell casting (see Chapter 26).

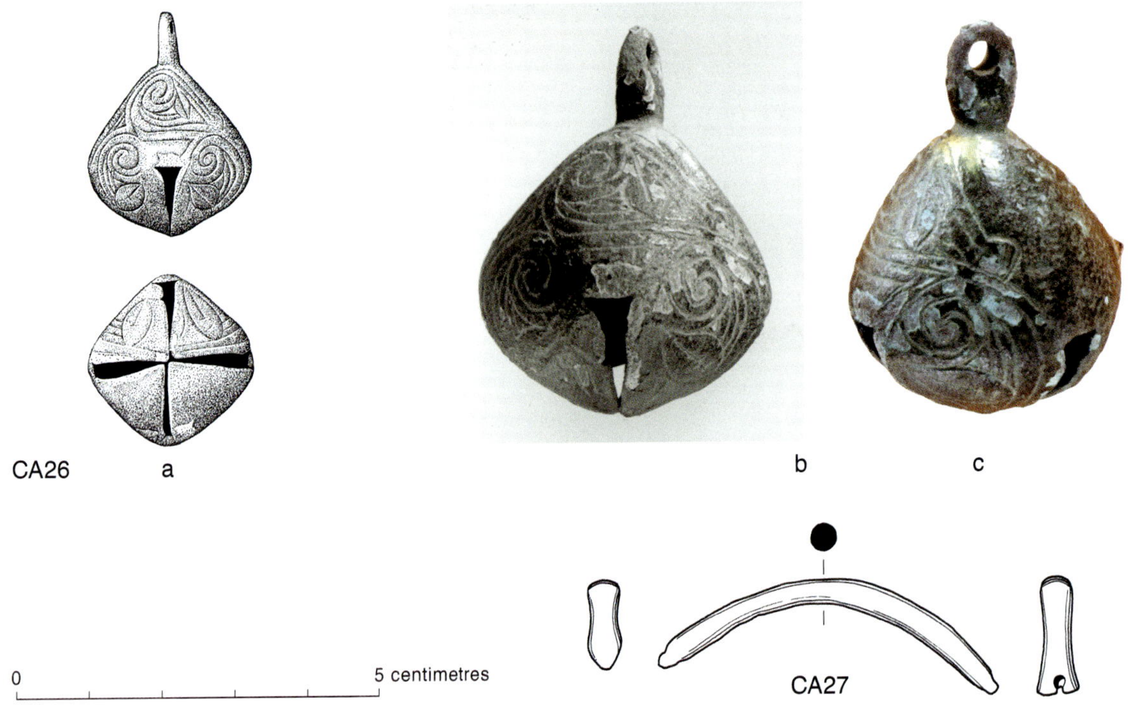

FIGURE 19.6
Decorated rumbler bell, CA26; pierced curved strip, CA27

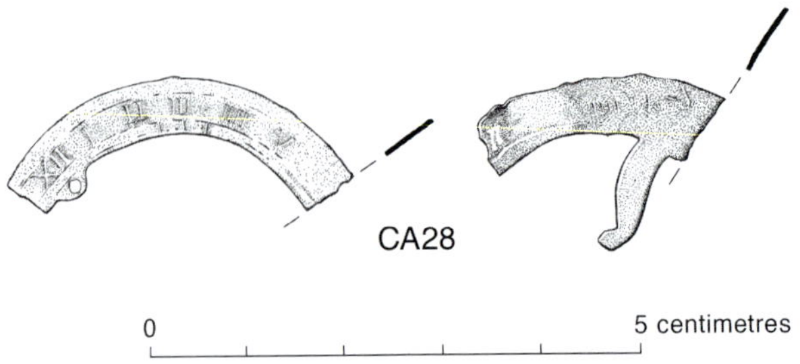

FIGURE 19.7
Rim fragments of a pocket sundial CA28

20
IRON
Belinda Burke

All the ironwork from The Hirsel was X-rayed. The quantity of ironwork prohibited the treatment of each item individually, but a selection of artefacts was cleaned and conserved. The assemblage was examined by Philip Clogg, and some of the notes from his record cards, particularly observations on tinning and brazing, have been incorporated into the catalogue.

Unfortunately much of the ironwork is badly degraded, and some has been lost or has disintegrated, so observations are frequently based on earlier listings, drawings, and X-rays.

Structural ironwork has been dealt with separately (see Chapter 12). But where nails were still attached to, or closely associated with an object, they are considered alongside that object in the catalogue. There were also several mounts from doors or chests, and padlocks which could have been used to secure doors, chests or furniture. There were ten knives, tools for use in craft and agriculture, and various artefacts relating to hunting and riding, but comparatively few domestic artefacts. In many cases the use of the object is unclear.

There was a heavy concentration of small finds in the extended nave of the church and the surrounding area. This included the vast majority of the nails and structural elements, as well as most of the arrowheads and tools. These were associated particularly with the final destructive phases; the latrine pit C1302 seems to have been filled with building debris, but also general waste including pottery and metalwork, iron finds consisted of a corner bracket (Fe6), an arrowhead (FeA2), a fish-hook (Fe91), part of a horseshoe (Fe97) and a total of 80 nails. This pattern seems to be repeated in the areas of more general burning in the church; C623 yielded 108 nails, as well as two arrowheads (FeA8–9), a twisted iron bar (Fe112) and a large quantity of pottery; C1135 yielded 24 nails, a blade (Fe55), and a possible tenterhook (Fe62), and C1159 yielded 62 nails. The hearth that sealed the latrine pit (C1227) yielded two further arrowheads (FeA3–4).

20.1 MOUNTS, FITTINGS, LOCKS AND KEYS

The importance of chests and caskets throughout the medieval period is well attested (Brenan 1998, 65–69), and it is reasonable to assume that the various smaller mounts from The Hirsel come from such portable furniture. This is also probably true of the majority of the security equipment; padlocks and hasps, possibly in conjunction with some of the staples (see Section 12.5), could have been used to secure chests and coffers, both in the church and in domestic contexts. Fe12 and Fe13 were from the western part of the site, and may be associated with elements of the post-medieval compound, but C8 yielded both medieval and post-medieval finds, so a precise attribution is not possible.

Corner bindings could have come from chests or coffins with corners reinforced with iron (Goodall 2011, 166), but while it is possible that Fe11 and Fe12 might have come from coffins (although neither was directly associated with a burial), Fe7 and Fe8 are less substantial, and may have come from a casket. Both come from the cemetery area to the north of the extended nave, Fe7 in a layer of rubble that covered most of the trench, and Fe6 in the layer of late medieval cemetery earth below it, but from their co-ordinates they were found quite close together, and may reasonably be assumed to form a pair.

Fe1 (Figure 20.1)
Strap hinge bent at a right angle, one end terminating in a looped eye, the other expanding around a nail hole, then curving inwards to a point at its terminal, similar to examples from Beeston Castle, found in post-medieval contexts, but considered to be either medieval or post-medieval (Courtney 1993, 137, fig 94.28, 36). The form is unusual, suggesting that the mount was bound around a substantial door or shutter that would have swung inwards on a hinge pivot, or possibly the right angle bend indicates where it was bound over the lid of a large chest. There are remains of four nails, three with large angular heads and one flat-headed nail in the terminal, as well as one empty nail hole, and traces of wood were observed adhering to it when it was found. Clearly the large-headed nails were for decorative effect. Since this was found in the stone dump over the line of the church, it seems likely that it was originally a structural fitting in the church, or the remains of a chest from within. The loose nail, Fe2, was found associated with this fitting, and may be assumed to belong to it. Found in the stone dump over the NW corner of the church (see Figure 5.3).
Arm with looped eye: L 240mm; W 40mm; Th 5mm.
Arm with pointed terminal: L 170mm; W 40mm; Th 5mm.
C404, Phase: 8 EPM, Findspot: 188.5/835.

Fe2 (Figure 20.1)
Nail, tapering, with a heavy rectangular head, square/rectangular shank. Found with Fe1, and similar to the nails

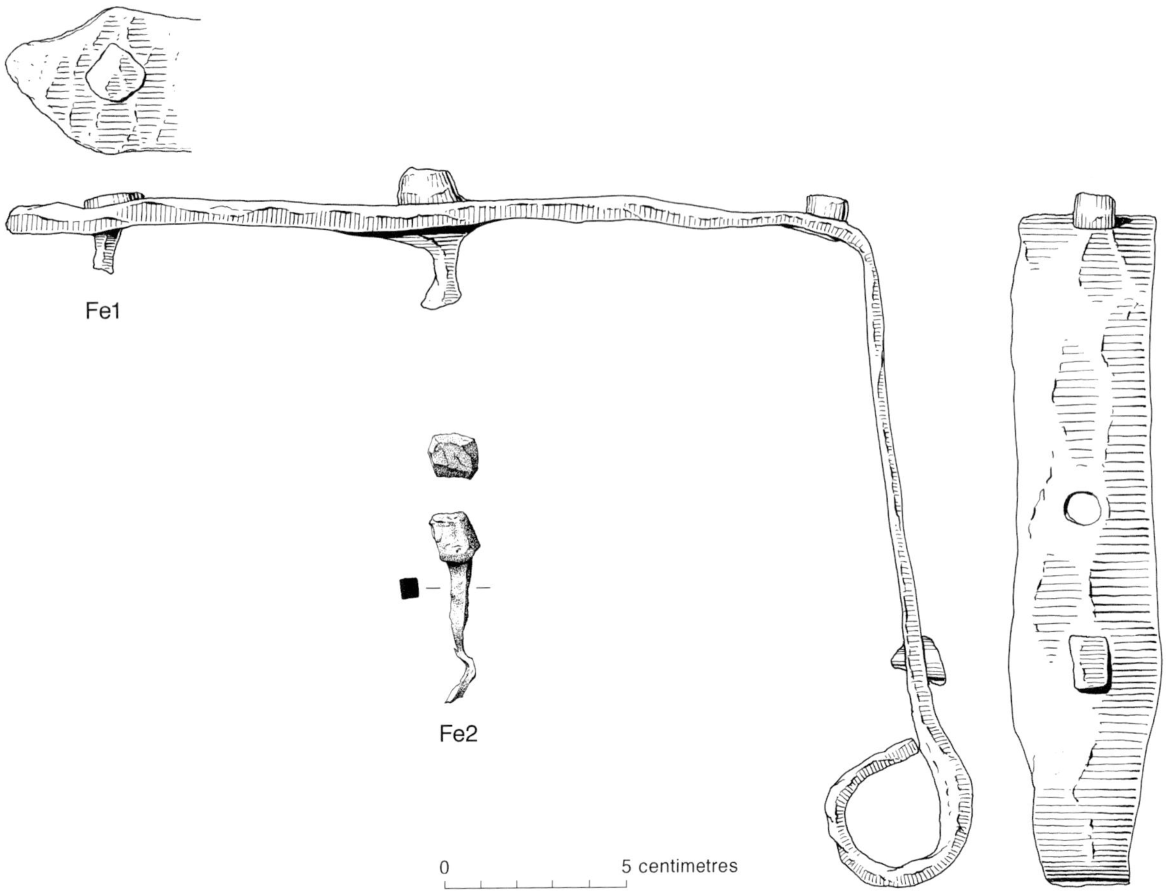

FIGURE 20.1
Strap hinge and nail, Fe1–2

still attached to the strap hinge, suggesting that it came from the empty nail hole.
L 55mm; Th 6mm; W(head) 13mm.
C404, Phase: 8 EPM, Findspot: 188.5/835.

Fe3 (Figure 20.2)
Part of a strip with a rivet hole and bifurcate terminal (incomplete), and two small fragments, possibly associated. Mount from a piece of furniture or chest?
From rubble over the church.
L 45mm; W 19>14mm; Th 2mm.
L 20mm; W 9mm; Th 7mm (not illustrated).
L 12mm; W 7mm; Th 6mm (not illustrated).
C902, Phase: 8 EPM, Findspot: 180.20/834.55.

Fe4 (Figure 20.2)
Fragment of mount with rivet in rounded terminal (now lost). This piece could be a terminal of a strip similar to Fe5 or Fe6, or it might be a strap end.
From medieval cemetery earth to the south of the east end of the church.
L 23mm; W 11>9mm; Th 2mm.
C710, Phase: 6 Med, Area: 208–10/820–2.

Fe5 (Figure 20.2)
Two fragments of a mount with three rivet holes. The largest portion of the strip has been folded, suggesting that it was to be reused as scrap. The smaller portion, now separate, tapers towards a slightly expanded round terminal with a rivet. This could be a mount from a box or small chest.
Found in a medieval layer to the north of the cemetery wall in a context that also yielded a large quantity of medieval pottery, and finds of metalwork; an iron ring (Fe15), the branch of a horseshoe (Fe101), and three lace chapes (CA12–14).
L (unwound) 135mm; W 12mm; Th 3mm.
L 32mm; W 12mm; Th 3mm (not illustrated).
C1003, Phase: 8 EPM, Area: 207.75–210/858–60.

Fe6 (Figure 20.2)
Corner bracket. The long arm is 105mm, with parallel sides and a nail hole towards the end where there was a pointed terminal, the shorter arm is 14mm with a nail hole and a squared end. Possible mount for a box or chest?
Found in the large pit (C1302) in the north of the extended nave.
Total length of strip: 119mm; W 17mm; Th 5mm.
C1305, Phase: 7 LM, Findspot: 191.45/831.70.

Fe7 (Figure 20.2)
Thin strip, bent sharply at a 90° angle. One arm is broken, the other tapers to a triangular point, similar in form to Fe8.
Found in cemetery earth.
L 58mm; W 10mm, Th 4mm.
C435, Phase: 7 LM, Area: 188–90/837–9.

Fe8 (Figure 20.2)
Thin strip, bent sharply at a 90° angle, of the same form as Fe7.
L 75mm; W 10mm; Th 3mm.
C428, Phase: 8 EPM, Area: 186–8/837–9.

Fe9 (Figure 20.2)
Object with one circular end and one spatulate end joined by a narrow shaft, of D-shaped section. Rivet hole in circular end, the spatulate end bent. Mount, originally hooked? Tinned.
From the fill of a robber trench.
L 98mm; Diam 25mm; W 13>4mm; Th 3mm.
C909, Phase: 7–8 LM–EPM, Findspot: 189.88/825.40.

Fe10 (Figure 20.2)
Part of a mount? Traces of non-ferrous plating and similar in form to Fe9, although more fragmentary. Similar to several examples of strips with flattened terminals from Late Saxon contexts at York (Ottaway 1992, 629).
Medieval domestic area to north of perimeter wall.
L 61mm; W 22mm; Th 2mm.
C240, Phase: 6 Med, Findspot: 194.970/854.90.

Fe11 (Figure 20.2)
Rectangular plate, slightly curved or bent, one possible rivet. Mount for chest or coffin.
Found in cemetery earth.
L 93mm; W 34mm; Th 3mm.
C908, Phase: 7 LM, Area: 175–83/825–37.

Fe12 (Figure 20.2)
Rectangular bracket with central angle of 90°, four rivet holes. From its context, it could be post-medieval.
L 90mm; W 33mm; Th 3>2mm.
C8, Phase: 9 LPM, Area: 178–9/842–3.

Fe13 (not illustrated)
Two fragments of plates with rivet holes, badly corroded and fragmentary. When found, this was a single object, although it looks as though it originally consisted of two very thin strips fused together. Pierced strip mount of similar dimensions to Fe12, from the same context, so they could have been mounts on a chest, and a copper-alloy boss, CA29, also came from this context. Found in association with ring Fe16.
L 105mm; W 35mm; Th 2mm.
L 35mm; W 30mm; Th 2mm.
C8, Phase: 9 LPM, Area: 174–5/840–1.

Collars/binding rings

Iron rings like Fe17 were used to strengthen vessels of wood or leather. Smaller examples could have bound wooden tubes or tool handles, preventing them from splitting, as well as performing a decorative function. Rings were also used on harnesses (Goodall 1993c). All these examples came from the north of the site (which is also the area where the possible bridle cheek piece Fe95 was found), apart from Fe16, which came from the westernmost trench, found with mount Fe13, suggesting that it could have been attached to a chest.

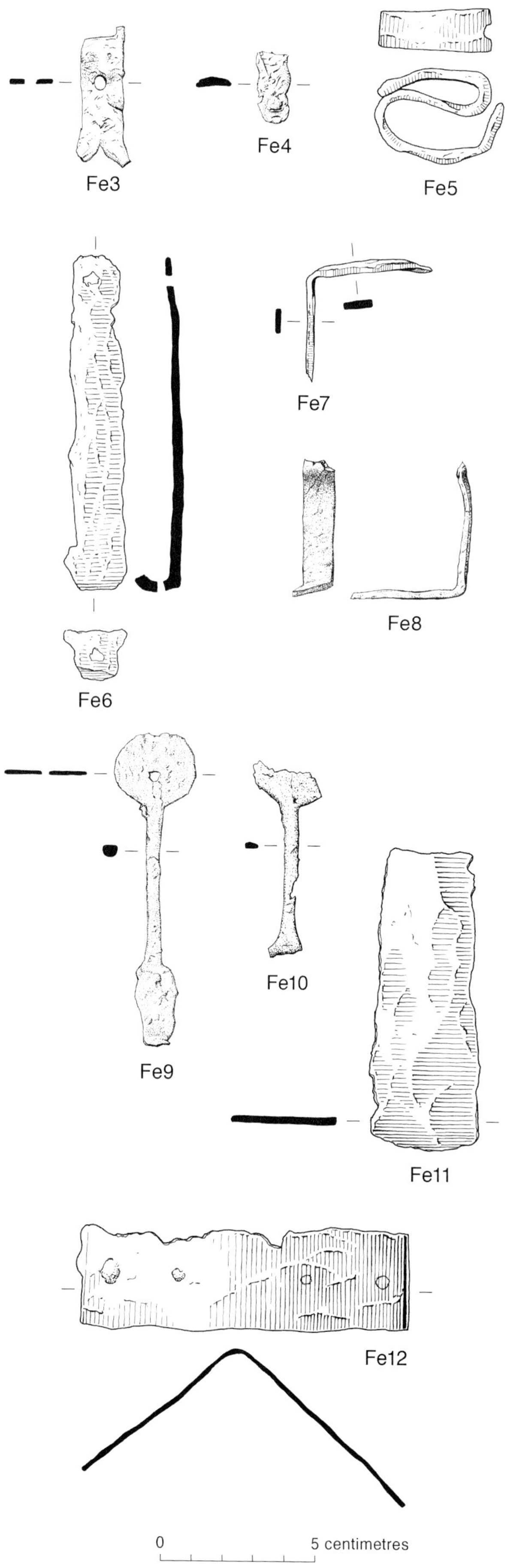

FIGURE 20.2
Mounts, Fe3–12

Fe14 (Figure 20.3)
Bent round to form a ring, the overlapping ends riveted together.
Diam 30mm; W 4mm; Th 16mm.
C1011, Phase: 6 Med, Findspot: 207.45/859.19.

Fe15 (Figure 20.3)
Ring with butted ends, incomplete.
Diam 32mm; W 13mm; Th 6>3mm.
C1003, Phase: 8 EPM, Area: 205–10/858–60.

Fe16 (Figure 20.3)
Ring with overlapping ends. Found in association with mount Fe13.
Diam 45mm; Th 7>4mm.
C8, Phase: 9 LPM, Area: 174–5/840–1.

Fe17 (Figure 20.3)
Circular binding, possibly the rim of a small wooden vessel. Flat iron strip bent into ring and welded (Phil Clogg pers comm).
Diam 68mm; W 22mm; Th 7>4mm.
C1001, Phase: 8 EPM, Area: 205.5–207.75/854–6.

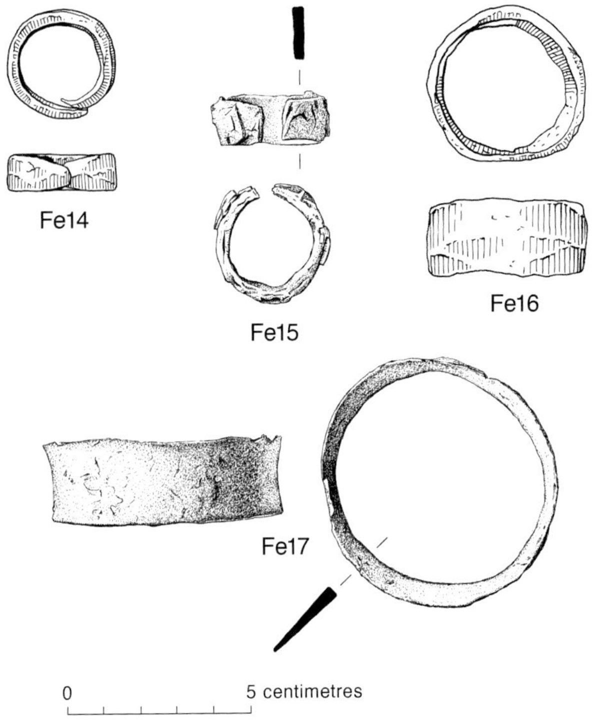

FIGURE 20.3
Rings, Fe14–17

Chains, swivel hooks/fittings and hasp

There were two swivel hooks from the site, which could have been used with a ring as a form of suspension for cooking, or as part of a harness (Egan 1998, fig 146; 2005, fig 83; I H Goodall 2007, 513, no. 86, fig 11.1.2; 2011, 302). The open hook (Fe20) could have ensured that suspended items could be removed and replaced, while Fe21 would have been a more permanent fitting.

Fe18 (Figure 20.4)
Ring or link in chain, oval in section, damaged and distorted (now lost). Possibly used for suspension.
From a disturbed cemetery level, which also yielded a spur (FeSp2) and a staple (FeS10).
L 45mm; W 30mm; Th 3mm.
C504, Phase: 7 LM (disturbed), Area: 196–8/848–50.

Fe19 (Figure 20.4)
Part of chain. Figure-of-eight twist holding two links in the same loop, presumably for additional strength. The shaping of these two links, which are themselves interlocked, suggests that they were held together by a further link or links. The spare loop of the figure of eight could have hooked onto a latch, or been secured by a padlock.
Found in topsoil, so date unknown.
L 100mm; W 40mm; Th 15mm (overall).
L 70mm; W 35mm (figure-of-eight).
C285, topsoil, Area: 202.9–205/852–4.

Fe20 (Figure 20.4)
Swivel hook, open, with square section and sub-rectangular head.
L 45mm; Th 4mm; W of head 8mm.
C625, Phase: 7 LM, Area: 196–9/830–5.

Fe21 (Figure 20.4)
Swivel hook, closed, with domed triangular head (now lost).
L 60mm; Th 5mm; W of head 11mm.
C203, Phase: 8 EPM, Area: 196–202/850–8.

Fe22 (not illustrated)
Small bolt with pierced shaft, similar to form to Fe23 (although much smaller; known from X-ray, now lost).
L 31mm; Th 5mm; W of head 17mm.
C105, Phase: 8 EPM, Area: 201–2/864–5.

Fe23 (Figure 20.4)
Large bolt with pierced sub-rectangular shaft similar to Fe22. The domed rectangular head appears to have been made separately and riveted into a hollow shaft, since there is a break visible at the top of the shaft, and possible traces of two rivets. This would mean that it could have been passed through the hole in a swivel loop before the head was attached, thereby fixing it securely. Probably post-medieval.
L 104mm; Th 12mm, the looped end broadening to 15mm; Head 30mm x 20mm.
C2, Phase: 8 EPM, Area: 176–7/842–3.

Fe24 (Figure 20.4)
Oval loop with rivet and washer. Handle, from chest? Context also yielded a 17th century coin and clay pipe, so probably post-medieval.
L 56; W 58; Th 11>6mm.
C911, Phase: 8 EPM, Area: 175–186/833–40.

Fe25 (Figure 20.4)
Figure-of-eight shaped looped hasp, bent over to form a hook at one end for grip. The profile is angled. A relatively common find, often used with padlocks and staples to secure doors or chests (Cox 1996, 781). In Norwich, a ratchet and pawl mechanism for suspending a pot over a hearth included a hasp to adjust the height of the hook for the cooking pot, found in a deposit dated to 1507 (from documentary evidence) (Goodall 1993b, 89, fig 55).
Post-medieval context, so could be post-medieval date.

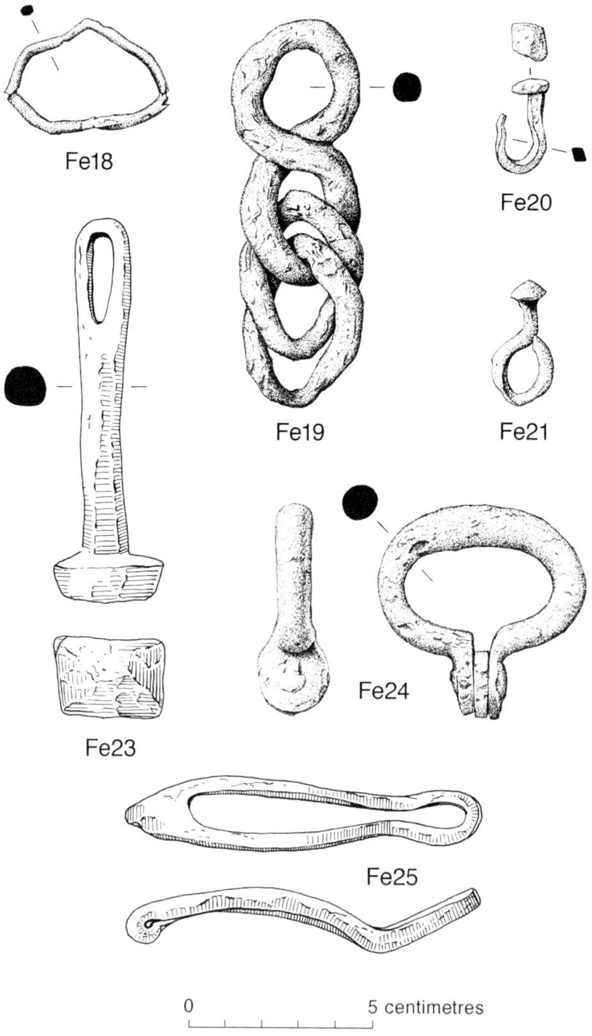

FIGURE 20.4
Chains and fastenings, Fe18–21, Fe23–25

L 98mm; W 19mm; Th 11mm.
C903, Phase: 8 EPM, Findspot: 179.43/834.5.

Padlocks

No padlock cases were identified, but 10 padlock bolts were found, some with leaf springs. One example, Fe27, may have been from a box padlock; a type that was in use until the 11th century, appearing in early- to mid-11th century contexts in Winchester (Goodall 1990d, 1001). It is not clear whether the other fragments came from box or barrel padlocks, since no other end plates survive. Fe26 is a fragment of a much smaller padlock, about half the size of the others, so it was probably used to secure a small box or casket, or maybe even a small aumbrey, since it was found on a possible surface in the apse of the church, while the larger padlocks could have been used on doors or large chests. They were found in later, more disturbed contexts. All except two were found in or around the church. Fe30 came from a fill of rubble in a pit (C1302) in the nave that also yielded arrowheads and other metalwork. Fe29, Fe31, Fe32 and Fe35 came from the cemetery area surrounding the nave; Fe31 being found in a layer that yielded architectural fragments, probably demolition debris from the church. Fe28 and Fe34 were found in plough soil in the northwesterly trenches of the site.

Fe30 has an expansion at the head of the spine and a step on the free arm, and Fe31 appears to be a fragment of a similar design. This places them within a category that Goodall dates to 13th–14th century (Goodall 2011, 232), the expansions performing the same function as closing plates.

Fe26 (Figure 20.5)
Very small padlock mechanism, twin bladed leaf spring.
From an early medieval surface or floor level in the apse.
L 45mm; W 5mm; Th 1mm.
C630, Phase: 6 Med, Findspot: 204.50/832.96.

Fe27 (Figure 20.5)
Padlock bolt with two spines, one with a double leaf spring, the other with a single spring (now fragmentary). The spines pass through a rectangular end plate, showing that this was probably part of a box padlock (Goodall 2011, 231 and nos I4 and I5), although a padlock with a small cylindrical case from London also has a rectangular bolt plate, as well as a similar arrangement of two spring strips (Egan 2010, 99, no. 256, fig 71).
Evidence of copper-alloy plating or brazing (Phil Clogg pers comm).
From the cemetery to south of church, associated with Sk153.
L 83; W 21>8mm; Plate: 21mm x 15mm.
C714, Phase: 6 Med, Findspot: 198.48/825.30.

Fe28 (Figure 20.5)
Part of a padlock, twin bladed leaf spring. Areas of copper alloy uncovered during cleaning.
From medieval cultivation in the NW of the site.
L 79mm; W 8mm; Th 10>2mm.
L 50mm; W 8mm; Th 2mm.
L 35mm; W 8mm; Th 2mm.
C240, Phase: 6 Med, Findspot: 190.72/855.20.

Fe29 (Figure 20.5)
Padlock mechanism. Twin bladed leaf spring. Iron rivets, with traces of copper alloy found around them.
From a late medieval occupation level to the north of the nave. (The context also yielded two arrowheads, FeA13 and Fe14.)
L 87mm; W 12m; Th 10mm.
C444, Phase: 7 LM, Area: 188–90/835–7.

Fe30 (Figure 20.5)
Loop and mechanism of barrel padlock. Traces of copper brazing were observed during conservation.
From a layer of stones within pit 1302 in the extended nave.
L 100mm; W 15mm; Th 5mm.
C1332, Phase: 7 LM, Findspot: 190.88/832.24.

Fe31 (Figure 20.5)
Fragment of padlock bolt.
L 67mm; W 25>14mm; Th 9>4mm.
C908, Phase: 7 LM, Area: 175–83/825–37.

Fe32 (Figure 20.5)
Loop, probably part of a padlock, although no evidence of spring remains.
From a trial trench in an area subsequently excavated at the SW corner of the church
L 92mm; W 35mm; Th 8mm.
C100, unstratified, Area: 189/825.

Fe33 (Figure 20.5)
Rectangular sectioned curved strip, with one straight arm, possibly incomplete, the other having a fine latch-like terminal. Fragment of a shackle from a padlock? If so, it probably belonged to a padlock operated by a revolving key of late medieval/post-medieval date (Goodall 2011, 234).
L 45mm; W 32mm; Th 4mm.
C428, Phase: 8 EPM, Area: 188–90/833–5.

Fe34 (not illustrated)
Fragment, with two possible fins. Probably part of a barrel padlock (now lost).
L 17mm; W 7>2mm.
C8, Phase: 9 LPM, Area: 176–7/844–5.

Fe35 (not illustrated)
Lock spring? (lost, known from X-ray).
From possible grave cut (context was interpreted as a grave cut, but no skeleton was found).
L 40mm; W 15mm; Th 2mm.
C442, Phase: 8 EPM, Area: 188–90/839.

Fe36 (not illustrated)
Two curved fragments, possibly part of a padlock case, made of thin sheet iron, re-enforced internally with strips 6mm wide. Traces of copper alloy were found both on the applied strips and the sheet to which they were attached. The form is suggestive of a barrel padlock, but it is strange that the applied strips are internal rather than on the outer face. The longer strip is less curved.
From a disturbed rubble and cobble spread in west of the terrace trench to the east of the site.
L 65mm; W 16mm; Th 2.5mm.
L 55mm; W 15mm; Th 2.5mm.
C801, Phase: 7 LM, Area: 211–12/834.5–836.

Fe37 (not illustrated)
Two fragments of a possible latch or lock. Distorted fragments of a box shape, the smaller of which has a slot formed by a folded sheet, re-enforced by a riveted band 7mm wide. It was found in association with Fe36.
L 42mm; W 20mm; Th 2–4mm.
L 15mm; W 37mm; Width of slot 3mm; Thickness of metal *c*3mm.
C801, Phase: 7 LM, Area: 211–12/834.5–836.

Fe38 (Figure 20.5)
Bent bar of semi-circular section, coated with copper alloy, in two fragments. Its similarity to the applied strips on Fe36 suggests that it was part of the same, or a similar object, although found in a different part of the site.
L 35mm; W 6mm; Th 5mm.
L 20mm; W 3mm; Th 1.5mm.
C146, Phase: 7 LM, Area: 200–1/866–8.

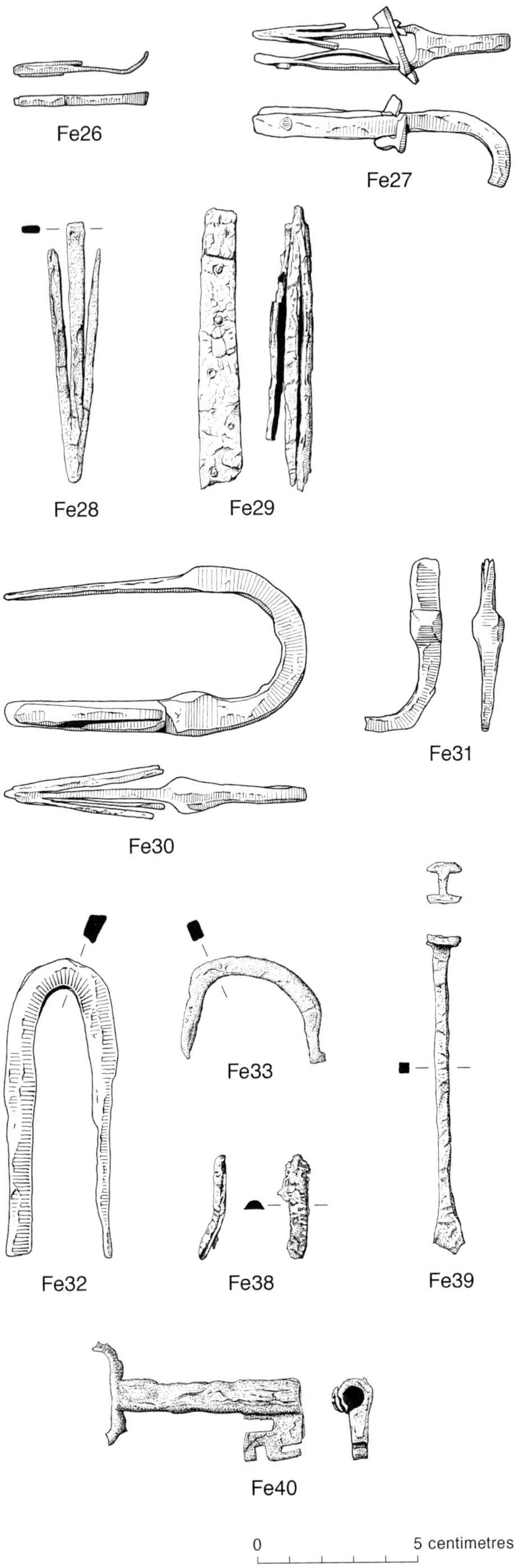

FIGURE 20.5
Locks and keys, Fe26–33, Fe38–40

Keys

Fe39 (Figure 20.5)
Padlock key. The shank is square in section with a flattened terminal, incomplete. The bit is set at a right angle to the shank, it is H-shaped, and therefore suitable for lock mechanisms with two leaf springs (Egan 2010, 99–100, no. 258). It corresponds to Goodall's type 4 'padlock keys with laterally set bits with radiating wards'; the expanding terminal suggesting type 4c (Goodall 2011, 237–238), although it is not certain whether the terminal was looped or hooked. Type 4 keys are found throughout the medieval period. This, like the leaf spring from padlock Fe28, was found to the north-west of the perimeter wall (C214), so may probably be associated with the evidence for domestic activity in that area.
From an early post-medieval layer to north of site.
L 97mm; W 13mm; Th 4mm.
C207, Phase: 8 EPM, Area: 196–200/850–9.

Fe40 (Figure 20.5)
Key with D-shaped bow and hollow stem, rolled in one with the bit, which is rectangular, with 3 ward cuts. This type of key would have been used in a lock with a sliding bolt (I H Goodall 1981, 60), and corresponds with Winchester type 3 (Goodall 1990d, 1007) or Goodall's type B (Goodall 2011, 241), found throughout the medieval period, reaching a peak in the 13th century.
From an agricultural surface, in northernmost trench.
L 65mm; W 40mm; Th 8mm.
C105, Phase: 8 EPM, Findspot: 202.29/869.0.

20.2 DRESS ACCESSORIES

Fe41–43 were all found together in the spread of stones south of the church (C715). The scale of the buckle (Fe41) suggests that it was used on a small strap or belt, and Fe42 and Fe43 could also have been a simple mount or mounts from a belt. A small pierced whetstone (SH2) came from within 20cm of these three items; it had an iron stain, and may well have been suspended from a ring like Fe42 on the same belt (a lace chape, Ca10, was found at the same spot as the buckle and mount and the context also yielded an arrowhead and several nails). Fe44–46 are larger, and might have belonged to horse harness rather than belts, but in the absence of firm evidence, they are considered here. Fe44 came from rubble in the same area, south of the chancel/nave 1, while Fe45 and Fe46 were from late medieval demolition layers.

Fe47 and Fe48 are simple pins without heads that could have been shroud pins, coming from the cemetery area to the west of the church, but neither was found in association with a skeleton.

Fe41 (Figure 20.6)
D-shaped buckle ring, with remains of a flanged pin (see Egan and Pritchard 1991, 74–75, no. 309, fig 45) and fragmentary remains of a plate attached to the bar.
L 20mm; W 28mm; Th 4>2mm.
C715, Phase: 7 LM, Findspot: 198.40/824.40.

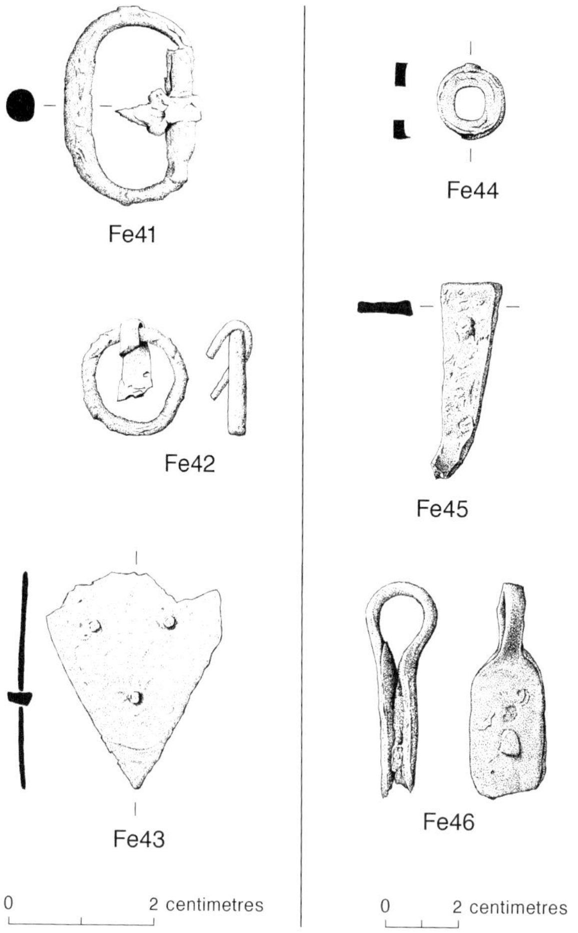

FIGURE 20.6
Dress accessories, Fe41–46

Fe42 (Figure 20.6)
Circular ring with looped clip folded over the ring. Possibly riveted onto belt or strap? Size suggests clothing. Similar to an example found in late medieval 14th–15th century contexts at Winchester (Hinton 1990b, fig 353).
L 17mm; Diam 15mm; Th 2mm.
C715, Phase: 7 LM, Findspot: 198.40/824.40.

Fe43 (Figure 20.6)
Triangular plate with three rivets. Shield shaped belt mount? It is possible that the 'clip' in Fe42 may have originally been part of this, since the metal is of similar thickness and appearance, so it could have been one side of a pendant mount, looped over a ring.
L 30mm; W 24mm; Th 1mm.
C715, Phase: 7 LM, Findspot: 198.40/824.40.

Fe44 (Figure 20.6)
Roughly circular mount with central hole. Slight rim on one side, corresponding projection on the other. This could be a belt mount or an eyelet for a large buckle pin (compare with an example from Meols (Egan 2007a, 113, no. 1011, pl 19), with two integral rivets, although the Meols example is lead/tin). Or an eyelet for a lace chape?
Found in the grave pit of Sk1.
Diam 20mm; Diam of hole 9mm; Th 3mm.
C219, Phase: 6 Med, Findspot: 199.44/851.55.

Fe45 (Figure 20.6)
?Tag end, possibly for a ribbon or leather lace or thong (see Hinton 1990a, 547). One rivet.
From late medieval demolition rubble over south of church.
L 52mm; W 18>9mm; Th 4mm.
C708, Phase: 7 LM, Area: 200–2/826–8.

Fe46 (Figure 20.6)
Loop with two rectangular strap ends held together by a single rivet. This could be part of a horse harness (Goodall 2011, 366–367, fig 13.8), or it might have been mounted on the rim of a leather bucket to hold a handle. Two rectangular straps held together by a single rivet.
From rubble in nave, west of cross wall C624.
L 59mm; W 20>10mm; Th 5mm.
C638, Phase: 7 LM, Findspot: 198.25/832.62.

Fe47 (not illustrated)
Pin; shroud pin?
From the upper fill of ditch C1386.
L 57mm; W 2mm.
C836, Phase: 5 EM2, Findspot: 182.20/825.50.

Fe48 (not illustrated)
Pin, found in lower fill of C928, the cut to the west of the cemetery platform.
L 23mm; W 3mm; Th 2mm.
C928, Phase: 8 EPM, Area: 175–186/830.

20.3 KNIVES AND SCISSORS

Knives would have been used for cutting food, or for craft activities such as leatherworking (Goodall 2011, 108). All the knives from The Hirsel were whittle tang as far as can be judged, although a possible handle for a scale tang knife was identified (see WB2, Chapter 21). Knives with bolsters (Fe59–60) are post-medieval; probably introduced around the middle of the 16th century (Goodall 2011, 109). Fe60 may have had a bone handle, but the association of some of the other blades with traces of wood, particularly where these were found on their tangs, suggests that wooden handles may have been more common.

Fe49 (Figure 20.7)
Knife blade with tapering whittle tang, almost in line with the back of the blade. Similar example from London from a 12th century context (Cowgill *et al* 1987, 78–79, no. 2).
From a layer covering perimeter wall C291.
L 97mm; W 14mm; Th 4mm.
C296, Phase: 7 LM, Findspot: 203.2/856.1.

Fe50 (Figure 20.7)
Knife blade, tang broken, but similarly positioned to above (Fe49). Traces of replaced wood on blade (Phil Clogg pers comm).
Found in cemetery earth, in layer associated with building debris.
L 84mm; W 16mm; Th 4mm.
C908, Phase: 7 LM, Findspot: 182.13/833.67.

Fe51 (Figure 20.7)
Knife blade, with angled shoulder and tang. The whittle tang is central on the tapering blade. The triangular shape would suggest a late 13th century date (Cowgill *et al* 1987, 80). Fe52 has a similar shape, but smaller.
Found in association with wall 291 (the northern perimeter of the churchyard), which C289 overlies.
L 148mm; W 20mm; Th 2mm.
C289, Phase: 6 Med, Findspot: 202.9/851.9.

Fe52 (Figure 20.7)
Knife blade, angled, with tang. In shape, it is similar to Fe51, but much smaller. Evidence of wood found on blade and handle (Phil Clogg pers comm).
From post-medieval rubble spread, disturbed by plough.
L 90mm; W 10mm; Th 4mm.
C502, Phase: 8 EPM, Area: 196–8/846–8.

Fe53 (Figure 20.7)
Knife blade, broken in 3 pieces, with long whittle tang central to the blade. What is left of the blade is parallel sided with a curved horizontal shoulder. Evidence of wood was found on the handle of the knife (Phil Clogg pers comm).
From a late hard packed surface to south of church.
L 81mm; W 17>4mm; Th 5mm.
C704, Phase: 8 EPM, Findspot: 201.8/822.18.

Fe54 (Figure 20.7)
Parallel-sided blade, tang broken.
L 83mm; W 13mm; Th 3mm.
C103, topsoil, Area: 199–200/862–3.

Fe55 (Figure 20.7)
Tapering blade, tang missing. Evidence of wood on the tang (Phil Clogg pers comm).
Found in late burning level within nave.
L 64mm; W 13mm; Th 9mm.
C1135, Phase: 7 LM, Findspot: 190.77/829.89.

Fe56 (Figure 20.7)
Blade fragment, with copper-alloy strips inlaid on either side.
Found in demolition layer to the south of church, which also yielded architectural fragments, lead cames and a range of pottery types including the reduced gritty ware (type 4.2).
Cowgill states that '14th and 15th century knives are more often decorated, but using simple techniques; usually a groove, which sometimes contains an inlay' (Cowgill *et al* 1987, 15), but the form is unusual. Could this be associated with the copper-alloy chape (CA25) found nearby, with similar co-ordinates (although the chape was from C701)?
From a demolition layer.
L 43mm; W 14mm; Th 3mm.
C708, Phase: 7 LM, Findspot: 197.15/827.13.

Fe57 (not illustrated)
Identified as the triangular point of a blade when found; fragmentary, so impossible to identify with certainty.
L 37mm; W 13>3mm; Th 3mm.
C845, Phase: 3–4 EM (disturbed), Findspot: 178.94/830.60.

Fe58 (not illustrated)
Flat plate. Tip of blade? Found with Sk329.
L 23mm; W 21mm; Th 7mm.
C1370, Phase: 5 EM2, Findspot: 184/827.

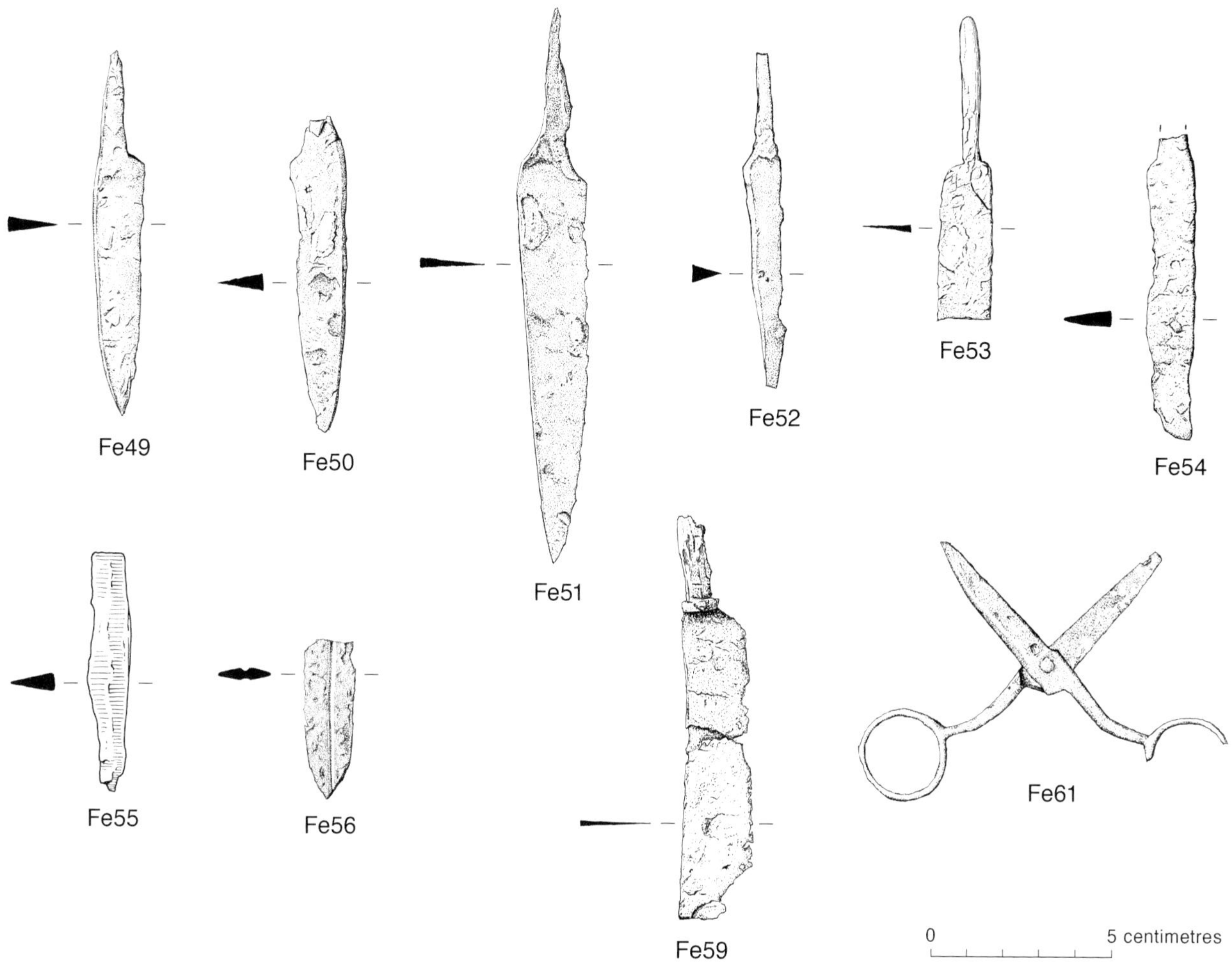

FIGURE 20.7
Knives and scissors, Fe49–56, Fe59, Fe61

Fe59 (Figure 20.7)
Parallel-sided blade, with bolster and tang, in three fragments, blade bent when found. Evidence of wood on tang found during conservation.
L 105mm; W 18mm; Th 1mm.
C6, Phase: 8 EPM, Area: 172–3/842–3.

Fe60 (not illustrated)
Blade and tang, in two parts, with a small disc shaped bolster. Possibly associated with bone handle WB3.
From a topsoil layer which yielded numerous finds.
L 86mm; W 19mm; Th 3mm.
L 39mm; W 17>4mm.
C901, topsoil, Findspot: 176.29/832.8.

Fe61 (Figure 20.7)
Small pair of scissors, with cutting edge 40mm long. Closed circular finger loops (one incomplete), set centrally on the stem. Possibly tin glazed?
L 100mm; W 8mm; Th 3mm; Diam of handle 24mm.
C428, Phase: 8 EPM, Findspot: 185.5/831.5.

20.4 CRAFT TOOLS

The craft tools provide evidence for textile and leatherworking (see also the rubbing stones CT18–25, Chapter 24). While the spokeshave would have been used for shaving wood, the awls could have been used to pierce leather or wood. There is no firm evidence for metalworking tools, except possibly Fe83 which could have been used for non-ferrous metalworking, but some smithing slag was identified by Phil Clogg.

Fe62 (not illustrated)
Small hook, with two ends tapering to points. Now lost, known from X-ray and sketch. Tenter hook, suitable for holding woollen cloth taut to dry, or for suspending a wall hanging (I H Goodall 1981, 54; 1993a, 174).
Found in an area of burning in the nave, so, like Fe63, it may be associated with the final phase of occupation of the nave of the church.
Long arm L 35mm; short arm L 17mm; Th 4mm.
C1135, Phase: 7 LM, Findspot: 191.41/829.93.

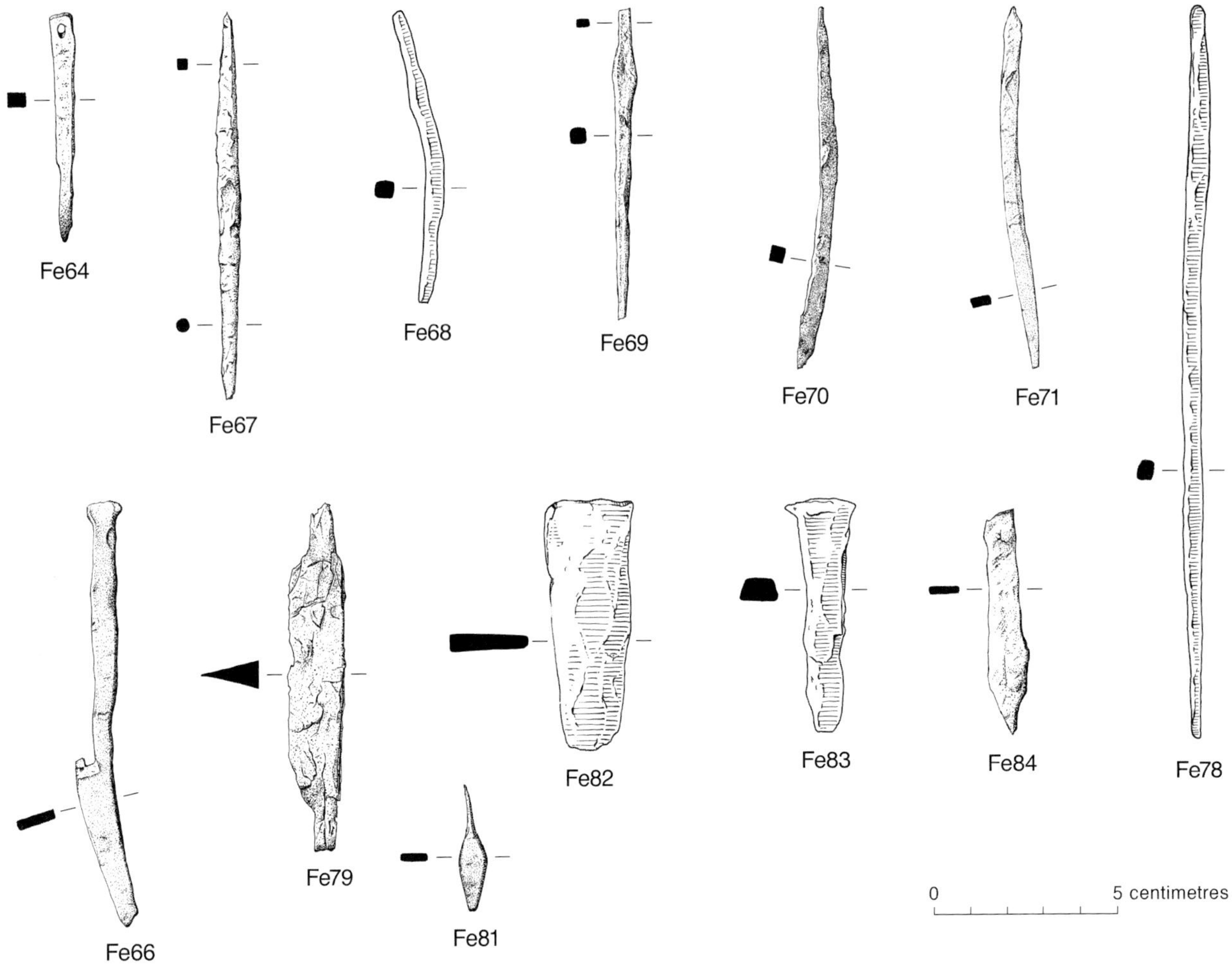

FIGURE 20.8
Craft tools, Fe64, Fe66–71, Fe78–79, Fe81–94

Fe63 (not illustrated)
Tenter hook? Not found, known from X-ray.
From the hearth that sealed pit 1302.
Long arm L 34mm; short arm L 13mm; Th 4mm.
C1227, Phase: 7 LM, Findspot: 191.61/831.75.

Fe64 (Figure 20.8)
Tapering iron bar with rectangular section and oval eye. Cloth or leather needle found with Sk1; possibly for a leather shroud? (see Chapter 6). Or possibly a tag end? It would fit through an eyelet hole found in same context (Fe44).
L 63mm, W: 5mm; Th 5mm.
C219, Phase: 6 Med, Findspot: 200.80/852.

Fe65 (not illustrated)
Pointed object, square in section, with possible hole at one end. Needle? (Missing, no measurements available.)
C428, Phase: 8 EPM, Findspot: 185.5/832.7.

Fe66 (Figure 20.8)
Tanged blade, the tang being flattened at the end of the handle. Leatherworking creaser, see examples from Barnard Castle (Goodall 2007, 512 and fig 11.1.1.8), Netherton and Winchester (Goodall 2011, 68, fig 6.2).
Found in the grave of Sk22.
L 113mm; W 12>6mm; Th 3mm.
C517, Phase: 6? Med, Findspot: 208.9/843.85.

Spikes/Awls

Several iron spikes were found, and while some may confidently be identified as awls, it is not clear whether they all served this purpose. Five were of a distinctive form, with pointed or flattened terminals. They were all found in the area of the nave, and the layers of rubble that surrounded it.

Fe67 (Figure 20.8)
Awl, tapering at both ends. One end rectangular in section, the other circular.
L 108mm; W 7mm; Th 3mm.
C626, Phase: 6 Med, Area: 202–4/836–8.

Fe68 (Figure 20.8)
Awl? The ends are blunter than other examples, it was found in the same context as Fe67.
L 80mm; W 6mm; Th 3mm.
C626, Phase: 6 Med, Area: 204–6/834–6.

Fe69 (Figure 20.8)
Awl, rectangular section tapering to a narrow point. It expands to a central shoulder, which would have provided a stop for a handle, before tapering into a short flattened tang (possibly incomplete). Similar to an example from Black

Friars, Newcastle (Vaughan 1987, 124, fig 30, no. 187). It is also similar in form to a metalworking graver from a 17th century context in London, but as described by Theophilus in the 12th century (see Egan 2005, 148–149, fig 142, no. 789).
From the fill of the robber trench of west wall of the church.
L 83mm; W 7>2mm; Th 6>2mm.
C909, Phase: 7–8 LM–EPM, Area: 184–90/825–34.

Fe70 (Figure 20.8)
Spike, slighly curved, pointed at both ends, one end flattened. Square section.
L 95mm; W 4mm; Th 4mm.
C437, Phase: 7 LM, Area: 184–6/836–8.

Fe71 (Figure 20.8)
Spike or tool, curved, square-sectioned, tapering to one pointed and one flattened end. Awl? (found associated with arrowhead and nails), similar in form to Fe70.
Found in compacted rubble over the church.
L 96mm; W 5mm; Th 5mm.
C902, Phase: 8 EPM, Area: 180–2/825–835.5.

Fe72 (not illustrated)
Spike with two flattened ends, one tapering to a point. Rectangular section, straight, similar to above.
L 84mm; W 5mm; Th 4mm.
C1198, Phase: 7 LM, Findspot: 193.49/829.61.

Fe73 (not illustrated)
Square/rectangular section, Spike, curved, very corroded, but one terminal flat, one pointed. Found while cleaning cobbles at the west end of the church.
L 100mm; W 5mm; Th 4mm.
C84/08, unstratified, Area: 184.5–186.5/826–829.5.

Fe74 (not illustrated)
Spike, tapering at both ends. Only known from X-ray, where it expands in the centre. Awl?
L 75mm; W 4mm.
C740, Phase: 5 EM2, Area: 196–8/820–2.

Fe75 (not illustrated)
Spike, bent, tapering at both ends (lost, from X-ray).
L 85mm; W 5mm.
C1122, Phase: 8 EPM, Area: 190–195.5/826–8.

Fe76 (not illustrated)
Long bent spike with rectangular section, flattened at one end, tapering slightly at the other (from conservation record and X-ray).
L 95mm; W 5mm; Th 4mm.
C1031, Phase: 8 EPM, Findspot: 183.24/836.32.

Fe77 (not illustrated)
Bent spike (from X-ray, 'piercer' on record card).
L 107mm; W 3mm; Th 3mm.
C911, Phase: 8 EPM, Findspot: 181.42/837.17.

Fe78 (Figure 20.8)
Long spike. Square section, tapering at both ends.
From the ditch surrounding the late compound.
L 195mm; W 7>2mm; Th 2mm.
C442, Phase: 8 EPM, Area: 188–90/839.

Other tools, probably associated with woodworking

Fe79 (Figure 20.8)
Blade with tangs at either end, a small spokeshave, similar to examples from Whaltham Abbey and Wharram Percy where, as here, the straight tangs are in line with the blade (Goodall 2011, 26, fig 3.8, B97 and B98).
Found in a post-medieval spread of cobbles to the north of the site.
L 92mm; W 15mm; Th 9mm.
C104, Phase: 8 EPM, Area: 199–200/866–8.

Fe80 (not illustrated)
Spoon auger, possibly square in section, with one curved and flattened end and one tapered square-sectioned end (now fragmentary).
L 122mm: W: 8mm; Th 5mm.
C714, Phase: 6 Med, Findspot: 197.55/827.56.

Fe81 (Figure 20.8)
Small tool with diamond-shaped head and tang (now lost). Possibly a small auger-bit (Goodall 1990b, 275 fig 59, no. 396, of similar dimensions), although the tang appears minimal, possibly incomplete. Similar to 'debris from ironworking' in York (Ottaway and Rogers 2002, 3026, fig 1318, no. 11250).
From the floor of the church (from the same context as fish-hook Fe93).
L 35mm; W 7mm; Th 3mm.
C559, Phase: 7 LM, Findspot: 188.8/830.8.

Fe82 (Figure 20.8)
Wood working wedge with burred head, comparable to those found at Winchester over a wide date range (Goodall 1990b, 276–277) or metalworking? (Goodall 1990a, 198–199).
Found in cemetery earth.
L 65mm; W 24mm; Th 4mm (head 24mm x 6mm).
C908, Phase: 7 LM, Area: 175–83/825–37.

Fe83 (Figure 20.8)
Tapering bar with burred head. Possible punch without a tang, its size suggests that it might have been used for non-ferrous metalworking (Ottaway 1992, 517).
L 61mm; W 15mm; Th 5mm (head 19mm x 7mm).
C902, Phase: 8 EPM, Area: 180–2/825–835.5.

Fe84 (Figure 20.8)
Tool, rectangular in section, with tang. Chisel?
L 60mm; W 12>8mm; Th 2mm.
C207, Phase: 8 EPM, Findspot: 195/859.

20.5 AGRICULTURAL AND FISHING EQUIPMENT

Two probable sickle blades were identified, as well as a possible plough tip, and a spade iron. One of the blades (Fe86) came from a disturbed cemetery layer, which also yielded other metalwork (CA6, Fe18, FeS10) including a spur (FeSp2). The other items came from beyond the cemetery area; Fe87 from a medieval level in an area of agricultural activity to the north of the site, and Fe85 and Fe88 from an area to the west that was probably cultivated through most of the medieval and post-medieval period.

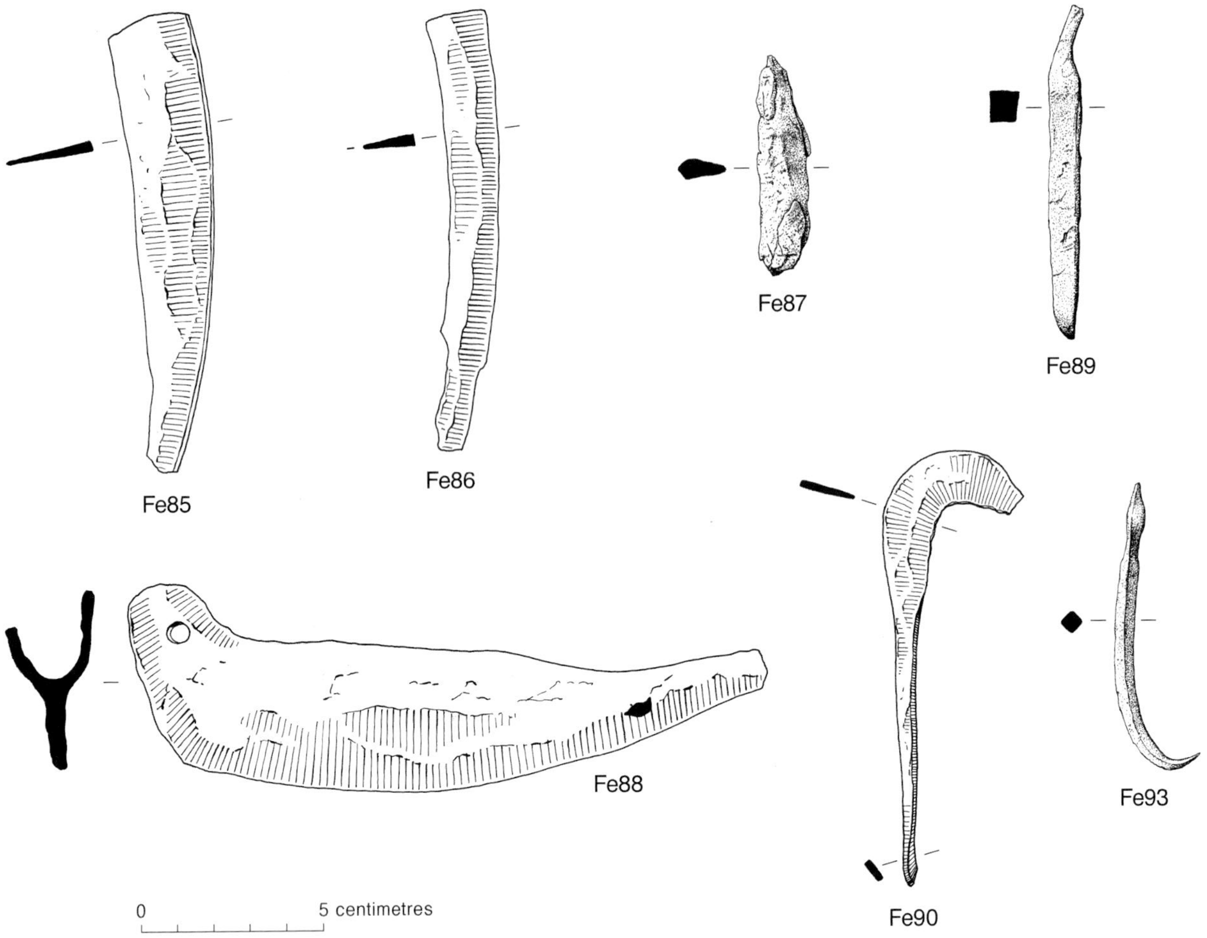

FIGURE 20.9
Agricultural and fishing equipment, Fe85–90, Fe93

Fe85 (Figure 20.9)
Curved, tapering blade, sickle.
L 127mm; W 26mm; Th 15mm.
C2, Phase: 8 EPM, Area: 172–3/846–7.

Fe86 (Figure 20.9)
Curved blade, sickle.
L 117mm; W 20mm; Th 2mm.
C504, Phase: 7 LM (disturbed), Area: 196–8/848–50.

Fe87 (Figure 20.9)
Flat tapering bar. Irregular edges. Two tabs attached on either side at one end. Bar slightly concave on one side, convex on other. Possible plough tip (Ian Riddler pers comm). Found in an agricultural context.
L 60mm; W 13mm; Th 7mm.
C128, Phase: 5? EM2, Area: 201–3/861–2.

Fe88 (Figure 20.9)
Fragment of rectangular spade iron, with a cleft to hold a wooden spade or shovel. There is no side arm, but one nail hole at one end shows where it was attached to the wooden blade; the rest of the iron having eroded away. Many examples have been found, both from medieval and post-medieval contexts (Goodall 2011, 77–79). Visual evidence for Scottish types is seen on tombstones dating back to the 17th century with representations of asymmetrical spades paired with square headed shovels; a shovel with a similar shaped shoe to this example being depicted on a tombstone from Mortlach Church, Banffshire (Fenton 1970, 157, fig 1.i). The Hirsel spade iron was found in topsoil, so a post-medieval date seems likely.
L 178mm; W 51mm; Th 12mm.
C1, topsoil, Area: 172–6/842–3.

Fe89 (Figure 20.9)
Rake tine, with tapering square section, tang broken (cf Goodall 2011, 90, fig 7.5, nos F30–34).
L 90mm; W 11mm; Th 10mm.
C502, Phase: 8 EPM, Area: 202–4/846–8.

Fe90 (Figure 20.9)
Small hooked knife with whittle tang, similar to those identified as weedhooks or pruning hooks, particularly Goodall's type 1A (Goodall 2011, 80–81, fig 7.6). The blade is crescent shaped, but the tang flattened, which suggests that it might have been inserted into masonry. It is of similar dimensions to a series from Whithorn (Nicholson 1997a, 428, fig 10.104), which came from contexts dated to the 11th–13th centuries and where it was suggested that they may have had a different function, in view of their distribution. Likewise the discovery of the example from The Hirsel, in a floor deposit at the west end of the church predating the secular occupation of the nave, would also suggest a non-agricultural use.
L 118mm; W 45mm; Th 14>3mm.
C1062, Phase: 6 Med, Findspot: 189.11/828.32.

Fish hooks

There are three probable fish hooks and one possible fragment (now lost). All are made of iron. Fe91 is barbed, and Fe92 was considered to have a trace of a possible barb when found. Fe93 and Fe94 do not have barbs.

Fe93 has evidence for a means of attachment to a line, where the tab is hammered flat and twisted (as seen in an example from Meols; Philpott 2007, 279). The terminal of Fe91 is also slightly expanded.

Fe93 and Fe94 may be compared with the series of 45 large hooks, also with splayed or thickened ends, found at Fullers Hill, Great Yarmouth, suitable for catching larger fish, such as spurdog, conger eel, ling, cod, large haddock, turbot or halibut (Steane and Foreman 1991, 92, fig 12.3). Being an inland site, the larger Hirsel hooks could have been for catching eels, but two contexts did yield bones from large cod, possible evidence for a fishing trip to the coast, and the pit in the nave (C1302) yielded a fish vertebra that had passed through a human gut. The Great Yarmouth hooks are dated to AD 1000–1200, but unfortunately the typology of fish hooks changed remarkably little between the Roman period and the 17th century (Philpott 2007, 280–281). Fe91 is more comparable in size and form to barbed examples from London sites, with an average length of around 55mm (Steane and Foreman 1991, 92), so it was probably used for catching smaller river fish.

Two hooks were found in the church; Fe91 came from a layer within the pit (C1302) in the nave of the church, and Fe93 was from a late floor level at the west end of the church. Fe94 was found in the cemetery to the north of the nave.

Fe91(not illustrated)
Straight, slender shanked fish-hook with barb. Expanded terminal for attachment to line. Corroded.
Found in one of the layers of pit C1302 in the nave of the church.
L 42mm; Span 19mm; Th 2mm.
C1305, Phase: 7 LM, Findspot: 191.16/831.35.

Fe92 (not illustrated)
Small curved fragment with possible barb, identified as a possible fish-hook similar to Fe91 (now lost).
Found in a cemetery level, with other metalwork.
L 11mm; Th 2mm.
C710, Phase: 6 Med, Findspot: 203.67/825.10.

Fe93 (Figure 20.9)
Curved shank with one end twisted and splayed, the hook terminating in a sharp point. Rectangular section, no barb. Its size suggests that it may have been for catching eels (Ian Riddler pers comm).
From a floor level in the church.
L 75mm; Span 22mm; Th 4mm.
C559, Phase: 6 Med, Findspot: 189.7/831.0.

Fe94 (not illustrated)
Fish-hook, straight, shank with square section, barbless. Incomplete, but possibly originally of similar dimensions to Fe93 although the gap is smaller, the hook less sharp. Means of attachment is missing, but the shank tapers slightly towards the terminal, possibly where it had been hammered into a tab.
L 53mm; Span 19mm; Th 4mm.
C449, Phase: 7 LM, Area: 183–5/837–9.

20.6 HORSE EQUIPMENT

There are a few fragments of horseshoes from the site, and with no complete examples it has sometimes proved difficult to define the type. We have followed Clark's classification (Clark 2004). There is only one specimen of Clark's type 2 (Fe96), and this is found in the north of the site redeposited in a grave in which the skeleton has a radiocarbon date of 1140–1280. Most belong to the high point of occupation of the site from the early 13th to 14th century. There are only two fragments of later shoes, Fe104 and Fe108, but these need not be later than the 17th century. Fe101 is remarkable in that it appears to have only two nail holes on the side, and all the examples are thin and heavily worn. The distribution of the fragments suggests casual losses, but there is a possible significance in that there is some concentration in the northern area of the site near, where it is considerable evidence for domestic occupation (RC).

Fe95 (Figure 20.10)
D-shaped ring with two flat L-shaped attachments either side. Probably the cheek piece of a snaffle bit (Clark 2004, 47–48, fig 33; similar, but not identical to Ward Perkins type D cheek piece, dated 14th–15th century; Ward Perkins 1940).
Found in the northern sector of the site, in a cobble spread related to possible robbing of the perimeter wall C291.
L 135mm; W 65mm; Th 7>2mm.
C1005, Phase: 7 LM, Findspot: 208.9/858.3.

Fe96 (Figure 20.10)
Heel of horseshoe. Two rectangular countersunk nail holes. Folded calkin, edge slightly wavey? Very worn, but possibly Clark's type 2b (Clark 2004, 86), in which case it would be 12th or early 13th century.
Found in grave of Sk1.
L 70mm; W 17mm; Th 4mm.
C219, Phase: 6 Med, Findspot: 201.5/851.

Fe97 (Figure 20.10)
Heel of horseshoe with a folded calkin. There is one countersunk nail hole, which contains a nail with a T-shaped head of the same thickness as the shank, a type seen as being contemporary with, but continuing later than fiddle-key headed nails at Whithorn (Nicholson 1997a, 407). The countersunk nail holes are similar to Clark's type 3 (2004, 86–88), dated 13th–14th century in London (Clark 2004, 96). The nail has a distinctive spiral clenching, also paralleled with type 3 shoes in finds from London in phase 9 (1270–1350), which Clark sees as allowing for the tightening of a nail that had worked loose, and compares with features on an

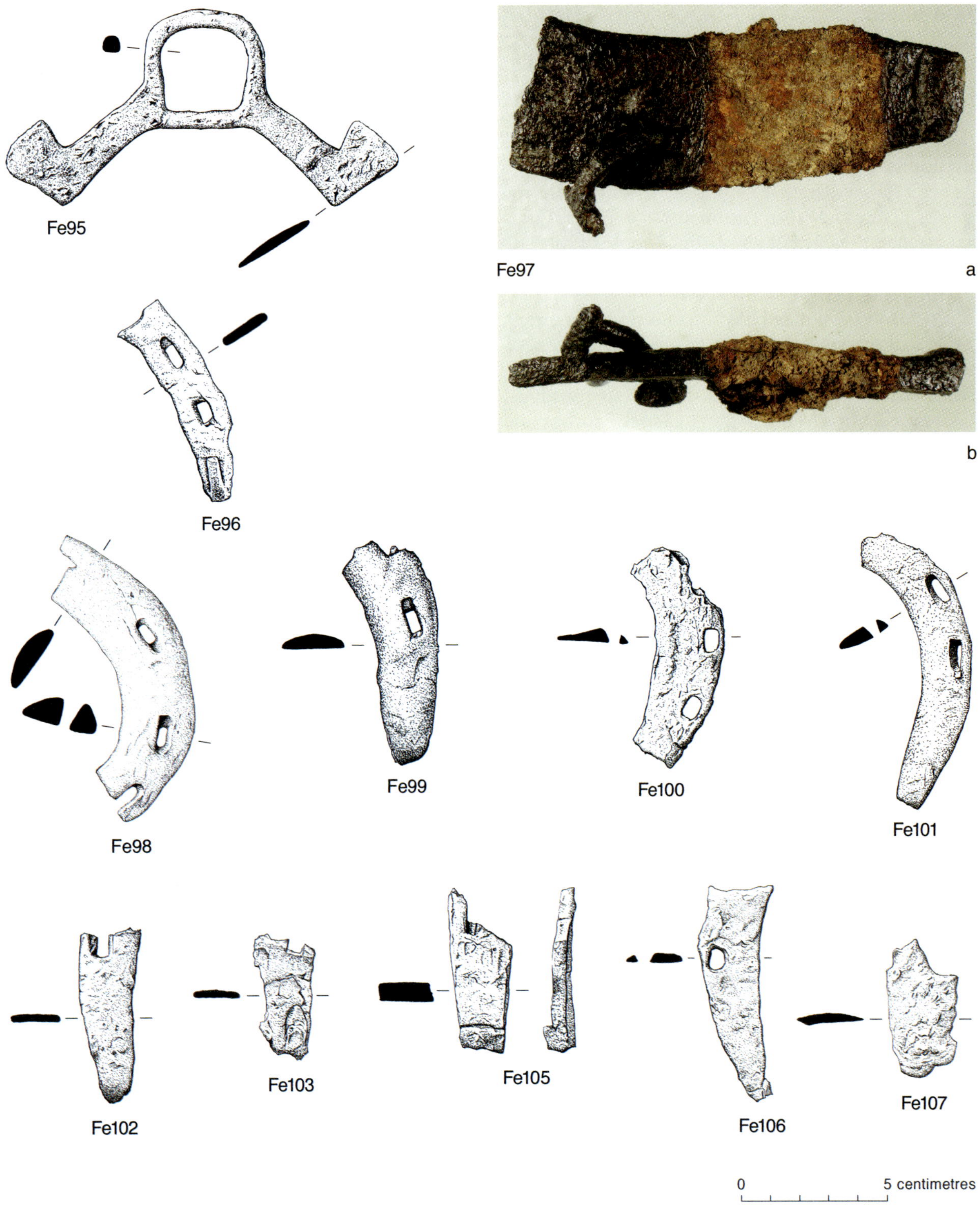

FIGURE 20.10
Horse equipment, Fe95–103, Fe105–107

early 14th century pilgrim badge of St Thomas Becket (Clark 2004, 87–88, fig 68).
The fragment was discovered, along with other metalwork, in a fill of the pit C1302 in the nave of the church.
L 75mm; W 24mm; Th 10mm.
C1305, Phase: 7 LM, Findspot: 191.44/831.92.

Fe98 (Figure 20.10)
Toe of horseshoe (now missing). Two complete rectangular nail holes, countersunk, two broken.
Found in fill of reburial pit C924 in church area.
L 95mm; W 25mm; Th 6mm.
C925, Phase: 8 EPM, Findspot: 186.8/827.6.

Fe99 (Figure 20.10)
Heel of horseshoe. One complete rectangular nail hole and one broken. Holes countersunk, type 3, as above.
L 74mm; W 23mm; Th 6mm.
C234, Phase: 6 Med, Findspot: 190.62/853.67.

Fe100 (Figure 20.10)
Horseshoe fragment with two nail holes. Nail holes fairly square and close to the outer edge of the shoe, implying that it was fitted close. Clark type 4 (2004, 88–91) or possibly later?
Found in the northern sector of the site. An arrowhead was also found in this context.
L 73mm; W 24mm; Th 4mm.
C1001, Phase: 8 EPM, Area: 207.75–210/852–4.

Fe101 (Figure 20.10)
Branch of a horseshoe, with two rectangular nail holes. It would appear to have had only two nail holes on one side.
Found in the northern sector of the site, in the layer underlying C1001 (see above).
L 95mm; W 23>11mm; Th 5mm.
C1003, Phase: 8 EPM, Findspot: 209.73/859.15.

Fe102 (Figure 20.10)
Heel of horseshoe, broken rectangular nail hole. Very thin, possibly worn down.
L 60mm; W 20mm; Th 4mm.
C620, Phase: 7 LM, Findspot: 204.78/836.75.

Fe103 (Figure 20.10)
Horseshoe fragment. Part of rectangular nail hole survives.
L 40mm; W 19mm; Th 8mm.
C53, Phase: 6 Med, Findspot: 196/843.

Fe104 (not illustrated)
Fragment of heel, bent, with remains of square or rectangular nail hole. Broad web. Clark type 4?
From a very disturbed context.
L 50mm; W 30mm; Th 5mm.
C207, Phase: 8 EPM, Findspot: 200.970/852.800.

Fe105 (Figure 20.10)
Part of horseshoe, with folded calkin, broken at the first nail hole. Context as above (Fe104).
L 54mm; W 20mm; Th 5mm.
C207, Phase: 8 EPM, Area: 196–200/850–9.

Fe106 (Figure 20.10)
Heel of horseshoe, with one squarish nail hole.
L 70mm; W 23mm; Th 4mm.
C502, Phase: 8 EPM, Area: 196–8/846–8.

Fe107 (Figure 20.10)
Curved fragment, possible heel of horseshoe?
L 46mm; W 25mm; Th 7>3mm.
C704, Phase: 8 EPM, Findspot: 201.251/823.52.

Fe108 (not illustrated)
Horseshoe fragment with one complete and one broken rectangular nail hole. Missing, known from X-ray. This could be Clark type 4.
Found in a layer of hill wash in the easternmost trench.
L 41mm; W 22mm; Th 4mm.
C803, Phase: 9 LPM, Area: 221–3/836–8.

20.7 POST-MEDIEVAL

While many items in the above catalogue are of uncertain date, the following are definitely from the post-medieval period.

Fe109 (Figure 20.11)
Complete triangular padlock, the body composed of two halves welded around the edge, late 16th to 17th century type (Nöel Hume 1991, 250). A similar example, although larger, was found at Caldecote in a period 4 context (*c*1360 to 1600) (Cool *et al* 2009, 206, fig 13.21). Evidence of brazing used in construction (Phil Clogg pers comm).
This context was considered medieval when excavated in 1979, but the padlock was found when cleaning in 1982, so may be regarded as intrusive.
L 53mm; W 33mm; Th 10mm.
C205, Phase: 7 LM, Area: 194–205/855–9.

Fe110 (not illustrated)
Folding bow corkscrew, of a type first produced in the 18th century.
(Measurements not available.)
C403, Phase: 8 EPM, Area: 186/832–8.

20.8 MISCELLANEOUS/UNIDENTIFIED

Fe111 (Figure 20.12)
Bar or strap.
L 80mm; W 23mm; Th 3mm.
C299, Phase: 6 Med, Findspot: 206.60/835.75.

Fe112 (Figure 20.12)
Twisted iron bar, rounded at one end, square-sectioned at the other. Possible staple? (cf Ludgershall Castle; Goodall 2000,

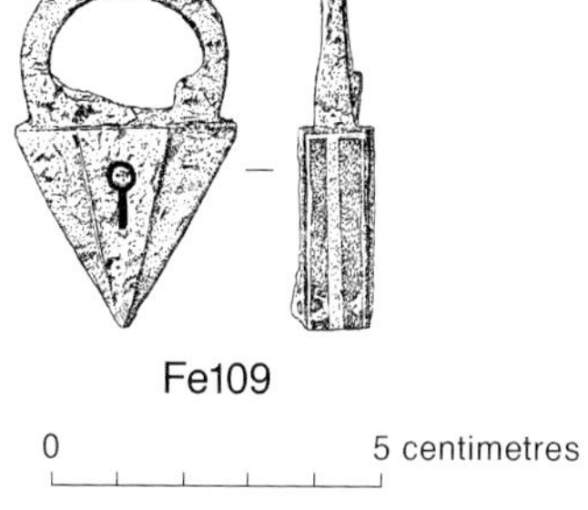

FIGURE 20.11
Post-medieval padlock, Fe109

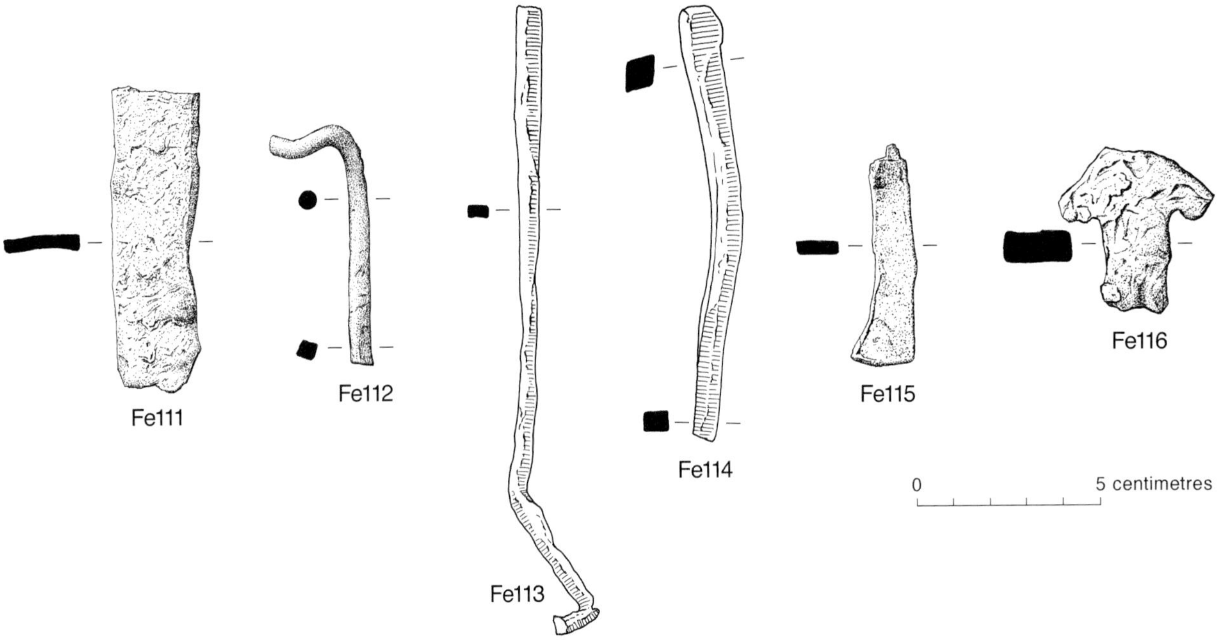

FIGURE 20.12
Miscellaneous/unidentified objects, Fe111–116

145–146, fig 6.20, no. 26; rectangular staple particularly suited to binding or joining timbers, with arms bent over to clench). From an area of burning in the nave of the church.
L 65mm; W 25mm; Th 6>4mm.
C623, Phase: 7 LM, Area: 198–200/830–2.

Fe113 (Figure 20.12)
Thin bar, square section, bent at one end. Similar dimensions to Fe78, but one end squared, the other bent. Scrap?
L 180mm; W 7mm; Th 4mm.
C302, Phase: 6 Med, Area: 202–5/858–9.

Fe114 (Figure 20.12)
Bar, rectangular section. Scrap?
L 105mm; W 8mm; Th 10>5mm.
C906, Phase: 8 EPM, Area: 175–178.5/835–839.5.

Fe115 (Figure 20.12)
Tool? Curved bar, rectangular in section, widening at one end and lipped. The other with remains of tang.
L 58mm; W 18>10mm; Th 4mm.
C2, Phase: 8 EPM, Area: 170–1/848–9.

Fe116 (Figure 20.12)
Fitting, head of timber strap, or latch?
L 43mm; W 42>16mm; Th 8mm.
C102, Topsoil, Area: 197–8/868–9.

20.9 SPURS
Blanche Ellis

All the spurs are iron and bear traces of non-ferrous plating (see Appendix 5). Tinning was frequently used to protect spurs from rust and to enhance their appearance (Jope 1956). FeSp1 is decorated with silver wire inlay.

The prick spurs FeSp1 and FeSp2 with their straight sides and minimal necks supporting large quadrangular goads are typical of the second half of the 12th century. The archaeological date of the low level from which FeS1 came supports this and an undecorated spur of this type came from a context dated 1050–1150 at Beverley, Yorkshire (Armstrong and Tomlinson 1987, no. BH77). The knight on the German tapestry *c*1180 from Baldishol church, Hedmark, Norway, wears a spur of the same form (Kunstindustrimuseet, Oslo; and Ellis 2002, fig 3, 13). The spur leathers were attached by two small rivets in the terminal worn to the outer side of the foot, while the inner terminal of FeSp1 and probably that of FeSp2 were each formed as a vertical slot through which the leather passed freely (for comparisons see Ellis 2002, nos 12, 13 and 14).

FeSp1 (Figure 20.13)
Prick spur, with piercing for strap, 8 x 5mm wide. Inlaid with silver wire.
From fill of feature 1386.
Overall length 80mm; Length of neck with goad 18mm; Span 85mm.
C1377, Phase: 4? EM1, Findspot: 183.0/826.19.

FeSp2 (Figure 20.13)
Prick spur.
From a disturbed medieval context.
Overall length 80mm; Length of neck with goad 18mm; Span originally *c*62mm.
C504, Phase: 7 LM (disturbed), Area: 200–2/844–6.

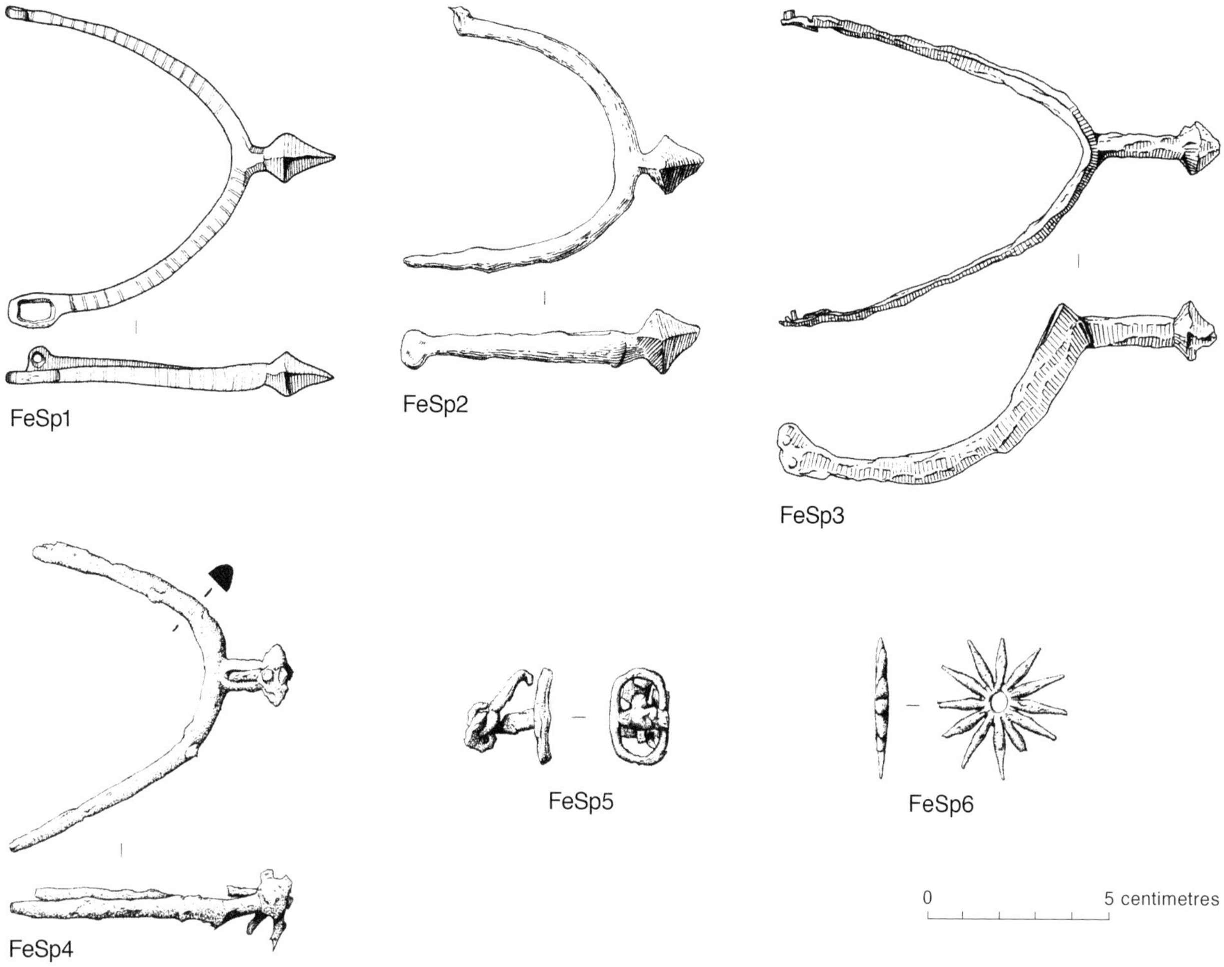

FIGURE 20.13
Spurs, FeSp1–6

FeSp3 (Figure 20.13)
Spur sides began to curve under the wearer's ankle in the 12th century and curved sides were common by the 13th century. This spur has damaged 2-rivet terminals which retained (2 and 1) rivets when excavated. Its quadrangular goad has a rounded blunt tip. 12th–13th century.
From a disturbed context near human skeletal material (Sk15 and Sk13).
Overall length 126mm; Length of neck with goad 37mm; Span 80mm.
C503, Phase: 6 Med, Findspot: 199.6/849.4.
Published: Ellis 2002, 6 and 7, no. 17.

FeSp4 (Figure 20.13)
Iron rowel spur, with the remains of a fairly large rowel between bold conical rowel bosses which appear typical of the 14th century, although its straight sides would have been rare at that time, when most spur sides were strongly curved. It was found in a context that yielded 13th–14th century pottery, but the area was contaminated with 17th century material. Comparable spurs with straight sides and quite large rowels appear on the monumental brass of Jan and Gerard van Heere, *c*1390–1395, from Heere near St Trond, Belgium, now in the Musées Royaux du Cinquantenaire, Brussels (Norris 1977, II, pl 56). The alabaster effigy of Lord Seagrave *c*1380 in Dorchester Abbey also wears spurs with straight sides. In the 17th century straight spur sides were more common, but usually such spurs had smaller rowels. Probably late 14th century.
Overall length *c*80mm; Length of neck 19mm; Length of rowel box 17mm; Length of remaining points of rowel *c*13mm, giving an original diameter of *c*26mm.
C105, Phase: 8 EPM, Area: 201–2/860–1.

FeSp5 (Figure 20.13)
Iron, detached spur terminal with an oval buckle and hook attachment, found associated with FeSp4.
Length of buckle 26mm; width of buckle 17mm; depth of fitting 24mm.
C105, Phase: 8 EPM, Area: 201–2/860–1.

FeSp6 (Figure 20.13)
Iron rowel of 12 points. The large diameter suggests a likely date of the second half of the 14th century.
Diam 40mm; Th 3mm.
C286, Phase: 8 EPM, Area: 204–205/850–2.

FeSp7 (Figure 20.14)
Iron rowel spur with straight sides tapered towards small figure-8 terminals, while its slightly curved rounded neck also tapers to a slender rowel box with a very small rowel. One terminal has two attachments, each with a mushroom stud to go into a slit in a spur leather. The opposite terminal

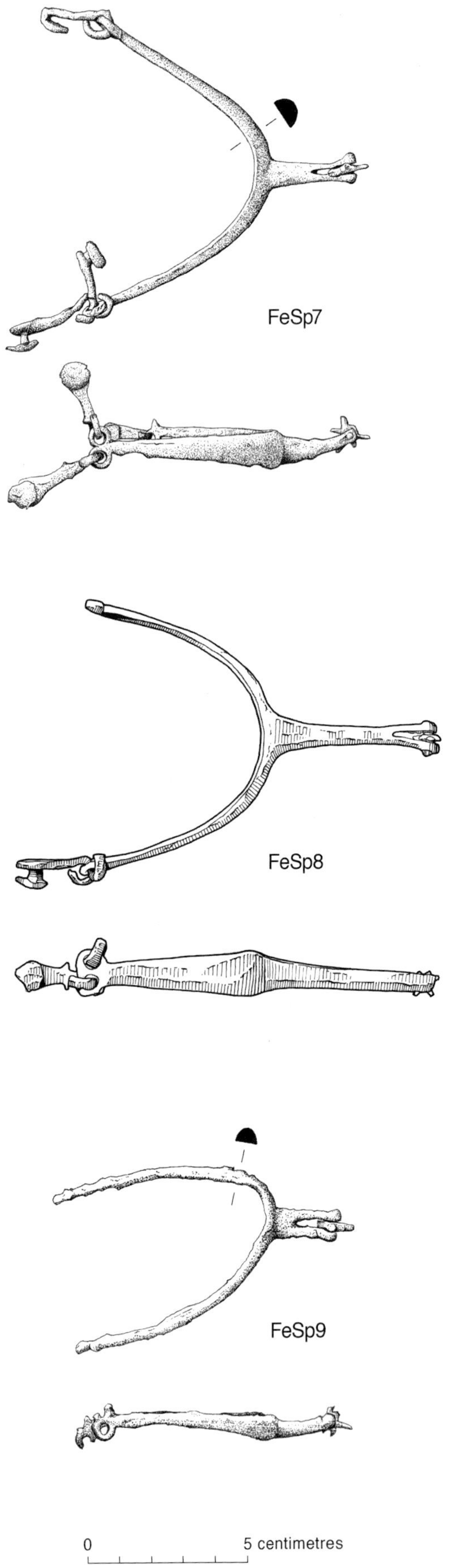

FIGURE 20.14
Spurs, FeSp7–9

is damaged and the buckle is lost, while one hook attachment remains. As buckles were worn to the outer side of the foot and in the top ring of a figure-8 terminal, the position of the surviving attachments indicates that this spur was worn with its neck curving upwards towards the rowel. Contemporary spurs were usually worn the other way up with down-curved necks. Compare the silver-gilt pair dated 1675 belonging to the Fief des Eperons and kept in the Greffe, Guernsey, the buckle position on these show that they were worn with their necks curved downward. Similarly the spurs of Sir William Penn 1621–1670 forming part of his funeral achievement in the church of St Mary Redcliffe, Bristol.
Date: 1640–1690.
Overall length *c*86mm; Length of neck 29mm; Span 86mm; Rowel diameter originally *c*15mm.
C3, Phase: 8 EPM, Findspot: 175.157/840.40.

FeSp8 (Figure 20.14)
Iron spur, similar form to FeSp7, but more slender, with tiny figure-8 terminals. It bears considerable traces of non-ferrous plating. The sides have become compressed, three terminal rings are broken, the buckle and attachments are lost. The short, rounded neck tapers as it curves gently towards the rowel box where conical rowel bosses flank the remains of a small six-point rowel. As stated above (FeSp7) contemporary spurs were usually worn with the neck curved downward towards the rowel.
Date: 1640–1690.
Overall length *c*88mm; neck 21mm.
C8, Phase: 9 LPM, Findspot: 176.10/840.85.

FeSp9 (Figure 20.14)
A post-medieval spur with straight sides and a long straight neck. One stud attachment and part of another survive, also a very small rowel.
Overall length 114mm; length of neck with goad 54mm; rowel diam *c*15mm; span *c*80mm.
C1122, Phase: 8 EPM, Findspot: 195.34/825.80.

20.10 ARROWHEADS
Graeme Rimer and John Waller

Identifying and dating

The dating of medieval European arrowheads is difficult to achieve without a reliable dating of the find context. Arrowheads do not exist within a precisely dateable chronology and, because of the very wide dating brackets for the pottery, the Hirsel site does not provide a very closely dated context for example as to the first ruination of the building, the subsequent secular use, and the final destruction and obliteration.

The arrowheads

The types and forms of arrowheads did not change dramatically during the Middle Ages. The most obviously military type of arrowhead, the 'bodkin'—a square-section slender spike intended to penetrate mail—was in widespread use by at least the 12th century, but many types of barbed and other heads used for both military and hunting purposes were already in use by then and changed very little until at least the 16th century, when military archery finally disappeared from British and European armies.

Any type of arrowhead on an arrow shot from a bow of suitable strength striking a human in the correct place will kill, but at the time when arrows or crossbow bolts were used for war and hunting there were many types and forms of arrowheads, each made for a specific purpose.

A barbed hunting arrowhead was usually kept extremely sharp on its long cutting edges since an arrow, even from a powerful bow, did not have the velocity to deliver a knock-down shock to an animal and instead was designed to penetrate as deeply and to cut as much soft tissue and as many blood vessels as possible. Barbed arrowheads generally took longer to manufacture than plainer military heads and unlike arrows used in war were expected to be reused, if they could be recovered. In the later Middle Ages most arrowheads intended for war were without barbs, although some forms retained small vestigial barbs. All but one of the arrowheads found on the Hirsel site are of a similar type and form: bladed, barbed and socketed.

A few other arrowheads which are similar to the majority of the Hirsel arrowheads have been identified from other archaeological assemblages. One, from the Thames at Hammersmith, is shown in the summary of arrowheads by Ward Perkins in his Medieval Catalogue of the London Museum (Ward Perkins 1940, pl XV, no. 25). Regrettably this means that it cannot be accurately dated. It is presumed to have been recovered from the foreshore, but finds recovered from strata in the banks of the Thames were not recorded as precisely in the past as they are now. Its length was 2.6 inches (65mm) but no other information was given. Ward Perkins however described it in his classification as a hunting head (Ward Perkins 1940, 70).

Another arrowhead relating to the Hirsel group was excavated in Winchester (Goodall 1990e, no. 4014). It is 62mm long and was identified as from the 15th century. Presumably the find context within the excavation made this dating possible (see also Jessop 1996, 194–195).

Nearer to The Hirsel, similar arrowheads were found in the excavations at Dunbar Castle, described as most closely paralleled in the Ward Perkins series by types from the 12th and 13th centuries (Cox 2000, 127, illus 97, 168), and similar arrowheads have also been found at Perth (Cox 1996, 772, no. 281).

Both the arrowheads from England have small holes in their socket allowing the arrowhead to be pinned to the arrow shaft. This practice is generally associated with barbed hunting heads, since the pin ensured that an arrow with a barbed head was not pulled off and lost when recovering the arrow. Ward Perkins (1940, 70) stated in his classification of figure 17 type 15 (which appears to be an illustration of the photograph of arrowhead 25 shown on plate 15) that it is a type exclusively used for hunting. He also added that the evolution of the barbed arrowhead was not clear, and that it is to the 14th and 15th centuries that the more elaborate examples belong. Ian Goodall, in his discussion of the Winchester arrowhead 4014, stated that 'the barbs are too small and the contours of the blade too smooth to make it a successful hunting head'. He went on to say that 'an arrow with such a head would tend to pass right through the animal with the minimum of laceration' (Goodall 1990e, 1073). This assumption, however, is not correct. Two of the most famous bow-hunters of the 20th century, Howard Hill and Fred Bear, both killed most of the different species of big game in America, including Grizzly Bear, while using arrows with arrowheads which had these attributes.

The function of barbs on an arrowhead

Barbs on an arrowhead ensured that the arrow could not be dislodged by the stricken animal as it ran from the archer. Movement of the animal as it ran, whether a deer in a forest or a horse on the battlefield, would cause massive internal damage. The bigger and sharper the wings on a hunting arrow the more damage would be caused to the quarry and the quicker it would die. The larger the arrowhead the heavier it was and the shorter its effective range. For this reason the large swallowtail arrowheads were intended to be shot at relatively short distances. To enable this deer were driven past a concealed hunter at a suitably short range. This method was called 'stable' and the position of the archer the 'set' or 'stand'. The smaller arrowheads found at The Hirsel would perhaps have been used when hunting by 'stalking'. This form of hunting was mostly carried out by trusted and skilled members of the lower class. The quarry would be found and then approached, by a single hunter, to a distance where a good shot was possible. This distance would generally be greater than the distances in the 'stable' and for this, a lighter arrowhead was desirable since it would enable shooting at longer ranges (Figure 20.15).

In the Middle Ages, deer were hunted as an important part of the diet of those entitled to shoot them. Members of the master's household, the master and those close to him also hunted for sport, but any deer killed also put food on their tables. Before the deer was butchered any arrowheads still within it would be recovered from the carcass in order that they could be fitted to fresh arrow shafts.

FIGURE 20.15
A late 14th-century image of a civilian archer: the poet John Gower shooting arrows with large barbed heads from a longbow. Gower is carrying three more arrows in his girdle ready for use. From Vox Clamantis and Chronica Tripertita, about 1400 © Glasgow University Library, MS Hunter 59 (T.2.17) folio 6v

Military arrowheads

Ward Perkins also stated that in the 14th century more compact types of arrowhead appeared in response to the development of plate armour (Ward Perkins 1940, 67). This is a rather general statement, but one which is essentially correct. Most arrowheads on military arrows, which were specifically intended to be shot at human targets, were generally glued to the arrow shaft and this also applied to those arrowheads which carried vestigial barbs. It was expected that a war arrow would be used only once. If the arrow struck its target and the arrowhead happened to come off in the body of the victim when it was being withdrawn, so much the better; it had done its job.

The Hirsel arrowheads

The group of arrowheads from The Hirsel site is interesting and unusual in that the heads recovered are of the same type and form and from within a small area. Fifteen arrowheads have been illustrated. All except one, FeA18, whatever their condition, have barbs or show where barbs would have been even if their wings had lost some of their length. The barbs, whatever their condition now, would have been substantial when new. All the heads are socketed and on five a hole has been pierced in the lower part of the ferrule, to take a small retaining nail. Although time has caused damage to some of the sockets, there is no reason to assume that the other heads did not also have holes for similar pins.

Some of the Hirsel arrowheads have a slightly convex curve to their wings (see FeA5). Four of the heads (FeA8, FeA12, FeA14 and FeA15) are what are sometimes referred to as 'swallowtails', and are larger than the others. These would be for use on the largest game, particularly deer or boar. 'Swallowtail' arrowheads are often shown in 15th century illustrations of battles. War horses became soft targets for these heavy headed arrows if they were ridden too close to enemy archers.

The other types of arrowheads recovered from the site are of a similar form to the swallowtails but of smaller dimensions. These were also suitable for larger game, for the reasons discussed above, but in times of conflict they could also be used against horses or men. While the larger swallowtail head is often shown in medieval illustrations, the smaller version is shown less frequently, which might suggest that it was a derivation of the larger form.

Why were there so many arrowheads of similar type all in one area?

Although some arrowheads had been moved by the ploughing the distribution was clearly focussed on the nave of the church (Figure 20.16). One reason might be that they may have been the tools of the trade of a person perhaps charged with keeping the larder well stocked with game for the lord's table. The old nave could have possibly been reused as a workshop as well as a barn and for temporary occupation (see Chapter 5). Here, if the property of the residents on the estate, the bows and arrows which were used to take game could have been kept in good order, to be ready at any time when required for hunting. Alternatively these arrows could have been deposited during a specific occupation when a hunting or raiding party sheltered in the building and re-shafted their arrows there.

Weapons for offence and defence, which would include bows and war arrows and crossbows and their quarrels or bolts, would normally be kept in the most secure place possible, probably in a nearby house (Chapter 2).

From the information available, it seems most likely that the arrowheads were made for hunting and were in use within the time scale of the pottery from the associated contexts. The most probable interpretation of these barbed arrowheads is, therefore, that they were primarily intended for

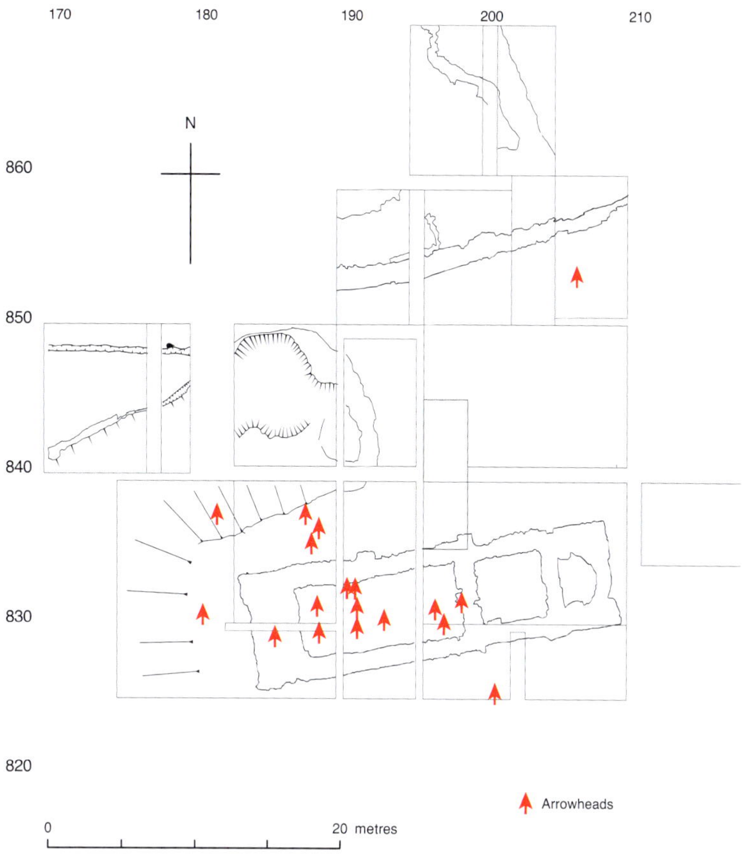

FIGURE 20.16
Site distribution of arrowheads

hunting rather than war and that they date from somewhere around the 14th–15th century.

Arrowhead FeA18

One arrowhead is different from the majority, however; a conical socket without wings or barbs. This arrowhead appears very similar to the 'type 5' arrowheads recovered from Holme Castle near Tewkesbury (Morris 1997, 156–161). It has a circular section conical socket and is slightly faceted towards the point. Thirty similar arrowheads were found in different locations around Holme Castle, none of which have any flanges or barbs and are simply described as 'plain, pointed, hollow metal tips for the ends of wooden arrow shafts'.

All but two of these heads were found within a 14th century find context, while the others were associated with a demolished medieval hall and could not be more precisely dated to nearer than a period from the mid-14th century to the late 16th century. The report on the Holme Castle excavations compares these heads to others found in other British medieval sites, but these give a date range from the 12th to the 14th century. They seem to be target arrows. The Hirsel arrowhead was found near to domestic buildings in the north of the site which were demolished by the 14th century, but it is not possible to date the arrowhead more closely than from the later 13th century to the late 15th century.

FeA1 (Figure 20.17)
Barbed arrowhead, point broken, with rivet hole in socket.
Found in a posthole in the west end of the church, last phase of use.
L 51mm; W 15mm; Diam of socket 10mm.
C917, Phase: 7 LM, Findspot: 188.95/829.

FeA2 (not illustrated)
Barbed arrowhead, found in lower fill of pit (C1302) in church.
L 67mm; W 18mm; Diam of socket 10>6mm.
C1305, Phase: 7 LM, Findspot: 191.44/831.92.

FeA3 (not illustrated)
Barbed arrowhead, angular, similar to Fe36.
Found in hearth on top of pit in church.
L 58mm; W 18mm; Max. diam of socket 9mm.
C1227, Phase: 7 LM, Findspot: 190.90/832.00.

FeA4 (Not illustrated)
Barbed arrowhead, with possible socket, broken tip.
From the same context same as FeA3.
L 40mm; W 18mm; Diam of socket 9>6mm.
C1227, Phase: 7 LM, Findspot: 191.36/832.08.

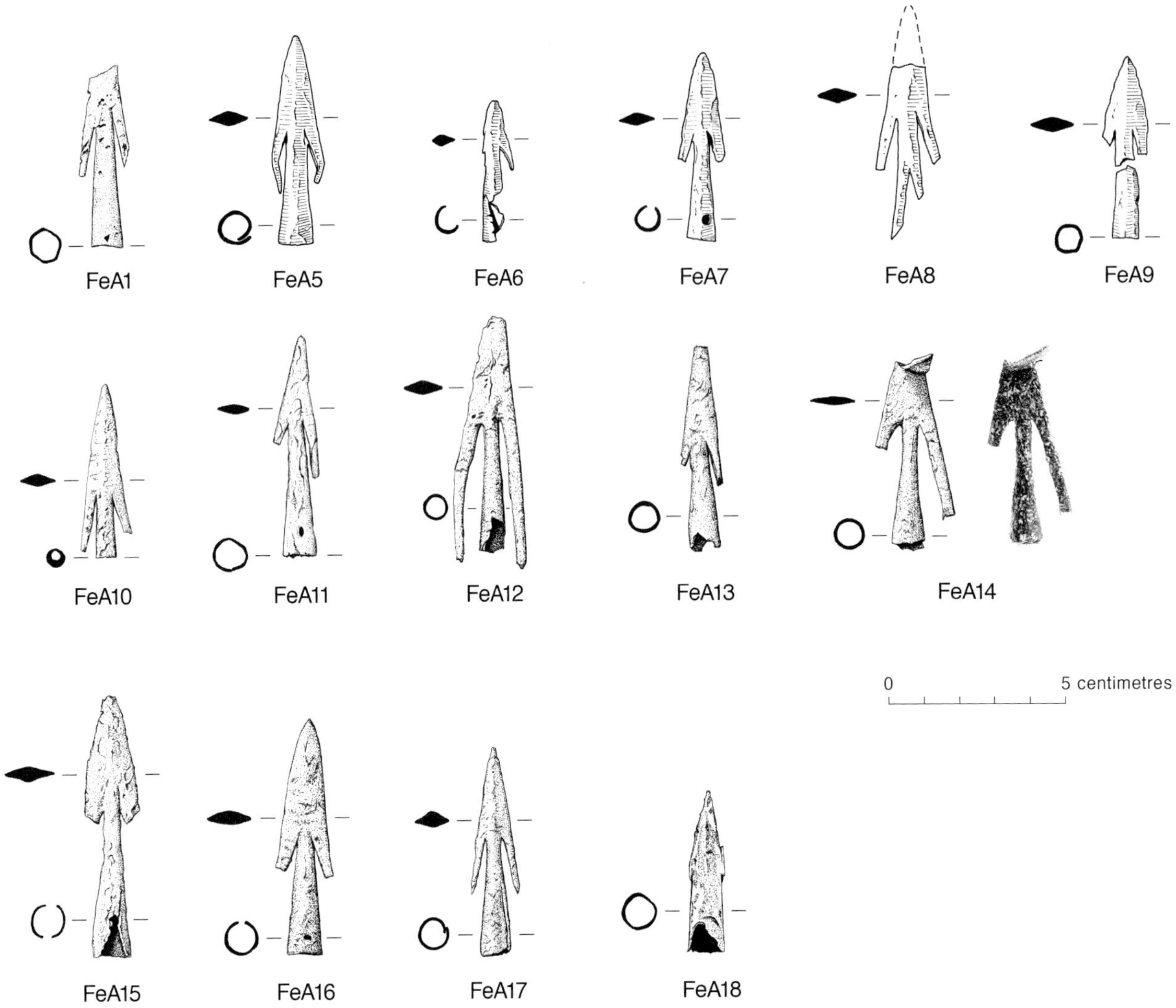

FIGURE 20.17
Arrowheads, FeA1, FeA5–18

FeA5 (Figure 20.17)
Barbed arrowhead, with a distinct central ridge.
Found in secular occupation level in nave.
L 60mm; W 15mm; Diam of socket 9mm.
C1158, Phase: 7 LM, Findspot: 193.39/829.87.

FeA6 (Figure 20.17)
Arrowhead with one barb and hollow circular socket. Very small arrowhead, tiny head, made of very thin metal.
Found in secular occupation level in nave.
L 35mm; W 8mm; Diam of socket 7mm.
C1135, Phase: 7 LM, Findspot: 191.53/829.34.

FeA7 (Figure 20.17)
Barbed arrowhead, with rivet hole, and trace of tinning? on socket.
Found in layer of burning in nave.
L 53mm; W 14mm; Diam of socket 8mm.
C1160, Phase: 7 LM, Findspot: 191.56/830.68.

FeA8 (Figure 20.17)
Barbed arrowhead, tip missing.
Found in layer of burning, east end of nave.
L 92mm; W 18mm; Diam of socket 8mm.
C623, Phase: 7 LM, Findspot: 198.64/831.09.

FeA9 (Figure 20.17)
Barbed arrowhead, broken in two.
Found in layer of burning, east end of nave.
L 50mm; W 13mm; Diam of socket 8mm.
C623, Phase: 7 LM, Findspot: 196.91/830.64.

FeA10 (Figure 20.17)
Barbed arrowhead, with broken socket.
Found in rubble, destruction of church.
L 48mm; W 15mm; Diam of socket 6mm.
C902, Phase: 8 EPM, Area: 180–2/825–835.5.

FeA11 (Figure 20.17)
Barbed arrowhead, bent, with rivet hole in rolled socket.
Found south of church in rubble spread cut by graves; spread could be from destroyed church.
L 62mm; W 13mm; Diam of socket 9mm.
C715, Phase: 7 LM, Area: 200–2/824–6.

FeA12 (Figure 20.17)
An iron arrowhead of slender barbed or 'broadhead' form, the outer edges and the barbs curving gently towards the socket. The extreme tip is lost through corrosion, but the area beneath it shows signs of sideways distortion compatible with impact damage. The tip of one barb, and part of the edge of the socket, are lost through corrosion. The slender socket contains a small amount of what may be the original shaft, and a hammer-welded seam is visible beneath the more complete barb. (GR)
Late medieval or early post-medieval spread from church.
L 71mm; W 22mm; Diam of socket 8mm.
C429, Phase: 7 LM, Area: 186–90/835–9.

FeA13 (Figure 20.17)
An iron arrowhead of barbed or 'broadhead' form, the narrow leaf-shaped head having small barbs (one largely lost through corrosion). The head is heavily corroded and somewhat distorted, being curved along its length. The extreme point is lost through corrosion. The socket is empty and somewhat misshapen, perhaps due to corrosion, and much of its rear edge is lost. A hammer-welded seam is visible in line with the stump of the lost barb. (GR)
Late medieval/early post-medieval occupation outside church.
L 55mm; W 13mm; Diam of socket 9mm.
C444, Phase: 7 LM, Area: 188–90/835–7.

FeA14 (Figure 20.17)
An iron arrowhead of elegant barbed or 'broadhead' form, the outer edges straight, the inner edges of the barbs slightly concave. One of the long thin barbs is broken off near its root. The slender socket is empty, and a hammer-welded seam is visible on the outside. The tip of the head is bent at approximately 90° to the rest of the head at about 23mm from the point, apparently having been bent after corrosion had taken place, the tip being attached only by a very small area of iron. (GR)
Context as above.
L 62mm; W 28mm; Diam of socket 8mm.
C444, Phase: 7 LM, Findspot: 188.5/835.

FeA15 (Figure 20.17)
Arrowhead, barbs broken, socket with rivet hole.
Abandonment layer, with a coin of Charles I.
L 74mm; W 16mm; Diam of socket 10mm.
C911, Phase: 8 EPM, Findspot: 181.92/836.95.

FeA16 (Figure 20.17)
An iron arrowhead of 'broadhead' or barbed form, the leaf-shaped head having relatively short barbs, the tips of which are now lost through corrosion. The point is bent to one side, possibly caused by impact. The socket has a visible hammer-welded seam, and near its rear edge is a small hole to enable the head to be pinned to the shaft. The socket is filled, apparently by burial concretion. Patches of copper alloy found on shaft, possibly from rivet. (GR)
Found in deposit of stones and mortar over church.
L 66mm; W 17mm; Diam of socket 10mm.
C402, Phase: 8 EPM, Findspot: 187.9/831.5.

FeA17 (Figure 20.17)
Barbed arrowhead, complete, with split socket and copper-alloy rivet.
Found in robbed wall trench of the south wall of the church.
L 58mm; W 13mm; Diam of socket 8mm.
C909, Phase: 7–8 LM–EPM, Findspot: 185.88/828.71.

FeA18 (Figure 20.17)
Possibly a flight arrow for target shooting? The socket runs right up into the head. The type is found within a wide date range.
From the domestic area in the north of the site, although the context is disturbed.
L 45mm; W 10mm; Diam of socket 10mm.
C1001, Phase: 8 EPM, Area: 205.5–207.75/852–4.

21

WORKED BONE

Ian Riddler and Belinda Burke

The finds of worked bone consist of three handles and a spindle whorl. The handles complement the collection of iron knives and tools found on the site; indeed WB3 could be associated with a specific blade found in the same context. However WB2 is the only evidence for a scale tang knife on the site. Animal bone identification was by James Rackham (JR) and Louisa Gidney (LG).

Handles produced from long bones of sheep (WB1) are a distinctive feature of the medieval period, occurring at Norwich, Winchester and York, amongst other sites (Riddler 2010, 278). They are usually undecorated and little modified from the original form of the bone. The scale tang knife handle (WB2) survives as a small fragment of a well manufactured implement, subsequently reworked with knife or saw marks on one side. Scale tang knife handles are common from the 14th century onwards, although there are examples from contexts extending back to the Early Anglo-Saxon period (Cowgill *et al* 1987, 26–27; Riddler 2010, 284; 2012, 127). In this case, the handle fits well with its late medieval context dating.

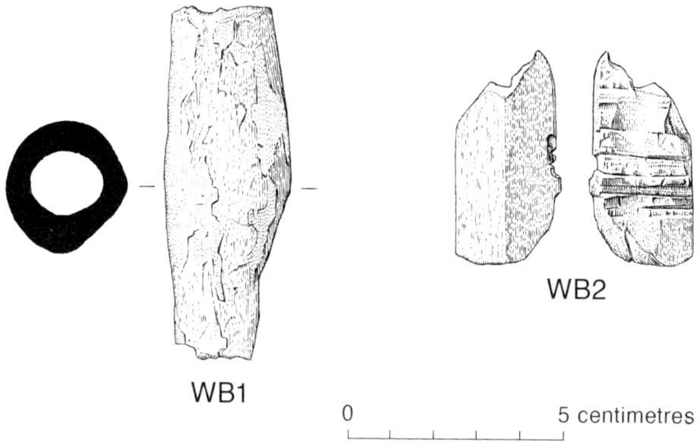

FIGURE 21.1
Bone knife handles, WB1–2

WB1 (Figure 21.1)
Handle for knife or awl in two fragments. There is evidence of working, but it is possibly unfinished. Sheep tibia, mid-shaft fragment, distal end worked (JR).
Found in a floor deposit, domestic area to north of church.
L 40mm; Cross section 19mm x 10mm.
C299, Phase: 6 Med, Findspot: 205.02/851.57.

WB2 (Figure 21.1)
Fragment, part of the handle of a scale tang knife, subsequently reworked, with knife or cut marks on one side. Originally well crafted. Shaft fragment from a large animal long bone (JR).
Found in a patch of pebbles to the south of the chancel.
L 22mm; W 11mm; Th 6mm.
C707, Phase 7 LM, Area: 200–2/826–8.

WB3 (not illustrated)
Handle, in eleven fragments (now lost). Iron stain. Possibly associated with iron blade Fe60, in which case it would be post-medieval.
Found in topsoil, beyond the west end of the church.
L 38mm; W 9mm; Th 2mm.
C901, topsoil, Area: 175–82.5/831–3.

WB4 (not illustrated)
Spindle whorl, of a similar form to an example from Goltho (MacGregor 1987, 191, no. 8, fig 161). Incomplete, but probably originally plano-convex. Cattle femoral head, teeth marks where chewed by a dog (LG).
From a rubble pack over the cemetery, to the north of the nave.
Diam 36mm; Th 15mm; Diam of hole 9mm.
C1122, Phase: 8 EPM, Area: 190.5–195.5/836–83.

22

PIERCED SCALLOP SHELLS

Rosemary Cramp

Two scallop shells were found in the cemetery to the north of the extended nave of the church. Sc1 was found in the grave of Sk222 near to the head, the radiocarbon date GU-1719 seems to peak in the 14th century. Sc2 was found in the disturbed cemetery earth in the same general area (see Figure 6.1). Both were Queen Scallops, *Pectinidae chlamys opercularis* (Louisa Gidney pers comm).

Both shells are characteristically pierced from the outer face with two perforations near to the bulbous top. Rather curiously the holes on both shells are not an exact pair, the one on the left being rectangular and on the right round, and both the holes are framed with a rectangular indent which was possibly the matrix for the point with which the shells were pierced. The holes on Sc1 are less carefully positioned than on Sc2.

As White Marshall and Walsh (2005) discuss in the account of the scallop shells excavated from the shrine and reliquary cists at the early medieval monastic site on the island of Illaunloughan, scallop shell motifs are found as ceremonial, symbolic imagery for centuries before the coming of Christianity and transcended religions, but the scallop formed an impressive feature of the entrance to the tomb of Christ at Jerusalem and figured later in many schematic renderings of that influential building. There is, then, a remote possibility that it may have inspired the placing of scallop shells in and on the shrine in Ireland. These are perforated in the centre of the shell with a single hole, as though they had been suspended either around the shrine or worn as ornament (White Marshall and Walsh 2005, illus 54a and 89–96). Their calibrated radiocarbon dates are given as AD 665–1048, which is earlier than the pilgrimage tokens associated with the apostle James, to which group the Hirsel shells belong.

Shells such as these (Figure 22.1) with two perforations for attachment to clothing or satchels are a not uncommon find in Western European medieval cemeteries, and are accepted as pilgrim badges, originally (from the 12th century) for those visiting the great shrine of St James at the church of Santiago de Compostela in Spain. Later these shells seem to have been obtained from other pilgrimage centres dedicated to St James. Such shells have been found in cemeteries in England from Winchester (Spencer 1990) to Durham where several recently excavated medieval burials in the Cathedral

FIGURE 22.1
Pierced scallop shell, Sc2

cemetery have been accompanied by scallop shells (Greenwell, 1906; Norman Emery pers comm). The discovery of a 14th–15th century burial in the church at St Etheran's monastery, Isle of May, in which a scallop shell had been wedged into the mouth of the corpse post-mortem, has provoked new comment concerning discoveries in Scotland and beyond (Yeoman 1999, 63; James and Yeoman 2008, illus 5.24, 180–181). Other finds in Scotland, which include one from the cemetery at Aberdeen (Cameron 2006), and a painted badge from High Street, Perth (Yeoman 1995, 26–28), indicate that such prophylactic tokens of pilgrimage were not uncommon. It seems reasonable to assume that the majority of the pilgrims who undertook the long journey from Scotland to Spain would have been of the upper ranks of the nobility and the clergy, and certainly these are the people who are recorded in surviving letters of commendation or licences granting immunity from civil and criminal proceedings until the pilgrim returned (Henderson 1997, 2–8). The list of pre-Reformation pilgrims recorded for Scotland begins in 1187 with Olaf Lord of Lewis and ends with George Donaldson, *c*1543 (Henderson 1997, 14–15). It is, however, not possible to deduce the status of the person buried at The Hirsel.

Sc1 (not illustrated)
Scallop shell with two perforations, from grave fill of Sk222.
68mm x 60mm.
C1091, Phase: 6 Med, Findspot: 184.25/835.00.

Sc2 (Figure 23.1)
Scallop shell with two perforations, found in cemetery earth.
59mm x 56mm.
C456, Phase: 6 Med, Area: 183–5/833–5.

23

LITHIC MATERIAL

Robert Young

Thirty-three pieces of lithic material, recovered over a five year period of excavation, were submitted for analysis from The Hirsel.

As the catalogue entries show, most of the lithic material has come from contexts that are the end result of processes such as ploughing, levelling and the construction of the chapel and the cemetery. Clearly all of these activities have disturbed an area of earlier prehistoric activity that may have been related to the putative Neolithic structure (C112, C116, C121, C126, C137, possibly C132/135) which has produced two Neolithic carinated bowls. The presence of this pottery and the Neolithic ceramic material from C851 might support the idea that all of the lithic material was of a similar date. The possibility that two sherds from C845 may be of Bronze Age date, confirms the fact that the material is clearly from a disturbed area of prehistoric activity. This is a point to which we will return below.

In this analysis all of the recovered material has been treated as one overall assemblage.

23.1 RAW MATERIAL

This can be broken down as shown in Figure 23.1. Four pieces retain hard, pitted, white/fawn pebble cortex and one piece retains a patch of hard grey pebble cortex. These raw material types are all common in the north and the Borders region (Mulholland 1970; Young 1985; 1987; 2000; 2007; Young and O'Sullivan 1993; 1995; Finlayson and Warren 2000; Waddington 2000). They would all be available from the gravel deposits of the Tweed valley. Finlayson and Warren note that in the lower reaches of the Tweed valley a number of raw materials are significant. These include flint, chert, agate and chalcedony and in some instances chalcedonies can make up some 30% of assemblages (Finlayson and Warren 2000, 138).

Raw material type	Number
Grey Mottled Flint	9
Light Grey Flint	8
Fawn/Pink Flint	1
Dark Grey Flint	2
Fawn Grey Flint	1
Grey Shiny Chert	4
Banded Chalcedony	4
Agate	1
Burnt flint	3
Total	**33**

FIGURE 23.1
Table of raw materials used

Artefact type	Number
Scraper	1
Awl	1
Serrated flake	1
? Oblique arrowhead fragment	1
Secondary flake (complete)	2
Secondary flake (broken) (includes one heavily calcined example)	2
Inner flake (complete)	2
Inner flake (broken)	6
Core trimming flake (broken)	1
Utilised/retouched blade segments	2
Retouched flake (broken)	1
Core fragment	1
Chips	6
Unworked chert pebble	2
Thermally spalled flake	1
Chunks	3
Total	**33**

FIGURE 23.2
Table of artefact types

23.2 TECHNOLOGY

The predominant method of flake removal would seem to have been hard hammer, direct percussion. In the six instances where bulbs of percussion survive, these are rounded and pronounced. Both plain (four examples) and facetted (two examples) butts are present in the assemblage. The presence of two blade segments and the occurrence of blade scars on the dorsal surfaces of at least two pieces indicates that blades may have been produced on the site.

Only one core fragment survives (Fl32) and this was recovered from the topsoil in association with post-medieval material. No primary flakes and only four secondary flakes were recorded.

23.3 TYPOLOGY

The artefact types recorded are listed in Figure 23.2. None of the recognised artefact types would seem to be truly diagnostic of any one period and all could, with the exception of the possible fragment from an oblique arrowhead discovered in 1980, fit into any regional date bracket from the Later Mesolithic to the Bronze Age. The occurrence of Neolithic pottery on the site should not blind us to the fact that whilst some lithic material may be Neolithic in date, there may be evidence for human activity on the site from the pre- and post-Neolithic periods.

The scraper (Fl6), for example, is a small 'thumbnail' type usually suggested as being of Early Bronze Age date and common in the north and in the Scottish Borders. Often these are associated with Beaker burials (Waddington 2004, 41). The present example comes from a context associated with two sherds of pottery of potential Bronze Age date.

The possible awl/borer was recovered in 1984 (Fl21) and is made on the distal end of a thick, light grey flake/blade. The working point has been made by steep almost abrupt retouch along approx 22mm of the right edge and the tip seems to be slightly rounded through use.

Of particular interest is the fragment from what may be an oblique arrowhead (Fl19). This was found in a disturbed context (C294). If the identification is correct then the piece appears to be the left edge of the projectile point, and exhibits very fine retouch similar to that observed on examples from Thirlings now in the Great North Museum and recovered through fieldwalking by the late Dr Joan Weyman (Museum of Antiquities Catalogue no. 1996.7; Waddington 2004, 46, fig 71 and 79). Another fine example was recovered from Haugh Head, Wooler, in 1946 when Dr E F Collingwood excavated a cist burial accompanied by a complete Yorkshire Vase type food vessel (Collingwood and Cowen 1948; Museum of Antiquities, Newcastle upon Tyne Catalogue no. 1946.25). Green has discussed the chronology of these projectile types, suggesting that they may be of Late Neolithic–Early Bronze Age date (Green 1980, i, 114–115).

23.4 GENERAL DISCUSSION

As highlighted above, none of this material is closely diagnostic of any one period of human activity. It may be that we have evidence here for every period from the Mesolithic to the Bronze Age represented in the flint assemblage. The possible Neolithic structure, as defined by C112, C116, C121, C126 and C137, produced pottery but only one lithic find (Fl1 from C126). C851 and C845, to the west of the church, also produced seeming Neolithic pottery (C851) and Bronze Age material (C851). C845 did produce six pieces of lithic material (Fl3–8), but only one of these, the 'thumbnail scraper' (Fl6), might be tentatively tied to a particular chronological period.

Overall, this small group of lithic artefacts would not be out of place anywhere on the gravel terraces of the River Tweed (Mulholland 1970; Finlayson and Warren 2000) and it can be paralleled by many similar groupings in the Milfield Basin (Waddington 2000) and the east coast of Northumberland (Young 2007).

Fl1 (Figure 23.3)
Fawn/pink flint chip with natural fault on underside.
10mm x 22mm x 3mm.
C126, Phase: 1 Neol (disturbed), Findspot: 199.81/868.49.

Fl2 (not illustrated)
Irregularly shattered light grey inner flint flake. Broken at bulbar end and transversely at distal end.
18mm x 13mm x 3mm.
C899, Phase: 3? Pre-med, Findspot: 188.3/831.6.

Fl3 (not illustrated)
Distal end of a grey mottled inner flake. Broken transversely at bulbar end.
18mm x 12mm.
C845, Phase: 3–4 Pre-med (disturbed), Findspot: 178.46/833.24.

Fl4 (not illustrated)
Dark grey flint chip.
13mm x 8mm.
C845, Phase: 3–4 Pre-med (disturbed), Findspot: 176.70/830.59.

Fl5 (not illustrated)
Pink/grey banded chalcedony chunk. Shows some signs of having been struck.
23mm x 20mm x 8mm.
C845, Phase: 3–4 Pre-med (disturbed), Findspot: 178.00/825.26.

Fl6 (not illustrated)
Small rounded 'thumbnail scraper'. Retains hard pitted cortex at bulbar end. Steep retouch around edges.
22mm x 20mm x 10mm.
C845, Phase: 3–4 Pre-med (disturbed), Findspot: 180.62/832.49.

Fl7 (not illustrated)
Irregular light grey flint chip.
18mm x 10mm.
C845, Phase: 3–4 Pre-med (disturbed), Findspot: 182.5/830.8.

Fl8 (not illustrated)
Light grey inner flint flake, broken transversely at bulbar end. Exhibits evidence for utilisation on left edge dorsal face.
15mm x 19mm x 3mm.
C845, Phase: 3–4 Pre-med (disturbed), Findspot: 178/834.

Fl9 (not illustrated)
Heavily calcined flake/blade. Crackled and crazed. Retains pronounced bulb and dorsal face exhibits hard grey cortex, very crackled and crazed. Broken irregularly at the distal end. Many small spall scars visible on dorsal and bulbar faces.
Found in the grave fill of Sk252.
30mm x 20mm x 8mm.
C691, Phase: 5? EM2, Findspot: 208.78/837.09.

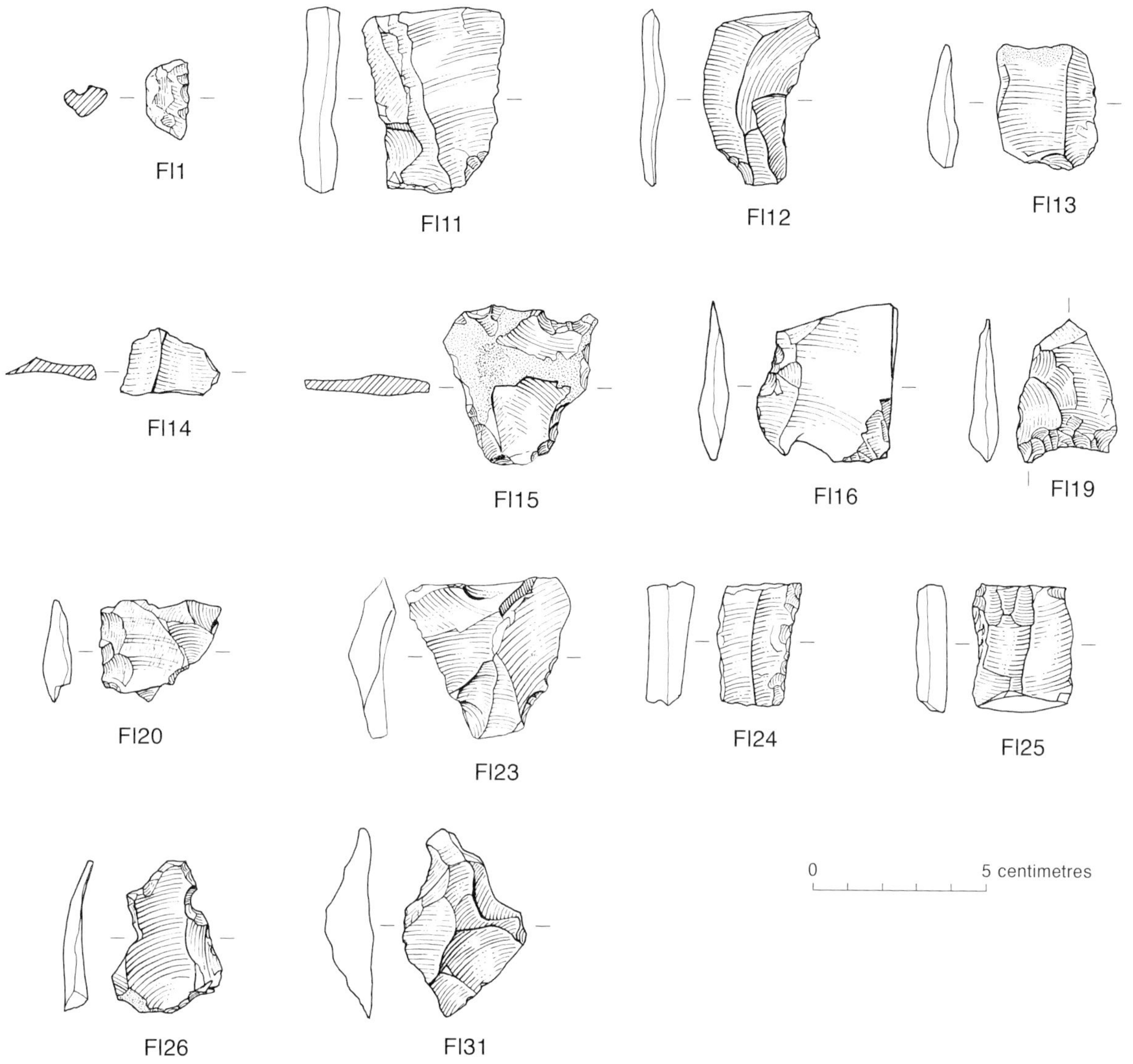

FIGURE 23.3
Lithic material

Fl10 (not illustrated)
Irregular banded chalcedony flake.
Found in the grave fill of Sk280.
32mm x 24mm x 8mm.
C781, Phase: 5? EM2, 192.3–193.2/825.5–826.

Fl11 (Figure 23.3)
Mottled grey inner blade/flake, broken transversely at distal end. Pronounced bulb, plain butt. Exhibits marked serrations on left edge and clear evidence for utilisation on right edge.
26mm x 20mm x 4mm.
C128, Phase: 5? EM2, Findspot: 203.74/862.86.

Fl12 (Figure 23.3)
Mottled grey inner blade like flint flake. Broken transversely at bulbar end. Pronounced hinge fracture at distal end.
24mm x 14mm x 3mm.
C456, Phase: 6 Med, Findspot: 184.05/833.

Fl13 (Figure 23.3)
Dark grey, shiny, chert flake from a blade core. Exhibits blade scars on dorsal face. Thin facetted butt, pronounced bulb of percussion and hinge fracture at distal end.
18mm x 15mm x 5mm.
C456, Phase: 6 Med, Findspot: 183.42/836.

Fl14 (Figure 23.3)
Distal end of a light grey inner flint flake/blade. Broken transversely at bulbar end.
10mm x 15mm x 2mm.
C1004, Phase: 6 Med, Area: 206–9/854–7.

Fl15 (Figure 23.3)
Grey mottled secondary flint flake, exhibiting hard fawn/grey pitted pebble cortex on dorsal face. Pronounced bulb, plain, thin butt. Pronounced hinge fracture at distal end, and retouched notch on left edge bulbar end.
26mm x 22mm x 4mm.
C295, Phase: 6 Med, Area: 202–5/857–8.

Fl16 (Figure 23.3)
Distal end of a mottled grey flake. Broken transversely at bulbar end slight hinge fracture at distal end.
23mm x 20mm x 4mm.
C1011, Phase: 6 Med, Findspot: 207.18/859.47.

Fl17 (not illustrated)
Small natural, dark grey, shiny, rounded chert pebble.
Found associated with Sk116.
With Sk116, Phase: 6 Med, Area: 198–9/827–8.

Fl18 (not illustrated)
Irregular, angular grey mottled flint chip shattered from a larger piece.
24mm x 12mm.
C955, Phase: 6 Med, Findspot: 182.5/834.8.

Fl19 (Figure 23.3)
Fawn grey flint fragment ?from oblique arrowhead, exhibits very fine retouch on dorsal face.
20mm x 14.5mm x 4mm.
C294, Phase: 6 Med (disturbed), Area: 202–5/853–6.

Fl20 (Figure 23.3)
Irregularly shattered mottled grey flint chip.
20mm x 15mm x 4mm.
C801, Phase: 7 LM, Area: 211–3/838–9.5.

Fl21 (not illustrated)
Awl/borer on a light grey flint blade. Broken transversely at bulbar end. Thick triangular cross section. Retouched on right edge at distal end; very steep and abrupt. Tip rounded and worn through use.
37mm x 12mm x 6mm.
C444, Phase: 7 LM, Findspot: 186.20/834.50.

Fl22 (not illustrated)
Irregular light grey flint chip.
Found associated with Sk129.
C444, Phase: 7 LM, Findspot: 188.54/836.68.

Fl23 (Figure 23.3)
Light grey inner flint flake, broken transversely at the bulbar end.
22mm x 24mm x 6mm.
C2, Phase: 8 EPM, Area: 178–9/842–3.

Fl24 (Figure 23.3)
Highly calcined grey/white thick blade segment. Very crackled and crazed but still exhibits some possible retouch/utilisation on left edge, dorsal face. Retains clear scars from previous blade removals on dorsal face.
18mm x 10mm x 6mm.
C2, Phase: 8 EPM, Area: 178–9/848–9.

Fl25 (Figure 23.3)
Mottled grey flint inner blade segment, broken transversely at distal end. Pronounced bulb, plain butt. Evidence for utilisation on both edges.
17mm x 14mm x 5mm.
C286, Phase: 8 EPM, Area: 202.4–205/852–4.

Fl26 (Figure 23.3)
Brick red agate flake possibly from blade core. Facetted butt, pronounced bulb. ?utilised across base. Retains a small patch of cortex like material on right edge, dorsal face.
21mm x 16mm x 3mm.
C909, Phase: 7–8 LM–EPM, Area: 184–90/825–34.

Fl27 (not illustrated)
Irregularly shattered chunk from dark grey flint pebble. Exhibits hard, pitted off white/fawn pebble cortex on one face.
C207, Phase: 8 EPM, Findspot: 185/854.

Fl28 (not illustrated)
Banded grey pink/red chalcedony fragment. Exhibits possible evidence for retouch/utilisation on one edge. Very bashed and battered.
C1002, Phase: 8 EPM, Area: 205.50–207.75/858–60.

Fl29 (not illustrated)
Irregularly shattered, banded chalcedony fragment. Not worked.
C1003, Phase: 8 EPM, Area: 205.50–207.75/854–6.

Fl30 (not illustrated)
Thermally spalled flint fragment, rounded, off white, retains hard fawn/off white cortex on outer surface. Found when cleaning back over contexts 1058/1027.
21mm x 15mm.
C013, unstratified, Area: 175–80/830–4.

Fl31 (Figure 23.3)
Grey mottled inner flint flake, broken transversely at the bulbar end. Exhibits a slight hinge fracture at distal end. A core trimming flake showing bi-polar working.
23mm x 17mm x 6mm.
C103, topsoil, Area: 195–6/864–5.

Fl32 (not illustrated)
Fragment from grey shiny chert pebble, utilised as a core. The piece has been split by a blow from a hard hammer and exhibits a small bulb of percussion on the fractured face. Evidence for several flake removals before splitting.
32mm x 20mm x 17mm.
C1000, topsoil, Area: 205.5–207.75/858–60.

Fl33 (not illustrated)
Small, dark grey, shiny chert pebble; unworked.
Disturbed context associated with 18th century material.
17mm x17mm x 16mm.
C1000, topsoil, Area: 205.50–207.75/858–60.

24
STONE ARTEFACTS

24.1 SMALL PIERCED HONES
Rosemary Cramp

SH1 (Figure 24.1)
Hone pierced for suspension, fine-grained sandstone, neatly shaped with sharp edges, and the hole is precisely drilled. It tapers from a squared end with the hole to a rounded tip. There is slight evidence of wear. Such small personal hones are found in Britain in domestic contexts over a wide period of time from the 6th/7th century throughout the medieval period. Four similar pierced hones were found at Jarrow, three in Anglo-Saxon contexts, one in a 14th/15th century context (Cramp 2006, WS 17–20). At Dunbar there were two small pierced hones in phases 13 and 20 (Perry 2000, illus 99, 309, 303). A similar small well shaped hone, but unpierced, was found in a structure at Barhobble (Cormack 1995, fig 35, 69). The Hirsel example is closest in type to Jarrow, but is probably later. It was found in the area of the 'priest's house' in the north-east of the site.
L 90mm; W 10>8mm; Th 11mm; Diam of hole 6mm.
C220, Phase: 6 Med, Findspot: 200.430/853.600.

SH2 (Figure 24.1)
Hone pierced for suspension, fine-grained siltstone. The hole end is narrow and squared and it tapers at both ends. There is an iron stain in the middle. For type see SH1. Found in a rubbish deposit in the southern cemetery, in association with a small iron buckle and a belt mount with a ring for suspension of medieval date, suggesting that this assemblage represents the remains of a belt to which the hone was attached.
L 114mm; W 18>4mm; Th 10mm.
C715, Phase: 7 LM, Findspot: 198.44/824.25.

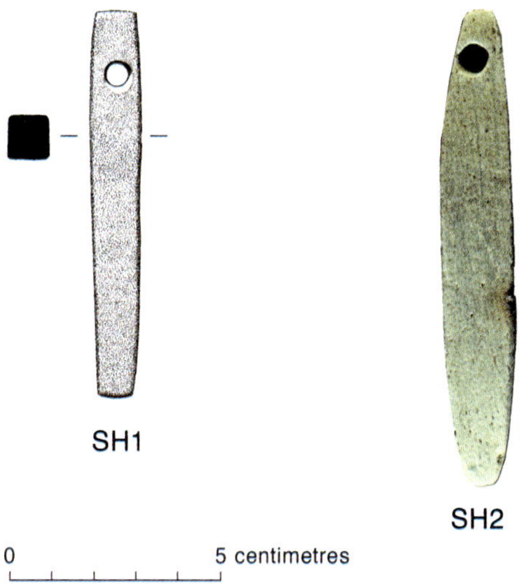

FIGURE 24.1
Small pierced hone stones, SH1–2

24.2 COBBLE TOOLS
Caroline R Wickham-Jones and Dawn McLaren
Geological identifications by Diane Dixon

These tools were reported on by Caroline Wickham-Jones in 1994, and some were later revised (with the author's consent) by Dawn McLaren in 2010 (see initialled entries).

Materials and provenance

Twenty-nine artefacts have been examined by the authors and are the subject of this report. They are made on rounded cobbles of a variety of local materials: sandstones, siltstones and tuffs. A range of different grain size is represented in the assemblage, from fine siliceous mudstone (CT9) to coarse sandstone (CT15). The materials blend into one another to some extent: sandstones may be more or less tuffaceous, or they may be very fine-grained and silty. The local stone resources of river and field cobbles clearly provided a variety of suitable materials and the past inhabitants of The Hirsel were able to exploit these and extract those pebbles that suited their different needs.

Manufacture

Few of the pieces show evidence of complex manufacturing techniques. In most cases it seems that the natural characteristics of the cobbles were quite suitable for various uses, and where necessary these were enhanced by grinding. This is very obvious on some pieces, e.g. CT15 and CT16, but on most pieces it is difficult to distinguish traces of deliberate alteration from traces of wear, particularly when both are faint and concentrate on the same areas of the stone. In many cases use-wear probably overlies and enhances the evidence for manufacture. With the exception of one artefact (CT26), none of the objects have been flaked, though traces of preliminary flaking may have been obliterated by later grinding and use. Further information on manufacture will be discussed under the individual tool types.

Artefact types

The assemblage has been divided into different artefact categories on the basis of a combination of shape and wear traces (Figure 24.2).

Tool type	Quantity
Hones	14
Rubbing stones	8
Ground wedge-shaped	3
Pestle	1
Weight	1
Miscellaneous ground pieces	2
Total	**29**

FIGURE 24.2
The composition of the assemblage by type

Hones

There are 14 probable hones. They are mainly made on sandstones (7) and tuffaceous sandstones (5), though there is one of siltstone and one of a fine siliceous mudstone. Most are made on naturally long, rounded blanks. All have one or more smoothed and often slightly concave surfaces; three have two used surfaces, one has three used surfaces. Concave, rubbed surfaces are characteristic of wear on a hone, and four also show marked striations. On most of the hones it is difficult to tell whether the sides were ground into shape prior to use; only two (CT5 and CT10) have clear signs of manufacture: both have been ground. These worked pieces are both finer; CT5 is made of a fine-grained mudstone and has been worked into a quadrilateral cross section, and CT10 has a more triangular cross section.

There is little difference in the size and shape of the cobble hones, although some are quite rounded and some are larger (see catalogue). It seems that suitable blanks were easily available, probably locally, and with use these would gradually become worn down into a more traditional, regular shape. A similar range of fine and coarse hones has been found on other sites for example Whithorn, Dumfries and Galloway, and here the excavators argued that 'fancier' well made hones were imported and reserved for more specific uses, while local blanks, where suitable, were collected and used for everyday tasks (Nicholson 1997b, 454–455). This would lead to a situation like that at The Hirsel where a range of hones from well-made perforated versions (see small pierced hones, above), through well-worn fine and irregular cobbles, to rounded cobble blanks has been found.

Both of the finer worked pieces (CT5 and CT10) are broken, and it has been suggested elsewhere (Nicholson 1997b, 455) that finer manufactured hones were used more intensively than their coarser counterparts and thus are more commonly found broken. The two from The Hirsel both show staining, indicating reuse in leatherworking and certainly, of the cruder hones from The Hirsel, only four are broken, all are larger and more irregular artefacts. CT11 and CT12 are made on naturally laminar cobbles, and have split along their horizontal planes. CT3 has a roughly flaked end, probably the result of natural breakage, and CT6 has also lost one end through breakage.

CT1 (Figure 24.3)
Tuffaceous sandstone hone. An elongated rounded pebble, with no signs of manufacture. Possible wear marks: one slightly smooth, concave surface. (CW-J)
L 112mm; W 45mm; Th 21mm.
C714, Phase: 6 Med, Area: 196–8/826–8.

CT2 (Figure 24.3)
Tuffaceous sandstone hone. An elongated round cobble, triangular cross section, slightly irregular shape. Broken, only one end survives. There are no signs of manufacture, but possible wear marks; one slightly smoothed surface, other marks probably modern, e.g. trowel? (CW-J)
L 125mm; W 50mm; Th 30mm.
C124, Phase: 6 Med, Findspot: 204.00/861.50.

CT3 (not illustrated)
Hone/pounder of tuffaceous sandstone; a fragment of a flattened ovoid sandstone cobble, both ends lost and one face damaged. A light band of abrasion is present on both elongated rounded edges, one associated with red-brown staining, the other overlapped by an oval facet of pitting (39.5mm x 12.5mm), possibly from expedient use as a pounder or working surface. One rounded face is slightly discoloured, perhaps from exposure to heat. The opposite rounded face has been flattened along one edge from use as a hone, the abrasion being associated with light use: polish and angled scratchmarks. (DMcL)
L 121mm; W 39.5–32mm; Th 19–22mm.
C503, Phase: 6 Med, Area: 200–2/848–50.

CT4 (not illustrated)
Small sandstone hone. An elongated rounded pebble, one flattish face, a natural v-shaped depression on one side. There are no signs of manufacture. Use marks: one slightly concave ?smoothed surface. (CW-J)
L 78mm; W 27mm; Th 15mm.
C456, Phase: 6 Med, Area: 183–6/833.5–7.4.

CT5 (Figure 24.3)
Small elongated hone of tuffaceous sandstone. Damaged at both ends and one face, possibly from heat damage. Both faces used as a whetstone. Abrasion on both edges. Secondary pitting: pounder/working surface. (DMcL)
L 92mm; W 35mm; Th 20mm.
C1195, Phase: 7 LM, Area: 199–202/835–8.

CT6 (Figure 24.3)
Hone of tuffaceous sandstone. An elongated, rounded cobble, roughly triangular cross section. No signs of manufacture, but possible use marks in the form of light striations and smoothing on one narrow face. (CW-J)
L 115mm; W 50mm; Th 30mm.
C1195, Phase: 7 LM, Area: 199–202/835–8.

CT7 (Figure 24.3)
Sandstone hone. Flattened elongated ovoid cobble, surfaces naturally smooth with small natural hollow on one face. One end is bifacially fractured (?from hammerstone use), resulting in the loss of one end and a large spall from one face has been detached. The opposite face is naturally smooth with a light sheen from use as a hone. (DMcL)
L 129mm; W 44.5mm; Th 22mm.
C1154, Phase: 7 LM, Findspot: 193.33/830.18.

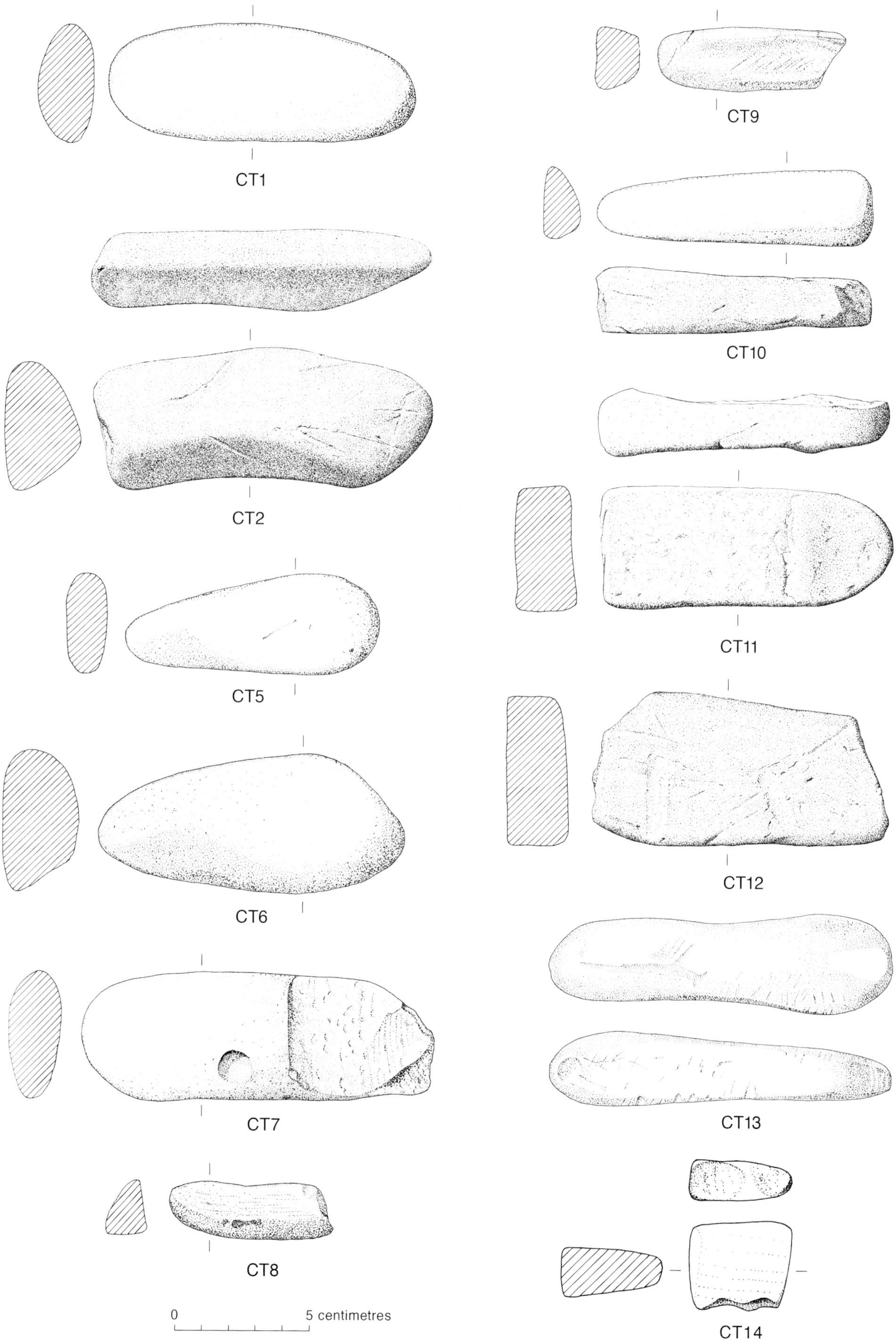

FIGURE 24.3
Hone stones, CT1–14

CT8 (Figure 24.3)
Sandstone hone/smoother. Small ovoid pebble, one end lost in antiquity prior to use. The other rounded end remains, but lacks any evidence of use. One face is slightly dished with light striations from whetting. The adjacent rounded end also displays light abrasion with associated use-polish and red-brown staining suggests secondary use as a smoother for leatherworking. (DMcL)
L 60mm; W 22.5mm; Th 15.5mm.
C705, Phase: 7–8 LM–EPM, Area: 198–200/822–4.

CT9 (Figure 24.3)
A small hone of slightly siliceous mudstone. Small elongated ovoid pebble, sub-square in section, one end broken in antiquity. Remaining end and surfaces are naturally smooth, both sides gently rounded with two naturally concave faces. One concave face is associated with diagonal abrasion and dark red-brown staining, which extends in irregular patches onto both edges. (DMcL)
L 69mm; W 21.5mm; Th 15–16.5mm.
C1031, Phase: 8 EPM, Area: 183–8/837–839.5.

CT10 (Figure 24.3)
Fine sandstone hone. A rounded elongated pebble, thin in cross section. One face is very smooth and concave indicating possible use. There are no obvious signs that the shape of the piece has been altered. (CW-J)
L 103mm; W 27mm; Th 13mm.
C902, Phase: 8 EPM, Area: 180–2/825–35.

CT11 (Figure 24.3)
Elongated hone stone of flaggy siltstone, broken. A split elongated pebble. One end is rounded, the other broken. There are two flat sides with possible wear marks, and two horizontal split surfaces — natural, but the sides may be ground. (CW-J)
L 110mm; W 42mm; Th 23mm.
C105, Phase: 8 EPM, Area: 201–2/864–5.

CT12 (Figure 24.3)
Sandstone hone. A split elongated pebble. One end has been rounded, the other is broken. One flat face, the other split surface seems to reflect the natural fracture pattern. Possible wear marks, the flat surface has some apparently recent damage, and may have slight diagonal striations as well, but no signs of manufacture. (CW-J)
L 110mm; W 55mm; Th 23mm.
C105, Phase: 8 EPM, Area: 203–4/862–3.

CT13 (Figure 24.3)
Hone/pounder/sharpening stone produced from an elongated ovoid sandstone cobble, unmodified prior to use. One edge is distinctly concave, with smoothing and polish from extensive use as a hone. A linear area of abrasion continues from this facet onto the tip of one rounded end, overlapping a small oval pitted area (15.5mm x 9mm) from expedient use as a pounder. A similar circular pitted facet (7mm x 5.5mm) is present on the opposite rounded end. Both faces have also been utilised: one flattened and one concave face have been lightly abraded and smoothed from use as a hone. A series of short sharpening grooves are present on three long edges, cross-cutting early use-wear. (DMcL)
L 128mm; W 29–35.5mm; Th 15.5–28mm.
C450, Phase: 8 EPM, Area: 182–4/847–9.

CT14 (Figure 24.3)
Possible hone in fine sandstone. Small flat tapering sub-rectangular fragment of a larger cobble, both ends and one side damaged in antiquity. The remaining surfaces are naturally flat, but with light surface striations, which may be the result of use. (DMcL)
L 39mm; W 34mm; Th 17mm.
C1121, Phase 9: LPM, Area: 190.25–5.75/844.5–6.5.

Ground wedge-shaped tools

There are three wedge-shaped pieces. Each is made on an angular piece of coarser sandstone, though there is considerable difference in the stones.

CT15 is double ended, but the ends are inclined to one another rather than on the same plane so that the tool is twisted, like a pivot, around a central point. It is made on a coarse sandstone and has clearly been carefully ground, but there is little sign of use, with the exception of a slight longitudinal groove on one face. Similar longitudinal grooves were noted on the faces of several hones from Whithorn, though no precise explanation could be found as to their origin (Nicholson 1997b, 455).

The other two pieces, CT16 and CT17, are more similar. CT16 is carefully worked, with a broad ground wedge end and a rougher, rounder butt. The butt-end has been ground and smoothed in one area, but it also has signs of much flaked damage. The wedge end is slightly flaked along the edge, perhaps as a result of use, but there is little other obvious damage from wear on this tool and it does not seem to have been subject to great pressure. CT17 is a smaller piece, in fine red sandstone. It is rectangular in shape and has been ground all over. The wedge end has no damage, but the opposite end is broken. The breakage of CT17 means that the original shape of the two artefacts cannot be compared, but it is interesting that the wedge ends are almost identical in size (76mm x 10mm). It is likely that these tools were used as hones.

The raw material of these pieces differs greatly from that of the other stone tools at The Hirsel. All three come from late contexts and it is possible that reworked masonry fragments were used for each. The form of CT16 is particularly suggestive of this, and the material is similar to other, larger masonry fragments from the site. CT16 and CT17 were found in close proximity to one another, CT15 was further away.

CT15 (Figure 24.4)
A coarse pink sandstone worked into an angular lozenge with two blunt axe-like ends. Twisted, the ends are slightly offset from one another. Size of ends: 46 x 10/44 x10mm. Only the final stages of manufacture are visible, when ground into shape. There is one slight groove running along one face. (CW-J)
Grinding stone, perhaps for smoothing timber? (DMcL)
L 154mm; W 42–64mm; Th 10–46.5mm.
C102, topsoil, Findspot: 202.78/861.16.

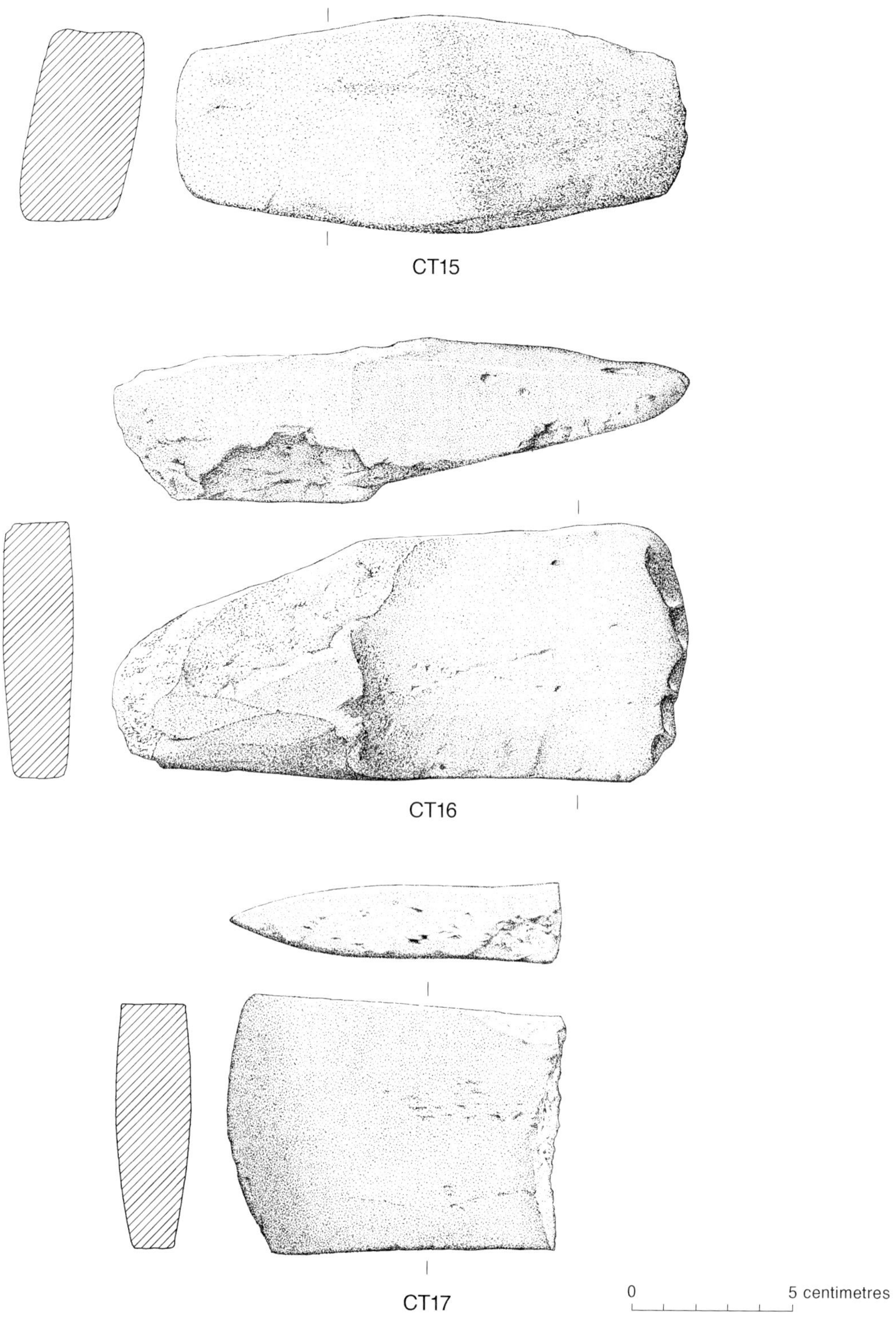

FIGURE 24.4
Wedge-shaped tools, CT15–17

CT16 (Figure 24.4)
Trapezoidal piece of medium yellow sandstone. Wedge shaped, round in section at one end, blunt wedge end at the other 76mm x 10mm, angle 80°: Only the final stages of manufacture can be seen. Smoothed or ground into shape, the rounded end shows faceting from the original smoothing, and the wedge end has some striations. Rough at the butt. Use marks: The 'blade', though blunt, has a series of small flakes removed from one face. An architectural piece, perhaps a window mullion, that has been reworked and used. Ground-stone wedge? (DMcL)
L 180mm; W 47–77mm; Th 16–44mm.
C1, topsoil, Area: 178–9/848–9.

CT17 (Figure 24.4)
Trapezoidal piece of medium red sandstone. Wedge shaped and broken, one end has been worked to a blunt 'blade', the other has fractured off. Size of the wedge end: 77mm x

10mm, angle 55°, ground or smoothed all over. The material is too smooth to have served as a woodworking wedge, and the lack of use-damage suggests that it was not used for heavy work. (CW-J)
L 103mm; W 76mm; Th 23mm.
C1, topsoil, Area: 174–5/846–7.

Rubbing stones

There are eight rubbing stones and they fall into two types: triangular and rounded. Three are made of tuff, three of tuffaceous sandstone and two of sandstone.

The rounded artefacts (CT18, CT20–22 and CT25) are larger and more irregular. They have less evidence of alteration prior to use, but each has a smoothed, striated surface. One (CT25) is very large and chunky; it is very smooth all over, though this may be due to natural rounding. CT20–22 are of a coarser stone, and each has an area of striations and smoothing. CT18 is also coarser and rounded, but it is broken, and one end is missing; it has a ground facet on each side at the broken end, and the other (complete) end is rounded. These pieces are quite heavy and chunky (see catalogue) and there are many uses to which they may have been put, from relatively 'soft' tasks such as leather- or linen-working to 'harder' tasks such as the working of bone or metal. It is, of course, possible that they served not one, but many purposes.

The triangular artefacts (CT19, CT23–24) are smaller and more particular in shape. They are flattish and triangular in plan, with one broad end and a blunt point opposite. The sides are flat, almost facetted, and may have been ground down. Despite the similarity of shape, there is less conformity of use-wear; one (CT24) has well developed longitudinal striations on both main faces, another (CT19) has possible slight striations on one face, running back from the broad blunt edge, and the third (CT23) has no clear signs of use. It seems that these tools have been used to different degrees for a similar task. Once again suggestions as to this use are pure speculation, though rubbing or smoothing were obviously involved.

The rubbing tools do not cluster in any particular period or area of the site, and there is no spatial grouping of the two types of tool.

CT18 (not illustrated)
Tuff rubbing stone. A rounded elongated cobble, oval cross section with two large faces. Broken, one end missing, side facets towards the break. The side facets may be ground. The rounded end is slightly smoothed and striated. (CW-J)
L 128mm; W 65mm; Th 37mm.
C715, Phase: 7 LM, Area: 196–8/824–6.

CT19 (not illustrated)
Sandstone rubber or smoothing stone. Rounded, triangular pebble, flat with two faces. Blunt point at one end and broad blunt edge at the other. Flat sides, facetted? Weight 105g. No signs of manufacture, the shape seems to be natural. Use marks: possible light diagonal striations run back from the broad edge on one face. (CW-J)
L 80mm; W 63mm; Th 17mm.
C715, Phase: 7 LM, Area: 198–200/824–6.

CT20 (not illustrated)
Sandstone smoothing stone or rubber. Elongated rounded pebble, broad at one end and pointed at the other. Two flattish surfaces. Weight 535g, no signs of intentional alteration, but longitudinal striations cover the larger of the flat surfaces.
L 133mm; W 59mm; Th 50mm.
C716, Phase: 6 Med, Area: 200–4/822–4.

CT21 (not illustrated)
Possible rubber (there are no signs of wear from hammering or pounding). Tuff. A rounded cobble, irregular shape, broader at one end than the other, rounded cross section. Weight 480g. No signs of manufacture. An area near to the narrower end is slightly smoothed and has faint striations round the tool. (CW-J)
L 124mm; W 58mm; Th 49mm.
C721, Phase: 6 Med, Area: 198–200/829–30.

CT22 (Figure 24.5)
Rubbing tool of tuffaceous sandstone. A rounded elongated cobble, oval cross section, wider at one end than the other, but not as exaggerated as some of the other pieces. Weight 595g. No signs of manufacture, but possible slight striations on the two faces. (CW-J)
L 120mm; W 65mm; Th 45mm.
C273, Phase: 6 Med, Area: 196–200/856–9.

CT23 (not illustrated)
Rubbing or smoother stone, tuffaceous sandstone. Rounded triangular pebble, two flattish faces, one end pointed, the other broad and blunt. Flat sides, facetted? No signs of manufacture, the shape seems to be natural, no signs of use. (CW-J)
L 94mm; W 62mm; Th 23mm.
C421, Phase: 8 EPM, Area: 188–90/845–7.

CT24 (Figure 24.5)
Possible grinding tool of tuffaceous sandstone. Ovoid sandstone cobble with round flattened widened end tapering to a narrow rounded tip. Both rounded convex faces are abraded, with irregular linear striations. This abrasion could be the result of use but is likely to be natural. (DMcL)
L 107mm; W 71mm; Th 32mm.
C803, Phase: 9 LPM, Area: 221–3/836–8.

CT25 (Figure 24.5)
Tuff rubbing stone, elongated irregular cobble, smoothed all over. Use marks: possible slight smoothing and striations. Weight 1035g. (CW-J)
L 180mm; W 60mm; Th 55mm.
C1, topsoil, Area: 170–1/842–3.

Pestle

This is a finely made tool of tuffaceous sandstone. It has been ground into a blunt conical shape with slight facets and areas of smoothing towards the point. It has apparently been broken across the

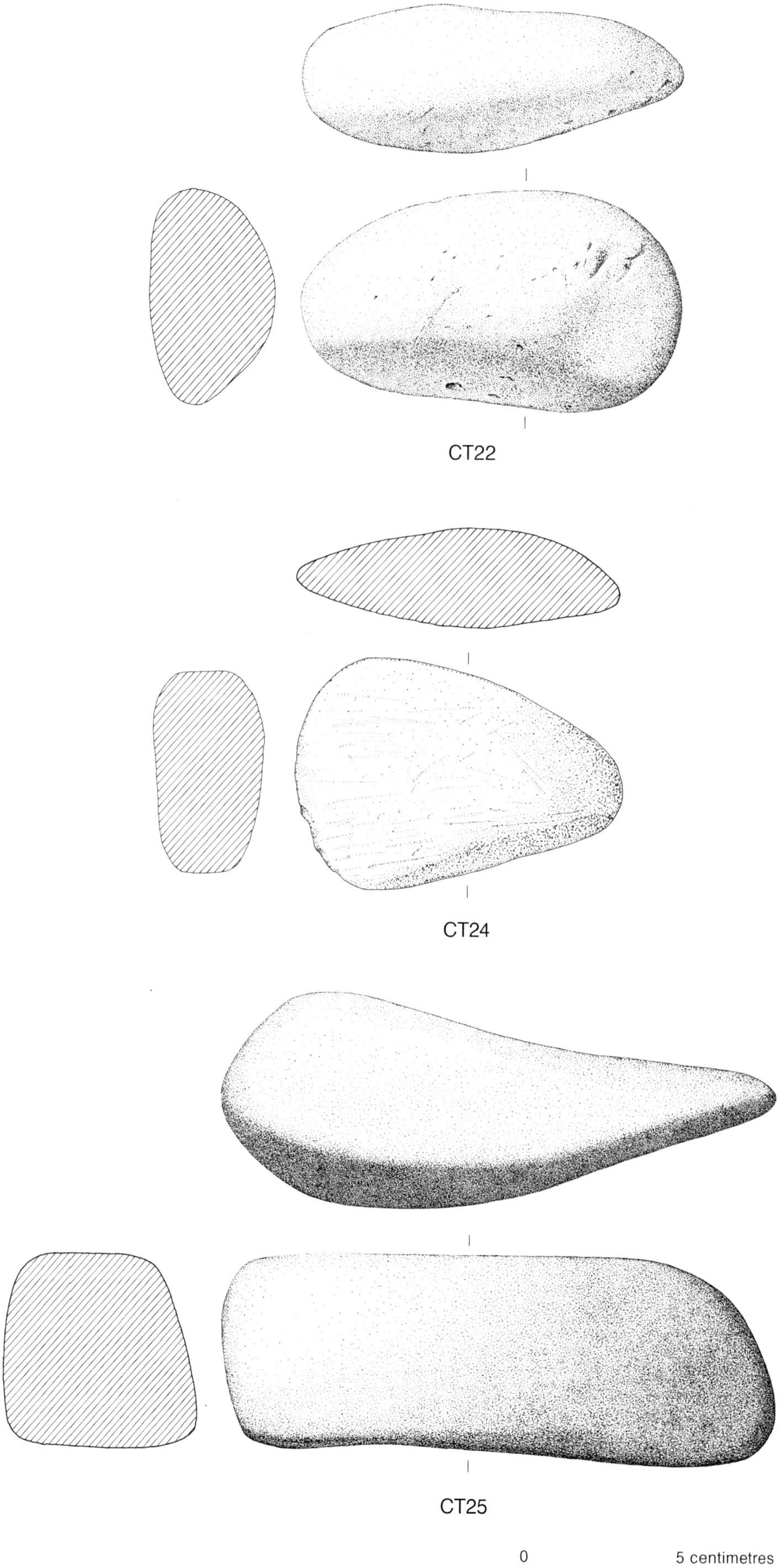

FIGURE 24.5
Rubbing stones, CT22–25

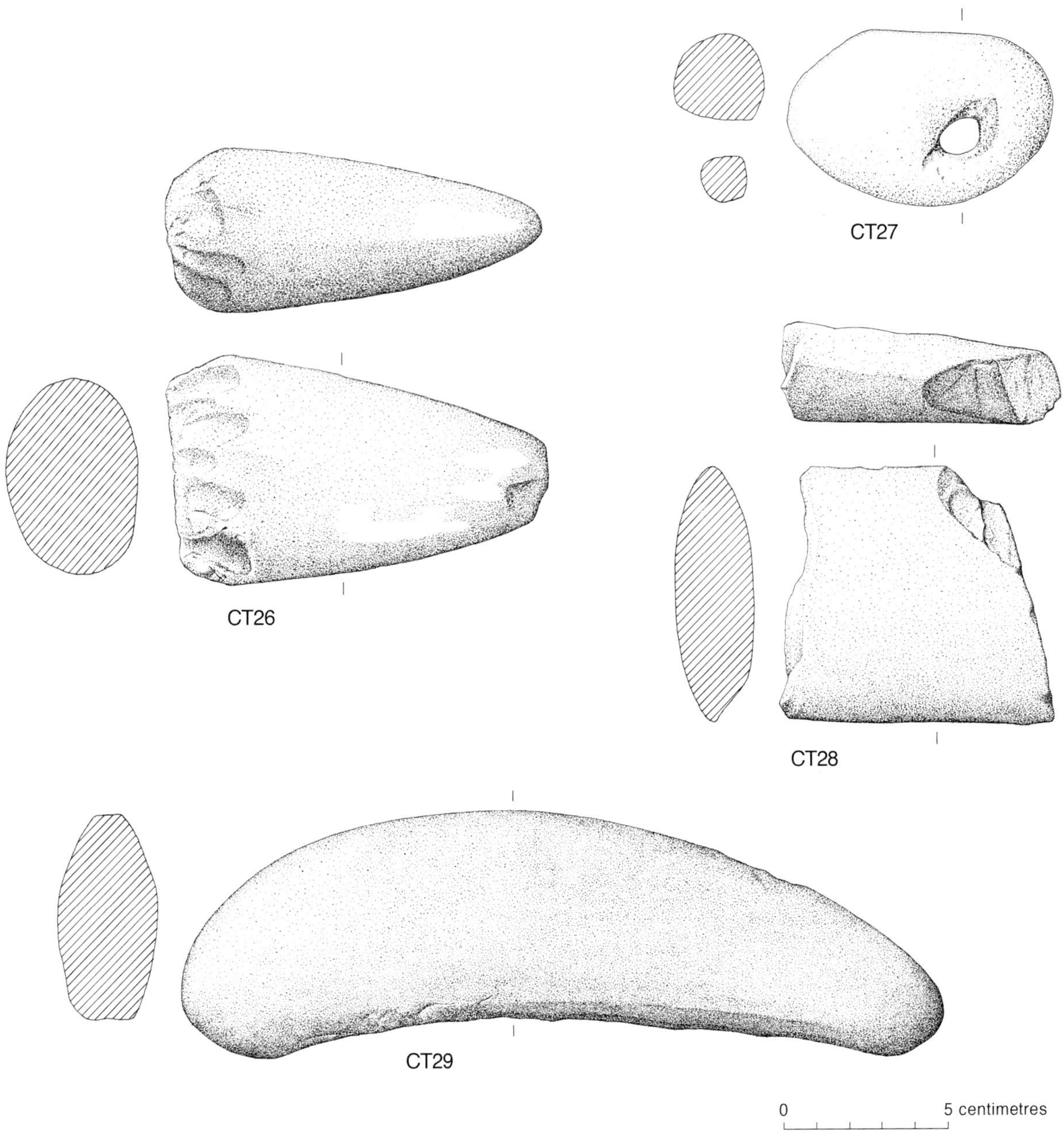

FIGURE 24.6
Reshaped Neolithic axehead CT26; weight for loom or fishing net CT27; broken ellipsoid bar, CT28; curved grinding tool, CT29

wider end, and subsequently flaked around the circumference of the tool, perhaps to modify the working end. Small flakes have also been removed from one side of the point, perhaps due to use. There is little other evidence of use-wear.

This is an enigmatic piece; the closest parallels come from Shetland, where similar pestles were found at Upper Scalloway, but they were made in a different manner (Ann Clarke pers comm). It is ard shaped, but it would be small for an ard point and the facets and smoothing are not characteristic of ards. It has been suggested that it may be a reworked prehistoric axe (Jill Harden pers comm); the material, shape, size and working would all be quite at home in this context. If this were so, the butt of the axe only is present, the blade has snapped away at about the level of the haft and the artefact was re-flaked round the break. The tool was recovered from an early medieval context with no other prehistoric material, though its reuse in later periods should not, of course, be ruled out.

CT26 (Figure 24.6)
Butt-end from Neolithic ground-stone axehead of tuffaceous sandstone, blade lost in antiquity and edge around fracture facet reworked. The butt-end of the axe forms a blunt oval tip which is pitted from later expedient use or damage. The surfaces of the stone at this end preserve the original facets

of the axehead with slight polish remaining despite later damage. Two distinct linear grooved facets on opposite edges (L 51mm; W 8–12mm) are surviving features of the axehead. The wide oval end created by the loss of the blade of the tool has been reshaped with the removal, by fracturing, of a series of regularly spaced flakes from the circumference of the break. This was clearly an attempt to reshape the stone, but for what purpose is unclear. It is likely that the original form and function of the stone was unknown at the time of its modification. (DMcL)
L 114mm; W 26.5–66mm; Th 12–45mm.
C248, Phase: 5 EM2, Area: 201–2/852–5.

Weight

There is one perforated weight, made on a small cobble of sandstone. There has been no attempt to round off the rather irregular shape of the pebble, and the perforation is to one end (taking advantage of a natural hollow in the piece), so that it could not have served as a drill-weight or spindle whorl. The perforation is very irregular. Likely functions include a net sinker or loom-weight.

The piece was found just outside the east end of the church structure and has been phased to the Early Medieval period, though it might also be related to the ploughing up of earlier prehistoric levels at this time. There is nothing chronologically significant about the weight.

CT27 (Figure 24.6)
Fine sandstone weight. A rounded irregular pebble. There are no obvious changes to the overall shape of the pebble. To one side, however, a natural hollow has been enlarged into a perforation. Interpretation: a weight, for a loom or fishing nets? As the piece is not symmetrical it cannot be a drill-weight, and it would be small for a thatch-weight. (CW-J)
L 83mm; W 52mm; Th 29mm.
C955, Phase: 6 Med, Findspot: 184.10/834.47.

Miscellaneous ground pieces

CT28 is a small broken artefact of fine-grained siltstone. It has been carefully ground all over to give two smooth curved faces and an oval cross section, but it is broken at both ends so that it is impossible to deduce the original shape or size. There is little wear that may have come from use.

CT29 is a large carefully made piece, also of a finer grained siltstone. It has been ground into a curved, 'boomerang' shape, with traces of faceting from the final shaping visible along the edges, though the inner curve has been subsequently slightly damaged; this may be an unfinished edge. The ends are slightly smoothed, possibly from use. This piece comes from a late context on the site, though the only parallel is a similar, smaller artefact of wood recovered from the much earlier (7th century) crannog site at Buiston, Ayrshire (Anne Crone pers comm). Various possible functions could be put forward for artefacts of this shape, but all are speculative.

CT28 (Figure 24.6)
Siltstone, angular in form, elipsoid in section, broken; both ends missing. Only the final phases are visible, finely ground and smoothed. There are a few striations visible that probably come from manufacture. No use marks, two grooves are probably more modern. Function unknown. (CW-J)
L 83mm; W 74mm; Th 28mm.
C207, Phase: 8 EPM, Area: 194–5/855–7.

CT29 (Figure 24.6)
Grinding tool/hone of flaggy siltstone. Flattened ovoid siltstone with rounded narrow tip, distinctly curved along length, expanding into a wide blunt end with faceted abrasion at the tip. Narrow bands of abrasion (W 16–20mm) from grinding are present on the external and internal curved edges of the rounded sides. This wear may be the result of shaping or smoothing of the edges but reasons for this are not clear. Curved bands of smoothing and light polish are present on both faces adjacent to the internal curved edge, probably the result of use as a hone. (DMcL)
L 230mm; W 60mm; Th 33mm; Weight 680g.
C51, topsoil, Findspot: 196/844.

Discussion

The assemblage comprises a variety of cobble tools of mixed functions. Some have made use of the natural shape of the original blanks, others have been carefully shaped by grinding, and in one case, flaking. The cobbles are of local materials, different grain sizes were apparently selected in accordance with the projected alteration and use of each artefact. There is no spatial or chronological clustering of the artefacts; they are spread across the site, and throughout its different periods.

Cobble tools like this occur on many sites, though they are rarely examined in detail, and the rougher versions may often be overlooked. Excavations where they are considered in detail are still few and far between, but one of the most useful studies has been that of the material from Whithorn where a variety of hones and other artefacts were recovered (Nicholson 1997b, 453–459). The finer hones are also known from other sites such as the excavations at Hoddom and Finlaggan, though their wider implications are discussed outwith this report.

Rubbing stones also occur on other sites such as Whithorn (Nicholson 1997b, 459), though there are no exact parallels for the pieces from The Hirsel. It may be that rubbing stones were usually made with a minimum of alteration on local blanks, and therefore reflect more local conditions. (CW-J)

Many of these cobble tools show multifunctional use (CT7, CT10, CT13, CT29). All had been used primarily as honestones, typically used for sharpening metal blades. Polish and staining indicates secondary use as smoothers for leatherworking, sharpening grooves from blade sharpening and pitting from pounding.

Few of the stone tools are chronologically distinctive. The honestones and multifunction tools produced from unmodified cobbles have a long currency of use from the prehistoric through to the post-medieval periods. One distinctive early prehistoric stone tool is present; a modified Neolithic ground-stone axe fragment (CT26). Only the butt-end of the axe now remains and has been significantly reshaped for an alternative function. The blade-end of the tool has been lost, probably in antiquity, long before it was rediscovered and modified. This object was recovered from an early medieval context and it is possible that the reshaping of the axe took place during this period. The function of the tool after the shape was modified is unclear as no later use-wear is present to identify its intended purpose. It may of course have had an amuletic role.

Several other enigmatic objects are present amongst the stone, including several ground-stone implements, possibly for use in carpentry or leatherworking (CT15, CT16 and CT29). This includes ground-stone wedges of varying textures such as CT15, a double sided wedge-shaped tool produced from coarse sandstone which may have been used as a grinder for smoothing flat timbers. An unusual flat curved siltstone tool (CT29) used as a honestone on both faces, has also been abraded in patches around the edges and at the tip of one end. It is unclear whether these ground facets represent an attempt to shape the stone, or have been formed as the result of use, but the level of smoothing and sheen on both faces may indicate use as a leatherworking tool.

Athough these tools are not datable on form alone, they are not typical of later prehistoric assemblages and are likely to be medieval or post-medieval in date. (DMcL)

Conclusion

The assemblage provides evidence for the use of cobble tools to fulfil a variety of tasks at The Hirsel. Local blanks were used for most of the tools, and in many cases the natural shape was left untouched. Some were altered before use, but many only became gradually worn into shape as they were used. A range of states of alteration and damage is therefore present.

These tools are likely to reflect artisanal craftwork; domestic, agricultural or industrial chores related to the everyday life of a rural community. As activity on site continued over a considerable period of time, the assemblage may be considered relatively small, and it is not surprising, perhaps, that there are no clear foci of spatial or temporal significance in the distribution of artefacts.

Predominant among the tasks carried out was honing or sharpening, presumably on a variety of objects of different sizes, functions and values. Rubbing or smoothing was also important and, for this, different types of cobble tool were necessary; precise details as to the types of material or task cannot be deduced. There are also several carefully shaped artefacts of uncertain function and it is likely that these relate to specific craftsman's duties that are no longer current or known to the author.

24.3 QUARTZ PEBBLES

Rosemary Cramp

The discovery of quartz pebbles on ecclesiastical sites, particularly in graves, is a well known phenomenon with their presence being seen as of possibly ritual significance by Crowe (1982), and this interpretation of their presence, including specifically Christian rites, has been considered in relation to most of the sites where quartz stones appear. Only a very few specimens were retrieved from The Hirsel in comparison with, for example, Whithorn where the massive deposition of such pebbles, some covering entire graves, has been fully discussed (Hill 1997, 472–473). At Barhobble, some 500 white quartz pebbles were recorded, some as strike-a-lights (Cormack 1995, 71, nos 41–43) and some associated with graves, and indeed they are described as 'the commonest grave good', with the numbers in each grave varying from nil to 20+ (Cormack 1995, 35). Some at that site are associated with the church structure, but, as at Whithorn, they seem to be widely dispersed throughout the site. At The Hirsel, the three from C691, C1253 and C785 are all from grave fills which could be from a range of dates: the fill of C691 also contained a flint, C1253 contained Tweed Valley Ware (type E3) pottery (12th–15th century). The graves from 1984 are probably some of the earliest excavated from the site and so far the earliest dated graves have been 11th century.

The presumption that this custom begins in the early Christian period and continues in a sporadic way throughout the Middle Ages is supported in Scotland not only at Whithorn and Barhobble but more recently at Inchmarnock as well as elsewhere in the Isle of Man and Ireland. Lowe in discussing the ten deposits at Inchmarnock points to the fact that in Ireland on sites such as Church Island and Reask such deposits point to a late medieval custom and he would date the Inchmarnock deposits as 'essentially post 12th century'(Lowe 2008, 268). This accords with the Hirsel evidence, but there is no doubt that the practice started earlier not only at Whithorn but also at Illaunloughan Island, Co. Kerry, where the deposition dates probably to the 7th to 8th centuries (White Marshall and Walsh 2005, 87–89). These authors come to the balanced conclusion: 'The deposition of white stones appears to be a spontaneous gesture rather than a formal ritual act, one based on popular belief, a cultural attitude that needed no discussion or official recognition' (White Marshall and Walsh 2005, 89). At The Hirsel, then, the appearance of such stones may be seen as a lingering conservative ritual.

It is difficult to be certain about the deliberate placing of other types of pebble in graves since the natural subsoil can be pebbly, but in nine other graves, pebbles are specifically recorded as being grave goods.

QP1 (not illustrated)
Quartz pebble. Elongated and irregular natural pebble.
35mm x 27mm.
C691, Phase: 5? EM2, grave fill of Sk252, Area: 205–7/836–8.

QP2 (not illustrated)
Quartz pebble. Elongated pebble with one rounded and one flattened broken end. Red ?haematite inclusion.
30mm x 20>12mm.
C1253, Phase: 6 Med, grave fill of Sk310, 191–2/835–6.

QP3 (not illustrated)
Quartz pebble. Irregular tapering pebble with one rounded and one broken end, with conspicuous red staining and veining.
The shape of this pebble with flat base and the flattened side suggest a tool and the hollowing on the broken tip could suggest a strike-a-light as at Barhobble where several such were found in graves. This pebble was the only inclusion in the fill of a grave which could belong to an early phase of the cemetery.
L 25mm; W 23>16mm; Th 22>10mm.
C785, Phase: 5? EM2, grave fill of Sk277, 200–2/825–6.

QP4 (not illustrated)
Quartz tool. Large pebble with signs of rubbing and wear on three faces and pitting on the end.
This piece fits neatly into the hand if used as a pounder as is evident also from the indentations in roughened end.
Found in graveyard soil containing disturbed burials and Scottish White Gritty ware.
63mm x 55mm x 45mm.
C740, Phase: 5 EM2, 196–8/822–4.

24.4 OTHER STONE OBJECTS

Rosemary Cramp

OS1 (Figure 24.7)
Gaming board. Local sandstone.
Fragment, with about half of the 'board' for merels incised with casual wavering lines on one face. These compose three concentric rectangles which are bisected on each side by lines at right angles and thus form a classic outline for the merels game of nine men's morris. The game is played with two players each using a set of nine, six, or three counters. The board for nine counters, as here, is the most complex: once the 18 pieces had been placed alternately on each intersection, the aim is to get three of one's pieces in a line (mill) (Parlett 1999, 109–112, fig 7.1g and fig 7.3). This allows the player then to remove one of his opponent's pieces. The game was popular from the 11th century throughout the Middle Ages, and because the board was easy to make and the pieces could have been simply small pebbles, such 'boards' are common on medieval sites throughout the British Isles. They are found in domestic and ecclesiastical settings, even on stone coffin lids (Mynard 1994, 156–157, fig 86; Croft 1987, 2, fig 3) and seemingly wherever workmen were present. In Scotland some of the earliest seem to be the three boards found on the island of Inchmarnock (Ritchie 2008, 119–123,127; for other sites in Scotland, see Robertson 1967). The Hirsel piece was found in the packing of a late posthole in the northern domestic area of the churchyard. Such boards are difficult to date, but the lack of diagonal lines linking the corners of the squares could mean that it was pre- *c*1400 (Parlett 1999, 118).
L 155>125mm; W 135mm; Th 35>25mm.
C209, Phase: 8 EPM, Findspot: 194.73/858.40.

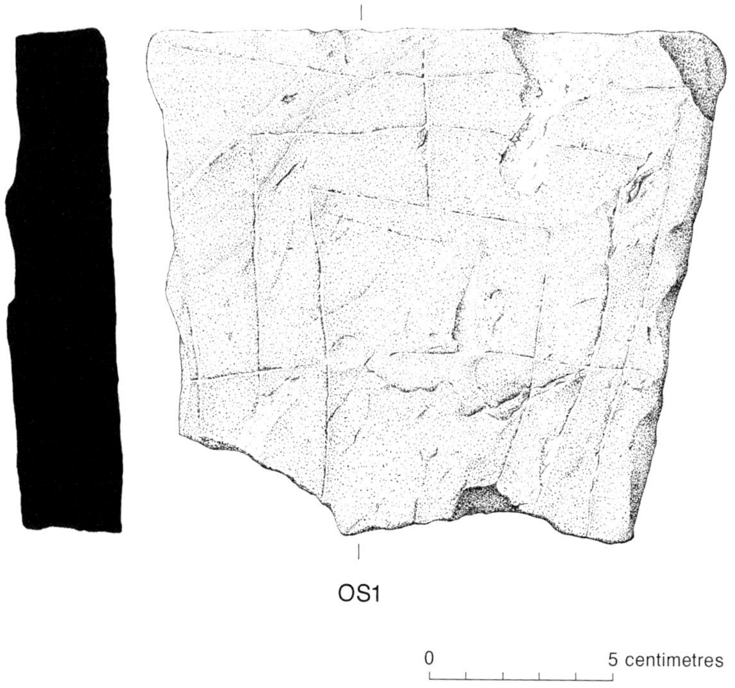

FIGURE 24.7
Gaming board for merels, OS1

FIGURE 24.8
Gaming board, OS2

FIGURE 24.9
Part of the upper stone of a rotary disc quern, OS4

OS2 (Figure 24.8)
Gaming Board of worn greyish sandstone.
Part of a rectangular block with two dressed and two broken faces. Slight traces of mortar cover what appears to be a board with squares and diagonals. The surface is broken off at one end and so the board out line may not be complete. There are small pecked holes near some intersections which may be intentional marks for the game.

This piece is like those boards found most recently at Inchmarnock, some of which were on the same stones as the merrels game (Ritchie 2008, fig 6.18). The boards with a grid of cells and diagonal lines have been identified by Ritchie as for the game of Alquerque, a predecessor of draughts (Ritchie 2008, 119; Parlett 1999, 121–123, 243–244). This piece had been built into the perimeter wall (C204) in the north of the site and in the same domestic area where the merrels board was also found.
L 365mm; W 210mm; Th 205mm.
C204, Phase: 7 LM, Findspot: 192.5/855.

OS3 (not illustrated)
?Gaming piece of dark black flecked sandstone.
Pebble, smooth and rounded. This could be a natural pebble but its size, distinctive colour and neat outline gives the impression of a made piece. It would be the right size to use as a counter in a board game, but it was not found in the same area of the site as OS1, although also in a secondary context in a spread of building rubble, medieval pottery and domestic objects south of the church.
Diam 22mm; Th 15mm.
C708, Phase: 7 LM, Area: 196–8/826–8.

OS4 (Figure 24.9)
Part of the upper stone of a rotary disc quern, coarse-grained sandstone with large quartz inclusions.

The stone has been roughly broken up and formed part of the foundation level of the dry-stone wall C646 where it met the north wall of the church. The upper surface and the rounded side are roughly finished with pecking and there

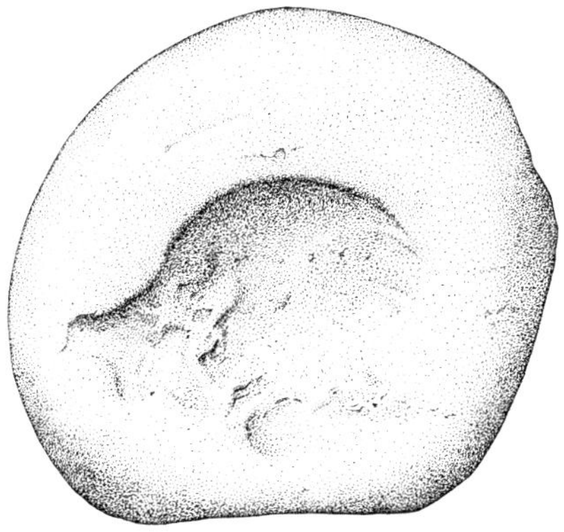

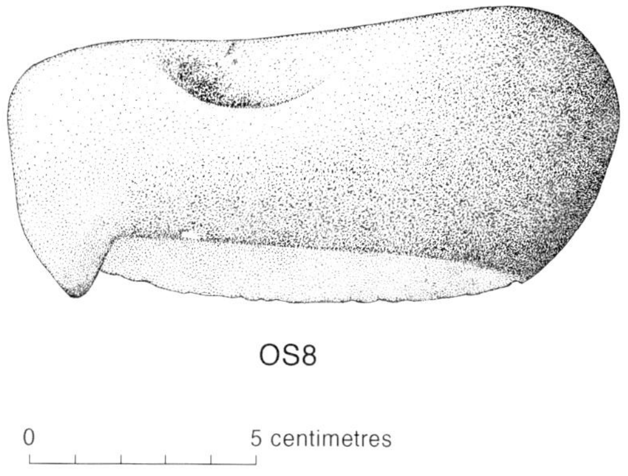

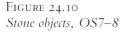

FIGURE 24.10
Stone objects, OS7–8

is a small shallow hole about 15mm deep near to the edge. The funnel-shaped central hole has been chipped out of shape, but on the smoothed lower surface of the stone is a lightly grooved concentric ring, about 30mm from the edge of the hole, which seems to be a wear-mark. This fragment has been interpreted as the upper stone because of the shallow hole in the top for a handle, and the slightly curved outline of the upper pecked surface. Such stones as part of disc rotary querns have been found in Scotland in contexts ranging from the Iron Age to early historic times. There is other evidence for prehistoric–early medieval activity on the site and this fragment is reminiscent of the stones found at Dunadd (Lane and Campbell 2000, 180–186), which are tentatively dated to the early medieval period. The study of the typological evolution of rotary querns has been mainly concentrated on the prehistoric to Roman periods (MacKie 1972, fig 3), but the later stones seem, like this one, to have larger funnels. Since this stone was found in the foundations of the earliest church on the site a date pre-10th century is appropriate.
L 225mm; W 240>160mm; Th 85>70mm.
Probable diam of hole: top 100mm< base 140mm.
C646, Phase: 5 EM2, Findspot: 204/837.

OS5 (not illustrated)
Grey sandstone, probably an erratic.
Pot lid, rounded, but tapering towards one corner. One face smooth and worked on part of the edge, the other face roughly tooled with indented sides. Such items are common on medieval sites and this piece was found with a large quantity of pottery and domestic rubbish amongst a patch of cobble in the northern domestic area of the site.
Diam 80>75mm; Th 24>12mm.
C1005, Phase: 7 LM, Area: 207.75–210/854–7.

OS6 (not illustrated)
Pot lid of local micaceous sandstone
A large, heavy lid crudely cut from a slab (possibly a stone tile) with two smooth faces. On the upper face are traces of an incised rectangle and on the lower some curving incised lines, the stone and tooling being typical of some of the architectural fragments of the Phase III church. It was found with a deposit of domestic rubbish in the upper surface of the SE section of the cemetery.
Diam 120>110mm; Th 300>250mm.
C710, Phase: 6 Med, Area: 203–10/820–30.

OS7 (Figure 24.10)
Possibly a lamp.
Smooth, irregularly shaped split pebble in coarse grit stone.
The base of the stone is rounded, and one side of the stone is flattened and indented as if by wear.
The cavity in the top is roughly pear shaped and the shaping appears to be man-made although this is not certain. Where the cavity tapers at a higher level there is a narrow runnel.
If this is a stone lamp it is a crude specimen, but the deeper cavity could be for oil and the runnel could have held the wick. Stone lamps such as this are known throughout the early medieval period and a 13th century specimen from Winchester (no. 3547; Barclay and Biddle 1990, 992–993) is a possible parallel since it is roughly hollowed to a D shape and has a similar narrow runnel. It has, however, a more stable base but the Hirsel specimen could have been hand held or set in a wall. There is no sign of burning on this piece, but Barclay notes that although pottery lamps from Winchester have signs of burning and some have visible residues, 'the stone lamps, by contrast, are rarely burnt and even more rarely encrusted with burnt residues'.
Found in a rubble and pebble spread at the west end of the site. The fact that this piece was found at the west end of the site with domestic rubbish could mean that it derives from a domestic context rather than from the church.
L 105mm; W 100mm; Th 45mm; Depth of cavity 15mm.
Date: Medieval, 12th–16th century.
C801, Phase: 7 LM, Area: 211–2/834.5–836.

OS8 (Figure 24.10)
Reworked river pebble.
The stone is curved with rounded ends. One face has been cut to a smooth flat surface, with a projecting 'stop' at one end, and on the opposite face, which is curved, there is a shallow depression with a rough base. This seems to be a tool, which if used in the other way up from the drawing could have served as a hammer with the first finger braced against the 'stop'.
Found in a spread of rubble over south wall of nave.
145mm x 60mm x 40mm.
Date: ?Late medieval.
C702, Phase: 7 LM, Area:198–200/828–829.5.

25
GLASS OBJECTS

25.1 ROMAN GLASS
Jennifer Price

A few fragments of Roman glass from the site supplemented the evidence from the pottery of the presence of Roman occupation nearby (see Section 16.2). RG3 was found in densely packed cobbles related to the robbing of the cemetery wall in the north. RG1 and RG2 were from grave fills which cut the earliest site levels investigated, to the west of the church. The context of RG1 (C845), early occupation level west of the church, disturbed by later graves and ploughing, also produced Roman and Bronze Age pottery and flint. The dates of these fragments, 1st to 2nd century AD, correspond well with the Roman pottery dating and that of the glass bangle (RG4).

The fragments RG1–3 come from the jars or bottles produced in vast numbers as containers for foodstuffs and other materials in the late 1st and 2nd centuries AD (see Price and Cottam 1998, 136–137; 191–202 for the forms and dates). Too little survives to be certain of the form of RG1, but RG3 is certainly from a bottle and RG2 comes from either a jar or a bottle with a square body or, less probably, a bottle with a rectangular body. Similar fragments have occasionally been noted in post-Roman monastic settlements, as at Whithorn (Price 1997) and also Wearmouth and Jarrow (Price 2006).

RG1 (not illustrated)
Blue/green thick-walled convex fragment, probably from shoulder of bottle.
24mm x 14mm x 7 mm.
C845, Phase 3–4 R–EM (disturbed), Findspot: 178.43/830.84.

RG2 (not illustrated)
Blue/green body fragment, prismatic, that is, square or rectangular body, probably a bottle, although it could be jar.
26mm x 8mm x 3mm.
C1287, Phase: 5 EM2, Findspot: 182.12/826.30.

RG3 (not illustrated)
Fragment of blue/green handle of bottle, the edge of an angular ribbon handle with vertical reeding. It could be a cylindrical or prismatic bottle.
18mm x 14mm x 7mm.
C1005, Phase: 7 LM, Area: 205.5–207.75/856–7.

RG4 (Figure 25.1)
Abraded fragment of a bangle in pale bluish green glass with dark blue and opaque white chevron trails marvered into the surface at the centre, and a half width trail along one edge. The type seems to be Kilbride-Jones 2 with dark blue and opaque white banding and is dated to the 1st–2nd century AD (Kilbride-Jones 1938), but the chevron form of the central band is not common, and is more like the decoration on decorative studs from post-Roman sites (Cramp 2006, 258–262). Bangles such as these are commonly found on native sites in northern England and Scotland (Price 1988), as well as in Anglo-Saxon graves and on later ecclesiastical sites such as Barhobble (Cormack 1995, 72 and fig 36/1); Whithorn (Price 1997, fig 10.1); Wearmouth (Cramp 2006, 31.4/1) or Whitby, where they have been considered either as cullet or as keepsakes (Price 1997, 294–295). Found in topsoil from the west of the site.
23mm x 14mm, D-shaped section, Width 8mm.
C901, topsoil, Area: 175–7/835–7.

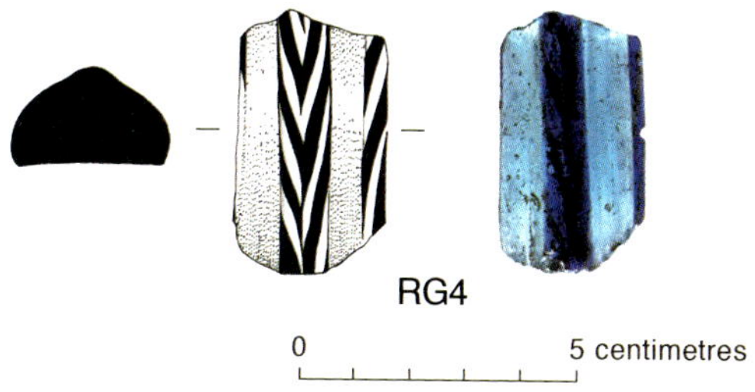

FIGURE 25.1
Roman glass bangle, RG4

25.2 MEDIEVAL AND POST-MEDIEVAL VESSEL GLASS
Rosemary Cramp

These fragments are too small and distorted to be closely dated, but Gl1 and Gl2 should be medieval, with Gl3 possibly 16th–17th century.

Gl1 (not illustrated)
Glass fragment, heat warped and discoloured in medium thick colourless metal.
From burnt level in the nave of the church.
22mm x 8mm x 2mm.
C1260, Phase: 7 LM, Findspot: 191.18/831.65.

Gl2 (not illustrated)
Two fragments of thin-walled glass vessel in clear colourless glass with ribbing, possibly part of a bowl.
Redeposited in curving stone feature.
21mm x 18mm x 2>1mm.
19mm x 17mm x 1mm.
C1124, Phase: 8 EPM, Area: 190.5–195.5/840.5–842.

Gl3 (not illustrated)
Part of the body of a thick-walled vessel in white/colourless glass, with attached coil, probably part of a drinking vessel.
Found in topsoil from the domestic area in the north of the site.
20mm x 20mm x 16mm.
C102, topsoil, Area: 197–8/864–5.

26

EXAMINATION AND ANALYSIS OF THE BELL MOULD

Philip Clogg

This report details the examination and analysis of 250 fired clay mould fragments and associated copper-alloy fragments from excavations in 1984 at The Hirsel. The material originates from two pits, C898 and C1348, cut through the floor at the western end of the church. Pit 898 was considered to be a bell-casting pit with associated flue and a ledge on which the mouth of the bell mould would have rested. The majority of the mould fragments were excavated from this pit. The second pit, C1348, contained the largest intact piece of mould, from the mouth of the bell, and a quantity of copper-alloy fragments.

26.1 MATERIAL DESCRIPTION

The fragments from C898 ranged in size from 10mm x 10mm, to 150mm x 130mm. The cross section of the fragments showed a clear colour change from a red/orange outer layer through light and dark grey to a final thin black inner layer. This black inner layer was covered in a series of very fine parallel striations. Traces of green copper corrosion product were visible on a number of fragments.

The large piece of mould fragment from C1347 was block-lifted on site to allow a more controlled excavation in the conservation laboratories at Durham University. The examination revealed the mould to be from the mouth of the bell, from an area where the inner and outer moulds would have joined. A quantity of copper-alloy waste was also retrieved from C1347 and much of it was in the form of 'dribbles' or runs, clearly the remains of a casting process.

26.2 ANALYSIS OF THE COPPER-ALLOY FRAGMENTS

Elemental analysis was undertaken to confirm that the material was of a bell metal composition and that the materials from C898 and C1347 were related in composition. Samples were taken of the copper alloy found in the crevices of the mould fragments from C898 and C1347 and from the more substantial fragments from C1347. Where possible, the samples were taken from the sound metallic portion of the fragments. Initial analysis was undertaken by atomic absorption spectrophotometry (AAS) by the Chemistry Department at Durham University for the elements copper, tin, lead and zinc. Later and more extensive analysis was undertaken by energy dispersive X-ray fluorescence (EDXRF) in the Archaeology Department at Durham using an Oxford Instruments ED2000 spectrometer. The analysis focussed on identifying the concentrations of the main alloying elements copper, tin and lead and the minor and trace components iron, zinc and antimony. The results are shown in Figure 26.1.

The compositional analysis of the copper alloy indicates that the material from both contexts is likely to be from the same casting event, there being little deviation in the levels of the main alloying elements and a similar minor/trace element pattern.

Sample	Date	Cu	Sn	Zn	Pb	Fe	Sb
Hirsel from 1347		72.16	25.1	n.d.	1.29	<0.1	0.35
Hirsel from 898		72.74	25.02	n.d.	0.97	<0.1	0.37
Hirsel from mould		72.29	25.27	n.d.	1.56	<0.1	0.38
Hirsel from mould		72.01	25.31	n.d.	1.24	<0.1	0.34
Hedeby	8th–11thC		17.37	0.09	6.56	n.a.	n.a.
Winchester	10thC		18.75	<0.1	4.35	n.a.	n.a.
Gloucester	*c*900	84.5	13.9	1.9	1	1.2	n.a.
Cheddar	12thC		20	n.a.	n.a.	n.a.	n.a.
Thurgarton	12thC		22–25.5	1–2	3.5–4.5	n.a.	n.a.
Winchester	13thC		23	n.a.	n.a.	n.a.	n.a.
Chichester	14thC		24	0.03	2.7	n.a.	n.a.
Norton Priory	Medieval		20	n.a.	n.a.	n.a.	n.a.

FIGURE 26.1
Results of the EDXRF analysis of the Hirsel samples and a comparison with other published results. n.d. = not detected, n.a. = no figures

The analysis also confirms that the metal used in the casting process was of a composition known as a 'bell metal'. Theophilus (Hawthorne and Smith 1979) gives a recipe for bell metal as 'four parts of copper and a fifth of tin' which equates to 20% tin, although it would appear that the level of tin can vary between 20 and 26% depending upon the preference of the bell founder (Hiscox 1916). Comparison with other analysis of archaeological bell metals shows the Hirsel material to have slightly elevated tin levels which appears to be consistent with it being 12th/13th century and lower lead levels would have imparted a resonance to the sound.

26.3 EXAMINATION OF THE MOULD FRAGMENTS

The majority of the mould fragments were too small to give any accurate information as regards the form or the curvature of the bell, however those that were clearly curved were concave and there was no evidence of any convex material suggesting an absence of material from the inner or core of the mould. A number did show an intact cross section and thus provide an indication that the thickness of the mould varied between 3cm and 5cm. The colour variation over the cross section reflects the firing conditions with the red oxidised layer on the outside and a gradual change to the black reducing conditions on the inside of the mould fragments.

Microscopic examination of the thin black inner surface revealed fine parallel striations which could be associated with the brushing on to the bell pattern of the first fine clay layer.

There was evidence in the form of impressions within the surface that the clay had been tempered with an organic material which would have allowed the hot gasses to escape during the casting process. However no organic material was recoverable for further analysis/identification.

The two largest fragments, one from C898 (referred to as fragment A) and one from C1347 (referred to as fragment B) were substantial enough to provide some metrical information on the form of the bell which, together with the dimensions of the casting pit, allows for a reasonably accurate dimensional reconstruction to be made.

The inner surface of the fragment A showed concave curvature in two planes at right angles to each other which suggests that the piece is from the outer mould (the cope) and from the shoulder area of the bell. This gives an indication that the outside diameter of the bell at the shoulder was in the region of 20cm.

Fragment B is more substantial and is clearly from the mouth of the bell where the inner and outer moulds join, that is, the core and the cope. From this, it is possible to obtain an indication that the diameter of the mouth of the bell was in the region of 40cm. This correlates well with the relevant dimensions from the plan of the excavated feature. Considering these two dimensions and assuming the form of the bell to be fairly standard provides an indication that the height of the bell would have been in the region of 35cm. Also of significant interest was the observation that the core and the cope extended beyond the bell mouth edge and here they were joined with additional clay, sealing the two together and thus preventing any separation of the core and the cope and the removal of any pattern before casting. This suggests therefore that manufacture was by the *cire perdue* or lost wax process as described by Theophilus (Hawthorne and Smith 1979).

26.4 MANUFACTURE OF BELLS

There are four main literary sources that provide descriptions of the production and manufacture of bells in antiquity: Theophilus (*c*1110–*c*1140), Biringuccio (1540), Agricola (1556) and Kricka (1570). In all sources the techniques are broadly similar with differences occurring mainly with the preparation of the pattern and mould. Biringuccio, for example, highlighted the fact that wax, especially for large bells, was expensive and therefore there is the establishment of the loam pattern technique in which a fine loam would be used in place of wax.

As it has been suggested that the Hirsel bell was cast using the *cire perdue* technique, then, in order to fully appreciate the evidence gathered, it is useful to review the main points of bell production as described by Theophilus. The process is as follows:

— A mould of desired shape was made of clay (the core) and hung from a spindle on two timber uprights. Sheets of tallow or wax were then laid over this mould to the required thickness and then covered with clay (the cope). The inner core was hollowed out to reduce the weight and permit the firing of the clay. The mould was then fitted with attachments for the clapper inside and the suspension outside and bound together for stability.

— A pit was dug and a foundation of stone and clay made at the base on which the bell mould would stand. The mould was lowered into the pit and fuel was heaped around the mould and fired. When the tallow had melted away, the furnace was covered and the mould fired for a day and a night to harden.

— The bell metal was melted and prepared nearby in a crucible.

— When all was ready the hot metal was poured or ladled swiftly into the mould aperture.

— When the metal had solidified the mould was removed from the pit and the inner mould was hacked out and the bell allowed to cool. The outer mould was then removed and the bell was smoothed down.

Evidence for bell production

A number of bell-casting pits, mould fragments and associated copper-alloy waste have been identified within the archaeological record. Some of this material has undergone detailed examination and the published studies are useful to review for considering the Hirsel material in its wider context.

Blagg (1974) suggests that the bell-casting 'pit' or furnace can take two forms, although there appears to be many local variations. The first type is described as the horizontal draught furnace where a channel runs all the way through a central area in which the bell mould is supported normally on stone blocks. Examples of this type are seen at Winchester, Exeter and Diever (Blagg 1974).

The second type consists of a circular pit with one flue and stoke-hole which operates as an up draught kiln rather than a through draught. Examples of this type are seen at Cheddar (Rahtz 1979), Gloucester (Bayley *et al* 1993) and San Paolo pit 1(Blagg 1974).

The feature excavated at The Hirsel is clearly of the second type with a raised ledge on which the bell mould would have been positioned, rather than standing on blocks of stone as was the case of the Gloucester bell pit. The position of the Hirsel bell pit in the western end of the church is also consistent with the held idea that the bell would have been cast as near as possible to where it would have been hung in order to cut down on transport and the possibility of damage.

27

SITE SUMMARY AND EVALUATION WITHIN THE WIDER BRITISH CONTEXT

Rosemary Cramp

27.1 INTRODUCTION

The interim reports of this excavation (Cramp 1980–85) concentrated on the phases of development of the church, and despite the lapse of time since, no close parallels for the development of the building plan for an estate church and the subsequent analysis of the sequences of its use have been forthcoming, although there have been many important excavations of ecclesiastical sites in Scotland in the last twenty years. Most evidence for the development of ecclesiastical architecture in Scotland has been derived either from monastic sites or from some of the cathedrals, and it is at these sites also where most excavation has taken place. The massive destruction of medieval churches of all types in Scotland has ensured that there are less standing examples of parish churches than there are in England (McRoberts 1959), although the ruins of many survive in the later kirkyards and more were recorded in the 19th century (Ferguson 1892). Indeed, targeted excavation at some of these sites could be very informative. However, recently an ongoing research project *Corpus of Scottish medieval parish churches* (published in the website Fawcett *et al* 2008) has revealed that more medieval fabric in churches in use has survived the zeal of the Reformation than had been thought hitherto. In addition, the excavation of sites such as Whithorn (Hill 1997), Barhobble (Cormack 1995), The Isle of May (James and Yeoman 2008), Auldhame (Hindmarsh and Melikian 2008; Crone *et al* forthcoming), Inchmarnock (Lowe 2008) and Portmahomack (Carver 2008), have all contributed valuable new evidence, which has informed this report and is considered further in the medieval section below, but the status and sequences of the buildings and their occupation on these sites are not closely comparable to the estate church at The Hirsel.

Despite the lack of documentary evidence for the church in Scotland in the 10th and 11th centuries, it is clear both from written and archaeological evidence that by the 12th century the monastic and parochial churches must have varied greatly in scale and the detail of their life history, and the rise and demise of the church at The Hirsel is probably to be seen as an individual rather than a typical case history, although there are parallels with the life history of the church at Barhobble, Mochrum, where the site may have originally been monastic, but later fell into lay hands and developed as a proprietory church with a burial ground (Cormack 1995, 54–55).

The burial ground, which was the other major feature of the site as excavated, is more closely paralleled on other sites in Britain. The release into the public domain of the pathological report on The Hirsel burials (Anderson 1994), as commissioned by Historic Scotland, provided an important body of comparative evidence for medieval rural communities in Scotland which has been well utilised by researchers, although more modern techniques of analysis have been used to refine data in subsequent reports from other sites such as that from Auldhame (forthcoming). The lapse of time since the excavation has then produced one beneficial effect, in that it has provided the opportunity to consider the wider context of the church and associated area of the cemetery with the help of more recent excavations, although the changing status and functions of this church, including its relationship to the surrounding community, still leave many unanswered questions. This is hardly surprising when one considers the limited area which was excavated, and the wider indications of settlement which the electronic surveys produced.

It seems likely, however, that the secular buildings of the community which this church and cemetery served were tantalisingly close at hand. There were, as noted in Chapter 2 (p 21), indications of secular occupation to the west and south-west of the church in all periods, and the phosphate survey (Section 3.4) provided high readings to the west and immediately south-west of the church, although these could not be related to a specific period. Neither could the features revealed in the geophysical surveys (Section 3.2), which suggest in addition that there was occupation well to the south of the site, in an area not otherwise investigated. The episodes of ploughing, and, in the post-medieval period, movement and dumping of soil and stone debris, have blurred the sequential picture, but it is possible to suggest broad periods of change on the site in which the activity of the population around the enclosed space of the church and cemetery impinged on the area excavated.

27.2 THE PREHISTORIC AND EARLY HISTORIC PERIODS

Phase 1, Neolithic

Evidence for occupation in this period is confined to a very limited area of the site, outside the cemetery enclosure in the north, but here the evidence for flimsy enclosures and the nature of the content of the pottery indicate occupation rather than burial (Chapters 4 and 15), and the site seems to fit into the pattern of others, more extensively explored in North Northumberland and the Borders (Miket *et al* 2009, illus 40; Johnson and Waddington 2009, illus 8). Barclay has reviewed the rather scanty evidence for Neolithic settlement in the Lowlands of Scotland, and his map (2003, fig 8.1) shows The Hirsel as a rather lonely outlier in the east. The scatter of small postholes on sites in the south-east, with some in curving arcs, such as Beckton, Biggar and Cowie, bear some resemblance to the features excavated at The Hirsel. Domestic activity could have been more extensive if one considers the artefact scatter of pottery and flints on the site (Figure 4.13). The flints are more widely scattered than the pottery, although they tend to cluster in the north and west, but cannot be more closely assigned a date than 'Later Neolithic to Bronze Age' (Chapter 23). Whether there was a break or continuation in occupation of this river bank site in the later prehistoric period is, however, not clear. There seems to be evidence for the growth of scrub and other vegetation (Figures 4.11 and 4.12) where the site was excavated to natural in the north and west, and prehistoric levels were not revealed under the cemetery and churches, but in places this was no doubt because the excavation was not deep enough. There are, however, a few sherds which could be Bronze Age in date (Chapter 15) and these could possibly indicate a continuing occupation nearby which might bridge the long gap between the Neolithic and the Roman Iron Age, but there is no close conjunction here between early prehistoric and early Christian remains, as for example on the site at Ardnadam (Rennie 1984, fig 15). There was no evidence to suggest any remembrance of a Neolithic focus, although the association of such with a later burial site is a not infrequent phenomenon elsewhere, but usually there are some visible surface remains such as barrows or henges (see Hope-Taylor 1977; O'Brien 1999, 60–70 and 76, maps 16 and 18). Whether the church was directly located over some earlier ritual focus, as has been suggested is commonly the case in Wales (see Edwards 1996, 52–53 and fig 3.2), is impossible to say without further excavation.

Phase 2, Late prehistory

Within the estate the evidence for activity in later prehistory is to be found in the hill-top enclosure of Hirsel Law which dominated the surrounding landscape and continued to influence estate divisions throughout the Middle Ages, as discussed in Chapter 2. Evidence for continuing settlement in the Bronze Age and Iron Age in the area excavated is too slight to postulate occupation on the site, as mentioned above, but there could have been a shift of settlement to the northern area of the estate where enclosures/hut circles have been noted by the Royal Commission (Figure 2.3), although only further intensive field work around Hirsel Law could clarify this. The transition found elsewhere from pagan 'Iron Age' to an early medieval Christian site (see for a recent summary Barrowman 2011, 192–194), was probably disrupted by the Roman intervention in the region.

Phase 3, Roman/sub-Roman

The evidence for a Roman presence in the vicinity was revealed in the incidental disturbances of the lower site levels, and artefacts (mainly pottery) have been scattered by the plough across the site, yet this remains a significant episode, as Bidwell points out, and the evidence includes not only pottery but a little vessel glass and a glass bangle (see Chapter 16 and Section 25.1). After the withdrawal of the Roman frontier further south, the region probably reverted to a native Iron Age life-style (Clarkson 2010, 18–27) and it is possible that Hirsel Law was occupied at this time, but, as Haselgrove has remarked in his survey and excavation of the Traprain Law environs, '...as the Whittingehame excavations demonstrated, sites occupied in the late and post-Roman periods are inherently difficult to recognise...' (Haselgrove 2009, 232). Indeed it would need as extensive an exploration of the estate in relation to Hirsel Law as he undertook in relation to Traprain Law in order to be able to test whether there were regular shifts in settlement areas within a defined territory over millennia. The after-life of hillforts in the Borders has been briefly considered recently (Oswald *et al* 2006, 101–118), but the rectangular buildings which cut across the enclosure at The Hirsel have only been identified by aerial photography and could be of any post-prehistoric date (Chapter 2). What is so remarkable, however, in the case of Hirsel Law, is not its structures but the documentary evidence for its use as an assembly place for the mustering and disbanding of armies, for legal activity and for executions which continued as late as the 16th century.

27.3 MEDIEVAL

The above is only broad brush evidence for a long period of time, the detailed investigation on this site was contained within a relatively short time scale, with a concentration on small changes of use and movement of focus in one building and its surrounding cemetery in the early historic and medieval periods (Phases 4–7). Although there is the same problem of plough movement as for all periods, where the artefactual evidence is more substantial, patterns of activity do seem to emerge. There are a few vestiges of gulleys and ditches which are cut by the church and cemetery which could be prehistoric or early historic (Figure 4.15). The early medieval period (Phases 4 and 5) is, however, characterised by the earliest medieval pottery (Group 1) and there is a marked concentration of this type in the west and north-east of the site and in the ditch/pit (C1386), which is the earliest identified medieval feature.

In Phase 6, which spans the 12th–14th centuries, the large concentrations of domestic pottery of groups 2 and 3 are focussed also on the west and north-east of the site, the latter area being where domestic buildings were identified and further activity has been postulated (Figure 7.6). The impression that on the west one is near to an occupation zone is strengthened, as noted above, by the distribution of animal bones on the site (see Section 10.2, Figure 10.11). In the pre- and early medieval periods the west of the site is the only area producing animal bone. In the mid-12th to early 14th century there is activity across the site but a marked concentration in the north and north-west of the site around the domestic buildings, but with continuing activity in the west. In the late medieval period only the western area is producing any significant quantity of animal bone. In the post-medieval phases the animal bone is spread around the site as rubbish.

27.4 THE CHURCH, ITS DEVELOPMENT AND SIGNIFICANCE

Phases 4–7

The nature of the site before the advent of the church and cemetery is, then, still uncertain. The topography of the site has been discussed in Chapter 2 where it is postulated that it was sited near to a river crossing and probably adjacent to an estate centre. Although, as stated above, there could be earlier levels beneath and around the west end of the Phase III church, where a reddish soil containing a good deal of carbon indicates occupation, it is equally possible that this deposit could be contemporary with the first church which lay further east, and there the sand and gravel into which the first church was cut seems to be virgin ground. In discussing the nature of this church, its antecedents in Scotland should be considered.

The earliest structures which have been claimed as churches in north Britain have been found in late Roman or sub-Roman contexts. Ian Smith (1990, 106–116) presented a detailed argument suggesting that the round-ended, single-cell structures found on native sites in north Britain, mainly in Cumbria and the Borders, could be churches. He noted especially one such structure at Traprain Law, period 2 IV (Smith 1990, 204–215, fig 5.5), and also postulated one on the native site of Dod Law, illustrating this with comparative plans of round-ended buildings on native sites (Smith 1990, fig 4.19). He was, however, careful to claim only that such buildings 'find a reasonable context alongside other small British and Irish churches, as too a number of Roman churches whose liturgical function has been demonstrated by excavation, and more often, an association with burials' (Smith 1990, 114). This does seem to be a form common to several types of Roman ritual buildings and Smith mentioned the forms of mithraea and mausolea in wall forts, including Newstead (Smith 1990, 109–110). The identification of at least some of such buildings as churches has, however, been claimed more recently for similar structures within forts along Hadrian's Wall. At Vindolanda, a round-ended building was constructed over the ruins of the Commanding Officer's courtyard and produced what may be a portable altar or a pax (Birley 2009, figs 106 and 107) and similar buildings have been found at South Shields and possibly Housesteads. This type of rectangular single-celled round-ended building cannot be seen as a model for The Hirsel, however, where the apsidal end is clearly an addition to a small squarish structure and in fact, as a type, the Roman form seems to reach a dead end in the early historic period.

In the period when the eastern shires in the Tweed basin formed part of the patrimony of St Cuthbert (Chapter 2), the earliest churches which can be positively identified are of timber, dating probably from the 7th–8th century, as excavated at Yeavering, Northumberland (Hope-Taylor 1977, figs 78 and 79) and as revealed by aerial photography at Whitmuirhaugh near Sprouston in the Tweed valley (Figure 1.1 and Smith 1990, 217–236). Their two-cell plans are similar to contemporary Anglo-Saxon secular buildings as for example at Yeavering, where both the suggested church and secular buildings consist of rectangular structures with squared annexes against the narrow ends. (Such a plan is also found in the earliest stone churches of Northumbria such as Wearmouth/Jarrow or Escomb.) Yeavering can be convincingly assigned to the 7th to 8th century, and it is noteworthy that both of these churches appear to have an associated cemetery. Yeavering was a royal site, but it can be suggested that Sprouston was an estate church, which in form mirrors the domestic architecture of its time and status. Its spaced post-construction could however have been more expensive to build than the earth-bonded river cobbles of the Phase I and II churches at The Hirsel, but these could equally well have mirrored the simple domestic buildings of the estate. The domestic building excavated near to the wall on the north of the site (Chapter 7) was indeed a dry-stone structure.

There is no evidence at The Hirsel for a timber predecessor before the Phase I church was built, as is suggested for some other churches in Scotland. For example at St Ethernan's monastery, Isle of May, it is suggested that there could have been a timber predecessor to the first stone church, which is dated to the 10th century and, like The Hirsel, is squarish (potentially measuring 3.2m N–S by at least 4m E–W) and with clay-bonded walls (James and Yeoman 2008, 38–39). At Ardwall, in western Scotland, the timber structure phase II was defined by four/possibly five postholes, and measured only around 11ft x 7.5ft (3.35m x 2.26m) (Thomas 1967, 139 and fig 26).

At The Hirsel, the first small single-celled structure has been compared in plan to a structure discovered by aerial photography at Inveresk (Aliaga-Kelly 1986, 256, 373, fig 7.7), but Hope-Taylor, the excavator of the site, considered with more plausibility that this was some sort of shrine and not necessarily Christian. On the other hand, small unicellular buildings, constructed with locally available materials, and either dry-stone or clay-bonded, are a form commonly found in western Scotland, the Isle of Man and parts of Ireland (Swift 1987, 234–255), although the dry-stone corbelled churches of Ireland seem to belong to a different tradition (Ó Carragáin 2010, 49–55). There are resemblances to the first phase of The Hirsel in western Scotland, for example the unicellular church at Chapel Finnian, Wigtownshire (Radford 1951, fig 1), usually dated 10th to 11th century, which also has projecting, buttress-like antae. Nearer to The Hirsel, Building 1 at the ecclesiastical site at Auldhame (Lothian), a rectangular building with slightly rounded corners, constructed with earth-bonded field stones is comparable to, but larger than, the Phase I church at The Hirsel, being 8.4m east–west and 6.0m north–south (Crone *et al* forthcoming, fig 10). In Ireland the 8th century oratory/shrine at Illaunloughan is very similar in scale to The Hirsel, and measures internally 3.2m east–west and 2.2m north–south (White Marshall and Walsh 2005, 112–122, 45). A group of churches from Islay were compared by Swift (1987) with churches in Ireland on the Dingle peninsula and those in the Isle of Man and, although her conclusions are tentative, since she sees no uniform specification, she is inclined to see the dry-stone churches with rounded corners and western entrances as earlier in the sequence than the larger rectilinear clay-bonded churches with north and south doors and associated burials, and the former group as possibly private estate churches serving small communities, but without burial rights, whilst the latter may have served more than one family, and with burial rights, suggesting a parochial or proto-parochial structure (Swift 1987, 250–258). It is of interest, however, that these larger rectangular structures excavated in the west of Scotland at sites such as Whithorn and Barhobble are subdivided internally into chancel and nave by screens and furnishings and do not develop a distinctive two-cell plan of a larger nave than chancel as occurs at The Hirsel and other parish churches in the east.

Such buildings are practically unknown in north-east Britain, but this may be because of the lack of excavated sites beneath existing churches. In a recent re-evaluation of the chapel and burial ground on St Ninian's Isle (Barrowman 2011), the author also comes to the conclusion that the lack of early stone churches in Scotland 'is probably because later sites were built directly on top of older ones so obliterating the earlier evidence' (Barrowman 2011, 198). Where churches have been excavated, there is normally evidence for a sequence of structures, although in the west and north the single-celled rectangular plan survives into the high Middle Ages. The first St Ninian's Isle chapel in dry-stone can be dated after the later 11th century, but it is a more substantial rectangular building than The Hirsel (Barrowman 2011, 114), measuring as it does 6.5m x 5m, and such unicameral churches are found also at Ardnadam measuring internally 5.18m x 3.23m (Rennie 1984, fig 15), or St Nicholas, Papa Stronsay, Orkney, measuring 5.32m x 3.9m (Barrowman 2011, 205). The medieval chapel at St Ninian's 'could have been built any time from the mid-11th century onwards, at the earliest' (Barrowman 2011, 204), and its dimensions are nave: 7m x 5.1m, and chancel: 4.5m x 3.8m.

Most of the other Scottish churches in clay-bonded stone are simple rectangles as at Ardwall, where the stone-walled (phase III) chapel lay almost exactly E–W and measured internally 23ft x 13ft (7m x 3.96m). It had a clay-bonded wall base of slabs and pebbles, and large stone blocks for the corner quoins and the door opening. It was suggested by the excavator that the upper walls were of timber. There was one western entrance (Thomas 1967, 134 and figs 22 and 23) and an 8th century date was suggested. The second church was an extension of the first, but still a simple rectangle (illus 5.3), and was bonded by creamy mortar. It was succeeded by a third church in the 11th–13th century with a square chancel (illus 10.1) and these small churches were then enclosed in the larger priory church, rectangular 14.5m x 7m, and this sequence is replicated elsewhere.

At Barhobble, the earliest church, dated *c*12th century, is a long rectangle, and the construction suggested is of clay-bonded stone and rubble plinths, possibly supporting stave work. The roof was constructed with crucks which were supported on pads at ground level (Cormack 1995, fig 10). At The Hirsel, there was no evidence for pads at ground level and it is assumed that the building could have had roof supports in the walls as in other buildings in north Britain, for example at Yeavering Old Palace (Figure 5.37). In stone then, simple rectangular buildings are the most common form so far distinguished in Scotland between the 8th and 12th centuries, although at the Isle of May a rectangular chancel had been added by the end of the 11th century (James and Yeoman 2008, illus 10.1).

As noted in Chapter 5, the additional dry-stone or clay-bonded apse is an unusual feature alongside a persistent unicameral tradition. At St Ninian's Isle, the sequence of an initial dry-stone building overlaid by a later structure of mortared stone is the same as The Hirsel, and both have added apses, but at The Hirsel this feature belongs to an earlier phase than the mortared church, whereas at St Ninian's Isle it is part of the mortared successor church. Apsidal east ends are also found in Orkney at Birsay and Orphir, both churches being founded by the Orkney earls. Fawcett has remarked that '...the semi-circular apse was one of the architectural elements brought up from England' (Fawcett 2002, 25) and, as discussed in Chapter 2, the families of Gospatrick and the earls of Dunbar, whose church this was, moved in high ranking English as well as Scottish circles and had possessions in what is now England.

The addition of the apse in Phase II does indeed seem to reflect a knowledge of the wider world, and a fashion which emanated from high ranking circles. The earliest apses appear in Scotland at the highest social levels such as Queen Margaret's chapel at Dunfermline, or her chapel at Edinburgh, and these should reasonably date before her death in 1093 (Fernie 1994, 27). The addition of the apse could, then, reflect the Dunbar family's and the Countess Derder's elitist status. Around 1100 has been suggested as a date when apses became more frequent, although Fawcett (2002, 25) has noted that there may have been earlier examples than Dunfermline and Coldingham. Both are rather more sophisticated structures than the cobbled apse here, and the church at Dalmeny, which has been described as the most important survival of a Romanesque church in Scotland, is very richly decorated (Fawcett 2011, 53–54, illus 56). A closer parallel to The Hirsel is the surviving apse of the nearby Berwickshire church at Bunkle (Figures 5.39 and 27.1), which Ferguson suggests could be even earlier than the 12th century; 'the excessive plainness — I had almost said rudeness of such features as it presents certainly indicates great antiquity... The arch which opened to the chancel is totally devoid of ornament, being a plain semi-circular-headed, square edged specimen, resting on slightly projecting imposts' (Ferguson 1892, 95–96). In the detailed account in the online *Corpus of Scottish medieval parish churches* (published in the website Fawcett *et al* 2008), Fawcett has assigned the church to a date 'by the early 1100s at the latest', and this does not preclude a date in the late 11th century.

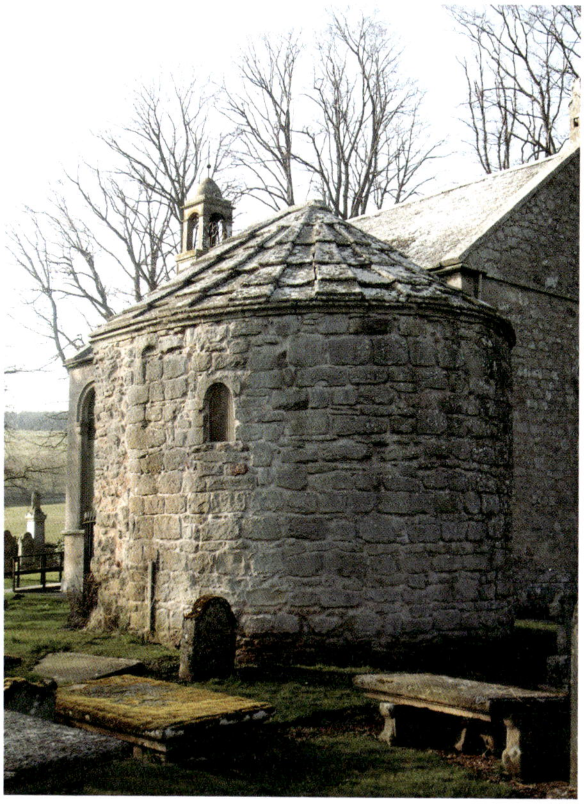

FIGURE 27.1
Bunkle old church, the apse

At The Hirsel, the dearth of decorative Norman sculpture, as noted above, inclines one to think that the openings in the Hirsel church must have been of a similar type, and that some of the simple chamfered blocks discovered in the dumps may have been imposts or bases. The two cobble packs on the chord of the apse may, however, have supported bases either for piers or for columns. Since the Phase II church was pulled down when the extended church was built, most of the surviving carved stone could well have come from the later structure. It is noteworthy that the apse was simply added in cobbles, in what may be presumed to be a local technique, and does not seem to be part of a campaign of rebuilding in a new technique like the addition of the extended nave in Phase III. According to Fawcett, round-ended chancels went out of use by the end of the 12th century, so the lengthened church of Phase III, with its squared-off apse, could have followed rapidly. Possibly the simple unicameral church which could be as early as 10th century in date could have been replaced by Phase II in the late 11th/early 12th century, before the transfer to Coldstream in 1165, and could be attributable to English Romanesque influence.

The more complex church of Hirsel Phases III and IV can be compared with some chronological exactitude to other examples in Scotland and England. The church of Dalmeny (see Fawcett 2002, figs 1.6 and 1.7), another Gospatrick church, could have had a similar development (Figure 27.2), and there are similarities to other 12th century Norman churches in the Borders and Northumberland, some of which like Chirnside (NT 869561), Edrom (NT 828559) or Old Bewick were on Dunbar estates.

It is unfortunate that key early Romanesque churches in Scotland have not been excavated in recent times, but with new investigation, more predecessors might emerge. Recent excavations at the monastic site of Portmahomack have revealed a sequence of buildings beneath St Colman's church. Nine phases of church building have been identified, the first being a simple rectangle dating to *c*1100, and the excavator has concluded that 'It must have had a simple belfry of some kind to house the bell-mould fragments'. The radiocarbon dating from the charcoal in the bell-casting pit provides a range of 1030–1270, and Carver suggests that late in the range would be appropriate (Carver 2008, 154–156 and fig 8.2). This evidence for a bell cote is the only recent example of an excavated casting pit other than that at The Hirsel (Figure 5.15 and Chapter 26).

In form, however, as well as dimensions, the Dunbar church at Old Bewick in Northumberland is closely similar to The Hirsel in its final plan, even to the squared-off apse (Figure 27.2). This church has been compared in detail with The Hirsel (Bettess 1991; 1995), but since this is still a standing church, and moreover one which has been extensively rebuilt, as the 1826 drawing in the Northumberland County History tellingly depicts (NCH 376–381 and illus p376), the sequence of its use or indeed detail is difficult to compare. Nevertheless the whole church, equivalent formally to The Hirsel Phase III, has been dated 'Norman' 12th century (Pevsner and Richmond 1992, 535).

Within Scotland then, St Margaret's chapel, the excavated plans of the early churches at Dunfermline *c*1070 and *c*1100 (Fernie 1994) and the mid-12th century church of Dalmeny, as well as the surviving apses at Bunkle and Leuchars (Fife), provide the main parallels for the 'Norman' plan, and the ruined church of Abbotrule (Borders) for the possible form of the west end. The church at Bassendean, which anciently belonged to Coldstream Priory, has some affinity with The Hirsel church in the dimensions

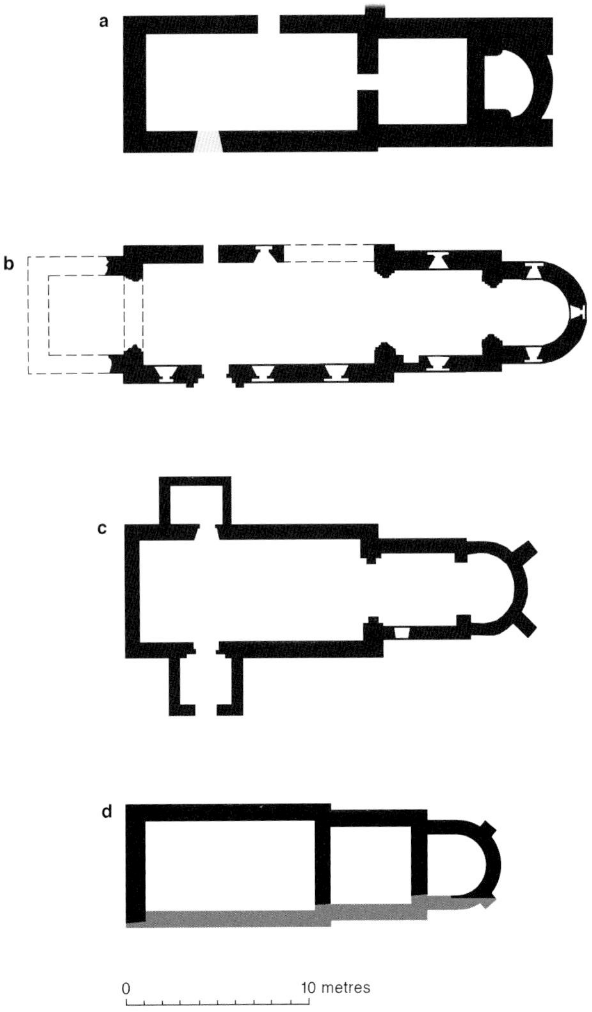

FIGURE 27.2
Comparative plans of a) The Hirsel, b) Dalmeny (after Fawcett 2002), c) Old Bewick (after Bettess 1991) and d) the excavated church of All Saints, Fishergate, York (after On-Site Archaeology)

of its nave, which was 54½ feet long (16.6m) and some 20 feet wide (6.10m) externally, according to Ferguson (1892, fig 37), while the ruined nave of the church at Lennel, which is now very badly overgrown (Figure 5.42) measured 'about 54 feet (16.46m) long by 22½ feet (6.86m) wide externally' (Ferguson 1892, 118) (the surviving west end of Lennel church when measured in 2010 was approximately 8.0m externally and 5.63m internally). Ferguson's measurements are all given as 'about', and The Hirsel measurements are at foundation level and are approximate also since there is variation along the line of the wall, with average measurement for the Phase IV nave being *c*16.80m x 8.0m externally and *c*12m x 5.0m internally. The nave of Old Bewick measures 12.08m x 5.34m internally, which is very close to The Hirsel, and its standing walls are 0.84m wide which would give an external width of only 7.02m, the discrepancy seemingly explained by the wider foundations at The Hirsel.

Comparable development to The Hirsel architectural sequence and internal evidence for its changing use is also revealed by excavation in England, the recently excavated and so far unpublished church at Fishergate, York, has a very similar plan (Figure 27.2). The history of the proprietary church at Raunds, Northamptonshire (Boddington 1996) is, however, particularly close, since it involved first a single-cell church, external length 5.5m, then the addition of a chancel and graveyard, followed by a second larger church and finally conversion to secular use (Boddington 1996, fig 5). Nevertheless, the forms of the Northamptonshire and Berwickshire churches subsequent to the first church are different, although the constructional sequence of Raunds is comparable in date, having been calculated as spanning a period from the late 9th/early 10th to the 13th century. Like Portmahomack, the chancel at Raunds was rectangular from the beginning but, as with The Hirsel, there was an additional wall at the west end which has been interpreted as a bell cote (Boddington 1996, figs 10 and 11). The foundations of bell cotes, which are essentially upward projections of walls, are not a frequent occurrence in excavated churches, but bell cotes were plausibly more frequent on small churches than western towers, and it has been noted above that the surviving west wall at Lennel is also a double structure (Figure 5.42).

Although what occasioned the enlargement of the church by the addition of the nave, and the rebuilding of the whole building in cut and mortared stone, remains uncertain, the presence of a team of masons in the vicinity and under the control of the lord of the manor could be one explanation. Certainly the crisp cutting of the few architectural details which remain in the distinctive stone of the Phase III church are confident and competent (see Chapter 12), in contrast with the cruder work which has been assigned to the fittings of the earlier church. Nevertheless, there is little evidence for the elaborate decoration which one finds on the openings at other Scottish Romanesque churches. The one fragment of chevron at The Hirsel could imply a single decorated opening as at small churches such as Gullane or Chirnside (see Fawcett 2002, illus 2.47). The very plainness of most of the church, however, could be a sign of either an early date or the status of the church. We have no firm evidence, however, for how short or long the interval was between the construction of the Phase II and Phase III churches. Equally difficult to establish is the interval between the construction of the Phase III church and the additional west wall in Phase IV.

The circumstances which explain the structural changes and the nature of the congregation which this church served can never be conclusively derived from archaeological evidence. The first church implies a relatively small or poor community or one with little aspiration. In discussing the small churches of Ireland, Ó Carragáin (2010, 213) has dismissed the long-held idea that the congregation could have stood outside small churches. Structurally though, such buildings seem to be part of an indigenous tradition, since nearby, on what may be earlier sites influenced by incoming Anglo-Saxon overlords, at Yeavering in Northumberland and Sprouston on the Tweed, the churches are bicameral and of cut timbers. The addition of an apse implies new external influence, although whether this demonstrates aspiration for a higher status building, or a liturgical development where the priest was facing the people or given his own private space, is uncertain. This remains however a simple building with minimum change. The complete rebuilding on a larger scale with professionally quarried and dressed stone and decorated architectural features could however imply a change of ownership or aspiration, a change of function or influence, or any combination of these, but seems to demand a change in context.

The Coldstream Cartulary records that a church at The Hirsel, with its supporting land holdings and tithes, was donated by the Earl of Dunbar to support Coldstream Priory in 1166, and this was confirmed in 1167 by the bishop of St Andrews, so at that date there was a parochial church, and, from the evidence of the burials, it had its own burial ground. Whether this was the Phase II church or Phase III church is a matter of debate. The Phase III church was a building of some pretension as the surviving sculptural fragments and glass indicate. No construction date was retrieved archaeologically, but the radiocarbon dates from the bell pit which cut the earliest floor of the nave (1015–1185), imply that it also had a bell before the late 12th century. The date assigned to the earliest decorative architectural sculpture is late 12th century, and this has the same tooling as the wall stones of the Phase III church. On the evidence of the sculpture, then, this church was built after it had been given over to Coldstream Priory, although the radiocarbon dates would allow for earlier construction. Its demise as a church would seem from the pottery evidence to be somewhere in the later 14th century, when there is evidence for robbing and a different type of use.

Phase 7 is the most obscure and intriguing period of use of the building, when the church apparently went out of use and its walls began to be robbed, but the nave seems to have been intensively used for various secular activities, and new flooring as well as new timber and rough stone structures appeared (Figures 5.26 and 5.27). It has been suggested from the botanical evidence that at some stage it may have been used as a barn, certainly a storage place for hay and corn, but the striking characteristic of the artefacts found within the church is their masculine character. There is a considerable number of arrowheads, a fish-hook, a horseshoe, much pottery including several large jugs and evidence for eating which included young lambs and oysters, as well as fish bone in the faecal material in the latrine pit C1302. There were also 80 nails from the pit. The arrowheads were primarily from hunting arrows and for this reason the idea that this was a military unit in occupation has not been seen as conclusive. Nevertheless, the specialist report does say that some could have been used effectively against horse and men (see Section 20.10) and a brief military use of the nave could have resulted in the deposit of both military and hunting arrows. The area suffered badly in the border troubles during the wars of independence and after March 1296 when Edward I encamped at Coldstream, with supposedly 5,000 horses and 30,000 infantry, the priory claimed compensation of £50 for wheat, rye, barley, malt and oats, and £62 15s for cattle, sheep, lambs and pigs, a demand which was partly compensated for by a return to the convent of 700 sheep (Rogers 1879, xiii–xiv). There could have been other similar raiding parties who would see a semi-ruined church as a useful billet, but in the lawless times of the late Middle Ages in this area, there could have been any number of reasons for the secular use of the building. Its final demise by the 15th century was by fire (Figure 5.32).

27.5 THE PAROCHIAL BACKGROUND

Throughout this report, I have followed the view set out by Morgan as early as 1947, and developed by Cowan in 1961, that the feudal unit — in this case the estate or vill — was coterminous with the parish. From the earliest charter evidence it is noted: 'Lay lords built and endowed churches on their estates: charters of Thor Longus describe (*c*1105) how, when King Edgar gave him Ednam as waste land, he peopled it at his own expense, built a church in honour of St Cuthbert, and endowed it with a carucate of land. From the time of the earliest records they distributed tithes at will' (Morgan 1947, 136). As Cowan has remarked, 'In certain instances moreover the grant of land to a religious house ensured that a church would be built and a parish brought into existence' (Cowan 1961, 52).

The initiatives of David I (1124–53) encouraged massive development, not only in the building of monastic houses, but for local churches. 'He fostered the establishment of an effective network of parishes and revived and expanded the system of dioceses' (Fawcett 1996, 85). This followed the pattern in England when in the 10th and 11th centuries 'much of England moved from a pastoral system based primarily on minsters to one based primarily on local churches' although the 'formal creation of the parochial system was the work of the 12th and early 13th centuries' (Blair 1996, 12). Whether the sitings of proprietorial churches in lowland Scotland were in long standing places of cult or were new initiatives of the local gentry, placed near to their homes and contending with the old established minsters for burial dues and tithes, is still open to debate. Nevertheless they seem to have existed in some numbers since, in the 11th and early 12th centuries, when the popularity of monastic foundations increased, many local proprietorial churches were donated to endow them.

It is possible that, as already mentioned, the Dunbar family used the team who had built the priory to rebuild some of their churches, as a matter of prestige to enhance the family gift for (as Fawcett has remarked in considering proprietary churches and the growth of parishes) when estates were granted to incomers to Scotland a requirement could be made that a church should be provided on the estate, and 'It may also have been the case that the church building activities of the new grantees spurred existing landowners to provide churches on their own estates, and in some cases they may have tried to outdo the newcomers in their architectural activities' (Fawcett 2011, 44). It seems indeed more likely that the earl rather than the priory community would pay for this much more elaborate church even if it were after the donation. As with other 12th century donations, the bishop swiftly confirmed the grant, thus maintaining his authority. Yet, despite ecclesiastical pressure that rights of patronage should be passed over from lay control to the newly endowed monasteries, it appears that there were residual interests so that the family maintained some control in estates such as The Hirsel.

As Elsa Hamilton has shown, the nunneries did not own land and churches outright, and the master of a house such as Coldstream 'would serve both the house and the earl' (Hamilton 2010, 229). Moreover, she envisages a close relationship between the nunnery and the founding family and has recently discussed the degree of control which a lay patron might continue to exercise over a church when it and its appurtenances had been surrendered to a religious house (Hamilton 2010, 67–68). In the case of The Hirsel, she notes that 'By the late twelfth or early thirteenth century Hirsel church, which had been given to Coldstream, apparently still had a parson, Adam, who witnessed Patrick I's charter confirming Lennel church to the nuns' (*Cold. Cart.*, 5–6, no. 7). Parsons had some status and could be drawn from the landowner's family, and in the area to the north of the cemetery where a domestic building has been demolished, the quality of the finds like the gilded bell suggest this may have been the parson's house (see Chapter 7).

Hamilton postulates, however, that William's charter given between 1203 and 1209 may indeed mark the full appropriation of Hirsel church by Coldstream' (Hamilton 2007, 28; *Cold. Cart.*, 11, 15 and 47, Appendix II). In that case, when the rededication took place in 1246, its parsonage and vicarage teinds would have been already annexed to the priory and the church would have been served by a mercenary chaplain. Cowan, in his listing of the medieval parishes of Scotland, notes for The Hirsel: 'Both parsonage and vicarage were apparently annexed, the cure of souls evidently being served by a chaplain' (Cowan 1967, 82). Perhaps there was still a close enough family interest in the Hirsel church for the priory to support it at that stage, but if later there was so much destruction of the priory resources during the Wars of Independence, then the community probably did not see its maintenance and the provision of a chaplain as a priority and allowed it to fall into ruin and subsequent lay use.

Although rents from lands at The Hirsel were still being paid to Coldstream Priory up to the time when the priory ceased to exist in the 16th century (Rogers 1879, xxxii–xxiii and Chapter 2 above), excavation has proved that the church had been destroyed long before that, and indeed later documents do not mention a church. Lennel seems to be, as today, the parish church for this area. We know from both documentary and archaeological evidence that the cemetery at The Hirsel existed for longer than the church (Robson 1896, 70, and Chapter 6 above), but the relationship between church and cemetery at the beginning of the ecclesiastical use of the site is still debatable.

27.6 THE CEMETERY

General discussion

Although the location of the cemetery had been lost by the beginning of the 19th century, there is a puzzling reference in the *New Statistical Account* (Goldie 1841, 207) to the 'great quantities of human bones' found 'in the grounds of Hirsel' as well as on the site of Coldstream Priory. Like the large stone coffin which exists on the site (Figure 13.1), the location where such bones were found is uncertain, although the coffin was once in the walled garden to the west of the site (Caroline Douglas-Home pers comm). It is possible that the cemetery once extended further west, but it is equally possible that the cemetery for Coldstream Priory may be the source of the coffin and large slab (FM2, now at The Hirsel). The lack of firm evidence for the full extent of The Hirsel cemetery means that any general statements can only apply to the unknown percentage excavated.

Differences of orientation as considered in Chapter 6 are not necessarily indicators of different periods of burial, but rather, as has been noted elsewhere, burial groupings, and the influence of topographic features such as the enclosing ditch and the slope (Rahtz 1978). But the line of the church does obviously exert an influence. Phases II and III of the church were not on a markedly different alignment (about 3°), and most burials align with them, although both to the south and the north of the church, those burials which appear earlier stratigraphically, such as the group around Sk317, Sk300, Sk269 to the south and Sk325, Sk324, Sk96 to the north, were buried more truly east–west than those that were later. Indeed the very late burials such as Sk56, with the 16th-century coins, seem to be quite casually placed.

The burial positions, supine and with hands to the sides or crossed on the pelvis are the norm in most medieval Christian cemeteries, but the crouched position with the head turned on the right cheek, as the female Sk14, and the child of 12–13 years Sk107, is also occasionally found. The orientation of Sk107 is also reversed and this has been noted also in the Coldingham cemetery where skeleton 009, also possibly female, had the head to the east (Stronach 2005, 404). In this cemetery the bent and twisted position of no. 007, also a female with head turned to the right, has been explained as possibly because the woman had suffered from some sort of paralysis or a condition such as cerebral palsy. A similar pathological symptom was noted in Sk107 at The Hirsel and although, as Anderson has noted, it is not a visible condition, it may have had some social consequence which resulted in a different treatment for this burial from the rest.

The proportion of males to females of almost 1:1 (Chapter 11) is comparable with other British sites, and indeed, except for the Isle of May Assemblage A (which may have been a monastic group), is similar to other Scottish sites (see James and Yeoman 2008, table 6.2), but the child/juvenile burials are more numerous than is commonly recorded (see Chapter 11). These are a group which has been accorded special care in burial, as is found elsewhere, most strikingly in the cemetery at Raunds in Northamptonshire (Boddington 1996, 54–55), and there seems to be similar treatment in the cemetery at Auldhame (Cook 2005; Hindmarsh and Melikian 2008; Craig 2007, 21–23).

The cemetery at Raunds had many similarities with The Hirsel, and is a useful parallel since it was completely excavated and dates from *c*900 to *c*1200 (Boddington 1996, fig 25). Moreover, since it is seemingly of a rural community, it is more relevant to The Hirsel than monastic or urban burial grounds which are nearer geographically. Its extent was similarly defined initially by a shallow ditch. There was a similar care in treating infants and very young children by providing them with complete cists, although the cists at Raunds are not the neat type which occurs at The Hirsel (Boddington

1996, 40 and fig 50). Boddington notes also that, from about the turn of the 11th century, children were customarily buried close to the church in the eaves drip position, and cites other examples: St Guthlac's, Hereford (Shoesmith 1980), Castle Bailey, Norwich (Ayers 1985), Wharram Percy (Mays *et al* 2007, 229), mentioning also The Hirsel (Boddington 1996, 69).

The favoured position for infants on the south of the church is supported by the tradition that the north side of the church was often considered less auspicious (Boddington 1996, 60). On the other hand, Boddington also notes that, as at The Hirsel, the north side of Raunds Furnells church was in use for burial from the outset, and wonders whether the desire to bury on the north side was because this was on the access route to the manorial enclosure which later developed there. This, as noted above, could be the situation at The Hirsel.

The most detailed analyses of Christian burials in Scotland have been accorded to the long cist graves which are particularly common in south-east Scotland and the Borders (A M Jones 1991; Dalland 1992, 204; Proudfoot 1996). James and Yeoman (2008, 74–76), in a recent summary of the position of the Isle of May cemetery, note that the earliest long cist burial there accords with the presently accepted inception date for long cist burials of the early 5th century, and that there was a period of transition between the 10th and 12th century when both long cists and dug graves appear to have been used, although there was one 'special cist' burial of a middle-aged woman which has a radiocarbon date of cal AD 1047–1280 (James and Yeoman 2008, 32 and illus 4.17). This accords well with the one substantial long cist burial from The Hirsel (Sk338), which is cut by the extended west wall of the church and has a radiocarbon date of cal AD 1150–1285 (GU-1901). However, as noted above, three infants were buried in tiny neat, box-shaped cists (see Figure 6.22), which do not seem to have parallels in Scotland. The Hirsel evidence then supplements the isolated occurrences recorded elsewhere in Scotland and Northumbria, and the evidence that there was sporadic use of long cists after the period of their main use. It is noteworthy at The Hirsel, however, that the older fashion for cists and quartz pebbles is mainly reserved for children in the area examined. It is conceivable that the sparsity of graves with quartz pebbles in comparison with sites such as Whithorn and the Isle of May, and the fact that there is only one long cist, but many types of stone arrangements in the graves, is a chronological indicator for the beginning of the cemetery, if these people were conforming to burial practices such as are found elsewhere in northern Britain.

It has been suggested by Reed (1995, 789) that as the fully stone-lined, long cist or lintel graves went out of use in the 11th century, other forms of stone arrangements within the graves, particularly stones flanking the skulls, became common. He also suggests that 'the inclusion of stones with the burial is a low status Christian ritual in this part of Scotland during the 11th and 12th century AD' (Reed 1995, 790). It is likely however, in the light of evidence elsewhere, that the fashion for stone arrangements in the graves began earlier and that it was widespread in Britain, extending to some places where there was no tradition of lintel or cist graves (Mays *et al* 2007, 238–241). Boddington (1996, 57 and 70, fig 44), in commenting on the many graves with stone arrangements at Raunds, suggests that it was between the 10th and 12th century that the practice was common in England. At Portmahomack monastic site, about half of the phase 2 burials (which succeeded those buried in cists) had head supports of stones and these have been dated 8th–9th century (Carver 2008, 76–79, illus 4.3 and 4.6). Such stone arrangements are quite common at The Hirsel, although because of the massive inter-cutting and disturbance of the burials, one can only be certain of 29 graves with intentional stone arrangements, with only nine examples of stones flanking the skull — 'ear muffs'. At Newhall Point, Balblair, mentioned above, the cemetery has many parallels with The Hirsel. Here, although only 38 graves were fully excavated, the inter-cutting was comparable to a long-lived Christian churchyard. There were 21 graves with stone arrangement in their fills and 11 of these had stones flanking the skull. This statistic is nearer to the situation at Raunds, where more than half the graves had stone arrangements (Boddington 1996, 38–44 and fig 52). Unlike at Raunds, complete lining of the grave cut with stones, as possible supports for wooden covers, is not found at The Hirsel, but flat plain stone grave covers and roughly shaped head or foot stones were found at both The Hirsel and Raunds. Whilst there was evidence for five or six stone coffins at Raunds, at The Hirsel the only complete coffin, and the massive grave cover which could have covered a stone coffin (FM5, Figure 13.6), were not found in the excavation.

One decorated grave cover was found *in situ* at Raunds (Boddington 1996, fig 62), but at The Hirsel all of the carefully shaped grave covers and markers (FM3, FM4, FM5) and the cross-head (FM7) emerged from the ploughing pre-excavation and were undecorated. The grave cover type can be paralleled in the Lincoln St Mark's cemetery where examples have been dated 11th–13th century (Gilmour and Stocker 1986, 69–71, illus 57). They may have been dragged from their position *in situ*, but it seems more likely, given the careful levelling off of the church and graveyard (see discussion of sequence), that they had been dumped on top of the stones in a large pit (Chapter 8), and dragged from there. Nevertheless, the fact that one standing cross was found at both sites could indicate the same tradition of marking the primary important grave. The shaft with no arris mouldings, and the shape of The Hirsel finial cross seem to be 12th century in date, and the well shaped plain grave cover with incised circles (FM5) is later in type than the flat grave covers with interlaced panels at Raunds and other British sites. Although there are other simple grave-markers with incised crosses at The Hirsel, which could be earlier, such sculpture is very difficult to date closely. The mound of stones and flat roughly shaped slabs discovered to the south of the Hirsel church (C708/715), as well as smaller scatters of stones, are also paralleled elsewhere, and Stocker remarked of St Mark's Lincoln: 'Graves covered with stones did not always employ a single slab. Indeed it was more common for the graves to be covered by an arrangement of several uncut or roughly shaped stones ...These stones may then have been buried under a mound of earth' (Gilmour and Stocker 1986, 55). There are therefore many features in the Hirsel grave morphology which can be paralleled quite widely in Britain.

The type of objects placed in the graves such as the folded coin (Figure 14.1) or the scallop shells (Figure 22.1) are noted by Gilchrist in various sites. Silver coins, usually folded and placed on the shoulders or near the head of the deceased, are found at British and French religious sites, including another in Scotland at Holyrood Abbey (Gilchrist and Sloane 2005, 100–102; Bain 1998, 1054). The significance of these folded coins is a matter for debate, but Gilchrist cites the explanation that the folding may represent the physical residue of a prayer in which a coin was placed over the body of a sick or dead person while a saint was invoked to help them, and suggests that it is conceivable that the use of a silver coin 'may be related to the Mass penny that was used during celebrations of the anniversaries of the dead' (Gilchrist and Sloane 2005, 101–102). Whatever the explanation of the deposition of silver coins, The Hirsel grave (of Sk336) fits the pattern of the others cited and, since these are practically all from high status monastic burial grounds, confirms the status of that burial.

The discovery of a burial (Sk222) with a pierced scallop shell and the loose scallop shell from the burial earth must also have been associated with a person of sufficient status to go on pilgrimage to Compostela, or another site dedicated to St James which could be much nearer. Such shells are relatively common in European graves. On the Isle of May a skeleton of a young man was buried in front of the position of the high altar with a scallop shell wedged into his mouth (James and Yeoman 2008, 181, illus 5.24). Scallop shells also occurred in graves in the cathedral cemeteries of Aberdeen, Winchester and Durham. At the last mentioned, near to the west front of the cathedral, a shell perforated with two holes was found in a cist grave (Greenwell 1906), and another was found with cist graves in the same location in 2007 (Norman Emery pers comm). In Ireland, shells with two perforations also occur with medieval graves, but have been found in an earlier context, with one perforation, in a shrine at the early medieval site at Llaunloughan (White Marshall and Walsh 2005, fig 54a).

The associated pottery

Valerie Dean in her pottery report has remarked that it is surprising to find so much pottery associated with a church and burial ground and it is worth considering why and when it could have been deposited and enclosed in the grave fill. Pottery could hardly have been deposited by manuring in a graveyard (although the cut between 840–850/204–210 could have been a cultivation terrace) but, if occurring in significant quantities, should denote domestic activity on or near the site.

Pottery from the grave fill of Sk335 and Sk338 has been assigned to the Early Gritty Wares (type 1.1) dated 10th–12th century, which matches the radiocarbon dates. It is of interest that the graves which contain this type of pottery alone are all at the west end and cut by the extended wall of the church (Sk311, Sk329, Sk335, Sk338). This pottery could have been deposited during the building activity of the earlier phases of the church. The predominant type of pottery from the site and in the graves is, however, from the local Tweed Valley Wares (group 2) dated 12th–15th century (Figures 17.1 and 17.2). An exception is the group of burials — many marked with head stones — in the north-east of the site. This pottery could have been dropped by the workmen building the Phase III church, or even during the occupation of the area for some secular activity. There are traces of domestic buildings in the north-east corner of the site and the pottery assemblage which is in the fill of the cultivation terrace (C131) to the north of the cemetery enclosure could have derived initially from the occupation of the adjacent house (see Chapter 7), but it is unlikely that material from this house would have been strewn across the churchyard even south of the church. Such deposits are more likely to derive from external lay activity. As noted in relation to the significant amount of pottery recorded from the medieval churchyard at Wharram Percy (North Yorkshire) there is extensive documentary evidence from the Middle Ages for churchyard activities such as social and sporting gatherings, fairs, or markets, and some of the large quantity of pottery from the upper cemetery levels, such as C444, could derive from such events. There was indeed a brief period when Edward I encamped with a huge army at Coldstream in 1296, after which, as discussed in Chapter 5, the nave of the church at least, probably ceased to function as a religious building. After that period the kirkyard may have had different uses, but although burial continued randomly on the site it did not cut into the area of the church, except for one redeposited burial (Sk46).

27.7 CHURCH AND CEMETERY

At The Hirsel there is no evidence for burial before the foundation of the earliest church or of a markedly different alignment from the churches when they were in use. Using all the evidence noted above, the earliest dated burials could probably be located in the late 11th century, although the radiocarbon dates for the burials sampled (Chapter 9) provide the bracket 1140–1275 for the beginning of the cemetery. A more detailed and structured series of radiocarbon dates as well as the determination of the full extent of the cemetery would be needed to provide a better sample. At present one of the earliest burials sampled is Sk3, dated 1035–1280 (GU-1310). No burials were discovered inside the church in any phase and, although there may have been a different burial ground in use with the first simple church, it seems plausible that burial rights were associated with the Phase II church, especially since in the gift to Coldstream Priory (see Chapter 2) appurtenances (probably including tithes) were part of the donation. Although this does not seem very large for a parish church, the rebuilt and extended church of Phase III has been ruled out as that of the Countess's gift of 1165/6 by the later dating of the architectural detail as noted above.

The surviving monumental stone cannot be dated precisely enough to resolve the issue. It is difficult to date any of the monumental stone earlier than the 11th century, although (see Chapter 13) the dating of any of the simple cross-incised monuments is very uncertain. The current hypothesis is, then, that this burial ground may have commenced with the apsidal church (Phase II), but was certainly in existence with the enlarged church in Phase III.

When the burial ground was closed is less uncertain. As already noted there are some more randomly aligned burials towards the end of the life of the cemetery, as if there were less oversight of the space. If after the church was ruined the church at Lennel assumed its later position as the main church for the Coldstream area, it is probable that some families moved to that burial ground (see Chapters 2 and 5). A life span of around late 11th to late 15th centuries is the closest possible estimate for the main occupation of the cemetery, with sporadic burial and especially burial of infants up to the 16th century; for that reason its location was remembered for longer than that of the church. In 1627 there is the reference to the kirkyard near to The Hirsel called Granton (see Chapter 2), and this is recorded on Robert Gordon's map of *c*1636–1652 (Figure 2.8), but at that scale it is difficult to pinpoint the exact position — it was certainly, like the excavated cemetery, located to the south of Hirsel House, and may be a new name for the cemetery.

There seems to have been a lull in site activity during the 16th century and the surge of secular activity in the north-west part of the site (Chapter 8) ignored and cut into the cemetery. The hard standings and the enclosure all contained fragmented architectural stones and are perhaps associated with the reworking of stone for building works. So far no convincing parallel has been found for the enclosure, but the activity may have been occasioned by an influx of workmen brought in for the building of the tower house which was the predecessor of the present Hirsel House. But the many bottles and clay pipes of 17th century date could equally have been dropped by soldiery encamped in the area. The coinage associated with this activity has a latest date of 1677–79, which is certainly a time of significant Border warfare. After that it seems the field may have been subjected to shallow ploughing and put down to grass until the deep ploughing of 1977 brought the grave stones to light.

27.8 THE PEOPLE OF THE HIRSEL

Finally, what manner of population used the church and was buried at The Hirsel? The general health of the population and the evidence for a fairly hard life-style is discussed in Sue Anderson's report (Chapter 11), and it could be that there is some evidence deriving from the traumatic evidence for social stratification in the burials, as well as for those whose graves contained spurs.

Although the Countess Derder and the earl of Dunbar may have been responsible for the building of the extended church, it is most likely that they would have been buried in a more prestigious centre, perhaps one of the Dunbar monastic foundations, such as Coldstream Priory or Eccles. A more junior branch of the family took over The Hirsel estate in the late 12th century, and later there were changes in holders of the estate, who also could have been buried elsewhere. The one cross shaft may have marked a founding grave, but was not *in situ*. Likewise the two cross-marked headstones could have marked special graves either for the resident priest or laity, but most graves, as was customary at that time, were anonymous. Presumably the people buried here worked on the estate, but could have been from differing social grades, and the relationship of burials to the domestic occupation in the north-east of the site and the evidence for further occupation on the west may indeed be significant in defining different occupational or family groups. It seems possible, however, that the churchyard was sporadically used in its last phase for infant burials and perhaps those who did not have a family plot in a new cemetery which might account for the randomly placed 17th century burial.

What has this excavation told us concerning the effect on the congregation of the appropriation of small parish churches to the great monastic houses of the high Middle Ages? In Cowan's words 'That the parochial system was seriously vitiated by the system of appropriation can scarcely be doubted' (Cowan 1961, 55), and the fate of the Hirsel church may be a concrete example of this. In times of hardship the maintaining of many churches gifted to a religious organisation may well have seemed a heavy price to pay for the incomings from land and teinds, especially if the church was in poor repair. The ravaging of the priory by Edward I and the depredations of his troops certainly caused the Coldstream prioress to plead poverty and, if the first phase of partial ruination of the building coincided with this event, then it could have seemed prudent to leave the church as a ruin and to cease support of a priest, diverting the congregation to one of the other churches nearby, probably Lennel, which remains the parish church. This is all supposition, but the destruction by stone robbing, reshaping for secular use, destruction by fire and eventual obliteration of the site and its location, are archaeologically proven. As late as 2011, Richard Oram has noted that the origins and development of Scotland's parish system remain understudied topics (Oram 2011, 347). The life story of this estate church (and the associated cemetery) relates to the nature of the pastoral provision for rural Scotland, and its rise and fall provides an interesting comment on the topic.

APPENDIX 1
SEED COUNTS FOR CLASSIFICATION GROUPS

Jacqui P Huntley

Two letter codes:

First letter refers to the preservation state: c=charred, m=mineralise.

Second letter refers to the broad habitat group:

a=arable weed	c=cereal grain	e=economic	g=grassland
h=heathland	m=maritime	r=ruderal	s=cereal chaff
t=woodland/scrub	w=wetland	x=broad	

Dominant taxa of the whole group

Constant but less abundant taxa

Twinspan group A

		C1227	C1151	C1226	C1195	C623
cs	Culm nodes	68	30	520	640	480
cs	*Secale* rachis internode	30	25	78	352	384
cc	*Avena* grain	528	187	1152	3024	3440
cc	*Triticum aestivum* grain	263	41	452	352	464
cc	*Secale cereale* grain	44	32	152	248	576
cx	Legume <4mm	19	21	106	224	144
cx	Gramineae undiff	17	26	920	320	80
cs	*Triticum aestivum* rachis node	67	9	264	64	32
ca	*Chrysanthemum segetum*	10	17	86	32	16
cr	*Rumex obtusifolius*-type	7	12	38	64	48
ca	*Centaurea cyanus*	14	2	32	80	64
ca	*Agrostemma githago*	12	9	44	64	48
cr	*Rumex acetosella*	1	194	758	416	240
cr	*Lapsana communis*	2	4	4	16	16
cs	*Triticum* brittle rachis internode	1	1	43	4	
cs	*Avena sativa* floret base	11	1	50	160	
cs	*Avena* awn	5	18	256	1424	
cg	*Rumex acetosa*	3	1	14	16	
cs	*Triticum aestivum* internode	16	1	16		16
cs	*Hordeum* rachis internode	3	5	34		32
ca	*Spergula arvensis*		7	12	16	
cx	*Galium verum/palustre/mollugo*		1	8	1	
cc	Cerealia undiff		346	1552	6720	4912
ca	*Anthemis cotula*		79	1036	528	32
cc	*Hordeum* hulled		17	176	48	32
cx	*Bromus* sp(p) grain		3	24	32	16
cg	*Plantago lanceolata*		1	18	16	16
ca	*Chenopodium album*		5	36	32	48
cx	*Trifolium* sp(p)		7	36	32	16
cr	Chenopodiaceae undiff		20	38	32	32
cg	*Vicia tetrasperma*-type		3	6	48	32
cg	*Vicia cracca*-type		8	30	96	80
cc	*Hordeum* indet		3	10		32
cs	*Hordeum* 6-row rachis internode	3	1			16
ce	*Pisum sativum*	18	2			
ca	*Scleranthus annuus* calyx	1		20		
ca	*Polygonum aviculare*	2		2		
cr	*Raphanus raphanistrum* pod fragment	8		14		
cx	*Veronica* sp(p)		1	2		
cw	*Carex* (trigonous)		2	8		
ca	*Chenopodium bonus-henricus*		1	8		
cr	*Vicia sativa*		1	25		

		C1227	C1151	C1226	C1195	C623
cg	*Hypochoeris radicata*		1	12	1	
cx	Indeterminate			22	32	48
cg	*Chrysanthemum leucanthemum*			6	48	16
cx	Legume >4mm			10	48	
cs	*Avena* sp(p) fl. base			84	416	
cs	*Avena fatua* floret base			8	16	
cr	*Conium maculatum*			3	1	
ca	*Cerastium arvense*			4	16	
ca	*Sinapis arvensis*				16	16
cx	Compositae undiff	3				
ca	*Polygonum lapth./persicaria*	3				
ce	*Lens culinaris*	4				
ca	*Matricaria matricariodes*		1		1	
cg	*Vicia tetrasperma*		4			
cg	*Pimpinella saxifraga*		1			
cc	*Hordeum* naked		1			
ca	*Polygonum periscaria*			30		
cx	*Vicia* sp(p)			16		
cs	*Avena strigosa* fl. base			8		
cr	*Brassica* sp(p)			8		
cw	*Polygonum amphibium*			6		
ca	*Stellaria media*			6		
cx	*Atriplex* sp(p)			6		
cr	*Urtica dioica*			4		
ca	*Fallopia convolvulus*			2		
cx	Labiatae undiff			2		
cg	*Linum catharticum*			2		
ch	*Sieglingia decumbens*				16	
cr	cf. *Antriscus sylvestris*				1	
ct	*Quercus* cupule/acorn fragment				1	
cr	*Veronica chamaedrys*				1	
cr	*Galium aparine*					16
wg	*Lathyrus pratensis*					16
cx	Caryophyllaceae undiff					16
ca	*Matricaria recutita*					16

Twinspan group B

		C1150	C1143	C1125
cc	Cerealia undiff	139	250	222
cc	*Avena* grain	89	123	67
cr	*Rumex acetosella*	69	114	27
cc	*Triticum aestivum* grain	14	40	43
cc	*Secale cereale* grain	18	20	34
ca	*Anthemis cotula*	20	26	17
cs	Culm nodes	11	29	20
cs	*Avena* awn	17	2	8
cx	Legume <4mm	7	16	25
ca	*Agrostemma githago*	6	7	6
cc	*Hordeum* hulled	4	11	12
cx	Gramineae undiff	8	12	7
cx	*Bromus* sp(p) grain	4	4	8
cr	*Rumex obtusifolius*-type	1	9	5
cs	*Triticum aestivum* rachis node	4	6	1
ca	*Chrysanthemum segetum*	3	7	4
cr	Chenopodiaceae undiff	4	7	4
cg	*Vicia cracca*-type	2	1	6
cx	*Trifolium* sp(p)	1	7	3
ca	*Centaurea cyanus*	1	7	1
ca	*Spergula arvensis*	1	1	2
ca	*Chenopodium album*	1	1	3
cr	*Lapsana communis*	1	1	1
cw	*Carex* (trigonous)	1		1
cs	*Secale rachis* internode	7	19	
cs	*Hordeum* rachis internode	3	9	
cc	*Hordeum* indet	3	2	
ca	*Polygonum periscaria*	2	2	
cx	*Polygonum* sp(p)	1	1	
cs	*Avena sativa* floret base	1	2	
cw	*Carex* (lenticular)	1	1	
ca	*Cerastium arvense*	1	1	
cw	*Polygonum amphibium*	1		1
cg	*Plantago lanceolata*	1		1
cr	*Prunella vulgaris*	1		
cx	Legume >4mm	1		
cg	*Rumex acetosa*		1	3
ce	*Pisum sativum*		2	6
cg	*Chrysanthemum leucanthemum*		2	1
ca	*Stellaria media*		1	1
cs	*Avena* sp(p) fl. base		3	
cs	*Hordeum* 6-row rachis internode		1	
cs	*Avena fatua* floret base		1	
cs	*Triticum* brittle rachis internode		1	
ch	*Sieglingia decumbens*		1	
ce	*Vicia faba*		1	
cr	*Plantago major*		1	
ca	*Polygonum lapathifolium*		1	
cr	*Vicia sativa*			4
cg	*Vicia tetrasperma*-type			2
cr	*Conium maculatum*			1
cc	*Hordeum* naked			1

Twinspan group C

		C1035	C1078	C1062	C1022	C908	C946	C1079	C1073	C1058	C955	C1063
cc	Cerealia undiff	255	132	137	358	666	158	389	186	547	889	205
cc	*Avena* grain	109	61	76	128	109	30	179	40	4	149	97
cs	*Avena* awn	41	115	52	52	17	19	281	122	211	134	223
cc	*Triticum aestivum* grain	8	8	12		16	11	15	6	43	22	6
cc	*Hordeum* indet	4	8		8	24	10	12	10	20	22	11
ca	*Chenopodium album*	1	1	4	4	2	1	19	9	11	8	
cc	*Secale cereale* grain	6	5	5	1	1	4	4	1	4	1	4
cs	*Avena sativa* floret base	1	4	5	2	2		1	8	1	1	2
cx	Legume <4mm	2	8	5	4	1		2		9		5
ca	*Polygonum periscaria*	2	2	1	2	3	1	11		9	4	1
cr	*Rumex acetosella*	2	3	16		2	3	5	9	4		5
cr	Chenopodiaceae undiff	2		4	3	1	2	4	3	14		25
cx	*Bromus* sp(p) grain	3	2			2		2		3	4	2
cs	Culm nodes		5	5	1	3		6	3	2	2	3
cr	*Rumex obtusifolius*-type		2	1	4	4	3	1	1	6	1	1
cc	*Hordeum* hulled		4	5	2	5	3	3	7	2	16	7
ca	*Spergula arvensis*		1	5	7	3	1	7	1	9	7	4
cx	Gramineae undiff		1	2	1		4	13	6	10	4	11
cs	*Avena fatua* floret base		2	1	1			1	4		8	2
ca	*Anthemis cotula*	1	1	1				1	2	1	3	6
cs	*Avena* sp(p) fl. base	1	1				1	8	2	4	9	
cg	*Rumex acetosa*			2		4	1	3	1	1		
cg	*Plantago lanceolata*				4	3	1	3	1	11	1	4
ca	*Fallopia convolvulus*		1		3	1				4	4	1
ca	*Sinapis arvensis*	2						2	1		1	3
cg	*Vicia cracca*-type								2	1	1	
cs	*Hordeum* rachis internode		1			1		2				
ce	*Linum usitatissimum*		3		1	1				1		
cx	Legume >4mm	1				1		1		2		
cs	*Secale rachis* internode		1	1				2	3			1
ca	*Agrostemma githago*		1	1						1		
ca	*Polygonum aviculare*		1				2	2		2		1
cg	*Vicia tetrasperma*					1		2	1			
cr	*Plantago media*							1		1		
cx	Polygonaceae undiff	1						1		1		2
ca	*Centaurea cyanus*	1	1	1					1	1		
cx	*Vicia* sp(p)	1										1
cx	*Veronica* sp(p)	1										
ce	*Pisum sativum*			1	9		1					
cg	*Chrysanthemum leucanthemum*		1	1								
cx	Indeterminate	6			1		1					3
cx	*Atriplex* sp(p)				1					1	1	
ca	*Stellaria media*									3	3	
cr	*Lapsana communis*									1	1	
cs	*Avena strigosa* fl. base					1						
cc	*Hordeum* naked	1										
cs	*Triticum aestivum* rachis node			1		1						
cw	*Polygonum amphibium*			1								1
cx	*Ranunculus* sp(p)			1				1				
cg	*Pimpinella saxifraga*			2								
cr	cf *Erysimum cheiranthoides*			1								
cx	*Trifolium* sp(p)				1			1				3
cx	Labiatae undiff		1									
cx	*Trifolium* sp(p) pod		1									
cw	*Polygonum hydropiper*		1						2			
ch	*Sieglingia decumbens*				1							
cr	*Raphanus raphanistrum* pod frag				1							
cx	*Polygonum* sp(p)					3						
cm	*Atriplex patula*						1					
cs	*Hordeum* 6-row rachis internode							1				
ct	*Corylus avellana* nut frag							2				
cg	*Centaurea nigra*							1				
cg	*Thalictrum minus*							1				
ca	*Polygonum lapathifolium*								1			1
cw	*Carex* (trigonous)									1		
wg	*Lathyrus pratensis*									1		1
ca	*Legousia hybrida*									2		1
ca	*Cerastium arvense*										1	
cr	*Brassica nigra*										1	
cr	*Vicia sativa*											1
ca	*Chrysanthemum segetum*											1
cr	*Prunella vulgaris*											1
cx	*Ranunculus repens*-type											1
cx	cf *Glechoma hederacea*											1
ca	*Papaver* sp(p)											1

Twinspan group D

		C1027	C441	C739	C740
cc	Cerealia undiff	2	36	19	8
cc	*Avena* grain	4	25	1	3
cs	*Avena* awn	2	72		2
cx	Legume <4mm	1	2		1
cs	Culm nodes	1	1		
cc	*Triticum aestivum* grain	1	4		
cr	*Rumex acetosella*	1	3		
cx	Gramineae undiff		9	1	1
cr	*Rumex obtusifolius*-type		3	1	
cg	*Plantago lanceolata*		3	1	
cx	*Veronica officinalis*		1	1	
cx	Indeterminate	2			
ca	*Agrostemma githago*	2			
cr	Chenopodiaceae undiff	1			
cx	*Ranunculus repens*-type	1			
cc	*Hordeum* indet		3		
cc	*Secale cereale* grain		5		
cs	*Avena fatua* floret base		1		
cr	*Plantago major*		1		
cx	Polygonaceae undiff		1		
cg	cf *Campanula rotundifolia*		2		
ca	*Legousia hybrida*		2		
cc	*Hordeum* naked		1		
ca	*Sinapis arvensis*		1		
ca	*Chenopodium bonus-henricus*		1		
ca	*Polygonum periscaria*		1		
ca	*Polygonum aviculare*		1		1
cg	*Vicia tetrasperma*			1	
cx	*Trifolium* sp(p)			1	
ca	*Spergula arvensis*			1	
ca	*Stellaria media*				2

Twinspan group E

		C1284	C1273	C1071	C1030	C1013	C986	C982	C568	C1131	C1123	C1031	C1025	C1012
cc	Cerealia undiff	24	5	11	99	21	131	28	17	11	61	30	1	45
cc	*Avena* grain	36	34	4	36	17	34	6	7	10	19	22	15	22
cc	*Triticum aestivum* grain	2	5	3	15	6	1	4	2		1	8	60	3
cc	*Hordeum* hulled	1		2	1	3		2	1		5	1		
cx	Gramineae undiff	2	2	1		1	1	1	1					1
cs	*Avena* awn	2			7	5	14		8		3		1	7
cc	*Hordeum* indet	4	7		3		1		4	1	1	1		1
cg	*Plantago lanceolata*	1			2	2	1			1		1		
cx	Legume <4mm			1	5	1						1	2	
cc	*Secale cereale* grain			1	1		1	1					1	
cr	*Rumex acetosella*			1	1					1	5		2	
cg	*Rumex acetosa*				1	1	1			1	1			
cr	Chenopodiaceae undiff				2	1	1			1		2	3	
ca	*Polygonum periscaria*				1			1	1	1	2			
ca	*Chenopodium album*	9				2				1	1		1	3
cx	*Bromus* sp(p) grain			2					1	3		1	1	
cs	*Hordeum* rachis internode							1				2	1	
cw	*Polygonum amphibium*									1	2			
cr	*Rumex obtusifolius*-type			1			1		1		1			
ca	*Spergula arvensis*	1				1								
cx	*Polygonum* sp(p)	1					1							
cs	*Avena sativa* floret base	1			1	1							1	
cg	*Vicia cracca*-type			1	2					1				
ca	*Stellaria media*			1	1		2					1		
cr	*Lapsana communis*										1		1	
ce	*Pisum sativum*		1					2						
cs	*Avena fatua* floret base		1							1		4		
cr	*Brassica* sp(p)										1		1	
ca	*Fallopia convolvulus*			1				1						
cw	*Carex* (trigonous)	3								1				1
cs	*Avena* sp(p) fl. base				1								2	
cr	*Raphanus raphanistrum* pod frag			1										
cx	*Trifolium* sp(p)				1									
cc	*Hordeum* naked			2										
cx	Indeterminate			1										
cx	Legume >4mm			1										
cg	*Hypochoeris radicata*				1									
cw	*Polygonum hydropiper*				1									
cr	*Brassica rapa*					1								
cw	*Carex* (lenticular)							1						
ca	*Sinapis arvensis*							1						
cx	Compositae undiff									1				
ca	*Centaurea cyanus*										1			
cx	*Veronica* sp(p)										1			
cr	*Cirsium* sp(p)											1		
ca	*Legousia hybrida*												2	
cw	*Apium nodiflorum/graveolens*												1	
cx	*Rumex* sp(p)													2
ca	*Polygonum lapth./persicaria*												1	
ca	*Cerastium arvense*													1
ca	*Anthemis cotula*													4
cs	*Avena strigosa* fl. base													1
ce	*Linum usitatissimum*													1
cs	Culm nodes													1

Twinspan group F

		C1305	C1260	C1244	C848
cc	*Avena* grain	31	4	89	40
cc	Cerealia undiff	7	1	5	17
cc	*Triticum aestivum* grain	13	7	12	4
cx	Legume <4mm	12	5	6	2
cc	*Secale cereale* grain	1	1	25	1
cs	Culm nodes	2	1	17	
cc	*Hordeum* hulled	8		4	4
cx	Gramineae undiff		1	2	1
cs	*Secale* rachis internode		1	63	3
cr	*Rumex obtusifolius*-type	2		2	2
mc	*Avena* grain	1	1		
cw	*Carex* (trigonous)	2		1	
cs	*Triticum* brittle rachis internode	1		2	
cx	Legume >4mm		2	2	
ca	*Chrysanthemum segetum*			3	1
ca	*Agrostemma githago*			1	1
cs	*Avena sativa* floret base			1	1
mx	Legume <4mm	2			
mw	*Carex* (trigonous)	2			
cx	*Galium verum/palustre/mollugo*	1			
cs	*Hordeum* rachis internode	1			
cg	*Plantago lanceolata*	2			1
ce	*Vicia faba*	4			
ca	*Spergula arvensis*	1			
cw	*Carex* (lenticular)		1		
ms	*Avena* swn		1		
cs	*Triticum aestivum* rachis node			13	
ca	*Polygonum lapth./persicaria*			1	

Twinspan group G

		C1403	C1216	C948	C883	C1278	C897	C881
cc	*Avena* grain	14	20	5	69	45	41	32
cc	Cerealia undiff	1	24	24	25	22		13
cc	*Hordeum* indet	2	2	1	3	12	7	
cc	*Triticum aestivum* grain		5	3	18	4	5	1
cs	*Avena* awn	1		2	1	2	2	2
cc	*Hordeum* hulled		2	1	2	2	5	10
cr	*Raphanus raphanistrum* pod frag	1	1		1	1		
cc	*Secale cereale* grain		3	2		1		1
cw	*Carex* (trigonous)			1	1	1	2	
ca	*Chenopodium album*				4	1	1	
cx	Gramineae undiff			1		3	3	
ca	*Polygonum lapth./persicaria*				5	7	5	
cs	Culm nodes	1		1		2		3
ch	*Sieglingia decumbens*				1		1	
cs	*Hordeum* rachis internode						2	
cr	*Rumex obtusifolius*-type		1		2	1		
cx	*Arrhenatherum elatius* - tuber		2					
ct	*Corylus avellana* nut frag			4				
cs	Avena sativa floret base			1			1	
cx	*Potentilla* sp(p)				1			
cx	*Bromus* sp(p) grain				1			
cs	*Triticum aestivum* rachis node				1			
cs	*Hordeum* 6-row rachis internode				2			
cr	*Galium aparine*				1			
cg	*Rumex acetosa*				1		1	
ca	*Anthemis cotula*					1		
cg	*Plantago lanceolata*					1		
cr	*Brassica* sp(p)						1	
ce	*Linum usitatissimum*						1	
cw	*Lychnis flos-cuculi*						1	
ca	*Galeopsis tetrahit*						1	

Twinspan group H

		C1349	C1341	C761	C1276	C984	C845	C836
cc	Cerealia undiff	3	2	3	47	8	40	1
cc	*Avena* grain	9	4	2	2	4	61	10
cs	*Avena* awn	14		3				1
cw	*Carex* (trigonous)	1	1	1				
ch	*Siglingia decumbens*	1	1					2
cs	Culm nodes		1				1	
cc	*Triticum aestivum* grain		1		4			
cc	*Hordeum* hulled			1	7		1	6
ca	*Polygonum lapth./persicaria*						1	2
cr	Chenopodiaceae undiff			1				
cm	*Fucus* - thallus/frond				1			
cx	Legume >4mm						1	
cx	*Ranunculus repens*-type						1	
cc	*Hordeum* indet						4	
cc	*Triticum* sp(p) grain						4	1
ca	*Fallopia convolvulus*							1
ct	*Corylus avellana* nut frag							1
cw	*Carex* pilulifera							1
cs	*Hordeum* basal internode							1

Twinspan constancy (percentage occurrence) data tables

	TWINSPAN group	A	B	C	D	E	F	G	H
cc	*Avena* grain	100	100	100	100	100	100	100	100
cc	Cerealia undiff	80	100	100	100	100	100	85.7	100
cc	*Triticum aestivum* grain	100	100	90.9	50	92.3	100	85.7	28.6
cs	Culm nodes	100	100	81.8	50	7.69	75	57.1	28.6
cc	*Hordeum* hulled	80	100	90.9		61.5	75	85.7	57.1
cc	*Secale cereale* grain	100	100	100	25	38.5	100	57.1	
cr	*Rumex obtusifolius*-type	100	100	90.9	50	30.8	75	42.9	
ca	*Spergula arvensis*	60	100	90.9	25	15.4	25		
cs	*Avena* awn	80	100	100	75	61.5		85.7	42.9
cc	*Hordeum* indet	60	66.7	90.9	25	69.2		85.7	14.3
cg	*Plantago lanceolata*	80	66.7	72.7	50	46.2	50	14.3	
cx	Legume >4mm	40	33.3	36.4		7.69	50		14.3
ca	*Agrostemma githago*	100	100	27.3	25		50		
cr	*Rumex acetosella*	100	100	81.8	50	38.5			
cr	Chenopodiaceae undiff	80	100	81.8	25	46.2			14.3
ca	*Polygonum periscaria*	20	66.7	90.9	25	38.5			
ca	*Stellaria media*	20	66.7	18.2	25	30.8			
cc	*Hordeum* naked	20	33.3	9.09	25	7.69			
cs	*Avena fatua* floret base	40	33.3	63.6	25	23.1			
cs	*Triticum aestivum* rachis node	100	100	18.2			25	14.3	
ca	*Chrysanthemum segetum*	100	100	9.09			50		
cg	*Chrysanthemum leucanthemum*	60	66.7	18.2					
ca	*Centaurea cyanus*	100	100	45.5		7.69			
cr	*Lapsana communis*	100	100	18.2		15.4			
ca	*Anthemis cotula*	80	100	72.7		7.69		14.3	
ca	*Chenopodium album*	80	100	90.9		46.2		42.9	
ca	*Cerastium arvense*	40	66.7	9.09		7.69			
cg	*Rumex acetosa*	80	66.7	54.5		38.5		28.6	
cg	*Vicia cracca*-type	80	100	27.3		23.1			
ce	*Pisum sativum*	40	66.7	27.3		15.4			
cs	*Avena sativa* floret base	80	66.7	90.9		30.8	50	28.6	
ch	Sieglingia decumbens	20	33.3	9.09				28.6	42.9
cw	*Carex* (trigonous)	40	66.7	9.09		23.1	50	57.1	42.9
ca	*Polygonum lapth./persicaria*	20				7.69	25	42.9	28.6
ca	*Sinapis arvensis*	40		45.5	25	7.69			
cg	*Vicia tetrasperma*	20		27.3	25				
ca	*Polygonum aviculare*	40		45.5	50				
cr	*Raphanus raphanistrum* pod frag	40		9.09		7.69		57.1	
cr	Vicia sativa	40	33.3	9.09					
cs	*Avena* sp(p) fl. base	40	33.3	63.6		15.4			
cs	*Hordeum* 6-row rachis internode	60	33.3	9.09				14.3	
cs	*Hordeum* rachis internode	80	66.7	27.3		23.1	25	14.3	
cs	*Secale* rachis internode	100	66.7	45.5			75		
cs	*Triticum* brittle rachis internode	80	33.3				50		
cw	*Polygonum amphibium*	20	66.7	18.2		15.4			
cx	Legume <4mm	100	100	72.7	75	38.5	100		
cx	Gramineae undiff	100	100	81.8	75	61.5	75	42.9	

TWINSPAN group		**A**	**B**	**C**	**D**	**E**	**F**	**G**	**H**
cx	*Trifolium* sp(p)	80	100	27.3	25	7.69			
cx	*Bromus* sp(p) grain	80	100	63.6		38.5		14.3	
cx	Indeterminate	60		36.4	25	7.69			
ca	*Legousia hybrida*			18.2	25	7.69			
ce	*Linum usitatissimum*			36.4		7.69		14.3	
ca	*Fallopia convolvulus*	20		54.5		15.4			14.3
cr	*Brassica* sp(p)	20				15.4		14.3	
cr	*Conium maculatum*	40	33.3						
cg	*Vicia tetrasperma*-type	80	33.3						
cx	*Polygonum* sp(p)		66.7	9.09		15.4			
cr	*Prunella vulgaris*		33.3	9.09					
ca	*Polygonum* lapathifolium		33.3	18.2					
cx	*Ranunculus repens*-type			9.09	25				14.3
cx	Polygonaceae undiff			36.4	25				
cx	*Veronica* sp(p)	40		9.09		7.69			
cx	*Vicia* sp(p)	20		18.2					
cx	*Atriplex* sp(p)	20		27.3					
wg	*Lathyrus pratensis*	20		18.2					
cg	*Pimpinella saxifraga*	20		9.09					
cx	Labiatae undiff	20		9.09					
cs	*Avena strigosa* fl. base	20		9.09		7.69			
cw	*Polygonum hydropiper*			18.2		7.69			
ct	*Corylus avellana* nut frag			9.09				14.3	14.3
cw	*Carex* (lenticular)		66.7			7.69	25		
ce	*Vicia faba*		33.3				25		
cr	*Plantago major*		33.3		25				
cg	*Hypochoeris radicata*	60				7.69			
ca	*Chenopodium bonus-henricus*	40			25				
cx	Compositae undiff	20				7.69			
cx	*Galium verum/palustre/mollugo*	60					25		
cr	*Galium aparine*	20						14.3	
cs	*Triticum aestivum internode*	*80*							
ca	*Matricaria matricariodes*	*40*							
ca	*Scleranthus annuus* calyx	40							
ce	*Lens culinaris*	20							
ct	*Quercus* cupule/acorn fragment	20							
cr	*Urtica dioica*	20							
cr	*Veronica* chamaedrys	20							
cx	Caryophyllaceae undiff	20							
cr	cf. *Anthriscus sylvestris*	20							
cg	*Linum catharticum*	20							
ca	*Matricaria recutita*	20							
cx	*Ranunculus* sp(p)			18.2					
cr	*Plantago media*			18.2					
cx	*Trifolium* sp(p) pod			9.09					
cx	cf. *Glechoma hederacea*			9.09					
cg	*Centaurea nigra*			9.09					
cg	*Thalictrum minus*			9.09					
cr	cf. *Erysimum cheiranthoides*			9.09					
cm	*Atriplex patula*			9.09					
cr	*Brassica nigra*			9.09					
ca	*Papaver* sp(p)			9.09					
cx	*Veronica officinalis*				50				
cg	cf. *Campanula rotundifolia*				25				
cw	*Apium nodiflorum/graveolens*					7.69			
cx	*Rumex* sp(p)					7.69			
cr	*Cirsium* sp(p)					7.69			
cr	*Brassica rapa*					7.69			
mc	*Avena* grain						50		
ms	*Avena* awn						25		
mx	Legume <4mm						25		
mw	*Carex* (trigonous)						25		
cw	*Lychnis flos-cuculi*							14.3	
cx	*Arrhenatherum elatius* - tuber							14.3	
cx	*Potentilla* sp(p)							14.3	
ca	*Galeopsis tetrahit*							14.3	
cc	*Triticum* sp(p) grain								28.6
cw	*Carex pilulifera*								14.3
cs	*Hordeum* basal internode								14.3
cm	*Fucus* - thallus/frond								14.3

Constancy groups showing taxa having value IV or more in at least one group of samples

TWINSPAN group	A	B	C	E	F	G	D	H
cc *Avena* grain	V	V	V	V	V	V	V	V
cc Cerealia undiff	IV	V	V	V	V	V	V	V
cc *Triticum aestivum* grain	V	V	V	V	V	V	IV	II
cs Culm nodes	V	V	V	I	IV	III	III	II
cc *Hordeum* hulled	IV	V	V	IV	IV	V		III
cx Gramineae undiff	V	V	V	IV	IV	III	IV	
cc *Secale cereale* grain	V	V	V	III	V	III	II	
cr *Rumex obtusifolius*-type	V	V	V	II	IV	III	III	
cr *Rumex acetosella*	V	V	V	II			III	
cx Legume <4mm	V	V	IV	II	V		IV	
ca *Agrostemma githago*	V	V	II		III		II	
ca *Chrysanthemum segetum*	V	V	I		III			
cs *Triticum aestivum* rachis node	V	V	I		II	I		
ca *Centaurea cyanus*	V	V	III	I				
cr *Lapsana communis*	V	V	I	I				
cs *Secale* rachis internode	V	IV	III		IV			
cg *Plantago lanceolata*	IV	IV	IV	III	III	I	III	
cw *Carex* (trigonous)	II	IV	I	II	III	III		III
cs *Avena sativa* floret base	IV	IV	V	II	III	II		
cs *Avena* awn	IV	V	V	IV		V	IV	III
cc *Hordeum* indet	III	IV	V	IV		V	II	I
cr Chenopodiaceae undiff	IV	V	V	III			II	I
ca *Spergula arvensis*	III	V	V	I	II		II	
ca *Chenopodium album*	IV	V	V	III		III		
ca *Anthemis cotula*	IV	V	IV	I		I		
cx *Bromus* sp(p) grain	IV	V	IV	II		I		
cx *Trifolium* sp(p)	IV	V	II	I			II	
cg *Vicia cracca*-type	IV	V	II	II				
cs *Hordeum* rachis internode	IV	IV	II	II	II	I		
cg *Rumex acetosa*	IV	IV	III	II		II		
ca *Polygonum periscaria*	I	IV	V	II			II	
ce *Pisum sativum*	II	IV	II	I				
ca *Cerastium arvense*	II	IV	I	I				
cs *Avena fatua* floret base	II	II	IV	II			II	
cs *Avena* sp(p) fl. base	II	II	IV	I				
cw *Polygonum amphibium*	I	IV	II	I				
cs *Triticum* brittle rachis internode	IV	II			III			
cg *Vicia tetrasperma*-type	IV	II						
cs *Triticum aestivum* internode	IV							
cx *Polygonum* sp(p)		IV	I	I				

APPENDIX 2
COUNTS OF ANATOMICAL ZONES

Louisa J Gidney

EM: Early medieval M: Medieval LM: Late medieval EPM: Early post-medieval

Cattle

	EM	M	LM	EPM
Skull				
1				
2				
3				
4				
5				
6				
7				
8			3	
9		1	1	1
0				
Jaw				
1		4	1	2
2	2	4		1
3	1	5	1	2
4	1	1		2
1	1	1		
2		2		
7	1	2	1	
8	1	1		1
Scapula				
1				
2	1	2	1	
3	1	1	1	1
4			2	
5				
6				
7				
Humerus				
1				
2		2		
3				
4				
5				
6	1	5		
7		3		
8		2		
9	1	3		

	EM	M	LM	EPM
Radius				
1		2		
2		2		
3	1	2		
4		1		
5		1		
6				
Ulna				
1	1	1		
2		2		1
3				
4				
Metacarpal				
1		3	3	2
2		4	3	2
3		3		1
4		3		
5		4		2
Innominate				
1				
2	1			2
3		1		4
4				1
5		1		
6				
7		2		
8				
9	1			1
0				1
Femur				
1		1	1	
2				1
3		2		1
4		2	2	
5		1	1	
6		1		
7				

	EM	M	LM	EPM
Tibia				
1			1	
2			1	
3			1	
4	1		1	2
5				2
6				
7		2		1
Calcaneum				
1		1		
2		2	2	
3		3	2	
Metatarsal				
1	1	2	1	2
2			5	5
3	1	2		1
4	1	2		1
5	1	5		1
Phalanx 1				
1	1	4	3	1
2		3	3	3
Phalanx 2		4	4	
1	1	3	2	2
Phalanx 3				
1		3		
Astragalus				
1	1		2	
				3
Centroquartal		3		
1		3		
Malleolus				
1	1	1		
Carpals		2	1	

Sheep/Goat

	EM	M	LM	EPM
Skull				
1				
2			1	
3				
4				
5			1	
6				
7				
8		2		
9		5	2	2
0				
		3		3
Jaw				
1		3	3	5
2	1	6	3	7
3	1	4	3	7
4	1	1	3	6
5	1	2	3	7
6	1	1	1	
7	1	3	3	5
8	1	1	1	4
Scapula				
1			1	3
2		1	3	6
3		5	4	6
4			1	1
5		3	4	5
6				
7				2
Humerus				
1		2	2	1
2		2	1	1
3			2	
4		2		
5		3	2	3
6		7	8	8
7	1	4	3	4
8		4	3	2
9		7	8	8

	EM	M	LM	EPM
Radius				
1		1	5	1
2		1	2	
3	1	6	13	7
4				
5				2
6				
Ulna				
1			1	1
2		2	4	3
4	3		2	
	4			
Metacarpal				
1		4	4	3
2		2	4	4
3			2	
4			2	
5			4	
Innominate				
1				
2		2		2
3	2	3	1	4
4	1	5	2	3
5		2	2	4
6				
7		4	8	5
8			4	2
9	2	5	3	5
0			2	
Femur				
1				1
2	1	2		
3				1
4		3	3	2
5		2	1	1
6		2		1
7		1	1	1

	EM	M	LM	EPM
Tibia				
1			2	1
2			2	1
3			2	
4	2	6	7	
5		3	5	3
6		3	5	3
7		11	12	13
Calcaneum				
1		1	2	
2	2			
3			2	2
Metatarsal				
1		3	2	4
2		3	2	4
3			1	1
4			1	1
5		1	1	1
Phalanx 1				
1		4	6	6
2		5	10	6
Phalanx 2				
1		3	1	2
Phalanx 3				
1		1	1	2
Astragalus				
1		4	4	1
Centroquartal				
1		1		1
Malleolus		2	3	2
1				
Carpals				

Pig

	EM	M	LM	EPM
Skull				
1			1	
2			1	
3				
4				
5				
6				
7				
8		2		
9		1		
0				
Jaw				
1		1	1	2
2		1		2
3		1		2
4		1		
5			1	
6			2	
7		1		
8				
Scapula				
1		1		
2		1		
3		3	1	3
4			1	
5		2	1	1
6				
7				
Humerus				
1				
2				
3				
4				
5		1	1	1
6		1	6	
7			2	
8			2	
9		1	5	

	EM	M	LM	EPM
Radius				
1		2	1	
2		2	1	
3		3	2	
4				
5				
6				
Ulna				
1				
2		2	1	
3		2	1	
4				
Metacarpal				
1				
2		2		
3				
4				
5				
Innominate				
1				
2			1	
3			2	
4				
5				
6				
7			1	
8			1	
9			1	
0				
Femur				
1				
2				
3				
4				
5				
6				
7				

	EM	M	LM	EPM
Tibia				
1				
2				
3				
4		2	3	1
5		1		
6		1		
7		2		
Calcaneum				
1				
2		2	1	1
3		1	1	1
Metatarsal				
1			1	
2		1		
3				
4				
5				
Phalanx 1				
1				
2		2	2	
Phalanx 2				
1	1			
Phalanx 3				
1			1	

APPENDIX 3
PHOSPHATE ANALYSIS OF PREHISTORIC POTTERY

Michael Alexander

The results of the phosphate analysis (carried out in 1980) are shown in Figure A3.1.

Pot 1: all three samples have very similar phosphorus concentrations and in all probability represent the general background or 'natural' soil phosphorus levels.

Pot 2: sample 1 submitted as a background sample shows rather higher phosphate concentration than the levels shown by the Pot 1 samples. However the difference is not sufficient to permit any categorical statement to be made as to the source of the phosphorus. Samples from the crushed sherd and the lining of the pot show very high phosphate levels strongly suggesting anthropogenic influence. However, in view of the small sample from the pot lining and the high phosphorus level in the sherd I would hesitate to suggest the possibility of the phosphorus levels indicating a cremation. It could well be that the use of such a pot for cooking over a period of time could impregnate the pot with phosphorous from the items being cooked.

		ppmP	
Pot 1	1	520.0	Soil outside of spread of pot
	2	420.0	Soil within spread of pot
	3	536.0	Soil outside spread of pot
Pot 2	1	800.0	Soil adjacent to sherds
	2	2048.0	Outer surface of a sherd
	3	3273.0*	Scraping of black material from inner surface of sherds

* Sample submitted only 0.44g therefore accuracy cannot be relied upon

FIGURE A3.1
Table of samples for phosphate analysis

APPENDIX 4

INVESTIGATION OF PRESERVED ORGANIC RESIDUES FROM EARLY NEOLITHIC SHERDS FROM THE HIRSEL USING LIPID ANALYSIS

Lucy Cramp

Preserved organic residues were investigated from the fabric of two sherds from Pot 1, and one sherd from Pot 2. Small fragments of these sherds were cleaned and crushed prior to solvent-extraction and analysis using gas chromatography (GC), GC/mass spectrometry (GC/MS) and GC-combustion-isotope ratio MS (GC/C/IRMS), in order to investigate the products processed in these vessels in prehistory. The distributions of preserved lipid components in pottery can be utilised to distinguish fats of various origins, including animal fats, plant waxes, oils and resins. Degraded animal fats, characterised by high abundances of saturated fatty acids, specifically palmitic ($C_{16:0}$) and stearic ($C_{18:0}$) acids, can be further classified by the stable carbon isotope composition of individual fatty acids. The $\delta^{13}C$ signature of fatty acids in animal tissues reflects both the source(s) of organic carbon and the metabolism of the organism, and thus may be exploited in order to assign archaeological fats to their origins. Milk fats are distinguished from adipose fats in ruminant species by more depleted $\delta^{13}C$ values of the $C_{18:0}$ fatty acids (Evershed *et al* 2002a; 2002b). It is also possible to discriminate between ruminant and non-ruminant (e.g. pig) fats from enriched values (+4 to +7‰) which characterise the latter (Evershed *et al* 1997; Mottram *et al* 1999), again resulting from metabolic and dietary differences (Koch *et al* 1994).

The pottery sherds were photographed and then the exterior surfaces of approximately 2g sherd were cleaned using a modelling drill, and crushed to powder. After addition of 20 μg *n*-tetratriacontane as an internal standard, the sherd was lipid extracted (2 x 10ml chloroform/methanol, 2:1 v/v, sonication x 20 min). The resultant total lipid extracts (TLEs) were filtered through a silica column and then treated with 40 μl *N,O*-bis(trimethylsilyl) trifluoroacetamide (70°, 1h). These derivatives were dissolved in an appropriate volume of hexane and screened using high temperature GC (HTGC). Aliquots of the three TLEs were then hydrolysed (2ml 0.5M NaOH/MeOH, 70°, 1h) and methylated (100 μl boron trifluoride in methanol with 1 % trichlorosilane; 75°, 1h), then analysed using GC/MS and GC/C/IRMS.

Pot 1

Two sherds (HS-1 and HS-3) from the belly of Pot 1 were investigated, with HS-3 deriving from the upper belly. Both contained significant concentrations of lipid, with the upper belly sherd containing the highest concentration of lipid (282 μg g^{-1}) compared with the other sherd (77 μg g^{-1}). This pattern is commonly observed in vessels used for boiling since lipids are wicked up through the vessel wall and will also float on the surface of water (Charters *et al* 1993). Both total lipid extracts (TLEs) resembled degraded animal fats, being dominated by high concentrations of saturated fatty acids ($C_{16:0}$ and $C_{18:0}$), along with significant concentrations of branched- and odd-carbon number fatty acids that occur in fats of ruminant origin (Christie 1978). The determination of the $\delta^{13}C$ values of individual fatty acids in these fats has confirmed that these residues originate from ruminant (i.e. cattle, sheep or goat) carcass fats. A distinctive distribution of mid-chain ketones (C_{31}–C_{35}) was observed in both lipid extracts, which is known to arise from heating of animal fats in excess of 300° (Evershed *et al* 1995; Raven *et al* 1997).

Pot 2

One sherd from the belly of this vessel (HS-2) was lipid-extracted, yielding 100 μg g^{-1} lipid. Again, this lipid extract was characterised by a predominance of saturated fatty acids, alongside branched- and odd carbon number fatty acids, thus resembling degraded ruminant fat. However, in contrast to Pot 1, the determination of the $\delta^{13}C$ values of individual fatty acids has revealed a dairy fat origin for this residue. In addition, a series of long-chain fatty acids (C_{20}–C_{26}) was also identified which occur in degraded waxes, although this would typically be accompanied by long-chain *n*-alkanes, *n*-alkanols and wax esters (Tulloch 1976).

APPENDIX 5
ANALYSIS OF THE SPURS

Philip Clogg

The following seven iron spurs and an iron rowel from The Hirsel were presented for investigative analysis: FeSp1, FeSp2, FeSp3, FeSp4, FeSp6, FeSp7, FeSp8 and FeSp9.

During cleaning and conservation, fragments of a white metal 'plating' were uncovered on the surface of the artefacts. An analytical scan of the surfaces of the arms and the points of each spur was undertaken using energy dispersive X-ray fluorescence (EDXRF) to identify the white metal coating.

The results are presented as spectrum plots in Figures A5.1–3. These show clearly defined energy peaks for the elements iron (Fe) and tin (Sn), indicating that a coating of tin had been applied to all sections of each of the iron spurs.

In addition, the iron rowel was also analysed (Figure A5.3) and the results also indicated the presence of a surface coating of tin.

The lack of any trace of lead within the analysis indicates that the plating material was pure tin rather than a tin-lead alloy. It has been suggested that this type of plating process consisted of first 'fluxing' the spurs, then sprinkling them with powdered tin and heating (Tylecote 1976).

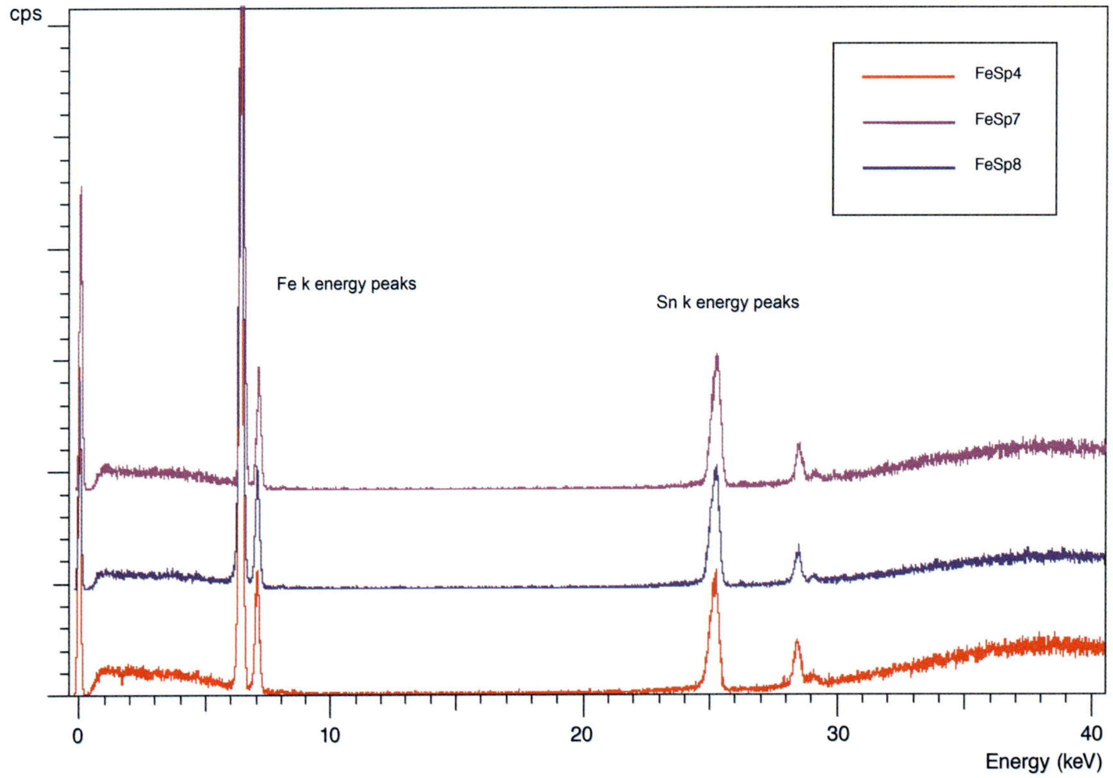

FIGURE A5.1
EDXRF Spectra from the surface of the Hirsel spurs FeSp7, FeSp8, FeSp4

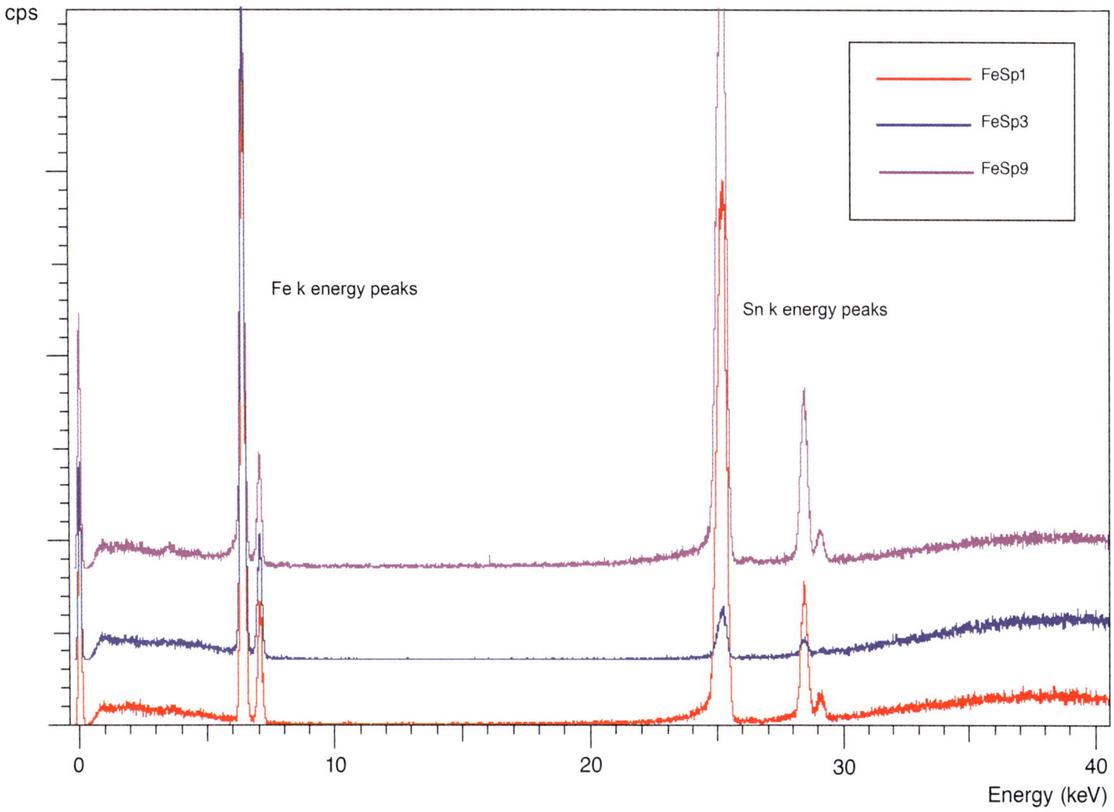

FIGURE A5.2
EDXRF Spectra from the surface of Hirsel spurs FeSp3, FeSp9, FeSp1

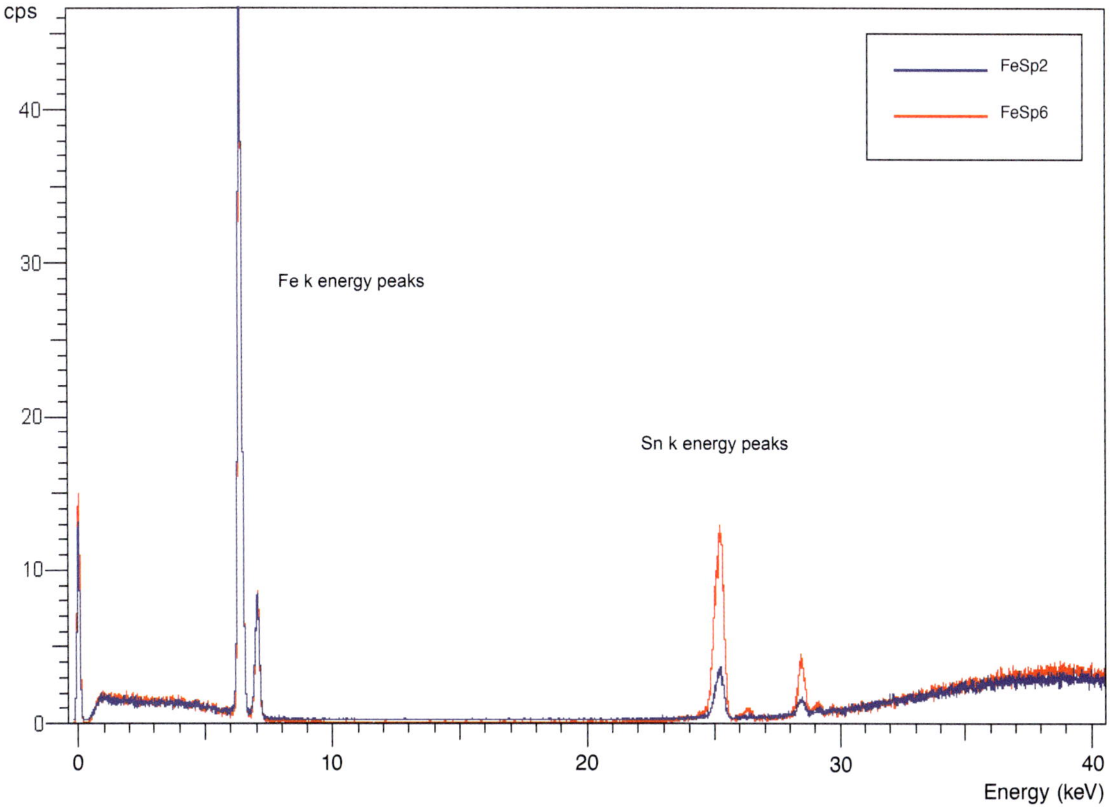

FIGURE A5.3
EDXRF Spectra from the surface of Hirsel spurs FeSp2, FeSp6

BIBLIOGRAPHY

Historic maps, National Library of Scotland

Armstrong, Andrew, 1700–1794; Armstrong, Mostyn, fl. 1769–1791 *South East section: Map of the County of Berwick* [EMS.s.316]

Blackadder, John, fl. 1793–1830 *Berwickshire* 1797 [EMS.s.46]

Gordon, Robert, 1580–1661 *A description of the province of the Merche. The Mers* [c1636–1652] [Gordon 58]

Greenwood, Christopher, 1786–1855; Fowler, William, fl. 1818–1863; Sharp, T, [nd]. *Right side: The County of Berwick* 1826 [EMS.s.322]

Pont, Timothy, 1560?–1614?; Blaeu, Joan, 1596–1673, *Mercia, vulgo vicecomitatus, Bervicensis/auct. Timothei Pont. Merce or Shirrefdome of Berwick* [1654] [WD3B/7

Abbreviations

BAR	British Archaeological Reports, Oxford
CDLHS	Coldstream and District Local History Society
Cold. Cart.	*Chartulary of the Cistercian Priory of Coldstream* (Grampian Club 1879), see Rogers 1879
HE	*Historia Ecclesiastica Gentis Anglorum*, see Plummer 1896
HMSO	Her Majesty's Stationery Office, London
NCH	*Northumberland County History*, see Northumberland County History Committee 1935
Reg. Mag. Sig.	*Regiam Magni Sigilii Regum Scotorum*, ed. Thomson and others, Edinburgh 1882–1914
Reg. Privy Council	*The Register of the Privy Council of Scotland*, Vol 1, see Burton 1877
RCAHMS	The Royal Commission on the Ancient and Historical Monuments of Scotland

References

Anon, 1984 'The Anglo-Saxon church', *Current Archaeology* 91, 249–250

Addis, L, 1979 'The pottery', in M O H Carver, 'Three Saxo-Norman tenements in Durham City', *Medieval Archaeology* 23, 39–47 (1–80)

Aitken, M J, 1985 *Thermoluminescence dating*, Academic Press, London

Algar, D, Light, A and Trehane, P, 1979 *The Verwood and district potteries: a Dorset industry*, C J Newsome, Ringwood

Aliaga-Kelly, C J, 1986 'The Anglo-Saxon occupation of south-east Scotland', unpublished PhD thesis, University of Glasgow

Allen, J R, 1903 'General results arrived at from the archaeological survey of the early Christian monuments of Scotland', in J R Allen and J Anderson, *The early Christian monuments of Scotland*, Edinburgh (reprint 1993, Balgavies) pt II, 1–419

Anderson, A O, 1922 *Early sources of Scottish history, AD 500 to 1286*, 2 vols, Oliver and Boyd, Edinburgh and London

Anderson, S M, 1989 'A comparative study of the human skeletal material from late first and early second millennium sites in the north-east of England', unpublished M Phil thesis, University of Durham

Anderson, S M, 1994 'The human skeletal remains from the Hirsel, Coldstream, 1979–1984', unpublished archive report

Anderson, S M, Wells, C and Birkett, D, 2006 'The human skeletal remains', in R Cramp, *Wearmouth and Jarrow monastic sites* 2, English Heritage, Swindon, 481–545

Arnold, T (ed), 1886 *Symeonis Monachi Opera Omnia: 1, Historia Ecclesiae Dunhelmensis*, Rerum Britannicarum medii aevi scriptores 75(1), Longman & Co and Trübner & Co, London

Armstrong, P and Tomlinson, D G, 1987 *Excavations at the Dominican priory, Beverley, 1960–83*, Humberside Heritage Publication 13, Humberside Leisure Services, Hull

Ash, M, 1975 'The lands and churches of the bishops of St Andrews', in P McNeill and R Nicholson (eds), *An historical atlas of Scotland, c400–c1600*, Atlas Committee of the Conference of Scottish Medievalists, St Andrews, 40–41

Ashmore P J, Cook, G T and Harkness, D D, 2000 'A radiocarbon database for Scottish archaeological samples', *Radiocarbon* 42, 41–48

Aspinall, A, 1985 'Geophysical survey on Hirsel Law 1982–84', *Universities of Durham and Newcastle Archaeological Reports for 1984*, 58–65

Aspinall, A and Lynam, J T, 1970 'An induced polarization instrument for the detection of near-surface features', *Prospezioni Archeologiche* 5, 67–75

Ayers, B, 1985 *Excavations within the north-east bailey of Norwich Castle, 1979*, East Anglian Archaeology 28, Gressenhall

Bailey, M, 1988 'The rabbit and the medieval East Anglian economy', *Agricultural History Review* 36(1), 1–20

Bailey, R N and Cramp, R, 1988 *Corpus of Anglo-Saxon stone sculpture, 2: Cumberland, Westmorland and Lancashire North-of-the-Sands*, Oxford University Press for the British Academy, Oxford

Bailiff, I K, 1991 'The pre-dose technique', in H Y Göksu, M Oberhofer and D Regulla (eds), *Scientific dating methods*, Euro Courses, Advanced Scientific Techniques 1, Kluwer Academic, Dordrecht and Boston, 155–173

Bailiff, I K, 2007 'Methodological developments in the luminescence dating of brick from English late-medieval and post-medieval buildings', *Archaeometry* 49, 827–851

Bain, S, 1998 'Excavation of a medieval cemetery at Holyrood Abbey, Edinburgh', *Proceedings of the Society of Antiquaries of Scotland* 128, 1047–1077

Bakkveig, S, 1980 'Phosphate analysis in archaeology and recent progress', *Norwegian Archaeological Review* 13, 73–100

Balfour Paul, J and Thomson, J M (eds), 1883 *Registrum Magni Sigilli Regum Scotorum: Register of the Great Seal of Scotland, 3, AD 1513–1546*, Her Majesty's General Register House, Edinburgh

Barclay, G J, 2003 'Neolithic settlement in the lowlands of Scotland: a preliminary survey', in I Armit, E Murphy, E Nelis and D Simpson (eds), *Neolithic settlement in Ireland and Western Britain*, Oxbow, Oxford, 71–83

Barclay, K and Biddle, M, 1990 'Stone and pottery lamps', in M Biddle (ed), *Winchester studies 7. Artefacts from medieval Winchester. Part ii: Object and economy in medieval Winchester*, Clarendon Press, Oxford, 983–1000

Barrow, G W S, 1973 *The kingdom of the Scots*, Edward Arnold, London

Barrow, G W S, 2003 *The kingdom of the Scots: government, church and society from the eleventh to the fourteenth century*, Edinburgh University Press, Edinburgh (2nd edn)

Barrowman, R C, 2011 *The chapel and burial ground on St Ninian's Isle, Shetland: excavations past and present*, The Society for Medieval Archaeology Monograph 32, London

Bass, W, 1971 *Human osteology: a laboratory and field manual*, Special Publications Missouri Archaeological Society 2, Columbia, MO

Bateson, J D, 1991 'The 1991 Kelso treasure trove', *British Numismatic Journal* 61, 82–89

Bayley, J, Bryant, R and Heighway, C, 1993 'A tenth-century bell-pit and bell-mound from St Oswald's Priory, Gloucester', *Medieval Archaeology* 37, 224–236

Beals, K L, Smith, C L and Dodd, S M, 1983 'Climate and the evolution of brachycephalisation', *American Journal of Physical Anthropology* 62, 425–437

Bell, J, 1792 'Parish of Coldstream (County of Berwick)', in J Sinclair (ed), *The statistical account of Scotland, drawn up from the communications of the ministers of the different parishes* 4, William Creech, Edinburgh, 410–420

Bettess, G, 1991 'Old Bewick church, graveyard and historical environment', unpublished BA dissertation, University of Newcastle upon Tyne

Bettess, G, 1995 'A new investigation of Old Bewick church', *History of the Berwickshire Naturalists' Club* 46(3), 223–236

Biddle, M, 1965 'Excavations at Winchester 1964: third interim report', *Antiquaries Journal* 45, 230–264

Biddle, M (ed), 1990 *Winchester studies 7. Artefacts from medieval Winchester. Part ii: Object and economy in medieval Winchester*, Clarendon Press, Oxford

Birley, R, 2009 *Vindolanda: a Roman frontier fort on Hadrian's Wall*, Amberley Publishing, Stroud

Blackwell, A, 2007 'An Anglo-Saxon figure-decorated plaque from Ayton (Scottish Borders), its parallels and implications', *Medieval Archaeology* 51, 165–172

Blagg, T F C, 1974 'The bell-casting', in T F C Blagg, A E Werner, P T Craddock, H McK Blake and A T Luttrell, 'An Umbrian abbey: San Paolo di Valdiponte, part two', *Papers of the British School at Rome* 42, 133–145 (98–178)

Blair, J, 1996 'Churches in the early English landscape: social and cultural contexts', in J Blair and C Pyrah (eds), *Church archaeology: research directions for the future*, Council for British Archaeology Research Report 104, York, 6–18

Blair, J, 2010 'The prehistory of English fonts', in M Henig and N Ramsay (eds), *Intersections: the archaeology and history of Christianity in England, 400–1200*, BAR British Series 505, 149–177

Boddington, A, 1980 'A Christian Anglo-Saxon graveyard at Raunds, Northamptonshire', in P Rahtz, T Dickinson and L Watts (eds), *Anglo-Saxon cemeteries 1979*, BAR British Series 82, 373–378

Boddington, A, 1996 *Raunds Furnells: the Anglo-Saxon church and churchyard, Raunds Area Project*, English Heritage Archaeological Report 7, London

Bown, L, 1985 'The pottery', in D M O'Sullivan, 'An excavation in Holy Island village, 1977', *Archaeologia Aeliana*, 5 ser, 13, 47–80 (27–116)

Bown, L, 1998 'Pottery', in P Dixon, 'A rural medieval settlement in Roxburghshire: excavations at Springwood Park, Kelso, 1985–6', *Proceedings of the Society of Antiquaries of Scotland* 128, 726–739 (671–751)

Brenan, J, 1998 'Furnishings', in G Egan, *The medieval household: daily living c1150–c1450*, Medieval Finds from Excavations in London 6, HMSO, 65–84

Bronk Ramsey, C, 2009 'Bayesian analysis of radiocarbon dates', *Radiocarbon* 51(4), 337–360

Brooks, C M, 1980 'Medieval pottery from the kiln site at Colstoun, East Lothian', *Proceedings of the Society of Antiquaries of Scotland* 110, 364–403

Brothwell, D R, 1960 'A possible case of mongolism in a Saxon population', *Annals of Human Genetics* 24, 141–150

Brothwell, D R, 1981 *Digging up bones: the excavation, treatment and study of human skeletal remains*, Oxford University Press, Oxford

Burton, J H, 1877 *The Register of the Privy Council of Scotland 1*, Her Majesty's General Register House, Edinburgh

Caldwell, D H and Dean, V E, 1992 'The pottery industry at Throsk, Stirlingshire, in the 17th and early 18th century', *Post-Medieval Archaeology* 26, 1–46

Caldwell, D H and Stewart, H, 1996 'The ceramics', in G Ewart and J Triscott, 'Archaeological excavations at Castle Sween, Knapdale, Argyll and Bute, 1989–90',

Proceedings of the Society of Antiquaries of Scotland 126, 546–550 (517–557)

Cameron, A, 2006 'The excavation', in A Cameron, C P Croly and J Stones, *East Kirk of St Nicholas project: initial report*, Aberdeen City Council Archaeology Unit, Aberdeen, 6–18

Cameron, A, Croly, C P and Stones, J, 2006 *East Kirk of St Nicholas Project: initial report*, Aberdeen City Council Archaeology Unit, Aberdeen

Campbell, E, 2009 'Anglo-Saxon/Gaelic interaction in Scotland', in J Graham-Campbell and M Ryan (eds), *Anglo-Saxon/Irish relations before the Vikings*, Proceedings of the British Academy 157, Oxford University Press, Oxford, 253–263

Caple, C, 1991 'The detection and definition of an industry: the English medieval and post-medieval pin industry', *Archaeological Journal* 148, 241–255

Carver, M O H, 2008 *Portmahomack: monastery of the Picts*, Edinburgh University Press, Edinburgh

CDLHS, 2010 'The Hirsel and the Homes, the Lees and the Marjoribanks family', in *Second to none: a history of Coldstream*, CDLHS, Coldstream, 208–220

Charters, S, Evershed, R P, Goad, L J, Leydon, A, Blinkhorn, P W and Denham, V, 1993 'Quantification and distribution of lipid in archaeological ceramics: implications for sampling potsherds for organic residue analysis and the classification of vessel use', *Archaeometry* 35, 211–223

Chenery, S, Phillips, E and Haggarty, G, 2001 'An evaluation of geochemical fingerprinting for the provenancing of Scottish red ware pottery', *Medieval Ceramics* 25, 45–53

Christie, W W, 1978 'The composition, structure and function of lipids in the tissues of ruminant animals', *Progress in Lipid Research* 17, 111–205

Clapham, A R, Tutin, T G and Warburg, E F, 1962 *Flora of the British Isles*, Cambridge University Press, Cambridge (2nd edn)

Clark, J (ed), 2004 *The medieval horse and its equipment c1150–c1450*, Medieval Finds from Excavations in London 5, Boydell Press, Woodbridge (2nd edn)

Clarkson, T, 2010 *The men of the north: the Britons of southern Scotland*, John Donald, Edinburgh

Clouston, R W M, 1998 'The bells of Berwickshire', *History of the Berwickshire Naturalists' Club* 47(3), 235–274

Coghlan, H H, 1977 *Notes on prehistoric and early iron in the Old World*, Occasional Papers in Technology 8, Pitt Rivers Museum, Oxford (2nd edn)

Collingwood, E F and Cowen, J D, 1948 'A prehistoric grave at Haugh Head, Wooler', *Archaeologia Aeliana*, 4 ser, 26, 47–54

Collins, E J T, 1975 'Dietary change and cereal consumption in Britain in the nineteenth century', *Agricultural History Review* 23, 97–115

Collins, R, 2011 'Military communities and transformation of the frontier from the fourth to the sixth centuries', in D Petts and S Turner (eds), *Early medieval Northumbria: kingdoms and communities*, Studies in the Early Middle Ages 24, Brepols, Turnhout, 15–34

Cook, M, 2005 'East Lothian, Auldhame', *Society for Church Archaeology Newsletter* 6, 13

Cool, H, Ellis, B, Pearce, J and Zeepvat, R, 2009 'Medieval and post-medieval artefacts', in G Beresford, *Caldecote, the development and desertion of a Hertfordshire village*, The Society for Medieval Archaeology Monograph 28, London, 179–209

Cormack, W F, 1995 'Barhobble, Mochrum: excavation of a forgotten church site in Galloway', *Transactions of the Dumfriesshire and Galloway Natural History and Antiquarian Society*, 3 ser, 70, 5–106

Cotta, H, 1980 *Orthopaedics: a brief textbook*, Year Book Medical, Chicago, IL

Courtney, P, 1993 'The medieval and post-medieval objects', in P Ellis (ed), *Beeston Castle, Cheshire: a report on the excavations 1968–85 by Laurence Keen and Peter Hough*, English Heritage Archaeological Report 23, London, 134–161

Cowan, I B, 1961 'The development of the parochial system in medieval Scotland', *Scottish Historical Review* 40, 43–55

Cowan, I B, 1967 *The parishes of medieval Scotland*, Scottish Record Society 93, Edinburgh

Cowan, I B, 1995 *The medieval Church in Scotland*, (ed J Kirk) Scottish Academic Press, Edinburgh

Cowgill, J, de Neergaard, M and Griffiths, N, 1987 *Knives and scabbards*, Medieval Finds from Excavations in London 1, HMSO

Cox, A, 1996 'Backland activities in medieval Perth: excavations at Meal Vennel and Scott Street', *Proceedings of the Society of Antiquaries of Scotland* 126(2), 733–821

Cox, A, 2000 'Iron objects', in D R Perry, *Castle Park, Dunbar: two thousand years on a fortified headland*, Society of Antiquaries of Scotland Monograph 16, Edinburgh, 127–136

Cox, E, 1984 'Notes on ceramic material from Jedburgh Abbey', unpublished manuscript held in the library of RCAHMS, Edinburgh

Cox, E, Haggarty, G and Hurst, J G, 1984 'Ceramic material', in C J Tabraham, 'Excavations at Kelso Abbey', *Proceedings of the Society of Antiquaries of Scotland* 114, 381–398 (365–404)

Craig, D, 1997 'The sculptured stones', in P Hill, *Whithorn and St Ninian: the excavation of a monastic town 1984–91*, Sutton Publishing, Stroud, 433–441

Craig, E, 2007 'The investigation of social identity in later Anglo-Saxon cemeteries', *Church Archaeology* 11, 19–34

Cramp, R, 1980a 'Excavations at the Hirsel, Coldstream, Berwickshire', *Universities of Durham and Newcastle Archaeological Reports for 1979*, 17–19

Cramp, R, 1980b 'The Hirsel (Coldingham p): early medieval church, cemetery, medieval domestic structure', *Discovery and Excavation in Scotland 1980*, 1

Cramp, R, 1981a 'Excavations at the Hirsel, Coldstream, Borders Region', *Universities of Durham and Newcastle Archaeological Reports for 1980*, 45–48

Cramp, R, 1981b 'The Hirsel, Coldsteam (Coldingham p): early medieval church, cemetery, domestic structures', *Discovery and Excavation in Scotland 1981*, 1

Cramp, R, 1982a 'Excavations at the Hirsel, Coldstream, Borders Region', *Universities of Durham and Newcastle Archaeological Reports for 1981*, 33–37

Cramp, R, 1982b 'The Hirsel (Coldstream p): early medieval church, cemetery, medieval domestic building', *Discovery and Excavation in Scotland 1982*, 1

Cramp, R, 1983 'Excavations at the Hirsel, Coldstream, Borders Region', *Universities of Durham and Newcastle Archaeological Reports for 1982*, 57–60

Cramp, R, 1984a 'Hirsel (Coldstream p): prehistoric, Romano-British occupation, medieval church, burials', *Discovery and Excavation in Scotland 1984*, 1

Cramp, R, 1984b *Corpus of Anglo-Saxon Stone Sculpture, 1: County Durham and Northumberland*, 2 vols, Oxford University Press, Oxford

Cramp, R, 1985 'Excavations at the Hirsel, Coldstream, Berwickshire', *Universities of Durham and Newcastle Archaeological Reports for 1984*, 52–57

Cramp, R, 2005 *Wearmouth and Jarrow monastic sites 1*, English Heritage, Swindon

Cramp, R, 2006 *Wearmouth and Jarrow monastic sites 2*, English Heritage, Swindon

Cramp, R and Douglas-Home, C, 1980 'New discoveries at the Hirsel, Coldstream, Berwickshire', *Proceedings of the Society of Antiquaries of Scotland* 109, 223–232

Crawford, B E (ed), 1998 *Conversion and Christianity in the North Sea world*, St John's House Papers 8, St Andrews

Croft, R A, 1987 *Graffiti gaming boards*, Finds Research Group AD700–1700, Datasheet 6

Crone, A, Hindmarch, E and Wolf, A, forthcoming *Living and dying at Auldhame, East Lothian; the excavation of an Anglian monastic settlement and medieval parish church*, Society of Antiquaries of Scotland Monograph Series, Edinburgh

Crowdy, A, 1986 'The pottery', in P Dixon, *Excavations in the fishing town of Eyemouth, 1982–1984*, Border Burghs Archaeology Project Monograph Series 1, Edinburgh, 38–55

Crowe, C J, 1982 'A note on white quartz pebbles found in early Christian contexts in the Isle of Man', *Proceedings of the Isle of Man Natural History and Antiquarian Society* 8(4), 413–415

Cruden, S, 1952 'Scottish mediaeval pottery: the Bothwell Castle collection', *Proceedings of the Society of Antiquaries of Scotland* 86, 140–170

Cruden, S, 1956 'Scottish mediaeval pottery', *Proceedings of the Society of Antiquaries of Scotland* 89, 67–82

Cruickshank, G, 1982 *Scottish saltglaze*, Scottish Pottery Studies 2, John Swain, Edinburgh

Dalland, M, 1992 'Long cist burials at Four Winds, Longniddry, East Lothian', *Proceedings of the Society of Antiquaries of Scotland* 122, 197–206

Davey, P (ed), 1987 *The archaeology of the clay tobacco pipe 10: Scotland*, BAR British Series 178

Davies, R M and Ovenden, P J, 1990 'Bell-founding in Winchester in the tenth to thirteenth centuries', in M Biddle (ed), *Winchester studies 7. Artefacts from medieval Winchester. Part ii: Object and economy in medieval Winchester*, part 1, Clarendon Press, Oxford, 100–123

Dawes, J D, 1980 'The human bones', in J D Dawes and J R Magilton, *The cemetery of St Helen-on-the-Walls, Aldwark*, The Archaeology of York 12/1, Council for British Archaeology, London, 19–82

Dean, V E, 1996 'The pottery vessel', in N M McQ Holmes, 'The Ednam, Roxburghshire, hoard, 1995', *British Numismatic Journal* 66, 43 (33–59)

Dean, V E, 2007 'Ceramic vessels associated with late 13th- to early 18th-century coin hoards', *Proceedings of the Society of Antiquaries of Scotland* 137, 433–460

Dean, V E, forthcoming a 'The pottery from excavations at Finlaggan, Islay'

Dean, V E, forthcoming b 'The pottery from Sillerholes, West Linton'

Dean, V E and Robertson, H G, 2001 'Scottish medieval and later pottery', in K L Mitchell, K R Murdoch and J R Ward, *Fast Castle: excavations 1971–86*, Edinburgh Archaeological Field Society, Edinburgh, 56–71

Dennell, R W, 1974 'Botanical evidence for prehistoric crop processing activities', *Journal of Archaeological Science* 1(3), 275–284

Dennell, R W, 1976 'The economic importance of plant resources represented on archaeological sites', *Journal of Archaeological Science* 3(3), 229–247

Dodwell, C R (ed), 1961 *Theophilus: De diversis artibus*, Nelson, London

Donaldson, G, 1985 *Scottish church history*, Scottish Academic Press, Edinburgh

Driscoll, S T, 2004 'The archaeological context of assembly in early medieval Scotland: Scone and its comparanda', in A Pantos and S Semple (eds), *Assembly places and practices in medieval Europe*, Four Courts Press, Dublin, 73–94

Duncan, A A M, 1976 'The battle of Carham, 1018', *Scottish Historical Review* 55(1), 20–28

Duncan, A A M, 2002 *The kingship of the Scots, 842–1292: succession and independence*, Edinburgh University Press, Edinburgh

Edwards, N, 1996 'Identifying the archaeology of the early church in Wales and Cornwall', in J Blair and C Pyrah (eds), *Church archaeology: research directions for the future*, Council for British Archaeology Research Report 104, York, 49–62

Egan, G, 1998 *The medieval household: daily living c1150–c1450*, Medieval Finds from Excavations in London 6, HMSO

Egan, G, 2005 *Material culture in London in the age of transition*, Museum of London Archaeology Service Monograph 19, London

Egan, G, 2007a 'Later medieval non-ferrous metalwork and evidence for metal working: AD 1050–1100 to 1500–50', in D Griffiths, R A Philpott and G Egan, *Meols: the archaeology of the north Wirral coast*, Oxford University School of Archaeology Monograph 68, Oxford, 77–188

Egan, G, 2007b 'Post-medieval non-ferrous metalwork and evidence for metal working: AD 1500–50 to 1800–50', in D Griffiths, R A Philpott and G Egan, *Meols: the archaeology of the north Wirral coast*, Oxford University School of Archaeology Monograph 68, Oxford, 213–228

Egan, G, 2007c 'Copper alloy items of uncertain date and significance', in D Griffiths, R A Philpott and G Egan, *Meols: the archaeology of the north Wirral coast*, Oxford University School of Archaeology Monograph 68, Oxford, 286–289

Egan, G, 2010 *The medieval household; daily living c. 1150–1450*, Medieval Finds from Excavations in London 6, Boydell Press, Woodbridge (2nd edn)

Egan, G and Pritchard, F, 1991 *Dress accessories c1150–c1450*, Medieval Finds from Excavations in London 3, HMSO, London

Eidt, R C, 1977 *Field and laboratory analysis of anthrosols*, Field Test Associates, Shorewood, Wisconsin

Elliott, W, 1872 'Address delivered at Berwick, on the 30th of September, 1869', *History of the Berwickshire Naturalists' Club* 6, 1–53

Ellis, B M A, 2002 *Prick spurs 700–1700*, Finds Research Group AD700–1700, Datasheet 30

Evershed, R P, Dudd, S N, Copley, M S and Mukherjee, A J, 2002a 'Identification of animal fats via compound specific δ^{13}C values of individual fatty acids: assessments of results for reference fats and lipid extracts of archaeological pottery vessels', *Documenta Praehistorica* 29, 73–96

Evershed, R P, Dudd, S N, Copley, M S, Stott, A W, Mottram, H R, Buckley, S A and Crossman, Z, 2002b 'Chemistry of archaeological animal fats', *Accounts of Chemical Research* 35, 660–668

Evershed, R P, Mottram, H R, Dudd, S N, Charters, S, Stott, A W and Lawrence, G J, 1997 'New criteria for the identification of animal fats preserved in archaeological pottery', *Naturwissenschaften* 84, 402–406

Evershed, R P, Stott, A W, Raven, A, Dudd, S N, Charters, S and Leyden, A, 1995 'Formation of long-chain ketones in ancient pottery vessels by pyrolysis of acyl lipids', *Tetrahedron Letters* 36, 8875–8878

Farmer, P G, 1979 *An introduction to Scarborough Ware and a re-assessment of knight jugs*, P G and N C Farmer, Hove

Fawcett, R, 1985 *Scottish medieval churches: an introduction to the ecclesiastical architecture of the 12th to 16th centuries in the care of the Secretary of State for Scotland*, HMSO, Edinburgh

Fawcett, R, 1996 'The archaeology of the Scottish church in the later Middle Ages', in J Blair and C Pyrah (eds), *Church archaeology: research directions for the future*, Council for British Archaeology Research Report 104, York, 85–101

Fawcett, R, 2002 *Scottish medieval churches: architecture and furnishings*, Tempus, Stroud

Fawcett, R, 2011 *The architecture of the Scottish medieval church 1100–1560*, Yale University Press, New Haven and London

Fawcett, R, Luxford, J and Oram, R, 2008 *A corpus of Scottish medieval parish churches*, http://arts.st-andrews.ac.uk/corpusofscottishchurches

Fenton, A, 1970 'Paring and burning and cutting of turf and peat in Scotland', in A Gailey and A Fenton (eds), *The spade in northern and Atlantic Europe*, Ulster Folk Museum and Queen's University, Belfast, 155–193

Ferguson, J, 1892 'Notices of remains of pre-Reformation churches, etc, in Berwickshire', *History of the Berwickshire Naturalists' Club* 13, 86–184

Ferguson, J, 1899 'Historical notices of early religious architecture in Berwickshire', *History of the Berwickshire Naturalists' Club* 16, 17–27

Fernie, E, 1994 'The Romanesque churches of Dunfermline Abbey', in J Higgitt (ed), *Medieval art and architecture in the Diocese of St Andrews*, British Archaeological Association Conference Transactions for the year 1986, 14, Leeds, 25–37

Finlayson, B and Warren, G, 2000 'The Mesolithic of eastern Scotland', in R Young (ed), *Mesolithic lifeways: current research from Britain and Ireland*, Leicester Archaeology Monographs 7, University of Leicester, Leicester, 133–142

Fisher, I, 2001 *Early medieval sculpture in the West Highlands and Islands*, RCAHMS and Society of Antiquaries of Scotland, Monograph 1, Edinburgh

Fisher, I, 2011 'The carved stones', in R C Barrowman, *The chapel and burial ground on St Ninian's Isle, Shetland: excavations past and present*, The Society for Medieval Archaeology Monograph 32, London, 121–124

Fogg, G E, 1950 'Biological flora of the British Isles: *sinapis arvensis* L', *Journal of Ecology* 38(2), 415–429

Ford, B and Walsh, A, 1987 'Iron nails', in P Holdsworth (ed), *Excavations in the medieval burgh of Perth 1979–81*, Society of Antiquaries of Scotland Monograph 5, Edinburgh, 139

Forsyth, K, 2005 '*Hic memoria perpetua:* the early inscribed stones of southern Scotland in context', in S M Foster and M Cross (eds), *Able minds and practised hands: Scotland's early medieval sculpture in the 21st century*, The Society for Medieval Archaeology Monograph 23, Leeds, 113–134

Fowler, J T (ed), 1903 *The Rites of Durham*, Publications of the Surtees Society 107, Durham and London

Franklin, J A, 1997 'Pottery', in D H Caldwell and G Ewart, 'Excavations at Eyemouth, Berwickshire, in a mid 16th-century *trace italienne* fort', *Post-Medieval Archaeology* 31, 96–103 (61–118)

Franklin, J A and Hall, D W, 2012 'Pottery', in D Perry, *Excavations in Ayr 1984–1987*, Ayrshire Archaeological and Natural History Society Monograph 37, Ayr, 36–69

Frere, S S, 1954 'Canterbury excavations, summer 1946. The Rose Lane sites', *Archaeologia Cantiana* 68, 101–143

Frodsham, P, 2004 *Archaeology in Northumberland National Park*, Council for British Archaeology Research Report 136, York

Furgol, E M, 1990 *A regimental history of the Covenanting armies 1639–1651*, John Donald, Edinburgh

Gidney, L J, 1986 'A report on the animal bones from The Hirsel', unpublished archive report

Gidney, L J, 1987 'Black Friars, Newcastle: the animal bone', unpublished archive report

Gidney, L J, 1991 *Leicester, the Shires 1988 excavations: the animal bones from the medieval deposits at Little Lane*, Ancient Monuments Laboratory Report 57/91

Gidney, L J, 1992 *Leicester, the Shires 1988 excavations: the animal bones from the post-medieval deposits at Little Lane*, Ancient Monuments Laboratory Report 24/92

Gilchrist, R and Sloane, B, 2005 *Requiem: the medieval monastic cemetery in Britain*, Museum of London Archaeology Service, London

Gilmour, B J J and Stocker, D A, 1986 *St Mark's church and cemetery*, The Archaeology of Lincoln 13-1, Council for British Archaeology, London

Goldie, T S, 1841 'Parish of Coldstream', in *The statistical account of Berwickshire*, Blackwood, Edinburgh and London, 199–214

Goodall, A R, 1981 'The medieval bronzesmith and his products', in D W Crossley (ed), *Medieval industry*, Council for British Archaeology Research Report 40, London, 63–71

Goodall, A R, 2007 'Non-ferrous metals', in D Austin, *Acts of perception: a study of Barnard Castle in Teesdale*, 2 vols, Architectural and Archaeological Society of Durham and Northumberland Research Report 6, Durham, II, 520–528

Goodall, I H, 1976 'The metalwork', in O Bedwin, 'The excavation of Ardingley fulling mill and forge 1975–76', *Post-Medieval Archaeology* 10, 60–64 (34–64)

Goodall, I H, 1981 'The medieval blacksmith and his products', in D W Crossley (ed), *Medieval industry*, Council for British Archaeology Research Report 40, London, 51–62

Goodall, I H, 1990a 'Metal-working tools', in M Biddle (ed), *Winchester studies 7. Artefacts from medieval Winchester. Part ii: Object and economy in medieval Winchester*, Clarendon Press, Oxford, 198–199

Goodall, I H, 1990b 'Wood-working tools', in M Biddle (ed), *Winchester studies 7. Artefacts from medieval Winchester. Part ii: Object and economy in medieval Winchester*, Clarendon Press, Oxford, 273–277

Goodall, I H, 1990c 'Building ironwork', in M Biddle (ed), *Winchester studies 7. Artefacts from medieval Winchester. Part ii: Object and economy in medieval Winchester*, Clarendon Press, Oxford, 328–349

Goodall, I H, 1990d 'Locks and keys', in M Biddle (ed), *Winchester studies 7. Artefacts from medieval Winchester. Part ii: Object and economy in medieval Winchester*, Clarendon Press, Oxford, 984–1036

Goodall, I H, 1990e 'Arrowheads', in M Biddle (ed), *Winchester studies 7. Artefacts from medieval Winchester. Part ii: Object and economy in medieval Winchester*, Clarendon Press, Oxford, 1070–1074

Goodall, I H, 1993a 'Iron (IR)', in G G Astill, *A medieval industrial complex and its landscape: the metalworking, watermills and workshops of Bordesley Abbey*, Council for British Archaeology Research Report 92, York, 165–181

Goodall, I H, 1993b 'Iron hearth equipment', in S Margeson, *Norwich households: the medieval and post-medieval finds from Norwich Survey excavations 1971–1978*, East Anglian Archaeology 58, Norwich, 86–89

Goodall, I H, 1993c 'Iron rings and washers', in S Margeson, *Norwich households: the medieval and post-medieval finds from Norwich Survey excavations 1971–1978*, East Anglian Archaeology 58, Norwich, 141

Goodall, I H, 2000 'Iron objects', in P Ellis (ed), *Ludgershall Castle, Wiltshire: a report on the excavations by Peter Addyman 1964–1972*, Wiltshire Archaeological and Natural History Society Monograph Series 2, Devizes, 143–156

Goodall, I H, 2007 'Iron', in D Austin, *Acts of perception: a study of Barnard Castle in Teesdale*, 2 vols, Architectural and Archaeological Society of Durham and Northumberland Research Report 6, Durham, II, 512–518

Goodall, I H, 2011 *Ironwork in medieval Britain: an archaeological study*, The Society for Medieval Archaeology Monograph 31, London

Grant, A, 1982 'The use of tooth wear as a guide to the age of domestic ungulates', in B Wilson, C Grigson and S Payne (eds), *Ageing and sexing animal bones from archaeological sites*, BAR British Series 109, 91–108

Graves, C P, 1985 'Scottish medieval stained and painted glass', unpublished MA dissertation, University of Glasgow

Graves, C P, 1994 'Medieval stained and painted window glass in the diocese of St Andrews', in J Higgitt (ed), *Medieval art and architecture in the Diocese of St Andrews*, British Archaeological Association Conference Transactions for the year 1986, 14, Leeds, 124–136

Green, H S, 1980 *The flint arrowheads of the British Isles*, 2 vols, BAR British Series 75

Green, R F, Suchey, J M and Gokhale, D V, 1979 'The statistical treatment of correlated bilateral traits in the analysis of cranial material', *American Journal of Physical Anthropology* 50, 629–634

Greenwell, W, 1906 In 'Meetings 1906', *Transactions of the Architectural and Archaeological Society of Durham and Northumberland* 6, i–xxi

Gregory, R A, 2001 'Excavation at Hayknowes Farm, Annan', *Transactions of the Dumfriesshire and Galloway Natural History and Antiquarian Society*, 3 ser, 75, 29–46

Hadley, D M, 2002 'Burial practices in northern England in the later Anglo-Saxon period', in S Lucy and A Reynolds (eds), *Burial in early medieval England and Wales*, The Society for Medieval Archaeology Monograph 17, London, 209–228

Haggarty, G, Hall, D and Chenery, S, 2011 *Sourcing Scottish Redwares*, Medieval Pottery Research Group Occasional Paper 5, London

Haggarty, G and Jennings, S, 1992 'The imported pottery from Fast Castle, near Dunbar, Scotland', *Medieval Ceramics* 16, 45–54

Haggarty, G and Will, R, 1995 'Ceramic material', in J H Lewis and G J Ewart, *Jedburgh Abbey: the archaeology and architecture of a Border abbey*, Society of Antiquaries of Scotland Monograph 10, Edinburgh, 98–105

Hall, D W, 1996 'Blind date: Scottish medieval pottery industries', *Tayside and Fife Archaeological Journal* 2, 126–129

Hall, D W, 1998a 'Pottery from Ladyhill', in D W Hall, A D S MacDonald, D R Perry and J Terry, 'The archaeology of Elgin: excavations on Ladyhill and in the High Street, with an overview of the archaeology of the burgh', *Proceedings of the Society of Antiquaries of Scotland* 128, 762–765 (753–829)

Hall, D W, 1998b 'Pottery', in D W Hall, A D S MacDonald, D R Perry and J Terry, 'The archaeology of Elgin: excavations on Ladyhill and in the High Street, with an overview of the archaeology of the burgh', *Proceedings of the Society of Antiquaries of Scotland* 128, 786–790 (753–829)

Hall, D W, 2001 'Pottery report', in R A Gregory, 'The excavation of a medieval ring-ditch enclosure at Hayknowes Farm, Annan, Dumfries and Galloway', *Scottish Archaeologial Journal* 23(2), 130–132 (119–139)

Hall, D W, 2007 'Excavations at the pottery production centre at Colstoun, East Lothian, 1939, 1969, 1971, 1977 and 1999/2000', *Medieval Ceramics* 28, 35–73

Hall, D W, 2009 'Recent excavations of pottery kilns and workshops at New Carron Road, Stenhousemuir, 2007', *Medieval Ceramics* 30, 3–20

Hall, D W and Hunter, D, 2001 'The rescue excavation of some medieval redware pottery kilns at Stenhousemuir, Falkirk, between 1954 and 1978', *Medieval Archaeology* 45, 97–168

Halliday, S P, 1988 'The pottery', in J Sherriff, 'A hut-circle at Ormiston farm, Newburgh, Fife', *Proceedings of the Society of Antiquaries of Scotland* 118, 104–108 (99–110)

Hamilton, E C, 2003 'The acts of the Earls of Dunbar relating to Scotland *c*1124–*c*1289: a study of lordship in Scotland in the twelfth and thirteenth centuries', unpublished PhD thesis, University of Glasgow

Hamilton, E C, 2007 'The Earls of Dunbar and the church in Lothian and the Merse', *Innes Review* 58(1), 1–34

Hamilton, E C, 2010 *Mighty subjects: the Dunbar earls in Scotland c1072–1289*, John Donald, Edinburgh

Harding, D W, 2001 'Later prehistory in south-east Scotland: a critical review', *Oxford Journal of Archaeology* 20(4), 355–376

Harding, D W, 2004 *The Iron Age in northern Britain: Celts and Romans, natives and invaders*, Routledge, London and New York

Haselgrove, C, 2009 *The Traprain Law Environs Project: fieldwork and excavations 2000–2004*, Society of Antiquaries of Scotland, Edinburgh

Hawthorne, J G and Smith, C S (eds), 1979 *Theophilus: on divers arts*, Dover, New York, NY

Hegi, G, 1924 *Illustrierte Flora von Mittel-Europa: mit besonderer Berücksichtigung von Deutschland, Osterreich und der Schweiz: zum Gebrauche in den Schulen und zum selbsunterricht*, J F Lehmann, Munich

Henderson, P, 1997 *Pre-reformation pilgrims from Scotland to Santiago de Compostela*, The Confraternity of Saint James, Occasional Papers 4, London

Herdman, J (ed), 1992 *The third statistical account of Scotland, 23: The county of Berwick*, Scottish Academic Press, Edinburgh

Hickman, M, 2010 'Coldstream Priory', in *Second to none: a history of Coldstream*, CDLHS, Coldstream, 23–44

Hill, M O, 1979a *DECORANA: de-trended correspondence analysis*, Cornell University Press, Ithaca, NY

Hill, M O, 1979b *TWINSPAN: a FORTRAN programme for multivariate analysis using Two Way Indicator species analysis*, Cornell University Press, Ithaca, NY

Hill, P H, 1997 *Whithorn and St Ninian: the excavation of a monastic town 1984–91*, Sutton Publishing, Stroud

Hillman, G, 1981 'Reconstructing crop husbandry practices from charred remains of crops', in R Mercer (ed), *Farming practice in British prehistory*, Edinburgh University Press, Edinburgh, 123–162

Hillman, G, 1983 'Interpretation of archaeological plant remains: the application of ethnographic model from Turkey', in W van Zeist and W A Casparie (eds), *VI Symposium of the International Work Group for Palaeoethnobotany*, Rotterdam, 1–41

Hindmarsh, E and Melikian, M, 2008 'Baldred's Auldhame: a medieval chapel and cemetery in East Lothian', *Church Archaeology* 10, 97–100

Hinton, D A, 1990a 'Tag ends', in M Biddle (ed), *Winchester studies 7. Artefacts from medieval Winchester. Part ii: Object and economy in medieval Winchester*, Clarendon Press, Oxford, 547

Hinton, D A, 1990b 'Clips', in M Biddle (ed), *Winchester studies 7. Artefacts from medieval Winchester. Part ii: Object and economy in medieval Winchester*, Clarendon Press, Oxford, 1094

Hiscox, G D, 1916 *Henley's twentieth century formulas, recipes and processes*, The Norman W Henley Publishing Company, New York, NY

Holden, T, 2006 'The botanical evidence', in C Lowe, *Excavations at Hoddom, Dumfriesshire: an early ecclesiastical site in south-west Scotland*, Society of Antiquaries of Scotland, Edinburgh, 150–155

Holmes, M R, 1951 'The so-called "Bellarmine" mask on imported Rhenish stoneware', *Antiquaries Journal* 31, 173–179

Hope-Taylor, B, 1977 *Yeavering: an Anglo-British centre of early Northumbria*, Department of the Environment Archaeological Report 7, HMSO

Hubbard, C E, 1968 *Grasses*, Pelican Books, Harmondsworth

Huntley, J P, 1984 *The Hirsel '82, Berwickshire. Analysis of carbonised plant remains*, Palaeoenvironmental Studies Service, Department of Botany, University of Durham

Huntley, J P, 1997 'The ninth-century carbonised plant remains', in P Hill, *Whithorn and St Ninian: the excavation of a monastic town 1984–91*, Sutton Publishing, Stroud, 592–595

Huntley, J P, 2008 'Quarry Farm QF03: analysis of charred plant remains from a Roman villa and settlement in the Tees valley, North Yorkshire', *Durham Environmental Archaeology Report* 3/2008, Durham

Hurst, J G, 1977 'Langerwehe stoneware of the fourteenth and fifteenth centuries', in M R Apted, R Gilyard-Beer and A D Saunders (eds), *Ancient monuments and their interpretation: essays presented to A J Taylor*, Phillimore, London, 219–238

Hurst, J G, Neal, D S and van Beuningen, H J E, 1986 *Pottery produced and traded in north-west Europe 1350–1650*, Rotterdam Papers 6, Het Nederlandse Gebruiksvoorwerp, Rotterdam

James, H F and Yeoman, P, 2008 *Excavations at St Ethernan's monastery, Isle of May, Fife 1992–1997*, Tayside and Fife Archaeological Committee Monograph 6, Perth

Jessop, O, 1996 'A new artefact typology for the study of medieval arrowheads', *Medieval Archaeology* 40, 192–205

Johnson, B and Waddington, C, 2008 'Prehistoric and Dark Age settlement remains from Cheviot Quarry, Milfield Basin, Northumberland', *Archaeological Journal* 165, 107–264

Johnson, B and Waddington, C, 2009 'Prehistoric and Dark Age settlement remains from Cheviot Quarry, Milfield Basin, Northumberland', in R Miket and B Edwards, with C O'Brien, B Johnson and C Waddington, *Neolithic and early historic settlement in north Northumberland*, Royal Archaeological Institute, London, 107–264

Johnson South, T (ed), 2002 *'Historia De Sancto Cuthberto': a history of Saint Cuthbert and a record of his patrimony*, D S Brewer, Woodbridge

Jones, A M, 1991 'Early Christianity, conversion and cemeteries: a study of long cist cemeteries and their use as a mortuary practice and symbol within southern Scotland', unpublished BSc dissertation, University of Glasgow

Jones, M K, 1980 'The plant remains', in M Parrington, *The excavation of an Iron Age settlement, Bronze Age ring ditch and Roman features at Ashville Trading Estate, Abingdon, (Oxfordshire) 1974–76*, Council for British Archaeology Research Report 28, 93–100

Jones, R, Will, R, Haggarty, G and Hall, D, 2003 'Sourcing Scottish white gritty ware', *Medieval Ceramics* 26–27, 45–84

Jones, R *et al* [nd], *Computer based osteometry*, Ancient Monuments Laboratory Report 3342

Jope, E M, 1956 'The tinning of iron spurs: a continuous practice from the tenth to the seventeenth century', *Oxoniensia* 21, 35–41

Kilbride-Jones, H E, 1938 'Glass armlets in Britain', *Proceedings of the Society of Antiquaries of Scotland* 72, 366–395

Kirk, J (ed), 1995 *The Books of Assumption of the Thirds of Benefices: Scottish ecclesiastical rentals at the Reformation*, British Academy Records of Social and Economic History, new series 1, Oxford University Press, Oxford

Koch, P L, Fogel, M L and Tuross, N, 1994 'Tracing the diets of fossil animal using stable isotopes', in K Lajtha and R H Michener (eds), *Stable isotopes in Ecology and Environmental Science*, Blackwell, London, 63–92

Kokeza, N, 2008 *Later prehistoric enclosed site evidence of southern Scotland: a study of the sites from Peebleshire, Berwickshire and E Dumfriesshire*, BAR British Series 469

Krogman, W M, 1978 *The human skeleton in forensic medicine*, C C Thomas, Springfield, IL

Laidlaw, W, 1905 'Sculptured and inscribed stones in Jedburgh and vicinity', *Proceedings of the Society of Antiquaries of Scotland* 39, 21–54

Lane, A and Campbell, E, 2000 *Dunadd, an early Dalriadic capital*, Oxbow, Oxford

Larsen, J, 1967 'Soil phosphorous', *Advances in Agronomy* 19, 151–209

Lever, C, 1977 *The naturalised animals of the British Isles*, Granada Publishing, London

Lewis, J and Ewart, G, 1995 *Jedburgh Abbey: the archaeology and architecture of a Border abbey*, Society of Antiquaries of Scotland Monograph 10, Edinburgh

Lowe, C, 2006 *Excavations at Hoddom, Dumfriesshire: an early ecclesiastical site in south-west Scotland*, Society of Antiquaries of Scotland, Edinburgh

Lowe, C, 2008 *Inchmarnock: an early historic island monastery and its archaeological landscape*, Society of Antiquaries of Scotland, Edinburgh

MacAskill, N L, 1987 'The pottery', in P Holdsworth (ed), *Excavations in the medieval burgh of Perth 1979–81*, Society of Antiquaries of Scotland Monograph 5, Edinburgh, 89–120

MacGregor, A, 1987 'Objects of bone and antler', in G Beresford, *Goltho: the development of an early medieval manor c850–1150*, English Heritage Archaeological Report 4, London, 188–192

MacGregor, G and McLellan, K, 2008 'A burning desire to build: excavations at Ewesford West and Pencraig Hill (3950–3380 BC)', in O Lelong and G MacGregor, *The lands of ancient Lothian. Interpreting the archaeology of the A1*, Society of Antiquaries of Scotland, Edinburgh, 15–45

Macinnes, L, 1982 'Pattern and purpose: the settlement evidence', in D W Harding (ed), *Later prehistoric settlement in south-east Scotland*, University of Edinburgh Department of Archaeology Occasional Papers 8, Edinburgh, 57–73

MacKie, E W, 1972 'Some new quernstones from brochs and duns', *Proceedings of the Society of Antiquaries of Scotland* 104, 137–146

McLaren, A, 1861 'Account of a stone coffin found in the old churchyard of Coldstream Abbey', *History of the Berwickshire Naturalists' Club* 4, 319–321

McNaught, J M, 2006 'A clinical and archaeological study of Schmorl's nodes: using clinical data to understand the past', 2 vols, unpublished PhD thesis, Durham University

McNeill, P G B and MacQueen, H L (eds), 1996 *Atlas of Scottish history to 1707*, The Scottish Medievalists and Department of Geography, University of Edinburgh

McNeill, T, 2000 'The iron nails', in P Ellis (ed), *Ludgershall Castle, Wiltshire: a report on the excavations by Peter Addyman 1964–1972*, Wiltshire Archaeological and Natural History Society Monograph 2, Devizes, 229–232

McOmish, D, 1999 'Wether Hill and Cheviots hillforts', in P Frodsham, P Topping and D Cowley (eds), *'We were always chasing time', Papers presented to Keith Blood*, Northern Archaeology special edition 17/18, 113–121

McRoberts, D, 1959 'Material destruction caused by the Scottish Reformation', *Innes Review* 10, 126–172

MacSween, A, 2009 'The coarse pottery', in C Haselgrove, *The Traprain Law Environs Project: fieldwork and excavations 2000–2004*, Society of Antiquaries of Scotland, Edinburgh, 117–123

Margeson, S, 1993 *Norwich households: the medieval and post-medieval finds from Norwich Survey excavations 1971–1978*, East Anglian Archaeology 58, Norwich

Margeson, S and Goodall, I H, 1993 'Weapons and armour', in S Margeson, *Norwich households: the medieval and post-medieval finds from Norwich Survey excavations 1971–1978*, East Anglian Archaeology 58, Norwich, 227–229

Mays, S, Harding, C and Heighway, C, 2007 *Wharram: a study of settlement on the Yorkshire Wolds, 11: The churchyard*, York University Archaeological Publications 13, York

Miket, R, Edwards, B with O'Brien, C, 2008 'Thirlings: a Neolithic site in Northumberland', *Archaeological Journal* 165, 1–106

Miket, R, Edwards, B with O'Brien, C, 2009 'Thirlings: a Neolithic site in Northumberland', in R Miket and B Edwards, with C O'Brien, B Johnson and C Waddington, *Neolithic and early historic settlement in north Northumberland*, Royal Archaeological Institute, London, 1–106

Millson, D, Marshall, P and Waddington, C, 2012 'Towards a sequence for Neolithic ceramics in the Milfield Basin and Northumberland', *Archaeologia Aeliana*, 5 ser, 40, 1–40

Mitchell, A, 1884 'On white pebbles in connection with pagan and Christian burials, a seeming survival of an ancient burial custom', *Proceedings of the Society of Antiquaries of Scotland* 18, 286–291

Morgan, M, 1947 'The organisation of the Scottish church in the twelfth century', *Transactions of the Royal Historical Society*, 4 ser, 29, 135–149

Morris, C, 1997 'Iron and copper-alloy objects', in A Hannan, 'Tewkesbury and the Earls of Gloucester: excavations at Holm Hill, 1974–5', *Transactions of the Bristol and Gloucestershire Archaeological Society* 115, 152–197 (79–231)

Morris, C D, 1977 'Northumbria and the Viking settlement: the evidence for land-holding', *Archaeologia Aeliana*, 5 ser, 5, 81–103

Mottram, H R, Dudd, S N, Lawrence, G J, Stott, A W and Evershed, R P, 1999 'New chromatographic, mass spectrometric and stable isotope approaches to the classification of degraded animal fats preserved in archaeological pottery', *Journal of Chromatography A* 833, 209–221

Mulholland, H, 1970 'The microlithic industries of the Tweed Valley', *Transactions of the Dumfriesshire and Galloway Natural History and Antiquarian Society*, 3 ser, 47, 81–110

Munsell, A H, 1975 *A color notation: an illustrated system defining all colors and their relations by measured scales of hue, value, and chroma*, Munsell Color Company, Baltimore, MD (12th edn)

Murray, J C, 1982 'The pottery', in J C Murray (ed), *Excavations in the medieval burgh of Aberdeen, 1973–81*, Society of Antiquaries of Scotland Monograph 2, Edinburgh, 116–176

Murray, J C, 1993 'The pottery', in H K Murray and J C Murray, 'Excavations at Rattray, Aberdeenshire: a Scottish deserted burgh', *Medieval Archaeology* 37, 148–169 (109–218)

Mynard, D C, 1994 *Excavations on medieval and later sites in Milton Keynes 1972–1980*, Buckinghamshire Archaeological Society Monograph 6, Aylesbury

Nicholson, A, 1997a 'The iron', in P Hill, *Whithorn and St Ninian: the excavation of a monastic town 1984–91*, Sutton Publishing, Stroud, 404–433

Nicholson, A, 1997b 'The stone artefacts', in P Hill, *Whithorn and St Ninian: the excavation of a monastic town 1984–91*, Sutton Publishing, Stroud, 447–474

Nicholson, A and Hill, P, 1997 'The non-ferrous metals', in P Hill, *Whithorn and St Ninian: the excavation of a monastic town 1984–91*, Sutton Publishing, Stroud, 360–404

Noël Hume, I, 1991 *Artifacts of colonial America*, Random House, New York

Norris, M, 1977 *Monumental brasses: the memorials*, 2 vols, Phillips and Page, London

Northumberland County History Committee, 1935 *A history of Northumberland 14: the parishes of Alnham, Chatton, Chillingham, Eglingham, Ilderton, Ingram and Whittingham; the chapelries of Lowick and Doddington*, A Reid, Newcastle upon Tyne

Oakley, G E and Webster, L E, 1979 'The copper-alloy objects', in J Williams, *St Peter's Street, Northampton: excavations 1973–1976*, Archaeological Monograph 2, Northampton Development Corporation, Northampton, 248–264

O'Brien, C, 2011 'Yeavering and Bernician kingship: a review of debate on the hybrid culture thesis', in D Petts and S Turner (eds), *Early medieval Northumbria: kingdoms and communities*, Studies in the Early Middle Ages 24, Brepols, Turnhout, 207–220

O'Brien, E, 1999 *Post-Roman Britain to Anglo-Saxon England: burial practices reviewed*, BAR British Series 289

Ó Carragáin, T, 2010 *Churches in Early Medieval Ireland: architecture, ritual and memory*, Yale University Press, New Haven and London

Oram, R, 2011 *Domination and lordship 1070–1230*, The New Edinburgh History of Scotland, vol 3, Edinburgh University Press, Edinburgh

Ortner, D and Putschar, W, 1981 *Identification of pathological conditions in human skeletal remains*, Smithsonian Institute, Washington DC

Orton, C, Tyers, P and Vince, A, 1993 *Pottery in Archaeology*, Cambridge University Press, Cambridge

Oswald, A, Ainsworth, S and Pearson, T, 2006 *Hillforts: prehistoric strongholds of Northumberland National Park*, English Heritage, Swindon

Ottaway, P, 1992 *Anglo-Scandinavian ironwork from 16–22 Coppergate*, The Archaeology of York, The Small Finds 17/6, Council for British Archaeology, London

Ottaway, P and Rogers, N, 2002 *Craft, industry and everyday life: finds from medieval York*, The Archaeology of York, The Small Finds 17/15, Council for British Archaeology, York

Pantos, A, 2004 'The location and form of Anglo-Saxon assembly-places: some "moot points"', in A Pantos and S Semple (eds), *Assembly places and practices in medieval Europe*, Four Courts Press, Dublin, 155–180

Pantos, A and Semple, S (eds), 2004 *Assembly places and practices in medieval Europe*, Four Courts Press, Dublin

Parlett, D, 1999 *The Oxford history of board games*, Oxford University Press, Oxford

Parsons, D, 1986 '*Sacrarium*: ablution drains in early medieval churches', in L A S Butler and R K Morris (eds), *The Anglo-Saxon Church: papers on history, architecture and archaeology in honour of Dr H M Taylor*, Council for British Archaeology Research Report 60, London, 105–120

Parsons, D, 1996 'Liturgical and social aspects', in A Boddington, *Raunds Furnells: the Anglo-Saxon church and churchyard, Raunds Area Project*, English Heritage Archaeological Report 7, London, 58–66

Passmore, D G and Waddington, C, 2012 *Archaeology and environment in Northumberland: Till-Tweed studies 2*, English Heritage and Oxbow, Oxford

Perizonius, W R K, 1979 'Non-metric cranial traits: sex difference and age dependence', *Journal of Human Evolution* 8, 679–684

Perry, D R, 2000 *Castle Park, Dunbar: two thousand years on a fortified headland*, Society of Antiquaries of Scotland Monograph 16, Edinburgh

Pevsner, N and Richmond, I, revised by Grundy, J, McCombie, G, Ryder, P and Welfare, H, 1992 *The buildings of England: Northumberland*, Penguin, London (2nd edn)

Philpott, R A, 2007 'Fishing equipment', in D Griffiths, R A Philpott and G Egan, *Meols: the archaeology of the north Wirral coast*, Oxford University School of Archaeology Monograph 68, Oxford, 279–286

Piggott, C M, 1949 'The Iron Age settlement at Hayhope Knowe, Roxburghshire: excavations 1949', *Proceedings of the Society of Antiquaries of Scotland* 83, 45–67

Plummer, C (ed), 1896 *Venerabilis Bedae Opera Historica,* 2 vols, Oxford University Press, Oxford

Potter, J F, 2006 'Stone emplacement in early Scottish churches: evidence of early Christian craftmanship', *Proceedings of the Society of Antiquaries of Scotland* 136, 227–236

Price, J, 1988 'Romano-British glass bangles from eastern Yorkshire', in J Price and P R Wilson, with C S Briggs and S J Hardman (eds), *Recent research in Roman Yorkshire*, BAR British Series 193, 339–366

Price, J, 1997 'The Roman glass', in P Hill, *Whithorn and St Ninian: the excavation of a monastic town 1984–91*, Sutton Publishing, Stroud, 294–295

Price, J, 2006 'Roman vessel glass', in R Cramp, *Wearmouth and Jarrow monastic sites 2*, English Heritage, Swindon, 313–314

Price, J and Cottam, S, 1998 *Romano-British glass vessels: a handbook*, Council for British Archaeology Practical Handbooks in Archaeology 14, York

Proudfoot, E, 1996 'Excavations at the long cist cemetery on the Hallow Hill, St Andrews, Fife 1975–7', *Proceedings of the Society of Antiquaries of Scotland* 126, 387–454

Proudfoot, E and Aliaga-Kelly, C, 1996 'Towards an interpretation of anomalous finds and place-names of Anglo-Saxon origin in Scotland', in D Griffiths (ed), *Anglo-Saxon Studies in Archaeology and History* 9, Oxford University Committee for Archaeology, Oxford, 1–13

RCAHMS, 1915 *Sixth report and inventory of monuments and constructions in the county of Berwick (revised issue)*, HMSO, Edinburgh

RCAHMS, 1977 *Air Photographs Unit 1977 catalogue*, Edinburgh

RCAHMS, 1978 *Air Photographs Unit 1978 catalogue*, Edinburgh

RCAHMS, 1980a *Air Photographs Unit 1980 catalogue*, Edinburgh

RCAHMS, 1980b *The archaeological sites and monuments of Berwickshire District, Borders Region*, Society of Antiquaries of Scotland Archaeological Field Survey 10, Edinburgh

RCAHMS, 1985 *Air Photographs Unit 1983 catalogue*, Edinburgh

RCAHMS, 1990 *Air Photographs Unit 1988 catalogue*, Edinburgh

Rackham, D J, 1978 'The use of diagnostic zones for considerations of quantification, preservation, levels of fragmentation, skeletal selection and butchery', unpublished archive report

Radford, C A R, 1951 'The excavations at Chapel Finnian Mochrum', *Transactions of the Dumfriesshire and Galloway Natural History and Antiquarian Society*, 3 ser, 28, 28–40

Rahtz, P A, 1978 'Grave orientation', *Archaeological Journal* 135, 1–14

Rahtz, P A, 1979 *The Saxon and medieval palaces at Cheddar: excavations 1960–62*, BAR British Series 65

Raven, A M, van Bergen, P F, Stott, A W, Dudd, S N and Evershed, R P, 1997 'Formation of long-chain ketones in archaeological pottery vessels by pyrolysis of acyl lipids', *Journal of Analytical and Applied Pyrolysis* 40–41, 267–285

Reed, D, 1995 'The excavation of a cemetery and putative chapel site at Newhall Point, Balblair, Ross and Cromarty', *Proceedings of the Society of Antiquaries of Scotland* 125(2), 779–791

Rees, H, Crummy, N, Ottaway, P J and Dunn, G, 2008 *Artefacts and society in Roman and medieval Winchester: small finds from the suburbs and defences, 1971–1986*, Winchester Museum Services, Winchester

Reid-Henry, D and Harrison, C, 1988 *The history of the birds of Britain*, Collins, London

Reimer, P J, Baillie, M G L, Bard, E, Bayliss, A, Beck, J W, Blackwell, P G, Bronk Ramsey, C, Buck, C E, Burr, G S, Edwards, R L, Friedrich, M, Grootes, P M, Guilderson, T P, Hajdas, I, Heaton, T J, Hogg, A G, Hughen, K A, Kaiser, K F, Kromer, B, McCormac, F G, Manning, S W, Reimer, R W, Richards, D A, Southon, J R, Talamo, S, Turney, C S M, van der Plicht, J and Weyhenmeyer, C E, 2009 'IntCal09 and Marine09 radiocarbon age calibration curves, 0–50,000 years cal BP', *Radiocarbon* 51(4), 1111–1150

Rennie, E, 1984 'Excavations at Ardnadam, Cowal, Argyll 1964–1982', *Glasgow Archaeological Journal* 11, 13–39

Reynolds, D M, 1982 'Aspects of later prehistoric timber construction in south-east Scotland', in D W Harding (ed), *Later prehistoric settlement in south-east Scotland*, University of Edinburgh Department of Archaeology Occasional Papers 8, Edinburgh, 44–56

Riddler, I D, 2010 'Bone, antler and ivory objects', in C Harding, E Marlow-Mann and S Wrathmell, *Wharram: a study of settlement on the Yorkshire Wolds, 12: The post-medieval vicarage sites*, York University Archaeological Publications 14, York, 275–286

Riddler, I D, 2012 'Knives', in S Boulter and P Walton Rogers, *Circles and cemeteries: excavations at Flixton Volume 1*, East Anglian Archaeology 147, Gressenhall, 124–127

Ritchie, A, 2008 'Gaming boards', in C Lowe, *Inchmarnock: an early historic island monastery and its archaeological landscape*, Society of Antiquaries of Scotland, Edinburgh, 116–128

Roberts, J E, 1988 'Tennant's pipe factory, Tweedmouth', *History of the Berwickshire Naturalists' Club* 44(2), 87–102

Robertson, W N, 1967 'The game of merelles in Scotland', *Proceedings of the Society of Antiquaries of Scotland* 98, 321–323

Robson, J, 1896 *The churches and churchyards of Berwickshire*, J & J H Rutherfurd, Kelso

Rodwell, J S (ed), 2000 *British plant communities, 5: Maritime communities and vegetation of open habitats*, Cambridge University Press, Cambridge

Rogers, C (ed), 1879 *Chartulary of the Cistercian Priory of Coldstream, with relative documents*, Grampian Club 18, London and Edinburgh

Runge, F, 1973 *Die Pflanzengesellschaften Deutschlands*, Verlag Aschendorff, Munich

Ryder, P, 2005 *The medieval cross slab grave covers in Cumbria*, Cumberland and Westmorland Antiquarian and Archaeological Society, extra series 32, Kendal

Salaman, R A, 1986 *Dictionary of leather-working tools, c1700–1950 and the tools of allied trades*, The Astragal Press, Lakeville, Minnesota

Salisbury, E H, 1961 *Weeds and aliens*, Collins, London

Semple, S, 2004 'Locations of assembly in early Anglo-Saxon England', in A Pantos and S Semple (eds), *Assembly places and practices in medieval Europe*, Four Courts Press, Dublin, 135–154

Sheridan, J A, 2007 'From Picardie to Pickering and Pencraig Hill? New information on the "Carinated Bowl Neolithic" in northern Britain', in A W R Whittle and V Cummings (eds), *Going over: the Mesolithic–Neolithic transition in north-west Europe*, Proceedings of the British Academy 144, Oxford University Press, Oxford, 441–492

Sheridan, J A, 2008a (i) 'Early Neolithic pottery from Pit 1 [019] to the S of Area 5, Eweford'; (ii) 'Early Neolithic pottery from Pit 2 [025] to the SE of Area 5, Eweford'; (iii) 'Traditional carinated bowl pottery from Area 5 Early Neolithic funerary monument', unpublished archive reports accompanying O Lelong and G MacGregor, *The lands of ancient Lothian: interpreting the archaeology of the A1*, Edinburgh

Sheridan, J A, 2008b 'The small finds assemblage from Pencraig Hill', unpublished archive report accompanying O Lelong and G MacGregor, *The lands of ancient Lothian: interpreting the archaeology of the A1*, Edinburgh

Sheridan, J A, 2010 'The Neolithisation of Britain and Ireland: the big picture', in B Finlayson and G Warren (eds), *Landscapes in transition*, Oxbow Books, Oxford, 89–105

Sheridan, J A, 2012 Review of A W R Whittle, F Healey and A Bayliss, *Gathering time: dating the Early Neolithic enclosures of southern Britain and Ireland*, *Antiquity* 86, 262–264

Shimwell, D W 1971 *Description and classification of vegetation*, Sidgwick and Jackson, London

Shoesmith, R 1980 *Hereford City excavations, 1: Excavations at Castle Green*, Council for British Archaeology Research Report 36, London

Silver, I A, 1969 'The ageing of domestic animals', in D Brothwell and E Higgs (eds), *Science in Archaeology*, Thames and Hudson, London, 283–302 (2nd edn)

Silverside, A J, 1977 'A phytosociological survey of British arable-weeds and related communities', 2 vols, unpublished PhD thesis, University of Durham

Sinclair, J (ed), 1792 *The statistical account of Scotland, drawn up from the communications of the ministers of the different parishes*, 4, William Creech, Edinburgh

Smith, I M, 1990 'The archaeological background to the emergent kingdoms of the Tweed Basin in the early historic period', 2 vols, unpublished PhD thesis, University of Durham

Smith, I M, 1996 'The origins and development of Christianity in north Britain and southern Pictland', in J Blair and C Pyrah (eds), *Church archaeology: research directions for the future*, Council for British Archaeology Research Report 104, York, 19–37

Smith, I M, 1992 'Sprouston, Roxburghshire: an early Anglian centre of the eastern Tweed Basin', *Proceedings of the Society of Antiquaries of Scotland* 121, 261–294

Smith, J A, 1881 'Notice of the discovery of a massive silver chain of plain double rings or links at Hordwell, Berwickshire, by the Hon Lord Dunglas, with notes of similar silver chains found in Scotland', *Proceedings of the Society of Antiquaries of Scotland* 15, 64–70

Spencer, B, 1990 'Pilgrims' badges', in M Biddle (ed), *Winchester studies 7. Artefacts from medieval Winchester. Part ii: Object and economy in medieval Winchester*, Clarendon Press, Oxford, 799–803

Spry, C, 1956 *The Constance Spry cookery book*, J M Dent, London

Steane, J M and Foreman, M, 1991 'The archaeology of medieval fishing tackle', in G L Good, R H Jones and M W Ponsford (eds), *Waterfront archaeology*, Council for British Archaeology Research Report 74, London, 88–101

Stewart, I H, 1967 *The Scottish coinage*, Spink & Son, London (2nd edn)

Stirland, A, 1986 *Human bones in Archaeology*, Shire Archaeology 46, Shire Publications, Princes Risborough

St Joseph, J K S, 1982 'Sprouston, Roxburghshire: an Anglo-Saxon settlement discovered by air reconnaissance', *Anglo-Saxon England* 10, 191–199

Stocker, D, 2007 'Stone associated with burial EE 120', in S Mays, C Harding and C Heighway, *Wharram: a study of settlement on the Yorkshire Wolds, 11: The churchyard*, York University Archaeological Publications 13, York, 293–294

Stronach, S, 2005 'The Anglian monastery and medieval priory of Coldingham: *Urbs Coludi* revisited', *Proceedings of the Society of Antiquaries of Scotland* 135, 395–422

Stroud, G 1993 'The human bones', in G Stroud and R L Kemp, *Cemeteries of the church and priory of St Andrew, Fishergate*, The Archaeology of York 12/2, Council for British Archaeology, London, 160–241

Swift, C, 1987 'Irish influence on ecclesiastical settlements in Scotland: a case study of the island of Islay', unpublished M Phil thesis, University of Durham

Thomas, A C, 1967 'An early Christian cemetery and chapel on Ardwall Isle, Kirkcudbright' *Medieval Archaeology* 11, 127–188

Thomas, A C, 1971 *The early Christian archaeology of north Britain*, Oxford University Press, Oxford

Thomas, A C, 1981 *Christianity in Roman Britain to AD 500*, Batsford, London

Thomas, A C, 1995 'The artist and the people: a foray into uncertain semiotics', in C Bourke (ed), *From the isles of the north: early medieval art in Ireland and Britain*, HMSO, Belfast, 1–7

Thomas, C, forthcoming 'The leather from Sillerholes, West Linton'

Tipping, R, 2004 'Palaeoecology and political history: evaluating driving forces in historic landscape change in southern Scotland', in I D Whyte and A J L Winchester (eds), *Society, landscape and environment in upland Britain*, Society for Landscape Studies Supplementary Series 2, London, 11–20

Trotter, M, 1970 'Estimation of stature from intact long limb bones', in T D Stewart (ed), *Personal identification in mass disasters*, Smithsonian Institute, Washington DC, 71–83

Tulloch, A P, 1976 'Chemistry of waxes of higher plants', in P E Kolattukudy (ed), *Chemistry and Biochemistry of Natural Waxes*, Elsevier, Amsterdam, 236–287

Tylecote, R F, 1976 *A history of metallurgy*, The Metals Society, London

Untracht, O, 1982 *Jewelry concepts and technology*, Doubleday, New York, NY

Vallance, A, 1920 *Old crosses and lynchgates*, Batsford, London

van der Veen, M, 1982 'Carbonised plant remains from The Hirsel', unpublished report, Department of Archaeology, University of Durham, Durham

van der Veen, M, 1987 'The plant remains', in D H Heslop, *The excavation of an Iron Age settlement at Thorpe Thewles, Cleveland, 1980–1982*, Council for British Archaeology Research Report 65, London, 93–99

van der Veen, M and Fieller, N J, 1982 'Sampling seeds', *Journal of Archaeological Science* 9, 287–298

van Zeist, W, 1970 'Prehistoric and early historic food plants in the Netherlands', *Palaeohistoria* 14, 41–173

Vaughan, J E, 1987 'Metalwork', in R B Harbottle and R Fraser, 'Black Friars, Newcastle upon Tyne, after the Dissolution of the Monasteries', *Archaeologia Aeliana*, 5 ser, 15, 122–124

Veale, E M, 1966 *The English fur trade in the later middle ages*, Clarendon Press, Oxford

Waddington, C, 1998 'Hambleton Hill hillfort survey', *Northern Archaeology* 15/16, 71–81

Waddington, C, 2000 'Recent research on the Mesolithic of the Milfield Basin, Northumberland', in R Young (ed), *Mesolithic lifeways: current research from Britain and Ireland*, Leicester Archaeology Monographs 7, University of Leicester, Leicester, 165–178

Waddington, C, 2004 *The joy of flint*, Museum of Antiquities, Newcastle upon Tyne

Waddington, C, 2009a 'A note on Neolithic, Bronze Age, Iron Age and Anglo-Saxon remains at Lanton Quarry near Milfield, Northumberland', *Archaeologia Aeliana*, 5 ser, 38, 23–29

Waddington, C, 2009b 'Uncovering the past: evaluation trial-trenching of cropmark sites', in D G Passmore and C Waddington, *Managing archaeological landscapes in Northumberland: Till-Tweed Studies 1*, Oxbow Books, Oxford, 172–264

Waddington, C, Marshall, P and Passmore, D G, 2011 'Towards synthesis: research and discovery in Neolithic north-east England', *Proceedings of the Prehistoric Society* 77, 279–319

Ward Perkins, J B 1940 *London Museum Medieval Catalogue*, HMSO

Welfare, H and Swan, V, 1995 *Royal Commission on the Historical Monuments of England. Roman camps in England: the field archaeology*, HMSO

White Marshall, J and Walsh, C, 2005 *Illaunloughan Island: an early medieval monastery in County Kerry*, Wordwell, Bray

Whittle, A W R, Healy, F and Bayliss, A, 2011 *Gathering time: dating the Early Neolithic enclosures of southern Britain and Ireland*, Oxbow Books, Oxford

Will, R and Haggarty, G, 2008 'The medieval and later pottery', in H F James and P Yeoman, *Excavations at St Ethernan's monastery, Isle of May, Fife, 1992–7*, Tayside and Fife Archaeological Committee Monograph 6, Perth, 136–149

Williams, S A and Curzon, M E J, 1985 'Dental caries in a Scottish medieval child population', *Caries Research* 19, 162

Williams, S A and Curzon, M E J, 1986 'Observations on dental caries in primary teeth in some medieval British skull material', in E Cruwys and R A Foley (eds), *Teeth and anthropology*, BAR International Series S291, 201–213

Williamson, M G, 1942 'The non-Celtic place-names of the Scottish Border counties', unpublished PhD thesis, School of Scottish Studies, University of Edinburgh

Wood, M, 2011 'Bernician transitions: place-names and archaeology', in D Petts and S Turner (eds), *Early medieval Northumbria: kingdoms and communities*, Studies in the Early Middle Ages 24, Brepols, Turnhout, 35–70

Wordsworth, C (ed), 1885 *Pontificale Ecclesiae S Andreae. The pontifical offices used by David de Bernham, Bishop of S Andrews*, Pitsligo Press, Edinburgh

Workshop of European Anthropologists, 1980 'Recommendations for age and sex diagnoses of skeletons', *Journal of Human Evolution* 9, 517–549

Yeoman, P, 1995 *Medieval Scotland: an archaeological perspective*, Batsford/Historic Scotland, London

Yeoman, P, 1999 *Pilgrimage in medieval Scotland*, Batsford/Historic Scotland, London

Young, R, 1985 'Potential sources of flint and chert in the north-east of England', *Lithics* 5, 1–6

Young, R, 1987 *Lithics and subsistence in north-eastern England*, BAR British Series 161

Young, R, 2000 'Aspects of the "coastal Mesolithic" of the north east of England', in R Young (ed), *Mesolithic lifeways: current research from Britain and Ireland*, Leicester Archaeology Monographs 7, University of Leicester, Leicester, 179–190

Young, R, 2007 '*I must go down to the sea again...* A review of early research on the coastal Mesolithic of the north-east of England', in C Waddington and K Pedersen (eds), *Mesolithic studies in the North Sea basin and beyond*, Oxbow Books, Oxford, 16–24

Young, R and O'Sullivan, D M, 1993 'Nessend, Lindisfarne and the "coastal" Mesolithic of northern England', *Archaeology North* 6, 9–15

Young, R and O'Sullivan, D M, 1995 *Lindisfarne: Holy Island*, Batsford/English Heritage, London

INDEX

Peter J Brown